AFRICA 68-69

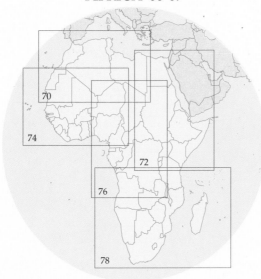

EUROPE 80-81

ESSENTIAL
WORLD
ATLAS

ESSENTIAL
WORLD
ATLAS

DORLING KINDERSLEY
LONDON • NEW YORK • STUTTGART • MOSCOW

A DK PUBLISHING BOOK

PROJECT CARTOGRAPHY AND DESIGN
Julia Lunn, Julie Turner

CARTOGRAPHERS
James Anderson, Sarah Baker-Ede, Roger Bullen, Bob Croser,
Martin Darlison, Stephen Flanagan, Sally Gable, Dieter Müller,
Simon Mumford, John Plumer, Andrew Thompson,
Scott Wallace, Peter Winfield

DATABASE MANAGER
Simon Lewis

DIGITAL CARTOGRAPHY CREATED IN DK CARTOPIA BY
Tom Coulson, Dan Gardiner, Phil Rowles, Rob Stokes

DESIGN
Katy Wall

INDEX-GAZETTEER
Debra Clapson, Natalie Clarkson, Ruth Duxbury,
Margaret Hynes, Margaret Stevenson

PRODUCTION
Hilary Stephens, David Proffit

CARTOGRAPHIC DIRECTOR
Andrew Heritage

ART DIRECTOR
Chez Picthall

10 9 8 7 6 5 4 3 2

First published in the United States as the Concise World Atlas in 1997
Reprinted with revisions 1998
95 Madison Avenue, New York, New York 10016

Library of Congress Cataloging-in-Publication Data
DK concise world atlas - 1st American ed.
        p.   cm.
    ISBN 0-7894-3250-1
    1. Atlases.   I. DK Publishing, Inc.
G1021 .E89   1998 <G&M>
912--DC21

KEY TO MAP SYMBOLS

BOUNDARIES

	Full international border
	Disputed de facto border
	Territorial claim border
	Ceasefire line
	Undefined boundary
	Internal administrative boundary

COMMUNICATION FEATURES

	Major road
	Minor road
	Railroad
	International airport

DRAINAGE FEATURES

	Major perennial river
	Minor perennial river
	Seasonal river
	Canal
	Waterfall
	Perennial lake
	Seasonal lake
	Wetland

ICE FEATURES

	Permanent ice cap/ice shelf
	Winter limit of pack ice
	Summer limit of pack ice

LANDSCAPE FEATURES

	Sandy desert
△	Spot height
▽	Spot depth
▲	Volcano
)(	Pass/tunnel
+	Site of interest

POPULATED PLACES

○	Less than 50,000
○	50,000-100,000
◉	100,000-500,000
◼	Greater than 500,000
●	Capital
◎	Internal administrative capital

NAMES

TAIWAN	Country
JERSEY (to UK)	Dependent territory
PARIS	Capital
KANSAS	Administrative region
Dordogne	Cultural region
Sahara	Landscape feature
Mont Blanc 4807ft	Mountain/pass
Blue Nile	Drainage feature
Sulu Sea	Ocean feature
Chile Rise	Underwater feature

INSET MAP SYMBOLS

	Urban area
	City
	Park
▪	Place of interest
▫	Suburb/district

CONTENTS

ESSENTIAL WORLD ATLAS

The Political World 8-9
The Physical World 10-11
Time Zones 12-13
Geology & Structure 14-15
World Climate 16-17
Ocean Currents 18-19
Life Zones 20-21
Population 22-23
Languages 24-25
Religion 26-27
The Global Economy 28-29
Global Conflict 30-31

THE WORLD'S REGIONS

NORTH & CENTRAL AMERICA

North & Central America 34-35
Western Canada & Alaska 36-37
Eastern Canada 38-39
USA: The Northeast 40-41
    Bermuda
USA: The Southeast 42-43
USA: Central States 44-45
USA: The West 46-47
    Los Angeles & Hawaii
USA: The Southwest 48-49
Mexico .50-51
Central America 52-53
The Caribbean 54-55
    Jamaica, St Lucia & Barbados

SOUTH AMERIC

South America 56-
Northern South America 58-
Western South America 60-
    Galapagos Islands
Brazil 62-
Southern South America 64-
The Atlantic Ocean 66-

AFRIC

Africa 68-
Northwest Africa 70-
Northeast Africa 72-
West Africa 74-
Central Africa 76-
    Sao Tome & Principe
Southern Africa . . . . . / 78-

EUROI

Europe 80-
The North Atlantic 82-
Scandinavia & Finland 84-
The Low Countries 86-
The British Isles 88-
    London
France, Andorra & Monaco 90-
    Paris, Andorra & Monaco

continued.

EUROPE *continued*

Spain & Portugal 92-93
  Azores & Gibraltar
Germany & the Alpine States 94-95
  Liechtenstein
Italy 96-97
  San Marino & Vatican City
Central Europe 98-99
The Western Balkans 100-101
  Bosnia & Herzegovina
The Mediterranean 102-103
  Malta & Cyprus
Bulgaria & Greece 104-105
The Baltic States & Belarus 106-107
Ukraine, Moldova & Romania .108-109
European Russia 110-111

NORTH & WEST ASIA

North & West Asia 112-113
Russia & Kazakhstan 114-115
Turkey & the Caucasus 116-117
The Near East 118-119
The Middle East 120-121
  West Bank
Central Asia 122-123

SOUTH & EAST ASIA

South & East Asia 124-125
Western China & Mongolia 126-127

Eastern China & Korea 128-129
  Hong Kong
Japan 130-131
  Tōkyō & Nansei-Shotō
South India & Sri Lanka 132-133
North India, Pakistan &
  Bangladesh 134-135
Mainland Southeast Asia 136-137
Maritime Southeast Asia 138-139
  Singapore
The Indian Ocean 140-141

AUSTRALASIA & OCEANIA

Australasia & Oceania 142-143
The Southwest Pacific 144-145
Western Australia 146-147
Eastern Australia 148-149
  Sydney
New Zealand 150-151
The Pacific Ocean 152-153
Antarctica 154
The Arctic Ocean 155

INDEX – GAZETTEER

Overseas Territories &
  Dependencies 156-159
Glossary of Geographical
  Terms 160-161
Index-Gazetteer of Places &
  Countries 162-256

THE POLITICAL WORLD

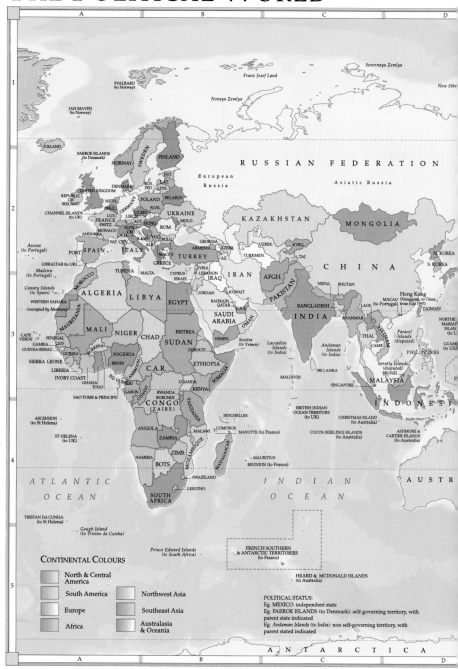

CONTINENTAL COLOURS

North & Central America

South America

Europe

Africa

Northwest Asia

Southeast Asia

Australasia & Oceania

POLITICAL STATUS:
Eg. MEXICO: independent state
Eg. FAEROE ISLANDS (to Denmark): self-governing territory, with parent state indicated
Eg. *Andaman Islands (to India)*: non self-governing territory, with parent stated indicated

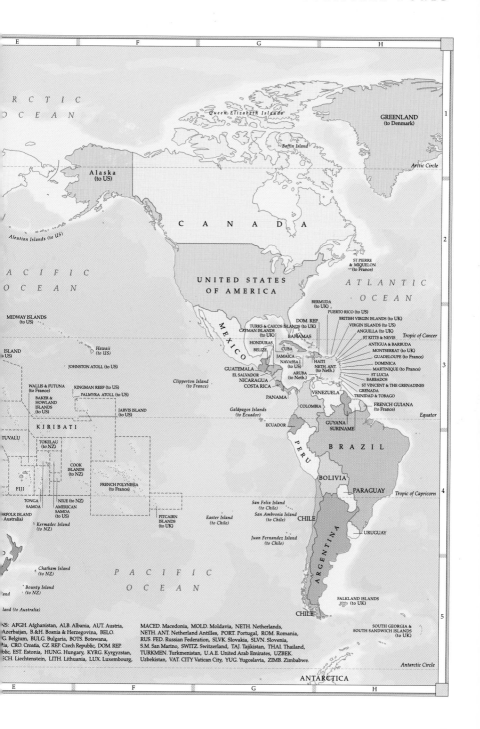

R C T I C

O C E A N

Queen Elizabeth Islands

GREENLAND
(to Denmark)

Baffin Island

Arctic Circle

Alaska
(to US)

Aleutian Islands (to US)

C A N A D A

A C I F I C

O C E A N

UNITED STATES
OF AMERICA

ATLANTIC

OCEAN

ST PIERRE
& MIQUELON
(to France)

MIDWAY ISLANDS
(to US)

ISLAND
(to US)

Hawaii
(to US)

JOHNSTON ATOLL (to US)

BERMUDA
(to UK)

PUERTO RICO (to US)

TURKS & CAICOS ISLANDS
(to UK)

CAYMAN ISLANDS
(to UK)

HONDURAS

BELIZE

DOM. REP.

BAHAMAS

CUBA

BRITISH VIRGIN ISLANDS (to UK)

VIRGIN ISLANDS (to US)

ANGUILLA (to UK)

ST KITTS & NEVIS

Tropic of Cancer

ANTIGUA & BARBUDA

MONTSERRAT (to UK)

GUADELOUPE (to France)

DOMINICA

MARTINIQUE (to France)

WALLIS & FUTUNA
(to France)

KINGMAN REEF (to US)

PALMYRA ATOLL (to US)

BAKER &
HOWLAND
ISLANDS
(to US)

JARVIS ISLAND
(to US)

K I R I B A T I

GUATEMALA

EL SALVADOR

NICARAGUA

COSTA RICA

PANAMA

JAMAICA

NAVASSA I.
(to US)

HAITI

NETH. ANT.
(to Neth.)

ARUBA
(to Neth.)

VENEZUELA

COLOMBIA

ST LUCIA

BARBADOS

ST VINCENT & THE GRENADINES

GRENADA

TRINIDAD & TOBAGO

FRENCH GUIANA
(to France)

Clipperton Island
(to France)

Galápagos Islands
(to Ecuador)

ECUADOR

GUYANA

SURINAME

Equator

TUVALU

TOKELAU
(to NZ)

COOK
ISLANDS
(to NZ)

FRENCH POLYNESIA
(to France)

P E R Ú

B R A Z I L

FIJI

BOLIVIA

PARAGUAY

Tropic of Capricorn

TONGA

SAMOA

NIUE (to NZ)

AMERICAN
SAMOA

PITCAIRN
ISLANDS
(to UK)

RFOLK ISLAND
Australia)

Kermadec Island
(to NZ)

San Felix Island
(to Chile)

San Ambrosia Island
(to Chile)

Easter Island
(to Chile)

CHILE

A R G E N T I N A

URUGUAY

Juan Fernandez Island
(to Chile)

Chatham Island
(to NZ)

P A C I F I C

O C E A N

Bounty Island
(to NZ)

land

land (to Australia)

CHILE

FALKLAND ISLANDS
(to UK)

SOUTH GEORGIA &
SOUTH SANDWICH ISLANDS
(to UK)

Antarctic Circle

ANTARCTICA

NS: AFGH. Afghanistan, ALB. Albania, AUT. Austria, Azerbaijan, B.&H. Bosnia & Herzegovina, BELO. G. Belgium, BULG. Bulgaria, BOTS. Botswana, ia, CRO. Croatia, CZ. REP. Czech Republic, DOM. REP. blic, EST. Estonia, HUNG. Hungary, KYRG. Kyrgyzstan, CH. Liechtenstein, LITH. Lithuania, LUX. Luxembourg,

MACED. Macedonia, MOLD. Moldavia, NETH. Netherlands, NETH. ANT. Netherland Antilles, PORT. Portugal, ROM. Romania, RUS. FED. Russian Federation, SLVK. Slovakia, SLVN. Slovenia, S.M. San Marino, SWITZ. Switzerland, TAJ. Tajikistan, THAI. Thailand, TURKMEN. Turkmenistan, U.A.E. United Arab Emirates, UZBEK. Uzbekistan, VAT. CITY Vatican City, YUG. Yugoslavia, ZIMB. Zimbabwe.

9

THE PHYSICAL WORLD

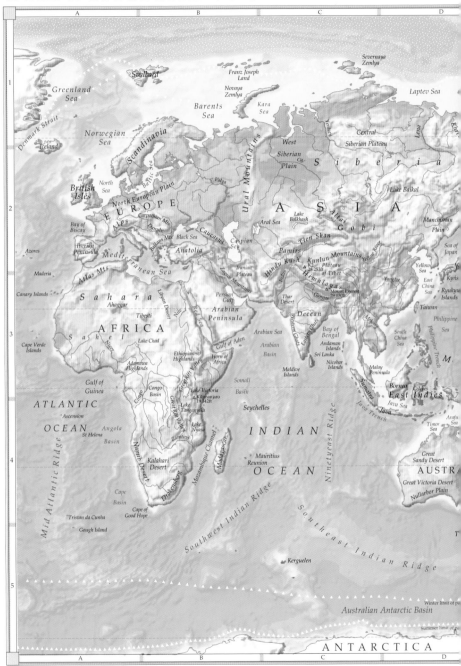

Greenland Sea

Svalbard

Franz Joseph Land

Novaya Zemlya

Severnaya Zemlya

Laptev Sea

Iceland

Denmark Strait

Barents Sea

Kara Sea

Norwegian Sea

Scandinavia

West Siberian Plain

Central Siberian Plateau

Lena

Ural Mountains

S i b e r i a

British Isles

North Sea

Baltic Sea

EUROPE

North European Plain

Volga

Ob'

Yenisey

ALPS

Carpathian Mts

Bay of Biscay

Danube

A S I A

Manchurian Plain

Azores

Iberian Peninsula

Balkans Mts

Black Sea

Caucasus

Aral Sea

Lake Balkhash

Altai

Gobi

Sea of Japan

Madeira

Atlas Mts

Mediterranean Sea

Anatolia

Caspian Sea

Pamirs

Tien Shan

Hindu Kush

Kunlun Mountains

Yellow River

Yellow Sea

Canary Islands

S a h a r a

Ahaggar

Libyan Desert

Nile

Iranian Plateau

Zagros Mountains

Plateau of Tibet

K2 8611m

Himalayas

Mount Everest 8848m

Yangtze

East China Sea

Kyushu

Ryukyu Islands

Cape Verde Islands

S a h e l

AFRICA

Lake Chad

Niger

Red Sea

Persian Gulf

Arabian Peninsula

Thar Desert

Decca n

Ganges

Indus

Mekong

Taiwan

Philippine Sea

Tibesti

Ethiopian Highlands

Gulf of Aden

Arabian Sea

Western Ghats

Eastern Ghats

Bay of Bengal

South China Sea

M

Adamawa Highlands

Great Rift Valley

Horn of Africa

Arabian Basin

Andaman Islands

Sri Lanka

Nicobar Islands

Malay Peninsula

Philippine Trench

Gulf of Guinea

Congo

Congo Basin

Somali Basin

Maldive Islands

Sumatra

Borneo

Celebes

East Indies

ATLANTIC

Ascension

Great Ruaha Valley

Lake Victoria

Kilimanjaro 5895m

Lake Tanganyika

Seychelles

Java Sea

Java

Java Trench

Arafu Sea

OCEAN

St Helena

Angola Basin

Lake Nyasa

Zambezi

I N D I A N

Timor Sea

Great Sandy Desert

AUSTRA

Namib Desert

Mozambique Channel

Madagascar

Mauritius

Reunion

Ninetyeast Ridge

OCEAN

Great Victoria Desert

Nullarbor Plain

Kalahari Desert

Drakensberg

Mid Atlantic Ridge

Cape Basin

Cape of Good Hope

Tristan da Cunha

Gough Island

Southwest Indian Ridge

Kerguelen

Southeast Indian Ridge

T

Winter limit of pa

Australian Antarctic Basin

Summer limit of p

A N T A R C T I C A

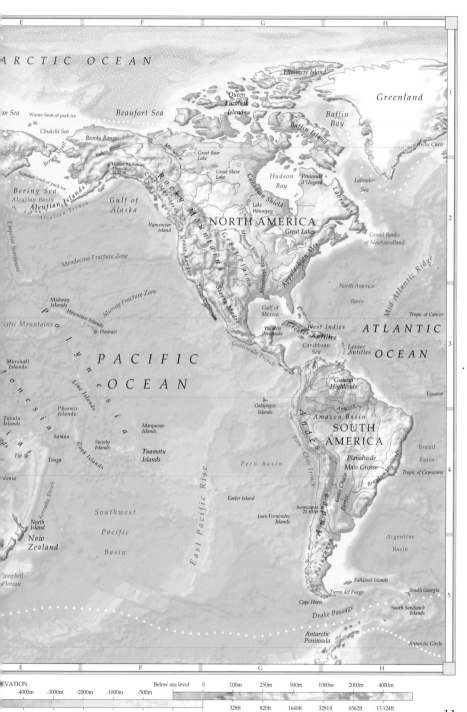

ARCTIC OCEAN

m Sea   Winter limit of pack ice

Beaufort Sea

Ellesmere Island

Queen
Elizabeth
Islands

Greenland

Baffin
Bay

Baffin Island

Arctic Circle

Chukchi Sea   Brooks Range

Yukon River

Bering Strait

Summer limit of pack ice

Bering Sea
Aleutian Basin
Aleutian Islands

Aleutian Trench

Emperor Seamount

△ Mount McKinley
(Denali)
20,320ft

Gulf of
Alaska

Vancouver
Island

Coast Ranges

Rocky Mountains

Great
Bear
Lake

Mackenzie

Great
Slave
Lake

Great Plains

Canadian Shield

Hudson
Bay

Péninsule
d'Ungava

Labrador

Labrador
Sea

Lake
Winnipeg

NORTH AMERICA

Great Lakes

Missouri River

Mississippi

Appalachian Mts

Grand Banks
of Newfoundland

Mid Atlantic Ridge

Mendocino Fracture Zone

Midway
Islands

Hawaiian Islands

Murray Fracture Zone

Sierra Madre

Lower California

North America
Basin

Tropic of Cancer

Marshall
Islands

cific Mountains

Hawaii

PACIFIC

OCEAN

Gulf of
Mexico

Yucatán
Peninsula

Guatemala Trench

Greater
Antilles

West Indies

Caribbean
Sea

Lesser
Antilles

ATLANTIC

OCEAN

P
o
l
y
n
e
s
i
a

Line Islands

Equator

Tuvalu
Islands

Phoenix
Islands

Samoa

Society
Islands

Marquesas
Islands

Galápagos
Islands

Guiana
Highlands

Amazon

Amazon Basin

SOUTH

Fiji

Tonga

Cook Islands

Tuamotu
Islands

Peru Basin

Peru Chile Trench

AMERICA

Andes

Gran Chaco

Pantanal

Planalto de
Mato Grosso

Brazil
Basin

Brazilian Highlands

Brazil
Basin

Tropic of Capricorn

edonia

Kermadec Trench

North
Island

New
Zealand

Southwest

Pacific

Basin

East Pacific Rise

Easter Island

Juan Fernández
Islands

Aconcagua
22,833ft

Argentine

Basin

Campbell
Plateau

Patagonia

Tierra del Fuego

Cape Horn

Falkland Islands

South Georgia

Drake Passage

South Sandwich
Islands

Antarctic
Peninsula

Antarctic Circle

EVATION
-4000m   -3000m   -2000m   -1000m   -500m   Below sea level   0   100m   250m   500m   1000m   2000m   4000m

-13 124ft   -9843ft   -6562ft   -3281ft   -1640ft   -820ft/-250m   0   328ft   820ft   1640ft   3281ft   6562ft   13 124ft

11

TIME ZONES

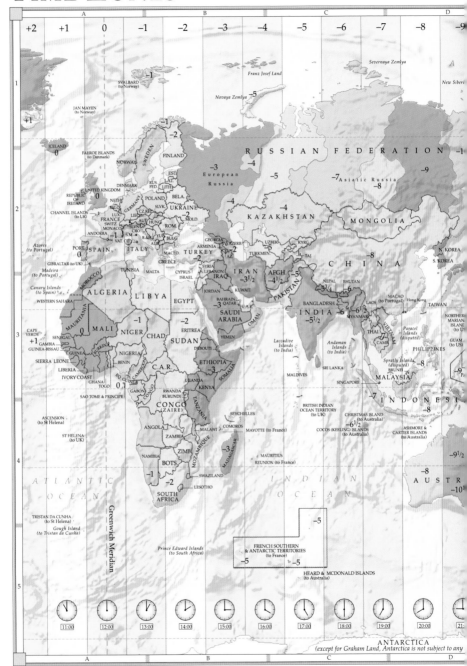

Numbers on the map indicate the number of hours which must be added or subtracted,
as appropriate, in that time zone to reach GMT (Greenwich Mean Time).

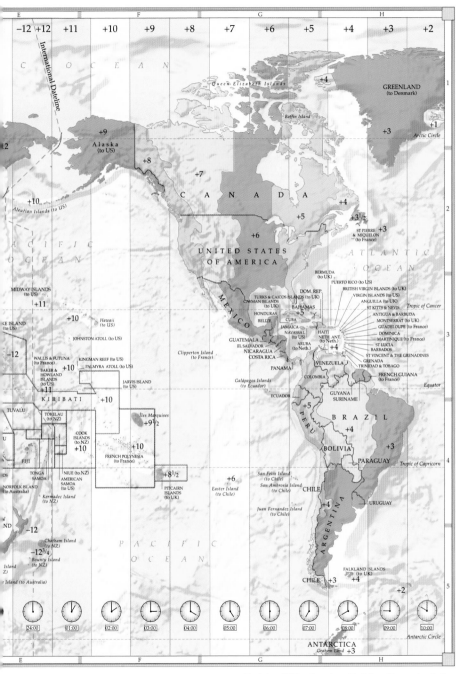

The clocks and 24 hour times given at the bottom of the map show the time in each time zone when it is 12:00 hours, or noon, at GMT.

GEOLOGY & STRUCTURE

Ural Mountains

EURASIAN PLATE

Alps

ANATOLIAN
PLATE

IRANIAN
PLATE

Himalayas

ARABIAN
PLATE

PHILIP
PLA

AFRICAN
PLATE

INDO-

AUSTRALIAN

PLATE

ANTARCTIC PLATE

GEOLOGICAL REGIONS				MOUNTAIN RANGES				M
	continental shield		igneous rock types				Hercynian (290 to 362 Ma)	
	sedimentary rocks		coral formation		Alpine (5 to 23 Ma)		Caledonian (386 to 439 Ma)	

14

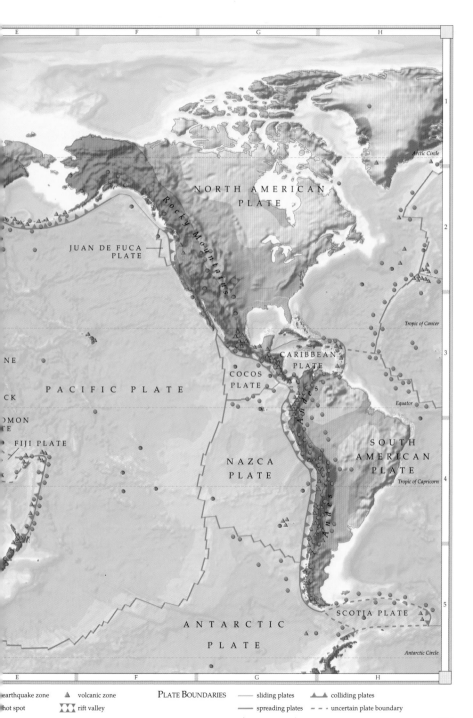

E   F   G   H

Arctic Circle

NORTH AMERICAN
PLATE

Rocky Mountains

JUAN DE FUCA
PLATE

Tropic of Cancer

CARIBBEAN
PLATE

NE

PACIFIC PLATE

COCOS
PLATE

Andes

Equator

MON
E

FIJI PLATE

NAZCA
PLATE

SOUTH
AMERICAN
PLATE

Tropic of Capricorn

Andes

SCOTIA PLATE

ANTARCTIC

PLATE

Antarctic Circle

E   F   G   H

earthquake zone   ▲ volcanic zone   PLATE BOUNDARIES   —— sliding plates   ▲▲ colliding plates

hot spot   〰 rift valley   —— spreading plates   - - - uncertain plate boundary

15

POLAR EASTERLIES

Arctic Circle

Buran

WESTERLIES

Mistral

Föhn

Bora

Etesian (Jun.-Oct.)

Bora

ATLANTIC OCEAN

Sirocco

Khamsin

Southwest Monsoon(Apr.-Sept.)

Tropic of Cancer

NORTH EAST TRADES

Harmattan

Haboob (Jan.)

Equator

SOUTH EAST TRADES

Northeast Monsoon(Oct.-Mar.)

Willy Willies

Tropic of Capricorn

SOUTH EAST TRADES

ATLANTIC OCEAN

INDIAN OCEAN

WESTERLIES

AVERAGE TEMPERATURE IN JANUARY

AVERAGE TEMPERATURE IN JULY

Antarctic Circle

Temperature	
°C	°F
30	86
20	68
10	50
0	32
-10	14
-20	-4
-30	-22

CLIMATE TYPES
(main map)

ice cap	subarctic	warm temperate	semi-arid	tropical
tundra	cool temperate	mediterranean	arid	humid equatorial

16

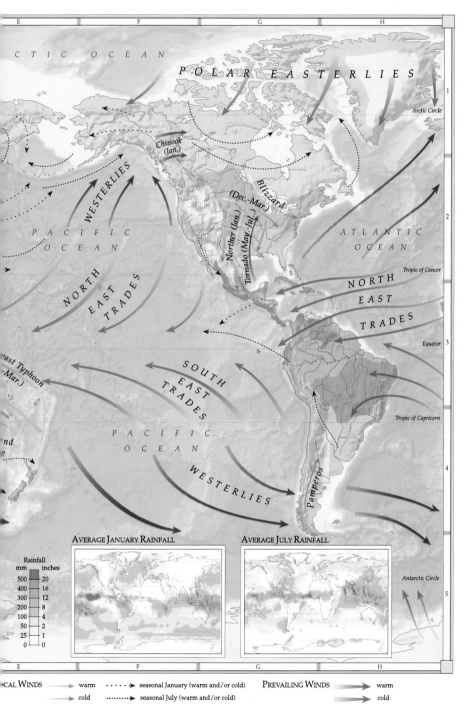

E   F   G   H

* C T I C   O C E A N*

P O L A R   E A S T E R L I E S

Arctic Circle

1

Chinook
(Jan.)

WESTERLIES

Blizzard
(Dec.–Mar.)

Norther (Jan.)

Tornado (May–Jul.)

*P A C I F I C
O C E A N*

*A T L A N T I C
O C E A N*

2

Tropic of Cancer

**N O R T H
E A S T
T R A D E S**

**N O R T H
E A S T
T R A D E S**

east Typhoon
–Mar.)

Equator   3

**S O U T H
E A S T
T R A D E S**

*nd
e*

*P A C I F I C
O C E A N*

Tropic of Capricorn

W E S T E R L I E S

Pamperos

4

AVERAGE JANUARY RAINFALL

AVERAGE JULY RAINFALL

Rainfall
mm	inches
500	20
400	16
300	12
200	8
100	4
50	2
25	1
0	0

Antarctic Circle

5

E   F   G   H

·CAL WINDS → warm ·····▸ seasonal January (warm and/or cold)   PREVAILING WINDS ➡ warm
            → cold ·····▸ seasonal July (warm and/or cold)   ➡ cold

OCEAN CURRENTS

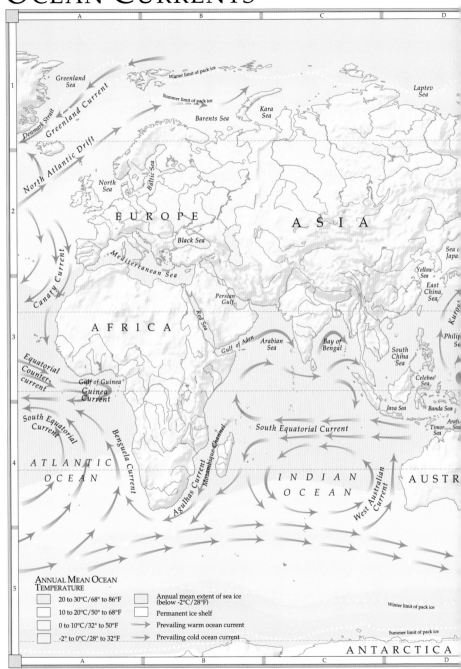

Greenland Sea
Denmark Strait
Greenland Current
Winter limit of pack ice
Summer limit of pack ice
Barents Sea
Kara Sea
Laptev Sea
North Atlantic Drift
North Sea
Baltic Sea
EUROPE
ASIA
Black Sea
Canary Current
Mediterranean Sea
Persian Gulf
Sea of Japan
Yellow Sea
East China Sea
Kuros
AFRICA
Red Sea
Gulf of Aden
Arabian Sea
Bay of Bengal
South China Sea
Phili Se
Equatorial Counter-current
Gulf of Guinea
Guinea Current
Celebes Sea
South Equatorial Current
Benguela Current
Java Sea
Banda Sea
Arai
Timor Sea
ATLANTIC OCEAN
Agulhas Current
Mozambique Channel
South Equatorial Current
INDIAN OCEAN
West Australian Current
AUSTR
Winter limit of pack ice
Summer limit of pack ice
ANTARCTICA

ANNUAL MEAN OCEAN TEMPERATURE

- 20 to 30°C/68° to 86°F
- 10 to 20°C/50° to 68°F
- 0 to 10°C/32° to 50°F
- -2° to 0°C/28° to 32°F
- Annual mean extent of sea ice (below -2°C/28°F)
- Permanent ice shelf
- Prevailing warm ocean current
- Prevailing cold ocean current

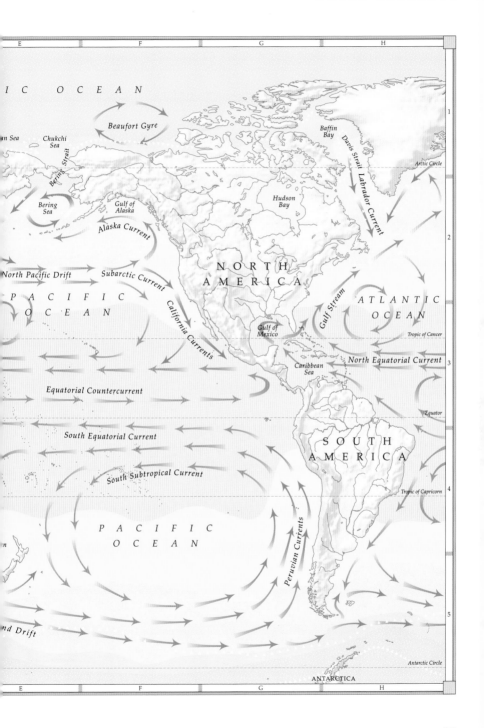

ARCTIC OCEAN

Beaufort Gyre

Baffin Bay

Davis Strait

an Sea

Chukchi Sea

Bering Strait

Arctic Circle

Bering Sea

Gulf of Alaska

Hudson Bay

Labrador Current

Alaska Current

North Pacific Drift

Subarctic Current

PACIFIC OCEAN

NORTH AMERICA

ATLANTIC OCEAN

California Currents

Gulf Stream

Tropic of Cancer

Gulf of Mexico

Caribbean Sea

North Equatorial Current

Equatorial Countercurrent

Equator

South Equatorial Current

SOUTH AMERICA

South Subtropical Current

Tropic of Capricorn

PACIFIC OCEAN

Peruvian Currents

nd Drift

Antarctic Circle

ANTARCTICA

LIFE ZONES

A R C T

Greenland Sea
Svalbard
Franz Joseph Land
Novaya Zemlya
Kara Sea
Severnaya Zemlya
Laptev Sea

Denmark Strait
Iceland

Norwegian Sea

Barents Sea

West Siberian Plain
Ob
Yenisey
Central Siberian Plateau
Lena

S i b e r i a

Scandinavia
Baltic Sea
North Sea
British Isles
North European Plain
EUROPE
Alps
Carpathian Mts
Danube
Balkans Mts
Black Sea
Caucasus
Volga
Ural Mountains
Aral Sea
Altai
Lake Baikal
A S I A
G o b i
Manchurian Plain

Bay of Biscay
Iberian Peninsula
Mediterranean Sea
Anatolia
Caspian Sea
Iranian Plateau
Zagros Mountains
Pamirs
Tien Shan
Hindu Kush
Indus
Kunlun Mountains
Plateau of Tibet
Himalayas
Yellow River
Yangtze
Sea of Japan
Yellow Sea
East China Sea
Ryukyu Islands
Kyu

Atlas Mts
S a h a r a
Ahaggar
Libyan Desert
Nile
Red Sea
Persian Gulf
Arabian Peninsula
Thar Desert
Ganges
Deccan
Western Ghats
Eastern Ghats
Taiwan

AFRICA
Tibesti
Lake Chad
Sahel
Niger
Ethiopian Highlands
Gulf of Aden
Horn of Africa
Arabian Sea
Bay of Bengal
Sri Lanka
South China Sea
Mekong
M

Adamawa Highlands
Gulf of Guinea
Congo
Congo Basin
Great Rift Valley
Lake Victoria
Malay Peninsula
East Indies
Borneo
Java Sea
Sumatra
Java

ATLANTIC OCEAN
Lake Tanganyika
Great Rift Valley
Lake Nyasa
Zambezi
Mozambique Channel
Madagascar
INDIAN OCEAN
Arafu Sea
Timor Sea
Great Sandy Desert
AUSTR

Namib Desert
Kalahari Desert
Drakensberg
Cape of Good Hope

Great Victoria Desert
Nullarbor Plain

Kerguelen

T

A N T A R C T I C A

LIFE ZONES

polar	mountain	broadleaf forest	temperate rainforest
tundra	needleleaf forest	temperate grassland	mediterranean

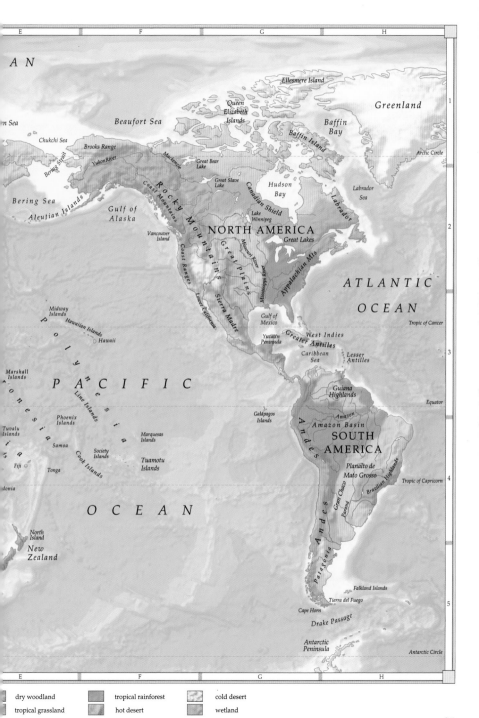

E   F   G   H

Ellesmere Island

Queen
Elizabeth
Islands

Greenland

Beaufort Sea

*Baffin
Bay*

Chukchi Sea

Baffin Island

Brooks Range

Arctic Circle

n Sea

YukonRiver

Mackenzie

Great Bear
Lake

Great Slave
Lake

*Labrador
Sea*

Bering Sea

Hudson
Bay

Canadian Shield

Labrador

Aleutian Islands

*Gulf of
Alaska*

Lake
Winnipeg

NORTH AMERICA

Great Lakes

Vancouver
Island

Missouri River

Appalachian Mts

ATLANTIC

Rocky Mountains

Great Plains

Coast Ranges

Mississippi River

OCEAN

*Midway
Islands*

Hawaiian Islands

Sierra Madre

Lower California

Tropic of Cancer

Hawaii

Gulf of
Mexico

Yucatán
Peninsula

West Indies

Greater Antilles

*Marshall
Islands*

P A C I F I C

Caribbean
Sea

Lesser
Antilles

Equator

Galápagos
Islands

Guiana
Highlands

*Phoenix
Islands*

Line Islands

Amazon

Amazon Basin

**SOUTH
AMERICA**

*Tuvalu
Islands*

Marquesas
Islands

Andes

Planalto de
Mato Grosso

Brazilian Highlands

Samoa

Society
Islands

Tuamotu
Islands

Tropic of Capricorn

Fiji

Tonga

Cook Islands

Gran Chaco

Paraná

donia

O C E A N

Andes

*North
Island*

*New
Zealand*

Patagonia

Falkland Islands

Tierra del Fuego

Cape Horn

Drake Passage

*Antarctic
Peninsula*

Antarctic Circle

E   F   G   H

dry woodland	tropical rainforest	cold desert
tropical grassland	hot desert	wetland

21

POPULATION

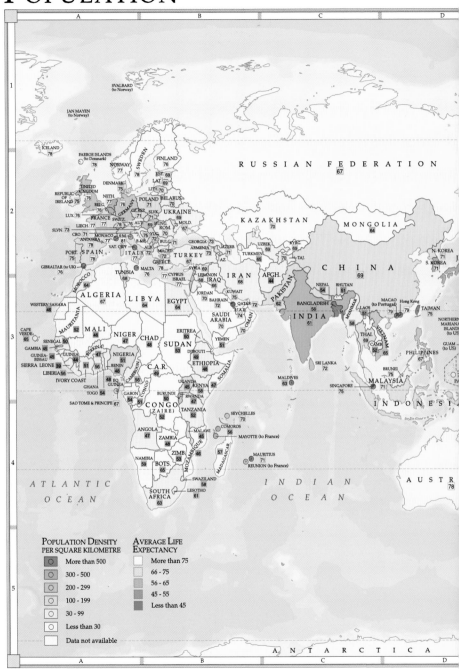

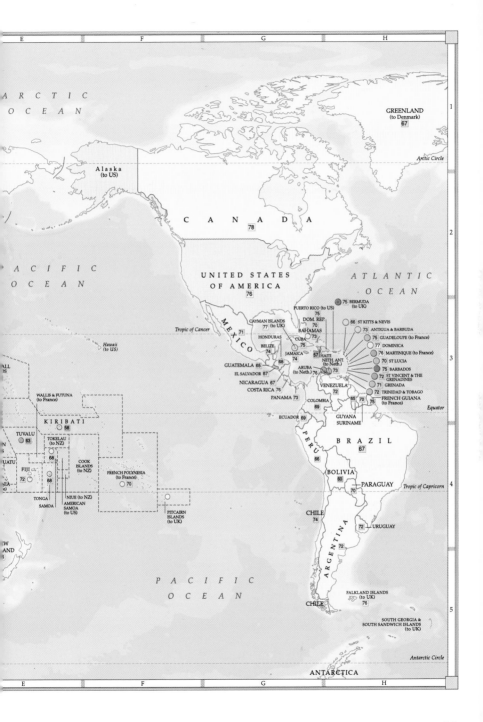

E   F   G   H

ARCTIC

OCEAN

GREENLAND
(to Denmark)
67

1

Arctic Circle

Alaska
(to US)

C A N A D A
78

2

P A C I F I C

O C E A N

UNITED STATES
OF AMERICA
76

A T L A N T I C

O C E A N

BERMUDA
75 (to UK)

PUERTO RICO (to US)
75

DOM. REP.
70

Tropic of Cancer

MEXICO
71

CAYMAN ISLANDS
77 (to UK)

BAHAMAS
73

ST KITTS & NEVIS
66

Hawaii
(to US)

HONDURAS

BELIZE
74

CUBA
75

ANTIGUA & BARBUDA
73

GUADELOUPE (to France)
75

ALL
DS

JAMAICA
74

DOMINICA
77

GUATEMALA 65

68

57

HAITI
NETH. ANT.
(to Neth.)

MARTINIQUE (to France)
76

ST LUCIA
70

EL SALVADOR 62

ARUBA
(to Neth.)
76

73

BARBADOS
75

WALLIS & FUTUNA
(to France)

NICARAGUA 67

ST VINCENT & THE
GRENADINES
72

COSTA RICA 76

PANAMA 73

VENEZUELA
72

GRENADA
71

KIRIBATI
58

COLOMBIA
69

TRINIDAD & TOBAGO
72

FRENCH GUIANA
(to France)
75

TUVALU
63

TOKELAU
(to NZ)

ECUADOR 69

GUYANA

SURINAME

Equator

68

COOK
ISLANDS
(to NZ)

PERÚ
86

B R A Z I L
67

FIJI
72

68

FRENCH POLYNESIA
(to France)
70

BOLIVIA
80

A

TONGA

NIUE (to NZ)

PARAGUAY
70

Tropic of Capricorn

SAMOA

AMERICAN
SAMOA
(to US)

PITCAIRN
ISLANDS
(to UK)

CHILE
74

A
R
G
E
N
T
I
N
A

URUGUAY
72

W
AND

P A C I F I C

O C E A N

CHILE

FALKLAND ISLANDS
(to UK)
76

5

SOUTH GEORGIA &
SOUTH SANDWICH ISLANDS
(to UK)

Antarctic Circle

ANTARCTICA

E   F   G   H

LANGUAGES

MAIN INTERNATIONAL LANGUAGES

◯ Chinese	Arabic/French	English/Spanish
◯ Spanish	French/other	Spanish/other
◯ Arabic	English/other	Portuguese/other
◯ Hindi	Arabic/other	Other Language
◯ English	Hindi/English/other	
◯ French	Chinese/other	**Bantu** Language Group
◯ Russian	Russian/other	*Mari* Other Language
◯ Portuguese	English/French	Uninhabited Land

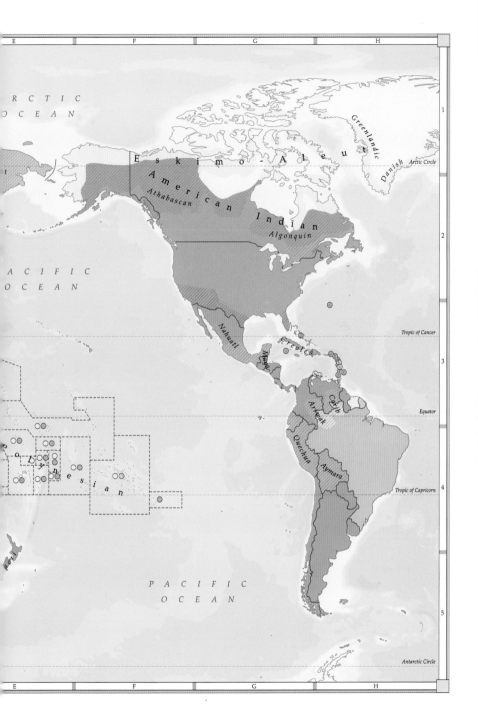

E   F   G   H

1

A R C T I C
O C E A N

Greenlandic

Danish   Arctic Circle

E s k i m o - A l e u

A m e r i c a n   I n d i a n

Athabascan

Algonquin

2

P A C I F I C
O C E A N

Tropic of Cancer

Nahuatl

Creoles

Maya

Carib

Equator

Arawak

P o l y n e s i a n

Quechua

Aymara

Tropic of Capricorn   4

Maori

P A C I F I C
O C E A N

5

Antarctic Circle

E   F   G   H

RELIGION

A | B | C | D

1

SVALBARD
(to Norway)

ICELAND

FAEROE ISLANDS
(to Denmark)

NORWAY

SWEDEN

FINLAND

RUSSIAN FEDERATION

European
Russia

Asiatic Russia

DENMARK

REPUBLIC
OF
IRELAND

UNITED KINGDOM

NETH.
LUX.
FRANCE
SWITZ.
MONACO
ANDORRA

GERMANY
LIECH.
AUT.
SLVN.
ITALY

POLAND
CZ.REP.
SLVK.
HUNG.
ROM.

EST.
LAT.
LITH.
BELARUS

UKRAINE

MOLD.

KAZAKHSTAN

MONGOLIA

N. KOREA
S. KOREA

RUS.
FED.

2

PORT.
SPAIN

VAT. CITY
S.M.
B.&H.
YUG.
MACED.
ALB.

BULG.

GEORGIA
ARMENIA
AZERB.
AZ.

UZBEK.
TURKMEN.

KYRG.
TAJ.

CHINA

GIBRALTAR (to UK)

TUNISIA

MALTA

GREECE
TURKEY

CYPRUS
ISRAEL
LEBANON
SYRIA
IRAQ

IRAN

AFGH.

NEPAL

BHUTAN

MACAO
(to Portugal)

Hong Kong

TAIWAN

MOROCCO

ALGERIA

LIBYA

EGYPT

JORDAN

KUWAIT

BAHRAIN
QATAR

U.A.E.

SAUDI
ARABIA

OMAN

PAKISTAN

BANGLADESH

INDIA

LAOS

MYANMAR

THAI.

VIETNAM

CAMB.

NORTHE
MARIA
ISLAN
(to U

WESTERN SAHARA

MAURITANIA

MALI

NIGER

CHAD

SUDAN

ERITREA

DJIBOUTI

YEMEN

Paracel
Islands
(disputed)

PHILIPPINES

CAPE
VERDE

SENEGAL

GAMBIA
GUINEA-BISSAU

GUINEA

BURKINA

NIGERIA

BENIN

CAMEROON

ETHIOPIA

SOMALIA

SRI LANKA

MALDIVES

Spratly Islands
(disputed)
BRUNEI

SINGAPORE

MALAYSIA

INDONESI

3

SIERRA LEONE

LIBERIA

IVORY COAST

GHANA
TOGO

SAO TOME & PRINCIPE

EQ. GUINEA

GABON

CONGO

C.A.R.

UGANDA

RWANDA
BURUNDI

KENYA

CONGO
(ZAIRE)

TANZANIA

SEYCHELLES

ANGOLA

ZAMBIA

MALAWI

COMOROS

MAYOTTE (to France)

ATLANTIC

OCEAN

NAMIBIA

ZIMB.

BOTS.

MOZAMBIQUE

MADAGASCAR

MAURITIUS
REUNION (to France)

INDIAN

OCEAN

AUSTR

4

SWAZILAND

LESOTHO

SOUTH
AFRICA

MAJORITY RELIGIONS

- Chinese
- Protestant Christianity
- Catholic Christianity
- Orthodox Christianity
- Shi'a Islam
- Sunni Islam
- Hinduism
- Judaism
- Theravada Buddhism
- Mahayana Buddhism
- Tibetan Buddhism
- Other

STATE POLICY

▲ Secular Ideologies governing
◉ Marxist states during 20th century
■ Non-pluralist states

ANTARCTICA
(uninhabited)

5

A | B | C | D

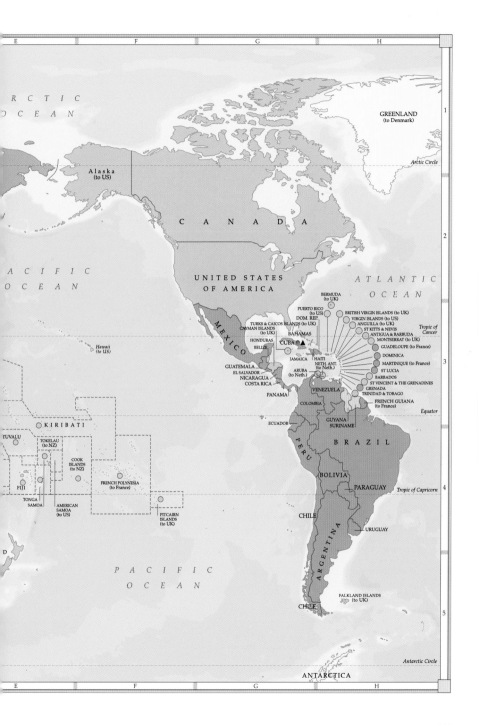

ARCTIC
OCEAN

GREENLAND
(to Denmark)

1

Arctic Circle

Alaska
(to US)

C A N A D A

2

P A C I F I C
OCEAN

A T L A N T I C
OCEAN

UNITED STATES
OF AMERICA

BERMUDA
(to UK)

Hawaii
(to US)

MEXICO

PUERTO RICO
(to US)
DOM. REP.
TURKS & CAICOS ISLANDS (to UK)
CAYMAN ISLANDS
(to UK)
BAHAMAS
HONDURAS
BELIZE
CUBA

BRITISH VIRGIN ISLANDS (to UK)
VIRGIN ISLANDS (to US)
ANGUILLA (to UK)
ST KITTS & NEVIS
ANTIGUA & BARBUDA
MONTSERRAT (to UK)
GUADELOUPE (to France)

*Tropic of
Cancer*

3

JAMAICA
GUATEMALA
EL SALVADOR
NICARAGUA
COSTA RICA
PANAMA

HAITI
NETH. ANT.
(to Neth.)
ARUBA
(to Neth.)

DOMINICA
MARTINIQUE (to France)
ST LUCIA
BARBADOS
ST VINCENT & THE GRENADINES
GRENADA
TRINIDAD & TOBAGO

VENEZUELA

COLOMBIA

FRENCH GUIANA
(to France)

Equator

K I R I B A T I

TUVALU

ECUADOR

GUYANA
SURINAME

TOKELAU
(to NZ)

COOK
ISLANDS
(to NZ)

P E R U

B R A Z I L

FIJI

FRENCH POLYNESIA
(to France)

BOLIVIA

TONGA
SAMOA

AMERICAN
SAMOA
(to US)

PITCAIRN
ISLANDS
(to UK)

PARAGUAY

Tropic of Capricorn

4

CHILE

URUGUAY

D

P A C I F I C
OCEAN

A R G E N T I N A

CHILE

FALKLAND ISLANDS
(to UK)

5

Antarctic Circle

E   F   G   H

ANTARCTICA

THE GLOBAL ECONOMY

ECONOMIC PERFORMANCE

GNP per capita, 1995 ($US)

- more than 20 000
- 10 000 to 20 000
- 5000 to 10 000
- 1000 to 5000
- 500 to 1000
- 250 to 500
- less than 250
- data not available

Human Development Index (HDI)

- high human development
- poor human development

HDI is one of the best indicators of economic development. The single index is reached by measuring life expectancy at birth, per capita purchasing power, literacy rates and years of schooling

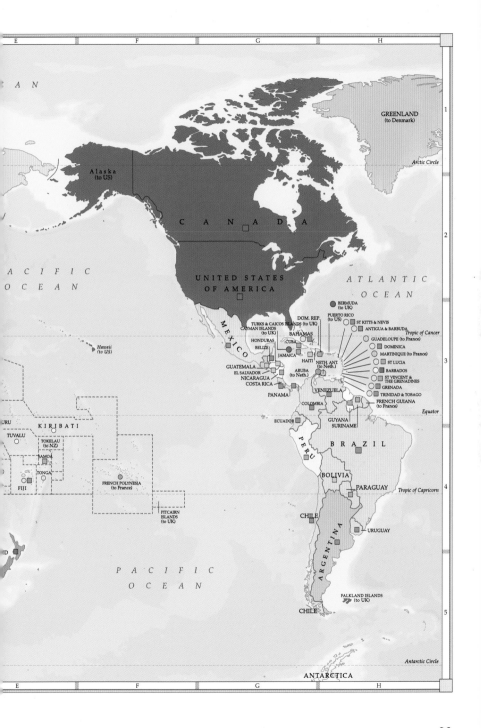

GREENLAND
(to Denmark)

Arctic Circle

Alaska
(to US)

C A N A D A

UNITED STATES
OF AMERICA

A T L A N T I C

O C E A N

P A C I F I C

O C E A N

BERMUDA
(to UK)

M E X I C O

TURKS & CAICOS ISLANDS (to UK)
CAYMAN ISLANDS
(to UK)
HONDURAS
BELIZE
GUATEMALA
EL SALVADOR
NICARAGUA
COSTA RICA
PANAMA

DOM. REP.
PUERTO RICO
(to US)
ST KITTS & NEVIS
ANTIGUA & BARBUDA
Tropic of Cancer
GUADELOUPE (to France)
DOMINICA
MARTINIQUE (to France)
ST LUCIA
BARBADOS
ST VINCENT &
THE GRENADINES
GRENADA
TRINIDAD & TOBAGO
FRENCH GUIANA
(to France)

BAHAMAS
CUBA
JAMAICA
HAITI
NETH. ANT.
(to Neth.)
ARUBA
(to Neth.)
VENEZUELA
COLOMBIA

*Hawaii
(to US)*

K I R I B A T I

URU
TUVALU

TOKELAU
(to NZ)
SAMOA
TONGA

FIJI

FRENCH POLYNESIA
(to France)

PITCAIRN
ISLANDS
(to UK)

ECUADOR

GUYANA
SURINAME

P E R U

B R A Z I L

BOLIVIA

PARAGUAY
Tropic of Capricorn

CHILE

URUGUAY

A R G E N T I N A

P A C I F I C

O C E A N

Equator

D

CHILE

FALKLAND ISLANDS
(to UK)

Antarctic Circle

ANTARCTICA

29

GLOBAL CONFLICT

KEY

▭	International conflict since 1975
↯	Civil unrest since 1975
◆	Disputed territories
⋯⋯	Disputed border
-- --	Undefined border

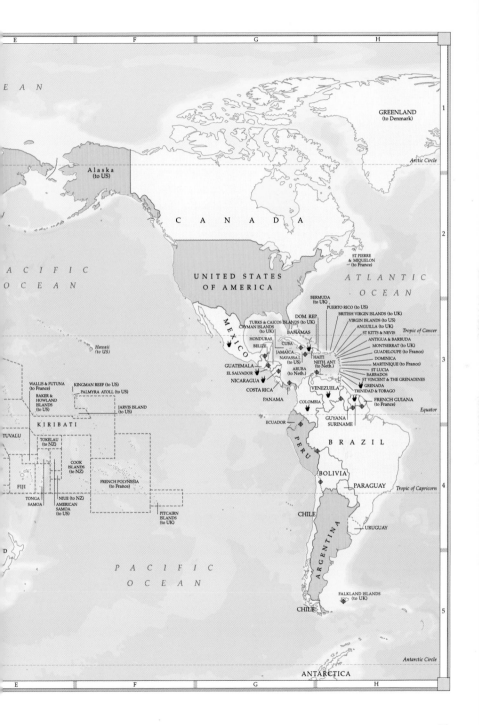

E F G H

1

GREENLAND
(to Denmark)

Arctic Circle

Alaska
(to US)

C A N A D A

2

UNITED STATES
OF AMERICA

ST PIERRE
& MIQUELON
(to France)

A T L A N T I C
O C E A N

P A C I F I C
O C E A N

Hawaii
(to US)

M E X I C O

BERMUDA
(to UK)

PUERTO RICO (to US)
BRITISH VIRGIN ISLANDS (to UK)
VIRGIN ISLANDS (to US)
ANGUILLA (to UK)
ST KITTS & NEVIS

DOM. REP.

TURKS & CAICOS ISLANDS (to UK)
CAYMAN ISLANDS
(to UK)

BAHAMAS

HONDURAS
BELIZE

CUBA

JAMAICA
NAVASSA I.

GUATEMALA
EL SALVADOR

NICARAGUA

COSTA RICA

PANAMA

ARUBA
(to Neth.)

HAITI
NETH. ANT.
(to Neth.)

Tropic of Cancer

ANTIGUA & BARBUDA
MONTSERRAT (to UK)
GUADELOUPE (to France)
DOMINICA
MARTINIQUE (to France)
ST LUCIA
BARBADOS
ST VINCENT & THE GRENADINES
GRENADA
TRINIDAD & TOBAGO

VENEZUELA

COLOMBIA

FRENCH GUIANA
(to France)

Equator

GUYANA
SURINAME

3

WALLIS & FUTUNA
(to France)

KINGMAN REEF (to US)

PALMYRA ATOLL (to US)

BAKER &
HOWLAND
ISLANDS
(to US)

JARVIS ISLAND
(to US)

K I R I B A T I

ECUADOR

TUVALU

TOKELAU
(to NZ)

COOK
ISLANDS
(to NZ)

FRENCH POLYNESIA
(to France)

P E R Ú

B R A Z I L

BOLIVIA

PARAGUAY

Tropic of Capricorn

4

FIJI

TONGA
SAMOA

NIUE (to NZ)
AMERICAN
SAMOA
(to US)

PITCAIRN
ISLANDS
(to UK)

CHILE

URUGUAY

A R G E N T I N A

P A C I F I C
O C E A N

CHILE

FALKLAND ISLANDS
(to UK)

5

Antarctic Circle

A N T A R C T I C A

E F G H

ATLAS *of the* WORLD'S REGIONS

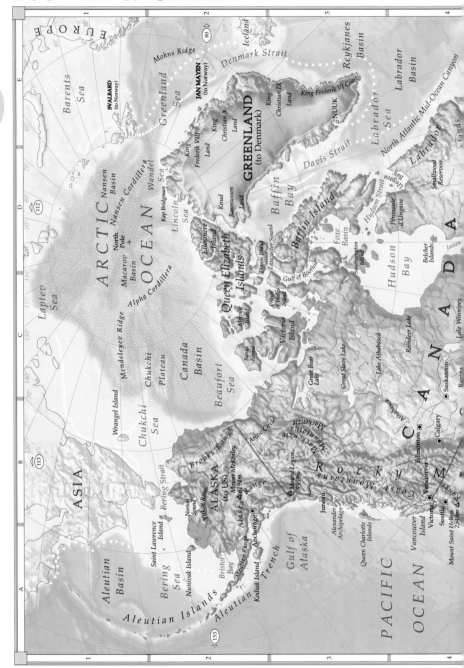

EUROPE

Barents
Sea

Mohns Ridge

Greenland
Sea

SVALBARD
(to Norway)

JAN MAYEN
(to Norway)

Iceland

Denmark Strait

Reykjanes
Basin

Labrador
Basin

80°

ARCTIC Nansen
Basin

Nansen Cordillera

Wandel

North
Pole

Macarov
Basin

Alpha Cordillera

OCEAN

Greenland
Sea

Kap Bridgman

Lincoln
Sea

King
Frederik VIII
Land

Knud
Rasmussen
Land

King
Christian X
Land

King
Christian IX
Land

King Frederik VI Coast

GREENLAND
(to Denmark)

NUUK

Davis Strait

Baffin
Bay

Labrador
Sea

North Atlantic Mid-Ocean Canyon

Labrador

Ungava
Bay

Smallwood
Reservoir

Péninsule
d'Ungava

Mendeleyev Ridge

Laptev
Sea

Chukchi
Plateau

Chukchi
Sea

Canada
Basin

Beaufort
Sea

Queen Elizabeth
Islands

Ellesmere
Island

Devon Island

Lancaster Sound

Prince
of Wales
Island

Gulf of Boothia

Melville
Island

Banks
Island

Victoria
Island

Foxe
Basin

Southampton
Island

Hudson

Bay

Belcher
Islands

James

Wrangel Island

Great Bear
Lake

Great Slave Lake

Lake Athabasca

Reindeer Lake

Lake Winnipeg

CANADA

Saskatoon

Regina

Calgary

Edmonton

ASIA

Saint Lawrence
Island

Bering
Sea

Bering Strait

Yukon Range

Brooks Range

ALASKA
(to US)

Mount McKinley
6194m

Alaska Range

Anchorage

Arctic Circle

Mackenzie

Mackenzie Mountains

Rocky
Mountains

Mount Logan
5959m

Coast Mountains

Vancouver

Victoria

Vancouver
Island

Seattle

Mount Saint Helens
2549m

Nunivak Island

Bristol
Bay

Norton
Sound

Juneau

Alexander
Archipelago

Queen Charlotte
Islands

Kodiak Island

Gulf of
Alaska

Aleutian Trench

Aleutian
Basin

Aleutian Islands

PACIFIC

OCEAN

M

112

113

153

0 km 1000

0 miles 1000

POPULATION

○ Less than 50,000   ○ 50,000 -100,000   ◉ 100,000 - 500,000   ■ Over 50

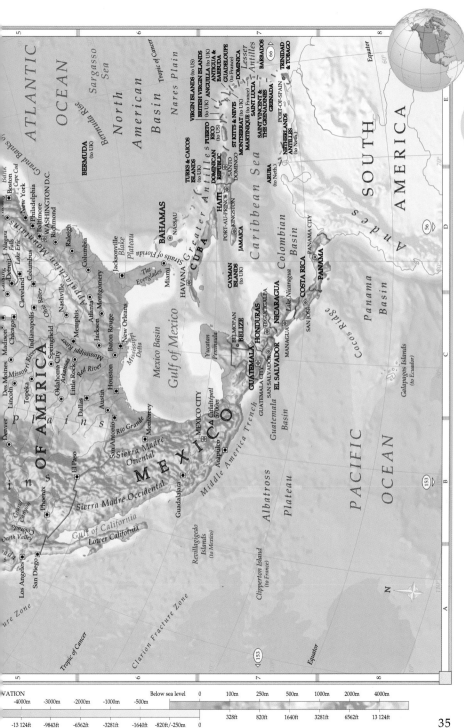

ATLANTIC OCEAN

Sargasso Sea

Bermuda Rise

North American Basin

Nares Plain

Tropic of Cancer

BERMUDA (to UK)

Grand Banks of Newfoundland

Bank

Boston
Cape Cod
New York
Philadelphia
Baltimore
WASHINGTON D.C.
Richmond
Raleigh
Columbia

Niagara Falls
Lake Erie
Detroit

Appalachian Mountains

Jacksonville
Blake Plateau

Columbus
Cleveland
Nashville
Atlanta
Montgomery
Memphis
Jackson
Baton Rouge
New Orleans

Lansing
Chicago
Indianapolis
Springfield
St Louis

Madison
Des Moines
Lincoln
Topeka

Denver

P l a i n s

O F   A M E R I C A

Oklahoma City
Little Rock
Dallas
Austin

Missouri River
Ohio River
Arkansas River
Mississippi River
Red River

Houston
San Antonio
Monterrey

Río Grande

El Paso

Sierra Madre Oriental

Phoenix

Sierra Madre Occidental

Guadalajara

M E X I C O

Acapulco

MEXICO CITY
Citlaltépetl
5700m

Revillagigedo Islands
(to Mexico)

Gulf of California

Lower California

Grand Canyon

Colorado
Death Valley

Los Angeles
San Diego

ure Zone

Tropic of Cancer

Clarion Fracture Zone

PACIFIC OCEAN

Albatross Plateau

Middle America Trench

Guatemala Basin

Cocos Ridge

Galapagos Islands
(to Ecuador)

Panama Basin

Colombian Basin

Caribbean Sea

Greater Antilles

Lesser Antilles

BAHAMAS
NASSAU

The Everglades
Miami

Straits of Florida

HAVANA
CUBA

CAYMAN ISLANDS
(to UK)

TURKS & CAICOS ISLANDS
(to UK)

DOMINICAN REPUBLIC
SANTO DOMINGO

HAITI
PORT-AU-PRINCE

JAMAICA
KINGSTON

PUERTO RICO
(to US)

VIRGIN ISLANDS (to US)
BRITISH VIRGIN ISLANDS (to UK)
ANGUILLA (to UK)
ANTIGUA & BARBUDA
GUADELOUPE (to France)
DOMINICA
MARTINIQUE (to France)
SAINT LUCIA
SAINT VINCENT & THE GRENADINES
GRENADA
BARBADOS
ST KITTS & NEVIS
MONTSERRAT (to UK)

ARUBA (to Neth.)
NETHERLANDS ANTILLES
(to Neth.)

TRINIDAD & TOBAGO
PORT-OF-SPAIN

BELMOPAN
BELIZE

GUATEMALA
GUATEMALA CITY

HONDURAS
TEGUCIGALPA

EL SALVADOR
SAN SALVADOR

NICARAGUA
MANAGUA
Lake Nicaragua

COSTA RICA
SAN JOSÉ

PANAMA
PANAMA CITY

Yucatan Peninsula

Mexico Basin

Gulf of Mexico

SOUTH AMERICA

Andes

66

56

153

153

N

Equator

Equator

60°
70°
110°
100°
90°
80°

Clipperton Island
(to France)

VATION

-4000m	-3000m	-2000m	-1000m	-500m	Below sea level	0	100m	250m	500m	1000m	2000m	4000m
-13 124ft	-9843ft	-6562ft	-3281ft	-1640ft	-820ft/-250m	0	328ft	820ft	1640ft	3281ft	6562ft	13 124ft

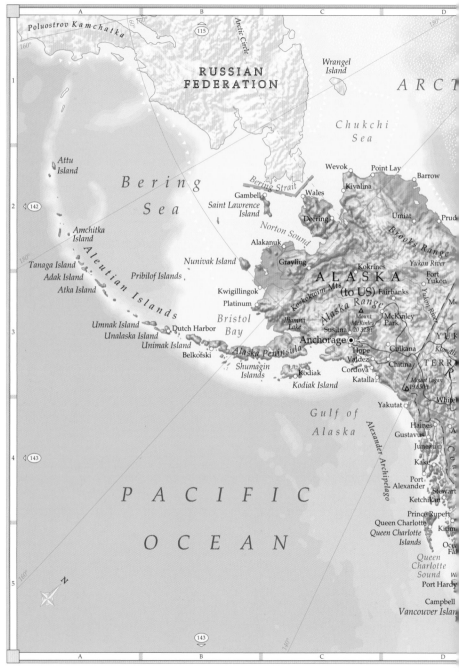

Poluostrov *Kamchatka*

115

Arctic Circle

RUSSIAN FEDERATION

Wrangel Island

ARCT

Chukchi Sea

Attu Island

Wevok
Point Lay
Barrow

B e r i n g

Gambell
Wales
Kivalina

Bering Strait

Umiat
Prud

142

Saint Lawrence Island

Deering

S e a

Norton Sound

Amchitka Island

Alakanuk

Grayling
Kokrines
Yukon River
Fort Yukon

A l e u t i a n   I s l a n d s

Tanaga Island
Adak Island
Atka Island

Nunivak Island

Pribilof Islands

Kwigillingok

A L A S K A
(to US) Fairbanks

Koskokwim Mts.

Platinum

Bristol Bay

Iliamna Lake

Alaska Range

Mount McKinley
20,323 ft

McKinley Park

M

Umnak Island
Unalaska Island
Unimak Island

Dutch Harbor

Susitna

YUK

Belkofski

Alaska Peninsula

Anchorage
Hope
Valdez
Gulkana
Chitina
Klondk
TERR

Shumagin Islands
Kodiak

Cordova
Katalla

Mount Logan
19,850 ft

Kodiak Island

Yakutat

White

G u l f   o f
A l a s k a

Haines
Gustavus
Juneau

Alexander Archipelago

Kake

P A C I F I C

Port Alexander
Stewart
Ketchikan

Prince Rupert
Queen Charlotte
Queen Charlotte Islands
Kitm

O C E A N

Oce
Fa

Queen Charlotte Sound W
Port Hardy

Campbell
Vancouver Islan

143

143

0 km   400

0 miles   400

POPULATION

○ Less than 50,000   ○ 50,000 -100,000   ◉ 100,000 - 500,000   ◼ Over 500

OCEAN

Alert

155

Knud Rasmussen Land

GREENLAND
(to Denmark)

Ellesmere Island

Axel Heiberg
Island

Eureka

Arctic Circle

Ellef Ringnes
Island
Isachsen

Amund
Ringnes
Island

Grise Fiord

Baffin
Bay

Prince Patrick
Island

Mould Bay

Queen Elizabeth Islands

Davis Strait

Devon Island

Bathurst
Island

Cornwallis
Island

82

Melville
Island

Resolute

Lancaster Sound

Viscount Melville
Sound

Somerset
Island

Arctic Bay

Baffin Island

Banks
Island

McClintock Channel

Prince of
Wales Island

Boothia
Peninsula

Gulf of Boothia

Amundsen
Gulf

Holman

Victoria
Island

Boothia
Peninsula

Igloolik

Melville
Peninsula

Iqaluit

Cambridge
Bay

King William
Island

Pelly Bay

Gjoa Haven

Coppermine

Repulse Bay

Great Bear Lake

Echo Bay

Southampton
Island

Coral
Harbour

Hudson Strait

Baker Lake

Péninsule
d' Ungava

NORTHWEST TERRITORIES

Rankin Inlet

Whale Cove

QUÉBEC

Rae-Edzo

Yellowknife

Reliance

Arviat

Fort
Simpson

Lutselk'e

Providence

Great Slave Lake

Hay River

Hudson

Fort Liard

Fort Smith

Bay

Nelson

Meander
River

Caribou

Churchill

Herchmer

Belcher
Islands

38

Fond-du-Lac

Fort
Vermilion

Lake
Athabasca

Wollaston
Lake

South
Indian Lake

James
Bay

Fort
McMurray

CANADA

ALBERTA

Buffalo
Narrows

Fox Mine

Thompson

Grande
Prairie

SASKATCHEWAN

Flin Flon

Ponton

Lake
Winnipeg

ONTARIO

Athabasca

Doré Lake

North Saskatchewan

Big River

The Pas

Edmonton

Leduc

Saskatchewan

Prince Albert

MANITOBA

Pine Dock

Provost

Red Deer

Hanna

Saskatoon

Barrows

Norquay

Lake
of the Woods

Great Lakes

Kindersley

Yorkton

Shoal Lake

Calgary

Vulcan

Regina

Brandon

Winnipeg

Lake Superior

Medicine
Hat

Elkford

Lethbridge

Weyburn

Melita

Lake
Michigan

Lake Huron

Milk River

Estevan

45

UNITED STATES OF AMERICA

ELEVATION

| -4000m | -3000m | -2000m | -1000m | -500m | Below sea level | 0 | 100m | 250m | 500m | 1000m | 2000m | 4000m |

| -13 124ft | -9843ft | -6562ft | -3281ft | -1640ft | -820ft/-250m | 0 | | 328ft | 820ft | 1640ft | 3281ft | 6562ft | 13 124ft |

EASTERN CANADA

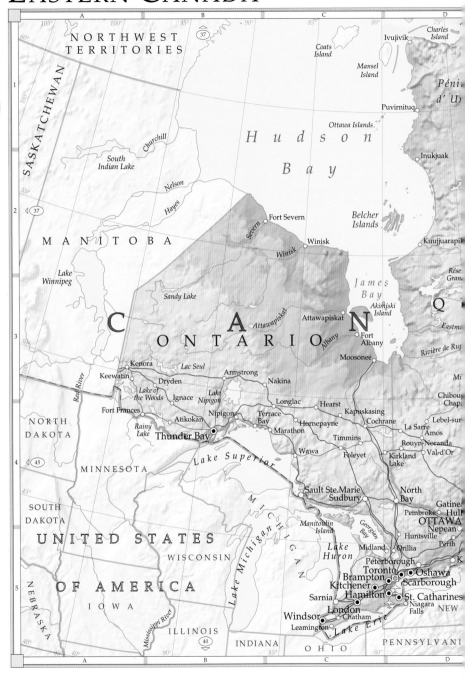

NORTHWEST TERRITORIES

SASKATCHEWAN

MANITOBA

Churchill

South Indian Lake

Nelson

Hayes

Lake Winnipeg

Coats Island

Mansel Island

Hudson Bay

Ottawa Islands

Belcher Islands

Ivujivik

Charles Island

Puvirnituq

Inukjuak

Kuujjuarapi

Péni d'U

Rése Gran

James Bay

Akimiski Island

Q

Fort Severn

Winisk

Winisk

Severn

Attawapiskat

Attawapiskat

Albany

Fort Albany

Moosonee

Eastma

Rivière de Ru

Sandy Lake

CANADA

ONTARIO

Kenora

Keewatin

Dryden

Lake of the Woods

Ignace

Fort Frances

Atikokan

Rainy Lake

Lac Seul

Armstrong

Nakina

Lake Nipigon

Nipigon

Thunder Bay

Longlac

Terrace Bay

Marathon

Hearst

Hornepayne

Wawa

Timmins

Foleyet

Kapuskasing

Cochrane

Kirkland Lake

La Sarre

Rouyn-Noranda

Lebel-sur

Amos

Val-d'Or

Mi

Chibou

Chapa

Red River

NORTH DAKOTA

MINNESOTA

SOUTH DAKOTA

UNITED STATES

OF AMERICA

NEBRASKA

WISCONSIN

IOWA

ILLINOIS

INDIANA

Mississippi River

Lake Superior

Lake Michigan

Michigan

Sault Ste.Marie

Sudbury

North Bay

Pembroke

OTTAWA

Nepean

Gatine

Hull

Manitoulin Island

Georgian Bay

Lake Huron

Midland

Orillia

Huntsville

Perth

Peterborough

Toronto

Brampton

Kitchener

Hamilton

Sarnia

Windsor

Leamington

London

Chatham

Oshawa

Scarborough

St. Catharines

Niagara Falls

Lake Erie

OHIO

PENNSYLVANI

NEW

K

NORTH & CENTRAL AMERICA

0 km   400

0 miles   400

POPULATION

○ Less than 50,000   ○ 50,000 -100,000   ◉ 100,000 - 500,000   ◼ Over 500

Resolution Island

Button Islands

Akpatok Island

ngava Bay

Hebron
Cod Island

Rivière à la Baleine

Nain

Labrador Sea

Hopedale
Makkovik
Cape Harrison

Cartwright

NEWFOUNDLAND & LABRADOR

Schefferville

Smallwood Reservoir
Lake Melville

Churchill

St.Anthony

C   D   A

Centian Highlands

Mingan
Havre-St-Pierre
Île d'Anticosti

Sept-Îles

Strait of Belle Isle

Gander
Grand Falls

St. John's

Newfoundland

Corner Brook

Cape Race

Baie-Comeau

Gaspé

Gulf of St. Lawrence

Channel-Port aux Basques

Péninsule de Gaspé

St. Lawrence

Chicoutimi

Matane

Rimouski

La Baie
quière   Rivière-du-Loup

Bathurst

Îles de la Madeleine

St Pierre

Cabot Strait

ST. PIERRE & MIQUELON
(to France)

PRINCE EDWARD ISLAND

Sydney Mines
Glace Bay
Sydney

Edmundston

NEW BRUNSWICK

Charlottetown

Cape Breton Island

Charlesbourg
Montmagny

Fredericton

Moncton
Amherst

New Glasgow

Québec
St-Georges

Oromocto

Truro

Rivières

McAdam

NOVA SCOTIA

al

MAINE

St. John

Digby

Dartmouth
Halifax

Sable Island

Sherbrooke

Bay of Fundy

Liverpool

NEW MPSHIRE

Yarmouth

Shelburne

Cape Sable

A T L A N T I C

HUSETTS

Cape Cod

O C E A N

N

RHODE ISLAND

CTICUT

ELEVATION

-4000m   -3000m   -2000m   -1000m   -500m   Below sea level   0   100m   250m   500m   1000m   2000m   4000m

-13 124ft   -9843ft   -6562ft   -3281ft   -1640ft   -820ft/-250m   0   328ft   820ft   1640ft   3281ft   6562ft   13 124ft

39

USA: THE NORTHEAST

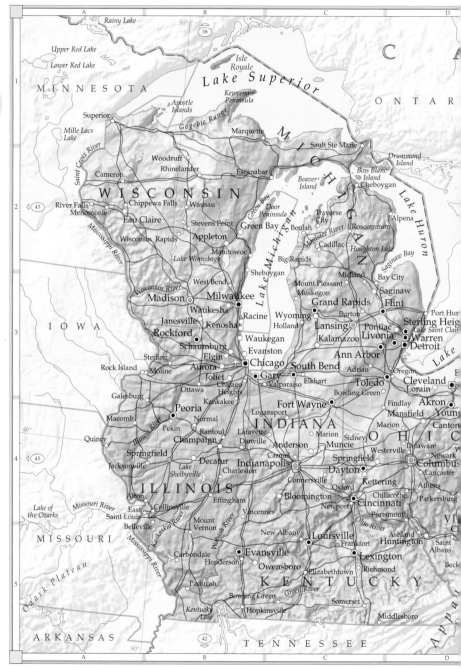

MINNESOTA

Rainy Lake

Upper Red Lake
Lower Red Lake

Isle
Royale

Lake Superior

ONTAR

Keweenaw
Peninsula

Superior

Apostle
Islands

Gogebic Range

Marquette

Sault Ste Marie

Drummond
Island

Mille Lacs
Lake

Saint Croix River

Cameron

Woodruff
Rhinelander

Escanabar

Bois Blanc
Island

Cheboygan

Beaver
Island

WISCONSIN

Chippewa Falls

Wausau

Green Bay

Door
Peninsula

Traverse
City

Roscommon

Alpena

Lake Huron

River Falls
Menomonie

Eau Claire

Stevens Point

Appleton

Beulah

Manistee River

Cadillac

Houghton Lake

Mississippi River

Wisconsin Rapids

Manitowoc

Big Rapids

Saginaw Bay

Lake Winnebago

Sheboygan

Midland

Bay City

MICHIGAN

Wisconsin River

West Bend

Mount Pleasant
Muskegon

Bay City

Saginaw

IOWA

Madison

Milwaukee

Waukesha

Racine

Grand Rapids

Burton

Flint

Port Hur

Janesville

Kenosha

Wyoming
Holland

Lansing

Pontiac
Livonia

Sterling Heig

Lake Saint Clair

Rockford

Waukegan

Kalamazoo

Ann Arbor

Warren
Detroit

Lake

Sterling

Schaumburg
Elgin

Evanston

Aurora

Chicago

South Bend

Adrian

Oregon

Cleveland

Rock Island
Moline

Joliet

Gary

Valparaiso

Elkhart

Toledo

Lorain

Ottawa

Chicago
Heights

Bowling Green

Findlay

Akron

Youn

Galesburg

Kankakee

Fort Wayne

Mansfield

Canton

Macomb

Peoria

Logansport

Marion

OHIC

Quincy

Normal
Pekin

Rantoul

Lafayette

Danville

INDIANA

Sidney

Westerville

Delaware

Newark

Springfield

Jacksonville

Champaign

Anderson

Muncie

Springfield

Columbus

Lancaster

Decatur

Indianapolis

Dayton

Kettering

Athens

Lake
Shelbyville

Charleston

Connersville

Oxford

Chillicothe

Parkersburg

ILLINOIS

Effingham

Bloomington

Newport

Cincinnati

Portsmouth

VI

Alton
East
Saint Louis

Collinsville

Vincennes

CI

Belleville

Mount
Vernon

New Albany

Louisville

Ohio River

Ashland

Huntington

Saint
Albans

MISSOURI

Lake of
the Ozarks

Missouri River

Kaskaskia River

Wabash River

Frankfort

Lexington

Beck

Mississippi River

Carbondale

Evansville

Owensboro

Elizabethtown

Richmond

Henderson

Paducah

KENTUCKY

Ozark Plateau

Kentucky
Lake

Bowling Green

Green River

Somerset

Hopkinsville

Middlesboro

ARKANSAS

TENNESSEE

Appa

| 0 km | 200 |
| 0 miles | 200 |

POPULATION

○ Less than 50,000   ○ 50,000 -100,000   ◉ 100,000 - 500,000   ◼ Over 50

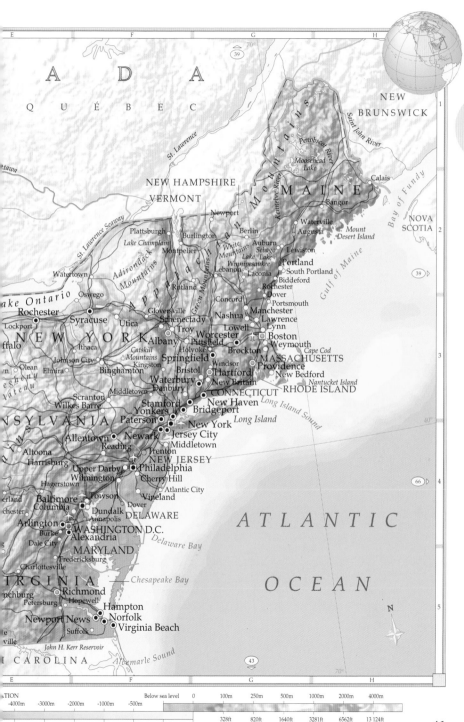

ADA

QUÉBEC

NEW
BRUNSWICK

1

St. Lawrence

awa

39

70

NOVA
SCOTIA

Penobscot River
Moosehead
Lake

Saint John River

Calais

MAINE

Bay of Fundy

39

NEW HAMPSHIRE

Kennebec River

VERMONT

Newport

Bangor

Waterville
Augusta

Mount
Desert Island

2

St. Lawrence Seaway

Plattsburgh

Lake Champlain

Burlington

Berlin

Montpelier

White
Mountains

Auburn
Lewiston

Portland

Gulf of Maine

Watertown

Adirondack
Mountains

Lebanon

Lake Lake
Sebago Winnipesaukee

South Portland
Biddeford

Rutland

Laconia

Rochester

Dover

ake Ontario

Oswego

Concord

Portsmouth

Rochester

Lockport

Syracuse

Utica

Gloversville
Schenectady

Nashua

Manchester

Lawrence

NEW YORK

ffalo

Ithaca

Johnson City

Albany

Troy
Pittsfield

Worcester

Lowell

Lynn

Boston

Weymouth

Catskill
Mountains

Elmira

Binghamton

Kingston

Springfield

Holyoke

Brockton

Cape Cod

Olean

eghe
ateau

Scranton

Middletown

Bristol

Waterbury

Danbury

Hartford

New Britain

Windsor

MASSACHUSETTS

Providence

New Bedford

RHODE ISLAND

Nantucket Island

NSYLVANIA

Wilkes Barre

Stamford
Yonkers

Paterson

New Haven

Bridgeport

CONNECTICUT

Long Island Sound

Altoona

Allentown

Reading

Newark

Jersey City

New York

Long Island

40°

Harrisburg

Trenton

Middletown

Hagerstown

Upper Darby

NEW JERSEY

Philadelphia

66

4

erland

Wilmington

Cherry Hill

Atlantic City

chester

Baltimore

Towson

Vineland

ATLANTIC

Columbia

Dundalk

DELAWARE

Arlington

Burke

WASHINGTON D.C.

Annapolis

Dale City

Alexandria

MARYLAND

Fredericksburg

Delaware Bay

Charlottesville

Chesapeake Bay

OCEAN

RGINIA

Richmond

nchburg

Hopewell

Petersburg

Hampton

N

5

Newport News

Norfolk

le

Suffolk

Virginia Beach

ville

John H. Kerr Reservoir

Albemarle Sound

43

CAROLINA

70°

E

F

G

H

USA: THE SOUTHEAST

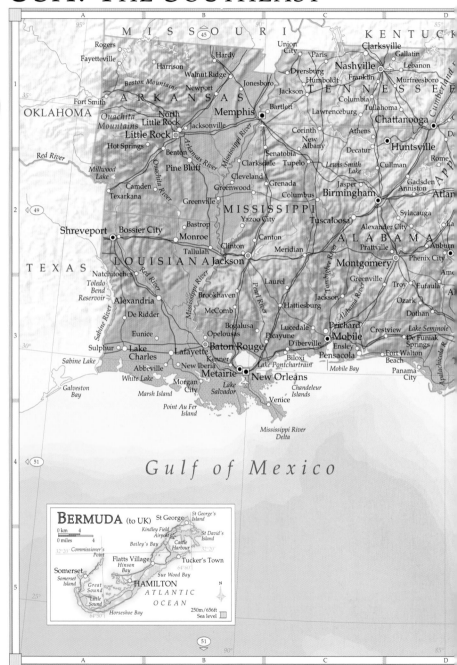

BERMUDA (to UK)

St George
St George's Island
Kindley Field Airport
St David's Island
Bailey's Bay
Castle Harbour
Commissioner's Point
Flatts Village
Hinson Bay
Tucker's Town
Somerset
Somerset Island
Sue Wood Bay
HAMILTON
Great Sound
Little Sound
Horseshoe Bay

ATLANTIC OCEAN

250m/656ft
Sea level

POPULATION

○ Less than 50,000   ○ 50,000 -100,000   ◉ 100,000 - 500,000   ◼ Over 5

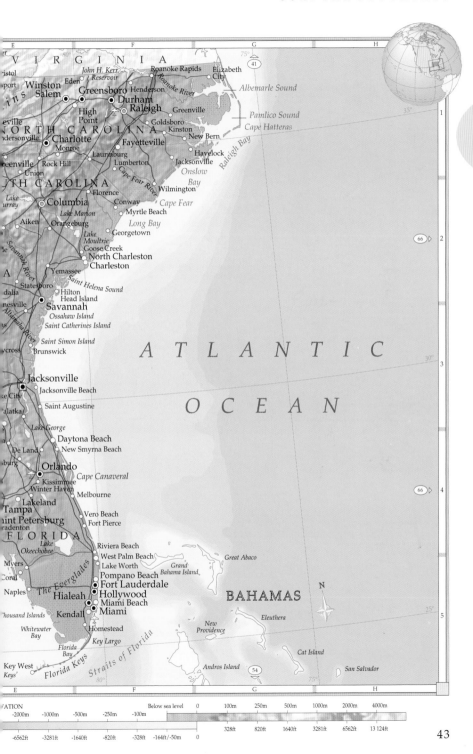

VIRGINIA
ristol
port   Winston   Eden   Greensboro
       Salem   Henderson
ns   High   Greensboro
                Point   Durham
              Raleigh
eville   ORTH CAROLINA   Greenville
ndersonville   Goldsboro
         Charlotte   Kinston
         Monroe   New Bern
              Fayetteville
         Rock Hill   Laurinburg   Havelock
eenville   Union   Lumberton   Jacksonville
UTH CAROLINA   Florence   Onslow
Lake   Bay
urray   Columbia   Conway   Cape Fear
              Myrtle Beach
   Aiken   Orangeburg   Long Bay
              Lake   Georgetown
              Moultrie
              Goose Creek
   le   North Charleston
              Charleston
   A   Yemassee   Saint Helena Sound
   Statesboro
dalia   Hilton
nesville   Head Island
         Savannah
         Ossahaw Island
         Saint Catherines Island
         Saint Simon Island
ycross   Brunswick

ATLANTIC

   Jacksonville
   Jacksonville Beach
ke City
         Saint Augustine
alatka

         Lake George
         Daytona Beach
De Land   New Smyrna Beach
sburg
   Orlando
   Kissimmee   Cape Canaveral
   Winter Haven
   Lakeland   Melbourne
Tampa
aint Petersburg
radenton   Vero Beach
         Fort Pierce
FLORIDA
   Lake
   Okeechobee   Riviera Beach
Myers   West Palm Beach
Coral   Lake Worth
         Pompano Beach
Naples   The Everglades   Fort Lauderdale
         Hialeah   Hollywood
         Miami Beach
housand Islands   Kendall   Miami
   Whitewater
   Bay   Homestead
   Florida   Key Largo
   Bay
Key West   Florida Keys
Keys

OCEAN

Roanoke Rapids   Elizabeth
              City
John H. Kerr
Reservoir
Roanoke River   75°
              41
         Albemarle Sound
         Pamlico Sound
         Cape Hatteras   35°
Raleigh Bay

Cape Fear River
Saint Helena Sound

66   2

30°   3

66   4

Great Abaco
Grand
Bahama Island

BAHAMAS   N

Eleuthera   25°
New
Providence
Cat Island

Andros Island   54
75°
80°   San Salvador
Straits of Florida

Savannah River
Altamaha River

E   F   G   H

VATION
-2000m   -1000m   -500m   -250m   -100m   Below sea level   0   100m   250m   500m   1000m   2000m   4000m

-6562ft   -3281ft   -1640ft   -820ft   -328ft   -164ft/-50m   0   328ft   820ft   1640ft   3281ft   6562ft   13 124ft

43

USA: Central States

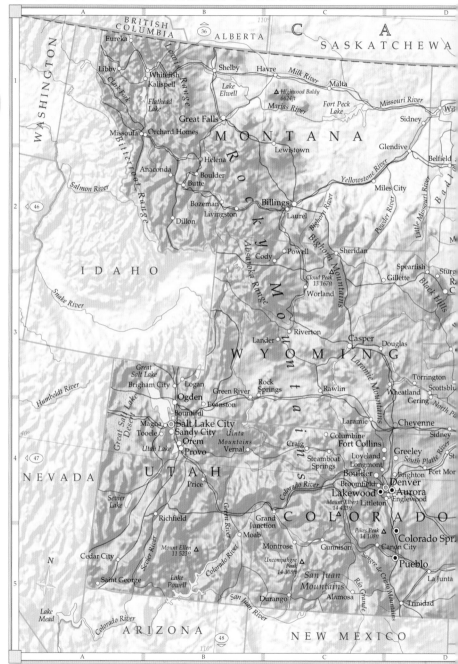

WASHINGTON

Eureka

Libby
Whitefish
Kalispell
Flathead
Lake
Lake
Elwell

Shelby
Havre
Milk River
Malta

Highwood Baldy
6624ft
Marias River
Fort Peck
Lake
Missouri River
Wil

Sidney

Great Falls

M O N T A N A

Missoula
Orchard Homes

Lewistown

Glendive

Belfield

Helena

Anaconda
Boulder
Butte

R

Yellowstone River
Miles City

Salmon River
Bitterroot Range

Bozeman
Livingston
Dillon

Billings

Laurel

Powell
Sheridan

Spearfish

Gillette
Sturg
R.

I D A H O

O

Cody

Cloud Peak
13 167ft
Worland

Bighorn Mountains
Absaroka Range
Bighorn River

Powder River
Little Missouri River
Black Hills

M

Snake River

c

k

y

Riverton

Lander

M

Douglas

o

W Y O M I N G

Casper

Torrington
Scottsblu
Gering

Humboldt River

u

Laramie Mountains

Great
Salt Lake

Brigham City
Logan

n

Green River
Rock
Springs

Rawlin

Wheatland

North Pla

Ogden
Evanston

t

Laramie

Cheyenne

Sidney

Magna
Bountiful
Salt Lake City
Tooele
Sandy City
Orem
Utah Lake
Provo

a

Columbine

Craig
Steamboat
Springs

Fort Collins
Loveland
Longmont
Boulder

Greeley

South Platte River
St

Uinta
Mountains
Vernal

i

Brighton
Fort Mor

Great Salt Lake Desert

N E V A D A

U T A H

Price

n

Broomfield
Lakewood
Littleton
Denver
Aurora
Englewood

Sevier
Lake

Mount Elbert
14 433ft

s

Richfield

Colorado River

Grand
Junction
Moab

C O L O R A D O

Pikes Peak
14 108ft

Colorado Spr.

Cedar City

Mount Ellen
11 523ft

Montrose

Gunnison

Cañon City

N

Sevier River

Green River

Uncompahgre
Peak
14 308ft

Pueblo

Saint George

Lake
Powell

Colorado River

San Juan
Mountains

San Juan River

Durango
Alamosa

Rio Grande

La Junta

Sangre de Cristo Mountains

Trinidad

Lake
Mead

Colorado River

A R I Z O N A

N E W M E X I C O

0 km   200
0 miles   200

POPULATION

O Less than 50,000   O 50,000 -100,000   ● 100,000 - 500,000   ■ Over 50

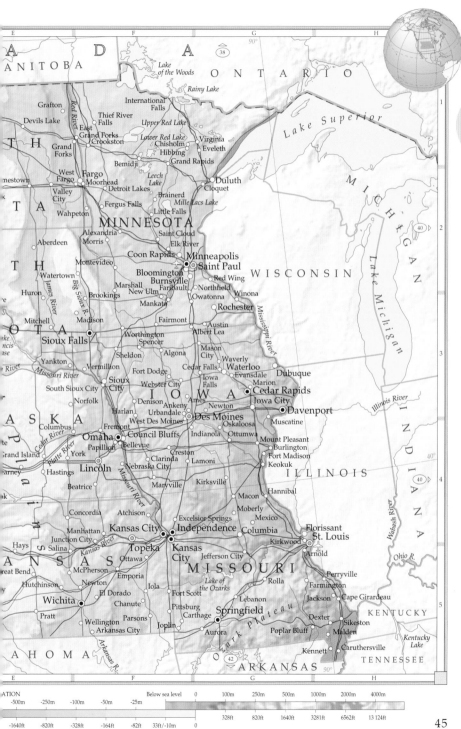

ATION

-500m	-250m	-100m	-50m	-25m		Below sea level	0	100m	250m	500m	1000m	2000m	4000m
-1640ft	-820ft	-328ft	-164ft	-82ft	33ft/-10m		0	328ft	820ft	1640ft	3281ft	6562ft	13 124ft

USA: THE WEST

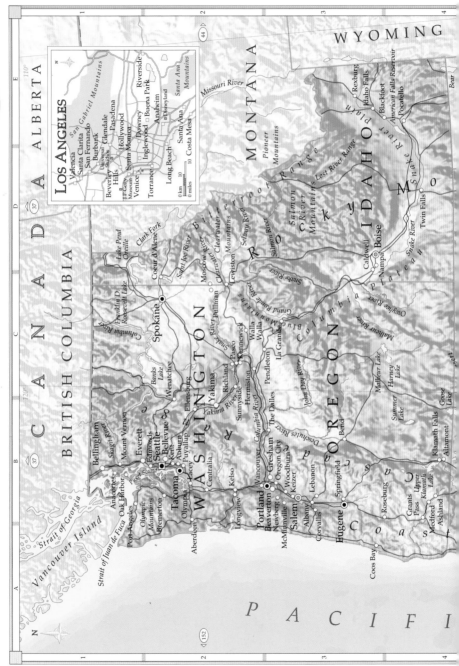

WYOMING

MONTANA

IDAHO

R O C K Y

M O

LOS ANGELES

Valencia
Santa Clarita
San Fernando
Burbank
San Gabriel Mountains
Glendale
Pasadena
Universal
Studios Hollywood
Beverley Santa Monica
Hills Getty
Museum
Venice Inglewood Downey
Torrance Buena Park
Anaheim
Long Beach Disneyland
Santa Ana
Costa Mesa
Riverside
Santa Ana Mountains

0 km 10
0 miles 10

CANADA

ALBERTA

BRITISH COLUMBIA

Missouri River

Bear

Rexburg
Idaho Falls
Blackfoot
American Falls Reservoir
Pocatello

Pioneer Mountains

Bitterroot Mountains

Salmon River Mountains

Clearwater Mountains

Lost River Range

Snake River Plain

Twin Falls

Caldwell
Nampa Boise

Salmon River

Selway River

Lochsa River

Snake River

Clark Fork

Lake Pend Oreille

Coeur d'Alene

St. Joe River

Moscow
Lewiston
Pullman

Palouse River

Columbia River

Grand Ronde River

Owyhee River

Malheur River

Franklin D. Roosevelt Lake

Columbia River

Banks Lake

Spokane

Wenatchee

Richland
Pasco
Kennewick
Walla Walla

Pendleton
La Grande

Blue Mountains

John Day River

Deschutes River

O R E G O N

Malheur Lake
Harney Lake

Summer Lake

Goose Lake

WASHINGTON

Bellingham
Anacortes
Skagit River
Mount Vernon
Everett
Edmonds Seattle
Bellevue
Kent Auburn
Tacoma Puyallup
Bremerton
Olympia Lacey
Centralia

Ellensburg
Yakima

Yakima River

Sunnyside
Hermiston

Kelso

Longview

Vancouver
Portland
Beaverton Gresham
Oregon City
Newberg Woodburn
McMinnville Keizer
Salem
Albany
Corvallis
Lebanon
Springfield
Eugene

Bend

Roseburg

Grants Pass

Medford

Klamath Falls
Altamont

Upper Klamath Lake

Ashland

Puget Sound

Olympic Mountains

Port Angeles

Aberdeen

Strait of Juan de Fuca Oak Harbor

Strait of Georgia

Vancouver Island

C o a s t
R a n g e

Coos Bay

Cascade Range

P A C I F I

0 km 200
0 miles 200

POPULATION
○ Less than 50,000
○ 50,000 -100,000
◉ 100,000 - 500,000
◼ Over 50

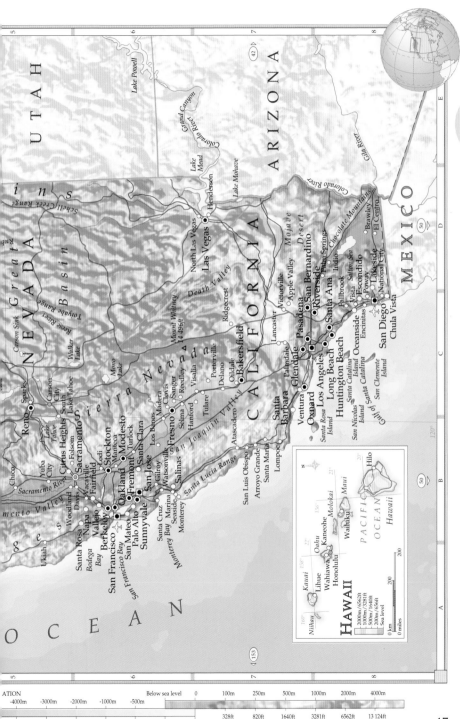

UTAH

NEVADA

Great Basin

Schell Creek Range

Carson Sink

Toiyabe Range

Reese River

Ruby

Walker Lake

Mono Lake

Carson City

Sparks
Reno
Carson City
South Lake Tahoe
Lake Tahoe
Curtis Heights
Folsom
Davis
Vacaville
Fairfield
Sacramento
Woodland
Napa
Santa Rosa
Ukiah
Chico
Yuba City
Sacramento River
Sacramento Valley
mento Valley
Bodega Bay
San Francisco
Berkeley
Oakland
San Mateo
Palo Alto
Sunnyvale
San Jose
Santa Clara
Fremont
San Francisco Bay
Monterey Bay
Marina
Seaside
Santa Cruz
Watsonville
Salinas
Monterey
Santa Lucia Range
Gilroy
Los Banos
Madera
Clovis
Fresno
Sanger
Reedley
Selma
Hanford
Tulare
Visalia
Porterville
Delano
Oildale
Bakersfield
San Joaquin Valley
Sierra Nevada
Lodi
Stockton
Manteca
Turlock
Modesto

Lake Powell

Grand Canyon

Colorado River

Lake Mead

Lake Mohave

ARIZONA

North Las Vegas
Las Vegas
Henderson

Death Valley

Mount Whitney
14 496ft

Ridgecrest

Lancaster
Palmdale
Victorville
Apple Valley

Mojave Desert

San Bernardino
Riverside
Santa Ana
Fallbrook
Vista
Oceanside
Encinitas
Poway
Lakeside
National City
San Diego
Chula Vista
Escondido

Chocolate Mountains

Colorado River

Brawley
El Centro

MEXICO

50

Pasadena
Glendale
Los Angeles
Long Beach
Huntington Beach
Ventura
Oxnard
Santa Barbara

CALIFORNIA

Santa Maria
Lompoc
Arroyo Grande
San Luis Obispo
Atascadero

Santa Catalina Island
Gulf of Santa Catalina
Santa Rosa Island
Santa Cruz Island
San Nicolas Island
San Clemente Island

Indio
Palm Springs

42

50

153

PACIFIC OCEAN

OCEAN

HAWAII

Niihau
Kauai
Lihue
Wahiawa
Oahu
Honolulu
Kaneohe
Molokai
Lanai
Wailuku
Maui
Hilo
Hawaii

PACIFIC OCEAN

2000m/6562ft
1000m/3281ft
500m/1640ft
200m/656ft
Sea level

0 km   200
0 miles   200

ATION
-4000m   -3000m   -2000m   -1000m   -500m   Below sea level   0   100m   250m   500m   1000m   2000m   4000m

-13 124ft   -9843ft   -6562ft   -3281ft   -1640ft   -820ft/-250ft   0   328ft   820ft   1640ft   3281ft   6562ft   13 124ft

USA: THE SOUTHWEST

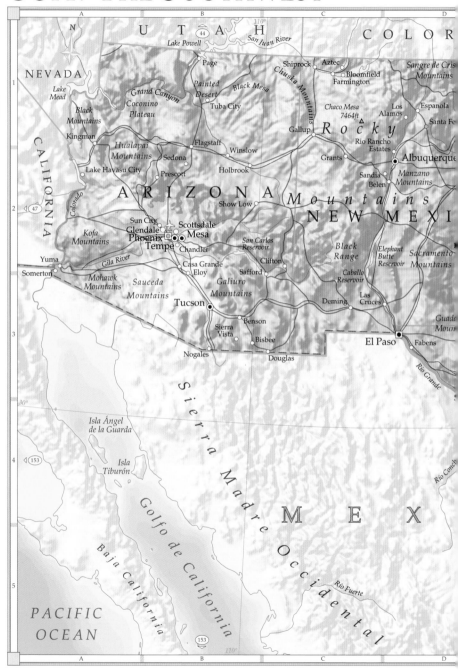

UTAH

Lake Powell

San Juan River

COLOR

NEVADA

Shiprock   Aztec
Page   Bloomfield
                              Farmington

Lake   Grand Canyon   Painted   Black Mesa   Chuska Mountains   Sangre de Cris
Mead   Coconino   Desert   Mountains
                    Plateau   Tuba City   Chaco Mesa
Black   7464ft   Los   Espanola
Mountains   Gallup   Rocky   Alamos
Kingman   Santa Fe
                    Hualapai   Flagstaff   Rio Rancho
                    Mountains   Winslow   Estates   Albuquerque
Lake Havasu City   Sedona   Grants
                    Prescott   Holbrook   Sandia   Manzano
                                                                      Belen   Mountains

A R I Z O N A   Show Low   M o u n t a i n s
                                                              NEW MEXI

Kofa   Sun City   Scottsdale   Black   Elephant   Sacramento
Mountains   Glendale   Mesa   San Carlos   Range   Butte   Mountains
                Phoenix   Reservoir   Reservoir
Yuma   Tempe   Chandler   Caballo
                            Casa Grande   Clifton   Reservoir
Somerton   Gila River Eloy   Safford
                Mohawk   Sauceda   Galiuro   Deming   Las   Guade
                Mountains   Mountains Mountains   Cruces   Moun

                            Tucson   El Paso   Fabens

                            Sierra   Benson
                            Vista   Bisbee   Rio Grande

                    Nogales   Douglas

30°

                    Isla Ángel
                    de la Guarda

                    Isla
                    Tiburón   Río Conch

S i e r r a   M E X

            B a j a   C a l i f o r n i a   G o l f o   d e   C a l i f o r n i a   M a d r e   O c c i d e n t a l

PACIFIC   Río Fuerte
OCEAN

                                    153
                    110°

0 km   200

0 miles   200

POPULATION

○ Less than 50,000   ○ 50,000 -100,000   ◉ 100,000 - 500,000   ■ Over 50

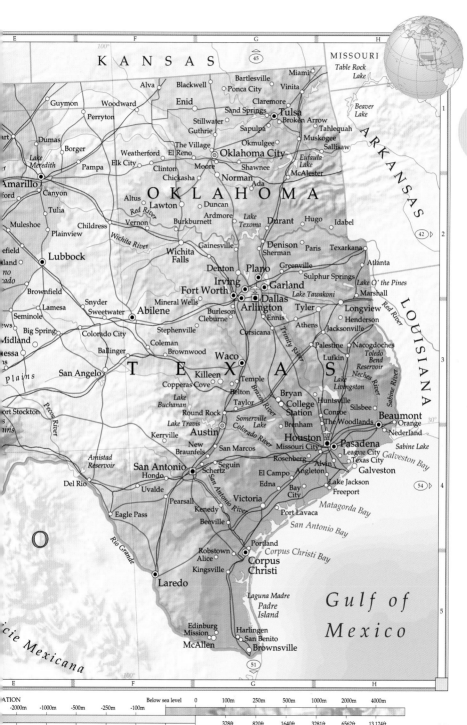

E   F   G   H

MISSOURI
Table Rock Lake

Guymon   Woodward   Alva   Blackwell   Bartlesville   Miami
Perryton   Enid   Ponca City   Vinita   Beaver Lake
Sand Springs   Claremore
Dumas   Stillwater   **Tulsa**
Borger   Weatherford   Guthrie   Sapulpa   Broken Arrow   Tahlequah
Lake Meredith   El Reno   The Village   Okmulgee   Muskogee   Sallisaw
Pampa   Elk City   **Oklahoma City**   Eufaula Lake
Canyon   Clinton   Moore   Shawnee   McAlester
Amarillo   Altus   **O K L A H O M A**   Norman   Ada
Tulia   Lawton   Duncan   Hugo   Idabel
Muleshoe   Childress   *Red River*   Ardmore   *Lake Texoma*   Durant
Plainview   Vernon   Burkburnett   Denison   Paris   Texarkana
Wichita River   Gainesville   Sherman   Atlanta
Lubbock   Wichita Falls   Denton   **Plano**   Greenville   *Lake O' the Pines*
Brownfield   Irving   Sulphur Springs   Marshall
Snyder   Mineral Wells   **Fort Worth**   **Garland**   *Lake Tawakoni*
Lamesa   Sweetwater   **Abilene**   Burleson   **Dallas**   Tyler   Longview
Seminole   Cleburne   **Arlington**   Henderson
Big Spring   Colorado City   Stephenville   Ennis   Athens   Jacksonville
Midland   Coleman   Corsicana   Palestine   Nacogdoches
Ballinger   Brownwood   Lufkin   *Toledo Bend Reservoir*
plains   **T E X A S**   **Waco**   *Neches River*   *Sabine River*
San Angelo   Killeen   Temple   *Lake Livingston*
Pecos River   Copperas Cove   Belton   Bryan   Huntsville
Lake Buchanan   Round Rock   Taylor   **College Station**   Conroe   Silsbee
Lake Travis   *Somerville Lake*   Brenham   The Woodlands   **Beaumont**
Kerrville   **Austin**   *Colorado River*   **Houston**   Orange
Fort Stockton   New Braunfels   San Marcos   Missouri City   **Pasadena**   Nederland
    San Antonio River   Rosenberg   League City   Texas City   *Sabine Lake*
Amistad Reservoir   **San Antonio**   Seguin   Alvin   *Galveston Bay*
Del Rio   Hondo   Schertz   El Campo   Angleton   Galveston
    Uvalde   Edna   Bay City   Lake Jackson
Eagle Pass   Pearsall   Kenedy   Victoria   Port Lavaca   Freeport
Rio Grande   Beeville   *Matagorda Bay*
    San Antonio Bay
    Portland   *Corpus Christi Bay*
    Robstown   **Gulf of Mexico**
    Alice   **Corpus Christi**
Laredo   Kingsville
    Laguna Madre Padre Island
    Edinburg   Mission
    McAllen   Harlingen   San Benito
    Brownsville

Sierra Mexicana

ATION
-2000m   -1000m   -500m   -250m   -100m   Below sea level   0   100m   250m   500m   1000m   2000m   4000m
-6562ft   -3281ft   -1640ft   -820ft   -328ft   -164ft/-50m   0   328ft   820ft   1640ft   3281ft   6562ft   13 124ft

49

MEXICO

POPULATION

○ Less than 50,000   ○ 50,000 -100,000   ◉ 100,000 - 500,000   ■ Over 50

0 km   400

0 miles   400

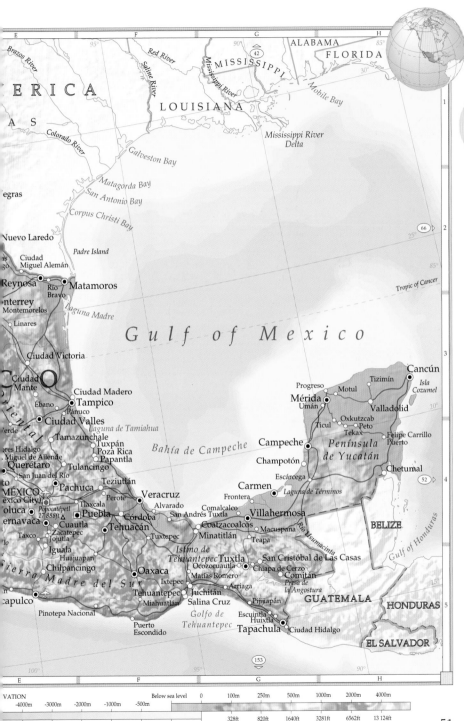

E F G H

95° 90° 85°

ALABAMA
FLORIDA

MISSISSIPPI

Red River

Saline River

Mississippi River

30°

ERICA

AS

LOUISIANA

Colorado River

1

Galveston Bay

Mississippi River
Delta

Matagorda Bay

San Antonio Bay

egras

Corpus Christi Bay

66

25° 85°

2

Nuevo Laredo

Padre Island

Ciudad
Miguel Alemán

Reynosa

Río
Bravo

Matamoros

Tropic of Cancer

nterrey
Montemorelos

Laguna Madre

Linares

Gulf of Mexico

Ciudad Victoria

3

Cancún

Ciudad
Mante

Progreso
Tizimín
Isla
Cozumel

Ciudad Madero

Mérida
Motul

Ébano
Tampico

Umán

20°

Pánuco

Valladolid

Ciudad Valles

Oxkutzcab

Tamazunchale

Laguna de Tamiahua

Ticul

Peto
Tekax

Felipe Carrillo
Puerto

res Hidalgo

Tuxpán
Poza Rica

Bahía de Campeche

Campeche

**Península
de Yucatán**

Miguel de Allende

Papantla

Champotón

Querétaro

Tulancingo

Chetumal

San Juan del Río

Teziutlán

Escárcega

52

to

Pachuca

MÉXICO
exico City)

Carmen

Frontera

Laguna de Términos

4

Perote

Veracruz

oluca

Tlaxcala

Alvarado

Comalcalco

Popocatépetl
17,888ft △

Puebla

Córdoba

San Andrés Tuxtla

Villahermosa

ernavaca

Cuautla

Tehuacán

Coatzacoalcos

Macuspana

BELIZE

Taxco

Zacatepec
Jojutla

Tuxtepec

Minatitlán

Teapa

Río Usumacinta

Gulf of Honduras

Iguala

Istmo de
Tehuantepec

Tuxtla

San Cristóbal de Las Casas

lo

Huajuapan

Ocozocuautla

Chiapa de Cerzo

Chilpancingo

Oaxaca

Matías Romero

Comitán

15°

Ixtepec

Sierra

Madre del Sur

Tehuantepec

Juchitán

Arriaga

Presa de
la Angostura

capulco

Miahuatlán

Salina Cruz

Pijijiapán

GUATEMALA

HONDURAS

Pinotepa Nacional

Golfo de
Tehuantepec

Escuintla
Huixtla

5

Puerto
Escondido

153

Tapachula
Ciudad Hidalgo

EL SALVADOR

100° 95° 90°

E F G H

CENTRAL AMERICA

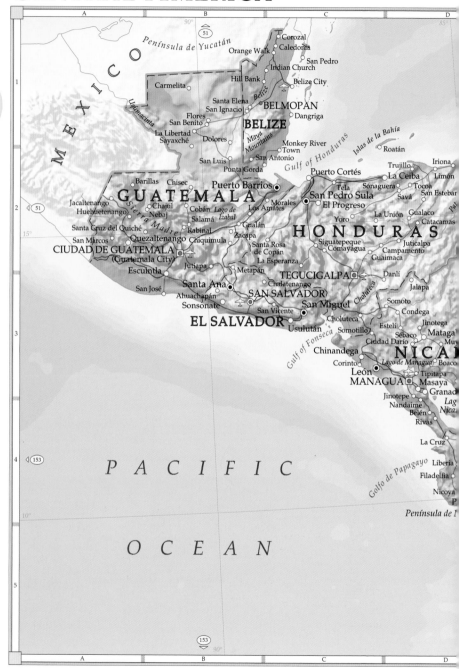

Península de Yucatán

MEXICO

90°

85°

A   B   C   D

51

Corozal
Orange Walk   Caledonia
San Pedro
Indian Church
Hill Bank   Belize City
Carmelita

Santa Elena
San Ignacio   BELMOPAN
Flores   BELIZE
San Benito   Dangriga
La Libertad   Dolores
Sayaxché   Maya Mountains
San Luis   Monkey River Town
San Antonio
Punta Gorda   Gulf of Honduras   Islas de la Bahía   Roatán

Barillas   Chisec   Puerto Barrios   Puerto Cortés   Trujillo   Iriona
GUATEMALA   Tela   La Ceiba   Limón
Chajul   Morales   San Pedro Sula   Sónaguera   Tocoa   San Esteban
Jacaltenango   Nebaj   Cobán   Lago de   Los Amates   El Progreso   Savá
Huehuetenango   Salamá   Izabal   Yoro   La Unión   Gualaco   Catacamas
Santa Cruz del Quiché   Rabinal   Gualán   HONDURAS
San Marcos   Chiquimula   Zacapa   Siguatepeque   Campamento
Quezaltenango   Santa Rosa   Comayagua   Guaimaca
CIUDAD DE GUATEMALA   de Copán   La Esperanza
(Guatemala City)   Jutiapa   Metapán   TEGUCIGALPA   Danlí
Escuintla   Chalatenango   Jalapa
San José   Santa Ana   Somoto
Ahuachapán   SAN SALVADOR   Condega
Sonsonate   San Vicente   San Miguel   Estelí   Jinotega
EL SALVADOR   San Vicente   Choluteca   Somotillo   Sébaco   Mataga
Usulután   Gulf of Fonseca   Ciudad Darío   NICA   Muy
Chinandega   Boaco
Corinto   Lago de Managua
León   Tipitapa
MANAGUA   Masaya   Granad
Jinotepe   Lag
Nandaime   Nica
Belén
Rivas
La Cruz
Liberia
Filadelfia
Nicoya
P
Península de l

Sierra Madre

Usumacinta   Belize

51

15°

10°

153

153

90°

P A C I F I C

O C E A N

0 km   200
0 miles   200

POPULATION

○ Less than 50,000   ○ 50,000 -100,000   ◉ 100,000 - 500,000   ◼ Over 50

52

N

54

Islas Santanilla
(to Honduras)

Bajo Nuevo
(to Colombia)

aratasca
Lempira

55

Cayos Miskitos

Tuapi
Puerto Cabezas

C a r i b b e a n

Isla de Providencia
(to Colombia)

Prinzapolka

Barra de Río Grande

S e a

aguna de Perlas

Islas del Maíz

luefields

Isla de San Andrés
(to Colombia)

Punta Gorda

Bahía de San Juan del Norte

San Juan del Norte

58

rto Viejo

COSTA RICA   Istmo de Panamá
edia   Siquirres   El Porvenir
AN JOSÉ   Limón   Portobelo
Cartago   Colón   Ailigandí   Gulf
ripó ▲   Guabito   Cristóbal   Cordillera de San Blas   of Darien
ande   Almirante   Panama Canal   Chepo
530ft   Laguna   Golfo de los   Lago Gatún   San Miguelito
os Aires   Talamanca   de Chiriquí   Mosquitos   Balboa   PANAMÁ   Puerto Obaldía
rtés ○   ▲ Volcán Barú 11 401ft   Capira   Bahía de Panamá   Chimán
mar Sur   Boquete   Serranía de Tabasará   Penonomé   La Palma
○   La Concepción   Aguadulce   Archipiélago   Isla   Yaviza
o   P A N A M A   de las Perlas   del Rey   El Real
de Osa   David   Santiago   Chitré   Garachiné
Golfo Dulce   Golfo   Ocú   Las Tablas
de Chiriquí   Guarumal   Jaqué
Isla de Coiba   Isla   Península de
Cébaco   Azuero   Golfo
de Panamá
58

COLOMBIA

Serranía del Darién

VATION   Below sea level   0   100m   250m   500m   1000m   2000m   4000m
-4000m   -3000m   -2000m   -1000m   -500m
328ft   820ft   1640ft   3281ft   6562ft   13 124ft
-13 124ft   -9843ft   -6562ft   -3281ft   -1640ft   -820ft/-250m   0

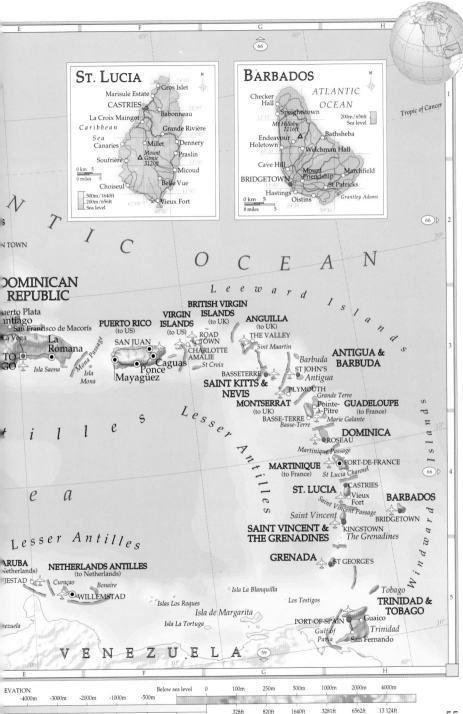

E F G H

65° 60°

66

ST. LUCIA

Gros Islet
Marisule Estate
CASTRIES
Babonneau
La Croix Maingot
Caribbean Grande Rivière
Sea Canaries Millet Dennery
Soufrière Mount Praslin
Ginnie
3120ft Micoud
Belle Vue
Choiseul
Vieux Fort

0 km 10
0 miles 5

■ 500m/1640ft
■ 200m/656ft
□ Sea level

14°05'
14°00'
13°55'
13°50'
13°45'
61°00' 61°55'

N

BARBADOS

Checker *ATLANTIC*
Hall *OCEAN*
Speightstown
Mt Hillaby 200m/656ft
1116ft Sea level
Endeavour Bathsheba
Holetown
Welchman Hall
Cave Hill
Mount Marchfield
BRIDGETOWN Friendship
Hastings St Patricks
Oistins Grantley Adams

0 km 5
0 miles 5

13°15'
13°10'
13°05'
13°00'
59°35' 59°30'

N

Tropic of Cancer

66

ATLANTIC OCEAN

N TOWN 20°

Leeward Islands

DOMINICAN
REPUBLIC

uerto Plata 3
ntiago
San Francisco de Macorís
La Vega
TO La BRITISH VIRGIN
Romana ISLANDS
Isla Saona (to UK)
Mona Passage VIRGIN ANGUILLA
PUERTO RICO ISLANDS (to UK)
Isla (to US) (to US) THE VALLEY
Mona SAN JUAN ROAD
TOWN Sint Maarten
CHARLOTTE
AMALIE Barbuda ANTIGUA &
Caguas St Croix BARBUDA
Mayagüez Ponce ST JOHN'S
BASSETERRE Antigua
SAINT KITTS & PLYMOUTH
NEVIS Grande Terre
MONTSERRAT Pointe- GUADELOUPE
(to UK) à-Pitre (to France)
BASSE-TERRE Marie Galante
Basse-Terre
DOMINICA
ROSEAU 15°

Lesser Antilles Martinique Passage

MARTINIQUE FORT-DE-FRANCE
(to France) St Lucia Channel
4
ST. LUCIA CASTRIES
Vieux
Fort
Saint Vincent Passage BARBADOS
Saint Vincent
BRIDGETOWN
SAINT VINCENT & KINGSTOWN
THE GRENADINES The Grenadines

e a GRENADA ST GEORGE'S *Windward Islands*

Lesser Antilles
Tobago

ARUBA NETHERLANDS ANTILLES
(Netherlands) (to Netherlands) Isla La Blanquilla
JESTAD Curaçao Bonaire Los Testigos
WILLEMSTAD Islas Los Roques TRINIDAD &
Isla de Margarita TOBAGO 5
Isla La Tortuga PORT-OF-SPAIN Guaico
ezuela Gulf of Trinidad 10°
Paria San Fernando

V E N E Z U E L A

59

E F G H

70° 60°

SOUTH AMERICA

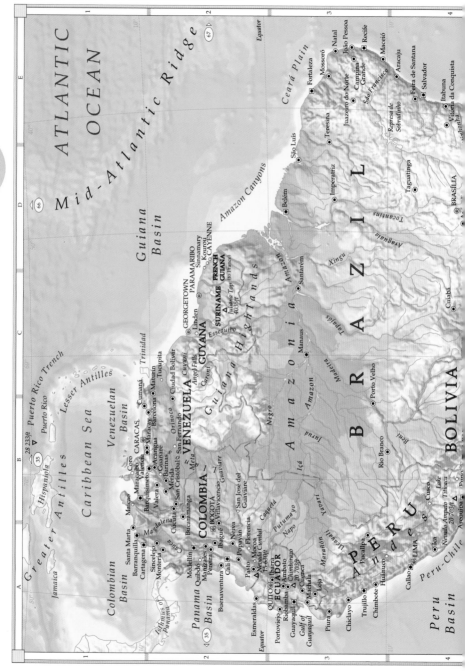

ATLANTIC OCEAN

Mid-Atlantic Ridge

Guiana Basin

Ceará Plain

Equator

Mossoró
Natal
João Pessoa
Fortaleza
Campina Grande
São Francisco
Recife
Maceió
Aracaju
Juazeiro do Norte
Feira de Santana
Salvador
Itabuna
Vitória da Conquista

Teresina
São Luís
Imperatriz
Represa de Sobradinho
Taguatinga
BRASÍLIA

Belém
Tocantins
Araguaia

Amazon Canyons

Guiana Basin

GEORGETOWN
PARAMARIBO
Sinnamary
CAYENNE
Kourou
Xingu
Cuiabá

SURINAME
FRENCH GUIANA
Juliana Top 4035ft

GUYANA
Linden
Essequibo
Courantyne
Demerara
Berbice

Caroni
Angel Falls
Cuyuni
Santarém
Amazon
Tapajós

Guiana Highlands

Trinidad
Cumaná
Barcelona
Maturín
Tucupita
Ciudad Bolívar
Orinoco
San Fernando

B R A Z I L

A m a z o n i a

Coro
Maracaibo
CARACAS
Maracay
Valencia
Aragua
Barinas
Guanare
VENEZUELA
Meta
Negro
Madeira
Manaus
Porto Velho
Beni
B O L I V I A

Puerto Rico Trench
28 233ft

Puerto Rico

Greater Antilles
Lesser Antilles
Caribbean Sea
Venezuelan Basin

Jamaica

Hispaniola

Santa Marta
Barranquilla
Cartagena
Sincelejo
Montería
Maicao
Valera
San Cristóbal
Bucaramanga
Cúcuta
Medellín
Quibdó
Manizales
Pereira
Buenaventura
Cali
Popayán
Pasto
San José del Guaviare
Villavicencio
Neiva
Florencia
Mocoa
COLOMBIA
BOGOTÁ
Ibagué
Guaviare
Caquetá
Putumayo
Napo
Içá
Juruá
Purus
Rio Branco
Madre

Iça
Yavarí
Ucayali
Marañón
Río Branco

Colombian Basin
Panama Basin

Isthmus of Panama

Equator

Esmeraldas
QUITO
Ibarra
ECUADOR
Portoviejo
Ambato
Riobamba
Chimborazo 20 703ft
Guayaquil
Gulf of Guayaquil
Cuenca
Machala
Loja
Cotopaxi
Nevada Cumbal 15 630ft
Nevado Ampato 20 703ft

Piura
Chiclayo
Chimbote
Trujillo
Pacasmayo
Huánuco
Pucallpa
LIMA
Callao
Ica
Cusco
Lake Titicaca
Arequipa
Nevado Ampato

P E R U

A n d e s

Peru Basin
Peru-Chile Trench

0 km 500
0 miles 500

POPULATION

○ Less than 50,000   ◌ 50,000 -100,000   ● 100,000 - 500,000   ■ Over 500

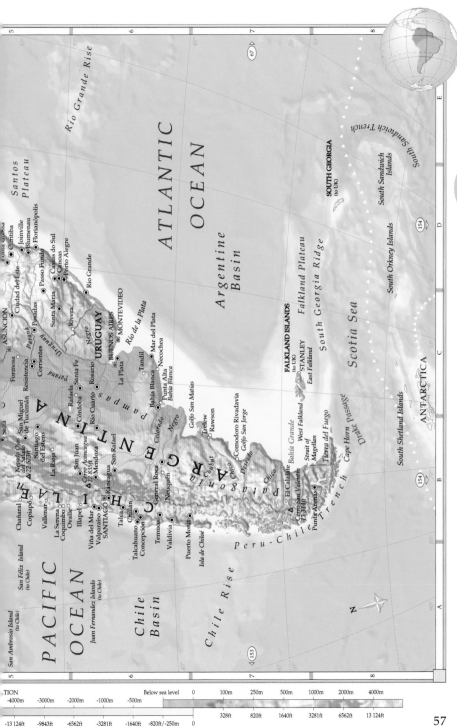

NORTHERN SOUTH AMERICA

POPULATION

○ Less than 50,000   ○ 50,000 -100,000   ◉ 100,000 - 500,000   ◼ Over 5

ATLANTIC

OCEAN

SAINT VINCENT & THE GRENADINES

BARBADOS

GRENADA

nquilla
de
rita
Los Testigos
La Asunción
Porlamar
Tobago
Carúpano
The Dragon's Mouth
TRINIDAD &
o La Cruz
Cariaco
Güiria
Gulf of
TOBAGO
lona
Paria
Mateo
Trinidad
co
Maturín
The Serpent's Mouth
aura
El Tigre
Tucupita
Morawhanna
Orinoco
Ciudad Guayana
Baramanni
d o
Upata
Charity
bar
Embalse de Guri
Matthews
Suddie
El Callao
Ridge
Baramita
Spring Garden
E L A
Parika
GEORGETOWN
El Dorado
Cuyuni
Aurora
New
Peters Mine
Bartica
Amsterdam
PARAMARIBO
Totness
Nieuw Amsterdam
St-Laurent-du-Maroni
Kamarang
Rockstone
Boskamp
Galibi
Sinnamary
Linden
Nieuw
W. J. van
Kourou
GUYANA
Nickerie
Apoera
Blommesteinmeer
CAYENNE
Mount Roraima
Orealla
9220ft
Serra Pacaraima
Kaaimanston
Grand-
Santi
Kurupukari
SURINAME
Cottica
FRENCH
Juliana Top
4037ft
GUIANA
Lethem
Kumaka
Teboe Top
(to France)
Camopi
Coroni
Coppename
Ouanary
St-Georges

a
n
a
Dadanawa
H
i
g
h
l
a
n
d
s
Isherton
Biloku
Acarai Mountains
Equator

R
A
Z
I
L

a
m
a
z
o
n
i
a
Amazon
Purus
Tapajós

ATION
-4000m -3000m -2000m -1000m -500m   Below sea level 0   100m 250m 500m 1000m 2000m 4000m

-13 124ft -9843ft -6562ft -3281ft -1640ft -820ft/-250m 0   328ft 820ft 1640ft 3281ft 6562ft 13 124ft

59

WESTERN SOUTH AMERICA

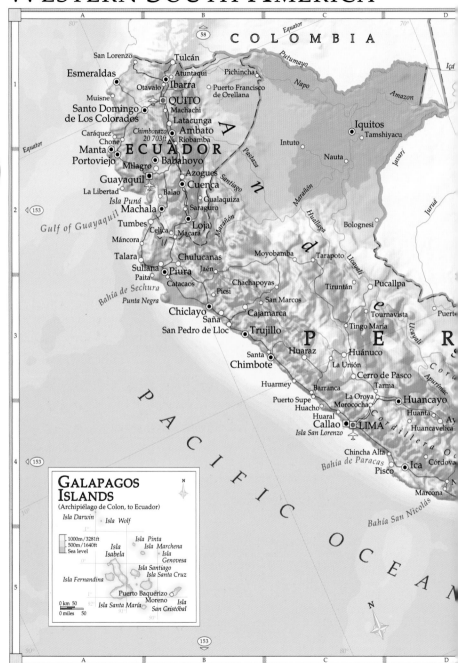

COLOMBIA

San Lorenzo
Tulcán
Esmeraldas
Atuntaqui
Pichincha
Muisne
Otavalo
Ibarra
Puerto Francisco
de Orellana
QUITO
Santo Domingo
Machachi
de Los Colorados
Latacunga
Caráquez
Chimborazo
Ambato
Chone
20 703ft
Riobamba
Manta
ECUADOR
Portoviejo
Milagro
Babahoyo
Azogues
Guayaquil
Cuenca
La Libertad
Balao
Isla Puná
Gualaquiza
Machala
Saraguro
Tumbes
Loja
Celica
Macará
Máncora
Talara
Chulucanas
Sullana
Jaén
Piura
Paita
Catacaos
Chachapoyas
Picsi
Bahía de Sechura
San Marcos
Punta Negra
Chiclayo
Cajamarca
Saña
San Pedro de Lloc
Trujillo
Santa
Huaraz
Chimbote
La Unión
Huarmey
Barranca
Puerto Supe
La Oroya
Huacho
Morococha
Huaral
Callao
LIMA
Isla San Lorenzo
Chincha Alta
Bahía de Paracas
Pisco
Ica

Putumayo
Napo
Amazon
Içá
Iquitos
Tamshiyacu
Intuto
Nauta
Pastaza
Santiago
Marañón
Bolognesi
Moyobamba
Tarapoto
Tiruntán
Pucallpa
Tournavista
Tingo María
Huánuco
Cerro de Pasco
Tarma
Huancayo
Huanta
Huancavelica
Córdova
Marcona

Jataeri
Juruá
Andes
Huallaga
Ucayali
PERÚ
Cordillera Oc
Apurímac
Bahía San Nicolás

PACIFIC OCEAN

Equator

Gulf of Guayaquil

GALAPAGOS ISLANDS
(Archipiélago de Colon, to Ecuador)

Isla Darwin
Isla Wolf

1000m/3281ft
500m/1640ft
Sea level

Isla Pinta
Isla Marchena
Isla
Isla
Isabela
Genovesa
Isla Santiago
Isla Santa Cruz
Isla Fernandina
Puerto Baquérizo
Moreno
Isla
Isla Santa María
San Cristóbal

0 km   50
0 miles   50

0 km   400
0 miles   400

POPULATION
○ Less than 50,000   ○ 50,000 -100,000   ◉ 100,000 - 500,000   ◼ Over 50

ATION

					Below sea level	0	100m	250m	500m	1000m	2000m	4000m
-4000m	-3000m	-2000m	-1000m	-500m								
-13 124ft	-9843ft	-6562ft	-3281ft	-1640ft	-820ft/-250m	0	328ft	820ft	1640ft	3281ft	6562ft	13 124ft

BRAZIL

58

VENEZUELA

Cordillera Occidental

Cordillera Oriental

A n d e s

COLOMBIA

Uraricoera
Boa Vista
Caracaraí

Guiana

Roraima

Hig

Pico da Neblina
3014m

Río Negro

R

Equator

ECUADOR

Napo

Putumayo

Japurá

Amazon

Tefé

Mana

Coari

Juruá

Galápagos Islands
(Archipiélago de Colón)
(to Ecuador)

Marañón

Javari

A m a z o

Amazonia

153

A n d e s

Ucayali

Japiim
Feijó

Acre

Purus

c e

Humaitá

B R

Madeira

Porto Vel

Rondôn

Ji

Chapada

PERU

Guaporé

Mamoré

Lake
Titicaca

BOLIVI

Cordillera Oriental

Lago Poopó

3

Desierto de Atacama

Cordillera Occidental

PACIFIC OCEAN

153

Pilco

Tropic of Capricorn

CHILE

Bermejo

A n d e s

Gran

Salado

N

153

ARGENT

POPULATION

O Less than 50,000   O 50,000 -100,000   ◉ 100,000 - 500,000   ▣ Over 50

0 km   600

0 miles   600

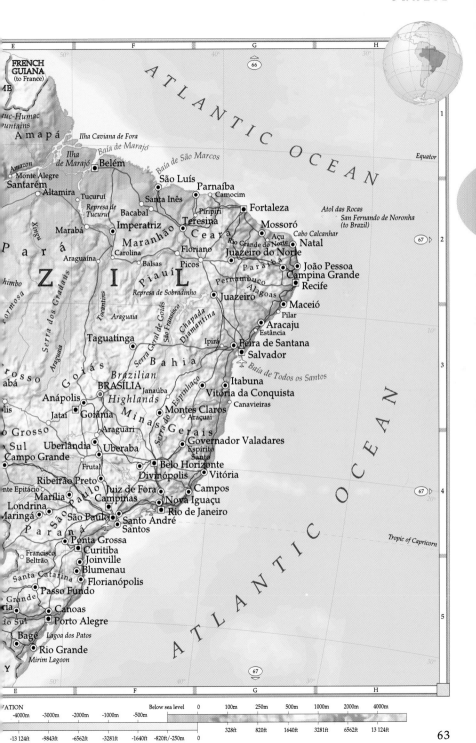

FRENCH GUIANA
(to France)
ME

uc-Humac
untains

A m a p á

Ilha Caviana de Fora

Baía de Marajó

Amazon
Monte Alegre
Santarém
Altamira

Ilha
de Marajó
Belém

Baía de São Marcos

Tucuruí
Represa de
Tucuruí
Bacabal

Santa Inês

São Luís

Parnaíba
Camocim

Piripiri
Teresina

Fortaleza

Atol das Rocas
San Fernando de Noronha
(to Brazil)

Equator

Marabá
Imperatriz

M a r a n h ã o
Carolina

C e a r á
Floriano

Mossoró
Açu
Rio Grande do Norte
Cabo Calcanhar
Natal

Araguaína

Balsas
Picos

Juazeiro do Norte

P a r a í b a
João Pessoa
Campina Grande
Recife

Z

P i a u í
L

P e r n a m b u c o
A l a g o a s
Pilar

Represa de Sobradinho

Juazeiro
Maceió

himbo

Serra dos Gradaús

Xingu

P a r á

rmosa

rosso
abá

Araguaia

Tocantins

Serra Gral de Goiás

São Francisco

Chapada
Diamantina

Aracaju
Estância

Taguatinga

B a h i a

Ipirá
Feira de Santana
Salvador

Baía de Todos os Santos

Serra do Espinhaço

Brazilian
BRASÍLIA
Highlands
Janaúba

M i n a s

Itabuna
Vitória da Conquista
Canavieiras

Anápolis
Jataí
Goiânia

Montes Claros
Araçuaí

o Grosso

Araguari
Uberlândia
Uberaba

G e r a i s
Espírito
Santo
Governador Valadares

Frutal
Belo Horizonte
Divinópolis
Vitória

Campo Grande
Sul

Ribeirão Preto

São Paulo

Juiz de Fora
Campinas

Campos
Nova Iguaçu
Rio de Janeiro

nte Epitácio
Londrina
Marília
Maringá

P a r a n á
São Paulo
Santo André
Santos

Tropic of Capricorn

Francisco
Beltrão

Ponta Grossa
Curitiba
Joinville
Blumenau
Florianópolis

Santa Catarina

Grande
ria
o Sul

Passo Fundo

Canoas
Porto Alegre

Bagé
Lagoa dos Patos

Y

Rio Grande
Mirim Lagoon

A T L A N T I C   O C E A N

A T L A N T I C   O C E A N

66

67

ATION
-4000m -3000m -2000m -1000m -500m

Below sea level 0 100m 250m 500m 1000m 2000m 4000m

328ft 820ft 1640ft 3281ft 6562ft 13 124ft

-13 124ft -9843ft -6562ft -3281ft -1640ft -820ft/-250m 0

SOUTHERN SOUTH AMERICA

0 km   200

0 miles   200

POPULATION

○ Less than 50,000   ○ 50,000 -100,000   ◉ 100,000 - 500,000   ◼ Over 50

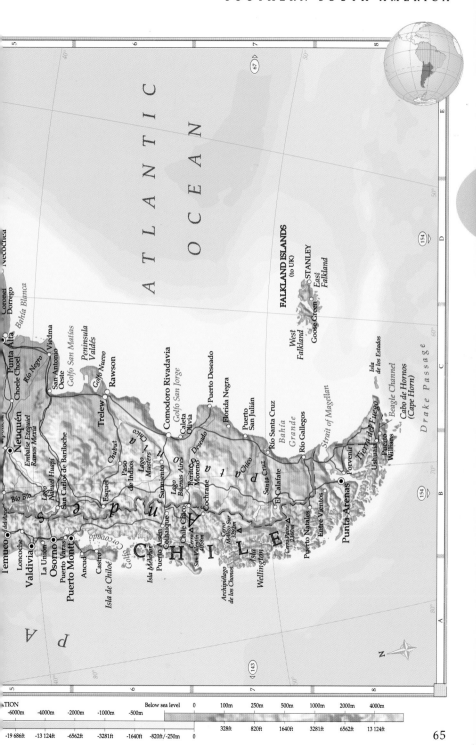

ATLANTIC

OCEAN

FALKLAND ISLANDS
(to UK)

STANLEY

West
Falkland

East
Falkland

Goose Green

Drake Passage

Isla
de los Estados

Cabo de Hornos
(Cape Horn)

Beagle Channel

Strait of Magellan

Tierra del Fuego

Porvenir

Ushuaia
Puerto
Williams

Punta Arenas

Río Gallegos

Río Santa Cruz

Bahía
Grande

Puerto Natales

Entre Vientos

Cerro Paine
2600m

Wellington

Isla

Archipiélago
de los Chonos

Cerro San Valentín
4058m

Cerro
Mellizo Sur
3292m

El Calafate

Santa Cruz

Perito
Moreno

Cochrane

Chile Chico

Lago
Buenos Aires

Paso
de Indios

Sarmiento

Lago
Musters

Coyhaique

Puerto Aisén

Corcovado

Golfo

Isla Melchor

Isla de Chiloé

Ancud

Castro

Puerto Montt

Puerto Varas

Osorno

La Unión

Valdivia

Loncoche

Temuco

Río Bío

Embalse Ezequiel
Ramos Mexía

Neuquén

San Carlos de Bariloche

Nahuel Huapi

Esquel

Chubut

Florida Negra

Puerto
San Julián

Puerto Deseado

Comodoro Rivadavia

Golfo San Jorge

Caleta
Olivia

Deseado

Río Chico

Río Chico

Rawson

Trelew

Golfo Nuevo

Península
Valdés

Golfo San Matías

San Antonio
Oeste

Viedma

Río Negro

Choele Choel

Punta Alta

Coronel
Dorrego

Bahía Blanca

Necochea

CHILE

PATAGONIA

S   e   p   r   ú   A   N   D   E   S

N

TION

	-6000m	-4000m	-2000m	-1000m	-500m	Below sea level	0	100m	250m	500m	1000m	2000m	4000m

-19 686ft   -13 124ft   -6562ft   -3281ft   -1640ft   -820ft/-250m   0   328ft   820ft   1640ft   3281ft   6562ft   13 124ft

THE ATLANTIC OCEAN

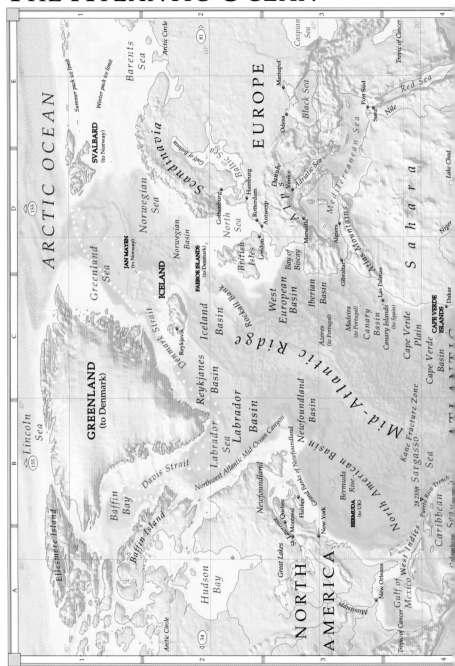

ARCTIC OCEAN

Barents Sea

EUROPE

Svalbard (to Norway)

Summer pack ice limit

Winter pack ice limit

Arctic Circle

Caspian Sea

Red Sea

Mariupol'

Black Sea

Port Said

Odesa

Nile

Suez

Scandinavia

Greenland Sea

Norwegian Sea

JAN MAYEN (to Norway)

Gulf of Bothnia

Baltic Sea

Danube

ALPS

Venice

Adriatic Sea

Hamburg

Mediterranean Sea

Sahara

Lake Chad

Gothenburg

North Sea

Rotterdam

Antwerp

Marseille

Atlas Mountains

Algiers

London

Niger

ICELAND

FAEROE ISLANDS (to Denmark)

Norwegian Basin

British Isles

Bay of Biscay

Gibraltar

Las Palmas

Denmark Strait

Reykjavik

Iceland Basin

Rockall Bank

West European Basin

Iberian Basin

Madeira (to Portugal)

Canary Basin

Cape Verde

CAPE VERDE ISLANDS

Dakar

GREENLAND (to Denmark)

Reykjanes Basin

Mid-Atlantic Ridge

Azores (to Portugal)

Canary Islands (to Spain)

Cape Verde Plain

Cape Verde Basin

ATLANTIC

Lincoln Sea

Baffin Bay

Davis Strait

Labrador Sea

Labrador Basin

Newfoundland Basin

Kane Fracture Zone

Sargasso Sea

Ellesmere Island

Baffin Island

Northwest Atlantic Mid-Ocean Canyon

Newfoundland

Grand Banks of Newfoundland

Bermuda Rise

North American Basin

Puerto Rico Trench

Hudson Bay

Great Lakes

Québec

Montreal

St. Lawrence

Halifax

New York

BERMUDA (to UK)

Caribbean Sea

Gulf of West Indies

NORTH AMERICA

Tropic of Cancer

Gulf of Mexico

New Orleans

Mississippi

Major ports

0 km 1000

0 miles 1000

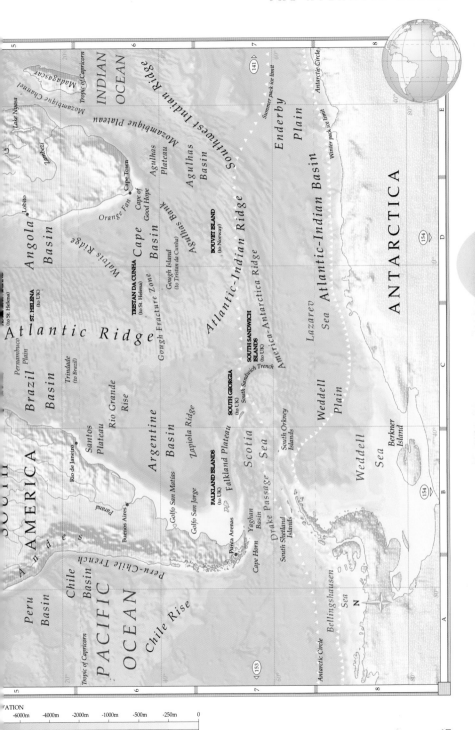

INDIAN OCEAN

Tropic of Capricorn

Madagascar

Lake Nyasa

Mozambique Channel

Zambezi

Mozambique Plateau

Southwest Indian Ridge

Summer pack ice limit

Winter pack ice limit

Antarctic Circle

Enderby Plain

Agulhas Plateau

Agulhas Basin

Cape Town

Cape of Good Hope

Orange Fan

Agulhas Bank

Angola Basin

Lobito

Walvis Ridge

Atlantic-Indian Ridge

BOUVET ISLAND (to Norway)

ANTARCTICA

Atlantic-Indian Basin

Lazarev Sea

Cape Basin

TRISTAN DA CUNHA (to St. Helena)

Gough Island (to Tristan da Cunha)

Gough Fracture Zone

ST. HELENA (to UK)

(to St. Helena)

Pernambuco Plain

Atlantic Ridge

Brazil Basin

Trindade (to Brazil)

Rio Grande Rise

America-Antarctica Ridge

SOUTH SANDWICH ISLANDS (to UK)

South Sandwich Trench

Weddell Plain

SOUTH GEORGIA (to UK)

Santos Plateau

Rio de Janeiro

Argentine Basin

Zapiola Ridge

FALKLAND ISLANDS (to UK)

Falkland Plateau

Scotia Sea

South Orkney Islands

Weddell Sea

Berkner Island

SOUTH AMERICA

Andes

Paraná

Buenos Aires

Golfo San Matías

Golfo San Jorge

Punta Arenas

Yaghan Basin

Cape Horn

Drake Passage

South Shetland Islands

Bellingshausen Sea

Peru Basin

Chile Basin

Chile-Chile Trench

Peru-Chile Trench

PACIFIC OCEAN

Chile Rise

Tropic of Capricorn

N

141

153

154

154

E

D

C

B

A

20°

30°

40°

50°

60°

70°

80°

VATION

| -6000m | -4000m | -2000m | -1000m | -500m | -250m | 0 |

| -19 686ft | -13 124ft | -6562ft | -3281ft | -1640ft | -820ft | 0 |

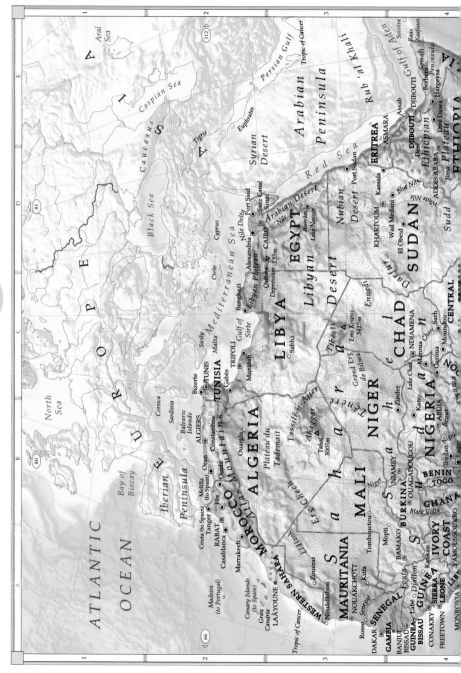

POPULATION

○ Less than 50,000   ○ 50,000 -100,000   ◉ 100,000 - 500,000   ▣ Over 50

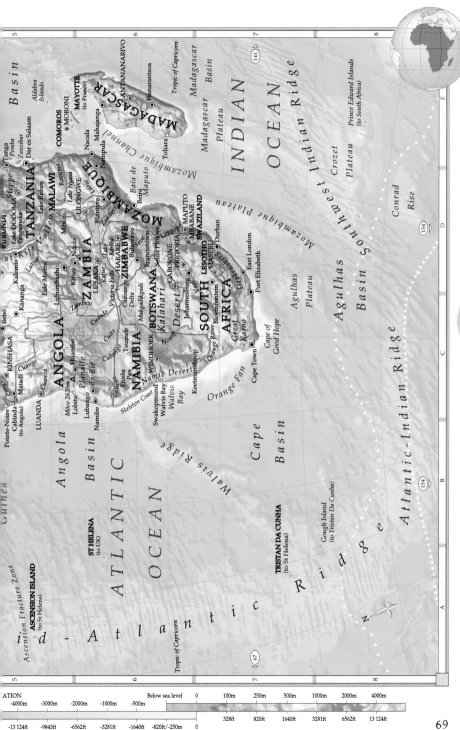

Basin

Aldabra
Islands

ANTANANARIVO

Flanarantsoa

Tropic of Capricorn

141

Madagascar
Basin

MAYOTTE
(to France)

Mahajanga

COMOROS
MORONI

MADAGASCAR

Nacala

Nampula

Madagascar
Plateau

INDIAN

OCEAN

Crozet

Prince Edward Islands
(to South Africa)

Tanga
Pemba
Zanzibar
Dar es Salaam

Toliara

Southwest Indian Ridge

Conrad
Rise

BURUNDI

Ilebo

KINSHASA
Matadi Cuango

Pointe-Noire
Cabinda
(to Angola)

LUANDA

Lobito
Lubango
Namibe

ST HELENA
(to UK)

TANZANIA

Lake DODOMA Steppe

Rift Valley MALAWI

LILONGWE

Lake Nyasa

Blantyre

Ruvuma

Lake Rukwa

Kalemie

Lake Tanganyika

Kananga

Lubumbashi

Lake Mweru

Luvua

Ndola

Kitwe

ZAMBIA

LUSAKA

Kabwe

Kafue

Zambezi

Victoria Falls

ANGOLA

Huambo

Planalto

Môco 2620m

lo Bié

Cuando

Cuito

Cubango

Cunene

Etosha
Pan

Tsumeb

WINDHOEK

NAMIBIA

Swakopmund
Walvis Bay

Walvis
Bay

Keetmanshoop

Skeleton Coast

Namib Desert

Bafa de
Maputo

Beira

MOZAMBIQUE

Mozambique Channel

Zambezi

Lake
Kariba

Mazowe

HARARE

ZIMBABWE

Bulawayo

Gwe

Gweru

Limpopo

MAPUTO

MBABANE

SWAZILAND

MASERU

LESOTHO

PRETORIA

Gaborone

CABORONE

Sehithwa

BOTSWANA

Makgadikgadi

Okavango
Delta

Kalahari
Desert

Nosob

Orange River

Francistown

Johannesburg

Bloemfontein

SOUTH

AFRICA

Great

Karoo

East London

Port Elizabeth

Durban

Cape of
Good Hope

Cape Town

Mozambique Plateau

Agulhas
Plateau

Agulhas Basin

Guinea

Ascension Fracture Zone

ASCENSION ISLAND
(to St Helena)

Angola

Basin

ATLANTIC

OCEAN

Walvis Ridge

Orange Fan

Cape

Basin

Atlantic-Indian Ridge

TRISTAN DA CUNHA
(to St Helena)

Gough Island
(to Tristan Da Cunha)

Mid-Atlantic Ridge

Tropic of Capricorn

67

154

154

N

ATION

					Below sea level	0	100m	250m	500m	1000m	2000m	4000m
-4000m	-3000m	-2000m	-1000m	-500m								
-13 124ft	-9843ft	-6562ft	-3281ft	-1640ft	-820ft/-250m	0		328ft	820ft	1640ft	3281ft	6562ft	13 124ft

Northwest Africa

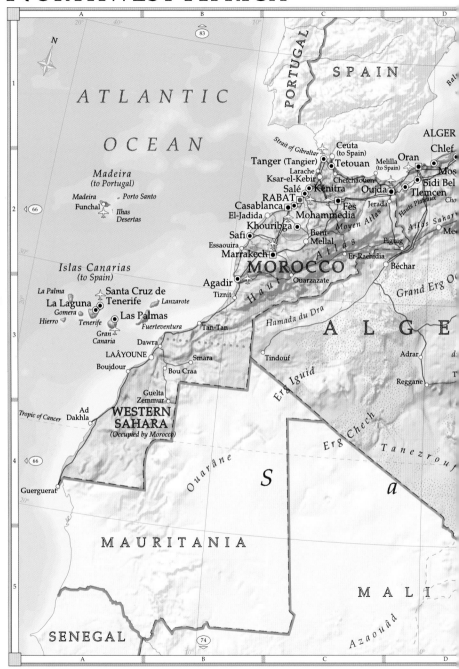

ATLANTIC

OCEAN

PORTUGAL

SPAIN

Madeira
(to Portugal)
Madeira • *Porto Santo*
Funchal ✈ • *Ilhas*
Desertas

Bal

ALGER

Chlef

Strait of Gibraltar Ceuta
(to Spain)
Tanger (Tangier) • Tetouan
Larache Melilla Oran Mos
Ksar-el-Kebir (to Spain) Sidi Bel
Chefchaouen
Salé Kenitra Oujda Tlemcen Cho
RABAT Jerada
Casablanca Fès
El-Jadida Mohammedia *Moyen Atlas* Hauts Plateaux
Safi Beni- *Atlas Sahar*
Essaouira Mellal Figuig Me
Marrakech Er-Rachidia
MOROCCO Béchar
Agadir Ouarzazate
Tiznit *Grand Erg O*
Haut
Hamada du Dra **ALGE**
Tan-Tan

Islas Canarias
(to Spain)
La Palma ✈ Santa Cruz de
La Laguna Tenerife *Lanzarote*
Gomera Tindouf Adrar d
Hierro *Tenerife* Las Palmas Reggane T
Gran
Canaria *Fuerteventura*
Dawra *Erg Iguid*
LAÂYOUNE Smara
Boujdour Bou Craa
Erg Chech
Guelta *Tanezrouf*
Zemmur
Tropic of Cancer Ad
Dakhla **WESTERN**
SAHARA S a
(Occupied by Morocco)
Ouarâne

Guerguerat

MAURITANIA

M A L I

SENEGAL

Azaouâd

0 km 400

0 miles 400

POPULATION

○ Less than 50,000   ○ 50,000 -100,000   ◉ 100,000 - 500,000   ◼ Over 50

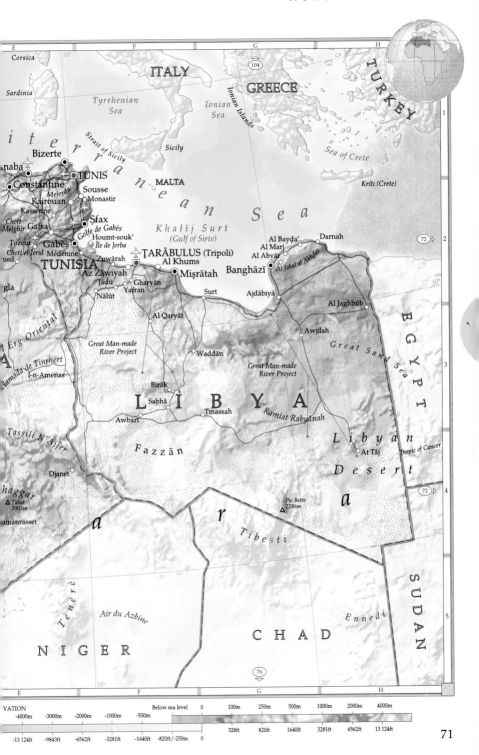

Corsica

Sardinia

ITALY

GREECE

TURKEY

Tyrrhenian
Sea

Ionian
Sea

Ionian Islands

Sicily

Sea of Crete

Kríti (Crete)

Bizerte

naba

Constantine

TUNIS

Sousse

Monastir

Kasserine

Kairouan

Chott
Melghir Gafsa

Sfax

Golfe de Gabès

Houmt-souk'

Île de Jerba

MALTA

Khalīj Surt
(Gulf of Sirte)

Tozeur

Chott el Jerid

Gabès

Médenine

ued

gla

TUNISIA

Zuwārah

Az Zāwiyah

ṬARĀBULUS (Tripoli)

Al Khums

Jādū

Gharyān

Yafran

Nālūt

Miṣrātah

Surt

Ajdābiyā

Al Bayda'

Al Marj

Al Abyār

Banghāzī

Al Jabal al Akhdar

Darnah

72

Al Qaryāt

Great Man-made
River Project

Waddān

Al Jaghbūb

Awjilah

Great Sand Sea

Alamadá de Tinrhert

I-n-Amenas

Great Man-made
River Project

L   I   B   Y   A

Birāk

Sabhā

Tmassah

Ramlat Rabyānah

Libyan

EGYPT

Tassili N'Ajjer

Awbārī

Fazzān

a

Desert

At Tāj

Tropic of Cancer

72

haggar

△Tahat
3005m

Djanet

r

Pic Bette
△ 2286m

Tibesti

20°

amanrasset

Ténéré

Air du Azbine

Ennedi

SUDAN

N   I   G   E   R

C   H   A   D

76

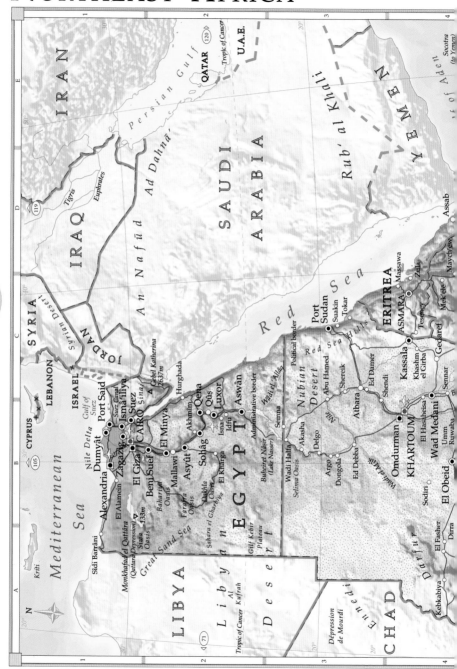

0 km 400

0 miles 400

POPULATION

○ Less than 50,000   ○ 50,000 -100,000   ◉ 100,000 - 500,000   ◼ Over 5

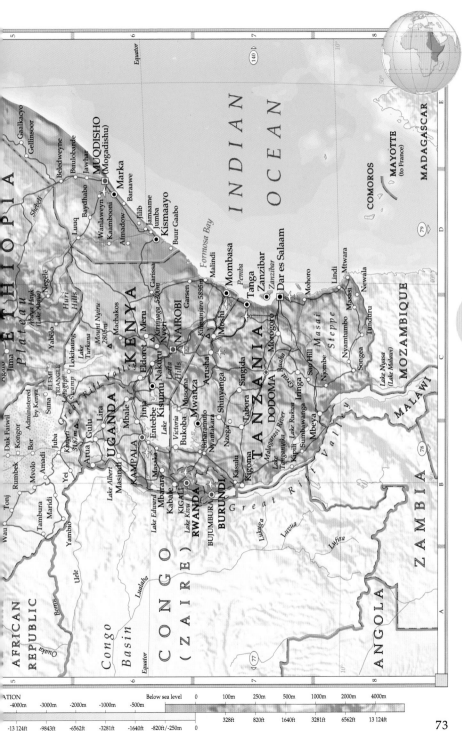

ETHIOPIA

Plateau

Jima

Gaalkacyo
Gellinsoor

MUQDISHO
(Mogadishu)
Marka
Baraawe

Beledweyne
Buulobarde
Jawhar

Negēlē
Yabēlo

Luuq
Baydhabo
Wanlaweyn
Kaambooni

Hilib
Jamaame
Jumba
Kismaayo
Buur Gaabo

Afmadow

INDIAN OCEAN

Huri
Hills

Formosa Bay

Malindi

Mombasa
Pemba
Tanga
Zanzibar
Zanzibar
Dar es Salaam

Mohoro

Lindi
Mtwara
Newala

MAYOTTE
(to France)

COMOROS

MADAGASCAR

Garissa
Garsen

KENYA

Machakos
Meru
Nyeri
NAIROBI
Kirinyaga 5200m
Kilimanjaro 5895m
Moshi

Mount Nyiru
2805m

Lake Turkana

Eldoret
Nakuru
Loita
Hills
Arusha

MOZAMBIQUE

Masai
Steppe

Nyamtumbo
Songea

Lake Nyasa
(Lake Malawi)

MALAWI

Tundru
Masasi

Negēlē

ILEMI
TRIANGLE
Administered
by Kenya

Lokitaung
Suna

Kisumu
Jinja
Entebbe
KAMPALA

Bukoba

Musoma
Mwanza
Biharamulo
Nyantakara

Shinyanga
Singida
DODOMA

Morogoro

Iringa

Sao Hill
Njombe

Great Ruaha

Lake
Eyasi

TANZANIA

CENTRAL
AFRICAN
REPUBLIC

Juba
Bor

Dk Faiwil
Kongor

Mvolo
Amadi

Rumbek

Toni
Tambura
Maridi

Wau
Yambio

Yei

Arua
Gulu

Kitgum
3187m

Lira

UGANDA

Lake
Albert

Masindi

Mbale

Masaka
Mbarara
Kabale

KIGALI
RWANDA

BUJUMBURA
BURUNDI

Kasulu
Kigoma

Kabwe

Lake Edward

Lake Kivu

Lake
Victoria

Lake
Tanganyika

Tabora
Nzega

Malagarasi River

Lake Rukwa
Sumbawanga
Mbeya
Kipili

CONGO
(ZAIRE)

Congo
Basin

Lualaba

Uele

Bomu

Ubangi

Equator

Great Rift Valley

Lukuga

Luvua

Lufira

ZAMBIA

ANGOLA

Equator

140

79

78

77

ATION

Below sea level								
-4000m	-3000m	-2000m	-1000m	-500m	0	100m	250m	500m	1000m	2000m	4000m
-13 124ft	-9843ft	-6562ft	-3281ft	-1640ft	-820ft/-250m	0	328ft	820ft	1640ft	3281ft	6562ft	13 124ft

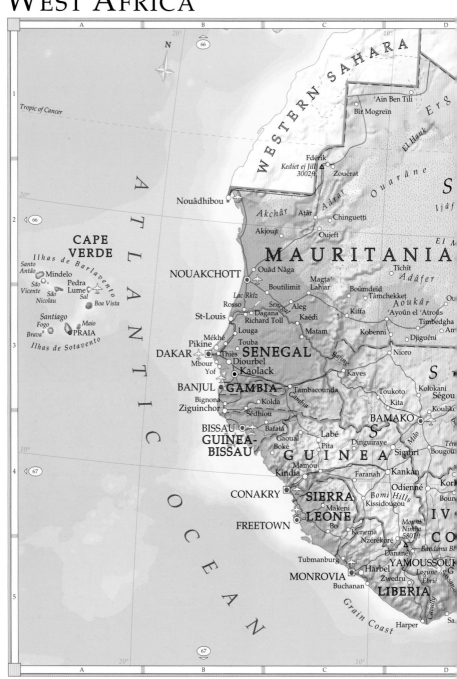

AFRICA

WESTERN SAHARA

N
66

Tropic of Cancer

'Aïn Ben Tili
Bîr Mogreïn

Fdérik
Kediet ej Jill
3002ft
Zouérat

El Hank
Erg

Ouarâne

Nouâdhibou

Akchâr Atâr *Adrar*
Chinguetti

S

Ijâf

CAPE
VERDE

Ilhas de Barlavento

Santo
Antão
Mindelo
São
Vicente
São
Nicolau
Pedra
Lume
Sal
Boa Vista

Santiago
Fogo
Brava
PRAIA
Maio

Ilhas de Sotavento

A
T
L
A
N
T
I
C

Akjoujt

NOUAKCHOTT
Ouâd Nâga
Boutilimit

Magta'
Lahjar

Oujeft

MAURITANIA

El M

Tîchît
Adâfer

Boûmdeïd
Tâmchekket

Aoukâr

'Ayoûn el 'Atroûs
Timbedgha

Ou

Am

Djiguéni

S

Senegal
Aleg
Kaédi

Rosso
Dagana
Richard Toll
Louga
Kiffa

Kobenni

Nioro

Lac Rkîz
St-Louis

Matam

Mékhé
Pikine
DAKAR
Mbour
Yof

Touba
Thiès
Diourbel
Kaolack

SENEGAL

Bafing

Kayes

BANJUL
GAMBIA
Bignona
Ziguinchor
Kolda
Sédhiou

Tambacounda

Gambia

Toukoto
Kita

Kolokani
Ségou

Koulik

BISSAU
GUINEA-
BISSAU
Bafatá
Boké
Gaoual
Labé
Pita

Dinguiraye

BAMAKO

S

Tén
Bougou

GUINEA

Siguiri

Kankan

Mamou
Kindia

Faranah

Odienné

Kor

Boun

CONAKRY

SIERRA

Bomi Hills
Kissidougou

IV
CO

Makeni

FREETOWN
LEONE
Bo

Kenema
Nzérékoré

Mount
Nimba
5801ft

Dananė

Bandama Bl

A

YAMOUSSOU
G

Tubmanburg
Harbel
Zwedru

*Lagune
Ébrié*

MONROVIA
Buchanan

LIBERIA

O
C
E
A
N

Grain Coast

Harper

Sa

Cavally

67

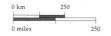

0 km   250

0 miles   250

POPULATION

○ Less than 50,000   ○ 50,000 -100,000   ◉ 100,000 - 500,000   ◼ Over 5

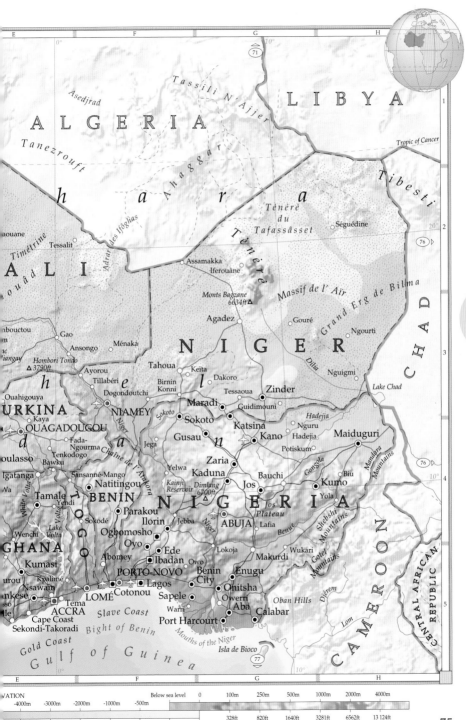

LIBYA

ALGERIA

Asedjrad

Tassili N'Ajjer

71

Tanezrouft

Tropic of Cancer

Tibesti

h   a   r   a

Ahaggar

Ténéré du Tafassâsset

Séguédine

20° 2

Adrar des Ifôghas

Timetrine

Tessalit

Assamakka

Iferouâne

76

MALI

aouâne

ALI

Ténéré

Massif de l'Air

Monts Bagzane 6634ft

Grand Erg de Bilma

Gouré

Ngourti

mbouctou m

Gao

Ansongo

Ménaka

Agadez

NIGER

CHAD

iangay

Hombori Tondo △ 3790ft

Ayorou

Tahoua

Keïta

Dakoro

Gouré

Ngourti

Nguigmi

Lake Chad

3

h

Tillabéri

Birnin Konni

e

Tessaoua

Zinder

l

Ouahigouya

Dogondoutchi

Maradi

Guidimouni

Hadejia

URKINA

Kaya

NIAMEY

Sokoto

Sokoto

Katsina

Nguru

Hadejia

Maiduguri

OUAGADOUGOU

Gusau

Kano

Potiskum

76

d

Fada-Ngourma

Jega

Chaîne de l'Atakora

a

oulasso

Tenkodogo

Bawku

Yelwa

Zaria

Congola

Biu

Mandara Mountains

10° 4

Igatanga

Sansanné-Mango

Kaduna

Bauchi

Kumo

Yola

Na

Natitingou

Kainji Reservoir

Dimlang 6700ft

Jos

Jos Plateau

Tamale

Yendi

BENIN

n

NIGERIA

ERIA

White Volta

Sokodé

Parakou

Ilorin

Jebba

ABUJA

Lafia

Benue

Shebshi Mountains

Wenchi

Lake Volta

TOGO

Oghomosho

Oyo

Lokoja

Wukari

Gotel Mountains

GHANA

Kumasi

Abomey

Ede

Ibadan

Owo

Makurdi

CAMEROON

urou

Kpalimé

PORTO-NOVO

Benin City

Enugu

nkese

Nsawam

LOMÉ

Cotonou

Lagos

Sapele

Onitsha

Oban Hills

Djèrem

CENTRAL AFRICAN REPUBLIC

sso

Tema

Slave Coast

Warri

Owerri

Aba

Calabar

Cape Coast

Port Harcourt

Lom

Sekondi-Takoradi

Bight of Benin

Mouths of the Niger

Gold Coast

Gulf of Guinea

Isla de Bioco

77

ATION

				Below sea level	0	100m	250m	500m	1000m	2000m	4000m
-4000m	-3000m	-2000m	-1000m	-500m							
						328ft	820ft	1640ft	3281ft	6562ft	13 124ft
-13 124ft	-9843ft	-6562ft	-3281ft	-1640ft	-820ft/-250m	0					

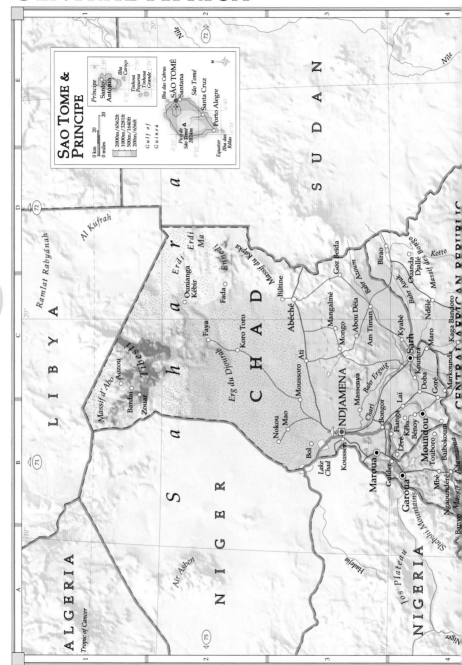

SAO TOME & PRINCIPE

0 km   20
0 miles   20

2000m / 6562ft
1000m / 3281ft
500m / 1640ft
200m / 656ft

Príncipe
Santo
António
Ilha
Caroço

Tinhosa
Pequena
Tinhosa
Grande

Ilha das Cabras
SÃO TOMÉ
Santana
São Tomé
Santa Cruz
Porto Alegre

Pico de
São Tomé
2024m

Gulf of
Guinea

Ilha das
Rolas
Equator

LIBYA

ALGERIA

Tropic of Cancer

NIGER

SUDAN

CHAD

CENTRAL AFRICAN REPUBLIC

NIGERIA

Ramlat Rabyānah

Al Kufrah

Sahara

Erdi Ma

Erdi

Ennedi

Massif du Kapka

Ounianga
Kébir

Fada

Biltine

Goz Beïda

Birao

Ouanda
Djallé

Bao
Bangoran

Kotto

Massif des

Aozou

Massif d'Abo

Bardaï

Zouar

Tibesti

Faya

Koro Toro

Abéché

Mangalmé

Mongo

Am Timan

Abou Déïa

Kyabé

Maro

Markounda

Kaga Bandoro

Ndélé

Bahr Aouk

Bahr Azoum

Sarh

Kountra

Erg du Djourab

Moussoro

Ati

NDJAMENA

Massenya

Bahr Erguig

Doba

Goré

Bongor

Chari

Fianga

Laï

Kélo

Bénoy

Touboro

Baïbokoum

Moundou

Nokou

Mao

Bol

Lake
Chad

Kousséri

Yéré

Guider

Mbé

Ngaoundéré

Maroua

Garoua

Banyo

Adamaoua

Massif de

Mandara Mountains

Jos Plateau

Shebshi Mountains

Hadejia

Niger

0 km   400
0 miles   400

POPULATION

○ Less than 50,000   ○ 50,000 -100,000   ◉ 100,000 - 500,000   ■ Over 50

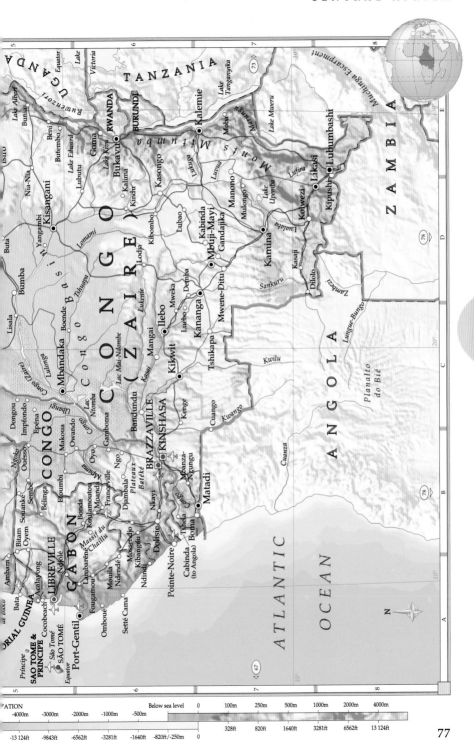

UGANDA
Lake Albert
Lake Edward
Lake Victoria
Equator
Ruwenzori
Bunia
Beni
Butembo
Nia-Nia
Kisangani
Yangambi
Buta
Lomami
Bumba
Lisala
Mbandaka
Lake Kivu
RWANDA
Goma
Bukavu
BURUNDI
Kalima
Kindu
Kasongo
Kibombo
Kalemie
Moba
Lukuga
Manono
Mulongo
Lake Upemba
Lake Mweru
Lake Tanganyika
Lake Tanganyika
Mitumba
Lualaba
Lufira
Lukuga
Likasi
Kolwezi
Kipushi
Lubumbashi
ZAMBIA
Mushinga Escarpment
Lubao
Lodja
Lukenie
Kabinda
Mbuji-Mayi
Gandajika
Kamina
Kasaji
Dilolo
Zambezi
Lungue-Bungo
Lubutu
CONGO (ZAIRE)
Mweka
Dembo
Sankuru
Demba
Mwene-Ditu
Kananga
Tshikapa
Luebo
Ilebo
Mangai
Kikwit
Lac Mai-Ndombe
Kwilu
ANGOLA
Planalto do Bié
Bumbo
Boende
Tshuapa
Congo Basin
Lac Ntomba
Luilaka
Lukonga
Lac Tumba
Bandundu
Kenge
Cuango
Kwango
Cuanza
Matadi
Mbanza-Ngungu
KINSHASA
BRAZZAVILLE
Kwilu
Kwango
Dongou
Impfondo
Epéna
Ouesso
Makoua
Owando
Sembé
Mossaka
Gamboma
Oyo
Ngo
Plateaux Batéké
Franceville
Djambala
Ngoko
Souanké
Bélinga
Bioumbi
Bonda
Koulamoutou
Moanda
Mossendjo
Kibangou
Dolisie
Tshela
Boma
Nkayi
Pointe-Noire
Cabinda (to Angola)
CONGO
Ubangi
Mbéné
GABON
Massif du Chaillu
Lambaréné
Ndjolé
LIBREVILLE
Oyem
Bitam
Ambam
Bata
Acalayong
Cocobeach
EQUATORIAL GUINEA
SÃO TOMÉ & PRÍNCIPE
São Tomé
Príncipe
Port-Gentil
Setté Cama
Omboué
Fougamou
Mouila
Ndendé
Kibangou
Ndindi
TANZANIA
Lake Kivu
Lake Victoria
ATLANTIC OCEAN
N

ATION
| -4000m | -3000m | -2000m | -1000m | -500m | Below sea level | 0 | 100m | 250m | 500m | 1000m | 2000m | 4000m |
| -13 124ft | -9843ft | -6562ft | -3281ft | -1640ft | -820ft/-250m | 0 | | 328ft | 820ft | 1640ft | 3281ft | 6562ft | 13 124ft |

SOUTHERN AFRICA

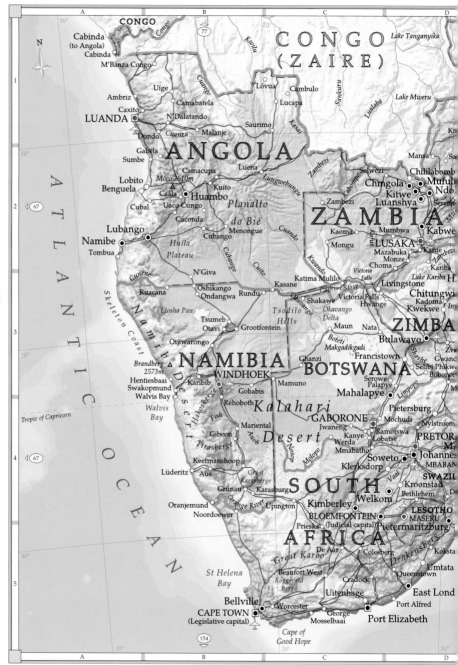

0 km   400

0 miles   400

POPULATION

○ Less than 50,000   ○ 50,000 -100,000   ◉ 100,000 - 500,000   ◼ Over 50

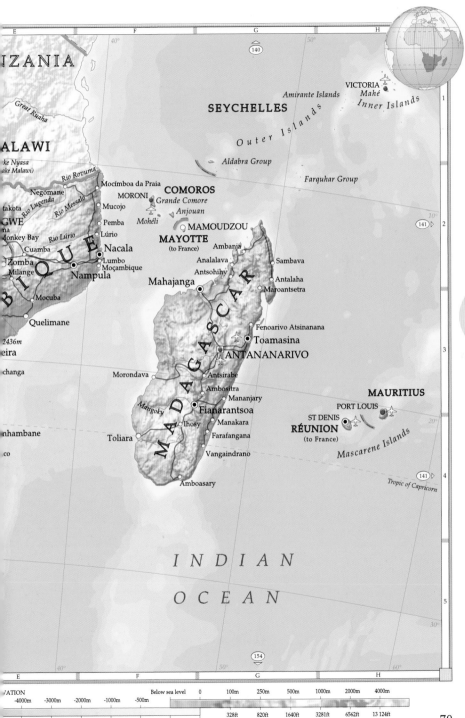

IZANIA

ALAWI

Great Ruaha

ke Nyasa
ake Malawi

GWE

Negómane
takota
Monkey Bay
Cuamba
Zomba
Milange
Nampula
Mocuba
Quelimane

2436m
eira

changa

nhambane

co

Rio Rovuma
Rio Messalo
Rio Lúrio

Mocímboa da Praia
Mucojo
Pemba
Lúrio
Lumbo
Moçambique
Nacala

BIQUE

Mahajanga

Morondava

Mangoky

Toliara

40°

SEYCHELLES

Amirante Islands

Outer Islands

Aldabra Group

COMOROS
MORONI Grande Comore
Anjouan
Mohéli
MAMOUDZOU
MAYOTTE
(to France)

140

VICTORIA
Mahé
Inner Islands

Farquhar Group

10°

141

Ambanja
Analalava
Antsohihy

Sambava

Antalaha
Maroantsetra

M A D A G A S C A R

Fenoarivo Atsinanana
Toamasina
ANTANANARIVO
Antsirabe
Ambositra
Mananjary
Fianarantsoa
Ihosy
Manakara
Farafangana
Vangaindrano

Amboasary

MAURITIUS

PORT LOUIS
ST DENIS
RÉUNION
(to France)

Mascarene Islands

20°

141

Tropic of Capricorn

I N D I A N

O C E A N

30°

154

60°

VATION
-4000m -3000m -2000m -1000m -500m

-13 124ft -9843ft -6562ft -3281ft -1640ft -820ft/-250m

Below sea level 0 100m 250m 500m 1000m 2000m 4000m

0 328ft 820ft 1640ft 3281ft 6562ft 13 124ft

REYKJAVÍK

ICELAND
Vatnajökull

Arctic Circle

Norwegian Basin

Norwegian Sea

Iceland Basin

Faeroe-Iceland Ridge

FAEROE ISLANDS
(to Denmark)

Trondhe

Faeroe-Shetland Trough
Shetland Islands

Rockall Bank

Outer Hebrides

Orkney Islands

Bergen

Stavanger

OSLO

Porcupine Plain

Glasgow

Edinburgh

British Isles

Belfast

REPUBLIC OF IRELAND

DUBLIN

UNITED KINGDOM

Liverpool

Manchester

North Sea

Gothenbur

Ålborg

Jylland

DENMARK

Odense

Celtic Sea

Birmingham

Cardiff

LONDON

NETHERLANDS

Hamb

Elb

Azores-Biscay Rise

ATLANTIC OCEAN

West European Basin

English Channel
Channel Islands

le Havre

AMSTERDAM

Rotterdam

BELGIUM

BRUSSELS

Liège

Bonn

Hannove

BERLIN

LUXEMBOURG

GERMANY

Rennes

PARIS

LUXEMBOURG

Frankfurt am Main

Nantes

Orléans

Loire

Strasbourg

Stuttgart

Mid-Atlantic Ridge

Biscay Plain

Bay of Biscay

Bordeaux

Lyon

Garonne

Munich

Zürich

LIECH.

Innsbruck

Iberian Plain

A Coruña

Bilbao

FRANCE

Mont Blanc
4807m

SWITZERLAND

BERN

SL(

Massif Central

Toulouse

Rhône

Milan

Po

Venice

Tri

Porto

Douro

Cordillera Cantábrica

Pyrénées

Turin

Bologna

PORTUGAL

Iberian Peninsula

Zaragoza

ANDORRA

Nice

MONACO

Appenni

SAN MARI

LISBON

MADRID

Tagus

Ebro

Marseille

Pisa

SPAIN

Guadalquivir

Barcelona

Corsica

VATICAN CITY

ROME

Madeira
(to Portugal)

Seville

Strait of Gibraltar

Málaga

Valencia

Mallorca

Menorca

Naples

Eivissa

Palma

Sardinia

Balearic Islands

GIBRALTAR
(to UK)

Ceuta
(to Spain)

Balearic Plain

Tyrrhenian Sea

Cagliari

Cos

Melilla
(to Spain)

M e d i t e r r a

Palerr

Canary Islands
(to Spain)

N

Sicily

AFRICA

Atlas Mountains

MALTA
VALLETTA

0 km   500

0 miles   500

POPULATION

○ Less than 50,000   ◎ 50,000 -100,000   ◉ 100,000 - 500,000   ◼ Over 50

E 30° 40° F 50° 60° G 70° H 80°

155

Barents Sea

North Cape

Ostrov Kolguyev

Arctic Circle

Ob'

80° 1

Murmansk
*Kola
Peninsula*

Irtysh

FINLAND

*White
Sea*

Archangel

Northern Dvina

R U S S I A N

112 2

Tampere

Lake Onega

Perm'

rku HELSINKI

Lake Ladoga

Vologda

F E D E R A T I O N 70°

TALLINN

Saint Petersburg

Yaroslavl'

Ufa

50°

ESTONIA

Nizhniy
Novgorod

Kazan'

LATVIA

MOSCOW

Ul'yanovsk

Orenburg

JANIA

Kaunas

Vitsyebsk

Samara

Ural

grad VILNIUS

MINSK

Volga

Babruysk

Voronezh

Aral Sea

Syr Darya

BELARUS

Homyel'

Brest

*Pripet
Marshes*

Don

Ural

Amu Darya

Bug

KIEV

*Dnieper
Lowland
Dnieper*

Kharkiv

Volgograd

L'viv

Dniester

UKRAINE

Dnipropetrovs'k

Donets'k

Astrakhan'

40°

Chernivtsi

Rostov-na-Donu

A

60° 112 4

rian Mountains

MOLDOVA

CHIŞINĂU

j-Napoca

Odesa

Stavropol'

S

OMANIA

Crimea

*Sea of
Azov*

C a u c a s u s

Braşov

Simferopol'

El'brus 5642m

Caspian Sea

E

BUCHAREST

Constanţa

Black Sea

I

Danube

BULGARIA

Varna

ountains

SOFIA

Burgas

*Aegean
Sea*

A n a t o l i a P l a t e a u

S

CE

ATHENS

Piraeus

A

Irákleio

Cyprus

*Syrian
Desert*

118

Tigris

Kūhhā-ye Zagros

Crete

30° 40° 50° H

E F G

ATION
-4000m -3000m -2000m -1000m -500m

Below sea level 0 100m 250m 500m 1000m 2000m 4000m

-13 124ft -9843ft -6562ft -3281ft -1640ft -820ft/-250m 0

328ft 820ft 1640ft 3281ft 6562ft 13 124ft

NORTHWEST TERRITORIES

Devon
Island

Ellesmere Is

Nares Strait

Siorapaluk *Inglefield*
Qaanaaq *Land*

Pituffik

Savissivik

Knud Rasmus

*Hudson
Bay*

*Southampton
Island*

*Foxe
Basin*

CANADA

Qimusseriarsuaq

*Baffin
Bay*

Kullorsuaq
Nuussuaq

Tasiusaq

Upernavik

Nettilling Lake
Amadjuak Lake

Baffin Island

*Péninsule
d'Ungava*

QUEBEC

Hudson Strait

Arnaud

Cumberland Sound

Frobisher Bay

Nuugaatsiaq

Uummannaq   Maarmovilik

Qeqertarsuaq

Qeqertarsuaq

Aasiaat   Ilulissat
Kangaatsiaq   Qasigianguit

Sisimiut

Davis Strait

Kong Frederik IX Land

Kangerlussuaq

GREENLA

(to Denm

*Ungava
Bay*

George

Maniitsoq

NUUK
Færingehavn

Qeqertarsuatsiaat

Paamiut

NEWFOUNDLAND & LABRADOR

Kong Frederik VI Kyst

Kong Christian

Mont Forel
11 024ft

Ammassalik

Ivittuut

*Labrador
Sea*

Narsaq
Qaqortoq
Nanortalik
Narsaq Kujallea
Uummannarsuaq

De

NORTH

ATLANT

OCEAN

0 km   400

0 miles   400

E F G H

155

ARCTIC OCEAN

Zemlya
Frantsa-Iosifa

1

*Peary
Land*

Kap Bridgman

*Wandel
Sea*

Kvitøya

Novaya
Zemlya

Nord

SVALBARD
(to Norway)

Nordaustlandet

*Kong
rederik VIII
Land*

Spitsbergen
Pyramiden
LONGYEARBYEN
Barentsberg

Kong Karls Land

Barentsøya

Edgeøya

Storfjorden

**Barents
Sea**

110

2

Danmark Havn

*Greenland
Sea*

Bjørnøya
(to Norway)

Nordkapp
(North Cape)

70°

X

Daneborg

**F
I
N
L
A
N
D**

3

Ittoqqortoormiit

ertittivaq

JAN MAYEN
(to Norway)

Arctic Circle

84

4

t

*Norwegian
Sea*

**S
W
E
D
E
N**

ICELAND

rvík
iglufjördhur Raufarhöfn
Húsavík
Akureyri
shólmur
YKJAVÍK
lfoss Djúpivogur
n *Vatnajökull*
*Hvannadalshnúkur
6952ft*
estmannaeyjar

Seydhisfjördhur
Neskaupstadhur

*Gulf
of
Bothnia*

60°

5

FAEROE ISLANDS
(to Denmark)

TÓRSHAVN

N

N O R W A Y

*Shetland
Islands*

85

E F G H

ATION -4000m -3000m -2000m -1000m -500m Below sea level 0 100m 250m 500m 1000m 2000m 4000m

328ft 820ft 1640ft 3281ft 6562ft 13 124ft

-13 124ft -9843ft -6562ft -3281ft -1640ft -820ft/-250m 0

SCANDINAVIA & FINLAND

Barents Sea

RUSSIAN FEDERATION

Arctic Circle

ARCTIC OCEAN

Varangerhalvøya
Varangerfjorden
Kirkenes
Tana
Nordkapp
(North Cape)
Magerøya
Sørøya
Laksely
Porsangen
Alta
Talvik
Kvaløya
Ringvassøy
Tromsø
Senja
Andøya
Harstad
Vesterålen
Lofoten
Vestfjorden
Bodø
Narvik
Fauske
Mo i Rana
Mosjøen
Vega
Namsos

Tana
Valjok
Karasjok
Kautokeino
Kaamanen
Ivalo
Saariselkä
Inari
Kaaresuvanto
Muonio
Kolari
Muonionjoki
Torneträsk
Kiruna
Kebnekaise
6946ft
Malmberget
Skalka
Jokkmokk
Arvidsjaur
Storuman
Storjuman
Umeälven
Vilhelmina
Lycksele
Kamberget
fjället
Borgefjellet
Ångermanna

Lapland
Finnmarksvidda

Saltanen
Sodankylä
Kitinen
Kemijärvi
Rovaniemen mlk
Kuusamo
Ounasjoki
Kolari
Tornionjoki
Kemijoki
Kemi
Tornio
Haparanda
Kalix
Boden
Luleå
Piteå
Skellefteå
Kokkola
Gällivare
Kalixälven
Luleälven

RUSSIAN FEDERATION

Suomussalmi
Kuhmo
Kajaani
Sotkamo
Oulujärvi
Oulu
Pudasjärvi
Kemijärvi
Lioki
Oulujoki
Kempele
Haukipudas
Raahe

FINLAND

Norwegian Sea

Arctic Circle

N

0 km   200
0 miles   200

POPULATION

○ Less than 50,000   ○ 50,000 -100,000   ◉ 100,000 - 500,000   ◼ Over 5

THE LOW COUNTRIES

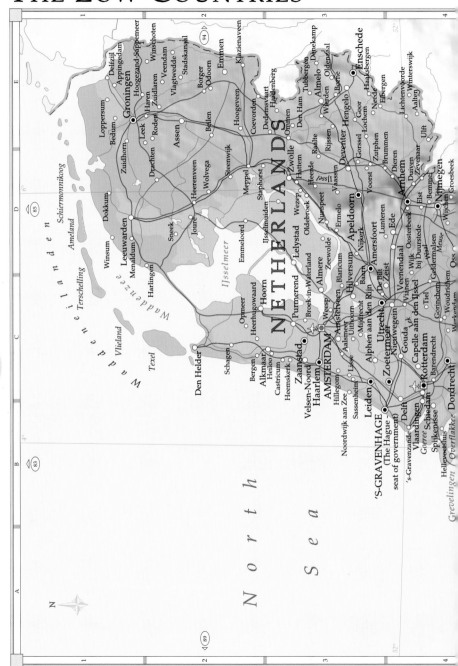

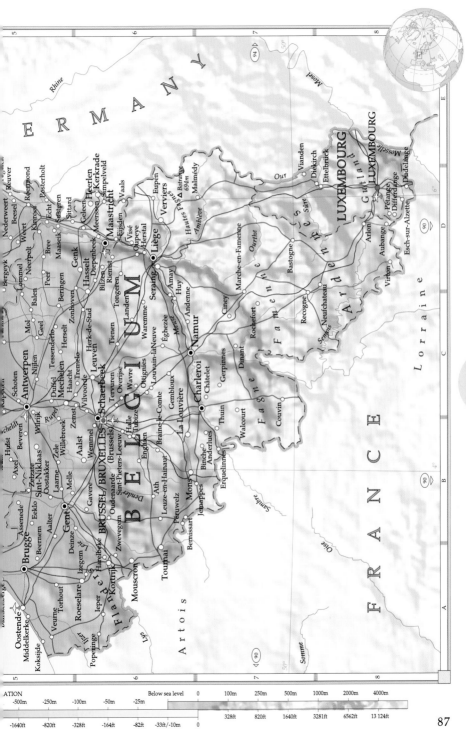

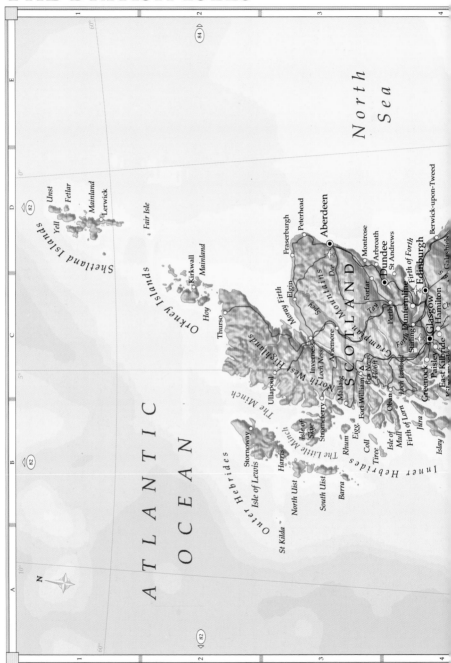

North Sea

ATLANTIC OCEAN

Shetland Islands

Unst
Fetlar
Yell
Mainland
Lerwick

Fair Isle

Orkney Islands

Kirkwall
Mainland
Hoy

Thurso

Fraserburgh
Peterhead
Aberdeen

Montrose
Arbroath
Dundee
St Andrews
Firth of Forth
Edinburgh
Berwick-upon-Tweed
Galashiels

Elgin
Dee
Moray Firth
Spey
Grampian Mountains
Forfar
Tay
Perth
Aviemore
Inverness
Loch Ness
SCOTLAND
Dunfermline
Stirling
Glasgow
Hamilton
East Kilbride
Paisley
Greenock

Ullapool
North West Highlands
Mallaig
Fort William
Ben Nevis 1406ft
Loch Lomond
Oban
Firth of Lorn
Isle of Lorn

The Minch
Isle of Skye
Stromeferry
Eigg
Rhum
Coll
Tiree
Isle of Mull
Jura
Islay

Stornoway
Harris
Isle of Lewis
The Little Minch
Outer Hebrides
Inner Hebrides

North Uist
South Uist
Barra
St Kilda

0 km   100
0 miles   100

POPULATION
○ Less than 50,000   ○ 50,000 -100,000   ◉ 100,000 - 500,000   ▣ Over

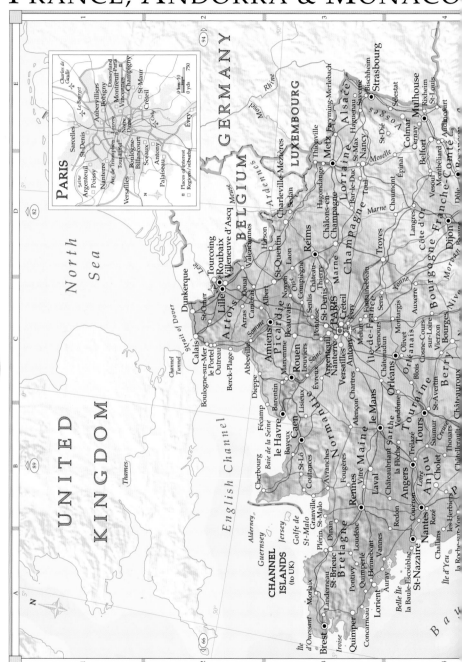

PARIS

Charles de Gaulle
Le Bourget
Sarcelles
St-Denis
Argenteuil
Poissy
Nanterre
Aubervilliers
Bobigny
Disneyland-Paris
Louvre
Montreuil-Paris
Champigny
Tour Eiffel
Notre Dame
St-Maur
Vincennes
Créteil
Versailles
Boulogne-Billancourt
Billancourt
Antony
Sceaux
Orly
Palaiseau
Evry

Seine

Places of interest
Regions/suburb

GERMANY

BELGIUM

LUXEMBOURG

Rhine

Ardennes

Thionville
Freyming-Merlebach
Metz
St-Max
Strasbourg
Bischheim
Sélestat
St-Dié
Colmar
Cernay
Mulhouse
Rixheim
St-Louis
Belfort
Montbéliard
Audincourt
Vesoul
Épinal
Dôle

Meuse
Moselle

Hagondange
Lorraine
Alsace
Savenne
Haguenau
Nancy
Bar-le-Duc
Toul

Champagne
Vosges

Côte d'Or
Bourgogne
Dijon
Franche-Comté

Charleville-Mézières
Sedan
Hirson
Vervins
Laon
St-Quentin
Noyon
Château-Thierry
Châlons-en-Champagne
Chaumont
Langres
Moreau

Marne
Marne
Yonne

Reims
St-Denis
Fontainebleau
Troyes
Sens
Auxerre
Montargis
Niève

Valenciennes
Tourcoing
Roubaix
Villeneuve d'Ascq
Lille
Douai
Cambrai
Arras
Albert
Amiens
Compiègne
Senlis
Beauvais
Pontoise
PARIS
Melun
Montereau
Montbéliard

North
Sea

UNITED

KINGDOM

Thames

Strait of Dover
Channel
Tunnel

Calais
Dunkerque
St-Omer
le Portel
Outreau
Berck-Plage
Abbeville
Dieppe
Fécamp
Somme
Artois
Picardie
St-Denis
Île-de-France
Créteil
Châteaudun
Orléanais
Berry
Vierzon
Bourges
Sancerre
Châteauroux

English Channel

Cherbourg
Baie de la Seine
le Havre
Barentin
Rouen
Louviers
Lisieux
Évreux
Chartres
Antony
Versailles
Argenteuil
Nanterre
Maromme

Alderney
Guernsey
Jersey
St-Malo
Golfe de St-Malo
Plérin
St-Brieuc
Dinan
Granville
Avranches
St-Lô
Bayeux
Caen
Coutances
Fougères
Alençon
le Mans
Vendôme
Blois
Olivet
Orléans

CHANNEL
ISLANDS
(to UK)

Île d'Ouessant
Brest
Morlaix
Landivisiau
Landerneau
Quimper
Concarneau
Lorient
Belle-Île
la Baule-Escoublac
St-Nazaire
Challans
Île d'Yeu
Rennes
Laval
Vitré
Châteaubriant
la Flèche
Sarthe
Maine
Anjou
Angers
Cholet
Redon
Coueron
Nantes
Rezé
les Herbiers
la Roche-sur-Yon

Bretagne
Normandie
Pontivy
Loudéac
Hennebont
Quimperlé
Auray
Vannes

Saumur
Thouars
Trélazé
Châtellerault
Tours
Touraine
St-Avertin
Loire
Creuse

Baie

Normandy

0 km   100

0 miles   100

POPULATION

○ Less than 50,000   ○ 50,000 -100,000   ⊙ 100,000 - 500,000   ■ Over 500

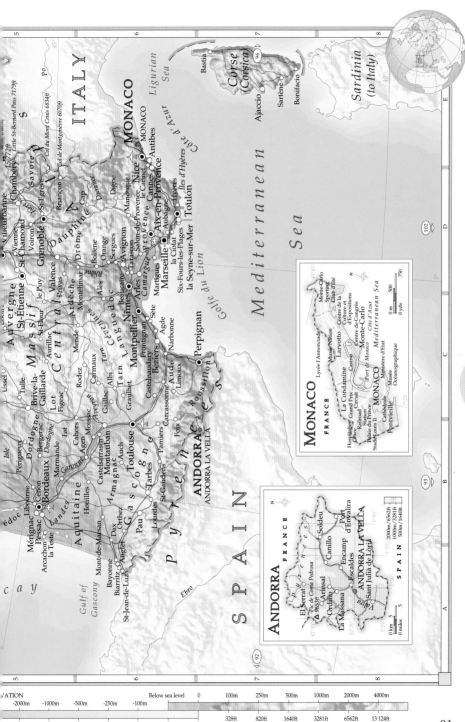

5   6   7   8

ITALY

15772ft
Little St-Bernard Pass 7179ft
Col du Mont Cenis 6834ft
Col de Montgenèvre 6070ft

SAVOIE

Vueulurbanne
Chambéry
St-Egrève
Vienne
St-Chamond
Grenoble
Voiron
Briançon
Gap
Digne
Drôme
Durance
Valence
Montélimar
Privas
Bollène
Orange
Sorgues
Avignon
Tarascon
Arles
Salon-de-Provence
Aix-en-Provence
Aubagne
Martigues
Marseille
la Ciotat
Six-Fours-les-Plages
la Seyne-sur-Mer
Toulon
Hyères
Îles d'Hyères
Fréjus
le Cannet
Cannes
Antibes
Nice
MONACO
MONACO

St-Étienne

Auvergne

Ussel
Tulle
Brive-la-Gaillarde
Aurillac
St-Flour
Mende
le Puy
Ardèche

Massif
Central

Rodez
Carmaux
Albi
Castres
Graulhet
Gaillac
Montpellier
Nîmes
Béziers
Agde
Narbonne
Sète
Frontignan
Camargue
Beaucaire

Tarn
Languedoc
Cévennes

Périgueux
Bergerac
Libourne
Cénon
Bordeaux
Pessac
Mérignac
Arcachon
la Teste
Dordogne
Lot
Figeac
Cahors
Moissac
Agen
Marmande
Villeneuve
Montauban
Castelsarrasin
Toulouse
Auch
Tarbes
St-Gaudens
Pamiers
Foix
Carcassonne
Castelnaudary
Limoux
Aude

Périgueux

Roussillon
Perpignan

Golfe du Lion

Mediterranean Sea

Ligurian Sea

Côte d'Azur

Corse
(Corsica)
Bastia
Ajaccio
Sartène
Bonifacio

Sardinia
(to Italy)

Aquitaine
Landes
Médoc

Gulf of
Gascony

Bayonne
Biarritz
Anglet
Dax
St-Jean-de-Luz
Hossiles
Pau
Lourdes
Mont-de-Marsan

Armagnac
Gascogne
Garonne

Pyrénées

ANDORRA
ANDORRA LA VELLA

SPAIN

Ebro

ELEVATION
-2000m -1000m -500m -250m -100m   Below sea level 0   100m 250m 500m 1000m 2000m 4000m
-6562ft -3281ft -1640ft -820ft -328ft 164ft/-50m 0   328ft 820ft 1640ft 3281ft 6562ft 13 124ft

MONACO

FRANCE

Lycée l'Annonciade
Musée National
Monte-Carlo
Sporting
Club d'Été
Larvotto
Centre de la
Culture et
d'Expositions
Centre de Congrès
Auditorium
La Condamine
Hospital
Casino
Grace
Railroad
Station
Palais du Prince
Stade Louis II
MONACO
Port de Monaco
Ministère d'État
Cathédrale
Musée
Océanographique
Fontvieille

Côte d'Azur
Mediterranean Sea

N

0 m   500   750
0 yds   500   750

ANDORRA

FRANCE

N

Pyrénées

Soldeu
Canillo
El Serrat
Tic de Coma Pedrosa
9653ft
Ordino
Arinsal
La Massana
Encamp
Port
d'Envalira
Escaldes
ANDORRA LA VELLA
Sant Julià de Lòria
SPAIN

0 km   5
0 miles   5

SPAIN & PORTUGAL

POPULATION

○ Less than 50,000 ○ 50,000 -100,000 ◉ 100,000 - 500,000 ◼ Over 500

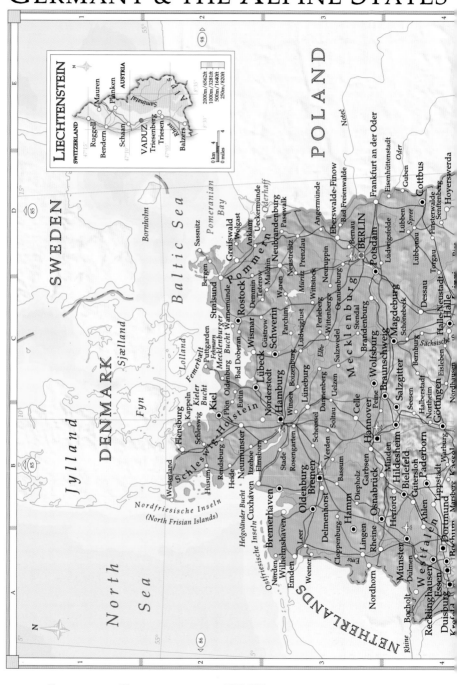

0 km 100

0 miles 100

POPULATION

○ Less than 50,000   ○ 50,000 -100,000   ◉ 100,000 - 500,000   ◼ Over 50

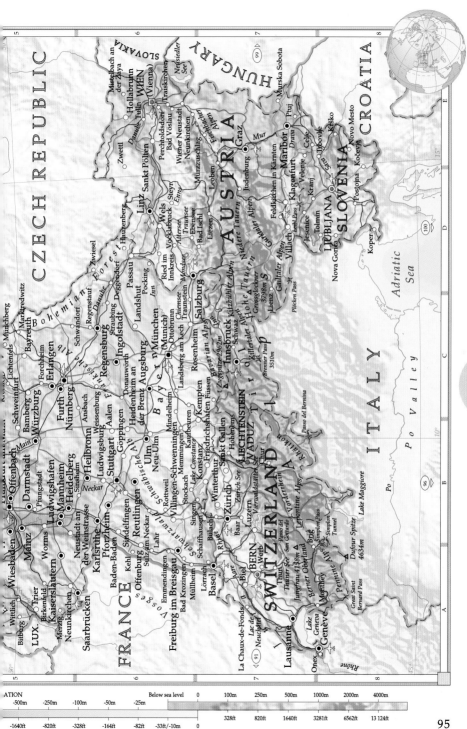

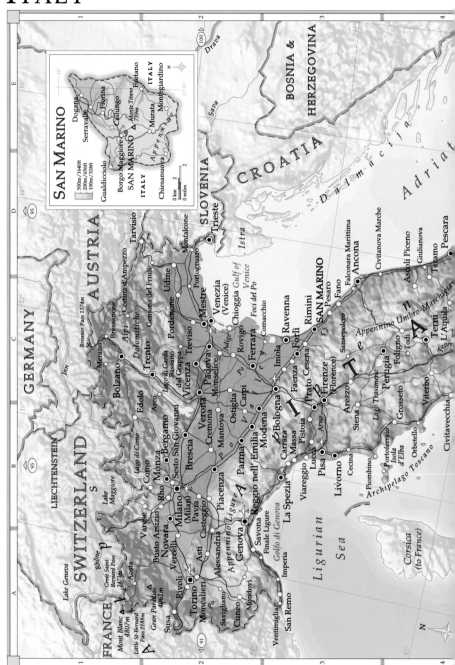

SAN MARINO

ITALY

Dogana
Serravalle
Fiorina
Gualdicciolo
Borgo Maggiore
SAN MARINO
ITALY
Tailungo
Faetano
Monte Titano
739m
Murata
Montegiardino
Chiesanuova

500m/1640ft
200m/656ft
100m/328ft

0 km   2
0 miles   2

Drava

BOSNIA &
HERZEGOVINA

Sava

CROATIA

Dalmacija

Adriat

SLOVENIA

Istra

Trieste
Monfalcone

GERMANY

AUSTRIA

LIECHTENSTEIN

Brenner Pass 1374m
Inn

Tarvisio
Cortina d'Ampezzo
Merano
Bressanone
Alpi
Dolomitiche
Bolzano
Edolo
Trento
Arco
Lago di Garda
Bassano
del Grappa
Gemona del Friuli
Udine
Pordenone
Portogruaro
Mestre
Venezia
(Venice)
Chioggia
Gulf of
Venice
Foci del Po
Comacchio

SWITZERLAND

Lake Geneva
Great Saint
Bernard Pass
2473m
Rhône
Lake
Maggiore
Lago di Como
Varese
Como
Monza
Rho
Bergamo
Sesto San Giovanni
Brescia
Vicenza
Verona
Cremona
Mantova
Ostiglia
Padova
Monselice
Rovigo
Adige
Ferrara
Po
Treviso
Ravenna
Forlì
Rimini
SAN MARINO
Pesaro
Fano
Ancona
Falconara Marittima
Civitanova Marche
Astoli Piceno
Giulianova
Teramo
Pescara

FRANCE

Mont Blanc
4807m
Little St-Bernard
Pass 2188m
Gran Paradiso
4061m
Susa
Rivoli
Torino
Moncalieri
Savigliano
Cuneo
Mondovì
Po

Aosta
Busto Arsizio
Novara
Vercelli
Pavia
Milano
(Milan)
Casteggio
Piacenza
Asti
Alessandria
Appennino (Ligure)
Genova
Savona
Finale Ligure
Golfo di Genova
La Spezia
Carrara
Massa
Reggio nell'Emilia
Modena
Parma
Bologna
Imola
Faenza
Cesena
Prato
Firenze
(Florence)
Arno
Pistoia
Lucca
Pisa
Viareggio
Livorno
Cecina

ITALY

Appennino Umbro-Marchigian
Sansepolcro
Perugia
Lago Trasimeno
Arezzo
Siena
Grosseto
Orbetello
Isola
d'Elba
Portoferraio
Piombino
Archipelago Toscano
Civitavecchia
Todi
Foligno
Viterbo
Terni
L'Aquila
Tevere

Ventimiglia
San Remo
Imperia

Ligurian
Sea

Corsica
(to France)

N

0 km   100
0 miles   100

POPULATION

○ Less than 50,000   ○ 50,000 -100,000   ◉ 100,000 - 500,000   ◼ Over 5

Brindisi
Lecce
Maglie
Penisola Salentina
Strait of Otranto
Taranto
Golfo di Taranto
Gallipoli
Molfetta
Bari
Bitonto
Matera
Altamura
Cerignola
Ofanto
Potenza
Sala Consilina
Appennino Lucano
Castrovillari
Rossano Calabro
Cirò Marina
Crotone
La Sila
Catanzaro
Ionian Sea
Aversa
Vesuvio 1277m
Avellino
Salerno
Capri
Lauria
Cosenza
Amantea
Lamezia
Siderno
Reggio di Calabria
Isole Ponziane
Gaeta
Isola d'Ischia
Napoli
Torre del Greco
Isola di Capri
Battipaglia
Golfo di Salerno
Agropoli
Isola di Stromboli
Isole Eolie
Isola Lipari
Isola Vulcano
Palmi
Messina
Stretto di Messina
Catania
Siracusa
Tyrrhenian Sea
Isola d'Ustica
Cefalù
Monte Etna 3340m
Simeto
Ragusa
Modica
Pozzallo
Palermo
Sicilia (Sicily)
Alcamo
Caltanissetta
Gela
Vittoria
Malta Channel
Ghaudex (Gozo)
MALTA
Malta
Trapani
Isole Egadi
Marsala
Castelvetrano
Agrigento
Isola di Pantelleria
Isole Pelagie
Mediterranean Sea
Sardegna (Sardinia)
Oristano
Villacidro
Iglesias
Carbonia
Cagliari
Quartu Sant'Elena
TUNISIA

VATICAN CITY

N
Main Entrance
Pigna Courtyard
Vatican Museums
Vatican Gardens
Radio Vatican
Sistine Chapel
Raphael Stanza
Saint Peter's Basilica
Papal Apartments
St Peter's Square
ROME
Vatican Railway Station
Monte Vaticano
Papal Heliport
ROME
0m 200 250
0 yds

ATION

-2000m	-1000m	-500m	-250m	-100m	Below sea level	0	100m	250m	500m	1000m	2000m	4000m
-6562ft	-3281ft	-1640ft	-820ft	-328ft	-164ft/-50m	0	328ft	820ft	1640ft	3281ft	6562ft	13 124ft

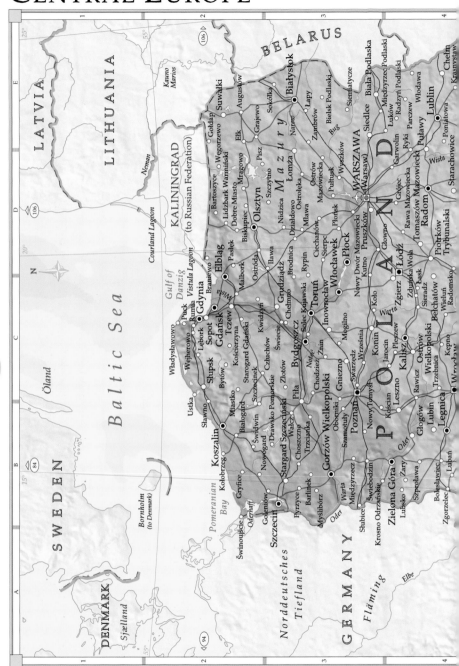

LATVIA

LITHUANIA

BELARUS

SWEDEN

DENMARK
Sjælland

Bornholm
(to Denmark)

Öland

Baltic Sea

Pomeranian
Bay

*Norddeutsches
Tiefland*

GERMANY

Fläming

Elbe

KALININGRAD
(to Russian Federation)

*Kauno
Marios*

Neman

Courland Lagoon

Gulf of
Danzig

Vistula Lagoon

POLAND

Mazury

WARSZAWA
(Warsaw)

Świnoujście
Szczecin
Goleniów
Gryfice
Pyrzyce
Myślibórz
Barlinek
Międzyrzecz
Krosno Odrzańskie
Gorzów Wielkopolski
Świebodzin
Zielona Góra
Lubsko
Żary
Szprotawa
Boleslawiec
Zgorzelec
Lubań
Luban
Głogów
Lubin
Legnica
Wrocław
Trzebnica
Kępno
Wieluń
Bełchatów
Radomsko
Piotrków
Trybunalski
Łódź
Pabianice
Zgierz
Łask
Sieradz
Zduńska Wola
Kalisz
Ostrów
Wielkopolski
Pleszew
Jarocin
Rawicz
Leszno
Kościan
Gostyń
Śrem
Koło
Konin
Turek
Września
Gniezno
Mogilno
Inowrocław
Żnin
Nowy Tomyśl
Poznań
Oborniki
Szamotuły
Swarzędz
Oleśnica

Warta
Odra
Oder
Warta
Odra

Ustka
Słupsk
Sławno
Koszalin
Kołobrzeg
Białogard
Świdwin
Nowogard
Stargard Szczeciński
Drawsko Pomorskie
Wałcz
Piła
Trzcianka
Czarnków
Choszczno
Miastko
Bytów
Szczecinek
Złotów
Chodzież

Władysławowo
Wejherowo
Puck
Rumia
Reda
Lębork
Sopot
Gdynia
Gdańsk
Tczew
Starogard Gdański
Kościerzyna
Kwidzyn
Malbork
Braniewo
Elbląg
Pasłęk
Ostróda
Iława
Chełmno
Świecie
Grudziądz
Bydgoszcz
Nakło
Solec Kujawski
Toruń
Chełmża
Włocławek
Brodnica
Rypin
Płock
Kutno
Gostynin
Głowno
Łowicz
Skierniewice
Sochaczew
Żyrardów
Pruszków
Nowy Dwór Mazowiecki
Grodzisk
Mazowiecki

Suwałki
Gołdap
Węgorzewo
Giżycko
Ełk
Olecko
Augustów
Grajewo
Sokółka
Białystok
Łapy
Wysokie Mazowieckie
Zambrów
Bielsk Podlaski
Hajnówka
Siemiatycze
Biała Podlaska
Międzyrzec Podlaski
Radzyń Podlaski
Włodawa
Chełm
Krasnystaw
Lublin
Poniatowa
Puławy
Ryki
Garwolin
Parczew
Łuków
Siedlce
Mińsk Mazowiecki
Otwock
Radom
Starachowice
Tomaszów Mazowiecki
Rawa Mazowiecka

Bartoszyce
Lidzbark Warmiński
Dobre Miasto
Biskupiec
Mrągowo
Mikołajki
Szczytno
Pisz
Kolno
Łomża
Ostrołęka
Ostrów
Mazowiecka
Pułtusk
Wyszków
Ciechanów
Mława
Działdowo
Nidzica
Olsztyn
Płońsk
Sierpc
Nowe Miasto
Nasielsk

Wisła
Narew
Bug
Wisła
Warta

N

0 km   100

0 miles   100

POPULATION

○ Less than 50,000   ○ 50,000 -100,000   ◉ 100,000 - 500,000   ◼ Over 50

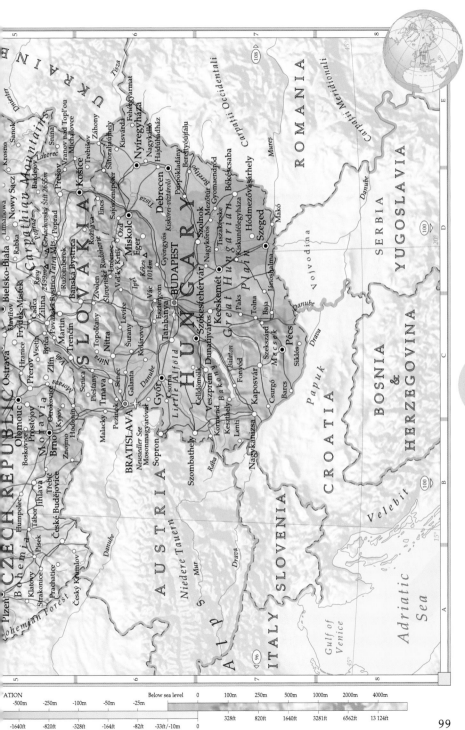

ATION

					Below sea level	0	100m	250m	500m	1000m	2000m	4000m
-500m	-250m	-100m	-50m	-25m								
-1640ft	-820ft	-328ft	-164ft	-82ft	-33ft/-10m	0		328ft	820ft	1640ft	3281ft	6562ft	13 124ft

THE WESTERN BALKANS

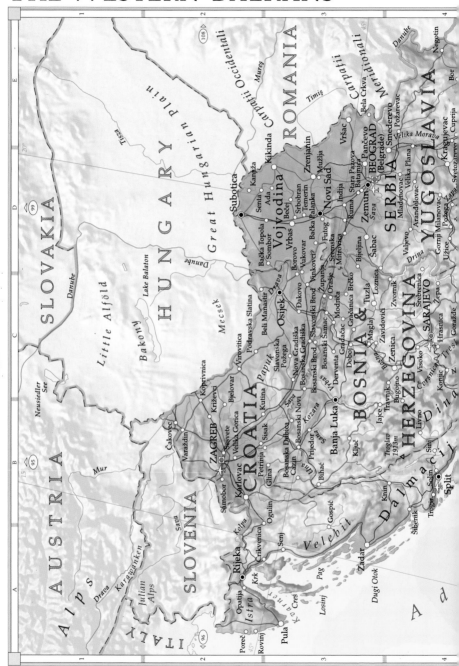

0 km 75
0 miles 75

POPULATION

○ Less than 50,000   ○ 50,000 -100,000   ◉ 100,000 - 500,000   ■ Over 50

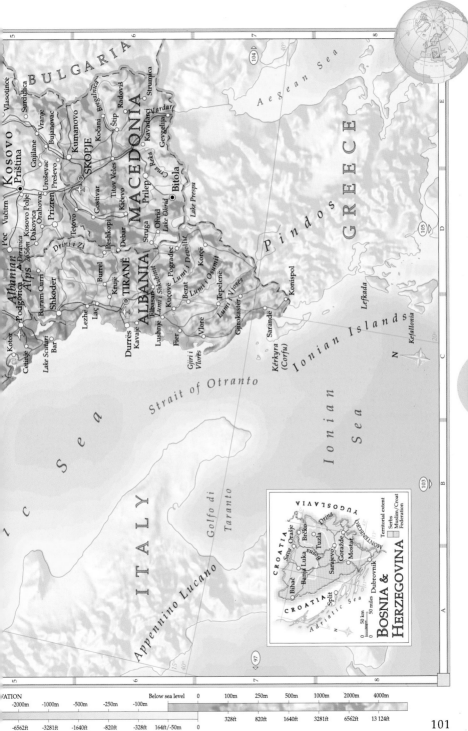

BULGARIA

Vlasotince
Surdulica
Vranje
Bujanovac
Gnjilane

KOSOVO
Priština

Vučitrn
Peć
A. Deravica
2656m
Kosovo Polje
Đakovica
Orahovac
Prizren
Preševo
Uroševac

Albanian Alps
Podgorica
Bajram Curri
Shkodër

Kotor
Cetinje
Lake Scutari
Bar

Drini i Zi

Kumanovo
Kočani
Bregalnica
Štip
Radoviš
Strumica

SKOPJE

MACEDONIA

Titov Veles
Prilep

Bitola

Lake Prespa

Vardar

Kavadarci
Gevgelija

Reka

Gostivar
Kičevo

Tetovo
Debar
Peshkopi
Struga
Ohrid
Lake Ohrid

Aegean Sea

GREECE

Burrel
Kruje
Lac
Lezhe

TIRANË
ALBANIA

Durrës
Kavaje

Lushnje
Fier

Gjiri i
Vlorës

Vlorë

Elbasan
Lumi i Shkumbit
Kuçovë
Pogradec
Berat
Lumi i Devollit
Lumi i Osumit

Korçë

Tepelenë
Lumi i Vjosës
Gjirokastër
Sarandë

Komispol

P i n d o s

Kérkyra
(Corfu)

Ionian Islands

Lefkada

Kefallonia

N

I

a

t

i

c

S

e

a

Strait of Otranto

ITALY

Golfo di
Taranto

Appennino Lucano

I o n i a n

S e a

BOSNIA &
HERZEGOVINA

CROATIA
YUGOSLAVIA

Sava
Orašje
Brčko
Tuzla
Drina

Bihać
Banja Luka
Bosna
Goražde
Sarajevo
Mostar

Split
Dubrovnik

CROATIA
MONTENEGRO

Adriatic Sea

Territorial extent
Serbs
Muslim/Croat
Federation

0   50 km
0   50 miles

ELEVATION

-2000m	-1000m	-500m	-250m	-100m	Below sea level	0	100m	250m	500m	1000m	2000m	4000m
-6562ft	-3281ft	-1640ft	-820ft	-328ft	164ft/-50m	0	328ft	820ft	1640ft	3281ft	6562ft	13 124ft

HUNGARY

Danube BUDAPEST

Great

Hungarian

Plain

ZAGREB

ROATIA

B. & H.

BELGRADE

SARAJEVO

Dinaric Alps

YUGOSLAVIA

Deravica
2656m

SKOPJE

TIRANA

MACED.

ALB.

Bari

277m

Lecce

Golfo di
Taranto

Ionian

Catanzaro

Sea

Kefallinía

Zákynthos

Corfu

Pindos

GREECE

ATHENS

Peiraías

Mirtóo
Pelagos

Kýthira

Irákleio

Crete

Carpathian Mountains

MOLD.

CHIȘINĂU

108

ROMANIA

Carpații Meridonali

BUCHAREST

Danube

Constanța

Balkan Mountains

SOFIA

Varna

BULGARIA

Burgas

Musala 2925m

Rhodope Mountains

Thessaloníki

Thásos

Límnos

Lésvos

Aegean

Skíros

Sea

Chíos

Ándros Sámos

Ikaría

Kikládes

Náxos

Kos

Sea of Crete

UKRAINE

Odesa

Dnieper

Sea of Azov

Krym
(Crimea)

Kerch

Sevastopol'

Novorossiysk

Black Sea

117

İstanbul
Boğazı Zonguldak

Küre Dağları

Samsun

Ordu

İstanbul

Marmara
Denizi

Bursa

ANKARA

TURKEY

İzmir

Tuz Gölü

Anatolia Plateau

Antalya

Toros Dağları

Adana

Rhodes

Antalya
Körfezi

İskenderun
Körfezi

SYRIA

Kárpathos

NICOSIA

CYPRUS

LEBANON

BEIRUT

DAMASCUS

119

Hefa

ISRAEL

Tel Aviv-Yafo

AMMAN

JERUSALEM

Gaza

Dead Sea

JORDAN

n
e
a
n

S
e
a

Banghāzī

Gulf of
Sirte

Libyan Plateau

Gulf of
Sollum

Nile Delta

Alexandria

Qattara
Depression ▽ -133m

Port Said

Suez
Canal

CAIRO

El Giza

Great Sand Sea

Sinai

SAUDI

ARABIA

IBYA

Libyan

Desert

EGYPT

Nile

Arabian Desert

Red
Sea

72

ATION

-4000m -3000m -2000m -1000m -500m

Below sea level 0 100m 250m 500m 1000m 2000m 4000m

-13 124ft -9843ft -6562ft -3281ft -1640ft -820ft/-250m 0

328ft 820ft 1640ft 3281ft 6562ft 13 124ft

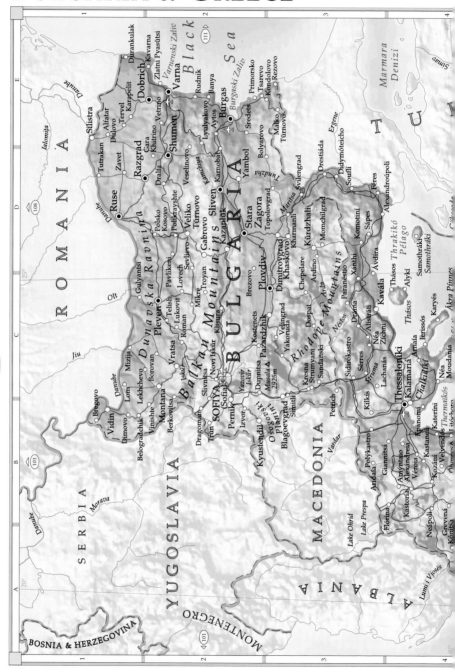

POPULATION

 Less than 50,000   50,000 -100,000   100,000 - 500,000   Over 5

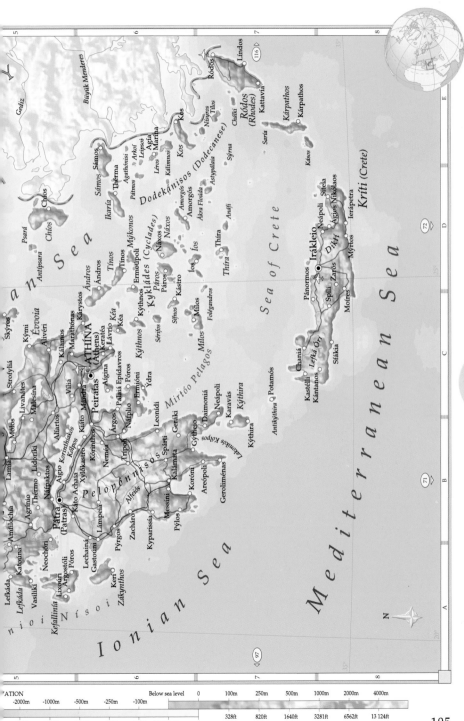

ELEVATION

-2000m	-1000m	-500m	-250m	-100m		Below sea level	0	100m	250m	500m	1000m	2000m	4000m
-6562ft	-3281ft	-1640ft	-820ft	-328ft	-164ft/-50m		0	328ft	820ft	1640ft	3281ft	6562ft	13 124ft

The Baltic States & Belarus

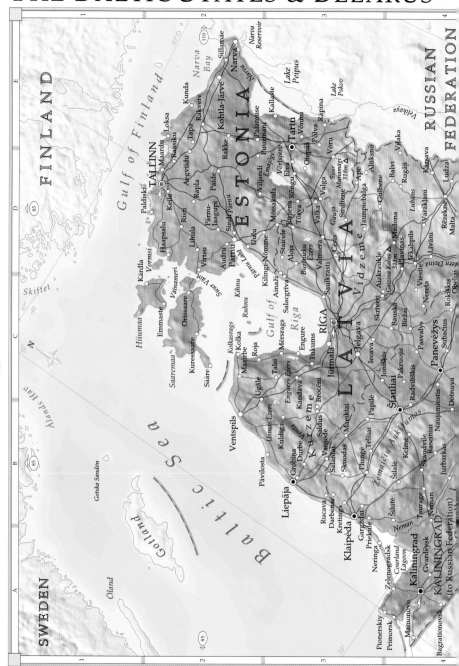

0 km 100

0 miles 100

POPULATION

○ Less than 50,000   ○ 50,000 -100,000   ◉ 100,000 - 500,000   Over 500

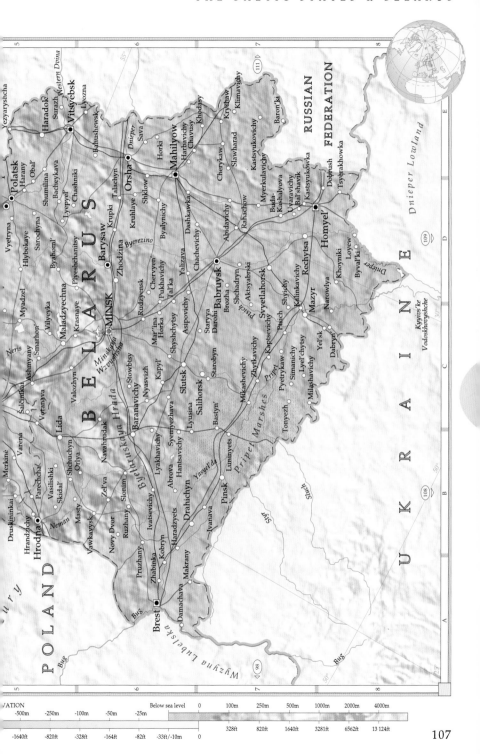

RUSSIAN FEDERATION

POLAND

BELARUS

UKRAINE

Dnieper Lowland

Kyгич'ke Vodoskhovyshche

Wyżyna Lubelska

Yezyaryshcha
Haradok
Suražh Western Dvina
Vitsyebsk
Lyozna
Klimavichy
Kryčaw
Abal'
Shumlina
Obal'
Bacheykava
Polatsk
Harany
Bahushewsk
Sava
Khodasy
Kastsyukovichy
Baron'ki
Chashniki
Dnieper
Horki
Mahilyow
Slawharad
Kastsyukowka
Vyetryna
Lyepyel'
Talachyn
Orsha
Shklow
Harbavichy Chavusy
Dolyrush
Hlybokaye
Sarodyna
Byahoml'
Krupki
Kruhlaye
Byalynichy
Cherykaw
Tsyerakhowka
Myadzel
Pyasheshanitsy
Barysaw
Zhodzina
Byerezino
Dashkawka
Homyel'
Vilyeyka
Maladzyechna
Krasnaye
Cheryven
Pukhavichy
Chachevichy
Abidavichy
Rahachow
Rechytsa
Loyew
Smarhon'
MINSK
Rudzyensk
Mar'ina Horka
Tal'ka
Yalizava
Babruysk
Brozha
Kashalyova
Byval'ki
Neris
Ashmyany
Minskaya Vzvyshsha
Shyshchytsy
Staryya Darohi
Shchadryn
Aktsyabrski
Budu-
Uravavichy Bal'shavik
Khoyniki
Vyerxuny
Salcininkai
Valozhyn
Starobyn
Svyetlahorsk
Narowlya
Merkinė
Lida
Mikashevichy
Shyichy
Pasich
Yel'sk
Druskininkai
Varena
Zel'va
Baranavichy
Nyasvizh
Slutsk
Zhytkavichy
Simanichy
Lyel'chytsy
Dabryn'
Hrandzichy
Parechcha'
Vasilishki
Shchuchyn
Kapyl'
Salihorsk
Bastyn'
Milashavichy
Hrodna
Skidal'
Orlya
Lyusina
Luninyets
Pyetrykaw Simanichy
Neman
Masty
Vawkavysk
Navahrudak
Bastyn'
Pinsk
Pripet
Pripet Marshes
Novy Dvor
Ruzhany
Slonim
Lyakhavichy
Abrova
Hantsavichy
Drahichyn
Ivanava
Ivatsevichy
Kobryn
Haradzyets
Pruzhany
Zhabinka
Damachava
Makrany
Yasyel'da
Sluch
Styr
Brest
Bug
Bug
Bug
Bjelaruskaya Hrada

VATION
-500m   -250m   -100m   -50m   -25m   Below sea level   0   100m   250m   500m   1000m   2000m   4000m
-1640ft   -820ft   -328ft   -164ft   -82ft   -33ft/-10m   0   328ft   820ft   1640ft   3281ft   6562ft   13 124ft

107

POPULATION

○ Less than 50,000　　○ 50,000 -100,000　　◉ 100,000 - 500,000　　◼ Over 50

RUSSIAN
FEDERATION

Horodnya
Shchors
Shostka
Hlukhiv
Chernihiv
Krolevets'
Konotop
Bakhmach
Nizhyn
Nosivka
Romny
Sumy
Pryluky
Lebedyn
Yahotyn
Okhtyrka
Zolochiv
Pyryatyn
Derhachi
Hrebinka
Lubny
Myrhorod
Kharkiv
Kaniv
Zolotonosha
Lyubotyn
Kup"yans'k
Merefa
Cherkasy
Hlobyne
Poltava
Starobil's'k
Smila
Svitlovods'k
Izyum
Kreminna
Rubizhne
Shpola
Kremenchuk
Syeverodonets'k
Oleksandrivka
Chyhyryn
Slov"yans'k
Lysychans'k
Znam"yanka
Oleksandriya
Kramators'k
Zolote
Luhans'k
Kirovohrad
Dniprodzerzhyns'k
Novomoskovs'k
Kostyantynivka
Zhovti Vody
Pavlohrad
Stakhanov
Vil'shanka
P"yatykhatky
Dnipropetrovs'k
Horlivka
Krasnodon
Pervomays'k
Dolyns'ka
Synel'nykove
Yenakiyeve
Krasnyy Luch
Arbyzynka
Bobrynets'
Pokrovs'ke
Makiyivka
Torez
Novyy Buh
Kryvyy Rih
Inhulets'
Donets'k
Amvrosiyivka
Voznesens'k
Ordzhonikidze
Nikopol
Zaporizhzhya
Dokuchayevs'k
Kam"yanka-Dniprovs'ka
Marhanets'
Orikhiv
Volnovakha
Mykolayiv
Dniprorudne
Polohy
Novoazovs'k
Zhovtneve
Nova Kakhovka
Tokmak
Mariupol'
Kherson
Kakhovka
Melitopol'
Hola Prystan'
Tsyurupyns'k
Yakymivka
Berdyans'k
Chaplynka
Novotroyits'ke
Prymors'k
Kalanchak
Armyans'k
Heniches'k
Krasnoperekops'k
Zatoka Syvash
Sea of Azov
Rozdol'ne
Dzhankoy
Chornomors'ke
Krasnohvardiys'ke
Kerch
Yevpatoriya
Nyzhn'ohirs'kyy
Kerch Strait
Saky
Krym
Lenine
Simferopol'
(Crimea)
Bakhchysaray
Feodosiya
Sevastopol'
Alushta
Yalta
Alupka

RUSSIAN
FEDERATION

Black Sea

Below sea level

-2000m -1000m -500m -250m -100m   0   100m   250m   500m   1000m 2000m 4000m

-6562ft -3281ft -1640ft -820ft -328ft -164ft/-50m 0   328ft 820ft 1640ft 3281ft 6562ft 13 124ft

EUROPEAN RUSSIA

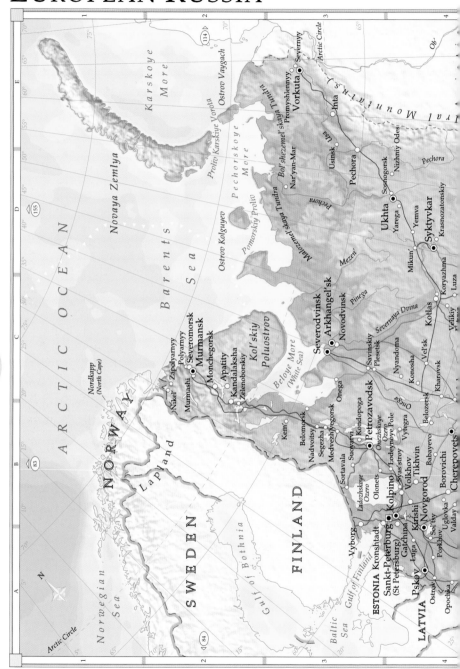

ARCTIC OCEAN

Norwegian Sea

Nordkapp (North Cape)

NORWAY

Lapland

SWEDEN

FINLAND

Gulf of Bothnia

Baltic Sea

ESTONIA
LATVIA

Vyborg
Kronshtadt
Sankt-Peterburg
(St Petersburg)
Gatchina
Pskov
Ostrov
Opochka

Karskoye More

Novaya Zemlya

Barents Sea

Ostrov Kolguyev

Ostrov Vaygach

Proliv Karskiye Vorota

Pomorskiy Proliv

Pechorskoye More

Kol'skiy Poluostrov

Beloye More (White Sea)

Polyarnyy
Zapolyarnyy
Severomorsk
Murmansk
Monchegorsk
Nikel'
Murmashi
Apatity
Kandalaksha
Zelenoborskiy

Kem'
Belomorsk
Nadvoitsy
Segezha
Medvezh'yegorsk
Suoyarvi
Sortavala
Olonets
Ladozhskoye Ozero

Kondopoga
Onega
Petrozavodsk
Onezhskoye Ozero
Lodeynoye Pole
Syas'stroy
Volkhov
Tikhvin

Severodvinsk
Arkhangel'sk
Novodvinsk

Vorkuta
Severnyy
Promyshlennyy
Inta
Naryan-Mar
Usinsk
Usa'
Pechora
Sosnogorsk
Nizhniy Odes
Pechora

Ukhta
Yarega
Yemva
Mikun'
Syktyvkar
Krasnozatonskiy

Bol'shezemel'skaya Tundra
Malozemel'skaya Tundra
Mezen'
Pinega
Severnaya Dvina

Koryazhma
Luza
Velikiy
Kotlas
Vel'sk
Kharovsk

Ural Mountains
Ob'
Arctic Circle

Savinskiy
Pleseetsk
Nyandoma
Konosha
Belozersk
Onega

Babayevo
Borovichi
Cherepovets

Valday
Uglovka
Solfisy
Porkhov
Luga
Krishi
Novgorod

Lodeynoye
Kolpino

Gulf of Finland

N

Arctic Circle

0 km   200

0 miles   200

POPULATION

○ Less than 50,000   ○ 50,000 -100,000   ◉ 100,000 - 500,000   ■ Over 50

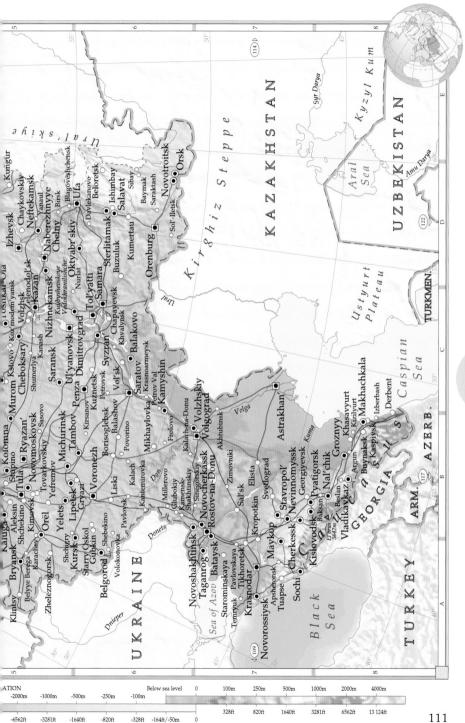

KAZAKHSTAN

UZBEKISTAN

Kirghiz Steppe

Ural'skiye

Kyzyl Kum

Aral Sea

Syr Darya

Amu Darya

TURKMEN.

Ustyurt Plateau

Caspian Sea

AZERB.

ARM.

GEORGIA

TURKEY

Black Sea

Sea of Azov

UKRAINE

Dnieper

Donets

Don

Volga

Kura

Kungur
Chaykovskiy
Neftekamsk
Izhevsk
Yanaul
Birsk
Blagoveshchensk
Davlekanovo
Ufa
Naberezhnyye Chelny
Ishimbay
Beloretsk
Salavat
Sterlitamak
Oktyabr'skiy
Buzuluk
Kumertau
Baymak
Sibay
Saraktash
Sol'-Iletsk
Novotroitsk
Orsk
Orenburg

Tosukar Ola
Murom
Kstovo
Koz'modem'yansk
Kazan'
Zelenodol'sk
Volzhsk
Cheboksary
Shumerlya
Kanash
Kuybyshevskoye Vodokhranilishche
Nurlat
Oktyabr'skiy
Tol'yatti
Samara
Chapayevsk
Khvalynsk
Balakovo
Vol'sk
Krasnoarmeysk
Kamyshin

Kolomna
Stupino
Ryazan'
Novomoskovsk
Tovarkovskiy
Michurinsk
Saransk
Nizhnekamsk
Ul'yanovsk
Penza
Syzran'
Saratov
Petrov Val

Kaluga
Aleksin
Tula
Shchekino
Kimovsk
Yefremov
Tambov
Kirsanov
Kuznetsk
Petrovsk
Balashov
Povorino
Frolovo
Mikhaylovka
Kalach-na-Donu
Volzhskiy
Volgograd
Akhtubinsk
Astrakhan'

Bryansk
Orël
Yelets
Lipetsk
Gryazi
Voronezh
Borisoglebsk
Volgodonsk

Klintsy
Belyye Berega
Karachev
Zheleznogorsk
Kursk
Starry Oskol
Gubkin
Shchigry
Liski
Kalach
Kantemirovka
Millerovo
Kamensk-Shakhtinskiy
Glubokiy
Kalach-na-Donu
Zimovniki
Svetlograd
Elista
Sal'sk

Shebekino
Pavlovsk
Belgorod
Volokonovka

Novoshakhtinsk
Taganrog
Batalysk
Novocherkassk
Rostov-na-Donu
Bataysk
Starominskaya
Pavlovskaya
Tikhoretsk
Krasnodar
Kropotkin
Stavropol'
Nevinnomyssk
Svetlograd
Georgiyevsk
Pyatigorsk
Mineral'nyye
Cherkessk
Kislovodsk
Maykop
Armavir

Temryuk
Apsheronsk
Tuapse
Sochi
Novorossiysk

Nal'chik
Beslan
Baksan
El'brus 5642m
Vladikavkaz
Grozny
Argun
Baynaksk
Buynaksk
Makhachkala
Khasavyurt
Kizilyurt
Kaspiysk
Izberbash
Derbent
Kizlyar

114
122
117
109

55°
50°
45°
40°

5
6
7
8

E
D
C
B
A

ATION

-2000m -1000m -500m -250m -100m

-6562ft -3281ft -1640ft -820ft -328ft -164ft/-50m 0

Below sea level 0 100m 250m 500m 1000m 2000m 4000m

328ft 820ft 1640ft 3281ft 6562ft 13 124ft

111

NORTH & WEST ASIA

POPULATION

○ Less than 50,000 ○ 50,000 -100,000 ◉ 100,000 - 500,000 ■ Over 5

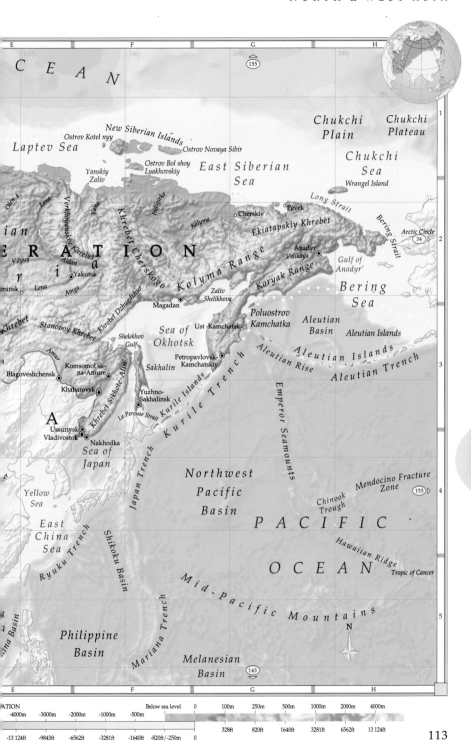

E   F   G   H

C E A N

1

Laptev Sea

New Siberian Islands

Ostrov Kotel nyy

Ostrov Novaya Sibir

Yanskiy Zaliv

Ostrov Bol shoy Lyakhovskiy

East Siberian Sea

Chukchi Plain

Chukchi Plateau

Chukchi Sea

Wrangel Island

Olen k

Lena

Verkhoyanskiy Khrebet

Yana

Indigirka

Kolyma

○ Cherskiy

○ Pevek

Long Strait

Bering Strait

70

Arctic Circle

34

2

Vilyuy

Khrebet

Aldan

○ Yakutsk

Khrebet Cherskogo

Kolyma Range

Ekiatapskiy Khrebet

Anadyr ○
Velikaya

Gulf of Anadyr'

60

R E R A T I O N

r   i   a

minsk

Lena

Amga

Khrebet Dzhugdzhur

Zaliv Shelikhova

Koryak Range

Bering Sea

Khrebet

Stanovoy Khrebet

● Magadan

Ust -Kamchatsk ○

Poluostrov Kamchatka

Aleutian Basin

Aleutian Islands

Sea of Okhotsk

Shelekhov Gulf

Petropavlovsk- ●
Kamchatskiy

Aleutian Rise

Aleutian Islands

3

● Blagoveshchensk

Komsomol sk-
na-Amure ●

Amur

Sakhalin

Aleutian Trench

50

Khabarovsk ●

Khrebet Sikhote-Alin'

Yuzhno-
Sakhalinsk ●

Kurile Islands

Emperor Seamounts

A

Ussuriysk ○
Vladivostok ○

La Perouse Strait

● Nakhodka

Sea of Japan

Kurile Trench

Northwest Pacific Basin

Mendocino Fracture Zone

153

4

Japan Trench

P A C I F I C

40

Yellow Sea

Chinook Trough

East China Sea

Ryukyu Trench

Shikoku Basin

O C E A N

Hawaiian Ridge

Tropic of Cancer

30

Mid - Pacific Mountains

5

na Basin

Philippine Basin

Mariana Trench

Melanesian Basin

143

N

E   F   G   H

RUSSIA & KAZAKHSTAN

0 km   800

0 miles   800

POPULATION

○ Less than 50,000 ○ 50,000 -100,000 ◉ 100,000 - 500,000 ◼ Over 5

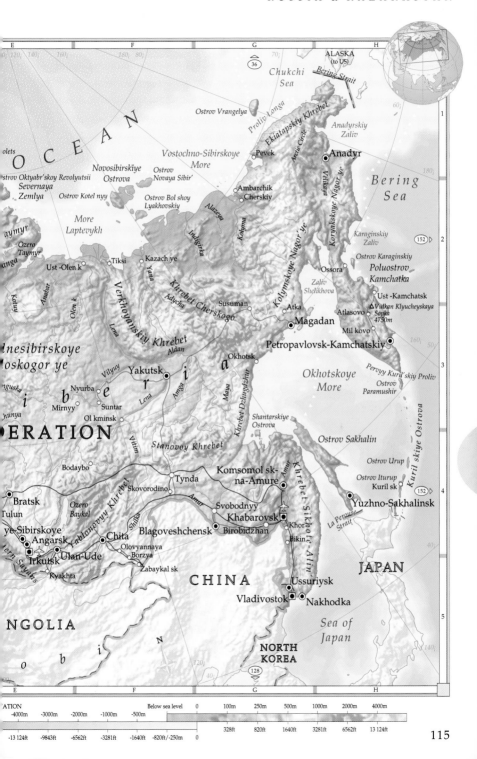

0| 120| 140| 160| 180| 80| 70| ALASKA   60|

OCEAN

36

Chukchi
Sea   Bering Strait

olets   Ostrov Vrangelya   Proliv Longa   Arctic Circle

strov Oktyabr'skoy Revolyutsii
Severnaya
Zemlya
Ostrov Kotel nyy

Novosibirskiye
Ostrova

Ostrov
Novaya Sibir'

Vostochno-Sibirskoye
More

Pevek

Ekiatapskiy Khrebet

Anadyrskiy
Zaliv

Anadyr

Bering
Sea

180|

aymyr

More
Laptevykh

Ozero
Taymyr

Ostrov Bol shoy
Lyakhovskiy

Ambarchik
Cherskiy

Alazeya

Korvakskoye Nagor ye

Karaginskiy
Zaliv

152

anga

Ust -Olen k

Tiksi

Kazach ye

Yana

Indigirka

Khrebet Cherskogo

Kolyma

Kolymskoye Nagor ye

Velikaya

Ostrov Karaginskiy
Poluostrov
Kamchatka

Kotuy

Anabar

Olen k

Lena

Adycha

Verkhoyanskiy Khrebet

Susuman

Atka

Ossora

Zaliv
Shelikhova

Ust -Kamchatsk

Vulkan Klyucheyskaya
Sopka
4750m

Magadan

Mil kovo

Atlasovo

Petropavlovsk-Kamchatskiy

160| 50|

nesibirskoye
oskogor ye

Yakutsk

Vilyuy

Aldan

Amga

Maya

Okhotsk

Okhotskoye
More

Pervyy Kuril'skiy Proliv
Ostrov
Paramushir

nguska

Nyurba

i   b   e   r   i   a

Lena

Khrebet Dzhugdzhur

Shantarskiye
Ostrova

Kuril skiye Ostrova

hunya

Mirnyy

Suntar

Ol kminsk

Ostrov Sakhalin

ERATION

Vitim

Stanovoy Khrebet

Ostrov Urup

Ostrov Iturup
Kuril sk

152

Bodaybo

Tynda

Komsomol sk-
na-Amure

Amur

Khrebet Sikhote Alin

Bratsk

Ozero
Baykal

Skovorodino

Amur

Svobodnyy

Khabarovsk

La Perouse
Strait

Yuzhno-Sakhalinsk

Tulun

Yablonovyy Khrebet

Chita

Blagoveshchensk

Birobidzhan

Khor

ye-Sibirskoye

Angarsk

Shilka

Olovyannaya

Bikin

40|

Irkutsk

Ulan-Ude

Borzya

tern Sayans

Kyakhta

Zabaykal sk

CHINA

Ussuriysk

Vladivostok

Nakhodka

Sea of
Japan

JAPAN

140|

NGOLIA

o   b   i

N

NORTH
KOREA

128

120|

40|

ATION
-4000m   -3000m   -2000m   -1000m   -500m

Below sea level   0   100m   250m   500m   1000m   2000m   4000m

-13 124ft   -9843ft   -6562ft   -3281ft   -1640ft   -820ft/-250m   0   328ft   820ft   1640ft   3281ft   6562ft   13 124ft

TURKEY & THE CAUCASUS

ROMANIA

Lacul Razim
Lacul Sinoie

Danube

N

K r y m
(C r i m e a)

BULGARIA

Varnenski Zaliv

B l a c k   S e a

Burgaski Zaliv

Maritsa

Edirne
Kırklareli
Ergene

İnebolu
Cide
Küre
Sinop
Gerze

Küre Dağları

Bafra
Sam

Zonguldak
Ereğli
Devrek
Karabük
Kastamonu
Kargı
Canık Dağla
Havza

Tekirdağ
Kâğıthane
İstanbul
Marmara Denizi
İzmit
Adapazarı
Yalova
İznik Gölü
Bolu
Gerede
Çankırı
Ilgaz
Kızıl Irmak
Çorum
Alaca
To

Çanakkale Boğazı
Bandırma
Çanakkale
Bursa
Bilecik
Bozüyük
Eskişehir
ANKARA
Kalecik
Kırıkale
Sorgun
Yıld

Edremit
Lésvos
Ayvalık
Balıkesir
Kütahya
Simav
Gediz
T U R
Hirfanli Baraji
Şarkışla
Gemerek

Chíos
Menemen
Akhisar
Manisa
Gediz
Uşak
Alaşehir
Afyon
Cihanbeyli
Kulu
Tuz Gölü
Nevşehir
Aksaray
İncesu
Bunyan
Kayseri
Göksun
G
Kahran

İzmir
Torbalı
Sámos
Söke
Büyük Menderes
Nazilli
Aydın
Denizli
Dinar
Burdur
Beyşehir Gölü
Anatolia Plateau
Konya
Niğde

Milas
Muğla
Tavas
Burdur Gölü
Isparta
Suğla Gölü
Ereğli
Karaman
Osmaniye
Tarsus
Mersin
Ceyhan
Adana
Kır

Bodrum
Marmaris
Dalaman
Fethiye
Antalya
Manavgat
Mut
Toros Dağ
İskenderun

Dodekánisos
Ródos (Rhodes)
Kas
Finike
Antalya Körfezi
Gazipaşa
Silifke
Anamur
Antakya

Kárpathos

TURKISH REPUBLIC
OF NORTHERN CYPRUS
(only recognized by Turkey)

CYPRUS

Orontes

M e d i t e r r a n e a n
S e a

LEBANON

0 km   200

0 miles   200

POPULATION

○ Less than 50,000   ○ 50,000 -100,000   ◉ 100,000 - 500,000   ◼ Over 5

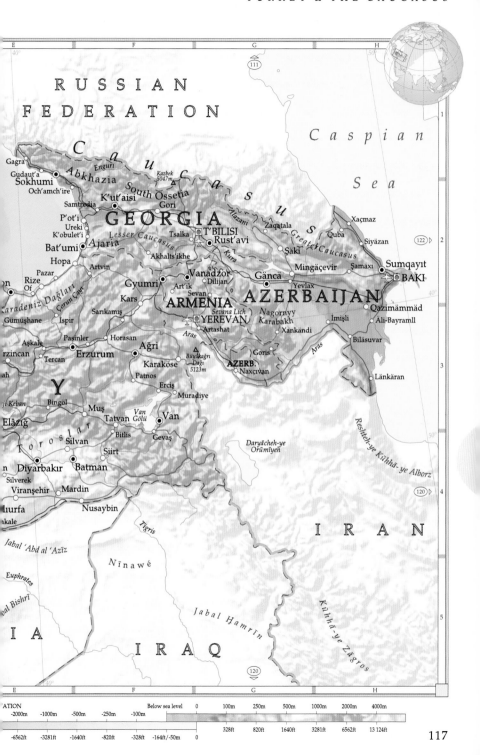

RUSSIAN
FEDERATION

Caspian

Sea

Gagra
Gudaut'a
Sokhumi
Och'amch'ire
Samtredia
P'ot'i
Ureki
K'obulet'i
Bat'umi
Hopa
Pazar
Rize
Of
Gümüşhane
Aşkale
Erzincan
Tercan

Abkhazia
Enguri
K'ut'aisi
South Ossetia
Gori
Tsalka
T'BILISI
Rust'avi
Akhalts'ikhe
Artvin
Gyumri
Kars
Sarıkamış
İspir
Pasinler
Horasan
Erzurum
Karaköse
Patnos

Kazbek 5047m.

GEORGIA

Lesser Caucasus

Ajaria

Vanadzor
Dilijan
Art'ik
Sevan

ARMENIA

Sevana Lich
YEREVAN
Artashat

Aras

Ağri

Büyükağrı Dağı 5123m

Erciş
Muradiye

Zaqatala
Kura
Şäki
Mingäçevir
Gäncä
Yevlax

AZERBAIJAN

Nagornyy
Karabakh
Xankändi

Goris

AZERB.
Naxçıvan

Aras

Xaçmaz
Quba
Siyäzan
Şamaxı
Sumqayıt
BAKI
Qäzimämmäd
Äli-Bayramll
Biläsuvar

Länkäran

İmişli

Elâzığ
Bingöl
Muş
Tatvan
Silvan
Bitlis
Siirt
Diyarbakır
Batman
Silverek
Viranşehir
Mardin
Nusaybin

Van
Van Gölü
Gevaş

Toroslar

Daryächeh-ye Orūmīyeh

IRAN

Tigris

Euphrates

Jabal 'Abd al 'Azīz

Nīnawé

IA

IRAQ

Jabal Ḥamrīn

Kūhhā-ye Zāgros

Reshteh-ye Kūhhā-ye Alborz

Caucasus
Alazani
Greater Caucasus
Çoruh Çayı
Karadeniz Dağları

ATION
-2000m -1000m -500m -250m -100m

Below sea level 0 100m 250m 500m 1000m 2000m 4000m

-6562ft -3281ft -1640ft -820ft -328ft -164ft/-50m 0 328ft 820ft 1640ft 3281ft 6562ft 13 124ft

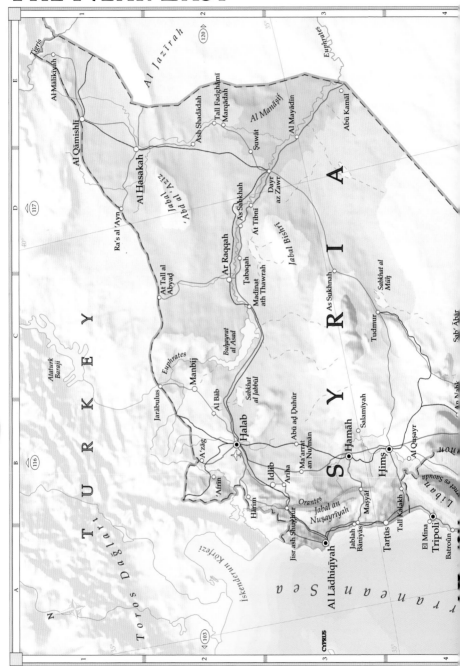

POPULATION
○ Less than 50,000   ○ 50,000 -100,000   ◉ 100,000 - 500,000   ◼ Over 5

0 km   100

0 miles   100

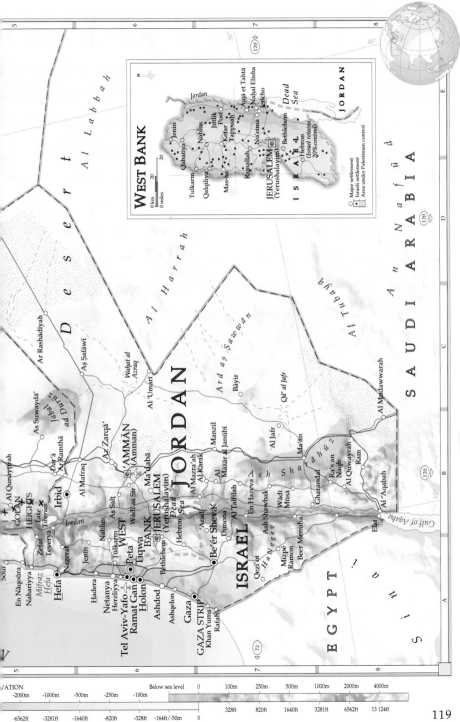

WEST BANK

Jordan

Jenin
Qabatiya
Tulkarm
Qalqilya
Mas-ha
Nablus
Jiftlik
Post
Kefar
Tappuah
Ramallah
Auja et Tahtā
Nuʿeima
Bethlehem
Nahal Elisha
Jericho

Dead Sea

JERUSALEM
(Yerushalayim)

Hebron

JORDAN

I S R A E L

(Israel retains
20% control)

0 km   20
0 miles   20

○ Major settlement
■ Israeli settlement
▨ Area under Palestinian control

A l   L a b b a h

A l   L a b b a h

D e s e r t

A l   H a r r a h

Ar Rashadiyah

As Safāwī

Waḥat al
Azraq

Al ʿUmāri

Bayir

Qaʿ al Jafr

Al Madawwarah

A r d   a ṣ   S a w w ā n

A n   N a f ū ḍ

S A U D I   A R A B I A

A t   T u b a y q

Jebal
ad Dūrūz

As Suwaydāʾ

Al Qunayṭirah

Darʿā
Ar Ramthā
Az Zarqāʾ

Irbid

Al Mafraq

AMMAN
(Amman)

As Salt

Mādabā

Manzil

Al Mazraʿah
Al Karak

Al Karak

Al
Mazār al Janūbī

Al Jafr

Maʿān

Ghatandal

Raʾs an
Naqb

Al Quwayrah

Ram

J O R D A N

Wādi as Sir

A s h   S h a r ā h

Aṭ Ṭafīlah

En Hazeva
Wādi
Shawbak
Wādi
Mūsā
Beer Menuḥa

Ghor es
Safi

GOLAN
HEIGHTS

Zefat
Teverya

Lake
Tiberias

Nahariyya

En Naqūra
Mifraẓ
Ḥefa

Hefa

Nazerat

Hadera

Netanya
Herzliyya
Tel Aviv-Yafo
Ramat Gan
Holon

Ashdod
Ashqelon

Gaza
GAZA STRIP
Khan Yunis
Rafaḥ

Nablus

Jenin

Tulkarm

Petaḥ
Tiqwa

WEST
BANK

JERUSALEM
(Yerushalayim)

Bethlehem

Hebron

Dead
Sea

ʿArad

Dimona

Beʾér Sheva

Qeziʿot

Mizpe
Ramon

Ha Negev

I S R A E L

Eilat
Al ʿAqabah

Gulf of Aqaba

E G Y P T

S i n a i

Jordan

× GOLAN
HEIGHTS

VATION

-2000m	-1000m	-500m	-250m	-100m	Below sea level	0	100m	250m	500m	1000m	2000m	4000m
-6562ft	-3281ft	-1640ft	-820ft	-328ft	-164ft/-50m	0	328ft	820ft	1640ft	3281ft	6562ft	13 124ft

THE MIDDLE EAST

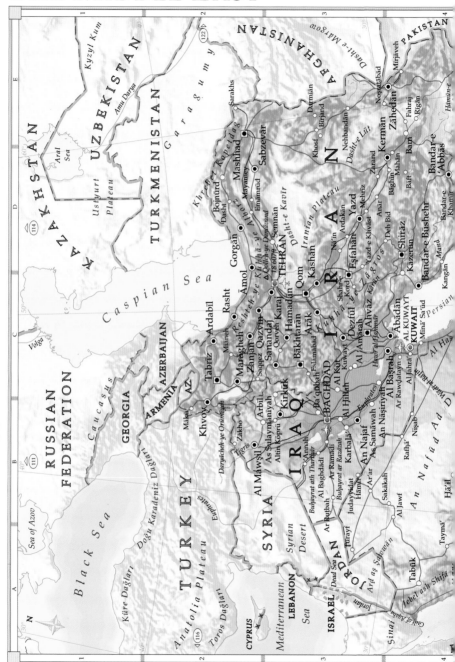

POPULATION

○ Less than 50,000 ○ 50,000 -100,000 ◉ 100,000 - 500,000 ◼ Over 5

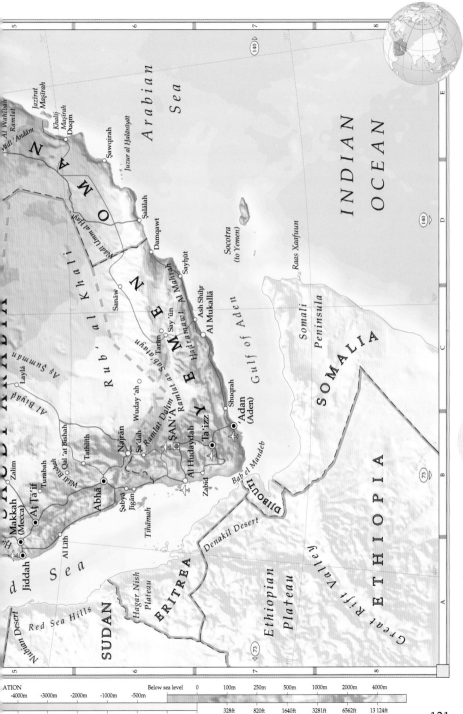

CENTRAL ASIA

RUSSIAN
FEDERATION

GEORGIA

Caspian

AZERBAIJAN

Sea

Ustyurt
Plateau

Aral
Sea

Mŭynoq

Chimboy

Takhtakŭpir

Kŭneŭrgench

Nukus

UZBEKIS

Gubadag

Ky

Takhiatosh

Il'yaly

Dashkhovuz

Uch

Zaliv
Kara-
Bogaz-Gol

Proliv Kara-
Bogaz-Gol

Urganch

Khiwa

Tŭrtkŭl

Dzhanak

Turkmenbashi

Gaz-Achak

Lebap

Krasnovodskiy
Zaliv

Cheleken

Nebitdag

Darvaza

Zaunguzskiye

Amu Darya

Gaz

Gazandzhyk

Karakumy

Bu

Turkmenskiy
Zaliv

TURKMENISTAN

Seydi

Deynau

Gyzylarbat

Chardzhev

Khrebet Kopetdag

Kara-Kala

Bakharden

Geok-Tepe

Byuzmeyin

Garagumy

Gaz

Reshteh-ye Kŭhhā-ye Alborz

Gora Reza
9653ft

ASHGABAT

Mary

Karak

Tedzhen

Kaakhka

Murgab

Bayrama

Kashaf Rūd

Serakhs

Vozvys

Murgab

Kar

Kŭhhā-ye Zāgros

Iranian

Plateau

IRAN

Bālā Morghāb

Dugo

Towraghoudī

Gushgy

Selseleh-ye S

Ghūrīān

Herāt

AFGH

Shīndand

Farāh

Kūh-e Chehe

Delār

Daryācheh-ye
Sīstān

Lashkar Gā

Zarghūn Shahr

Zaranj

Dasht-e Mārgow

Chahār Borjak

Daryā-ye Helmand

R

Bahrām Chāh

0 km   200

0 miles   200

POPULATION

○ Less than 50,000   ○ 50,000 -100,000   ◉ 100,000 - 500,000   ◼ Over 50

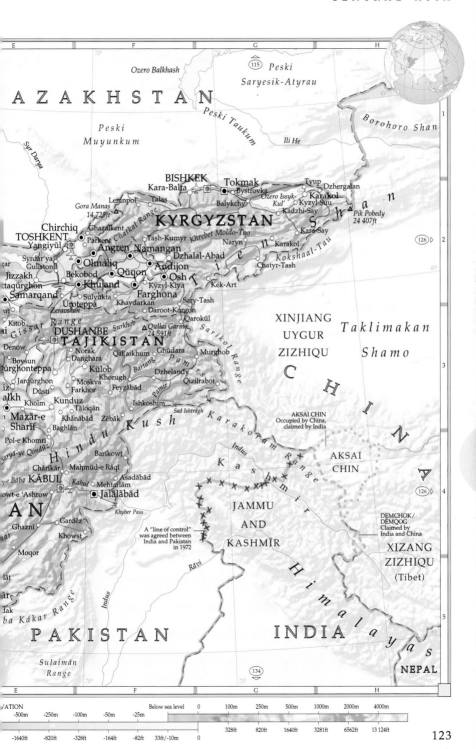

AZAKHSTAN

KYRGYZSTAN

TAJIKISTAN

CHINA

PAKISTAN

INDIA

NEPAL

Ozero Balkhash

Peski Saryesik-Atyrau

Peski Taukum

Peski Muyunkum

Syr Darya

Ili He

Borohoro Shan

XINJIANG UYGUR ZIZHIQU

Taklimakan Shamo

BISHKEK
Kara-Balta
Tokmak
Bystrovka
Tyup Dzhergalan
Ozero Issyk-Kul' Karakol
Kyzyl-Suu
Balykchy
Kadzhi-Say
Kara-Say
Pik Pobedy
24 407ft
Gora Manas
14 725ft
Leninpol' Talas
Ghazalkent
Chirchiq
TOSHKENT
Yangiyŭl
Parkent Tash-Kumyr Khrebet Moldo-Too
Angren Namangan
Syrdar'ya Olmaliq Qŭqon Andijon Naryn Karakol
Guliston
Jizzakh Bekobod Khujand Osh Kokshaal-Tau
taqŭrghon Sulyukta Kyzyl-Kiya Kěk-Art
Samarqand Ŭroteppa Farghona Chatyr-Tash
Zeravshan Khaydarkan Sary-Tash
Kitob Daroot-Korgon
Gissar Range Qarokŭl
Denow DUSHANBE Surkhob Qullai Garma Sarikol Range Pamirs
Boysun Norak 24 591ft
ŭrghontteppa Danghara Qal'aikhum Ghŭdara Murghob
Jardŭrghon Külob Khorugh Bartang Dzhelandy Qizilrobot
Farkhor Feyzābād Pamir
Dŭsti Moskva Ishkoshim Sad Ishtrāgh
alkh Kunduz Zēbāk Karakoram Range
Mazār-e Khānābād Tāloqān Indus
Sharif Baghlān AKSAI CHIN
Occupied by China,
claimed by India
arya-ye Qondŭz Barīkowt Kashmir AKSAI CHIN
-e Bāba Chārīkār Mahmūd-e Rāqī Asadābād
KĀBUL Kabul Mehtarlām DEMCHOK/
owt-e 'Ashrow Jalālābād DÉMQOG
Claimed by
India and China
AN Khyber Pass JAMMU XIZANG
Ghaznī Gardēz AND ZIZHIQU
Khowst KASHMĪR (Tibet)
Moqor A "line of control"
was agreed between
India and Pakistan
in 1972
lāt Ravi Himalayas
ba Kākar Range Indus
ak

PAKISTAN INDIA

Sulaimān
Range

NEPAL

Chatkal Range

Tien Shan

Tajik

115

126

126

134

ATION
-500m -250m -100m -50m -25m Below sea level 0 100m 250m 500m 1000m 2000m 4000m

-1640ft -820ft -328ft -164ft -82ft 33ft/-10m 0 328ft 820ft 1640ft 3281ft 6562ft 13 124ft

SOUTH & EAST ASIA

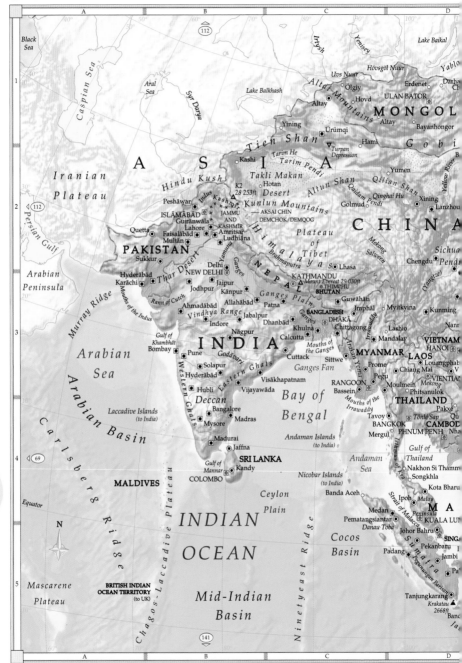

Black Sea

Caspian Sea

Aral Sea

Syr Darya

Lake Balkhash

112

Irtysh

Yenisey

Lake Baikal

Uvs Nuur

Hövsgöl Nuur

Yablo

Olgiy

Erdenet

Darha

Cr

Hovd

ULAN BATOR

MONGOL

Altay

Tien Shan

Altay Mountains

Altay

Bayanhongor

Yining

Ürümqi

Hami

Gobi

Iranian Plateau

112

Kashi

Tarim He

Tarim Pendi

Turpan Depression

Yumen

Qilian Shan

Yellow River

Hindu Kush

Takli Makan Desert

Altun Shan

Qaidam Pendi

Qinghai Hu

Xining

Lanzhou

CHINA

Persian Gulf

Peshāwar

Indus

K2 28 253ft

Kunlun Mountains

Kashmir

AKSAI CHIN

Golmud

Sichua

Pendi

ISLĀMĀBĀD

JAMMU AND KASHMIR

DEMCHOK/DEMQOG

Plateau of Tibet

Chengdu

(Yangtze)

Arabian Peninsula

Quetta

Gujrānwāla

Lahore

Amritsar

Ludhiāna

Himalaya

Lhasa

Mekong

Salween

Faisalābād

Multān

PAKISTAN

Sukkur

Delhi

Yamuna

Ganges

NEPAL

KATHMANDU

Mount Everest 29 030ft

THIMPHU

Guwāhāti

Brahmaputra

Nanr

Hyderābād

NEW DELHI

Jaipur

Kānpur

Ganges Plain

BHUTAN

Imphāl

Myitkyina

Kunming

Karāchi

Jodhpur

Allahābād

Patna

Ganges

Lashio

Mandalay

VIETNAM

Mouths of the Indus

Thar Desert

Ahmadābād

Vindhya Range

Jabalpur

BANGLADESH

DHĀKĀ

Chittagong

HANOI

Murray Ridge

Rann of Cutch

Indore

Nāgpur

Dhanbād

Ganges

Khulnā

Calcutta

Arakan Yoma

LAOS

Gulf of Khambhāt

Bombay

Pune

Godāvari

INDIA

Cuttack

Mouths of the Ganges

MYANMAR

Louangphab

Arabian Sea

Hyderābād

Solapur

Eastern Ghats

Sittwe

Prome

Chiang Mai

VIENTIAN

Ganges Fan

Pegu

V

Visākhapatnam

RANGOON

Moulmein

Mekong

Arabian Basin

Hubli

Western Ghats

Vijayawāda

Bay of Bengal

Bassein

Mouths of the Irrawaddy

THAILAND

Pakxé

Deccan

Bangalore

Madras

BANGKOK

CAMBOL

Carlsberg Ridge

Laccadive Islands (to India)

Mysore

Tônlé Sap

Tavoy

Qu

Madurai

Jaffna

Andaman Islands (to India)

Mergui

PHNOM PENH

Nha

SRI LANKA

Gulf of Mannar

Kandy

Andaman Sea

Gulf of Thailand

Isthmus of Kra

COLOMBO

MALDIVES

Nicobar Islands (to India)

Nakhon Si Thamm

Songkhla

Equator

Ceylon Plain

Banda Aceh

Kota Bharu

Ipoh

Malay

MA

Chagos-Laccadive Plateau

N

Medan

Strait of Malacca

Peninsula

KUALA LUI

INDIAN OCEAN

Danau Toba

Pematangsiantar

Cocos Basin

Johor Bahru

Pekanbaru

SING

Sumatra

Padang

Jambi

I

Pa

Mascarene Plateau

BRITISH INDIAN OCEAN TERRITORY (to UK)

Mid-Indian Basin

Ninetyeast Ridge

Pegunungan Barisan

Tanjungkarang

Krakatau 2668ft

Banc

141

Ja

0 km   1000

0 miles   1000

POPULATION

○ Less than 50,000   ○ 50,000 -100,000   ◉ 100,000 - 500,000   ▣ Over 50

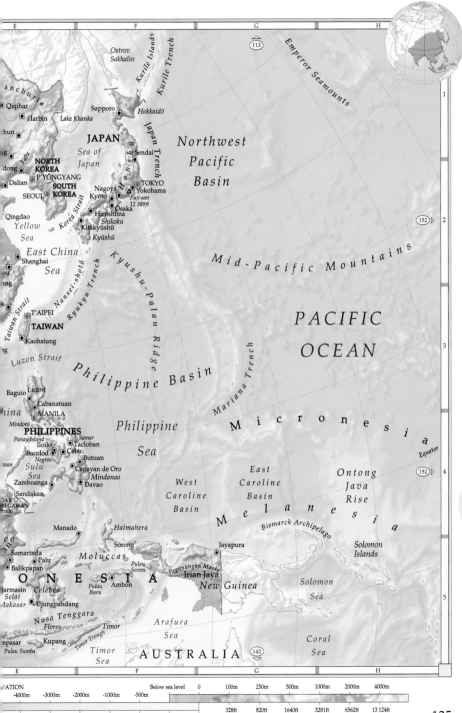

E F G H

113

Emperor Seamounts

Ostrov
Sakhalin

Kurile Islands

Kurile Trench

1

Qiqihar

Harbin Lake Khanka Sapporo Hokkaidō

152

2

chun

anchuria

dong

Dalian

Qingdao

JAPAN

Sea of
Japan

NORTH
KOREA
P'YŎNGYANG
SOUTH
KOREA
SEOUL

Honshū

Sendai

TOKYO
Yokohama
Fuji-san
12 389ft

Sendai Trench

Japan Trench

Northwest
Pacific
Basin

Nagoya
Kyōto
Ōsaka
Hiroshima
Shikoku
Kitakyūshū
Kyūshū

Korea Strait

Yellow
Sea

East China
Sea

Shanghai

ou

ang

Nansei-shotō

Kyushu-Palau Ridge

Ryukyu Trench

Mid-Pacific Mountains

PACIFIC
OCEAN

Taiwan Strait

T'AIPEI
TAIWAN
Kaohsiung

Luzon Strait

Philippine Basin

Mariana Trench

152

3

g

Baguio Luzon
Cabanatuan
MANILA

Mindoro

PHILIPPINES

Panay Island
Iloilo
Bacolod
Negros

Samar
Tacloban
Cebu
Butuan

Philippine

Sea

M i c r o n e s i a

Equator

4

hina

Sulu
Sea

Zamboanga

Sandakan

EGAWAN

AR

bah

Cagayan de Oro
Mindanao
Davao

West
Caroline
Basin

East
Caroline
Basin

M e l a n e s i a

Ontong
Java
Rise

wan

Manado

Samarinda
Palu
Balikpapan

Halmahera

Sorong

Moluccas

Pulau
Seram

ONESIA

Celebes

Ujungpandang

jarmasin

Selat

Makasar

Nusa Tenggara
Flores

Pulau
Buru
Ambon

Pegunungan Maoke
Irian Jaya
New Guinea

Jayapura

Bismarck Archipelago

Solomon
Sea

Solomon
Islands

5

npasar
Pulau Sumba

Kupang

Timor

Timor Trough

Timor
Sea

Arafura
Sea

AUSTRALIA

142

Coral
Sea

E F G H

ATION

-4000m -3000m -2000m -1000m -500m

Below sea level 0 100m 250m 500m 1000m 2000m 4000m

-13 124ft -9843ft -6562ft -3281ft -1640ft -820ft/-250m 0

328ft 820ft 1640ft 3281ft 6562ft 13 124ft

125

WESTERN CHINA & MONGOLIA

RUSSIAN F

KAZAKHSTAN

Kazakhskiy

Melkosopochnik

Kulunda Steppe

Ozero Zaysan

Ozero Balkhash

Ozero Issyk-Kul'

KYRGYZSTAN

TAJIKISTAN

AFGH.

PAKISTAN

JAMMU AND KASHMIR

Demchok/ Dèmqog Claimed by India and China

INDIA

Zapadnyy Sayan

Bol'shoy Yenisey

Malyy Yenisey

Hovs Ni

Uvs Nuur

Ulaangom Hanhöhiy Uul

Ölgiy

Altay

Altai Mountains

Har Us Nuur

Hovd

Hyargas Nuur

Har Nuur

Hangayn

Tse

MON

Altay

Bayanhor

Irtysh

Ulungur Hu

Karamay

Dzungaria *Gurbantünggüt*

Kuytun *Shamo* Fukang Jimsar

Baruun Huuray

Aj Bogd Uul 12 474ft

Atas Bogd 8865ft

Boharo Shan

Yining

Shihezi

Kuytun Ürümqi

Qitai

Turpan

Hami

Tien Shan

Pik Pobedy 24 407ft

Turpan Pendi

Korla *Bosten Hu*

Kuruktag

Xingxingxia

Bei Shan

Bor

Toxkan He

Tarim He *Tarim Basin*

Lop Nur

GANSU

Qilian S

Kashi

Yengisar

Shache

Yecheng

Pishan

XINJIANG UYGUR

ZIZHIQU

Ruoqiang

Altun Shan

Karakoram Range

K2 28 253ft

Kashmir

Moyu Qira

Taklimakan *Shamo*

Hotan

Kunlun Shan

Qimantag Shan

Golmud

Qaidam Pendi

Qi

Qinghu

Burhan Budai Shan

AKSAI CHIN

Aksai Chin Occupied by China, claimed by India

Rutog

CH

QINGHA

XIZANG

ZIZHIQU

(Tibet)

Bayan Har

Yushu

Mekong

Ch

Indus

Gar Xincun

Shiquanhe

Zanda X

Moincêr

Tongtian He

Tangra Yumco

Nyima

Tanggula Shan

Siling Co

Amdo

Gyaring Hu

Nam Co Nagqu

Damxung

Salween

Qam

Ngangzê Co

Yamuna

Brahmaputra

Plateau

of

Tibet

Nyainqêntanglha Shan

Hengd

NEPAL

Himalayas

Lhazê Xigazê

Mount Everest 29 030ft

Gyangzê

Maizhokunggar X

Lhasa

Gonggar X

INDIA

BHUTAN INDIA

MYANMA

0 km 400

0 miles 400

POPULATION

○ Less than 50,000   ○ 50,000 -100,000   ◉ 100,000 - 500,000   ◉ Over 50

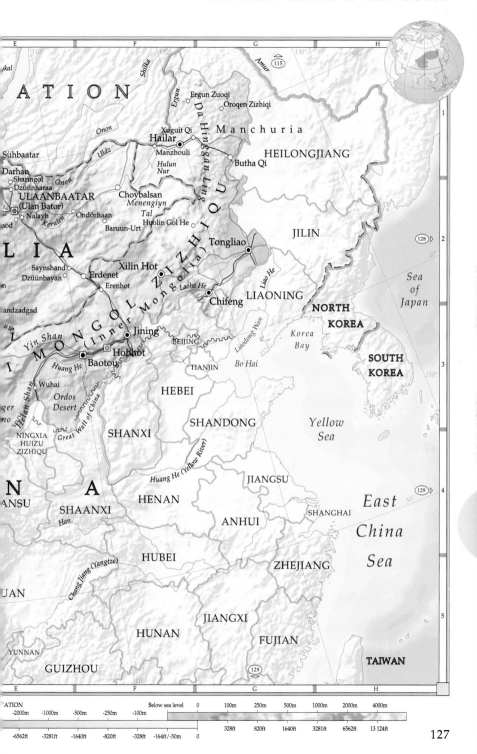

E   F   G   H

Amur 115

ykal

Shilka

A T I O N

Onon

Ergun

Ergun Zuoqi

Oroqen Zizhiqi

M a n c h u r i a

Xuguit Qi

Uldz

Hailar

Manzhouli

Butha Qi

HEILONGJIANG

Sühbaatar

Hulun Nur

Darhan

Sharingol

Onon

Dzüünharaa

ULAANBAATAR
(Ulan Bator)

Choybalsan

Menengiyn Tal

Nalayh

Kerulen

Ondörhaan

Huolin Gol He

Baruun-Urt

JILIN

Tongliao

L I A

Saynshand

Xilin Hot

Dzüünbayan

Erdenet

Erenhot

Laoha He

Liao He

Chifeng

LIAONING

andzadgad

Jining

BEIJING

Lindong Wan

NORTH KOREA

I

Yin Shan

Huang He

Hohhot

Baotou

TIANJIN

Korea Bay

SOUTH KOREA

Wuhai

Ordos Desert

Great Wall of China

HEBEI

Bo Hai

Helan Shan

SHANXI

SHANDONG

Yellow Sea

NINGXIA HUIZU ZIZHIQU

ger

no

N

A

SHAANXI

HENAN

Han

Huang He (Yellow River)

JIANGSU

East

China

Sea

ANSU

SHANGHAI

ANHUI

HUBEI

Chang Jiang (Yangtze)

UAN

ZHEJIANG

JIANGXI

HUNAN

FUJIAN

GUIZHOU

129

TAIWAN

Sea of Japan

M O N G O L   (Inner Mongolia)   Z I Z H I Q U

Da Hinggan Ling

128

129

129

E   F   G   H

ATION

					Below sea level	0	100m	250m	500m	1000m	2000m	4000m
-2000m	-1000m	-500m	-250m	-100m								
-6562ft	-3281ft	-1640ft	-820ft	-328ft	-164ft/-50m	0		328ft	820ft	1640ft	3281ft	6562ft	13 124ft

EASTERN CHINA & KOREA

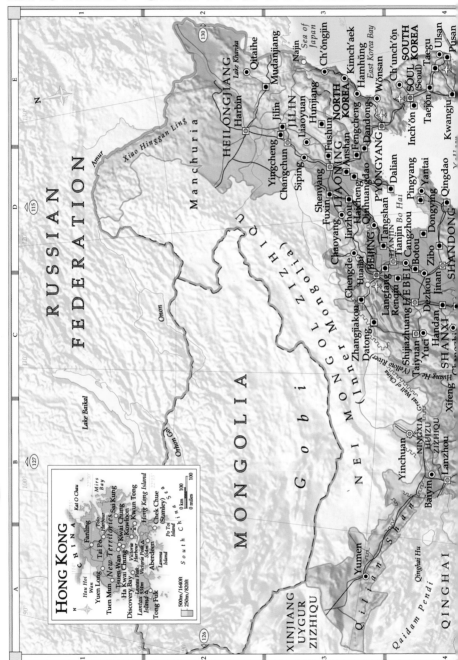

N

RUSSIAN FEDERATION

Xiao Hinggan Ling

Amur

Manchuria

Onon

Orhon Gol

Lake Baikal

HEILONGJIANG

Lake Khanka

Qitaihe

Mudanjiang

Sea of Japan

Najin

Ch'ŏngjin

Kimch'aek

East Korea Bay

Hunjiang

Harbin

Jilin

JILIN

Liaoyuan

Changchun

Yingcheng

Siping

Fushun

Anshan

Hamhŭng

NORTH KOREA

Fengcheng

Dandong

Wŏnsan

Ch'unch'ŏn

SOUTH KOREA

Ulsan

Taegu

Pusan

SŎUL (Seoul)

Inch'ŏn

Taejŏn

Kwangju

Shenyang

LIAONING

Jinzhou

Haicheng

Benxi

Fuxin

Chaoyang

Chengde

Huailai

Qinhuangdao

Dalian

Pyongyang

P'YŎNGYANG

Pingyang

Yantai

Qingdao

SHANDONG

Tangshan

TIANJIN

Tianjin

Bo Hai

Cangzhou

Botou

Dongying

Zibo

Jinan

BEIJING

Langfang

HEBEI

Renqiu

Zhangjiakou

Datong

Shijiazhuang

Handan

Dezhou

SHANXI

Xifeng

Qinghai Hu

QINGHAI

Qaidam Pendi

Qilian Shan

Yumen

Yinchuan

NINGXIA HUIZU ZIZHIQU

HUIZU ZIZHIQU

Baiyin

Lanzhou

Lanzhou

Yuci

Taiyuan

Great Wall of China (Yellow River)

Huang He

NEI MONGOL ZIZHIQU

(Inner Mongolia)

Gobi

MONGOLIA

QINGHAI ZIZHIQU

XINJIANG UYGUR ZIZHIQU

HONG KONG

CHINA

Hau Hoi Wan

Kat O Chau

Mirs Bay

Fanling

Yuen Long

Tai Po

Tolo Harbour

Sai Kung

Tuen Mun

New Territories

Kwai Chung

Tsuen Wan

Kowloon

Kwun Tong

Hong Kong Island

Victoria Peak 552m

Ha Kwai Chung

Discovery Bay

Victoria Harbour

Lantau Island 934m

Lantau Peak

Aberdeen

Chek Chue (Stanley)

Po Toi Island

Lamma Island

Tong Fuk

South China Sea

N

0 km   100
0 miles   100

500m/1640ft
250m/820ft

0 km   200
0 miles   200

POPULATION

○ Less than 50,000   ○ 50,000 -100,000   ◉ 100,000 - 500,000   ■ Over 5

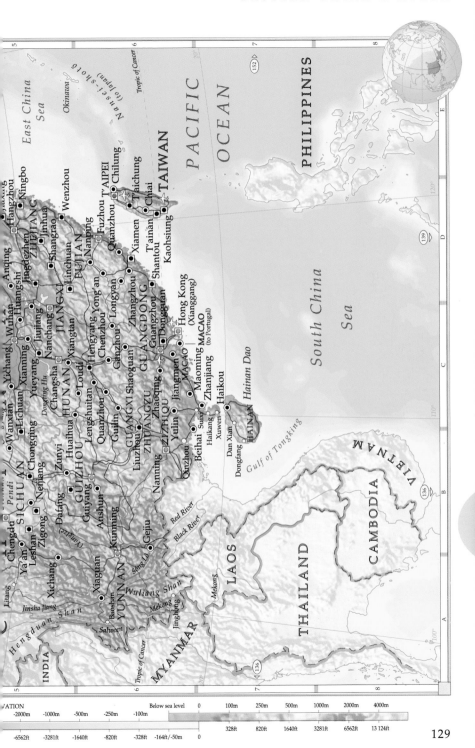

JAPAN

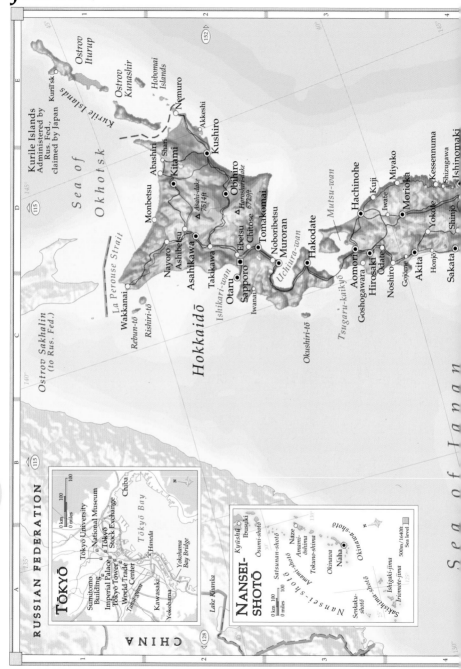

Ostrov Iturup

Ostrov Kunashir

Kurile Islands Administered by Rus. Fed., claimed by Japan

Kuril'sk

Hobomai Islands

Nemuro

Akkeshi

Kushiro

Sea of Okhotsk

Abashiri

Shari

Kitami

Monbetsu

Obihiro

△ Asahi-dake 7514ft

Hiroshiri-dake 6729ft △

Ebetsu

Chitōse

Tomakomai

Noboribetsu

Muroran

Uchiura-wan

Hakodate

Mutsu-wan

Hachinohe

Kuji

Iwate

Miyako

Morioka

Kessennuma

Shizugawa

Ishinomaki

Nayoro

Ashibetsu

Asahikawa

Takikawa

Otaru

Sapporo

Iwanai

Aomori

Goshogawara

Hirosaki

Odate

Noshiro

Gojome

Akita

Honjō

Yokode

Shinjō

Sakata

Wakkanai

Rebun-tō

Rishiri-tō

La Perouse Strait

Ishikari-wan

Hokkaidō

Okushiri-tō

Tsugaru-kaikyō

Ostrov Sakhalin (to Rus. Fed.)

Kurile Islands

Sea of Japan

RUSSIAN FEDERATION

CHINA

Lake Kitaku

TŌKYŌ

Chiba

Tōkyō University

National Museum

Tōkyō Stock Exchange

Sumitomo Building

Imperial Palace

Tōkyō Tower

World Trade Center

Tōkyō

Tama-gawa

Haneda

Kawasaki

Yokohama

Yokohama Bay Bridge

Tōkyō Bay

NANSEI-SHOTŌ

Kyūshū

Ibusuki

Ōsumi-shotō

Satsunan-shotō

Amami-shotō

Amami-Ōshima

Naze

Tokuno-shima

Okinawa

Naha

Okinawa-shotō

Nansei-shotō

Sakishima-shotō

Ishigaki-jima

Iriomote-jima

Senkaku-shotō

500m / 1640ft Sea level

POPULATION

○ Less than 50,000   ○ 50,000 -100,000   ◉ 100,000 - 500,000   ◼ Over 500,000

0 km 200
0 miles 200

PACIFIC OCEAN

East China Sea

SOUTH KOREA

Place names and labels:

Choshi
Utsunomiya
Mito
TOKYO
Oyama
Chiba
Yokohama
Kawagoe
Kawasaki
Omiya
Nagano
Ueda
Kofu
Maebashi
Matsumoto
Hamamatsu
Toyama
Fuji-san 3,389 △
Shizuoka
Itoigawa
Takaoka
Gifu
Toyota
Kanazawa
Komatsu
Nakatsugawa
Okazaki
Fukui
Ogaki
Nagoya
Ise
Tsuruga
Kyōto
Ōtsu
Tsu
Owase
Osaka
Shingū
Takefu
Wakayama
Gobō
Kōbe
Himeji
Tottori
Okayama
Kurashiki
Tokushima
Matsue
Yonago
Kure
Niihama
Matsuyama
Kōchi
Nakamura
Sukumo
Iwakuni
Nobeoka
Gōtsu
Hiroshima
Hōfu
Ōita
Hamada
Ube
Masuda
Kurume
Yamaguchi
Ōmuta
Yatsushiro
Nagato
Shimonoseki
Miyazaki
Kitakyūshū
Fukuoka
Kumamoto
Miyakonojō
Sasebo
Sendai
Nagasaki
Kagoshima

Shikoku
Kyūshū

Izu-shotō
Hachijō-jima
Miyake-jima
Mikura-jima
Nii-jima
Kōzu-shima
Ō-shima
Bosō-hantō
Sagami-wan
Suruga-wan
Ise-wan
Kii-suidō
Tosa-wan
Bungo-suidō
Iyo-nada
Harima-nada
Kii-sanchi
Chūgoku-sanchi
Hida-sammyaku
Toyama-wan
Wakasa-wan
Biwa-ko
Tanega-shima
Yaku-shima
Shibushi-wan
Kagoshima-wan
Koshikijima-rettō
Amakusa-shotō
Gotō-rettō
Iki
Kō-saki
Tsushima
Korea Strait
Liancourt Rocks
(claimed by Japan & South Korea)
Oki-shotō
Dōgo
Dōzen
Ōsumi-shotō

35°
30°
135°
140°

ATION

-4000m	-3000m	-2000m	-1000m	-500m	Below sea level	0	100m	250m	500m	1000m	2000m	4000m

| -13 124ft | -9843ft | -6562ft | -3281ft | -1640ft | -820ft/-250m | 0 | 328ft | 820ft | 1640ft | 3281ft | 6562ft | 13 124ft |

131

SOUTH INDIA & SRI LANKA

N

Bombay
(Mumbai)
Pune
Ahmadnagar
Nānded
134
Godavari
Jagd
Bārāmati
Nizāmābād
Karīmnagar
Vizianagar
Andhra Pradesh
INDIA
Solapur
Sāngli
Secunderābād
Visāk
Kolhāpur
Gulbarga
Hyderābād
Rāja
Western Ghats
Belgaum
Karnātaka
Rāichūr
Kurnool
Vijayawāda
Machilī
Panaji
(Goa)
Dhārwād
Nandyāl
Chīrāla
Hubli
Krishna
Ongole
Kāvali
Deccan
Tungabhadra
Reservoir
Tādpatri
Anantapur
Nellore
Dāvangere
Shimoga
Cuddapah
Bhadrāvati
Udupi
Tumkūr
Mangalore
Bangalore
Vellore
Madras
Kāsaragod
Mandya
Krishnagiri
Kānchīpuram
Cannanore
Mysore
Tiruppattūr
Erode
Salem
Pondicherry
Calicut
Neyveli
Eastern Ghats
Coromandel Coast
Coimbatore
Tamil Nādu
Trichūr
Tiruchchirāppalli
Ernākulam
Dindigul
Cochin
Madurai
Jaffna
Alleppey
Rājapālaiyam
Mannar
Vavuniya
Trincomale
Quilon
SRI LA
Trivandrum
Tuticorin
Anuradhapura
Eravur
Batti
Nāgercoil
Puttalam
Gulf of
Mannar
Matale
Kandy
Negombo
COLOMBO
Sri Jayawardan
Moratuwa
Ratnapura
Kalutara
Galle
Matara
Malabar Coast
Kerala
Palk Strait

Arabian
Sea

Amīndivi
Islands

Lakshadweep
(Laccadive Islands)
(to India)

Kavaratti
Island

Kalpeni
Island

Nine Degree Channel

Minicoy Island

Eight Degree Channel

Ihavandippolhu
Atoll

MALDIVES

Faadhippolhu
Atoll

Horsburgh
Atoll

Ari Atoll
MALE'

Male'Atoll

Felidhu Atoll

Mulaku Atoll

Kolhumadulu
Atoll

Hadhdhunmathi Atoll

North Huvadhu Atoll

Equator

South Huvadhu
Atoll

Gan

Addu Atoll

140

INDIA

0 km   400

0 miles   400

POPULATION

○ Less than 50,000   ○ 50,000 -100,000   ◉ 100,000 - 500,000   ◼ Over 5

E · 90° · F · 95° · G · 100° · H

Bay

MYANMAR

THAILAND

of Bengal

15° · 1

Mouths of the Irrawaddy

136

North Andaman

Andaman Islands
(to India)

Middle Andaman

137 · 2

10°

South Andaman

Port Blair

Mergui Archipelago

A n d a m a n

Little Andaman

S e a

Isthmus
of Kra

Car Nicobar

3

Katchall Island

Strait of Malacca

Little Nicobar

Nicobar Islands
(to India)

Great Nicobar

Sumatera

138 · 4

INDONESIA

Pulau
Simeulue

Kepulauan Banyak

C E A N

Pulau Nias

Equator

5

Pulau Siberut

141

E · F · 90° · G · 95° · H

ATION

Below sea level · 0 · 100m · 250m · 500m · 1000m · 2000m · 4000m

-4000m · -3000m · -2000m · -1000m · -500m

328ft · 820ft · 1640ft · 3281ft · 6562ft · 13 124ft

-13 124ft · -9843ft · -6562ft · -3281ft · -1640ft · -820ft/-250m · 0

133

NORTH INDIA, PAKISTAN & BANGLADI

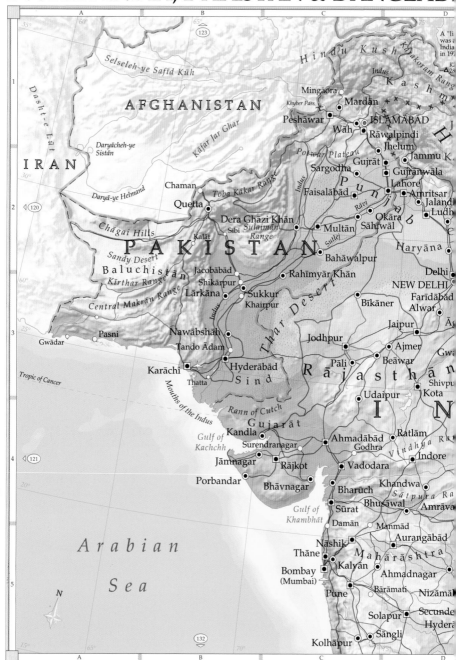

0 km   300

0 miles   300

POPULATION

○ Less than 50,000   ○ 50,000 -100,000   ◉ 100,000 - 500,000   ◼ Over 50

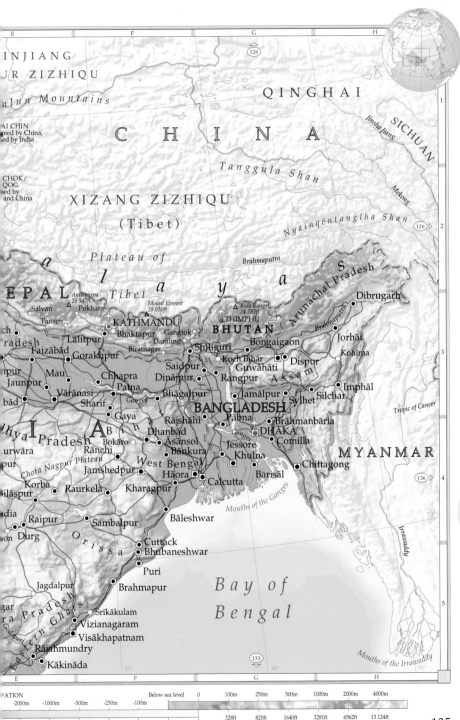

E   F   G   H

126

INJIANG
JR ZIZHIQU

nlun Mountains   QINGHAI   Jinsha Jiang   SICHUAN   1

AI CHIN
pied by China,
ed by India   C   H   I   N   A

Tanggula Shan   Mekong

CHOK/
QOG
ed by
and China   XIZANG ZIZHIQU   Nyainqêntanglha Shan   126   2

(Tibet)

a   Plateau of   Brahmaputra   s   2

EPAL   Tibet   Mount Everest   Kula Kangri   Arunāchal Pradesh   Dibrugarh
              Annapurna   29 030ft   ▲   24 785ft   Brahmaputra
              26 547ft △   △   Jorhāt
Salyan   Pokhara   KATHMANDU   Bhaktapur   THIMPHU   Kohima
    Tansen   Bhaktapur   Gangtok   BHUTAN   Bongaigaon
rades h   Lalitpur   Darjiling   Imphāl   3
    Faizābād   Gorakhpur   Biratnagar   Shiliguri   Koch Bihār   Guwāhāti   Dispur
npur   Mau   Saidpur   Rangpur   Assam
Jaunpur   Vārānasi   Chhapra   Dinājpur   Jamālpur   Sylhet   Silchar
bād   Sharif   Patna   Bhāgalpur   BANGLADESH   Tropic of Cancer
        Gaya   Ganges   Pābna   Brāhmanbāria
hya   I   A   Rājshāhi   DHĀKA   Comilla
Pradesh   Bokaro   Dhanbād   Āsansol   Ganges   Jessore   Khulna   MYANMAR
urwāra   Ranchi   Bānkura   West Bengal   Barisāl   Chittagong   136
pur   Chota Nagpur Plateau   Jamshedpur   Hāora   Calcutta   4
Korba   Raurkela   Kharagpur   Mouths of the Ganges
lāspur   Bāleshwar
dia   Raipur   Sambalpur
n   Durg   Orissa   Cuttack
        Jagdalpur   Bhubaneshwar   Bay of
                Puri
ar   Brahmapur   Bengal   Irrawaddy   5
ra Pradesh   Srīkākulam
    Vizianagaram   Mouths of the Irrawaddy
    Visākhapatnam
Rājahmundry
Kākināda   133

E   F   G   H

MAINLAND SOUTHEAST ASIA

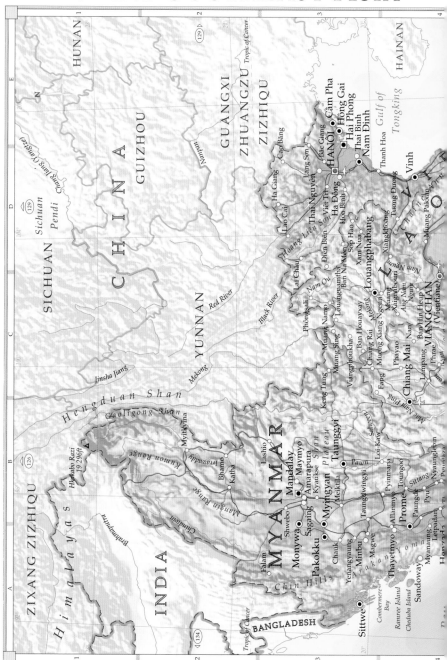

HUNAN

HAINAN

GUIZHOU

GUANGXI
ZHUANGZU
ZIZHIQU

C H I N A

SICHUAN

Sichuan
Pendi

Chang Jiang (Yangtze)

ZIXANG ZIZHIQU

Jinsha Jiang

YUNNAN

Red River

Mekong

Black River

Hoang Lien Son

Gulf of
Tongking

Cẩm Pha
Cao Bằng   Hồng Gai
                  Hải Phòng
Bắc Giang   HANOI Thái Bình
Hà Giang Lạng Sơn Nam Định
          Thái Nguyên
Lào Cai   Viêt Trì   Thanh Hoa   Vinh
Lai Châu Hà Đông
          Hòa Bình
Điện Biên Sơn La
          Ban Na Môn   Xam Nua
Phôngsali Nam Ou Sốp Hao
Nam Nam   Louangnamtha   Muong Pakxan
Muang Sing Ban Na Môn   Xiangkhoang
Louangphabang
Ban Houayxay Muong Xiangkhoang   Tương Dương
Chiang Rai Xiang Ngeun
Fang   Muong Xiang Ngeun   Ang Nam
Phayao   Muang Magetuburi Ngum
Chiang Mai Nan Ban Hin Heup VIANGCHAN
Lampang Phrae   (Vientiane)
                    Mae Nam Mun

L A O S

Mường
Khoua

Nam Nua

Hengduan Shan

Gaoligong Shan

Myitkyina

Bhamo
Katha

Kunlun Range

Mangin Range

Hkakabo Razi
19,296ft

Himalayas

Brahmaputra

INDIA

Chindwin

Irrawaddy

Lashio
Mandalay
Amarapura
Maymyo
Kyaukse Taunggyi
Mongywa Myingyan Plateau
Sagaing Meiktila Shan
Shwebo   Pakokku Loi-Kaw
Monywa Chauk Pawn
Falam   Yenangyaung Pyinmana Satween
Minbu Taungdwingyi Toungoo Sittang
Magwe Allanmyo Paungde
Thayetmyo Prome Pyu
Myanaung Letpadan

M Y A N M A R

Chin Hills

Arakan Yoma

Bago Yoma

Sandoway

Combermere
Bay

Ramree Island

Cheduba Island

Sittwe

BANGLADESH

Tropic of Cancer

Tropic of Cancer

0 km   200

0 miles   200

POPULATION

○ Less than 50,000   ○ 50,000 -100,000   ◉ 100,000 - 500,000   ■ Over

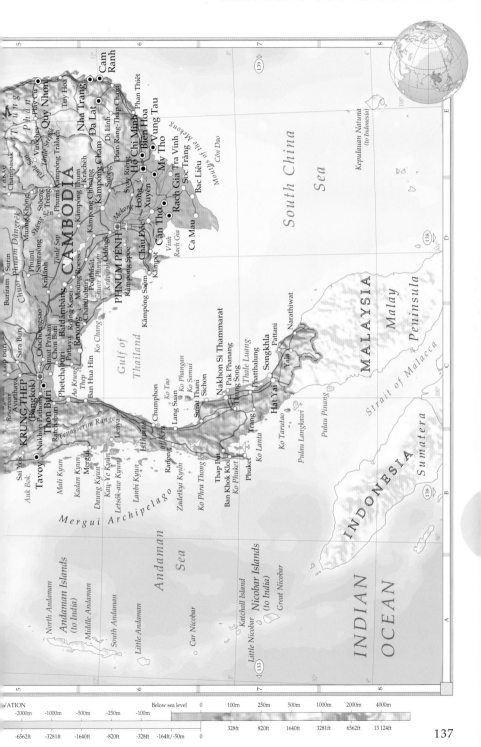

MARITIME SOUTHEAST ASIA

POPULATION

○ Less than 50,000 ○ 50,000 -100,000 ● 100,000 - 500,000 ■ Over 500

THE INDIAN OCEAN

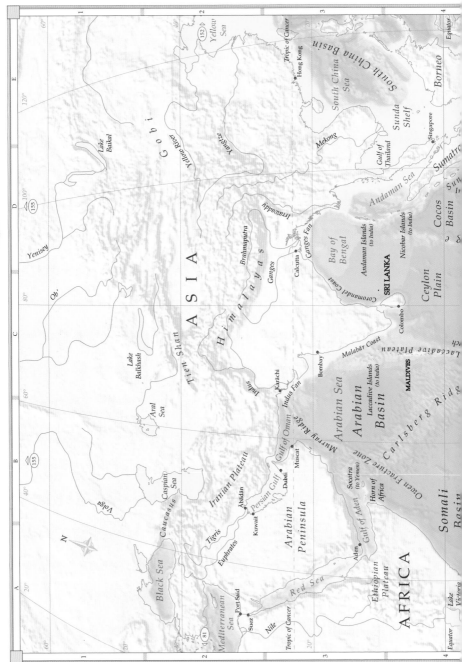

Tropic of Cancer
Equator
Equator

Yellow Sea
152
South China Basin
Hong Kong
Borneo
Sunda Shelf
South China Sea
Singapore
Sumatra
Gobi
Yellow River
Yangtze
Mekong
Gulf of Thailand
Andaman Sea
Sunda
Cocos Basin
Lake Baikal
155
Irrawaddy
Andaman Islands (to India)
Nicobar Islands (to India)
Yenisey
Brahmaputra
Ganges Fan
Bay of Bengal
SRI LANKA
Ceylon Plain
Ob'
A S I A
Himalayas
Ganges
Calcutta
Coromandel Coast
Colombo
Lake Balkhash
Tien Shan
Indus
Karachi
Indus Fan
Bombay
Malabar Coast
Laccadive Plateau
Laccadive Islands (to India)
MALDIVES
Carlsberg Ridge
Aral Sea
Arabian Sea
Arabian Basin
Murray Ridge
Owen Fracture Zone
155
Caspian Sea
Iranian Plateau
Gulf of Oman
Muscat
Dubai
Socotra (to Yemen)
Horn of Africa
Somali Basin
Volga
Caucasus
Ābādān
Persian Gulf
Kuwait
Arabian Peninsula
Gulf of Aden
Aden
N
Tigris
Euphrates
Black Sea
Ethiopian Plateau
AFRICA
Mediterranean
Port Said
Suez
Nile
Red Sea
Tropic of Cancer
81
Lake Victoria

0 km   1500
0 miles   1500

• Major ports

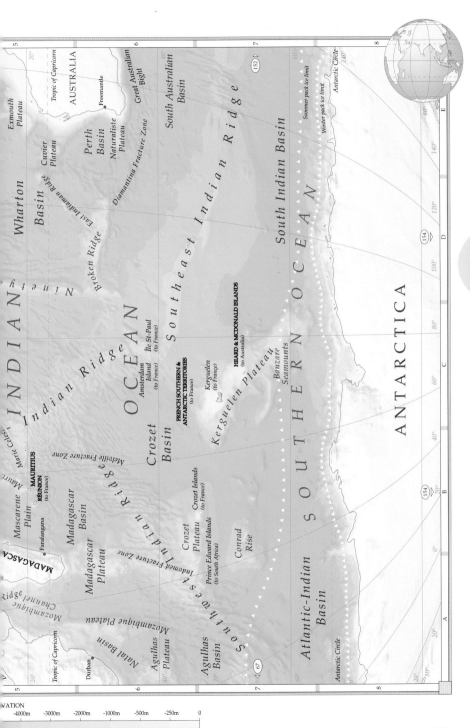

INDIAN OCEAN

Wharton Basin

Exmouth Plateau

AUSTRALIA

Tropic of Capricorn

20°

Freemantle

Cuvier Plateau

Perth Basin

Naturaliste Plateau

Great Australian Bight

South Australian Basin

Diamantina Fracture Zone

East Indian Ridge

Broken Ridge

Ninety

Indian Ridge

Southeast Indian Ridge

South Indian Basin

Île St-Paul (to France)

Amsterdam Island (to France)

FRENCH SOUTHERN & ANTARCTIC TERRITORIES (to France)

HEARD & McDONALD ISLANDS (to Australia)

Kerguelen (to France)

Kerguelen Plateau

Banzare Seamounts

SOUTHERN OCEAN

ANTARCTICA

Summer pack ice limit

Winter pack ice limit

Antarctic Circle

Mascarene Plain

Marie Celeste

Mauri...

MAURITIUS

RÉUNION (to France)

Farafangana

MADAGASCAR

Madagascar Basin

Madagascar Plateau

Mozambique Channel Ridge

Tropic of Capricorn

20°

Durban

Natal Basin

Agulhas Plateau

Mozambique Plateau

Agulhas Basin

Metdie Fracture Zone

Crozet Basin

Crozet Plateau

Crozet Islands (to France)

Conrad Rise

Prince Edward Islands (to South Africa)

Indomed Fracture Zone

Southwest Indian Ridge

Atlantic-Indian Basin

Antarctic Circle

152

154

154

67

...VATION

-4000m	-3000m	-2000m	-1000m	-500m	-250m	0
-13 124ft	-9843ft	-6562ft	-3281ft	-1640ft	-820ft	0

AUSTRALASIA & OCEANIA

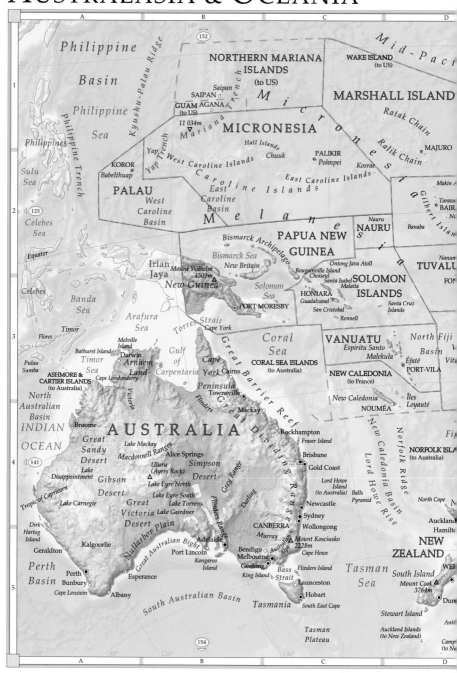

Philippine

Basin

Philippine

Sea

Philippines

Sulu
Sea

Celebes
Sea

Celebes

Equator

Banda
Sea

Timor

Flores

Pulau
Sumba

Bathurst Island

Timor

North
Australian
Basin

INDIAN

OCEAN

NORTHERN MARIANA
ISLANDS
(to US)

Saipan
SAIPAN
GUAM AGANA
(to US)
11 034m

MICRONESIA

Hall Islands
Chuuk
PALIKIR
Pohnpei
Kosrae

KOROR
Babelthuap

Yap

PALAU

West
Caroline
Basin

West Caroline Islands

Caroline Islands

East Caroline Islands

East
Caroline
Basin

WAKE ISLAND
(to US)

Mid-Paci

MARSHALL ISLAND

Ratak Chain

Ralik Chain

MAJURO

Makin

Tarawa
BAIR
N

Nauru

Banaba

NAURU

TUVALU
FON

Melane

Bismarck Archipelago

PAPUA NEW
GUINEA

Bismarck Sea
New Britain

Irian
Jaya
Mount Wilhelm
4509m
New Guinea

Solomon
Sea

PORT MORESBY

Bougainville Choiseul
Santa Isabel
Malaita

HONIARA
Guadalcanal
San Cristobal
Rennell

Ontong Java Atoll

SOLOMON
ISLANDS

Santa Cruz
Islands

Nanum

si

North Fiji

Basin

VANUATU
Espiritu Santo
Malekula
Éfaté

NEW CALEDONIA
(to France)

PORT-VILA

Vit

Arafura
Sea

Torres Strait
Cape York

Melville
Island
Darwin
Arnhem
Land
Cape Londonderry

ASHMORE &
CARTIER ISLANDS
(to Australia)

Gulf
of
Carpentaria

Cape
York
Peninsula

Cairns

Townsville

Flinders

Victoria

Coral
Sea

CORAL SEA ISLANDS
(to Australia)

New Caledonia

NOUMÉA

Îles
Loyauté

New Caledonia Ridge

New Caledonia Basin

Lord Howe Rise

Norfolk Ridge

Fi

Broome

AUSTRALIA

Great
Sandy
Desert

Lake Mackay
Macdonnell Ranges

Alice Springs

Lake
Disappointment

Gibson
Desert

Uluru
(Ayers Rock)

Simpson
Desert

Great Barrier Reef
Great Dividing Range

Mackay

Rockhampton
Fraser Island

Brisbane
Gold Coast

Lord Howe
Island
(to Australia)

Balls
Pyramid

NORFOLK ISLA
(to Australia)

North Cape

Auckland
Hamilto

N

Lord Howe Basin

Tropic of Capricorn

Lake Carnegie

Dirk
Hartog
Island

Geraldton

Perth
Basin

Perth

Bunbury

Cape Leeuwin

Albany

Great
Victoria
Desert

Lake Eyre North

Lake Eyre South
Lake Torrens
Lake Gairdner

Grey Range

Darling

Flinders Range

Newcastle
Sydney
CANBERRA
Wollongong
Mount Kosciusko
2228m
Cape Howe

NEW
ZEALAND

WE

South Island

Mount Cook
3764m

Dun

Kalgoorlie

Nullarbor Plain
Great Australian Bight

Adelaide
Port Lincoln

Kangaroo
Island

Bendigo
Melbourne
Geelong

King Island

Australian Alps
Murray

Esperance

Tasman
Sea

South Australian Basin

Bass
Strait

Flinders Island

Launceston

Hobart

Tasmania

South East Cape

Stewart Island

Anti

Tasman
Plateau

Auckland Islands
(to New Zealand)

Camp
(to N

0 km   1000

0 miles   1000

POPULATION

○ Less than 50,000   ○ 50,000 -100,000   ◉ 100,000 - 500,000   ■ Over 50

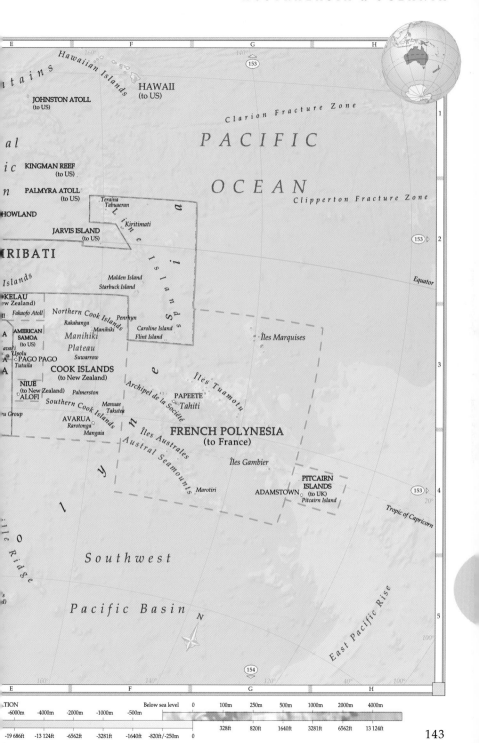

HAWAII
(to US)

JOHNSTON ATOLL
(to US)

Hawaiian Islands

Clarion Fracture Zone

PACIFIC

OCEAN

Clipperton Fracture Zone

KINGMAN REEF
(to US)

PALMYRA ATOLL
(to US)

HOWLAND

Teraina
Tabuaeran

Kiritimati

JARVIS ISLAND
(to US)

KIRIBATI

Equator

Islands

Malden Island

Starbuck Island

TOKELAU
(New Zealand)

Fakaofo Atoll

Northern Cook Islands

Penrhyn

Rakahanga

Manihiki

Caroline Island

Flint Island

AMERICAN
SAMOA
(to US)

Apia

Upolu

PAGO PAGO

Tutuila

Manihiki
Plateau

Suwarrow

Îles Marquises

COOK ISLANDS
(to New Zealand)

NIUE
(to New Zealand)
ALOFI

Palmerston

Southern Cook Islands

Manuae
Takutea

Archipel de la Société

PAPEETE
Tahiti

Îles Tuamotu

AVARUA
Rarotonga

Mangaia

Îles Australes

FRENCH POLYNESIA
(to France)

Tonga Group

Austral Seamounts

Îles Gambier

Marotiri

PITCAIRN
ISLANDS
(to UK)

ADAMSTOWN

Pitcairn Island

Tropic of Capricorn

Kermadec Ridge

Southwest

Pacific Basin

East Pacific Rise

N

ELEVATION

Below sea level

-6000m -4000m -2000m -1000m -500m

-19 686ft -13 124ft -6562ft -3281ft -1640ft -820ft/-250m 0

0 100m 250m 500m 1000m 2000m 4000m

328ft 820ft 1640ft 3281ft 6562ft 13 124ft

THE SOUTHWEST PACIFIC

NORTHERN MARIANA ISLANDS (to US)

Saipan
SAIPAN · Tinian
Rota

GUAM (to US) · AGANA

MARSHALL ISLANDS

Ra

Ralik Chain

Bikini Atoll
Rongelap Atoll
Enewetak Atoll

Micro

Yap

MICRONESIA

Hall Islands
Chuuk
Oroluk Atoll

West Caroline Islands

Ujelang Atoll
Kwajalein Atoll
Ebeye
Namu
Ailinglaplap Atoll
Jaluit Atoll
Ebon Atoll

PALIKIR
Pohnpei
Kosrae

nesia

KOROR
Babelthuap

PALAU

Caroline Islands

East Caroline Islands

M

139

Equator

Abe

PAPUA NEW GUINEA

Nauru

NAURU

Admiralty Islands
Mussau Island

Bismarck Sea
Bismarck Archipelago

New Guinea

New Ireland

INDONESIA

Madang
New Britain

Central Range
△ Mount Wilhelm 4500m
Lae

Bougainville Island

Me
lan

Owen Stanley Range

Solomon Sea

Choiseul
Santa Isabel

Kiriwina Islands

New Georgia Islands

SOLOMON ISLANDS

Malaita

HONIARA
Guadalcanal

Gulf of Papua

PORT MORESBY

Torres Strait

Arafura Sea

Louisiade Archipelago

San Cristobal
Rennell

Santa Cruz Islands

Coral Sea

VANUATU

Banks Is

Arnhem Land
Groote Eylandt

Gulf of Carpentaria

Cape York Peninsula

CORAL SEA ISLANDS (to Australia)

Espiritu Santo

Maev
Pent
Amb
Épi

Malekula

146

Barkly Tableland

Great Barrier Reef

PO
Éfaté
E

NEW CALEDONIA (to France)

NORTHERN TERRITORY

Great Dividing Range

Ouvéa
Lifou
New Caledonia
Maré

Îles Loyauté

NOUMÉA

Tropic of Capricorn
Macdonnell Ranges

QUEENSLAND

AUSTRALIA

149

0 km · 750
0 miles · 750

POPULATION
○ Less than 50,000
○ 50,000 -100,000
◉ 100,000 - 500,000
◼ Over 5

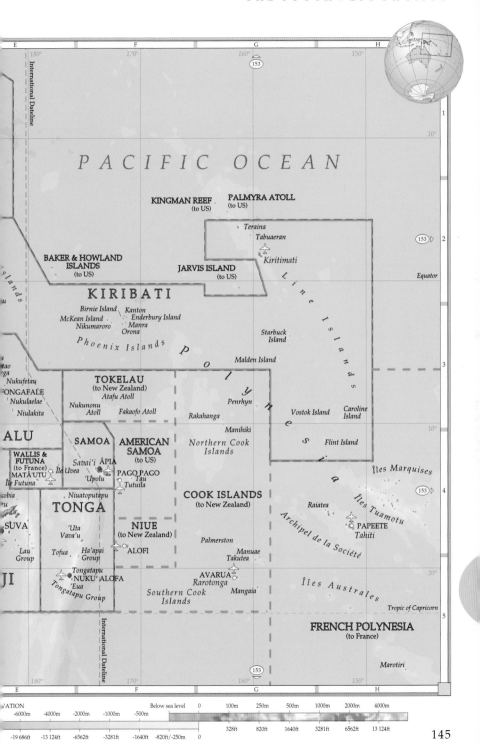

E   180°   170° F   160° G   150° H

(153)

International Dateline

1

10°

PACIFIC OCEAN

KINGMAN REEF   PALMYRA ATOLL
(to US)   (to US)

Teraina
Tabuaeran   (153) 2

BAKER & HOWLAND   ✈ Kiritimati
ISLANDS
(to US)   JARVIS ISLAND   Equator
(to US)

KIRIBATI   Line Islands

Birnie Island   Kanton
McKean Island   Enderbury Island
Nikumaroro   Manra   Starbuck
Orona   Island

Phoenix Islands   P   Malden Island   3

o
Nukufetau   l   10°
FONGAFALE   TOKELAU   y
Nukulaelae   (to New Zealand)   Penrhyn   n
Niulakita   Atafu Atoll   e   Vostok Island   Caroline
Nukunonu   s   Island
ALU   Atoll   Fakaofo Atoll   Rakahanga   i
SAMOA   AMERICAN   Manihiki   a
WALLIS &   SAMOA   Northern Cook   Flint Island   Îles Marquises
FUTUNA   Savai'i ĀPIA   (to US)   Islands
(to France)   Île Uvea   PAGO PAGO   (153) 4
MATA'UTU   'Upolu   Tau
Île Futuna   Tutuila   Îles Tuamotu
Niuatoputapu   COOK ISLANDS   Raiatea
SUVA   TONGA   (to New Zealand)   ✈ PAPEETE
'Uta   Tahiti
Vava'u   NIUE   Archipel de la Société
Tofua   Ha'apai   (to New Zealand)   Palmerston
Lau   Group   ALOFI   Manuae   20°
Group   Takutea   Îles Australes
JI   Tongatapu   AVARUA
NUKU'ALOFA   Rarotonga   Mangaia   Tropic of Capricorn
'Eua   Manua
Tongatapu Group   Southern Cook
Islands   FRENCH POLYNESIA
(to France)   5

International Dateline   Marotiri

(153)

E   180°   170° F   160° G   150° H

WESTERN AUSTRALIA

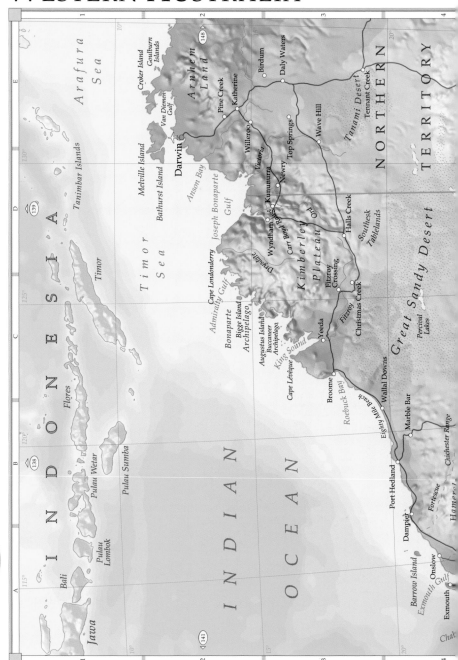

Arafura Sea

Arnhem Land

Croker Island
Goulburn Islands
148

Van Diemen Gulf

Melville Island

Bathurst Island

Croker Island

Pine Creek
Katherine

Birdum
Daly Waters

Darwin

Anson Bay

Willeroo
Victoria
Newry
Top Springs
Wave Hill

Tennant Creek

Tanami Desert

Joseph Bonaparte Gulf

Wyndham
Kununurra
Carr Boyd Range

Halls Creek

NORTHERN

TERRITORY

Cape Londonderry

Admiralty Gulf

Bonaparte

Bigge Island
Buccaneer Archipelago

Drysdale

Ord

Southesk
Tablelands

Kimberley Plateau

Fitzroy Crossing

Augustus Island

King Sound

Cape Leveque

Yeeda

Fitzroy

Christmas Creek

Percival Lakes

Great Sandy Desert

Broome

Roebuck Bay

Wallal Downs

Eighty Mile Beach

Marble Bar

Chichester Range

Port Hedland

Dampier
Onslow

Fortescue

Hamersley

Barrow Island

Exmouth Gulf

Exmouth

Chab

Timor Sea

Timor

Tanimbar Islands

138
139
148
141

Pulau Wetar

Flores

Pulau Sumba

Pulau Lombok

Bali

Jawa

I N D O N E S I A

I N D I A N   O C E A N

0 km   400

0 miles   400

POPULATION

○ Less than 50,000   ○ 50,000 -100,000   ◉ 100,000 - 500,000   ◼ Over 50

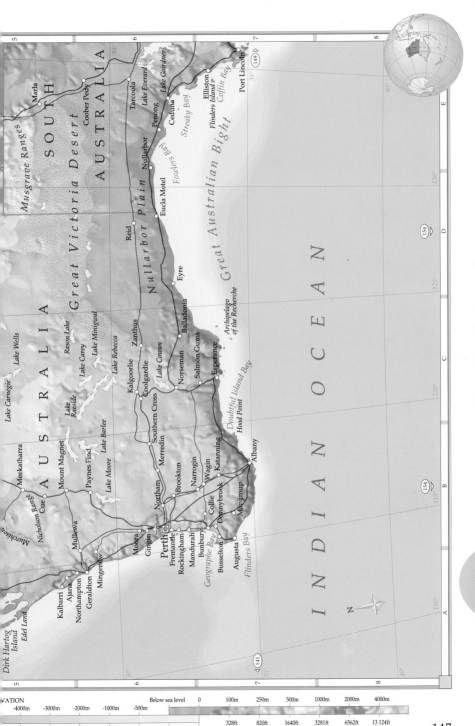

SOUTH AUSTRALIA

AUSTRALIA

Musgrave Ranges

Great Victoria Desert

Nullarbor Plain

Great Australian Bight

INDIAN OCEAN

Marla
Coober Pedy
Tarcoola
Lake Everard
Lake Gairdner
Penong
Nullarbor
Ceduna
Elliston
Flinders Island
Coffin Bay
Port Lincoln
Fowlers Bay
Streaky Bay
Eucla Motel
Reid
Eyre
Balladonia
Zanthus
Kalgoorlie
Coolgardie
Lake Cowan
Norseman
Salmon Gums
Esperance
Southern Cross
Merredin
Archipelago of the Recherche
Doubtful Island Bay
Hood Point
Brookton
Narrogin
Wagin
Katanning
Albany
Northam
Perth
Fremantle
Rockingham
Mandurah
Bunbury
Busselton
Collie
Donnybrook
Augusta
Manjimup
Geographe Bay
Flinders Bay
Moora
Gingin
Meekatharra
Mount Magnet
Paynes Find
Cue
Mullewa
Mingenew
Geraldton
Northampton
Ajana
Kalbarri

Lake Carnegie
Lake Wells
Raeson Lake
Lake Carey
Lake Minigwal
Lake Rebecca
Lake Raeside
Lake Barlee
Lake Moore

Nicholson Range
Murchison
Dirk Hartog Island
Edel Land

N

VATION

-4000m	-3000m	-2000m	-1000m	-500m	Below sea level	0	100m	250m	500m	1000m	2000m	4000m
-13 124ft	-9843ft	-6562ft	-3281ft	-1640ft	-820ft/-250m	0		328ft	820ft	1640ft	3281ft	6562ft	13 124ft

EASTERN AUSTRALIA

0 km   400

0 miles   400

POPULATION

○ Less than 50,000   ○ 50,000 -100,000   ◉ 100,000 - 500,000   ■ Over 50

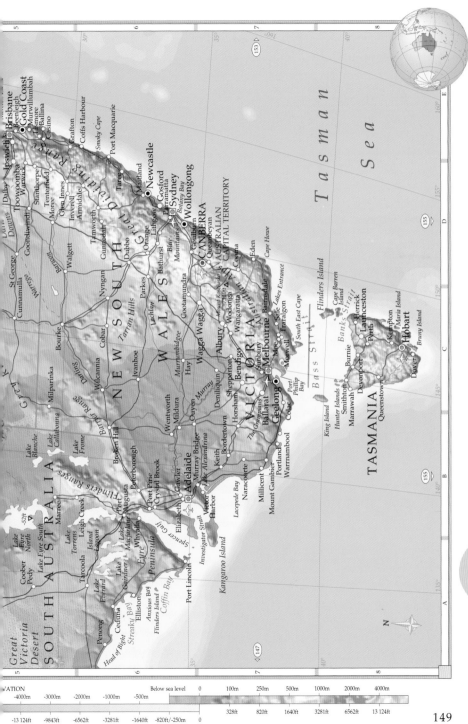

ELEVATION

-4000m	-3000m	-2000m	-1000m	-500m	Below sea level	0	100m	250m	500m	1000m	2000m	4000m
-13 124ft	-9843ft	-6562ft	-3281ft	-1640ft	-820ft/-250m	0	328ft	820ft	1640ft	3281ft	6562ft	13 124ft

NEW ZEALAND

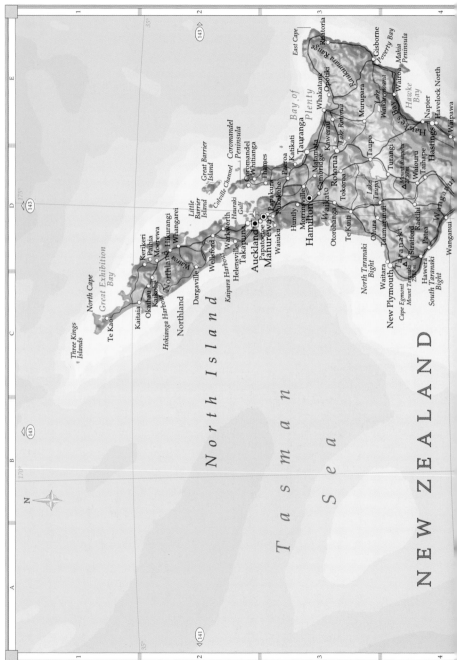

Three Kings Islands

North Cape

Te Kao

Kaitaia

Okaihau

Kaikohe

Kerikeri

Paihia

Moerewa

Hokianga Harbour

Dargaville

Kaipara Harbour

Northland

Whangarei

Pikurangi

Whangarei

Great Exhibition Bay

North Island

T a s m a n   S e a

Wellsford

Helensville

Takapuna

Warkworth

Hauraki Gulf

Manukau

Little Barrier Island

Great Barrier Island

Coromandel Channel

Coromandel Peninsula

Coromandel

Whitianga

Thames

Paeroa

Katikati

Tauranga

Auckland

Papatoetoe

Mahurewa

Papakura

Waiuku

Pukekohe

Morrinsville

Huntly

Hamilton

Cambridge

Matamata

Waikato

Te Aroha

Rotorua

Lake Rotorua

Kawerau

Opotiki

Whakatane

Bay of Plenty

Raukumara Range

East Cape

Rotoria

Gisborne

Poverty Bay

Mahia Peninsula

Murupara

Lake Waikaremoana

Taupo

Lake Taupo

Wairoa

Napier

Hastings

Havelock North

Waipawa

Hawke Bay

Turangi

Mount Ruapehu 2797m

Waiouru

Taihape

Raetihi

Ohura

Taumarunui

Te Kuiti

Otorohanga

Tokoroa

Wanganui

North Taranaki Bight

New Plymouth

Cape Egmont

Mount Taranaki 2518m

Taranaki

Stratford

Hawera

Patea

South Taranaki Bight

Waitara

Wanganui

NEW ZEALAND

N

0 km   100
0 miles   100

POPULATION

○ Less than 50,000   ○ 50,000 -100,000   ◉ 100,000 - 500,000   ◼ Over 500

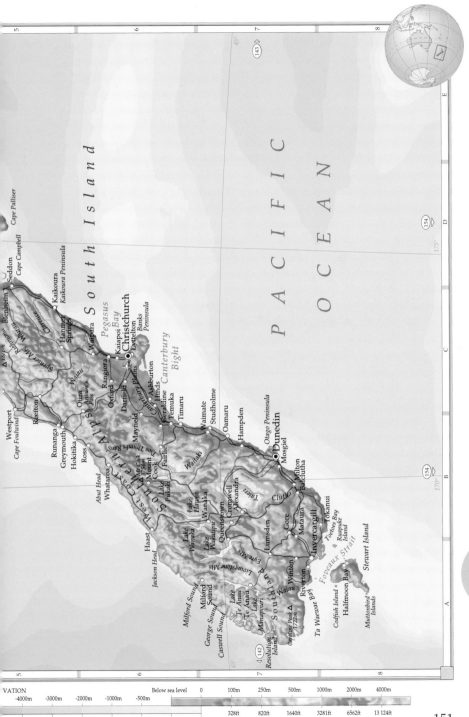

South Island

Cape Palliser
Cape Campbell
Seddon
Blenheim
Kaikoura
Kaikoura Peninsula
Spenser Mts
Hanmer
Springs
Rai
Chrome
Waiau
Waipara
Pegasus Bay
Kaiapoi Bay
Christchurch
Lyttelton
Banks
Peninsula
Rangiora
Oxford
Darfield
Canterbury Plains
Ashburton
Hinds
Mayfield
Geraldine
Temuka
Canterbury Bight
Mount
Fairlie
Timaru
Waimate
Studholme
Oamaru
Waitaki
Hampden
Otago Peninsula
Dunedin
Mosgiel
Milton
Balclutha

Westport
Cape Foulwind
Runanga
Greymouth
Hokitika
Ross
Reefton
Otira
Arthur's
Pass
Abut Head
Whataroa
Southern Alps
Mt Cook
3754m
Cook
Two Thumbs Range
Lake
Pukaki
Lake
Tekapo
Lake
Hawea
Lake
Wanaka
Cromwell
Alexandra
Taieri
Clutha
Clyde
Haast
Jackson Head
Lake
Wanaka
Lake
Wakatipu
Queenstown
Eyre Mts
Lumsden
Gore
Mataura
West Coast
South West Plain
Lake
Te Anau
Caroline Peak
1722m
Winton
Waiau
Invercargill
Riverton
Toetoes Bay
Tokanui
Mataura
Ruapuke
Island
Foveaux Strait
Stewart Island
Codfish Island
Halfmoon Bay
Muttonbird
Islands
Ta Waewae Bay
Milford Sound
Milford
Sound
George Sound
Caswell Sound
Lake
Manapouri
Resolution
Island
Livingstone Mts

PACIFIC OCEAN

143
154
154
142

45°
175°
170°
45°

5
6
7
8

E
D
C
B
A

THE PACIFIC OCEAN

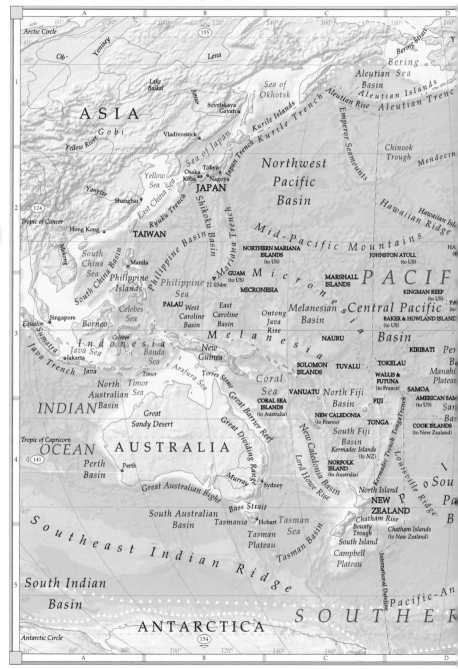

Arctic Circle

155

Ob'
Yenisey
Lena

Bering Strait

Bering

Lake
Baikal

Aleutian Basin

Amur

Sovetskaya
Gavan

Aleutian Rise
Aleutian Islands
Aleutian Trench

A S I A
Gobi

Vladivostock

Yellow River

Kurile Islands

Emperor Seamounts

Chinook
Trough

Mendocin

Yellow
Sea

Osaka Tōkyō
Kōbe Nagoya
JAPAN

Japan Trench
Kurile Trench

Northwest
Pacific
Basin

Yangtze

Shanghai

Sea of Japan

Sea of
Okhotsk

Hawaiian Ridge

Hawaiian Isl

Tropic of Cancer

124

East China Sea

Ryukyu Trench

Shikoku Basin

Mid-Pacific Mountains

HA

Hong Kong

TAIWAN

South
China
Sea

Manila

Philippine Basin

Philippine Basin

Mariana Trench

NORTHERN MARIANA
ISLANDS
(to US)

JOHNSTON ATOLL
(to US)

HA

Mekong

South China Basin

Philippine
Islands

Philippine
Sea

GUAM
(to US)

11 034m

MICRONESIA

M i c r o n e s i a

PACIF

MARSHALL
ISLANDS

KINGMAN REEF
(to US)

Singapore

Celebes
Sea

PALAU
West
Caroline
Basin

East
Caroline
Basin

Ontong
Java
Rise

Melanesian
Basin

Central Pacific

PA

Equator

Borneo

Sumatra

Java Sea
Jakarta

Celebes

Banda
Sea

Indonesia
New
Guinea

M e l a n e s i a

BAKER & HOWLAND ISLAND
(to US)

Basin

NAURU

KIRIBATI

Per

Java Trench

Java

Timor

North
Australian
Basin

Arafura Sea

Torres Strait

Great Barrier Reef

Coral
Sea

SOLOMON
ISLANDS

TUVALU

TOKELAU

B

Manahi
Platea

WALLIS &
FUTUNA
(to France)

SAMOA

INDIAN Basin

Great
Sandy Desert

CORAL SEA
ISLANDS
(to Australia)

VANUATU North Fiji
Basin

NEW CALEDONIA
(to France)

FIJI

AMERICAN SAM
(to US)

San

Ba

Tropic of Capricorn

OCEAN AUSTRALIA

Perth
Basin

Perth

Great Dividing Range

New Caledonia Basin

Lord Howe Rise

TONGA

South Fiji
Basin

Kermadec Islands
(to NZ)

COOK ISLANDS
(to New Zealand)

Sou

141

NORFOLK
ISLAND
(to Australia)

Kermadec Trench

Tonga Trench

Louisville Ridge

Pa

B

Great Australian Bight

Murray

Sydney

North Island

NEW
ZEALAND

P

Bass Strait

South Australian
Basin

Tasmania

Hobart

Tasman
Sea

Tasman
Plateau

Tasman
Basin

Chatham Rise

Bounty
Trough

Chatham Islands
(to New Zealand)

South Island

Campbell
Plateau

International Dateline

S o u t h e a s t I n d i a n R i d g e

South Indian
Basin

Pacific-An

S O U T H E R

Antarctic Circle

ANTARCTICA

154

0 km   2000

0 miles   2000

● Major ports

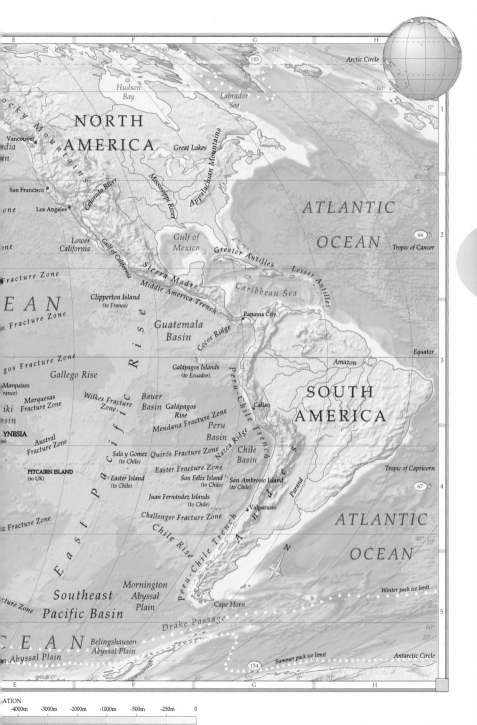

E   F   G   H

Arctic Circle

Hudson
Bay   *Labrador*
                Sea

NORTH
AMERICA   *Great Lakes*

Vancouver

San Francisco

Los Angeles   *Lower*   *Appalachian Mountains*
                   California

Fracture Zone   *Gulf of*   *Greater Antilles*   **ATLANTIC**
                               Mexico   **OCEAN**   Tropic of Cancer

n Fracture Zone   Clipperton Island   *Sierra Madre*   *Lesser Antilles*
                     (to France)   *Middle America Trench*   *Caribbean Sea*

EAN   **Guatemala**   *Cocos Ridge*   Panama City
           Basin

gos Fracture Zone   Gallego Rise   Galápagos Islands   *Amazon*   Equator
                                           (to Ecuador)

Marquises
(*rance*)   Marquesas   Wilkes Fracture   Bauer   *Peru-Chile Trench*   **SOUTH**
iki   Fracture Zone   Zone   Basin Galápagos   Callao   **AMERICA**
sin   Rise
YNESIA   Mendana Fracture Zone   Peru
e)   Austral   Sala y Gomez   Quirós Fracture Zone   Basin   *Nazca Ridge*
             Fracture Zone   (to Chile)   Chile   Tropic of Capricorn
PITCAIRN ISLAND   Easter Island   Easter Fracture Zone   Basin
(to UK)   (to Chile)   San Félix Island
                                                 San Ambrosto Island   (to Chile)
                                                 (to Chile)

z Fracture Zone   Juan Fernández Islands   Valparaíso   **ATLANTIC**
                     (to Chile)
                     Challenger Fracture Zone   **OCEAN**

                     East Pacific Rise   *Chile Rise*   *Peru-Chile Trench*   *Andes*   *Paraná*

ture Zone   **Southeast**   Mornington
               Pacific Basin   Abyssal   *Cape Horn*   Winter pack ice limit
                                  Plain
OCEAN   Belingshausen   *Drake Passage*
             Abyssal Plain
Abyssal Plain   Summer pack ice limit   Antarctic Circle

E   F   G   H

POLAR REGIONS

ANTARCTICA

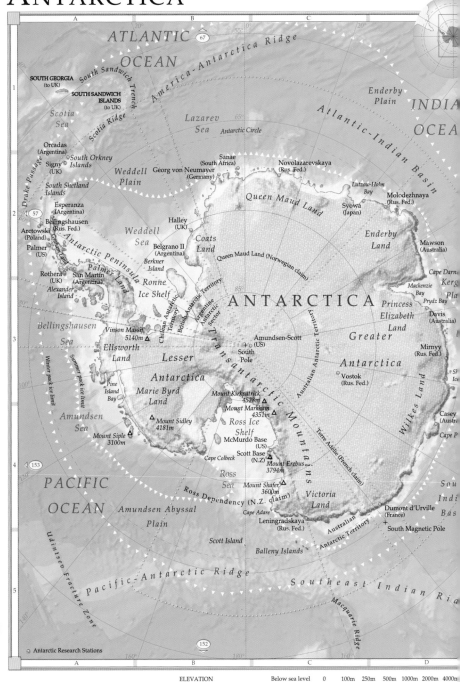

ATLANTIC OCEAN

America-Antarctica Ridge

SOUTH GEORGIA
(to UK)

SOUTH SANDWICH
ISLANDS
(to UK)

Scotia
Sea

Lazarev
Sea

Antarctic Circle

Enderby
Plain

INDIA

OCEA

Atlantic-Indian Basin

Orcadas
(Argentina)

Signy
(UK)

South Orkney
Islands

Weddell
Plain

Georg von Neumayer
(Germany)

Sanae
(South Africa)

Novolazarevskaya
(Rus. Fed.)

Lutzow-Holm
Bay

Molodezhnaya
(Rus. Fed.)

Queen Maud Land

South Shetland
Islands

Esperanza
(Argentina)

Bellingshausen
(Rus. Fed.)

Arctowski
(Poland)

Palmer
(US)

Rothera
(UK)

San Martin
(Argentina)

Alexander
Island

Weddell
Sea

Halley
(UK)

Belgrano II
(Argentina)

Berkner
Island

Coats
Land

Ronne
Ice Shelf

Syowa
(Japan)

Enderby
Land

Mawson
(Australia)

Cape Darn

Mackenzie
Bay

Kerg

Pla

Prydz Bay

Queen Maud Land (Norwegian claim)

ANTARCTICA

Princess
Elizabeth
Land

Davis
(Australia)

Bellingshausen
Sea

Vinson Massif
5140m

Ellsworth
Land

Lesser
Antarctica

Marie Byrd
Land

Amundsen-Scott
(US)

South
Pole

Greater
Antarctica

Mirnyy
(Rus. Fed.)

Vostok
(Rus. Fed.)

Casey
(Austra

Cape P

Sou
Indi
Bas

Pine
Island
Bay

Mount Sidley
4181m

Mount Siple
3100m

Mount Kirkpatrick
4528m

Mount Markham
4351m

Ross Ice
Shelf

McMurdo Base
(US)

Scott Base
(N.Z)

Mount Erebus
3794m

Cape Colbeck

Amundsen
Sea

Winter pack ice limit

Summer pack ice limit

PACIFIC

OCEAN

Amundsen Abyssal
Plain

Ross
Sea

Ross Dependency (N.Z. claim)

Cape Adare

Mount Shafer
3600m

Victoria
Land

Leningradskaya
(Rus. Fed.)

Dumont d'Urville
(France)

South Magnetic Pole

Scott Island

Balleny Islands

Pacific-Antarctic Ridge

Southeast Indian Ria

Macquarie Ridge

Antarctic Research Stations

Drake Passage

Scotia Ridge

South Sandwich Trench

Antarctic Peninsula

Graham Land

Palmer Land

Chilean Antarctic Territory

British Antarctic Territory

Argentine Antarctic Sector

Transantarctic Mountains

Australian Antarctic Territory

Terre Adélie (French claim)

Wilkes Land

Australian Antarctic Territory

Udintsev Fracture Zone

ELEVATION   Below sea level   0   100m 250m 500m 1000m 2000m 4000m
-4000m -3000m -2000m -1000m -500m

-13 124ft -9843ft -6562ft -3281ft -1640ft -820ft/-250m   328ft   820ft 1640ft 3281ft 6562ft 13 124

0 km   500

0 miles   500

154

RCTIC OCEAN

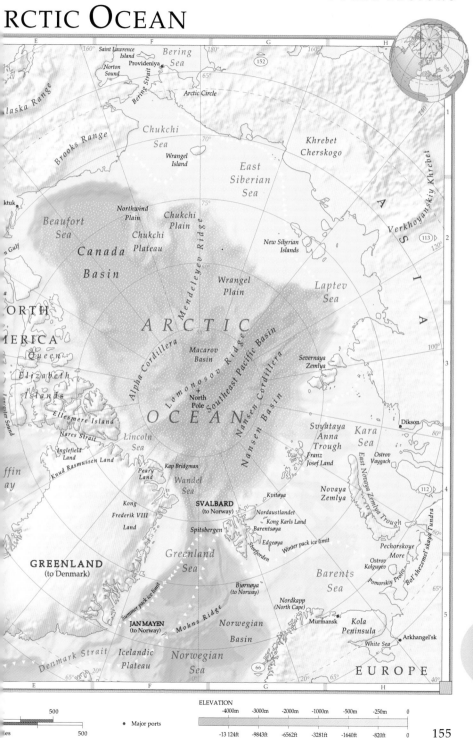

Saint Lawrence Island
Norton Sound
Providéniya
Bering Strait
Bering Sea
152
65°
Arctic Circle

Chukchi Sea
Wrangel Island
70°

Khrebet Cherskogo

East Siberian Sea

laska Range
Brooks Range
ktuk

Northwind Plain
Chukchi Plain
75°

New Siberian Islands

Beaufort Sea
n Gulf

Canada Basin
Chukchi Plateau

Mendeleyev Ridge
60°

Wrangel Plain

Laptev Sea

Verkhoyanskiy Khrebet
120°
113
A
S
I
A
100°

A R C T I C

Macarov Basin
85°
Alpha Cordillera
Lomonosov Ridge
Southeast Pacific Basin
+ North Pole
Nansen Cordillera
Nansen Basin

Severnaya Zemlya
80°
Dikson

Kara Sea
Ostrov Vaygach
East Novaya Zemlya Trough
112

ORTH
ERICA
Queen
Elizabeth
Islands
Ellesmere Island
Lancaster Sound

O C E A N

Svyataya Anna Trough
Franz Josef Land

Nares Strait
Inglefield Land
Knud Rasmussen Land
Lincoln Sea

ffin
ay

Peary Land
Kap Bridgman
Wandel Sea

Kvitøya

Novaya Zemlya

Kong Frederik VIII Land
SVALBARD (to Norway)
Nordaustlandet
Kong Karls Land
Barentsøya
Spitsbergen
Edgeøya
Storfjorden
Winter pack ice limit

Pechorskoye More
Ostrov Kolguyev
Bol'shezemel'skaya Tundra
Pomorskiy Proliv
65°

GREENLAND (to Denmark)

Greenland Sea

Barents Sea

Summer pack ice limit
JAN MAYEN (to Norway)
Mohns Ridge
Bjørnøya (to Norway)
Nordkapp (North Cape)
Murmansk
White Sea
Kola Peninsula
Arkhangel'sk

Norwegian Basin

Denmark Strait
65°
20°
Icelandic Plateau
Norwegian Sea
66
20°
65°
40°

EUROPE

ELEVATION

-4000m	-3000m	-2000m	-1000m	-500m	-250m	0

500

• Major ports

les

500

-13 124ft	-9843ft	-6562ft	-3281ft	-1640ft	-820ft	0

155

DESPITE THE RAPID process of decolonization since World War II, around 10 million people in 59 territories around the world continue to live under the protection of France, Australia, Denmark, Norway, Portugal, New Zealand, the UK, the USA, or the Netherlands. These remnants of former colonial empires may have persisted for economic, strategic, or political reasons and are now administered in a variety of ways.

AUSTRALIA

AUSTRALIA'S OVERSEAS TERRITORIES have not been an issue since Papua New Guinea became independent in 1975. Consequently there is no overriding policy toward them. Norfolk Island is inhabited by descendants of the HMS Bounty mutineers and more recent Australian migrants.

ASHMORE & CARTIER ISLANDS
Indian Ocean
STATUS: External territory
CLAIMED: 1978
CAPITAL: Not applicable
POPULATION: None
AREA: 2 sq miles
(5.2 sq km)

CHRISTMAS ISLAND
Indian Ocean
STATUS: External territory
CLAIMED: 1958
CAPITAL: Flying Fish Cove
POPULATION: 2,871
AREA: 52 sq miles
(134.6 sq km)

COCOS ISLANDS
Indian Ocean
STATUS: External territory
CLAIMED: 1955
CAPITAL: No official capital
POPULATION: 555
AREA: 5.5 sq miles
(14.24 sq km)

CORAL SEA ISLANDS
South Pacific
STATUS: External territory
CLAIMED: 1969
CAPITAL: None
POPULATION: 8 (meteorologists)
AREA: 1.16 sq miles
(Less than 3 sq km)

HEARD & MCDONALD IS.
Indian Ocean
STATUS: External territory
CLAIMED: 1947
CAPITAL: Not applicable
POPULATION: None
AREA: 161 sq miles
(417 sq km)

NORFOLK ISLAND
South Pacific
STATUS: External territory
CLAIMED: 1913
CAPITAL: Kingston
POPULATION: 2,637
AREA: 13.3 sq miles
(34.4 sq km)

DENMARK

THE FAEROE ISLANDS have been under Danish administration since Queen Margrethe I of Denmark inherited Norway in 1380. The Home Rule Act of 1948 gave the Faeroese control over all their internal affairs. Greenland first came under Danish rule in 1380. Today, Denmark remains responsible for the island's foreign affairs and defense.

FAEROE ISLANDS
North Atlantic
STATUS: External territory
CLAIMED: 1380
CAPITAL: Tórshavn
POPULATION: 47,310
AREA: 540 sq miles
(1,399 sq km)

GREENLAND
North Atlantic
STATUS: External territory
CLAIMED: 1380
CAPITAL: Nuuk
POPULATION: 55,385
AREA: 840,000 sq miles
(2,175,516 sq km)

FRANCE

FRANCE HAS DEVELOPED economi ties with its overseas territories, thereby stressing interdepender over independence. Overseas *départements*, officially part of France, have their own governments. Territorial *collectiv* and overseas *territoires* have varying degrees of autonomy.

CLIPPERTON ISLAND
East Pacific
STATUS: Dependency of French Polynesia
CLAIMED: 1930
CAPITAL: Not applicable
POPULATION: None
AREA: 2.7 sq miles
(7 sq km)

FRENCH GUIANA
South America
STATUS: Overseas departmen
CLAIMED: 1817
CAPITAL: Cayenne
POPULATION: 135,000
AREA: 35,135 sq miles
(90,996 sq km)

FRENCH POLYNESIA
South Pacific
STATUS: Overseas territory
CLAIMED: 1843
CAPITAL: Papeete
POPULATION: 211,000
AREA: 1,608 sq miles
(4,165 sq km)

GUADELOUPE
West Indies
STATUS: Overseas departmen
CLAIMED: 1635
CAPITAL: Basse-Terre
POPULATION: 413,000
AREA: 687 sq miles
(1,780 sq km)

ARTINIQUE
Indies
STATUS: Overseas department
CLAIMED: 1635
CAPITAL: Fort-de-France
POPULATION: 371,000
AREA: 425 sq miles
(00 sq km)

MAYOTTE
an Ocean
STATUS: Territorial collectivity
CLAIMED: 1843
CAPITAL: Mamoudzou
POPULATION: 97,088
AREA: 144 sq miles
(4 sq km)

NEW CALEDONIA
Pacific
STATUS: Overseas territory
CLAIMED: 1853
CAPITAL: Noumeá
POPULATION: 179,000
AREA: 7,374 sq miles
(103 sq km)

REUNION
an Ocean
STATUS: Overseas department
CLAIMED: 1638
CAPITAL: Denis
POPULATION: 632,000
AREA: 970 sq miles
(12 sq km)

ST PIERRE & MIQUELON
th America
STATUS: Territorial collectivity
CLAIMED: 1604
CAPITAL: Saint-Pierre
POPULATION: 6,000
AREA: 93.4 sq miles
(2 sq km)

WALLIS & FUTUNA
th Pacific
STATUS: Overseas territory
CLAIMED: 1842
CAPITAL: Matā'Utu
POPULATION: 14,000
AREA: 106 sq miles
(4 sq km)

NETHERLANDS

THE COUNTRY'S TWO remaining overseas territories were formerly part of the Dutch West Indies. Both are now self-governing, but the Netherlands remains responsible for their defense.

ARUBA
West Indies
STATUS: Autonomous part of the Netherlands
CLAIMED: 1643
CAPITAL: Oranjestad
POPULATION: 69,000
AREA: 75 sq miles
(194 sq km)

NETHERLANDS ANTILLES
West Indies
STATUS: Autonomous part of the Netherlands
CLAIMED: 1816
CAPITAL: Willemstad
POPULATION: 195,000
AREA: 308 sq miles
(800 sq km)

NEW ZEALAND

NEW ZEALAND'S GOVERNMENT has no desire to retain any overseas territories. However, the economic weakness of its dependent territory Tokelau and its freely associated states, Niue and the Cook Islands, has forced New Zealand to remain responsible for their foreign policy and defense.

COOK ISLANDS
South Pacific
STATUS: Associated territory
CLAIMED: 1901
CAPITAL: Avarua
POPULATION: 19,000
AREA: 113 sq miles
(293 sq km)

NIUE
South Pacific
STATUS: Associated territory
CLAIMED: 1901
CAPITAL: Alofi
POPULATION: 2,000
AREA: 102 sq miles
(264 sq km)

TOKELAU
South Pacific
STATUS: Dependent territory
CLAIMED: 1926
CAPITAL: Not applicable
POPULATION: 2,000
AREA: 4 sq miles
(10.4 sq km)

NORWAY

IN 1920, 41 nations signed the Spitsbergen treaty recognizing Norwegian sovereignty over Svalbard. There is a NATO base on Jan Mayen. Bouvet Island is a nature reserve.

BOUVET ISLAND
South Atlantic
STATUS: Dependency
CLAIMED: 1928
CAPITAL: Not applicable
POPULATION: None
AREA: 22 sq miles
(58 sq km)

JAN MAYEN
North Atlantic
STATUS: Dependency
CLAIMED: 1929
CAPITAL: Not applicable
POPULATION: None
AREA: 147 sq miles
(381 sq km)

PETER I. ISLAND
Southern Ocean
STATUS: Dependency
CLAIMED: 1931
CAPITAL: Not applicable
POPULATION: None
AREA: 69 sq miles
(180 sq km)

NORWAY *continued*

SVALBARD
Arctic Ocean
STATUS: Dependency
CLAIMED: 1920
CAPITAL: Longyearbyen
POPULATION: 3,431
AREA: 24,289 sq miles
(62,906 sq km)

PORTUGAL

AFTER A COUP in 1974, Portugal's overseas possessions were rapidly granted sovereignty. Macao is the only one remaining and it is to become a Special Administrative Region of China in 1999.

MACAO
South China
STATUS: Special territory
CLAIMED: 1557
CAPITAL: Macao
POPULATION: 388,000
AREA: 7 sq miles
(18 sq km)

UNITED KINGDOM

THE UK STILL has the largest number of overseas territories. Locally-governed by a mixture of elected representatives and appointed officials, they all enjoy a large measure of internal self-government, but certain powers, such as foreign affairs and defense, are reserved for Governors of the British Crown.

ANGUILLA
West Indies
STATUS: Dependent territory
CLAIMED: 1650
CAPITAL: The Valley
POPULATION: 8,960
AREA: 37 sq miles
(96 sq km)

ASCENSION
South Atlantic
STATUS: Dependency of St. Helena
CLAIMED: 1673
CAPITAL: Not applicable
POPULATION: 1,099
AREA: 34 sq miles (88 sq km)

BERMUDA
North Atlantic
STATUS: Crown colony
CLAIMED: 1612
CAPITAL: Hamilton
POPULATION: 60,686
AREA: 20.5 sq miles
(53 sq km)

BRITISH INDIAN OCEAN TERRITORY
STATUS: Dependent territory
CLAIMED: 1814
CAPITAL: No official capital
POPULATION: 3,400
AREA: 23 sq miles
(60 sq km)

BRITISH VIRGIN ISLANDS
West Indies
STATUS: Dependent territory
CLAIMED: 1672
CAPITAL: Road Town
POPULATION: 16,644
AREA: 59 sq miles
(153 sq km)

CAYMAN ISLANDS
West Indies
STATUS: Dependent territory
CLAIMED: 1670
CAPITAL: George Town
POPULATION: 25,355
AREA: 100 sq miles
(259 sq km)

FALKLAND ISLANDS
South Atlantic
STATUS: Dependent territory
CLAIMED: 1832
CAPITAL: Stanley
POPULATION: 2,121
AREA: 4,699 sq miles
(12,173 sq km)

GIBRALTAR
Southwest Europe
STATUS: Crown colony
CLAIMED: 1713
CAPITAL: Gibraltar
POPULATION: 28,074
AREA: 2.5 sq miles
(6.5 sq km)

GUERNSEY
Channel Islands
STATUS: Crown dependency
CLAIMED: 1066
CAPITAL: St Peter Port
POPULATION: 58,000
AREA: 25 sq miles
(65 sq km)

ISLE OF MAN
British Isles
STATUS: Crown dependency
CLAIMED: 1765
CAPITAL: Douglas
POPULATION: 71,000
AREA: 221 sq miles
(572 sq km)

JERSEY
Channel Islands
STATUS: Crown dependency
CLAIMED: 1066
CAPITAL: St. Helier
POPULATION: 84,082
AREA: 45 sq miles
(116 sq km)

MONTSERRAT
West Indies
STATUS: Dependent territory
CLAIMED: 1632
CAPITAL: Plymouth
POPULATION: 11,000
AREA: 40 sq miles
(102 sq km)

PITCAIRN ISLANDS
South Pacific
STATUS: Dependent territory
CLAIMED: 1887
CAPITAL: Adamstown
POPULATION: 66
AREA: 1.35 sq miles (3.5 sq km)

HELENA
h Atlantic
rUS: Dependent territory
.MED: 1673
'ITAL: Jamestown
'ULATION: 6,000
A: 47 sq miles (122 sq km)

UTH GEORGIA & E SANDWICH ISLANDS
h Atlantic
rUS: Dependent territory
.MED: 1775
ULATION: No permanent
dents
A: 1,387 sq miles
92 sq km)

ISTAN DA CUNHA
h Atlantic
rUS: Dependency of St. Helena
.MED: 1612
ULATION: 297
A: 38 sq miles (98 sq km)

RKS & CAICOS ISLANDS
* *Indies*
rUS: Dependent territory
.MED: 1766
ITAL: Cockburn Town
ULATION: 13,000
A: 166 sq miles (430 sq km)

NITED STATES F AMERICA

ERICA'S OVERSEAS TERRITORIES have
1 seen as strategically useful, if
ensive, links with its
ckyards." The US has, in most
s, given the local population a
in deciding their own status. A
Commonwealth territory, such
uerto Rico has a greater level of
pendence than that of a US
acorporated or external territory.

ERICAN SAMOA
h Pacific
rUS: Unincorporated
itory
IMED: 1900
ITAL: Pago Pago
ULATION: 51,000
A: 75 sq miles (195 sq km)

BAKER & HOWLAND ISLANDS
South Pacific
STATUS: Unincorporated
territory
CLAIMED: 1856
CAPITAL: Not applicable
POPULATION: None
AREA: 0.54 sq miles (1.4 sq km)

GUAM
West Pacific
STATUS: Unincorporated
territory
CLAIMED: 1898
CAPITAL: Agaña
POPULATION: 144,000
AREA: 212 sq miles
(549 sq km)

JARVIS ISLAND
South Pacific
STATUS: Unincorporated
territory
CLAIMED: 1856
CAPITAL: Not applicable
POPULATION: None
AREA: 1.7 sq miles (4.5 sq km)

JOHNSTON ATOLL
Central Pacific
STATUS: Unincorporated
territory
CLAIMED: 1858
CAPITAL: Not applicable
POPULATION: 327
AREA: 1 sq mile (2.8 sq km)

KINGMAN REEF
Central Pacific
STATUS: Administered territory
CLAIMED: 1856
CAPITAL: Not applicable
POPULATION: None
AREA: 0.4 sq miles (1 sq km)

MIDWAY ISLANDS
Central Pacific
STATUS: Administered territory
CLAIMED: 1867
CAPITAL: Not applicable
POPULATION: 453
AREA: 2 sq miles (5.2 sq km)

NAVASSA ISLAND
West Indies
STATUS: Unincorporated territory
CLAIMED: 1856
CAPITAL: Not applicable
POPULATION: None
AREA: 2 sq miles (5.2 sq km)

NORTHERN MARIANA ISLANDS
West Pacific
STATUS: Commonwealth
territory
CLAIMED: 1947
CAPITAL: Saipan
POPULATION: 47,000
AREA: 177 sq miles (457 sq km)

PALMYRA ATOLL
Central Pacific
STATUS: Unincorporated territory
CLAIMED: 1898
CAPITAL: Not applicable
POPULATION: None
AREA: 5 sq miles (12 sq km)

PUERTO RICO
West Indies
STATUS: Commonwealth
territory
CLAIMED: 1898
CAPITAL: San Juan
POPULATION: 3.6 million
AREA: 3,458 sq miles
(8,959 sq km)

VIRGIN ISLANDS
West Indies
STATUS: Unincorporated territory
CLAIMED: 1917
CAPITAL: Charlotte Amalie
POPULATION: 104,000
AREA: 137 sq miles (355 sq km)

WAKE ISLAND
Central Pacific
STATUS: Unincorporated territory
CLAIMED: 1898
CAPITAL: Not applicable
POPULATION: 302
AREA: 2.5 sq miles (6.5 sq km)

GLOSSARY OF GEOGRAPHICAL TER

THE GLOSSARY FOLLOWING lists all geographical terms occuring on the maps and in the main-entry names in the Index–Gazetteer. These terms may precede, follow or be run together with the proper elements of the name; where they precede it the term is reversed for indexing purposes – thus Poluostov Yamal is indexed as Yamal, Poluostrov.

A

Å *Danish, Norwegian,* River
Alpen *German,* Alps
Altiplanicie *Spanish,* Plateau
Älv(en) *Swedish,* River
Anse *French,* Bay
Archipiélago *Spanish,* Archipelago
Arcipelago *Italian,* Archipelago
Arquipélago *Portuguese,* Archipelago
Aukštuma *Lithuanian,* Upland

B

Bahía *Spanish,* Bay
Baía *Portuguese,* Bay
Baḥr *Arabic,* River
Baie *French,* Bay
Bandao *Chinese,* Peninsula
Banjaran *Malay,* Mountain range
Batang *Malay,* Stream
-berg *Afrikaans, Norwegian,* Mountain
Birket *Arabic ,* Lake
Boğazı *Turkish,* Lake
Bucht *German,* Bay
Bugten *Danish,* Bay
Buḥayrat *Arabic,* Lake, reservoir
Buḥeiret *Arabic,* Lake
Bukit *Malay,* Mountain
-bukta *Norwegian,* Bay
bukten *Swedish,* Bay
Burnu *Turkish,* Cape, point
Buuraha *Somali,* Mountains

C

Cabo *Portuguese,* Cape
Cap *French,* Cape
Cascada *Portuguese,* Waterfall
Cerro *Spanish,* Mountain
Chaîne *French,* Mountain range
Chau *Cantonese,* Island
Chāy *Turkish,* River
Chhâk *Cambodian,* Bay
Chhu *Tibetan,* River
-chôsuji *Korean,* Reservoir

Chott *Arabic,* Salt lake, depression
Ch'ün-tao *Chinese,* Island group
Cordillera *Spanish,* Mountain range
**Cambodian,* Mountains
Costa *Spanish,* Coast
Côte *French,* Coast
Cuchilla *Spanish,* Mountains

D

Dağı *Azerbaijani, Turkish,* Mountain
Dağları *Azerbaijani, Turkish,* Mountains
-dake *Japanese,* Peak
Danau *Indonesian,* Lake
Đao *Vietnamese,* Island
Daryā *Persian,* River
Daryācheh *Persian,* Lake
Dasht *Persian,* Plain, desert
Dawḥat *Arabic,* Bay
Dere *Turkish,* Stream
Dili *Azerbaijani,* Spit
-do *Korean,* Island
Dooxo *Somali,* Valley
Düzü *Azerbaijani,* Steppe
-dwīp *Bengali,* Island

E

Embalse *Spanish,* Reservoir
Erg *Arabic,* Dunes
Estany *Catalan,* Lake
Estrecho *Spanish,* Strait
-ey *Icelandic,* Island
Ezero *Bulgarian, Macedonian,* Lake

F

Fjord *Danish,* Fjord
-fjorden *Norwegian,* Fjord
-fjørdhur *Faeroese,* Fjord
Fleuve *French,* River
Fliegu *Maltese,* Channel
-fljór *Icelandic,* River

G

-gang *Korean,* River
Ganga *Nepali, Sinhala,* River
Gaoyuan *Chinese,* Plateau
-gawa *Japanese,* River
Gebel *Arabic,* Mountain

-gebirge *German,* Mountains
Ghubbat *Arabic,* Bay
Gjiri *Albanian,* Bay
Gol *Mongolian,* River
Golfe *French,* Gulf
Golfo *Italian, Spanish,* Gulf
Gora *Russian, Serbian,* Mountain
Gory *Russian,* Mountains
Guba *Russian,* Bay
Gunung *Malay,* Mountain

H

Ḥadd *Arabic,* Spit
-haehyŏp *Korean,* Strait
Haff *German,* Lagoon
Hai *Chinese,* Sea, bay
Ḥammādat *Arabic,* Plateau
Hāmūn *Persian,* Lake
Hawr *Arabic,* Lake
Hāyk' *Amharic,* Lake
He *Chinese,* River
Helodrano *Malagasy,* Bay
-hegység *Hungarian,* Mountain range
Hka *Burmese,* River
-ho *Korean,* Lake
Hô *Korean,* Reservoir
Ḥolot *Hebrew,* Dunes
Hora *Belarussian,* Mountain
Hrada *Belarussian,* Mountains, ridge
Hsi *Chinese,* River
Hu *Chinese,* Lake

I

Île(s) *French,* Island(s)
Ilha(s) *Portuguese,* Island(s)
Ilhéu(s) *Portuguese,* Islet(s)
Irmak *Turkish,* River
Isla(s) *Spanish,* Island(s)
Isola (Isole) *Italian,* Island(s)

J

Jabal *Arabic,* Mountain
Jāl *Arabic,* Ridge
-järvi *Finnish,* Lake
Jazīrat *Arabic,* Island
Jazīreh *Persian,* Island
Jebel *Arabic,* Mountain

Jezero *Serbo-Croatian,* Lake
Jiang *Chinese,* River
-joki *Finnish,* River
-jökull *Icelandic,* Glaci
Juzur *Arabic,* Islands

K

Kaikyō *Japanese,* Stra
-kaise *Lappish,* Mountain
Kali *Nepali,* River
Kalnas *Lithuanian,* Mountain
Kalns *Latvian,* Mountain
Kang *Chinese,* Harbo
Kangri *Tibetan,* Mountain(s)
Kaôh *Cambodian,* Isl
Kapp *Norwegian,* Ca
Kavīr *Persian,* Deser
K'edi *Georgian,* Mountain range
Kediet *Arabic,* Mountain
Kepulauan *Indonesian Malay,* Island group
Khalîg, Khalīj *Arabi* Gulf
Khawr *Arabic,* Inlet
Khola *Nepali,* River
Khrebet *Russian,* Mountain range
Ko *Thai,* Island
Kolpos *Greek,* Bay
-kopf *German,* Peak
Körfäzi *Azerbaijani,* Körfezi *Turkish,* Bay
Kõrgustik *Estonian,* Upland
Koshi *Nepali,* River
Kowtal *Persian,* Pass
Kūh(hā) *Persian,* Mountain(s)
-kundo *Korean,* Islar group
-kysten *Norwegian,* Coast
Kyun *Burmese,* Islan

L

Laaq *Somali,* Watercourse
Lac *French,* Lake
Lacul *Romanian,* Lake
Lago *Italian, Portugu Spanish,* Lake
Laguna *Spanish,* Lagoon, Lake

t *Estonian*, Bay
t *Indonesian*, Sea
nbalemba *Malagasy*,
lateau
r *Armenian*,
lountain
rnashght'a *Armenian*,
lountain range
Czech, Forest
n *Armenian*, Lake
eni *Albanian*, Lake
ni *Albanian*, River
nan *Ukrainian*,
stuary

e Nam *Thai*, River
gi *Estonian*, Hill
ja *Albanian*,
lountain
n *Korean*, Bay
rios *Lithuanian*,
ake
er *Dutch*, Lake
lkosopochnik
ussian, Plain
eri *Estonian*, Sea
fraz *Hebrew*, Bay
nkhafad *Arabic*,
epression
nt(s) *French*,
lountain(s)
nte *Italian*,
rrtuguese, Mountain
re *Russian*, Sea
rön *Mongolian*, River

gor'ye *Russian*,
pland
hal *Hebrew*, River
hr *Arabic*, River
m *Laotian*, River
hri *Turkish*, River
vado *Spanish*,
lountain (snow-
apped)
oi *Greek*, Islands
mennost' *Russian*,
owland, plain
sy *Malagasy*, Island
r *Mongolian*,
ruu *Mongolian*,
lountains
ur *Mongolian*, Lake
zovyna *Ukrainian*,
owland, plain

trov(a) *Russian*,
sland(s)
ed *Arabic*,
Watercourse
Faeroese, Island
(a) *Norwegian*,
sland
a *Sinhala*, River
ero *Russian*,
krainian, Lake

P

Passo *Italian*, Pass
Pegunungan *Indonesian*,
Malay, Mountain range
Pelagos *Greek*, Sea
Penisola *Italian*,
Peninsula
Peski *Russian*, Sands
Phanom *Thai*,
Mountain
Phou *Laotian*,
Mountain
Pic *Catalan*, Peak
Pico *Portuguese*,
Spanish, Peak
Pik *Russian*, Peak
Planalto *Portuguese*,
Plateau
Planina, Planini
Bulgarian, *Macedonian*,
Serbo-Croatian,
Mountain range
Ploskogor'ye *Russian*,
Upland
Poluostrov *Russian*,
Peninsula
Potamos *Greek*, River
Proliv *Russian*, Strait
Pulau *Indonesian*,
Malay, Island
Pulu *Malay*, Island
Punta *Portuguese*,
Spanish, Point

Q

Qā' *Arabic*, Depression
Qolleh *Persian*,
Mountain

R

Raas *Somali*, Cape
-rags *Latvian*, Cape
Ramlat *Arabic*, Sands
Ra's *Arabic*, Cape,
point, headland
Ravnina *Bulgarian*,
Russian, Plain
Rēcif *French*, Reef
Represa (Rep.) *Spanish*,
Portuguese, Reservoir
-rettō *Japanese*, Island
chain
Riacho *Spanish*,
Stream
Riban' *Malagasy*,
Mountains
Rio *Portuguese*, River
Río *Spanish*, River
Riu *Catalan*, River
Rivier *Dutch*, River
Rivière *French*, River
Rowd *Pashtu*, River
Rūd *Persian*, River
Rudohorie *Slovak*,
Mountains
Ruisseau *French*,
Stream

S

Sabkhat *Arabic*, Salt
marsh
Şaḩrā' *Arabic*, Desert
Samudra *Sinhala*,
Reservoir
-san *Japanese*, *Korean*,
Mountain
-sanchi *Japanese*,
Mountains
-sanmaek *Korean*,
Mountain
Sarīr *Arabic*, Desert
Sebkha, Sebkhet *Arabic*,
Salt marsh, depression
See *German*, Lake
Selat *Indonesian*, Strait
-selkä *Finnish*, Ridge
Selseleh *Persian*,
Mountain range
Serra *Portuguese*,
Mountain
Serranía *Spanish*,
Mountain
Sha'īb *Arabic*,
Watercourse
Shamo *Chinese*, Desert
Shan *Chinese*,
Mountain(s)
Shan-mo *Chinese*,
Mountain range
Shaṭṭ *Arabic*,
Distributary
-shima *Japanese*, Island
Shui-tao *Chinese*,
Channel
Sierra *Spanish*,
Mountains
Sơn *Vietnamese*,
Mountain
Sông *Vietnamese*, River
-spitze *German*, Peak
Štít *Slovak*, Peak
Stoeng *Cambodian*,
River
Stretto *Italian*, Strait
Su Anbarı *Azerbaijani*,
Reservoir
Sungai *Indonesian*,
Malay, River
Suu *Turkish*, River

T

Tal *Mongolian*, Plain
Tandavan' *Malagasy*,
Mountain range
Tangorombohitr'
Malagasy, Mountain
massif
Tao *Chinese*, Island
Tassili *Berber*, Plateau,
mountain
Tau *Russian*,
Mountain(s)
Taungdan *Burmese*,
Mountain range
Teluk *Indonesian*,
Malay, Bay

Terara — W

Terara *Amharic*,
Mountain
Tog *Somali*, Valley
Tônlé *Cambodian*,
Lake
Top *Dutch*, Peak
-tunturi *Finnish*,
Mountain
Tur'at *Arabic*,
Channel

V

Väin *Estonian*, Strait
-vatn *Icelandic*, Lake
-vesi *Finnish*, Lake
Vinh *Vietnamese*, Bay
Vodokhranilishche
(Vdkhr.) *Russian*,
Reservoir
Vodoskhovyshche
(Vdskh.) *Ukrainian*,
Reservoir
Volcán *Spanish*,
Volcano
Vozvyshennost'
Russian, Upland,
plateau
Vrh *Macedonian*,
Peak
Vysochyna *Ukrainian*,
Upland
Vysočina *Czech*,
Upland

W

Waadi *Somali*,
Watercourse
Wādī *Arabic*,
Watercourse
Wāḩat, Wâhat *Arabic*,
Oasis
Wald *German*, Forest
Wan *Chinese*, Bay
Wyżyna *Polish*,
Upland

X

Xé *Laotian*, River

Y

Yarımadası *Azerbaijani*,
Peninsula
Yazovir *Bulgarian*,
Reservoir
Yoma *Burmese*,
Mountains
Yü *Chinese*, Island

Z

Zaliv *Bulgarian*,
Russian, Bay
Zatoka *Ukrainian*, Bay
Zemlya *Russian*, Bay

GLOSSARY OF ABBREVIATIONS

THIS GLOSSARY provides a comprehensive guide to the abbreviations used in this Atlas, and in the Index-Gazetteer.

A
abbrev. abbreviation
Afr. Afrikaans
Alb. Albanian
Amh. Amharic
anc. ancient
Ar. Arabic
Arm. Armenian
Az. Azerbaijani

B
Basq. Basque
Bel. Belarussian
Ben. Bengali
Bibl. Biblical
Bret. Breton
Bul. Bulgarian
Bur. Burmese

C
Cam. Cambodian
Cant. Cantonese
Cast. Castilian
Cat. Catalan
Chin. Chinese
Cro. Croat
Cz. Czech

D
Dan. Danish
Dut. Dutch

E
Eng. English
Est. Estonian
est. estimated

F
Faer. Faeroese
Fij. Fijian
Fin. Finnish
Flem. Flemish
Fr. French
Fris. Frisian

G
Geor. Georgian
Ger. German
Gk. Greek
Guj. Gujarati

H
Haw. Hawaiian
Heb. Hebrew
Hind. Hindi
hist. historical
Hung. Hungarian

I
Icel. Icelandic
Ind. Indonesian
Inuit Inuit
Ir. Irish
It. Italian

J
Jap. Japanese

K
Kaz. Kazakh
Kir. Kirghiz
Kor. Korean
Kurd. Kurdish

L
Lao. Laotian
Lapp. Lappish
Lat. Latin

Latv. Latvian
Lith. Lithanian
Lus. Lusatian

M
Mac. Macedonian
Mal. Malay
Malg. Malagasy
Malt. Maltese
Mong. Mongolia

N
Nepali. Nepali
Nor. Norwegian

O
off. officially

P
Pash. Pashtu
Per. Persian
Pol. Polish
Port. Portuguese
prev. previously

R
Rmsch. Romansch
Roman. Romanian
Rus. Russian

S
SCr. Serbian and Croatian
Serb. Serbian
Slvk. Slovak
Slvn. Slovene
Som. Somali
Sp. Spanish
Swa. Swahili
Swe. Swedish

T
Taj. Tajik
Th. Thai
Tib. Tibetan
Turk. Turkish
Turkm. Turkmenistan

U
Uigh. Uighur
Ukr. Ukrainian
Uzb. Uzbek

V
var. variant
Vtn. Vietnamese

W
Wel. Welsh

X
Xh. Xhosa

Y
Yugo. Yugoslavia

Key to country factboxes within the index:

Date of formation
This denotes the country's date of independence or the date when its current borders were established.

Languages
Official language(s) are denoted with an asterisk.

162

INDEX

A

Aa *see* Gauja
Aachen 94 A 4 *Dut.* Aken, *Fr.* Aix-la-Chapelle; *anc.* Aquae Grani, Aquisgranum. W Germany
Aaiún *see* Laâyoune
Aalborg Bugt *see* Ålborg Bugt
Aalen 95 B 6 S Germany
Aalsmeer 86 C 3 C Netherlands
Aalst 87 B 6 *Fr.* Alost. C Belgium
Aalten 86 E 4 E Netherlands
Aalter 87 B 5 NW Belgium
Äänekoski 85 D 5 C Finland
Aar *see* Aare
Aare 95 A 7 *var.* Aar. River, W Switzerland
Aarhus *see* Århus
Aasiaat 82 C 3 *var.* Ausiait, *Dan.* Egedesminde. W Greenland
Aat *see* Ath
Aba 75 G 5 S Nigeria
Aba 77 E 5 NE Congo (Zaire)
Abā as Su'ūd *see* Najrān
Abaco Island *see* Great Abaco
Ābādān 120 C 4 SW Iran
Abagnar Qi *see* Xilin Hot
Abakan 114 D 4 C Russian Federation
Abancay 60 D 4 SE Peru
Abashiri 130 D 2 *var.* Abasiri. Hokkaidō, NE Japan
Abasiri *see* Abashiri
Ábaya Häyk' 73 C 5 *Eng.* Lake Margherita, *It.* Abbaia. Lake, SW Ethiopia
Abbatis Villa *see* Abbeville
Abbazia *see* Opatija
Abbeville 90 C 2 *anc.* Abbatis Villa. N France
Abbeville 42 B 3 Louisiana, S USA
'Abd al 'Azīz, Jabal 118 D 2 mountain range, NE Syria
Abéché 76 C 3 *var.* Abécher, Abeshr. SE Chad
Abellinum *see* Avellino
Abemama Atoll 144 D 2 *var.* Apamama; *prev.* Roger Simpson Island. Island, W Kiribati
Abengourou 75 E 5 E Ivory Coast
Aberbrothock *see* Arbroath
Abercorn *see* Mbala
Aberdeen 88 D 3 *anc.* Devana. E Scotland, UK
Aberdeen 128 A 2 S Hong Kong
Aberdeen 46 B 2 Washington, NW USA
Aberdeen 45 E 2 South Dakota, N USA
Abergwaun *see* Fishguard
Abertawe *see* Swansea
Aberystwyth 89 C 6 W Wales, UK
Abhā 121 B 6 SW Saudi Arabia
Abidavichy 107 D 7 *Rus.* Obidovichi. E Belarus
Abidjan 75 E 5 S Ivory Coast
Abilene 49 F 3 Texas, S USA
Abingdon *see* Pinta, Isla
Abkhazia 117 F 2 region, NW Georgia
Åbo *see* Turku
Aboisso 75 E 5 SE Ivory Coast
Abo, Massif d' 76 B 1 mountain range, N Chad
Abomey 75 F 5 S Benin
Abou-Déïa 76 C 3 SE Chad
Aboudouhour *see* Abū aḑ Ḑuhūr
Abou Kémal *see* Abū Kamāl
Abrantes 92 B 3 *var.* Abrántes. C Portugal

Abrántes *see* Abrantes
Abrashlare *see* Brezovo
Abrolhos Bank 57 E 4 undersea bank, W Atlantic Ocean
Abrova 107 B 6 *Rus.* Obrovo. SW Belarus
Abrud 108 B 4 *Hung.* Abrudbár SW Romania
Abrudbánya *see* Abrud
Abruzzese, Appennino 96 C 4 mountain range, C Italy
Absaroka Range 44 B 2 mount range, NW USA
Abū aḑ Ḑuhūr 118 B 3 *Fr.* Aboudouhour. NW Syria
Abu Dhabi *see* Abū Ẓaby
Abu Hamed 72 C 3 N Sudan
Abuja 75 G 4 country capital, C Nigeria
Abū Kamāl 118 E 3 *Fr.* Abou Kémal. E Syria
Abuná 61 E 2 *var.* Río Abuná. R Bolivia/Brazil
Abuná, Río *see* Abunã
Abut Head 151 B 6 headland, South Island, SW New Zealan
Ābuyē Mēda 73 D 5 mountain, C Ethiopia
Abū Ẓaby 121 D 5 *var.* Abū Ẓat *Eng.* Abu Dhabi. Country cap C United Arab Emirates
Acalayong 77 A 5 SW Equatorial Guinea
Acaponeta 50 C 4 C Mexico
Acapulco 51 E 5 *var.* Acapulco de Juárez. S Me
Acapulco de Juárez *see* Acapulco
Acarai Mountains 59 F 4 *var.* Serra Acaraí. Mountain ra Brazil/Guyana
Acaraí, Serra *see* Acarai Mounta
Acarigua 58 D 2 N Venezuela
Acay, Abra del 64 C 2 pass, N Argentina
Accra 75 E 5 country capital, SE Ghana
Achacachi 61 F 4 W Bolivia
Acklins Island 54 D 2 island, SE Bahamas
Aconcagua, Cerro 64 B 4 mountain, W Argentina
Acora 61 E 4 SE Peru
A Coruña 92 B 1 *Cast.* La Coruñ *Eng.* Corunna; *anc.* Caronium NW Spain
Acre 62 C 2 *off.* Estado do Acre. State, W Brazil
Acre 60 D 2 cultural region, W E
Acre, Estado do *see* Acre
Açu 63 G 2 NE Brazil
Ada 100 D 3 N Yugoslavia
Ada Bazar *see* Adapazarı
Adâfer 74 D 2 plateau, C Mauri
Adak Island 36 A 3 island, Alaska, NW USA
Adamaoua, Massif d' 76 B 4 *Eng.* Adamawa Highlands. Mountain range, NW Camerc
Adamawa 68 B 4 province, N Cameroon
Adamawa Highlands *see* Adamaoua, Massif d'
Adam-jo-Tando *see* Tando Ãdan
Adamstown 143 G 4 dependent territory capital, Pitcairn Islan SW Pacific Ocean
'Adan 121 B 7 *Eng.* Aden. SW Ye
Adana 116 D 4 *var.* Seyhan. S Turkey
Adapazarı 116 B 3 *prev.* Ada Ba NW Turkey

e, Cape 154 B 4 headland,
tarctica
ahnā' 120 B 4 desert,
audi Arabia
akhla 70 A 4 var. Dakhla;
?. Villa Cisneros.
W Morocco
alanj see Dilling
amazīn see Ed Damazin
āmūr see Damoûr
awhah 120 D 4 Eng. Doha.
untry capital, C Qatar
iffah see Libyan Plateau
s Ababa see Ādīs Ābeba
Atoll 132 B 5 island,
Maldives
aide 149 B 6
ath Australia, S Australia
see 'Adan
, Gulf of 121 C 7
Badyarada 'Adméd. Gulf,
Indian Ocean
e 96 C 2 Ger. Etsch. River,
Italy
ondack Mountains 41 F 2
ountain range, New York,
USA
Ābeba 73 C 5 var. Addis
aba. Country capital,
Ethiopia
aman 117 E 4 SE Turkey
d 108 C 4 E Romania
ralty Gulf 146 C 2 gulf,
ndian Ocean
ralty Islands 144 B 3 island
oup, N Papua New Guinea
93 E 5 S Spain
r 74 C 2 mountainous region,
Mauritania
r 70 D 3 mountain range,
Algeria
an 40 C 3 Michigan, N USA
atic Sea 103 E 2 Alb. Deti
riatik, It. Mare Adriatic, SCr.
Jransko More, Slvn. Jadransko
orje. Sea, N Mediterranean Sea
tha 115 F 2 river,
C Russian Federation
an Sea 103 F 3 Gk. Aigaío
lagos, Aigaion Pelagos,
rk. Ege Denizi. Sea,
Mediterranean Sea
iidu 106 D 2
r. Charlottenhof. NW Estonia
k see Ailuk Atoll

anistan
2 D 4 Per. Dowlat-e Eslāmī-ye
ghānestān; prev. Republic of
ghanistan. Islamic state, C Asia

ial name: Islamic State
anistan Date of formation:
Capital: Kābul
lation: 20.5 million Total Area:
70 sq miles (652,090 sq km)
Languages: Persian*, Pashtu*
ions: Sunni Muslim 84%, Shi'a
im 15%, other 1% Ethnic mix:
tun 38%, Tajik 25%, Hazara
Uzbek 6%, other 12%
rnment: Mujahideen coalition
ency: Afghani = 100 puls

adow 73 D 6 S Somalia
a 66 D 4 continent
a 118 B 2 NW Syria
an 116 B 3
v. Afyonkarahisar. W Turkey
nkarahisar see Afyon
ès see Agadez
ez 75 G 3 prev. Agadès.
Niger
ir 70 B 3 SW Morocco

Agana 144 B 1 var. Agaña.
   Dependent territory capital,
   NW Guam
Agaña see Agana
Āgaro 73 C 5 W Ethiopia
Agassiz Fracture Zone 153 E 4
   fracture zone, S Pacific Ocean
Agatha see Agde
Agathónisi 105 D 6 island,
   Dodekánisos, SE Greece
Agde 91 C 6 anc. Agatha. S France
Agen 91 B 6 anc. Aginnum.
   SW France
Agiá 104 B 4 var. Ayiá. C Greece
Agía Marína 105 E 6 Leros,
   SE Greece
Aginnum see Agen
Ágios Nikólaos 105 D 8 var.
   Áyios Nikólaos. Kríti, SE Greece
Āgra 134 D 3 N India
Ağrı 117 F 3 var. Karaköse;
   prev. Karakılısse. NE Turkey
Agrigento 97 C 7 Gk. Akragas;
   prev. Girgenti . SW Italy
Agrínio 105 B 5 prev. Agrinion.
   W Greece
Agrinion see Agrínio
Agriovótano 105 C 5 C Greece
Agropoli 97 D 5 Italy
Aguachica 58 B 2 N Colombia
Aguadulce 53 F 5 S Panama
Agua Prieta 50 B 1 NW Mexico
Aguascalientes 50 D 4 C Mexico
Aguilas 93 E 5 SE Spain
Aguililla 50 D 4 SW Mexico
Agulhas Bank 67 D 6 undersea
   bank, SW Indian Ocean
Agulhas Basin 67 E 6 undersea
   basin, SW Indian Ocean
Agulhas Plateau 67 E 6 undersea
   plateau, SW Indian Ocean
Ahaggar 68 B 3 mountain range,
   SE Algeria
Ahlen 94 B 4 W Germany
Ahmadābād 134 C 4
   var. Ahmedabad. W India
Ahmadnagar 134 C 5
   var. Ahmednagar. W India
Ahmedabad see Ahmadābād
Ahmednagar see Ahmadnagar
Ahuachapán 52 B 3 W El Salvador
Ahvāz 120 C 3 var. Ahwāz;
   prev. Nāsiri. SW Iran
Aígina 105 C 6 var. Aíyina.
   C Greece
Aígio 105 B 5 prev. Aíyion.
   C Greece
Aiken 43 E 2
   South Carolina, SE USA
Ailao Shan 129 A 6 mountain
   range, S China
Ailigandí 53 G 4 NE Panama
Ailinglaplap Atoll 144 D 2
   var. Aelōñlaplap, Ailinglapalap.
   Island, S Marshall Islands
Ailuk Atoll 144 D 1 var. Aelok.
   Island, NE Marshall Islands
Ainaži 106 C 3 Est. Heinaste,
   Ger. Hainasch. N Latvia
'Aïn Ben Tili 74 D 1 N Mauritania
Aiquile 61 F 4 C Bolivia
Air du Azbine see Aïr, Massif de l'
Aïr, Massif de l' 75 G 3 var. Aïr,
   Air du Azbine, Asben. Mountain
   range, NC Niger
Aiud 108 B 4 Ger. Strassburg,
   Hung. Nagyenyed; prev. Engeten.
   W Romania
Aix-en-Provence 91 D 6 var. Aix;
   anc. Aquae Sextiae. SE France
Aizkraukle 106 C 4 S Latvia

Ajaccio 91 E 7 SE France
Ajana 147 A 5 W Australia
Ajaria 117 F 2 region, SW Georgia
Aj Bogd Uul 126 D 2 mountain,
   SW Mongolia
Ajdābiyā 71 G 2 var. Agedabia,
   Ajdābiyah. NE Libya
Ajmer 134 D 3 var. Ajmere.
   N India
Ajmere see Ajmer
Akasha 72 B 3 N Sudan
Akçakale 117 E 4 Turkey
Akchâr 74 C 2 desert,
   W Mauritania
Akdar, Jebel see Akhḍar al Jabal
Akhalts'ikhe 117 F 2 SW Georgia
Akhḍar, Al Jabal al 121 D 5
   var. Jabal al Akhdar. Mountain
   range, NW Oman
Akhdar, Jabal al see Akhḍar,
   Al Jabal al
Akhisar 116 A 3 W Turkey
Akhmîm 72 B 2 anc. Panopolis.
   C Egypt
Akhtubinsk 111 C 7
   SW Russian Federation
Akhtyrka see Okhtyrka
Akimiski Island 38 C 3 island,
   Northwest Territories, C Canada
Akita 130 D 4 Honshū, C Japan
Akjoujt 74 C 2 prev. Fort-Repoux.
   W Mauritania
Akkeshi 130 E 2 Hokkaidō,
   NE Japan
Aklavik 36 D 3 North West
   Territories, NW Canada
Akmola see Astana
Akpatok Island 39 E 1 island,
   Northwest Territories, E Canada
Akron 40 D 4 Ohio, N USA
Akrotiri see Akrotírion
Aksai Chin 126 A 4
   Chin. Aksayqin. Disputed region,
   China/India
Aksaray 116 C 4 C Turkey
Aksayqin see Aksai Chin
Aktash see Oqtosh
Aktau 114 A 4 Kaz. Aqtaū; prev.
   Shevchenko. W Kazakhstan
Aktsyabrski 107 D 7
   Rus. Oktyabr'skiy; prev.
   Karpilovka. SE Belarus
Aktyubinsk 114 B 4 Kaz. Aqtöbe.
   NW Kazakhstan
Akureyri 83 E 5 N Iceland
Akyab see Sittwe
Alabama 42 C 2 off. State of
   Alabama; nicknames Camellia
   State, Heart of Dixie,
   The Cotton State, Yellowhammer
   State. State, S USA
Alabama River 42 C 3 river,
   S USA
Alagoas 63 G 2 off. Estado de
   Alagoas. State, E Brazil
Alagoas, Estado de see Alagoas
Alais see Alès
Alajuela 53 E 4 C Costa Rica
Alakanuk 36 B 2 Alaska, USA
Al 'Alamayn see El 'Alamein
Al 'Amārah 120 C 3 var. Amara.
   E Iraq
Alamosa 44 C 5 Colorado, C USA
Åland 106 D 6 var. Aland Islands,
   Fin. Ahvenanmaa. Island group,
   SW Finland
Aland Sea see Ålands hav

Ålands Hav 85 C 6 var. Aland Sea.
   Strait, C Baltic Sea
Al 'Aqabah 119 B 8 var. Akaba,
   Aqaba, 'Aqaba; anc. Aelana,
   Elath. SW Jordan
Alaşehir 116 A 4 W Turkey
Alaska 36 C 3 off. State of Alaska;
   nicknames Land of the
   Midnight Sun, Seward's Folly,
   The Last Frontier; prev.
   Russian America. State, NW USA
Alaska, Gulf of 152 D 1 gulf,
   NE Pacific Ocean
Alaska Peninsula 36 C 3 peninsula,
   Alaska, NW USA
Alaska Range 36 C 3 mountain
   range, Alaska, NW USA
Alattio see Alta
Alazani 117 G 2 var. Qanıx. River,
   Azerbaijan/Georgia
Alazeya 115 G 2 river,
   NE Russian Federation
Al Bāb 118 B 2 NW Syria
Albacete 93 E 4 C Spain
Al Baghdādī 120 B 3 var. Khān al
   Baghdādī. SW Iraq
Alba Iulia 108 B 4 Ger. Weissenburg,
   Hung. Gyulafehérvár;
   prev. Bálgrad, Karlsburg,
   Károly-Fehérvár. W Romania
Albania see Aubagne

Albania
   101 C 6 Alb. Republika e
   Shqipqërisë, Shqipëria;
   prev. People's Socialist Republic
   of Albania. Republic, SE Europe

   Official name: Republic of Albania
   Date of formation: 1912/1913
   Capital: Tiranë Population: 3.3
   million Total Area: 11,100 sq miles
   (28,750 sq km) Languages:
   Albanian*, Greek Religions: Muslim
   70%, Greek Orthodox 20%, Roman
   Catholic 10% Ethnic mix: Albanian
   96%, Greek 2%, other 2%
   Government: Multiparty republic
   Currency: Lek = 100 qindars

Albany 42 D 3 Georgia, SE USA
Albany 41 F 3 state capital,
   New York, NE USA
Albany 46 B 3 Oregon, NW USA
Albany 41 F 3 Eng. Basra;
   hist. Busra, Bussora. SE Iraq
Albatross Bay 148 C 2 bay,
   SE Arafura Sea
Albatross Plateau 35 B 7 undersea
   plateau, E Pacific Ocean
Al Batrūn see Batroûn
Al Baydā' 71 G 2 var. Beida.
   NE Libya
Albemarle Island see Isabela, Isla
Albemarle Sound 43 G 1 inlet,
   W Atlantic Ocean
Albergaria-a-Velha 92 B 2
   W Portugal
Albert 90 C 3 N France
Albert, Lake 77 E 5 var. Albert
   Nyanza, Lac Mobutu Sese Seko.
   Lake, Uganda/Zaire (Zaire)/Uganda
Albert Lea 45 G 3
   Minnesota, N USA
Albertville see Kalemie
Albi 91 C 6 anc. Albiga. S France
Albiga see Albi

Al Biyāḍ 121 C 5 desert, C Saudi Arabia
Ålborg 85 B 7 *var.* Aalborg, Ålborg-Nørresundby; *anc.* Alburgum. N Denmark
Ålborg Bugt 85 B 7 *var.* Aalborg Bugt. Bay, E North Sea
Alborz, Reshteh-ye Kuhhā-ye 120 C 2 *Eng.* Elburz Mountains. Mountain range, N Iran
Albuquerque 48 D 2 New Mexico, SW USA
Albury 149 C 7 New South Wales, SE Australia
Alcácer do Sal 92 B 4 W Portugal
Alcalá de Henares 93 E 3 *Ar.* Alkal'a; *anc.* Complutim, Complutum. C Spain
Alcamo 97 C 7 SW Italy
Alcañiz 93 F 2 NE Spain
Alcántara, Embalse de 92 C 3 reservoir, W Spain
Alcaudete 92 D 4 S Spain
Alcoi *see* Alcoy
Alcoy 93 F 4 *var.* Alcoi. E Spain
Aldabra Group 79 G 2 island group, SW Seychelles
Aldan 115 F 3 river, E Russian Federation
al Dar al Baida *see* Rabat
Alderney 89 D 8 island, N Channel Islands
Aleg 74 C 3 SW Mauritania
Aleksandriya *see* Oleksandriya
Aleksandrovka *see* Oleksandrivka
Aleksin 111 B 5 W Russian Federation
Aleksinac 100 E 4 E Yugoslavia
Alençon 90 B 3 N France
Alenquer 63 E 2 NE Brazil
Aleppo *see* Ḥalab
Alert 37 F 1 Ellesmere Island, Canada
Alès 91 D 6 *prev.* Alais. S France
Aleşd 108 B 3 *Hung.* Élesd. SW Romania
Alessandria 96 B 2 *Fr.* Alexandrie. N Italy
Ålesund 85 A 5 S Norway
Aleutian Basin 152 C 1 undersea basin, SW Pacific Ocean
Aleutian Islands 36 A 3 island group, Alaska, NW USA
Aleutian Range 34 A 2 mountain range, Alaska, NW USA
Aleutian Rise 152 C 1 undersea rise, NW Pacific Ocean
Aleutian Trench 152 D 1 trench, SW Pacific Ocean
Alexander Archipelago 36 C 4 island group, Alaska, NW USA
Alexander City 42 D 2 Alabama, S USA
Alexander Island 154 A 3 island, Antarctica
Alexandra 151 B 7 South Island, SW New Zealand
Alexandra Bay 148 D 2 bay, NE Coral Sea
Alexándreia 104 B 4 *var.* Alexándria. N Greece
Alexandretta *see* İskenderun
Alexandretta, Gulf of *see* İskenderun Körfezi
Alexandria 82 B 3 Louisiana, S USA
Alexandria 41 E 4 Virginia, NE USA
Alexandria 108 C 5 S Romania
Alexandria 45 F 2 Minnesota, N USA
Alexandria 72 B 1 *Ar.* Al Iskandarīyah. N Egypt
Alexándria *see* Alexándreia

Alexandrie *see* Alessandria
Alexandrina, Lake 149 B 7 lake, South Australia, SE Australia
Alexandroúpoli 104 D 3 *var.* Alexandroúpolis, *Turk.* Dedeagaç, Dedeagach. NE Greece
Al Fāshir *see* El Fasher
Alfatar 104 E 1 NE Bulgaria
Alfeiós 105 B 6 *prev.* Alfiós, *anc.* Alpheius, Alpheus. River, S Greece
Alga 114 B 4 *Kaz.* Algha. NW Kazakhstan
Algarve 92 B 4 cultural region, S Portugal
Algeciras 92 C 5 SW Spain
Algeciras, Bahía de *see* Gibraltar, Bay of
Algemesí 93 F 3 E Spain
Alger 70 D 1 *var.* Algiers, Al Jazair, El Djazaïr. Country capital, N Algeria

Algeria 70 C 3 NW Africa
Official name: Democratic and Popular Republic of Algeria **Date of formation:** 1962 **Capital:** Algiers **Population:** 27.1 million **Total area:** 919,590 sq miles (2,381,740 sq km) **Languages:** Arabic*, Berber, French **Religions:** Muslim 99%, Christian and Jewish 1% **Ethnic mix:** Arab and Berber 99% European 1% **Government:** Military regime **Currency:** Dinar = 100 centimes

Algerian Basin *see* Balearic Plain
Algha *see* Alga
Alghero 97 A 5 W Italy
Algiers *see* Alger
Al Golea *see* El Goléa
Algona 45 F 3 Iowa, C USA
Al Hasā 120 C 4 desert, NE Saudi Arabia
Al Ḥasakah 118 D 1 *var.* Al Hasijah, El Haseke, *Fr.* Hassetché. NE Syria
Al Ḥillah 120 B 3 *var.* Hilla. C Iraq
Al Hudaydah 121 B 6 *Eng.* Hodeida. W Yemen
Al Hufūf 121 C 5 *var.* Hofuf. NE Saudi Arabia
Aliártos 105 C 5 C Greece
Äli-Bayramll 117 H 3 *Rus.* Ali-Bayramly. SE Azerbaijan
Ali-Bayramly *see* Äli-Bayramlı
Alicante 93 F 4 *Cat.* Alacant; *Lat.* Lucentum. SE Spain
Alice 49 G 5 Texas, S USA
Alice Springs 148 A 4 Northern Territory, C Australia
Aliki *see* Alykí
Alindao 76 C 4 S Central African Republic
Aliquippa 40 D 4 Pennsylvania, NE USA
Al Iskandarīyah *see* Alexandria
Alistráti 104 C 3 NE Greece
Alivéri 105 C 5 *var.* Alivérion. Évvoia, C Greece
Alivérion *see* Alivéri
Al Jabal al Akhḍar 71 G 2 *var.* Jebel Akdar. Mountain range, NE Libya
Al Jafr 119 B 7 S Jordan
Al Jaghbūb 71 H 3 NE Libya
Al Jahrā' 120 C 4 *var.* Al Jahrah, Jahra. C Kuwait
Al Jawf 120 B 4 *var.* Jauf. NW Saudi Arabia
Al Karak 119 B 7 *var.* El Kerak, Karak, Kerak; *anc.* Kir Moab, Kir of Moab. W Jordan

Al Khārijah *see* El Khârga
Al-Khobar *see* Al Khubar
Al Khubar 120 C 4 *var.* Al-Khobar. NE Saudi Arabia
Al Khums 71 F 2 *var.* Homs, Khoms, Khums. NW Libya
Alkmaar 86 C 3 NW Netherlands
Al Kufrah 72 A 2 *var.* Kufra Oasis, *It.* Cufra. Oasis, W Libya
Al Kūt 120 C 3 *var.* Kūt al 'Amārah, Kut al Imara. E Iraq
Al Kuwayt 120 C 4 *var.* Kuwait City, Al-Kuwait, *Eng.* Kuwait; *prev.* Qurein. Country capital, E Kuwait
Al Lādhiqīyah 118 A 3 *Eng.* Latakia, *Fr.* Lattaquié; *anc.* Laodicea, Laodicea ad Mare. W Syria
Allahābād 135 E 3 N India
Allanmyo 136 B 4 W Myanmar
'Allāq, Wādi el 72 C 3 dry watercourse, Egypt/Sudan
Allegheny Plateau 41 E 3 mountain range, NE USA
Allenstein *see* Olsztyn
Allentown 41 F 4 Pennsylvania, NE USA
Alleppey 132 C 3 *var.* Alappuzha; *prev.* Aleppi. SW India
Alliance 44 D 3 Nebraska, C USA
Al Lith 121 B 5 SW Saudi Arabia
Alma 39 E 4 Québec, SE Canada
Alma-Ata *see* Almaty
Almada 92 B 4 W Portugal
Al Madīnah 121 B 5 *Eng.* Medina. W Saudi Arabia
Al Mafraq 119 B 6 *var.* Mafraq. N Jordan
Al Mahrah 121 C 6 mountain range, E Yemen
Al Majma'ah 120 C 4 C Saudi Arabia
Al Mālikīyah 118 E 1 *var.* Dayrīk, Malkiye, *Fr.* Malkieh. NE Syria
Almalyk *see* Olmaliq
Al Manāmah 120 C 4 *Eng.* Manama. Country capital, N Bahrain
Al Manāşif 118 E 3 mountain range, E Syria
Almansa 93 E 4 C Spain
Al Marj 71 G 2 *var.* Barka, *It.* Barce. NE Libya
Almaty 114 C 5 *var.* Alma-Ata. SE Kazakhstan
Al Mawşil 120 B 2 *Eng.* Mosul. N Iraq
Al Mayādīn 118 E 3 *var.* Mayadin, *Fr.* Meyadine. E Syria
Al Mazār al Janūbī 119 B 7 *var.* Mazar. W Jordan
Al Mazra'ah 119 B 7 *var.* Al Mazra', Mazra'a. W Jordan
Almelo 86 E 3 E Netherlands
Almendra, Embalse de 92 C 2 reservoir, NW Spain
Almendralejo 92 C 4 W Spain
Almere 86 C 3 *var.* Almere-stad. C Netherlands
Almere-stad *see* Almere
Almería 93 E 5 *Ar.* Al-Mariyya; *anc.* Unci, *Lat.* Portus Magnus. S Spain
Al Mīnā' *see* El Mina
Almirante 53 F 5 NW Panama
Al Mubarraz 121 C 5 E Saudi Arabia
Al Mudawwarah 119 B 8 SW Jordan
Al Mukallā 121 C 7 *var.* Mukalla. SE Yemen
Al Munastīr *see* Monastir
Alofi 145 F 5 dependent territory capital, W Niue

Aloja 106 D 3 N Latvia
Alónnisos 105 C 5 island, Vóre Sporádes, E Greece
Álora 92 D 5 S Spain
Alor, Kepulauan 139 E 5 island group, E Indonesia
Alost *see* Aalst
Alpena 40 D 2 Michigan, N US
Alpha Cordillera 155 F 3 *var. A* Ridge. Seamount range, Arctic Ocean
Alphen *see* Alphen aan den Rijn
Alphen aan den Rijn 86 C 3 *var.* Alphen. C Netherlands
Alpine 49 E 4 Texas, S USA
Alps 80 D 4 *Fr.* Alpes, *Ger.* Alp *It.* Alpi. Mountain range, C Europe
Al Qāmishlī 118 E 1 *var.* Kamis Qamishly. NE Syria
Al Qaryāt 71 F 3 NW Libya
Al Qaşrayn *see* Kasserine
Al Qayrawān *see* Kairouan
Al Qunayţirah 119 B 5 *var.* El Kuneitra, El Quneitra, Kuneitra, Qunaytra. SW Syri
Al Quşayr 118 B 4 *var.* El Quse Quayr, *Fr.* Kousseir. W Syria
Al Quwayrah 119 B 8 *var.* El Quweira. SW Jordan
Alsace 90 E 3 cultural region, NE France
Alsdorf 94 A 4 W Germany
Alta 84 D 2 *Fin.* Alattio. N Nor
Altai Mountains 124 C 1 *var. A* Shan. Mountain range, E Asi
AltaY Shan *see* Altai Mountains
Al Ţalfilah 119 B 7 *var.* Et Tafil. Tafila. W Jordan
Altamaha River 43 E 3 river, Georgia, SE USA
Altamira 63 E 2 NE Brazil
Altamont 46 B 4 Oregon, NW U
Altamura 97 E 5 *anc.* Lupatia. SE Italy
Altar, Desierto de 50 A 1 dese Mexico/USA
Altay 126 D 2 W Mongolia
Altay 126 C 2 *Chin.* A-le-t'ai, *M* Sharasume; *prev.* Ch'eng-hua Chenghwa. NW China
Altin Köprü 120 B 3 *var.* Altun Kupri. Iraq
Alton 40 B 4 Illinois, N USA
Altoona 41 E 4 Pennsylvania, NE USA
Alto Paraná *see* Paraná
Alt-Schwanenburg *see* Gulbene
Altun Kupri *see* Altin Köprü
Altun Shan 126 C 4 *var.* Altyn Mountain range, NW China
Altus 49 F 2 Oklahoma, C USA
Altyn Tagh *see* Altun Shan
Alūksne 106 D 3 *Ger.* Marienb NE Latvia
Al 'Umarī 119 C 6 E Jordan
Alupka 109 F 5 S Ukraine
Al Uqşur *see* Luxor
Alushta 109 F 5 S Ukraine
Alva 49 F 1 Oklahoma, C USA
Alvin 49 H 4 Texas, S USA
Al Wahībah, Ramlat 121 E 5 *var.* Ramlat Ahl Wahībah, Ra *It.* Wahaybah, Wahībah Sand Desert, N Oman
Al Wajh 120 A 4 NW Saudi Ara
Alwar 134 D 3 N India
Alykí 104 C 4 *var.* Aliki. Tháso N Greece

s 107 B 5 *Pol.* Olita.
thuania
eus, Lake 147 E 5 lake,
th Australia, S Australia
i 73 B 5 SW Sudan
juak Lake 82 A 2 lake,
'anada
usa-shotō 131 A 8
nd group, Japan
85 B 6 S Sweden
ıi-ōshima 130 A 3 island,
ısei-shotō, S Japan
ıi-shotō 130 A 3 island group,
an
tea 97 D 6 SW Italy
ıá 63 E 1 *off.* Território de
ıapá. State, NE Brazil
ı *see* Al 'Amārah
ıpura 136 B 3 C Myanmar
ıllo 49 E 2 Texas, S USA
87 C 6 E Belgium
ıon 56 C 3 *Sp.* Amazonas.
ıer, Brazil/Peru
ıonas 62 D 2 *off.* Estado do
azonas.
ıonas *see* Amazon
ıonas, Estado do *see* Amazonas
ıon Canyons 56 D 2 trough,
ıtlantic Ocean
ıon Fan 67 B 5 undersea fan,
Atlantic Ocean
ıonia 56 B 3 physical region,
ıouth America
ım 77 A 5 S Cameroon
ınja 79 G 2 N Madagascar
ırchik 115 G 2
   Russian Federation
ıto 60 B 1 C Iceland
ırieu-en-Bugey 91 D 5 E France
ève 87 D 7 river, E Belgium
ıasary 79 F 4 S Madagascar
ın 139 F 4 *prev.* Amboina,
ıboyna. Pulau Seram,
ıdonesia
ısitra 79 G 3 C Madagascar
ıacia *see* Arta
ıim *see* Ambrym
ıiz 78 A 1 NW Angola
ıym 144 D 4 *var.* Ambrim.
ınd, C Vanuatu
ıitka Island 36 A 2 island,
ıska, NW USA
ı 126 C 5 W China
ıand 86 D 1 *Fris.* It Amelân.
ıand, N Netherlands
ıica-Antarctica Ridge 67 C 7
ıdersea ridge, S Atlantic Ocean
ıican Falls Reservoir 46 E 4
ıervoir, Idaho, NW USA
ıican Samoa 145 F 4
   unincorporated territory,
ıacific Ocean
ıicus 42 D 3 Georgia, SE USA
ısfoort 86 D 3 C Netherlands
ı 45 F 3 Iowa, C USA
ılochia 105 B 5 *var.* Amfilokhía.
ıreece
ılokhía *see* Amfilochía
ı 115 F 3 river,
ıussian Federation
ırst 79 F 4 Nova Scotia,
ıanada
ırst *see* Kyaikkami
ıns 90 C 3 *anc.* Ambianum,
ınarobriva. N France
ıdīvi Islands 132 B 2 island
ıup, Lakshadweep, SW India
ıante Bank *see* Amirante Ridge
ıante Islands 79 G 1
ı. Amirantes Group. Island,
ıeychelles

Amirantes Group *see*
   Amirante Islands
Amistad, Presa de la *see*
   Amistad Reservoir
Amistad Reservoir 49 F 4
   var. Presa de la Amistad.
   Reservoir, Texas, S Mexico/USA
Amisus *see* Samsun
'Ammān 119 B 6 *var.* Amman;
   anc. Philadelphia, *Bibl.* Rabbah
   Ammon, Rabbath Ammon.
   Country capital, NW Jordan
Amman *see* 'Ammān
Ammassalik 82 D 4
   var. Angmagssalik. SE Greenland
Amoentai *see* Amuntai
Āmol 120 D 2 *var.* Amul. N Iran
Amorgós 105 D 6 Amorgós,
   SE Greece
Amorgós 105 D 6 island, Kykládes,
   SE Greece
Amos 38 D 4 Québec, SE Canada
Amourj 74 D 3 SE Mauritania
Ampato, Nevado 61 E 4 mountain,
   S Peru
Amposta 93 F 3 NE Spain
Amraoti *see* Amrāvati
Amrāvati 134 D 4 *prev.* Amraoti.
   C India
Amritsar 134 D 2 N India
Amstelveen 86 C 3 C Netherlands
Amsterdam 86 C 3 country capital,
   C Netherlands
Amsterdam Island 141 C 6 island,
   NE French Southern
   & Antarctic Territories
Am Timan 76 C 3 SE Chad
Amu Darya 122 D 2
   Rus. Amudar'ya, *Taj.* Dar"yoi
   Amu, *Turkm.* Amyderya,
   Uzb. Amudaryo; *anc.* Oxus.
   River, C Asia
Amu-Dar'ya 123 E 3
   SE Turkmenistan
Amul *see* Āmol
Amund Ringnes Island 37 F 2
   island, N Canada
Amundsen Abyssal Plain 154 B 4
   abyssal plain, S Pacific Ocean
Amundsen Gulf 37 E 3 gulf,
   SE Beaufort Sea
Amundsen-Scott 154 B 3 research
   station, Antarctica
Amundsen Sea 154 A 4 sea,
   S Pacific Ocean
Amuntai 138 D 4 *prev.* Amoentai.
   Borneo, C Indonesia
Amur 120 D 1 *Chin.* Heilong
   Jiang. River, China/
   Russian Federation
Amvrosiyevka *see* Amvrosiyivka
Amvrosiyivka 109 H 3
   var. Amvrosiyevka. SE Ukraine
Amýntaio 104 B 4 *prev.* Amíndaion.
   N Greece
Anabar 115 E 2 river,
   N Russian Federation
An Abhainn Mhór *see* Blackwater
Anaco 59 E 2 NE Venezuela
Anaconda 44 B 2
   Montana, NW USA
Anacortes 46 B 1
   Washington, NW USA
Anadolu Dağları *see* Doğu
   Karadeniz Dağları
Anadyr' 115 H 1
   NE Russian Federation
Anadyr, Gulf of *see*
   Anadyrskiy Zaliv
Anadyrskiy Zaliv 115 H 1
   Eng. Gulf of Anadyr. Gulf,
   N Bering Sea

Anáfi 105 D 7 *anc.* Anaphe. Island,
   Kykládes, SE Greece
'Ānah *see* 'Annah
Analalava 79 G 2 N Madagascar
Anamur 116 C 5 S Turkey
Anantapur 132 C 2 S India
Anaphe *see* Anáfi
Anápolis 63 F 3 C Brazil
Anār 120 D 3 C Iran
Anatolia *see* Anadolu
Anatolia Plateau 116 C 4 plateau,
   C Turkey
Anatom 144 D 5 *var.* Aneityum,
   prev. Kéamu. Island, S Vanuatu
Añatuya 64 C 3 N Argentina
An Bhearú *see* Barrow
Anchorage 36 C 3
   Alaska, NW USA
Ancona 96 C 3 C Italy
Ancud 65 B 6 *prev.* San Carlos de
   Ancud. S Chile
Åndalsnes 85 A 5 S Norway
Andalucía 92 D 4 cultural region,
   S Spain
Andaman Islands 133 E 2 island
   group, SE India
Andaman Sea 133 G 2 sea,
   NE Indian Ocean
'Andām, Wādī 121 E 5 river,
   NE Oman
Andenne 87 C 6 SE Belgium
Anderlues 87 B 7 S Belgium
Anderson 40 C 4 Indiana, N USA
Andes 57 B 5 mountain range,
   South America
Andhra Pradesh 135 E 5
   cultural region, E India
Andhra Pradesh 132 D 1 state,
   SE India
Andijon 123 F 2 *Rus.* Andizhan.
   E Uzbekistan
Andikíthira *see* Antikýthira
Andipaxi *see* Antípaxi
Andípsara *see* Antipsara
Ándissa *see* Ántissa
Andizhan *see* Andijon
Andkhvoy 122 D 3 N Afghanistan
Andorra
   91 A 7 *Cat.* Valls d'Andorra,
   Fr. Vallée d'Andorra. Monarchy,
   SW Europe
Official name: Principality of
Andorra Date of formation: 1278
Capital: Andorra la Vella
Population: 58,000
Total area: 181 sq miles (468 sq km)
Languages: Catalan*, Spanish
Religions: Roman Catholic 86%,
other 14% Ethnic mix: Catalan 61%,
Spanish Castilian 30%, other 9%
Government: Parliamentary
democracy Currency: French franc,
Spanish peseta
Andorra la Vella 91 B 7
   var. Andorra, *Fr.* Andorre la
   Vielle, *Sp.* Andorra la Vieja.
   Country capital, C Andorra
Andover 89 D 7 S England, UK
Andøya 84 C 3 island, C Norway
Andrews 49 E 3 Texas, S USA
Andria 97 E 5 S Italy
An Droichead Nua *see* Newbridge
Ándros 105 D 6 Ándros, SE Greece
Ándros 105 D 6 island, Kykládes,
   SE Greece
Andros Island 54 C 2 island,
   NW Bahamas
Andros Town 54 C 1 NW Bahamas

Angara 112 D 3 river,
   C Russian Federation
Angarsk 115 E 4
   C Russian Federation
Ånge 85 C 5 C Sweden
Ángel de la Guarda, Isla 50 B 2
   island, NW Mexico
Angeles 139 E 1 *off.* Angeles City.
   Luzon, N Philippines
Angeles City *see* Angeles
Angel Falls *see* Ángel, Salto
Ángel, Salto 59 E 3 *Eng.* Angel
   Falls. Waterfall, E Venezuela
Angerburg *see* Węgorzewo
Ångermanälven 84 C 4 river,
   N Sweden
Angermünde 94 D 3 NE Germany
Angers 90 B 4 *anc.* Juliomagus.
   NW France
Anglesey 89 C 5 island,
   NW England, UK
Anglet 91 A 6 SW France
Angleton 49 H 4 Texas, S USA
Anglia *see* England
Angmagssalik *see* Ammassalik
Ang Nam Ngum 136 C 4 lake,
   N Laos

Angola
   78 B 2 *prev.* People's Republic of
   Angola, Portuguese West Africa.
   Republic, S Africa
Official name: Republic of Angola
Date of formation: 1975 Capital:
Luanda Population: 10.3 million
Total area: 481,551 sq miles
(1,246,700 sq km) Languages:
Portuguese* Religions: Roman
Catholic/Protestant 64%, traditional
beliefs 34%, other 2% Ethnic mix:
Ovimbundu 37%, Kimbundu 25%,
Bakongo 13%, other 25%
Government: Multiparty republic
Currency: Kwanza = 100 lwei

Angola Basin 67 D 5 undersea
   basin, E Atlantic Ocean
Angostura *see* Ciudad Bolívar
Angostura, Presa de la 51 G 5
   reservoir, SE Mexico
Angoulême 91 B 5 *anc.* Iculisma.
   W France
Angoumois 91 B 5 cultural region,
   W France
Angra Pequena *see* Lüderitz
Angren 123 F 2 E Uzbekistan
Anguilla 55 G 3 UK dependent
   territory, E Caribbean Sea
Anhui 129 C 5 *var.* Anhwei,
   Wan. Province, E China
Anina 108 A 4 *Ger.* Steierdorf,
   Hung. Stájerlakanina;
   prev. Steierdorf-Anina,
   Steyerlak-Anina.
   SW Romania
Anjou 90 B 4 cultural region,
   NW France
Anjouan 79 F 2 *var.* Johanna Island,
   Nzwani. Island, Mozambique
   Channel/Pacific Ocean
Ankara 116 C 3 *prev.* Angora,
   anc. Ancyra. Country capital,
   C Turkey
Ankeny 45 F 3 Iowa, C USA
Anklam 94 D 2 NE Germany
An Mhuir Cheilteach *see* Celtic Sea
Annaba 71 E 1 *prev.* Bône.
   NE Algeria
An Nabk 118 B 4 *var.* El Nebk,
   Nabk, Nebk, *Fr.* Nébeck.
   SW Syria

An Nafūd 120 B 4 desert,
NW Saudi Arabia
'**Annah** 120 B 3 *var.* 'Ānah. NW Iraq
An Najaf 120 B 3 *var.* Najaf. S Iraq
Annamitique, Chaîne 136 D 4
mountain range, Laos
Annapolis 41 F 4 state capital,
Maryland, NE USA
Annapurna 135 E 3
mountain, C Nepal
An Nāqūrah *see* En Nâqoûra
Ann Arbor 40 C 3 Michigan, N USA
An Nāşirīyah 120 C 3 *var.* Nasiriya.
SE Iraq
Anneciacum *see* Annecy
Annecy 91 D 5 *anc.* Anneciacum.
E France
Anniston 42 D 2 Alabama, S USA
Annotto Bay 54 B 5 C Jamaica
An Ómaigh *see* Omagh
Anqing 129 D 5 E China
Ansbach 95 C 6 SE Germany
Anshan 128 D 3 NE China
Anshun 129 B 6 S China
Anson Bay 146 D 2 inlet,
W Pacific Ocean
Ansongo 75 E 3 E Mali
An Srath Bán *see* Strabane
Antakya 116 D 5 *anc.* Antioch,
Antiochia. S Turkey
Antalaha 79 G 2 NE Madagascar
Antalya 116 B 4 *prev.* Adalia, *anc.*
Attaleia, *Bibl.* Attalia. SW Turkey
Antalya Körfezi 116 B 4 *var.* Gulf of
Adalia, *Eng.* Gulf of Antalya.
Gulf, NE Mediterranean Sea
Antananarivo 79 G 3
prev. Tananarive. Country capital,
C Madagascar
Antarctica 154 B 3 continent,
Antarctic Peninsula 154 A 2
peninsula, Antarctica
Antequera 92 D 5 *anc.* Anticaria,
Antiquaria. S Spain
Antibes 91 E 6 *anc.* Antipolis.
SE France
Anticosti, Île d' 39 F 3
Eng. Anticosti Island. Island,
Québec, E Canada
Antigua 55 G 3 island,
S Antigua & Barbuda

Antigua & Barbuda
55 H 3 Commonwealth republic,
E Caribbean Sea

Official name: Antigua and
Barbuda **Date of formation:** 1981
Capital: St. John's **Population:**
65,000 **Total area:** 170 sq miles
(440 sq km) **Languages:** English*,
English Creole **Religions:** Protestant
87%, Roman Catholic 10%,
other 3% **Ethnic mix:** Black 98%,
other 2% **Government:**
Parliamentary democracy
Currency: E Caribbean $ = 100 cents

Antikýthira 105 C 7
var. Andikíthira. Island, S Greece
Anti-Lebanon 118 B 4 *var.* Jebel esh
Sharqî, *Ar.* Al Jabal ash Sharqī,
Fr. Anti-Liban. Mountain range,
Lebanon/Syria
Antípaxoi 105 A 5 *var.* Andipaxi.
Island, Iónioi Nísoi, W Greece
Antipodes Islands 142 D 5 island
group, S New Zealand
Antipolis *see* Antibes
Antípsara 105 D 5 *var.* Andípsara.
Island, E Greece
Ántissa 105 D 5 *var.* Ándissa.
Lésvos, E Greece

An tIúr *see* Newry
Antivari *see* Bar
Antofagasta 64 B 2 N Chile
Antony 90 C 3 N France
An tSionainn *see* Shannon
Antsirabe 79 G 3 C Madagascar
Antsohihy 79 G 2 N Madagascar
Antwerp *see* Antwerpen
Antwerpen 87 C 5 *Eng.* Antwerp,
Fr. Anvers. N Belgium
Anuradhapura 132 D 3 C Sri Lanka
Anxious Bay 149 A 6 bay,
E Great Australian Bight
Anyang 128 C 4 NE China
A'nyêmaqên Shan 126 D 4
mountain range, C China
Anykščiai 106 C 4 E Lithuania
Anzio 97 C 5 C Italy
Aomori 130 D 3 Honshū, C Japan
Aosta 96 A 1 *anc.* Augusta
Praetoria. NW Italy
Aoukâr 74 D 3 *var.* Aouker. Plateau,
C Mauritania
Aouk, Bahr 76 C 4 river,
Central African Republic/Chad
Aouker *see* Aoukâr
Aozou 76 C 1 N Chad
Apalachee Bay 42 D 3 bay,
NE Gulf of Mexico
Apalachicola River 42 D 3 river,
Florida, SE USA
Apartadó 58 B 2 NW Colombia
Apatity 110 C 2
NW Russian Federation
Ape 106 D 3 NE Latvia
Apeldoorn 86 D 3 E Netherlands
Apennines *see* Appennino
Äpia 145 F 4 country capital,
Savai'i, E Samoa
Apoera 59 G 3 NW Suriname
Apollinopolis Parva *see* Qûs
Apostle Islands 40 B 1 island
group, Wisconsin, N USA
Appalachian Mountains 35 C 5
mountain range, E USA
Appennino 96 C 3 *Eng.* Apennines.
Mountain range, C Italy/
San Marino
Appennino Lucano 97 D6
Mountain range, S Italy
Appingedam 86 E 1
NE Netherlands
Appleton 40 B 2 Wisconsin, N USA
Apple Valley 47 C 7
California, W USA
Apsheronsk 111 A 7
SW Russian Federation
Apure 58 C 2 river, W Venezuela
Apurímac 60 D 3 river, S Peru
Aputiteeq 82 D 4 *var.* Aputitêq.
Greenland
Aputitêq *see* Aputiteeq
Aqaba, Gulf of 120 A 4 *var.* Gulf of
Elat, Sinus Aelaniticus, *Ar.* Khalíj
al 'Aqabah. Gulf, Red Sea/
Indian Ocean
Äqchah 123 E 3 *var.* Āqcheh.
N Afghanistan
Āqcheh *see* Äqchah
Aquae Flaviae *see* Chaves
Aquidauana 63 E 4 S Brazil
Aquitaine 91 B 6 cultural region,
SW France
Arabian Basin 140 B 3 undersea
basin, N Indian Ocean
Arabian Desert 68 D 3 desert,
E Egypt
Arabian Peninsula 140 A 3
peninsula, Iran/Jordan
Arabian Sea 140 B 3 sea,
NW Indian Ocean

Aracaju 63 G 3 E Brazil
Araçuai 63 F 3 SE Brazil
Arad 108 A 4 W Romania
'**Arad** 119 B 7 S Israel
Arafura Sea 152 B 3 sea,
W Pacific Ocean
Aragón 93 E 2 cultural region,
E Spain
Araguaia, Río 63 E 3
var. Araguaya. River, C Brazil
Araguaína 63 F 2 E Brazil
Araguari 63 F 4 SE Brazil
Araguaya *see* Araguaia, Río
Ara Jovis *see* Aranjuez
Arāk 120 C 3 *prev.* Sultānābād.
W Iran
Arakan Yoma 136 A 3
mountain range, W Myanmar
Aral *see* Aral'sk
Aral Sea 122 D 1 *Kaz.* Aral Tengizi,
Rus. Aral'skoye More,
Uzb. Orol Dengizi. Inland sea,
Kazakhstan/Uzbekistan
Aral'sk 114 B 4 *Kaz.* Aral.
SW Kazakhstan
Aranda de Duero 92 D 2 N Spain
Aranđelovac 100 D 4 *prev.*
Arandjelovac. C Yugoslavia
Arandjelovac *see* Aranđelovac
Aranjuez 92 D 3 *anc.* Ara Jovis.
C Spain
Araouane 75 E 2 N Mali
'**Ar'ar** 120 B 3 N Saudi Arabia
Ararat, Mount *see* Büyükağri Baği
Aras 117 F 3 *Arm.* Arak's, *Az.* Araz,
Per. Rūd-e Aras, *Rus.* Araks,
Turk. Aras Nehri; *prev.* Araxes.
River, SW Asia
Arauca 58 C 2 NE Colombia
Arauca 58 D 2 river,
Colombia/Venezuela
Arausio *see* Orange
Arbíl 120 B 3 *var.* Erbil, Irbil, Kurd,
Hawlêr; *anc.* Arbela. N Iraq
Arbroath 88 D 4 *anc.*
Aberbrothock. E Scotland, UK
Arbuzinka *see* Arbyzynka
Arcachon 91 A 5 SW France
Arcata 47 A 5 California, W USA
Archangel *see* Arkhangel'sk
Archidona 92 D 5 S Spain
Arco 96 C 2 N Italy
Arco, Paso del 65 B 5 pass,
Argentina
Arctic Bay 37 G 2 Baffin Island,
Canada
Arctic Ocean 155 F 3 ocean,
Arctowski 154 A 2 research station,
Antarctica
Arda 104 C 3 *var.* Ardhas,
Gk. Ardas. River, Bulgaria/Greece
Ardabīl 120 C 2 *var.* Ardebil.
NW Iran
Ardakān 120 D 3 C Iran
Ardèche 91 C 5 cultural region,
E France
Ardennes 87 D 8 plateau, W Europe
Ardh es Suwwān *see*
Arḑ aş Şawwān
Ardino 104 D 3 S Bulgaria
Ard Mhacha *see* Armagh
Ardmore 49 G 2 Oklahoma, C USA
Arendal 85 A 6 S Norway
Arenys de Mar 93 G 2 NE Spain
Areópoli 105 B 7 *prev.* Areópolis.
S Greece

Areópolis *see* Areópoli
Arequipa 61 E 4 SE Peru
Arezzo 96 C 3 *anc.* Arretium. C
Argalastí 105 C 5 C Greece
Argenteuil 90 C 3 N France

Argentina
65 B 5 Republic,
S South America

Official name: Argentine Repu
Date of formation: 1816/1925
Capital: Buenos Aires **Populati**
33.5 million **Total area:** 1,068,29
miles (2,766,890 sq km) **Langua**
Spanish*, Italian, English, Germ
French, Indian languages
Religions: Roman Catholic 90%
Jewish 2%, other 8% **Ethnic mi**
White 85%, other (including me
and Indian) 15% **Government:**
Multiparty republic
Currency: Peso = 100 centavos

Argentina Basin *see* Argentine
Argentina, Republic of *see*
Argentina
Argentine Antarctic Sector 154
Argentine territorial claim,
Antarctica
Argentine Basin 67 B 6 *var.*
Argentina Basin. Undersea b
SW Atlantic Ocean
Argentine Rise *see* Falkland Pla
Argo 72 B 3 N Sudan
Árgos 105 B 6 S Greece
Argostóli 105 A 5 *var.* Argostól
Kefallinía, W Greece
Argostólion *see* Argostóli
Argun 111 B 8 SW Russian Feder
Århus 85 B 7 *var.* Aarhus.
C Denmark
Ari Atoll 132 A 4 island,
C Maldives
Arica 64 B 1 *hist.* San Marcos
de Arica. N Chile
Aridaía 104 B 3 *var.* Aridhaía.
N Greece
Ariha 118 B 3 *var.* Arīhā. W Syr
Arīhā *see* Ariha
Ariminum *see* Rimini
Arinsal 91 A 8 NW Andorra
Arizona 48 B 2 *off.* State of Ariz
nicknames Copper State, Gran
Canyon State. State, SW USA
Arkansas 42 A 1 *off.* State of
Arkansas; nickname Land of
Opportunity. State, S USA
Arkansas City 45 F 5
Kansas, C USA
Arkansas River 42 B 2 river, C
Arkhangel'sk 110 C 3
var. Arcangelo, *Eng.* Archange
NW Russian Federation
Arkoi 105 E 6 island, Dodekán
SE Greece
Arles 91 C 6 *var.* Arles-sur-Rhô
anc. Arelas, Arelate. SE Franc
Arlington 49 G 3 Texas, S USA
Arlington 41 E 4
Virginia, NE USA
Arlon 87 D 8 *Dut.* Aarlen, *Ger.*
Lat. Orolaunum. SE Belgium
Armagh 89 B 5 *Ir.* Ard Mhacha.
SE Northern Ireland, UK
Armagnac 91 B 6 cultural regio
S France

Armenia
117 F 3 *var.* Ajastan,
Arm. Hayastani Hanrapetut'y
prev. Armenian Soviet Socialis
Republic. Republic, SW Asia

al name: Republic of
nia Date of formation: 1991
al: Yerevan Population: 3.6
6
n Total area: 11,505 sq miles
0 sq km) Languages:
nian*, Azerbaijani, Russian,
sh Religions: Armenian
olic 90%, other Christian and
m 10% Ethnic mix: Armenian
Azerbaijani 3%, Russian,
sh 4% Government:
party republic
ncy: Dram = 100 louma

nia 58 B 3 W Colombia
dale 149 D 6
w South Wales, SE Australia
trong 38 B 3 Ontario,
anada
ansk see Armyans′k
ans′k 109 F 4 Rus. Armyansk.
kraine
a 104 C 4 N Greece
ud 82 A 3 river, E Canada
a see Arnaía
do 93 E 2 N Spain
em 86 D 4 SE Netherlands
em Land 148 A 2 physical
ion, Northern Territory,
Australia
96 B 3 river, C Italy
see Arno Atoll
d 45 G 5 Missouri, C USA
valde see Choszczno
e 145 E 3 island, W Kiribati
ahad see Er Rahad
amādī 120 B 3 var. Ramadi,
amadiya. SW Iraq
amthā 119 B 5 var. Ramtha.
lordan
a, Isle of 88 C 4 island,
′ Scotland, UK
aqqah 118 C 2 var. Rakka;
r. Nicephorium. N Syria
. 90 C 2 anc. Nemetocenna.
France
ashādīyah 119 C 5 NE Jordan
awdatayn 120 C 4
. Raudhatain. N Kuwait
ium see Arezzo
ga 51 G 5 SE Mexico
iyād 121 C 5 Eng. Riyadh.
untry capital, C Saudi Arabia
yo Grande 47 B 7
lifornia, W USA
ustāq 121 E 5 var. Rostak,
staq. N Oman
utbah 120 B 3 var. Rutba.
′ Iraq
105 A 5 anc. Ambracia.
Greece
hat 117 G 3 S Armenia
nisa 54 B 2 W Cuba
ia 48 D 3 New Mexico,
′ USA
ur′s Pass 151 C 6 pass,
uth Island, C New Zealand
as 64 D 3 prev. San Eugenio,
1 Eugenio del Cuareim.
Uruguay
k 117 F 2 W Armenia
s 90 C 2 cultural region,
France
rz 108 D 4 Rus. Artsiz.
′ Ukraine
n 117 F 2 NE Turkey
73 B 6 NW Uganda
a 55 E 5 var. Oruba. Dutch
tonomous region,
Caribbean Sea
a 58 C 1 island,
Caribbean Sea

Aru, Kepulauan 139 G 4 Eng.
Aru Islands; prev. Aroe Islands.
Island group, E Indonesia
Arunāchal Pradesh 135 H 3
cultural region, NE India
Arusha 73 C 7 N Tanzania
Arviat 37 G 4 prev. Eskimo Point.
North West Territories, C Canada
Arvidsjaur 84 C 4 N Sweden
Arys′ 114 B 5 Kaz. Arys.
S Kazakhstan
Asadābād 123 F 4 var. Asadbād;
prev. Chaghasarāy. E Afghanistan
Asad, Buhayrat al 118 C 2 Eng.
Lake Assad. Reservoir, N Syria
Asahi-dake 130 D 2 mountain,
Hokkaidō, NE Japan
Asahikawa 130 D 2 Hokkaidō,
NE Japan
Asamankese 75 E 5 SE Ghana
Āsānsol 135 F 4 NE India
Ascension Fracture Zone 67 C 5
fracture zone, C Atlantic Ocean
Ascension Island 69 A 5 island,
E Atlantic Ocean
Ascoli Piceno 96 C 4 anc. Asculum
Picenum. C Italy
Asculum Picenum see Ascoli Piceno
Ashburton 151 C 6 South Island,
SW New Zealand
Ashburton 146 B 4 river, Western
Australia, W Australia
Ashdod 119 A 6 anc. Azotos,
Lat. Azotus. W Israel
Asheville 43 E 1
North Carolina, SE USA
Ashgabat 122 C 3 prev. Ashkhabad,
Poltoratsk. Country capital,
C Turkmenistan
Ashibetsu 130 D 2 var. Asibetu.
Hokkaidō, NE Japan
Ashkelon see Ashqelon
Ashland 40 D 5 Kentucky, E USA
Ashland 46 B 4 Oregon, NW USA
Ashmore & Cartier Islands 142 A 3
Australian external territory,
E Indian Ocean
Ashmyany 107 C 5
Rus. Oshmyany. W Belarus
Ashqelon 119 A 6
var. Ashkelon. C Israel
Ash Shadādah 118 E 2 var. Ash
Shaddādah, Jisr ash Shadadi
Shaddādī, Shedadi, Tell Shedadi.
NE Syria
Ash Sharāh 119 B 7 var. Esh Sharā.
Mountain range, W Jordan
Ash Shawbak 119 B 7 W Jordan
Ash Shihr 121 C 7 SE Yemen
Asia 112 D 3 continent
Asibetu see Ashibetsu
Asipovichy 107 D 6
Pol. Mahilyowskaya Voblasts′,
Rus. Osipovichi. C Belarus
Aşkale 117 M 1 NE Turkey
Askersund 85 C 6 C Sweden
Asmara 72 C 4 Amh. Āsmera.
Country capital, C Eritrea
Āsmera see Asmara
Aspinwall see Colón
Assab 72 D 4 Amh. Āseb. SE Eritrea
As Sabkhah 118 D 2 var. Sabkha.
NE Syria
Assad, Lake see Asad, Buhayrat al
As Safāwī 119 C 6 N Jordan
As Salamīyah see Salamīyah
As Salt 119 B 5 var. Salt. NW Jordan
Assam 135 G 3 cultural region,
NE India
Assamaka see Assamakka
Assamakka 75 F 2 var. Assamaka.
NW Niger

As Samāwah 120 B 3
var. Samawa. S Iraq
Assen 86 E 2 NE Netherlands
Assenede 87 B 5 NW Belgium
Assling see Jesenice
As Sukhnah 118 D 3 var. Sukhne,
Fr. Soukhné. C Syria
As Sulaymānīyah 120 C 3
var. Sulaimaniya, Kurd. Slēmānī.
NE Iraq
As Sulayyil 120 B 4 S Saudi Arabia
Aş Şummān 121 C 5 desert,
N Saudi Arabia
As Suwaydā′ 119 B 5
var. El Suweida, Es Suweida,
Suweida, Fr. Soueida. SW Syria
Astana 114 C 4 prev. Akmola,
Akmolinsk, Tselinograd Kaz.
Aqmola. country capital,
N Kazakhstan
Asten 87 D 5 SE Netherlands
Asti 96 A 2 anc. Asta Colonia,
Asta Pompeia, Hasta Colonia,
Hasta Pompeia. NW Italy
Astigi see Écija
Astorga 92 C 2 anc. Asturica
Augusta. N Spain
Astrakhan′ 111 C 7
SW Russian Federation
Asturias 92 C 1 cultural region,
NW Spain
Asturias see Oviedo
Asturica Augusta see Astorga
Astypálaia 105 D 7 var. Astipálaia,
It. Stampalia. Island,
Dodekánisos, SE Greece
Asunción 64 D 2 country capital,
S Paraguay
Aswān 72 B 2 var. Assouan,
Assuan; anc. Syene. SE Egypt
Asyūt 72 B 2 var. Assiout, Assiut,
Siut; anc. Lycopolis. C Egypt
Atacama Desert see
Atacama, Desierto de
Atacama, Desierto de 64 B 1 Eng.
Atacama Desert. Desert, N Chile
Atafu Atoll 145 F 3 island,
NW Tokelau
Atakora, Chaîne de l′ 75 F 4
var. Atakora Mountains.
Mountain range, N Benin
Atakora Mountains see
Atakora, Chaîne de l′
Atâr 74 C 2 NW Mauritania
Atas Bogd 126 D 3 mountain,
SW Mongolia
Atascadero 47 B 7 California, W USA
Atbara 72 C 3 var. ′Atbārah.
NE Sudan
Atbasar 114 C 4 N Kazakhstan
Atchison 45 F 4 Kansas, C USA
Ath 87 B 6 var. Aat. SW Belgium
Athabasca 37 E 5 Alberta,
SW Canada
Athabasca 37 E 5 var. Athabaska.
River, Alberta. SW Canada
Athabasca, Lake 37 F 4 lake,
SW Canada
Athabaska see Athabasca
Athens 42 C 1 Alabama, S USA
Athens 42 D 1 Tennessee, S USA
Athens 43 E 2 Georgia, SE USA
Athens 49 G 3 Texas, S USA
Athens 40 D 4 Ohio, N USA
Athens see Athína
Atherton 148 D 3 Queensland,
NE Australia
Athína 105 C 6 Eng. Athens;
prev. Athínai, anc. Athenae.
Country capital, C Greece
Athlone 89 B 6 Ir. Baile Átha Luain.
C Ireland

Ath Thawrah see
Madīnat ath Thawrah
Ati 76 C 3 C Chad
Atikokan 38 B 4 Ontario, S Canada
Atka 115 G 3
E Russian Federation
Atka Island 36 A 3 island, Alaska,
NW USA
Atlanta 49 H 2 Texas, S USA
Atlanta 35 C 6 state capital,
Georgia, SE USA
Atlantic City 41 F 4 New Jersey,
NE USA
Atlantic-Indian Basin 67 D 8
undersea basin, SW Indian Ocean
Atlantic-Indian Ridge 67 D 7
undersea ridge, SW Indian Ocean
Atlantic Ocean 66 C 4
var. Atlantshaf. Ocean,
Atlas Mountains 68 B 2 mountain
range, N Africa
Atlasovo 115 H 3
E Russian Federation
Atlas Saharien 70 D 2
var. Saharan Atlas. Mountain
range, Algeria/Morocco
Atlin 36 D 4 British Columbia,
W Canada
At Tā′if 121 B 5 W Saudi Arabia
At Tāj 71 H 4 SE Libya
At Tall al Abyad 118 C 2
var. Tall al Abyad, Tell Abyad,
Fr. Tell Abiad. N Syria
Attapu 137 E 5 var. Attopeu.
SE Laos
Attawapiskat 38 C 3 Ontario,
C Canada
Attawapiskat 38 C 3 river,
S Canada
Attersee 95 D 6 lake, N Austria
At Tibnī 118 D 2 var. Tibnī. NE Syria
Attopeu see Samakhixai
Attu Island 36 A 2 island, Alaska,
NW USA
Atuntaqui 60 B 1 N Ecuador
Atyrau 114 B 4 prev. Gur′yev.
W Kazakhstan
Aubagne 91 D 6 SE France
Aube 90 D 4 cultural region,
SE France
Auburn 42 D 2 Alabama, S USA
Auburn 41 G 2 Maine, NE USA
Auburn 46 B 3 Washington,
NW USA
Auch 91 B 6 Lat. Augusta
Auscorum, Elimberrum.
S France
Auckland 150 D 3 North Island,
N New Zealand
Auckland Islands 142 D 5 island
group, S New Zealand
Aude 91 C 6 cultural region,
S France
Audenarde see Oudenaarde
Audern see Audru
Audincourt 90 E 4 E France
Audru 106 D 2 Ger. Audern.
SW Estonia
Augila see Awjilah
Augsburg 95 C 6 Fr. Augsbourg;
anc. Augusta Vindelicorum.
S Germany
Augusta 43 E 2 Georgia, SE USA
Augusta 147 B 7 Western Australia,
SW Australia
Augusta 41 G 2 state capital,
Maine, NE USA
Augusta Emerita see Mérida
Augusta Praetoria see Aosta
Augusta Trajana see Stara Zagora
Augustobona Tricassium see Troyes
Augustodurum see Bayeux

Augustów 98 E 2 *Rus.* Avgustov.
NE Poland
Augustus Island 146 C 3 island,
NW Australia
'Aujā et Tahtā 119 E 7 *var.* Khirbet
el 'Aujā et Taḥtā. E West Bank
Auk Bok 137 B 5 *var.* South Island.
Island, S Myanmar
Auob 78 B 4 *var.* Oup.
River,
E Namibia/South Africa
Aurangābād 134 D 5 W India
Aur Atoll 144 D 1 island,
E Marshall Islands
Auray 90 A 4 NW France
Aurelia Aquensis *see*
Baden-Baden
Aurelianum *see* Orléans
Aurillac 91 C 5 C France
Aurora 40 B 3 Illinois, N USA
Aurora 45 G 5 Missouri, C USA
Aurora 44 D 4 Colorado, C USA
Aurora 59 F 2 NW Guyana
Aurora *see* Maewo
Aus 78 B 4 SW Namibia
Aussig *see* Ústí nad Labem
Austin 35 C 6 state capital,
Texas, S USA
Austin 45 G 3
Minnesota, N USA
Australes, Îles 145 H 5 island
group, SW French Polynesia
Austral Fracture Zone 153 E 4
fracture zone, S Pacific Ocean

Australia
142 A 4 Commonwealth
republic, Indian Ocean/
Pacific Ocean

Official name: Commonwealth of
Australia **Date of formation:** 1901
Capital: Canberra **Population:** 17.8
million **Total area:** 2,967,893 sq miles
(7,686850 sq km) **Languages:** English*,
Greek, Italian, Malay, Aboriginal
languages **Religions:** Protestant 60%,
Roman Catholic 26%, other 14%
Ethnic mix: Caucasian 92%, Asian
4%, Aboriginal and other 1%
Government: Parliamentary
democracy **Currency:** Australian
$ = 100 cents

Australian Alps 149 C 7 mountain
range, SE Australia
Australian Antarctic Territory 154
C 3 Australian territorial claim,
Antarctica
Australian Capital Territory 149 D 7
prev. Federal Capital Territory.
Territory, SE Australia
Australie, Bassin Nord de l' *see*
North Australian Basin
Austral Seamounts 152 D 4
seamount range,
S Pacific Ocean
Austrava *see* Ostrov

Austria
95 D 7 *Ger.* Österreich. Republic,
C Europe

Official name: Republic of Austria
Date of formation: 1918/1945
Capital: Vienna **Population:** 7.8
million **Total area:** 32,375 sq miles
(83,850 sq km) **Languages:** German*,
Croatian, Slovene, Hungarian
(Magyar) **Religions:** Roman Catholic
85%, Protestant 6%, other 9%
Ethnic mix: German 99%, other
(inc. Hungarian, Slovene, Croat) 1%
Government: Multiparty republic
Currency: Schilling = 100 groschen

Ausuitoq *see* Grise Fiord
Auvergne 91 C 5 cultural region,
S France
Auxerre 90 C 4 *anc.* Autesiodorum,
Autissiodorum. C France
Avaricum *see* Bourges
Avarua 145 G 5 dependent territory
capital, Rarotonga, S Cook Islands
Ávdira 104 D 3 NE Greece
Aveiro 92 B 3 *anc.* Talabriga.
W Portugal
Avellino 97 D 5 *anc.* Abellinum. S Italy
Avenio *see* Avignon
Aversa 97 D 5 S Italy
Avesta 85 C 6 C Sweden
Aveyron 91 C 6 river, S France
Avezzano 96 C 4 C Italy
Avgustov *see* Augustów
Aviemore 88 C 3 N Scotland, UK
Avignon 91 D 6 *anc.* Avenio. SE France
Ávila 92 D 3 *var.* Avila; *anc.* Abela,
Abula, Abyla, Avela. C Spain
Avilés 92 C 1 NW Spain
Avranches 90 B 3 N France
Awaji-shima 131 C 6 island, Japan
Āwash 73 D 5 C Ethiopia
Awbārī 71 F 3 SW Libya
Awjilah 71 G 3 *lt.* Augila. NE Libya
Awled Djellal *see* Ouled Djellal
Axel 87 B 5 SW Netherlands
Axel Heiberg Island 37 F 1 *var.*
Axel Heiburg. Island, N Canada
Axel Heiburg *see* Axel Heiberg Island
Axiós *see* Vardar
Ayacucho 60 D 4 S Peru
Ayaguz 114 C 5 *Kaz.* Ayaköz;
prev. Sergiopol. E Kazakhstan
Ayamonte 92 B 5 S Spain
Ayaviri 61 E 4 S Peru
Aydarkül 123 E 2 *Rus.* Ozero
Aydarkul'. Lake, C Uzbekistan
Aydarkul', Ozero *see* Aydarkül
Aydın 116 A 4 *var.* Aïdin;
anc. Tralles. SW Turkey
Ayers Rock *see* Uluru
Ayeyarwady *see* Irrawaddy
Ayiá *see* Agiá
Ayia Napa *see* Agía Nápa
Ayorou 75 F 3 W Niger
'Ayoûn el 'Atroûs 74 D 3 *var.* Aïoun
el Atroûss, Aïoun el Atrous.
SE Mauritania
Ayr 88 C 4 SW Scotland, UK
Ayr 148 D 3 Queensland,
E Australia
Aytos 104 E 2 E Bulgaria
Ayutthaya 137 C 5 *var.* Phra
Nakhon Si Ayutthaya. C Thailand
Ayvalık 116 A 3 W Turkey
A'zāg 118 B 2 NW Syria
Azahar, Costa del 93 F 3 coastal
region, E Spain
Azaouâd 75 E 3 plateau, SW Mali

Azerbaijan
117 G 2 *Az.* Azärbaycan,
Azärbaycan Respublikasi; *prev.*
Azerbaijan SSR. Republic, SE Asia

Official name: Republic of
Azerbaijan **Date of formation:** 1991
Capital: Baku **Population:** 7.3
million **Total area:** 33,436 sq miles
(86,600 sq km) **Languages:**
Azerbaijani*, Russian, Armenian
Religions: Muslim 83%, Armenian
Apostolic, Russian Orthodox 17%
Ethnic mix: Azerbaijani 83%,
Russian 6%, Armenian 6%, other 5%
Government: Multiparty republic
Currency: Manat = 100 gopik

Azimabad *see* Patna
Azogues 60 B 2 S Ecuador
Azores 92 A 5 *var.* Açores, Ilhas dos
Açores, *Port.* Arquipélago dos
Açores. Island group, W Portugal
Azores-Biscay Rise 80 A 3
undersea rise, E Atlantic Ocean
Azoum, Bahr 76 C 3 river, SE Chad
Azov, Sea of 109 G 4 *Rus.*
Azovskoye More, *Ukr.* Azovs'ke
More. Sea, N Black Sea
Azraq, Waḥat al 119 C 6 oasis,
N Jordan
Aztec 48 C 1 New Mexico, SW USA
Azuaga 92 C 4 W Spain
Azuero, Península de 53 F 5
peninsula, S Panama
Azul 65 D 5 E Argentina
Azur, Côte d' 91 C 6 coastal region,
SE France
Aẕ Ẕahrān 120 C 4 *Eng.* Dhahran.
NE Saudi Arabia
Az Zaqāzīq *see* Zagazig
Az Zarqā' 119 B 6 *var.* Zarqa.
NW Jordan
Az Zāwiyah 71 F 2 *var.* Zawia.
NW Libya
Az Zilfī 120 B 4 N Saudi Arabia
Az Zubayr *see* Isernia

B

Baabda 118 A 4 *var.* B'abdā.
C Lebanon
Baalbek 118 B 4 *var.* Ba'labakk;
anc. Heliopolis. E Lebanon
Baar 95 B 7 N Switzerland
Baarle-Nassau 87 C 5
enclave, N Belgium
Baarn 86 C 3 C Netherlands
Babadag 108 D 5 SE Romania
Babahoyo 60 B 2 *prev.* Bodegas.
C Ecuador
Babajevo *see* Babayevo
Bābā, Kūh-e 123 E 4 mountain
range, C Afghanistan
Babayevo 110 B 4 *var.* Babajevo.
NW Russian Federation
B'abdā *see* Baabda
Bab el Mandeb 121 B 7 strait,
Arabian Sea/Red Sea
Babelthuap 144 A 2 island, E Palau
Babonneau 55 F 1 N Saint Lucia
Babruysk 107 D 7 *Rus.* Bobruysk.
E Belarus
Babuyan Channel 139 E 1 channel,
Philippine Sea/South China Sea
Babuyan Islands 139 E 1 island,
N Philippines
Bacabal 63 F 2 E Brazil
Bacău 108 C 4 *Hung.* Bákó.
NE Romania
Bắc Giang 136 D 3 N Vietnam
Bacheykava 107 D 5
Rus. Bocheykovo. N Belarus
Bačka Palanka 100 D 3
prev. Palanka. NW Yugoslavia
Bačka Topola 100 D 3
Hung. Topolya; *prev.* Bácstopolya.
NW Yugoslavia
Bac Liêu 137 D 6
var. Vinh Loi. S Vietnam
Bacolod 139 E 2 *off.* Bacolod City.
Negros, C Philippines
Bacolod City *see* Bacolod
Bactra *see* Balkh
Badain Jaran Shamo 126 D 3
desert, N China
Badajoz 92 C 4
anc. Pax Augusta. W Spain
Bad Doberan 94 C 2 N Germany

Baden-Baden 95 B 6 *anc.* Aurel
Aquensis. SW Germany
Bad Freienwalde 94 D 3
NE Germany
Bad Hersfeld 94 B 4 C German
Bad Homburg *see* Bad Hombu:
vor der Höhe
Bad Homburg vor der Höhe 95
var. Bad Homburg. W Germa
Bad Ischl 95 D 7 C Austria
Bad Krozingen 95 A 6
SW Germany
Badlands 44 D 2 physical regio
North Dakota, N USA
Badu Island 148 C 1 island,
Queensland, NE Australia
Bad Vöslau 95 E 6 NE Austria
Badyarada 'Adméd *see* Aden, C
Bafatá 74 C 4 C Guinea-Bissau
Baffin Bay 82 C 2 bay,
NW Atlantic Ocean
Baffin Island 37 G 2 island,
Northwest Territories, NE Ca
Bafing 74 C 3 river, NW Afric;
Bafoussam 76 A 4 W Cameroc
Bafra 116 D 2 N Turkey
Bāft 120 D 4 S Iran
Bagaces 52 D 4 NW Costa Rica
Bagé 63 E 5 S Brazil
Baghdād 120 B 3 *var.* Bagdad, *
Baghdad. Country capital, C
Baghdad *see* Baghdād
Bāghīn 120 D 4 Iran
Baghlān 123 E 4 NE Afghanist
Bago *see* Pegu
Bagoé 74 D 4 river, Ivory
Coast/Mali
Bagrationovsk 106 A 4
Ger. Preussisch Eylau.
W Russian Federation
Bagrax Hu *see* Bosten Hu
Baguio 139 E 1 *off.* Baguio City
Luzon, N Philippines
Baguio City *see* Baguio
Bagzane, Monts 75 G 3 mount
N Niger
Bahama Islands *see* Bahamas

Bahamas
54 C 2 Commonwealth repu
N Caribbean Sea

Official name: The Commonwe
of the Bahamas **Date of formati**
1973 **Capital:** Nassau **Populatio**
300,000 **Total area:** 5,359 sq mile
(13,880 sq km) **Languages:**
English*, English Creole Religi
Protestant 76%, Roman Catholic
19%, other 5% **Ethnic mix:** Blac
85%, White 15% **Government:**
Parliamentary democracy **Curre**
Bahamian $ = 100 cents

Bahamas 35 D 6 *var.* Bahama
Islands. Island group,
W Atlantic Ocean
Bahariya Oasis 72 B 2 *var.* Wāḥ
el Baharīya. Oasis, C Egypt
Bahāwalpur 134 C 2 E Pakistar
Bahia 63 F 3 *off.* Estado da Bahi
State, E Brazil
Bahía, Estado da *see* Bahia
Bahía, Islas de la 52 C 1
Eng. Bay Islands. Island grou
N Honduras
Bahía Blanca 65 C 5 E Argenti
Bahir Dar 72 C 4 *var.* Bahr Dar,
Bahrdar Giyorgis. NW Ethio;
Bahraich 135 E 3 N India

rain
20 C 4 *Ar.* Al Baḥrayn;
prev. Bahrein, *anc.* Tylos or Tyros.
Monarchy, SW Asia

ficial name: State of Bahrain **Date
formation:** 1971 **Capital:** Manama
ulation: 500,000 **Total area:**
sq miles (680 sq km) **Languages:**
abic*, English, Urdu **Religions:**
slim (Shi'a majority) 85%,
ristian 7%, other 8% **Ethnic mix:**
ab 73%, South Asian 14%, Persian
, other 5% **Government:**
solute monarchy (emirate)
rrency: Dinar = 1,000 fils

ır al Milḥ *see* Razāzah, Buḥayrat ar
ırām Chāh 122 D 5
W Afghanistan
ıushewsk 107 E 6
Rus. Bogushëvsk. NE Belarus
a Mare 108 B 3 *Ger.* Frauenbach,
Hung. Nagybánya;
prev. Neustadt. NW Romania
a Sprie 108 B 3 *Ger.* Mittelstadt,
Hung. Felsőbánya. NW Romania
bokoum 76 B 4 SW Chad
coi 108 C 5 SE Romania
e-Comeau 39 E 4 Québec,
SE Canada
kal, Lake *see* Baykal, Ozero
le Átha Luain *see* Athlone
lén 92 D 4 S Spain
le na Mainistreach *see*
Newtownabbey
leşti 108 B 5 SW Romania
ley's Bay 42 A 5 bay,
W Atlantic Ocean
nbridge 42 D 3 Georgia, SE USA
ir *see* Bāyir
reuth *see* Bayreuth
riki 144 D 2 country capital,
Tarawa, W Kiribati
rnsdale 149 C 7 Victoria,
SE Australia
yin 128 B 4 N China
a 99 C 7 S Hungary
a California 48 A 5
Eng. Lower California. Peninsula,
NW Mexico
a California 50 A 2 state,
NW Mexico
o Boquete *see* Boquete
ram Curri 101 C 5 N Albania
kala 76 C 4
C Central African Republic
ker & Howland Islands 145 F 2
US unincorporated territory,
C Pacific Ocean
ker Lake 37 F 3 C Canada
kersfield 47 C 7 California, W USA
kharden 122 C 3 *Turkm.*
Bakherden; *prev.* Bakherden.
Bäherden; *prev.* Bakherden.
C Turkmenistan
khchisaray *see* Bakhchysaray
khchysaray 109 F 5
Rus. Bakhchisaray. S Ukraine
khmach 109 F 1 N Ukraine
khtarān 120 C 3 *prev.*
Kermānshāh, Qahremānshahr.
W Iran
ki 117 H 2 *Rus.* Baku. Country
apital, E Azerbaijan
kó *see* Bacău
kony 99 C 7 *Eng.* Bakony
Mountains, *Ger.* Bakonywald.
Mountain range, W Hungary
ksan 111 B 8
SW Russian Federation
ku *see* Baki
ku 112 B 4 country capital,
E Azerbaijan

Bakwanga *see* Mbuji-Mayi
Balabac, Selat *see* Balabac Strait
Balabac Strait 138 D 3 *var.* Selat
Balabac. Strait, W Pacific Ocean
Balaguer 93 F 2 NE Spain
Balakovo 111 C 6
W Russian Federation
Bālā Morghāb 122 D 4
NW Afghanistan
Balao 60 B 2 S Ecuador
Balashov 111 B 6
W Russian Federation
Balasore *see* Bāleshwar
Balaton 99 C 7 *var.* Lake Balaton,
Ger. Plattensee. Lake, W Hungary
Balbina, Represa 62 D 1 reservoir,
NW Brazil
Balboa 53 G 5 C Panama
Balcarce 65 D 5 E Argentina
Balclutha 151 B 7 South Island,
SW New Zealand
Baldy Mountain 44 C 1 mountain,
Montana, NW USA
Baleares, Islas 93 H 4 *Eng.* Balearic
Islands. Island group, E Spain
Balearic Islands *see* Baleares, Islas
Balearic Plain 80 C 5 *var.* Algerian
Basin. Undersea basin,
E Atlantic Ocean
Baleine, Rivière à la 39 E 2 river,
Québec, E Canada
Balen 87 C 5 N Belgium
Bāleshwar 135 F 4 *prev.* Balasore.
E India
Bali 138 D 5 island, C Indonesia
Balıkesir 116 A 3 W Turkey
Balıkpapan 138 D 4 Borneo,
C Indonesia
Balkan Mountains 104 C 2
Bul./Scr. Stara Planina. Mountain
range, Bulgaria/Yugoslavia
Balkh 123 E 3 *anc.* Bactra.
N Afghanistan
Balkhash 114 C 5 *Kaz.* Balqash.
SE Kazakhstan
Balkhash, Lake *see* Balkhash, Ozero
Balkhash, Ozero 114 C 5 *Eng.* Lake
Balkhash, *Kaz.* Balqash. Lake,
SE Kazakhstan
Balladonia 147 C 6 Western
Australia, S Australia
Ballarat 149 C 7 Victoria,
SE Australia
Balleny Islands 154 B 5 island
group, Antarctica
Ballina 149 E 5 New South Wales,
SE Australia
Ballinger 49 F 3 Texas, S USA
Balls Pyramid 142 C 4 island,
E Australia
Balqash *see* Balkhash
Balş 108 B 5 S Romania
Balsas 63 F 2 E Brazil
Balsas, Río 51 E 5 *var.* Río Mexcala.
River, S Mexico
Bal'shavik 107 D 7 *Rus.* Bol'shevik.
NE Belarus
Balta 108 D 3 SW Ukraine
Bălţi 108 D 3 *Rus.* Bel'tsy.
N Moldova
Baltic Sea 66 D 2 *Ger.* Ostee,
Rus. Baltiskoye More. Sea,
NE Atlantic Ocean
Baltimore 41 F 4 Maryland, NE USA
Baluchistān 134 A 3
var. Balochistan, Beluchistan.
Province, SW Pakistan
Balvi 106 D 4 NE Latvia
Balykchy 123 G 2 *Kir.* Ysyk-Köl;
prev. Issyk-Kul', Rybach'ye.
NE Kyrgyzstan
Balzers 94 E 2 S Liechtenstein

Bam 120 E 4 SE Iran
Bamako 74 D 4 country capital,
SW Mali
Bambari 76 C 4
C Central African Republic
Bamberg 95 C 5 SE Germany
Bamenda 76 A 4 W Cameroon
Banaba 144 D 2 *var.* Ocean Island.
Island, W Kiribati
Banc St.Lazarus *see* St.Lazarus Bank
Banda Aceh 138 A 3 *var.* Banda
Atjeh; *prev.* Koetaradja, Kutaradja,
Kutaraja. Sumatera, W Indonesia
Banda, Laut 139 F 5 *Eng.* Banda
Sea. Sea, W Pacific Ocean
Bandama 74 D 5 *var.* Bandama
Fleuve. River, S Ivory Coast
Bandama Blanc 74 D 5 river,
C Ivory Coast
Bandama Fleuve *see* Bandama
Bandar-e 'Abbās 120 D 4 *var.*
Bandar'Abbās; *prev.* Gombroon.
S Iran
Bandar-e Büshehr 120 C 4 *var.*
Büshehr, Bushire. S Iran
Bandar-e Khamīr 120 D 4 S Iran
Bandar-e Langeh 120 D 4 *var.*
Bandar-e Lengeh, Lingeh. S Iran
Bandarlampung 138 C 4 Sumatera,
W Indonesia
Bandar Maharani *see* Muar
Bandar Penggaram *see* Batu Pahat
Bandar Seri Begawan 138 D 3 *prev.*
Brunei Town. Country capital,
N Brunei
Banda Sea *see* Banda, Laut
Bandırma 116 A 3 *var.* Penderma.
NW Turkey
Bandjarmasin *see* Banjarmasin
Bandoeng *see* Bandung
Bandundu 77 C 6 *prev.*
Banningville. SW Congo (Zaire)
Bandung 138 C 5 *prev.* Bandoeng.
Jawa, C Indonesia
Bangalore 132 C 2 state capital,
S India
Bangassou 77 D 5
S Central African Republic
Banggai, Kepulauan 139 E 4 island
group, C Indonesia
Banghāzī 71 G 2 *Eng.* Bengazi,
Benghazi, *It.* Bengasi. NE Libya
Bangka 138 C 4 island, W Indonesia
Bangkok *see* Krung Thep
Bangkok, Bight of *see* Krung Thep, Ao
Bangladesh
135 F 3 *prev.* East Pakistan.
Republic, S Asia

Official name: People's Republic of
Bangladesh **Date of formation:** 1971
Capital: Dhaka **Population:** 122.2
million **Total Area:** 55,598 sq miles
(143,998 sq km) **Languages:** Bangla*,
Urdu, Chakma **Religions:** Muslim
83%, Hindu 16%, 1% **Ethnic mix:**
Bengali 98%, other 2%

Bangor 89 C 6 NW Wales, UK
Bangor 89 C 5 *Ir.* Beannchar.
E Northern Ireland, UK
Bangor 41 H 2 Maine, NE USA
Bang Pla Soi *see* Chon Buri
Bangui 77 C 5 country capital,
SW Central African Republic
Ban Hat Yai *see* Hat Yai
Ban Houayxay 136 C 4 C Laos
var. Ban Houayxay. N Laos
Ban Houei Sai *see* Houayxay

Ban Hua Hin 137 C 6 *var.* Hua Hin.
C Thailand
Bani 74 D 3 river, S Mali
Banī Suwayf *see* Beni Suef
Bāniyās 118 A 3 *var.* Banias,
Baniyas, Paneas. W Syria
Banjak, Kepulauan *see*
Banyak, Kepulauan
Banja Luka 101 A 7
NW Bosnia & Herzegovina
Banjarmasin 138 D 4 *prev.*
Bandjarmasin. Borneo, C Indonesia
Banjul 74 B 3 *prev.* Bathurst.
Country capital, W Gambia
Ban Khok Kloi 137 B 7 S Thailand
Banks, Îles *see* Banks Islands
Banks Island 37 E 2 island,
NW Canada
Banks Islands 144 D 4 *Fr.* Îles
Banks. Island group, N Vanuatu
Banks Lake 46 C 2 reservoir,
Washington, NW USA
Banks Peninsula 151 C 6 peninsula,
South Island, C New Zealand
Banks Strait 149 C 8 strait,
SW Tasman Sea
Bānkura 135 F 4 NE India
Banmo *see* Bhamo
Ban Na Môn 136 D 3 NE Laos
Banningville *see* Bandundu
Bañolas *see* Banyoles
Ban Pak Phanang *see* Pak Phanang
Banská Bystrica 99 C 6 *Ger.*
Neusohl, Hung. Besztercebánya.
C Slovakia
Bantry Bay 89 A 7 *Ir.* Bá Bheanntraí.
Bay, NE Atlantic Ocean
Banya 104 E 2 E Bulgaria
Banyak, Kepulauan 138 A 3 *prev.*
Kepulauan Banjak. Island group,
NW Indonesia
Banyo 76 B 4 W Cameroon
Banyoles 93 G 2 *var.* Bañolas. NE Spain
Banzare Seamounts 141 C 7
seamount range, S Indian Ocean
Baoji 128 B 4 *var.* Pao-chi, Paoki.
C China
Baoro 76 C 4
W Central African Republic
Baoshan 126 A 6 *var.* Pao-shan.
SW China
Baotou 127 F 3 *var.* Pao-t'ou,
Paotow. N China
Ba'qûbah 120 B 3 *var.* Baquba. C Iraq
Baquerizo Moreno *see* Puerto
Baquerizo Moreno
Bar 101 C 5 *It.* Antivari.
SW Yugoslavia
Baraawe 73 D 6 *It.* Brava. S Somalia
Baraji, Hirfanli 116 C 3 lake,
C Turkey
Bărămati 134 C 5 W India
Baramita 59 F 2 N Guyana
Baranavichy 107 B 6 *Pol.* Baranowicze,
Rus. Baranovichi. SW Belarus
Barbados
55 G 1 Commonwealth republic,
E Caribbean Sea

Official name: Barbados **Date of
formation:** 1966 **Capital:**
Bridgetown **Population:** 260,000
Total area: 166 sq miles (430 sq km)
Religions: Protestant 94%, Roman
Catholic 5%, other 1% **Ethnic mix:**
Black 80%, mixed 15%, White 4%,
other 1% **Government:**
Parliamentary democracy
Currency: Barbados $ = 100 cents

Barbados 59 F 1 island,
W Atlantic Ocean
Barbastro 93 F 2 NE Spain
Barbate de Franco 92 C 5 S Spain
Barbuda 55 G 3 island,
N Antigua & Barbuda
Barcaldine 148 C 4 Queensland,
E Australia
Barcelona 93 G 2 anc. Barcino,
Barcinona.
E Spain
Barcelona 59 E 2 NE Venezuela
Barcoo 148 C 4 river, E Australia
Barcs 99 C 7 SW Hungary
Bardaï 76 C 1 N Chad
Bardejov 99 D 5 Ger. Bartfeld,
Hung. Bártfa. NE Slovakia
Bardina, Gora see Bardin Seamount
Barduli see Barletta
Bareilly 135 E 3 var. Bareli.
N India
Bareli see Bareilly
Barendrecht 86 C 4 SW Netherlands
Barentin 90 B 3 N France
Barentsburg 83 G 2 W Svalbard
Barentsøya 83 G 2 island,
E Svalbard
Barents Sea 155 H 5 Nor. Barents
Havet, Rus. Barentsevo More. Sea,
Arctic Ocean
Bari 97 E 5 var. Bari delle Puglie;
anc. Barium. S Italy
Barikot see Barīkowt
Barīkowt 123 F 4 var. Barikot.
NE Afghanistan
Barillas 52 A 2 var. Santa Cruz
Barillas. NW Guatemala
Barinas 58 C 2 W Venezuela
Barīsāl 135 G 4 S Bangladesh
Barisan, Pegunungan 138 B 4
mountain range, Sumatera,
W Indonesia
Barito 138 D 4 river, Borneo,
C Indonesia
Barkly Tableland 148 B 3 plateau,
N Australia
Bårlad 108 D 4 prev. Bîrlad.
E Romania
Barlavento, Ilhas de 74 A 2 var.
Windward Islands. Island group,
N Cape Verde
Bar-le-Duc 90 D 3 var. Bar-sur-
Ornain. NE France
Barlee, Lake 147 B 6 lake, Western
Australia, W Australia
Barlee Range 146 B 4 mountain
range, Western Australia,
W Australia
Barletta 97 E 5 anc. Barduli. S Italy
Barlinek 98 B 3 Ger. Berlinchen.
W Poland
Barmen-Elberfeld see Wuppertal
Barmouth 89 C 6 W Wales, UK
Barnaul 114 D 4
C Russian Federation
Barnstaple 89 C 7 SW England, UK
Baroda see Vadodara
Baron'ki 107 E 7 Rus. Boron'ki.
E Belarus
Barquisimeto 58 C 2
NW Venezuela
Barra 88 B 3 island, W Wales, UK
Barra de Río Grande 53 E 3
E Nicaragua
Barranca 60 C 3 W Peru
Barrancabermija 58 B 2
N Colombia
Barranquilla 58 B 1 N Colombia
Barreiro 92 B 4 W Portugal
Barrier Range 149 B 6 hill range,
New South Wales, SE Australia
Barrow 89 B 6 Ir. An Bhearú. River,
SE Ireland
Barrow 36 D 2 Alaska, NW USA

Barrow-in-Furness 89 C 5
NW England, UK
Barrow Island 146 A 4 island,
W Australia
Barrows 37 F 5 Manitoba, S Canada
Bar-sur-Ornain see Bar-le-Duc
Bartang 123 F 3 river,
SE Tajikistan
Bartenstein see Bartoszyce
Bartica 59 F 3 N Guyana
Bartlesville 49 G 1
Oklahoma, C USA
Bartlett 42 C 1 Tennessee, S USA
Bartoszyce 98 D 2 Ger. Bartenstein.
N Poland
Baruun Huuray 126 C 2 wetland,
E Mongolia
Baruun-Urt 127 F 2 E Mongolia
Barú, Volcán 53 E 5 var. Volcán de
Chiriquí. Volcano, W Panama
Barwon 149 D 5 river,
New South Wales, SE Australia
Barysaw 107 D 6 Rus. Borisov.
NE Belarus
Basarabeasca 108 D 4
Rus. Bessarabka. SE Moldova
Basel 95 A 7 Eng. Basle, Fr. Bâle.
NW Switzerland
Basilan Island 139 E 3 island,
SW Philippines
Basra see Al Baṣrah
Bassano del Grappa 96 C 2 NE Italy
Bassein 136 A 4 var. Pathein
SW Myanmar
Basse-Terre 55 G 4 island,
E Guadeloupe
Basse-Terre 55 G 4 dependent
territory capital, SW Guadeloupe
Basseterre 55 G 3 country capital,
C Saint Kitts & Nevis
Bassikounou 74 D 3 SE Mauritania
Bass, Îlots de see Marotiri
Bass Strait 152 B 4 strait, Indian
Ocean/Pacific Ocean
Bassum 94 B 3 NW Germany
Bastia 91 E 7 SE France
Bastogne 87 D 7 SE Belgium
Bastrop 42 B 2 Louisiana, S USA
Bastyn' 107 C 7 Rus. Bostyn'.
SW Belarus
Bata 77 A 5 NW Equatorial Guinea
Batabanó, Golfo de 54 B 2 gulf,
NW Cuba
Batae Coritanorum see Leicester
Batajnica 100 D 3 N Yugoslavia
Batangas 139 E 2 off. Batangas City.
Luzon, N Philippines
Batangas City see Batangas
Bataysk 111 B 7 SW Russian Federation
Bâtdâmbâng 137 D 5
prev. Battambang. NW Cambodia
Batéké, Plateaux 77 B 6 plateau,
S Congo
Bath 89 D 7 hist. Akermanceaster,
anc. Aquae Calidae, Aquae Solis.
S England, UK
Bathsheba 55 H 1 E Barbados
Bathurst 149 F 4 New Brunswick,
SE Canada
Bathurst 149 D 6 New South Wales,
SE Australia
Bathurst see Banjul
Bathurst Island 37 F 2 island,
N Canada
Bathurst Island 146 D 2 island,
Northern Territory, N Australia
Bāṭin, Wādī al 120 C 4
dry watercourse, SW Asia
Batman 117 F 4 var. İluh. SE Turkey
Baton Rouge 42 B 3
Louisiana, S USA

Batroûn 118 A 4 var. Al Batrūn.
N Lebanon
Battambang see Bâtdâmbâng
Batticaloa 132 D 3 E Sri Lanka
Battipaglia 97 D 5 S Italy
Bat'umi 117 E 2 W Georgia
Batu Pahat 138 B 3 prev. Bandar
Penggaram. W Malaysia
Baturaja 138 B 4 W Indonesia
Bauchi 75 G 4 NE Nigeria
Bauer Basin 153 F 3 undersea
basin, E Pacific Ocean
Baumann, Pic see Agou, Mont
Bauru 57 D 5 S Brazil
Bauska 106 C 4 Ger. Bauske.
S Latvia
Bauske see Bauska
Bautzen 94 D 4 Lus. Budyšin.
E Germany
Bavarian Alps 95 C 7
Ger. Bayerische Alpen. Mountain
range, Austria/Germany
Bawku 75 E 4 N Ghana
Bayamo 54 C 3 E Cuba
Bayan Har Shan 126 D 4 var. Bayan
Khar. Mountain range, C China
Bayanhongor 126 D 2 C Mongolia
Bayan Khar see Bayan Har Shan
Bay City 49 G 4 Texas, S USA
Bay City 40 C 3 Michigan, N USA
Baydhabo 73 D 6 var. Baydhowa,
Isha Baydhabo, It. Baidoa.
SW Somalia
Bayern 95 C 6 cultural region,
SE Germany
Bayeux 90 B 3 anc. Augustodurum.
N France
Bāyir 119 C 7 var. Bā'ir. S Jordan
Bay Islands see Bahía, Islas de la
Baykal, Ozero 115 E 4 Eng. Lake
Baikal. S Russian Federation
Baymak 111 D 6 W Russian Federation
Bayonne 91 A 6 anc. Lapurdum.
SW France
Bayram-Ali see Bayramaly
Bayramaly 122 D 3
prev. Bayram-Ali. S Turkmenistan
Bayreuth 95 C 5 var. Baireuth.
SE Germany
Bayrische Alpen see Bavarian Alps
Baysun see Boysun
Baza 93 E 4 S Spain
Beagle Channel 65 C 8 channel,
Atlantic Ocean/Pacific Ocean
Béal Feirste see Belfast
Beannchar see Bangor
Bear Island see Bjørnøya
Bear Lake 46 E 4 lake, NW USA
Beas de Segura 93 E 4 S Spain
Beata, Isla 55 E 3 island,
SW Dominican Republic
Beatrice 45 F 4 Nebraska, C USA
Beatton River 37 E 4 British
Columbia, W Canada
Beaucaire 91 C 6 S France
Beaufort Island see Beaufort West
Beaufort West 78 C 5 Afr.
Beaufort-Wes. SW South Africa
Beaumont 49 H 4 Texas, S USA
Beaune 90 D 4 C France
Beauvais 90 C 3 anc. Bellovacum,
Caesaromagus. N France
Beaver Island 40 C 2 island,
Michigan, N USA
Beaverton 46 B 3
Oregon, NW USA
Beāwar 134 C 3 N India
Bečej 100 D 3 Ger. Altbetsche,
Hung. Óbecse. Rácz-Becse;
prev. Magyar-Becse, Stari Bečej.
N Yugoslavia

Béchar 70 D 2
prev. Colomb-Béchar. W Algeri
Beckley 40 D 5
West Virginia, NE USA
Bedford 89 E 6 E England, UK
Bedford, Cape 148 D 2 headland
Queensland, NE Australia
Bedum 86 E 1 NE Netherlands
Beenleigh 149 F 8 E Australia
Beer Menuha 119 B 7 S Israel
Beernem 87 A 5 NW Belgium
Be'ér Sheva' 119 A 7 var. Beershe
Ar. Bir es Saba. S Israel
Beesel 87 D 5 SE Netherlands
Beeville 49 G 4 Texas, S USA
Begoml' see Byahoml'
Behar see Bihār
Beida see Al Bayḍā'
Beihai 129 C 6
var. Peihai. S China
Beijing 128 D 3 var. Pei-ching,
Eng. Peking; prev. Pei-p'ing.
Country capital, E China
Beilen 86 E 2 NE Netherlands
Beira 79 E 3 C Mozambique
Beirut see Beyrouth
Bei Shan 126 D 3 mountain rang
C China
Beiuş 108 B 3 Hung. Belényes.
NW Romania
Beja 92 B 4 anc. Pax Julia.
SE Portugal
Béjar 92 C 3 N Spain
Békás see Bicaz
Békéscsaba 99 D 7
Rom. Bichiş-Ciaba. SE Hungary
Bekobod 123 E 2 Rus. Bekabad;
prev. Bekabad, Uzb. Uzbekistan
Bela Crkva 100 E 3
Ger. Weisskirchen, Hung.
Fehértemplom. E Yugoslavia

Belarus
107 C 6 var. Belarus, Latv.
Baltkrievija, Rus. Belorusskaya
SSR; prev. Belorussian SSR.
Republic, E Europe

Official name: Republic of Belaru
Date of formation: 1991 **Capital:**
Minsk **Population:** 10.3 million
Calling code: 375 **Total area:**
80,154 sq miles
(207,600 sq km) **Languages:**
Belarussian*, Russian **Religions:**
Russian Orthodox 60%, Roman
Catholic 8%, other 32% **Ethnic m**
Belarussian 78%, Russian 13%,
Polish 4%, other 5% **Governmen**
Multiparty republic **Currency:**
Rouble = 100 kopeks

Belau see Palau
Belaya Tserkov' see Bila Tserkva
Belchatow see Bełchatów
Bełchatów 98 D 4 var. Belchatow.
C Poland
Belcher, Îles see Belcher Islands
Belcher Islands 38 C 2
Fr. Îles Belcher. Island group,
Northwest Territories, NE Canada
Beledweyne 73 D 5 var. Belet Hu
Belém 63 F 1 var. Pará. N Brazil
Belen 48 D 2 New Mexico, SW U
Belén 52 D 4 W Nicaragua
Belényes see Beiuş
Belfast 89 B 5 Ir. Béal Feirste.
E Northern Ireland, UK
Belfield 44 D 2 North Dakota, N U
Belgard see Białogard
Belgaum 132 B 1 W India

gium
7 B 6 *Dut.* België, *Fr.* Belgique.
Monarchy, W Europe

icial name: Kingdom of Belgium
e of formation: 1830
ital: Brussels **Population:** 10
ion **Total area:** 12,780 sq miles
100 sq km) **Languages:**
nch*, Dutch*, Flemish
igions: Roman Catholic 75%,
er 25% **Ethnic mix:** Flemish 58%,
lloon 32%, other European 6%,
er 4% **Government:**
stitutional monarchy
rency: Franc = 100 centimes

gorod 111 A 6
N Russian Federation
grade *see* Beograd
grano II 154 B 2 research
tation, Antarctica
Manastir 100 C 2 *Hung.*
élmonostor; *prev.* Monostor.
E Croatia
nga 77 B 5 NE Gabon
tung, Pulau 138 C 4 island,
W Indonesia

ze
2 B 1 *Sp.* Belice; *prev.* Colony of
Belize, British Honduras.
ommonwealth republic, Belize

icial name: Belize Date of
mation: 1981 Capital: Belmopan
pulation: 200,000 Total area:
5 sq miles (22,960 sq km)
guages: English*, English
le, Spanish Religions: Christian
, other 13% Ethnic mix: *mestizo*
, Creole 30%, Indian 11%,
afuna 8%, other 7% Government:
liamentary democracy
rency: Belizean $ = 100 cents

ze 52 B 1 river,
elize/Guatemala
ze City 52 C 1 *var.* Belize,
p. Belice . NE Belize
ak *see* Villach
kofski 36 B 3 Alaska, NW USA
le Île 90 A 4 island, NW France
le Isle, Strait of 39 G 3 strait,
Newfoundland and Labrador,
JW Gulf of St.Lawrence
leville 40 B 5 Illinois, N USA
le Vue 55 F 2 S Saint Lucia
evue 46 B 2 Washington, NW USA
evue 45 F 4 Nebraska, C USA
ingham 46 B 1
Washington, NW USA
ing Hausen Mulde *see*
outheast Pacific Basin
ingshausen 154 A 2 research
tation, Antarctica
ingshausen Abyssal Plain *see*
ellingshausen Plain
ingshausen Sea 154 A 3
ea, SE Pacific Ocean
o 58 B 2 W Colombia
o Horizonte *see* Belo Horizonte
ville 78 C 5 SW South Africa
mopan 52 C 1 country capital,
Belize
gradchik 104 B 1
ar. Belogradčik. NW Bulgaria
gradčik *see* Belogradchik
o Horizonte 63 F 4
rev. Bello Horizonte. SE Brazil
morsk 110 B 3
N Russian Federation
pretsk 111 D 6
W Russian Federation

Belorusskaya Gryada *see*
Byelaruskaya Hrada
Belovár *see* Bjelovar
Beloye More 110 C 3
Eng. White Sea. Sea,
Arctic Ocean/Barents Sea
Belozersk 110 B 4 *var.* Beloz'orsk.
NW Russian Federation
Beloz'orsk *see* Belozersk
Belton 49 G 3 Texas, S USA
Bel'tsy *see* Bălţi
Belynichi *see* Byalynichy
Belyye Berega 111 A 5
W Russian Federation
Belyy, Ostrov 114 D 2 island,
N Russian Federation
Bemidji 45 F 1 Minnesota, N USA
Bemmel 86 D 4 SE Netherlands
Benavente 92 C 2 N Spain
Bend 46 B 3 Oregon, NW USA
Bendern 94 E 1
NW Liechtenstein
Bendigo 149 C 7 Victoria,
SE Australia
Beneschau *see* Benešov
Benešov 99 B 5 *Ger.* Beneschau.
W Czech Republic
Benevento 97 D 5 *anc.*
Beneventum, Malventum. S Italy
Bengal, Bay of 133 E 1 bay,
N Indian Ocean
Bengbu 129 D 5 *var.* Peng-pu.
E China
Benghazi *see* Benghazi
Bengkulu 138 B 4 *prev.* Bengkoeloe,
Benkoelen, Benkulen. Sumatera,
W Indonesia
Benguela 78 B 2 *var.* Benguella.
W Angola
Benguella *see* Benguela
Beni 77 E 5 E Congo (Zaire)
Beni 61 E 3 river, N Bolivia
Benidorm 93 F 4 SE Spain
Beni-Mellal 70 C 2 C Morocco

Benin
52 F 4 *prev.* Dahomey. Republic,
W Africa

Official name: Republic of Benin
Date of formation: 1960 Capital:
Porto-Novo Population: 5.1 million
Total area: 43,480 sq miles
(112,620 sq km) Languages: French*,
Fon, Bariba, Yoruba, Adja Religions:
Traditional beliefs 70%, Muslim
15%, Christian 15%
Ethnic mix: Fon 39%, Yoruba 12%,
Adja 10%, other 39%
Government: Multiparty republic
Currency: CFA franc = 100 centimes

Benin, Bight of 75 F 5 bay,
N Gulf of Guinea
Benin City 75 G 5 SW Nigeria
Beni Suef 72 B 2 *var.* Banī Suwayf.
N Egypt
Ben Nevis 88 C 3 mountain,
W Scotland, UK
Bénoué *see* Benue
Bénoy 76 B 4 S Chad
Benson 48 B 3 Arizona, SW USA
Benton 42 B 2 Arkansas, C USA
Benue 68 B 4 *Fr.* Bénoué. River,
Cameroon/Nigeria
Beograd 100 D 3 *Eng.* Belgrade,
Ger. Belgrad; *anc.* Singidunum.
Country capital, N Yugoslavia
Berat 101 C 6 *var.* Berati,
SCr. Belgrad. C Albania
Berau, Teluk 139 G 4 *var.* MacCluer
Gulf. Gulf, W Pacific Ocean
Berbera 72 D 4 NW Somalia

Berbérati 77 B 5
SW Central African Republic
Berck-Plage 90 C 2 N France
Berdichev *see* Berdychiv
Berdyans'k 109 G 4
Rus. Berdyansk; *prev.* Osipenko.
SE Ukraine
Berdychiv 108 D 2 *Rus.* Berdichev.
N Ukraine
Berehove 108 B 3 *Cz.* Berehovo,
Hung. Beregszász, *Rus.* Beregovo.
W Ukraine
Berettyó 99 D 7 *Rom.* Barcău;
prev. Berătău, Beretău. River,
Hungary/Romania
Berettyóújfalu 99 E 6 E Hungary
Berezhany 108 C 2 *Pol.* Brzeżany
W Ukraine
Berezina *see* Byerezino
Berezniki 111 D 5
NW Russian Federation
Berga 93 G 2 NE Spain
Bergamo 96 B 2
anc. Bergomum. N Italy
Bergara 93 E 1 N Spain
Bergen 85 A 5 S Norway
Bergen 94 D 2 NE Germany
Bergen 86 C 2 NW Netherlands
Bergen *see* Mons
Bergerac 91 B 5 SW France
Bergeyk 87 D 5 S Netherlands
Bergomum *see* Bergamo
Beringen 87 C 5 NE Belgium
Beringov Proliv *see* Bering Strait
Bering Sea 152 D 1 sea,
N Pacific Ocean
Bering Strait 152 D 1 *Rus.* Beringov
Proliv. Strait, N Pacific Ocean
Berja 93 E 5 S Spain
Berkeley 47 B 6 California, W USA
Berkner Island 154 B 2 island,
Antarctica
Berkovitsa 104 C 2 NW Bulgaria
Berlin 94 D 3 country capital,
NE Germany
Berlin 41 G 2 Maine, NE USA
Berlinchen *see* Barlinek
Bermejo 64 C 2 river, N Argentina
Bermeo 93 E 1 N Spain
Bermuda 35 E 6 *var.* Bermuda
Islands, Bermudas; *prev.* Somers
Islands. UK crown colony,
W Atlantic Ocean
Bermuda Rise 66 B 3 undersea rise,
W Atlantic Ocean
Bern 95 A 7 *Fr.* Berne. Country
capital, W Switzerland
Bernau 94 D 3 NE Germany
Bernburg 94 C 4 C Germany
Berne *see* Bern
Berner Alpen 95 A 7 *var.* Berner
Oberland, *Eng.* Bernese Oberland.
Mountain range, SW Switzerland
Bernier Island 147 A 5 island,
W Australia
Bernina, Passo del 95 B 7
Eng. Bernina Pass.
SE Switzerland
Béroubouay *see* Béroubouay
Berón de Astrada *see* Berón
Berry Islands 54 C 1 island group,
N Bahamas
Bertoua 77 B 5 C Cameroon
Beru 145 F 3 *var.* Peru. Island,
W Kiribati
Berwick-upon-Tweed 88 D 4
N England, UK
Besançon 90 D 4 *anc.* Besontium,
Vesontio. E France

Beslan 111 B 8
SW Russian Federation
Bessarabka *see* Basarabeasca
Betanzos 92 B 1 NW Spain
Betanzos 61 F 4 S Bolivia
Bethlehem 78 D 4 C South Africa
Bethlehem 119 E 7 *Ar.* Bayt Laḥm,
Heb. Bet Leḥem. C West Bank
Bético, Sistema 92 D 5 mountain
range, S Spain
Bétou 77 C 5 N Congo
Bette, Pic 71 G 4 *var.* Bikkū Bīttī,
It. Picco Bette. Mountain, S Libya
Beulah 40 C 2 Michigan, N USA
Beveren 87 B 5 N Belgium
Beverley 89 D 5 NE England, UK
Beyrouth 118 A 4 *var.* Bayrūt,
Eng. Beirut; *anc.* Berytus. Country
capital, W Lebanon
Beyşehir Gölü 116 B 4 lake,
C Turkey
Béziers 91 C 6 *anc.* Baeterrae,
Baeterrae Septimanorum,
Julia Beterrae. S France
Bezwada *see* Vijayawada
Bhadrāvati 132 C 2 SW India
Bhāgalpur 135 F 3 NE India
Bhaktapur 135 F 3 C Nepal
Bhamo 136 B 2 *var.* Banmo.
N Myanmar
Bharūch 134 C 4 W India
Bhaunagar *see* Bhāvnagar
Bhāvnagar 134 C 4
prev. Bhaunagar. W India
Bheanntraí, Bá *see* Bantry Bay
Bhopāl 134 D 4 state capital,
C India
Bhubaneshwar 135 F 5 *prev.*
Bhubaneswar, Bhuvaneshwar.
State capital, E India
Bhusaval *see* Bhusāwal
Bhusāwal 134 D 4 *prev.* Bhusaval
C India

Bhutan
135 G 3 *var.* Druk-yul. Monarchy,
S Asia

Official name: Kingdom of Bhutan
Date of formation: 1865 Capital:
Thimphu Population: 1.7 million
Total Area: 418,147 sq miles
(7,000 sq km) Languages:
Dzongkha*, Nepali Religions:
Mahayana Buddhist 70%, Hindu 24%,
Muslim 5%, other 1% Ethnic mix:
Bhutia 61%, Gurung 15%, Assamese
13%, other 11% Government:
Constitutional monarchy
Currency: Ngultrum = 100 chetrum

Biak, Pulau 139 G 4 island,
E Indonesia
Biała Podlaska 98 E 3 E Poland
NW Poland
Białogard 98 B 2 *Ger.* Belgard.
NW Poland
Białystok 98 E 3 *Rus.* Belostok,
Bielostok. E Poland
Bianco, Monte *see* Blanc, Mont
Biarritz 91 A 6 SW France
Bicaz 108 C 4 *Hung.* Békás.
NE Romania
Bichis-Ciaba *see* Békéscsaba
Biddeford 41 G 2 Maine, NE USA
Bideford 89 C 7 SW England, UK
Biel 95 A 7 *Fr.* Bienne.
W Switzerland
Bielefeld 94 B 4 NW Germany
Bielsko-Biała 99 C 5 *Ger.* Bielitz,
Bielitz-Biala. S Poland
Bielsk Podlaski 98 E 3 E Poland
Biên Hoa 137 E 6 S Vietnam
Bienne *see* Biel

Bienville, Lac 38 D 2 lake, Québec, C Canada
Bié, Planalto do 69 C 6 *var.* Bié Plateau. Plateau, C Angola
Bié Plateau *see* Bié, Planalto do
Bigge Island 146 C 2 island, W Australia
Bighorn Mountains 44 C 2 mountain range, Wyoming, C USA
Bighorn River 44 C 2 river, NW USA
Bight, Head of 149 A 6 bay, NE Great Australian Bight
Bight, The 54 C 1 C Bahamas
Bignona 74 B 3 SW Senegal
Bigorra *see* Tarbes
Bigosovo *see* Bihosava
Big Rapids 40 C 2 Michigan, N USA
Big River 37 F 5 Saskatchewan, C Canada
Big Sioux River 45 F 3 river, N USA
Big Spring 49 E 3 Texas, S USA
Bihać 101 A 7 NW Bosnia & Herzegovina
Bihār 135 F 4 *prev.* Behar. State, N India
Biharamulo 73 B 7 NW Tanzania
Bihosava 107 D 5 *Rus.* Bigosovo. NW Belarus
Bijeljina 100 D 3 NE Bosnia & Herzegovina
Bijelo Polje 101 D 5 W Yugoslavia
Bīkāner 134 C 3 NW India
Bikin 115 G 4 SE Russian Federation
Bikini Atoll 144 D 1 *var.* Pikinni. Island, NW Marshall Islands
Bilāspur 135 E 4 C India
Bilāsuvar 117 H 3 *Rus.* Bilyasuvar; *prev.* Pushkino. SE Azerbaijan
Bila Tserkva 109 E 2 *Rus.* Belaya Tserkov'. N Ukraine
Bilbao 93 E 1 *Basq.* Bilbo. N Spain
Bilbo *see* Bilbao
Bilecik 116 B 3 NW Turkey
Billings 44 C 2 Montana, NW USA
Biloela 148 D 4 Queensland, E Australia
Biloku 59 G 4 S Guyana
Biloxi 42 C 3 Mississippi, S USA
Bilpa Morea Claypan 148 B 4 lake, C Australia
Biltine 76 C 3 E Chad
Bilwi *see* Puerto Cabezas
Bilzen 87 D 6 NE Belgium
Bimini Islands 54 C 1 island group, W Bahamas
Binche 87 B 7 S Belgium
Bindloe Island *see* Marchena, Isla
Binga, Monte 79 E 3 mountain, C Mozambique
Bingerville 75 E 5 SE Ivory Coast
Binghamton 41 F 3 New York, NE USA
Bingöl 117 E 3 E Turkey
Bintulu 138 D 3 Borneo, E Malaysia
Bío Bío 65 B 5 river, C Chile
Bioco, Isla de 77 A 5 *var.* Bioko, *Eng.* Fernando Po, *Sp.* Fernando Póo; *prev.* Macías Nguema Biyogo. Island, NW Equatorial Guinea
Birāk 71 F 3 *var.* Brak. C Libya
Birao 76 D 3 NE Central African Republic
Biratnagar 135 F 3 SE Nepal
Birdum 148 A 2 Northern Territory, N Australia
Bireuen 138 A 3 W Indonesia
Bīrjand 120 E 3 E Iran
Birkenfeld 95 A 5 SW Germany
Birkenhead 89 C 6 NW England, UK
Birlad *see* Bârlad

Birmingham 89 C 6 W England, UK
Birmingham 42 C 2 Alabama, S USA
Bîr Mogreïn 74 C 1 *var.* Bir Moghrein; *prev.* Fort-Trinquet. N Mauritania
Birnie Island 145 F 3 island, C Kiribati
Birni-Nkonni *see* Birnin Konni
Birnin Konni 75 F 3 *var.* Birni-Nkonni. SW Niger
Birobidzhan 115 G 4 SE Russian Federation
Birsen *see* Biržai
Birsk 111 D 5 W Russian Federation
Biržai 106 C 4 *Ger.* Birsen. NE Lithuania
Bisbee 48 B 3 Arizona, SW USA
Biscay, Bay of 66 D 3 *Fr.* Golfe de Gascogne, *Sp.* Golfo de Vizcaya. Bay, NE Atlantic Ocean
Biscay Plain 80 B 4 abyssal plain, E Atlantic Ocean
Bischheim 90 E 3 NE France
Bischofsburg *see* Biskupiec
Bishah, Wādī 121 B 5 dry watercourse, W Saudi Arabia
Bishkek 123 G 2 *var.* Pishpek; *prev.* Frunze. Country capital, N Kyrgyzstan
Bishrī, Jabal 118 D 3 mountain range, E Syria
Biskra 71 E 2 *var.* Beskra, Biskara. NE Algeria
Biskupiec 98 D 2 *Ger.* Bischofsburg. N Poland
Bislig 139 F 2 Mindanao, S Philippines
Bismarck 45 E 2 state capital, North Dakota, N USA
Bismarck Archipelago 144 C 3 island group, NE Papua New Guinea
Bismarck Sea 144 B 3 sea, SW Pacific Ocean
Bissau 74 B 4 country capital, W Guinea-Bissau
Bistrita 108 B 3 *Ger.* Bistritz, *Hung.* Beszterce; *prev.* Nösen. N Romania
Bitam 77 B 5 N Gabon
Bitburg 95 A 5 SW Germany
Bitlis 117 F 4 SE Turkey
Bitoeng *see* Bitung
Bitola 101 D 6 *Turk.* Monastir; *prev.* Bitolj. S Macedonia
Bitonto 97 E 5 *anc.* Butuntum. SE Italy
Bitterroot Range 46 D 2 *Port.* Cadeia Bitterroot. Mountain range, NW USA
Bitung 139 F 3 *prev.* Bitoeng. Celebes, C Indonesia
Biu 75 H 4 E Nigeria
Biwa-ko 131 C 6 lake, Honshū, SW Japan
Biy-Khem *see* Bol'shoy Yenisey
Bizerte 71 E 1 *Ar.* Banzart, *Eng.* Bizerta. N Tunisia
Bjelovar 100 B 2 *Hung.* Belovár. N Croatia
Björneborg *see* Pori
Bjørnøya 83 G 3 *Eng.* Bear Island. Island, N Norway
Blackall 148 C 4 Queensland, E Australia
Blackfoot 46 E 4 Idaho, NW USA
Black Forest *see* Schwarzwald
Black Hills 44 D 3 mountain range, N USA
Black Mesa 48 B 1 mountain, Arizona, SW USA

Black Mountains 48 A 1 mountain range, Arizona, SW USA
Blackpool 89 C 5 NW England, UK
Black Range 48 C 2 mountain range, New Mexico, SW USA
Black River 54 A 5 W Jamaica
Black River 136 C 3 *Chin.* Lixian Jiang, *Fr.* Rivière Noire, *Vtn.* Sông Đa. River, China/Vietnam
Black Rock Desert 46 C 4 *Port.* Deserto Black Rock. Desert, Nevada, W USA
Blacksburg 40 D 5 Virginia, NE USA
Black Sea 81 F 4 *Bul.* Cherno More, *Eng.* Euxine Sea, *Rom.* Marea Neagrã, *Rus.* Chernoye More, *Turk.* Karadeniz, *Ukr.* Chorne More. Sea, SE Atlantic Ocean
Black Sea Lowland *see* Prychornomors'ka Nyzovyna
Black Volta 75 E 4 *var.* Borongo, Mouhoun, Moun Hou, *Fr.* Volta Noire. River, NW Africa
Blackwater 89 B 6 *Ir.* An Abhainn Mhór. River, S Ireland
Blackwell 49 G 1 Oklahoma, C USA
Blagoevgrad 104 C 3 *prev.* Gorna Dzhumaya. W Bulgaria
Blagoveshchensk 111 D 5 W Russian Federation
Blagoveshchensk 115 G 4 SE Russian Federation
Blake Plateau 35 D 6 *var.* Blake Terrace. Undersea plateau, W Atlantic Ocean
Blake Terrace *see* Blake Plateau
Blanca, Bahía 65 C 5 bay, SW Atlantic Ocean
Blanca, Costa 93 F 4 physical region, SE Spain
Blanche, Lake 149 B 5 lake, South Australia, S Australia
Blanc, Mont 80 C 4 *It.* Monte Bianco. Mountain, France/Italy
Blanes 93 G 2 NE Spain
Blankenberge 87 A 5 NW Belgium
Blankenheim 95 A 5 W Germany
Blanquilla, Isla 59 E 1 *var.* La Blanquilla. Island, N Venezuela
Blantyre 79 E 2 *var.* Blantyre-Limbe. S Malawi
Blantyre-Limbe *see* Blantyre
Blaricum 86 C 3 C Netherlands
Blenheim 151 D 5 South Island, C New Zealand
Blesae *see* Blois
Blida 70 D 2 *var.* El Boulaïda, El Boulaïda. N Algeria
Bloemfontein 78 C 4 *var.* Mangaung. C South Africa
Blois 90 C 4 *anc.* Blesae. C France
Bloomfield 48 C 1 New Mexico, SW USA
Bloomington 40 C 4 Indiana, N USA
Bloomington 45 F 2 Minnesota, N USA
Bluefields 53 E 3 SE Nicaragua
Blue Mountain Peak 54 B 5 mountain, E Jamaica
Blue Mountains 149 D 6 mountain range, New South Wales, SE Australia
Blue Mountains 46 C 3 *Port.* Montanha Azuis. Mountain range, NW USA
Blue Mud Bay 148 B 2 bay, Gulf of Carpentaria/Arafura Sea
Blue Nile 72 C 4 *var.* Bahr el Azraq, *Amh.* Abai, Ābay Wenz, *Ar.* An Nīl al Azraq. River, Ethiopia/Sudan
Blumenau 63 F 5 S Brazil

Bo 74 C 4 S Sierra Leone
Boaco 52 D 3 W Nicaragua
Boa Vista 74 A 3 island, E Cape Verde
Boa Vista 62 D 1 state capital, NW Brazil
Bobo-Dioulasso 75 E 4 SW Burkina
Bobonong 78 D 3 E Botswana
Bobrinets *see* Bobrynets'
Bobruysk *see* Babruysk
Bobrynets' 109 E 3 *Rus.* Bobrinets. C Ukraine
Bocay 52 D 2 N Nicaragua
Bocheykovo *see* Bacheykava
Bocholt 94 A 4 W Germany
Bochum 94 A 4 W Germany
Bocsca 108 A 4 *Ger.* Bokschen, *Hung.* Boksánbanyá. SW Roma[...]
Bodaybo 115 F 4 E Russian Federation
Bodega Bay 47 A 6 bay, E Pacific Ocean
Bodegas *see* Babahoyo
Boden 84 D 3 N Sweden
Bodensee *see* Lake Constance
Bodmin 89 C 7 SW England, UK
Bodø 84 C 3 C Norway
Bodrum 116 A 4 SW Turkey
Boeloekoemba *see* Bulukumba
Boende 77 C 5 C Congo (Zaire)
Boeroe *see* Buru, Pulau
Bogale 137 B 5 S Myanmar
Bogalusa 42 B 3 Louisiana, S USA?
Bogatynia 98 B 4 *Ger.* Reichenau. SW Poland
Bogendorf *see* Łuków
Bogor 138 C 5 *Dut.* Buitenzorg. Jawa, C Indonesia
Bogotá 58 B 3 *prev.* Santa Fe, Sant[...] Fe de Bogotá. Country capital, C Colombia
Bogushëvsk *see* Bahushewsk
Boguslav *see* Bohuslav
Bo Hai 128 D 4 *var.* Gulf of Chihli Gulf, Yellow Sea/Pacific Ocean
Bohemia 99 A 5 *Cz.* Čechy, *Ger.* Böhmen. Cultural region, W Czech Republic
Bohemian Forest 95 C 5 *Cz.* Česk[...] Les, Šumava, *Ger.* Böhmerwald Mountain range, C Europe
Bohol Sea 139 E 2 *var.* Mindanao Sea. Sea, W Pacific Ocean
Bohoro Shan 126 B 2 mountain range, NW China
Bohuslav 109 E 2 *Rus.* Boguslav. N Ukraine
Bois Blanc Island 40 C 2 island, Michigan, N USA
Boise 46 D 3 *var.* Boise City. State capital, Idaho, NW USA
Boise City *see* Boise
Bois, Lac des *see* Woods, Lake of
Boizenburg 94 C 3 N Germany
Bojador *see* Boujdour
Bojnūrd 120 D 2 *var.* Bujnurd. N I[...]
Boké 74 C 4 W Guinea
Boknafjorden 85 A 6 fjord, NE North Sea
Bol 76 B 3 W Chad
Bolesławiec 98 B 4 *Ger.* Bunzlau. SW Poland
Bolgatanga 75 E 4 N Ghana
Bolgrad *see* Bolhrad
Bolhrad 108 D 4 *Rus.* Bolgrad. SW Ukraine
Bolívar, Pico 58 C 2 mountain, W Venezuela

via
F 4 Republic,
South America

cial name: Republic of Bolivia
e of formation: 1825/1938
tal: La Paz **Population:** 7.8
on **Total area:** 424,162 sq miles
8,580 sq km) Languages:
ish*, Quechua*, Aymará*
gions: Roman Catholic 95%,
r 5% **Ethnic mix:** Indian 55%,
zo 27%, White 10%, other 8%
ernment: Multiparty republic
rency: Boliviano = 100 centavos

ene 91 D 6 SE France
näs 85 C 5 C Sweden
gna 96 B 3 N Italy
gnesi 60 C 2 E Peru
goye 110 B 4
Russian Federation
sezemelskaja Tundra see
ol'shezemel'skaya Tundra
shevik see Bal'shavik
shevik, Ostrov 115 E 2 island,
evernaya Zemlya,
Russian Federation
shezemel'skaya Tundra 110 E 3
r. Bol'sezemelskaja Tundra.
hysical region,
W Russian Federation
shoy Lyakhovskiy, Ostrov 115
2 island, N Russian Federation
on 89 C 5 prev. Bolton-le-Moors.
W England, UK
on-le-Moors see Bolton
u 116 B 3 NW Turkey
angarvík 83 E 4 NW Iceland
varovo 104 D 3
rev. Pashkeni. SE Bulgaria
zano 96 C 1 Ger. Bozen;
ac. Bauzanum. N Italy
a 77 B 7 W Congo (Zaire)
abay 134 C 5 Guj. Mumbai.
tate capital, W India
ai Hills 74 D 4 hill range,
W Liberia
u 76 D 4 var. M'Bomu,
bomou, Mbomu. River, Central
frican Republic/Congo (Zaire)
aire 58 D 1 island,
Netherlands Antilles
anza 52 D 2 NE Nicaragua
aparte Archipelago 146 C 2
land group, NW Australia
da 77 B 6 C Gabon
doukou 75 E 4 E Ivory Coast
e see Watampone
e see Annaba
e, Teluk 139 E 4 bay,
Pacific Ocean
gaigaon 135 G 3 NE India
go, Massif des 76 D 4
ar. Chaîne des Mongos.
ountain range,
E Central African Republic
gor 76 B 4 SW Chad
ifacio 91 E 7 SE France
n 95 A 5 W Germany
onia see Vidin
thia Felix see Boothia Peninsula
thia, Gulf of 37 F 2 inlet,
rctic Ocean
thia Peninsula 37 F 2
rev. Boothia Felix. Peninsula,
orthwest Territories,
E Canada
pard 95 A 5 W Germany
uete 53 F 5 var. Bajo Boquete.
Panama
100 E 4 E Yugoslavia

Bor 73 B 5 S Sudan
Borås 85 B 7 S Sweden
Bordeaux 91 B 5 anc. Burdigala.
SW France
Bordertown 149 B 7
South Australia, S Australia
Borgå see Porvoo
Borgefjellet 84 C 4 mountain range,
C Norway
Borger 49 E 1 Texas, S USA
Borger 86 E 2 NE Netherlands
Borgholm 85 C 7 S Sweden
Borgo Maggiore 96 E 1
NW San Marino
Borisoglebsk 111 B 6
W Russian Federation
Borisov see Barysaw
Borlänge 85 C 6 C Sweden
Borne 86 E 3 E Netherlands
Borneo 138 C 4 island, SE Asia
Bornholm 85 B 8 var. Bornholms
Amt. Island group, E Denmark
Bornholm 94 D 2 island,
E Denmark
Bornholms Amt see Bornholm
Boron'ki see Baron'ki
Borovan 104 C 2 NW Bulgaria
Borovichi 110 B 4 var. Borovichi
W Russian Federation
Boroviči see Borovichi
Borovo 100 D 3 NE Croatia
Borşa 108 C 3 Hung. Borsa.
N Romania
Borsa see Borşa
Bor Ul Shan 126 D 3 mountain
range, N China
Boryslav 108 B 2 Pol. Boryslaw,
Rus. Borislav. NW Ukraine
Borzya 115 F 5
S Russian Federation
Bosanska Dubica 100 B 3
NW Bosnia & Herzegovina
Bosanska Gradiška 100 C 3
N Bosnia & Herzegovina
Bosanski Brod 100 C 3
N Bosnia & Herzegovina
Bosanski Novi 100 B 3
NW Bosnia & Herzegovina
Bosanski Šamac 100 C 3
N Bosnia & Herzegovina
Boskamp 59 G 3 N Suriname
Boskovice 99 B 5 Ger. Boskowitz.
SE Czech Republic
Boskowitz see Boskovice
Bosna 101 A 8 river,
N Bosnia & Herzegovina

Bosnia & Herzegovina
100 A 8 Republic, SE Europe

Official name: The Republic of
Bosnia and Herzegovina **Date of**
formation: 1992 **Capital:** Sarajevo
Population: 3.5 million **Total area:**
19,741 sq miles (51,130 sq km)
Languages: Serbian*, Croatian*
Religions: Muslim 40%, Orthodox
Catholic 31%, other 29% **Ethnic mix:**
Bosnian 44%, Serb 31%, Croat 17%,
other 8% **Government:** Multiparty
republic **Currency:** Dinar = 100 para

Bōsō-hantō 131 D 6 peninsula,
Honshū, S Japan
Bossangoa 76 C 4
C Central African Republic
Bossembélé 76 B 4
C Central African Republic
Bossier City 42 A 2 Louisiana, S USA
Bosten Hu 126 C 3 var. Bagrax Hu.
Lake, NW China
Boston 89 D 6 prev. St.Botolph's
Town. E England, UK

Boston 41 G 3 state capital,
Massachusetts, NE USA
Boston Mountains 42 B 1 mountain
range, Arkansas, C USA
Bostyn' see Bastyn'
Botany Bay 149 D 6 bay,
W Tasman Sea
Boteti 78 C 3 var. Botletle. River,
N Botswana
Bothnia, Gulf of 66 D 2
Fin. Pohjanlahti, Swe. Bottniska
Viken. Gulf, N Baltic Sea
Botletle see Boteti
Botoşani 108 C 3 Hung. Botosány.
NE Romania
Botosány see Botoşani
Botou 128 D 4 NE China
Botrange 87 D 6 mountain,
E Belgium

Botswana
78 C 3 Republic, S Africa

Official name: Republic of
Botswana **Date of formation:** 1966
Capital: Gaborone **Population:**
1.4 million **Total area:** 224,600 sq
miles (581,730 sq km) **Languages:**
English*, Tswana, Shona, San
Religions: Traditional beliefs 50%,
Christian 50% **Ethnic mix:** Tswana
75%, Shona 12%, San 3%, other 10%
Government: Multiparty republic
Currency: Pula = 100 thebe

Bouar 76 B 4
W Central African Republic
Bou Craa 70 B 3
N Western Sahara
Bougainville Island 144 C 3 island,
NE Papua New Guinea
Bougouni 72 D 4 SW Mali
Boujdour 70 A 3 var. Bojador.
W Western Sahara
Boulder 44 B 2 Montana, NW USA
Boulder 44 C 4 Colorado, C USA
Boulogne-sur-Mer 90 B 2
var. Boulogne; anc. Bononia,
Gesoriacum, Gesoriacum.
N France
Boûmdeïd 74 C 3 var. Boumdeït.
S Mauritania
Boumdeït see Boûmdeïd
Boundiali 74 D 4 N Ivory Coast
Bountiful 44 B 4 Utah, W USA
Bounty Basin see Bounty Trough
Bounty Islands 142 D 5 island
group, S New Zealand
Bounty Trough 152 C 5 var. Bounty
Basin. Trough, S Pacific Ocean
Bourbonnais 90 C 4 cultural region,
C France
Bourgas see Burgas
Bourg-en-Bresse 91 D 5 var. Bourg,
Bourg-en-Bresse. E France
Bourges 90 C 4 anc. Avaricum.
C France
Bourgogne 90 C 4 Eng. Burgundy.
Cultural region, E France
Bourke 149 C 5 New South Wales,
SE Australia
Bournemouth 89 D 7 S England, UK
Boutilimit 74 C 3 SW Mauritania
Bowen 148 D 3 Queensland,
NE Australia
Bowling Green 40 D 3 Ohio, N USA
Bowling Green 40 C 5
Kentucky, E USA
Bowling Green, Cape 148 D 3
Queensland, NE Australia
Boxmeer 86 D 4 SE Netherlands
Boyarka 109 E 2 N Ukraine

Boysun 123 E 3 Rus. Baysun.
S Uzbekistan
Bozeman 44 B 2 Montana, NW USA
Bozüyük 116 B 3 NW Turkey
Brač 100 B 4 var. Brach, It. Brazza;
anc. Brattia. Island, S Croatia
Bracara Augusta see Braga
Bradenton 43 E 4 Florida, SE USA
Bradford 89 D 5 NW England, UK
Braga 92 B 2 anc. Bracara Augusta.
NW Portugal
Bragança 92 C 2 Eng. Braganza;
anc. Julio Briga. NE Portugal
Brahestad see Raahe
Brāhmanbāria 135 G 4 E Bangladesh
Brahmapur 135 F 5 E India
Brahmaputra 124 C 2 var. Tsangpo,
Ben. Jamuna, Chin. Yarlung
Zangbo Jiang. River, S Asia
Brăila 108 D 4 E Romania
Braine-le-Comte 87 B 6
SW Belgium
Brainerd 45 F 2 Minnesota, N USA
Brak see Birāk
Brampton 38 D 5 Ontario, S Canada
Brandberg 78 B 3 mountain,
NW Namibia
Brandenburg 94 C 3
var. Brandenburg an der Havel.
NE Germany
Brandenburg an der Havel see
Brandenburg
Brandon 37 F 5 Manitoba, S Canada
Braniewo 98 C 2 Ger. Braunsberg.
N Poland
Brasília 63 F 3 country capital,
C Brazil
Braşov 108 C 4 Ger. Kronstadt,
Hung. Brassó; prev. Oraşul Stalin.
C Romania
Brasstown Bald 42 D 1 mountain,
Georgia, SE USA
Bratislava 99 C 6 Ger. Pressburg,
Hung. Pozsony. Country capital,
SW Slovakia
Bratsk 115 E 4 C Russian Federation
Braunsberg see Braniewo
Braunschweig 94 C 4
Eng./Fr. Brunswick. N Germany
Brava 74 A 3 island, SW Cape Verde
Brava see Baraawe
Brava, Costa 93 H 2 coastal region,
NE Spain
Bravo del Norte see Grande, Río
Brawley 47 D 8 California, W USA

Brazil
62 C 2 var. República Federativa
do Brasil, Sp. Brasil; prev. United
States of Brazil. Federal republic,
NE South America

Official name: Federative Republic
of Brazil **Date of formation:**
1822/1929 **Capital:** Brasília
Population: 164.4 million **Total area:**
3,286,472 sq miles (8,511,970 sq km)
Languages: Portuguese*, German,
Italian **Religions:** Roman Catholic
90%, other 10% **Ethnic mix:** White
(Portuguese, Italian, German) 55%,
mixed 38%, Black 6%, other 1%
Government: Multiparty republic
Currency: Real = 100 centavos

Brazil Basin 67 C 5 var. Brazilian
Basin, Brazil'skaya Kotlovina.
Undersea basin, W Atlantic Ocean
Brazilian Highlands 63 F 3 var.
Planalto Central. Mountain range,
E Brazil
Brazos River 49 G 3 river,
Texas, S USA

Brazzaville 77 B 6 country capital, S Congo
Brčko 101 B 7 NE Bosnia & Herzegovina
Brecht 87 C 5 N Belgium
Brecon Beacons 89 C 6 mountain range, S Wales, UK
Breda 86 C 4 S Netherlands
Bree 87 D 5 NE Belgium
Bregalnica 101 E 6 river, E Macedonia
Bregovo 104 B 1 NW Bulgaria
Brême *see* Bremen
Bremen 94 B 3 *Fr.* Brême. NW Germany
Bremerhaven 94 B 3 NW Germany
Bremerton 46 B 2 Washington, NW USA
Brenham 49 G 4 Texas, S USA
Brenner Pass 95 C 7 *var.* Col du Brenner, Brenner Sattel, *Ger.* Brennerpass, *It.* Passo del Brennero. Pass, Austria/Italy
Brescia 96 B 2 *anc.* Brixia. N Italy
Breslau *see* Wrocław
Bressanone 96 C 1 *Ger.* Brixen. Italy
Brest 90 A 3 NW France
Brest 107 A 6 *Pol.* Brześć nad Bugiem, *Rus.* Brest-Litovsk; *prev.* Brześć Litewski. SW Belarus
Bretagne 90 A 3 *Eng.* Brittany; *Lat.* Britannia Minor. Cultural region, NW France
Brezhnev *see* Naberezhnyye Chelny
Brezovo 104 D 2 *prev.* Abrashlare. C Bulgaria
Bria 76 D 4 C Central African Republic
Briançon 91 D 5 *anc.* Brigantio. SE France
Bribie Island 149 E 5 island, Queensland, SE Australia
Bricgstow *see* Bristol
Bridgeport 41 F 3 Connecticut, NE USA
Bridgetown 55 G 2 country capital, SW Barbados
Bridgman, Kap 83 E 1 headland, NE Greenland
Bridlington 89 E 5 NE England, UK
Bridport 89 C 7 SW England, UK
Brig 95 B 7 *Fr.* Brigue, *It.* Briga. SW Switzerland
Brigantio *see* Briançon
Brigham City 44 B 3 Utah, W USA
Brighton 89 E 7 SE England, UK
Brighton 44 D 4 Colorado, C USA
Brindisi 97 E 5 *anc.* Brundisium, Brundusium, SE Italy
Brisbane 149 E 5 state capital, Queensland, E Australia
Bristol 89 D 7 *anc.* Bricgstow. S England, UK
Bristol 43 E 1 Tennessee, S USA
Bristol 40 D 5 Rhode Island, NE USA
Bristol 41 F 3 Connecticut, NE USA
Bristol Bay 36 B 3 bay, SE Bering Sea
Bristol Channel 89 C 7 inlet, Atlantic Ocean/Celtic Sea
British Antarctic Territory 154 B 3 UK territorial claim, Antarctica
British Columbia 36 D 4 *Fr.* Colombie-Britannique. Province, SW Canada
British Indian Ocean Territory 124 B 5 UK dependent territory, C Indian Ocean
British Indian Ocean Territory 140 C 4 *var.* Chagos Islands. Island group, C Indian Ocean
British Isles 66 D 2 island group, NE Atlantic Ocean

British Solomon Islands Protectorate *see* Solomon Islands
British Virgin Islands 55 G 3 *var.* Virgin Islands. UK dependent territory, Caribbean Sea
Brive-la-Gaillarde 91 C 5 *prev.* Brive, *anc.* Briva Curretia. C France
Brixen *see* Bressanone
Brixia *see* Brescia
Brno 99 B 5 *Ger.* Brünn. SE Czech Republic
Broad Sound 148 D 4 sound, SE Coral Sea
Brocēni 106 B 3 SW Latvia
Brockton 41 G 3 Massachusetts, NE USA
Brockville 38 D 5 Ontario, SE Canada
Brodeur Peninsula 37 F 2 peninsula, Baffin Island, NE Canada
Brodnica 98 D 3 *Ger.* Buddenbrock. N Poland
Broek-in-Waterland 86 C 3 C Netherlands
Broken Arrow 49 G 1 Oklahoma, C USA
Broken Hill 149 B 6 New South Wales, SE Australia
Broken Ridge 141 D 6 undersea plateau, S Indian Ocean
Bromberg *see* Bydgoszcz
Brookhaven 42 B 3 Mississippi, S USA
Brookings 45 F 3 South Dakota, N USA
Brookton 147 B 6 Western Australia, W Australia
Brooks Range 36 D 2 mountain range, Alaska, NW USA
Broome 146 C 3 Western Australia, NW Australia
Broomfield 44 C 4 Colorado, C USA
Brovary 109 E 2 N Ukraine
Brownfield 49 E 2 Texas, S USA
Brownsville 49 G 5 Texas, S USA
Brownwood 49 F 3 Texas, S USA
Brozha 107 D 7 E Belarus
Brozha *see* Brozha
Bruce, Mount 146 B 4 mountain, Western Australia, W Australia
Bruges *see* Brugge
Brugge 87 A 5 *Fr.* Bruges. NW Belgium
Brummen 86 D 4 E Netherlands

Brunei 138 D 3 *Mal.* Negara Brunei Darussalam. Monarchy, Borneo, SE Asia

Official name: The Sultanate of Brunei **Date of formation:** 1984 **Capital:** Bandar Seri Begawan **Population:** 300,000 **Total Area:** 2,228 sq miles (5,770 sq km) **Languages:** Malay*, English, Chinese **Religions:** Muslim 63%, Buddhist 14%, Christian 10%, other 13% **Ethnic mix:** Malay 69%, Chinese 18%, other 13% **Government:** Absolute monarchy **Currency:** Brunei $ = 100 cents

Brunei Town *see* Bandar Seri Begawan
Brünn *see* Brno
Brunswick 43 E 3 Georgia, SE USA
Brunswick *see* Braunschweig
Bruny Island 149 C 8 island, Tasmania, SE Australia
Brus Laguna 52 D 2 E Honduras

Brüx *see* Most
Bruxelles 87 C 6 *var.* Brussels, *Dut.* Brussel, *Ger.* Brüssel; *anc.* Broucsella. Country capital, C Belgium
Bryan 49 G 3 Texas, S USA
Bryansk 111 A 5 W Russian Federation
Brzeg 98 C 4 *Ger.* Brieg; *anc.* Civitas Altae Ripae. SW Poland
Brzeżany *see* Berezhany
Bucaramanga 58 B 2 N Colombia
Buccaneer Archipelago 146 C 3 island group, W Australia
Buchanan 74 C 5 *prev.* Grand Bassa. SW Liberia
Buchanan, Lake 49 F 3 reservoir, Texas, S USA
Bucharest *see* Bucharest
Bu Craa *see* Bou Craa
Bucuresti 108 C 5 *Eng.* Bucharest, *Ger.* Bukarest, Gross Schlatten, *Hung.* Abrudbánya, *Rom.* Bucureti; *prev.* Altenburg, *anc.* Cetatea Damboviței. Country capital, S Romania
Buda-Kashalyova 107 D 7 *Rus.* Buda-Koshelëvo. SE Belarus
Buda-Koshelëvo *see* Buda-Kashalyova
Budapest 99 D 6 *off.* Budapest Főváros, *SCr.* Budimpešta. Country capital, N Hungary
Budaun 135 E 3 N India
Budweis *see* České Budějovice
Budyšin *see* Bautzen
Buenaventura 58 A 3 W Colombia
Buena Vista 93 H 5 S Gibraltar
Buena Vista 61 G 4 C Bolivia
Buenos Aires 64 D 4 *hist.* Santa Maria del Buen Aire. Country capital, E Argentina
Buenos Aires 53 E 5 SE Costa Rica
Buenos Aires, Lago 65 B 6 *var.* Lago General Carrera. Lake, Argentina/Chile
Buffalo 41 E 3 New York, NE USA
Buffalo Narrows 37 F 4 Saskatchewan, C Canada
Buff Bay 54 B 5 E Jamaica
Buftea 108 C 5 S Romania
Bug 81 E 3 *Bel.* Zakhodni Buh, *Eng.* Western Bug, *Rus.* Zapadnyy Bug, *Ukr.* Zakhidnyy Buh. River, E Europe
Buga 58 B 3 W Colombia
Bughotu *see* Santa Isabel
Bugojno 100 B 4 C Bosnia & Herzegovina
Buhayrat ath Tharthār 120 B 3 lake, C Iraq
Buheiret Nâsir 72 B 3 *var.* Buíayrat Náir, *Eng.* Lake Nasser. Lake, Egypt/Sudan
Buitenzorg *see* Bogor
Bujalance 92 D 4 S Spain
Bujanovac 101 E 5 SE Yugoslavia
Bujnurd *see* Bojnürd
Bujumbura 73 B 7 *prev.* Usumbura. Country capital, W Burundi
Bukavu 77 E 6 Costermansville. E Congo (Zaire)
Bukhoro 122 D 2 *var.* Bokhara, *Rus.* Bukhara. C Uzbekistan
Bukit Panjang 138 A 1 C Singapore
Bukoba 73 B 6 NW Tanzania
Bülach 95 B 7 NW Switzerland
Bulawayo 79 D 3 *var.* Buluwayo. SW Zimbabwe
Buldur *see* Burdur
Bulgan 127 E 2 N Mongolia

Bulgaria 104 C 2 *var.* Bulgariya, *Bul.* Bŭlgariya; *prev.* People's Repu of Bulgaria. Republic, SE Euro

Official name: Republic of Bulga **Date of formation:** 1908/1923 **Capital:** Sofia **Population:** 8.9 million **Total area:** 42,822 sq mile (110,910 sq km) **Languages:** Bulgarian*, Turkish, Macedonian Romany **Religions:** Christian 85% Muslim 13%, Jewish 1%, other 1% **Ethnic mix:** Bulgarian 85%, Turk 9%, Macedonian 3%, Gypsy 3% **Government:** Multiparty republic **Currency:** Lev = 100 stotinki

Bulukumba 139 E 5 *prev.* Boeloekoemba. Celebes, C Indonesia
Buluwayo *see* Bulawayo
Bumba 77 D 5 N Congo (Zaire)
Bunbury 147 B 7 Western Austra SW Australia
Bundaberg 148 D 4 Queensland E Australia
Bungo-suidō 131 B 7 strait, NW Pacific Ocean
Bunia 77 E 5 NE Congo (Zaire)
Bunyan 116 D 3 C Turkey
Bunzlau *see* Bolesławiec
Buraida *see* Buraydah
Buraydah 120 B 4 *var.* Buraida. N Saudi Arabia
Burdigala *see* Bordeaux
Burdur 116 B 4 *var.* Buldur. SW Turkey
Burē 72 C 4 NW Ethiopia
Burgas 104 E 2 *var.* Bourgas. E Bulgaria
Burgaski Zaliv 104 E 2 gulf, W Black Sea
Burgos 92 D 2 N Spain
Burgundy *see* Bourgogne
Burhan Budai Shan 126 D 4 mountain range, C China
Buriram 137 D 5 *var.* Buri Ram, Puriramya. E Thailand
Burjassot 93 F 3 E Spain
Burkburnett 49 F 2 Texas, S USA
Burke 41 E 4 Virginia, NE USA

Burkina 75 E 3 *prev.* Upper Volta. Republic, NW Africa

Official name: Burkina Faso **Date of formation:** 1960 **Capital:** Ouagadougou **Population:** 9.8 mill **Total area:** 105,870 sq miles (274,200 sq km) **Languages:** Frenc Mossi, Fulani **Religions:** Tradition beliefs 65%, Muslim 25%, Christia 10% **Ethnic mix:** Mossi 45%, Mane 10%, Fulani 10%, other 35% **Government:** Multiparty republi **Currency:** CFA franc = 100 centir

Burleson 49 G 3 Texas, S USA
Burlington 41 F 2 Maine, NE USA
Burlington 45 G 4 Iowa, C USA
Burnie 149 C 8 Tasmania, SE Australia
Burnsville 45 F 2 Minnesota, N L
Burrel 101 D 6 *var.* Burreli. C Albania
Burreli *see* Burrel
Burriana 93 F 3 E Spain
Bursa 116 B 3 *var.* Brusa; *prev.* Brusa, *anc.* Prusa. NW Turkey
Bür Sa'īd *see* Port Said
Burtnieks *see* Burtnieku Ezers

nieku Ezers 106 D 3
r. Burtnieks. Lake, N Latvia
on 40 C 3 Michigan, N USA

ndi
8 B 7 *prev.* Kingdom of Burundi,
rundi. Republic, NE Africa

cial name: Republic of Burundi
e of formation: 1962
ital: Bujumbura **Population:** 5.8
on Total area: 10,750 sq miles
30 sq km) **Languages:**
ndi*, French*, Swahili
gions: Christian 68%, traditional
fs 32% **Ethnic mix:** Hutu 85%,
i 13%, Twa pygmy 1%, other 1%
ernment: Multiparty republic
ency: Franc = 100 centimes

, Pulau 139 F 4 *prev.* Boeroe.
land, E Indonesia
selton 147 B 7 Western
ustralia, SW Australia
o Arsizio 96 B 2 N Italy
i 77 D 5 N Congo (Zaire)
mbo 77 E 5 NE Congo (Zaire)
ia Qi 127 G 1 *var.* Zalantun.
E China
er 41 E 4 Pennsylvania, NE USA
w *see* Bytów
e 44 B 2 Montana, NW USA
erworth 138 B 3 W Malaysia
on Islands 39 E 1 island group,
orthwest Territories, NE Canada
an 139 F 2 *off.* Butuan City.
indanao, S Philippines
an City *see* Butuan
ntum *see* Bitonto
lobarde 73 D 6 *var.* Buulo
erde. C Somalia
lo Berde *see* Buulobarde
e Gaabo 73 D 6 S Somalia
naksk 111 B 8
W Russian Federation
likağrı Dağı 117 G 3 *var.* Aghri
agh, Agri Dagi, Koh I Noh,
asis, *Eng.* Mount Ararat,
eat Ararat. Mountain, E Turkey
uk Menderes 116 A 4 river,
W Turkey
iu 108 C 5 SE Romania
uluk 111 D 6
Russian Federation
oml' 107 D 5 *Rus.* Begoml'.
Belarus
ynichy 107 D 6 *Rus.* Belynichi.
Belarus
goszcz 98 C 3 *Ger.* Bromberg.
Poland
aruskaya Hrada 107 B 6
us. Belorusskaya Gryada. Ridge,
Belarus
ezino 107 D 6 *Rus.* Berezina.
ver, E Belarus
anga, Gora 115 E 2 mountain
nge, N Russian Federation
rovka *see* Kemin
rovka 123 G 2 N Kyrgyzstan
a 99 C 5 NW Slovakia
w 98 C 2 *Ger.* Bütow.
W Poland
meyin 122 C 3
rkm. Büzmeyin; *prev.* Bezmein.
Turkmenistan
l'ki 107 D 8 SE Belarus

a 78 B 2 *var.* Kaala, Robert
illiams, *Port.* Vila Robert
illiams. C Angola
apá 64 D 3 S Paraguay

Caballo Reservoir 48 C 3 reservoir,
New Mexico, SW USA
Cabañaquinta 92 D 1 N Spain
Cabanatuan 139 E 1 *off.* Cabanatuan
City. Luzon, N Philippines
Cabanatuan City *see* Cabanatuan
Cabillonum *see* Chalon-sur-Saône
Cabimas 58 C 1 NW Venezuela
Cabinda 77 B 6 *var.* Kabinda.
Province, NW Angola
Cabinda 78 A 1 *var.* Kabinda
NW Angola
Cabora Bassa, Lake *see* Cahora
Bassa, Albufeira de
Caborca 50 B 1 NW Mexico
Cabot Strait 39 G 4 strait Atlantic
Ocean/Gulf of St.Lawrence
Cabras, Ilha das 76 E 2 island,
E Atlantic Ocean
Cabrera 93 G 3 *anc.* Capraria.
E Spain
Čačak 100 D 4 C Yugoslavia
Cáceres 92 C 3 *Ar.* Qazris. W Spain
Cachimbo, Serra do 63 E 2
mountain range, C Brazil
Caconda 78 B 2 C Angola
Čadca 99 C 5 *Hung.* Csaca.
N Slovakia
Cadillac 40 C 2 Michigan, N USA
Cadiz 139 E 2 *off.* Cadiz City.
Negros, C Philippines
Cádiz 92 C 5 *anc.* Gades, Gadier,
Gadir, Gadire. SW Spain
Cadiz City *see* Cadiz
Cádiz, Golfo de 92 B 5 gulf,
NE Atlantic Ocean
Cadiz, Gulf of *see* Cádiz, Golfo de
Cadurcum *see* Cahors
Caen 90 B 3 N France
Caerdydd *see* Cardiff
Caer Gybi *see* Holyhead
Caesena *see* Cesena
Cafayate 64 C 2 N Argentina
Cagayan de Oro 139 F 2 *off.*
Cagayan de Oro City. Mindanao,
S Philippines
Cagayan de Oro City *see*
Cagayan de Oro
Cagliari 97 A 6 *anc.* Caralis. W Italy
Caguas 55 F 3 E Puerto Rico
Cahora Bassa, Albufeira de 78 D 2
var. Lake Cabora Bassa. Reservoir,
NW Mozambique
Cahors 91 B 6 *anc.* Cadurcum.
S France
Cahul 108 D 4 *Rus.* Kagul. S Moldova
Caicos Passage 54 D 2 channel,
N Caribbean Sea
Cailungo 96 E 1 N San Marino
Cairns 148 D 3 Queensland,
NE Australia
Cairo 72 B 1 *Ar.* Al Qāhirah,
El Qâhira. Country capital,
N Egypt
Caisleán an Bharraigh *see* Castlebar
Cajamarca 60 B 3 *prev.* Caxamarca.
NW Peru
Čajovskij *see* Chaykovskiy
Čakovec 100 B 2 *Ger.* Csakathurn,
Hung. Csáktornya; *prev.*
Tschakathurn. N Croatia
Calabar 75 G 5 S Nigeria
Calabozo 58 D 2 C Venezuela
Calafat 108 B 5 SW Romania
Calafate *see* El Calafate
Calahorra 93 E 2 N Spain
Calais 90 C 2 N France
Calais 41 H 2 Maine, NE USA
Calama 64 B 2 N Chile
Călăraşi 108 D 3 *var.* Călăras,
Rus. Kalarash. C Moldova

Călăraşi 108 C 5 SE Romania
Calatayud 93 E 2 NE Spain
Calbayog 139 F 2 *off.* Calbayog City.
Samar, C Philippines
Calbayog City *see* Calbayog
Calcanhar, Cabo 63 G 2 headland,
NE Brazil
Calcutta 135 G 4 state capital,
NE India
Caldas da Rainha 92 A 3
W Portugal
Caldera 64 B 3 N Chile
Caldwell 46 D 3 Idaho, NW USA
Caledon Bay 148 B 2 bay, Gulf of
Carpentaria/Arafura Sea
Caledonia 52 C 1 N Belize
Caleta *see* Catalan Bay
Caleta Olivia 65 B 6 SE Argentina
Calgary 37 E 5 Alberta, SW Canada
Cali 58 A 3 W Colombia
Calicut 132 C 2 *var.* Kozhikode.
SW India
Calida, Costa 93 F 5
physical region, SE Spain
California 47 C 7 *off.* State of
California; *nicknames* El Dorado,
The Golden State. State, W USA
California, Golfo de *see* California,
Gulf of
California, Gulf of 153 F 2
var. Golfo de California; *prev.* Sea
of Cortez. Gulf, E Pacific Ocean
Călimăneşti 108 B 4 SW Romania
Callabonna, Lake 149 B 5 lake,
South Australia, S Australia
Callao 60 C 4 W Peru
Callatis *see* Mangalia
Callosa de Segura 93 F 4 E Spain
Calmar *see* Kalmar
Caloundra 149 E 5 Queensland,
E Australia
Caltanissetta 97 C 7 SW Italy
Caluula 72 E 4 NE Somalia
Camabatela 78 B 1 NW Angola
Camacupa 78 B 2 *var.* General
Machado, *Port.* Vila General
Machado. C Angola
Camagüey 54 C 2 *prev.* Puerto
Príncipe. C Cuba
Camagüey, Archipiélago de 54 C 2
island group, C Cuba
Camaná 61 E 4 *var.* Camaná. SW Peru
Camaná *see* Camana
Camargue 91 D 6 physical region,
SE France
Ca Mau 137 D 6 *var.* Quan Long,
Quanlong; *prev.* Camau.
S Vietnam
Cambay, Gulf of *see*
Khambhāt, Gulf of
Camberia *see* Chambéry

Cambodia
137 D 5 *var.* Democratic
Kampuchea, Roat Kampuchea,
Cam. Kampuchea; *prev.* People's
Democratic Republic of
Kampuchea. Republic, SE Asia

Official name: State of Cambodia
Date of formation: 1953
Capital: Phnom Penh **Population:**
9 million **Total Area:** 69,000 sq miles
(181,040 sq km) **Languages:** Khmer*,
French **Religions:** Buddhist 88%,
Muslim 2%, other 10% **Ethnic mix:**
Khmer 94%, Chinese 4%,
other 2% **Government:** Constitutional
monarchy **Currency:** Riel = 100 sen

Cambrian Mountains 89 C 6
mountain range, C Wales, UK
Cambridge 89 E 6 *Lat.* Cantabrigia.
E England, UK
Cambridge 54 A 5 W Jamaica
Cambridge 150 D 3 North Island,
N New Zealand
Cambridge Bay 37 F 3
Victoria Island, NW Canada
Cambulo 78 C 1 NE Angola
Camden 42 B 2
South Carolina, SE USA
Cameron 40 A 2 Wisconsin, N USA

Cameroon
76 B 4 *Fr.* Cameroun. Republic,
C Africa

Official name: Republic of Cameroon
Date of formation: 1960 **Capital:**
Yaoundé **Population:** 13.6 million
Total area: 183,570 miles (475,440 sq
km) **Languages:** English*, French*,
Fang, Bulu **Religions:** Traditional
beliefs 51%, Christian 33%, Muslim
16% **Ethnic mix:** Bamileke and
Manum 20%, Fang 19%, other 61%
Government: Multiparty republic
Currency: CFA franc = 100 centimes

Camiri 61 G 4 S Bolivia
Camocim 63 G 2 E Brazil
Camopi 59 H 3 E French Guiana
Campamento 52 C 2 C Honduras
Campbell, Cape 151 D 5 headland,
South Island, SW New Zealand
Campbell Island 142 D 5 island,
S New Zealand
Campbell Plateau 152 C 5 undersea
plateau, SW Pacific Ocean
Campbell River 36 D 5 Vancouver
Island, Canada
Campeche 51 G 4 SE Mexico
Campeche, Bahía de 51 F 4
Eng. Bay of Campeche. Bay,
Gulf of Mexico
Campeche, Bay of *see* Campeche,
Bahía de
Câm Pha 136 E 3 N Vietnam
Câmpina 108 C 5 *prev.* Cîmpina.
SE Romania
Campina Grande 63 G 2 E Brazil
Campinas 63 F 4 S Brazil
Campobasso 97 D 5 S Italy
Campo Criptana *see* Campo de
Criptana
Campo de Criptana 93 E 3
var. Campo Criptana. C Spain
Campo dos Goitacazes *see* Campos
Campo Grande 63 E 4 state capital,
SW Brazil
Campos 63 F 4 *var.* Campo dos
Goitacazes. SE Brazil
Câmpulung 108 B 4
prev. Câmpulung-Muşcel,
Cîmpulung. S Romania
Cam Ranh 137 E 6 SE Vietnam

Canada
34 C 4 Commonwealth republic,
N North America

Official name: Canada **Date of
formation:** 1867/1949 **Capital:**
Ottawa **Population:** 27.8 million
Total area: 3,851,788 sq miles
(9,976,140 sq km) **Languages:**
English*, French* Chinese, Italian,
German, Ukrainian **Religions:** Roman
Catholic 46%, Protestant 30%, other
24% **Ethnic mix:** British origin 40%,
French origin 27%, other 33%
Government: Parliamentary state
Currency: Canadian $ = 100 cents

175

Canada Basin 155 F 2 undersea basin, Arctic Ocean
Canadian River 49 E 2 river, S USA
Çanakkale 116 A 3 var. Dardanelli; prev. Chanak, Kale Sultanie. W Turkey
Çanakkale Boğazı 116 A 2 Eng. Dardanelles. Strait, Marmara Denizi/Mediterranean Sea
Cananea 50 B 1 NW Mexico
Canarias, Islas 70 A 2 autonomous community, SW Spain
Canaries 55 F 1 W Saint Lucia
Canarreos, Archipiélago de los 54 B 2 island group, W Cuba
Canary Basin 66 C 3 var. Canaries Basin, Monaco Basin. Undersea basin, E Atlantic Ocean
Canary Islands 70 A 3 island group, SW Spain
Cañas 52 D 4 NW Costa Rica
Canaveral, Cape 43 F 4 headland, Florida, SE USA
Canavieiras 63 G 3 E Brazil
Canberra 149 D 7 country/territory capital, Australian Capital Territory, SE Australia
Cancún 51 H 3 SE Mexico
Cangzhou 128 D 4 NE China
Caniapiscau 39 E 2 river, Québec, E Canada
Caniapiscau, Réservoir de 39 E 2 reservoir, Québec, C Canada
Canik Dağları 116 D 2 mountain range, N Turkey
Canillo 91 A 8 C Andorra
Çankırı 116 C 3 var. Chankiri; anc. Gangra, Germanicopolis. N Turkey
Cannanore 132 B 2 var. Kananur, Kannur. SW India
Cannes 91 D 6 SE France
Canoas 63 E 5 S Brazil
Canon City 44 D 5 Colorado, C USA
Cantabria 92 D 1 cultural region, N Spain
Cantábrica, Cordillera 92 C 1 mountain range, N Spain
Cantabrigia see Cambridge
Cantaura 59 E 2 NE Venezuela
Canterbury 89 E 7 hist. Cantwaraburh, anc. Durovernum, Lat. Cantuaria. SE England, UK
Canterbury Bight 151 C 6 sea area, S Pacific Ocean
Canterbury Plains 151 C 6 plain, South Island, SW New Zealand
Cần Thơ 137 D 6 S Vietnam
Canton see Guangzhou
Canton 42 B 2 Mississippi, S USA
Canton 40 D 4 Ohio, N USA
Canyon 49 E 2 Texas, S USA
Cao Bǎng 136 D 3 var. Caobang. N Vietnam
Caobang see Cao Bǎng
Cap-Breton, Île de see Cape Breton Island
Cape Barren Island 149 C 8 island, Tasmania, SE Australia
Cape Basin 67 D 6 undersea basin, SW Atlantic Ocean
Cape Breton Island 39 G 4 Fr. Île du Cap-Breton. Island, Nova Scotia, SE Canada
Cape Coast 75 E 5 prev. Cape Coast Castle. S Ghana
Cape Coast Castle see Cape Coast
Cape Coral 43 E 5 Florida, SE USA
Cape Fear River 43 F 2 river, North Carolina, SE USA
Cape Girardeau 45 H 5 Missouri, C USA

Capelle aan den IJssel 86 C 4 SW Netherlands
Cape Palmas see Harper
Cape Town 78 B 5 var. Ekapa, Afr. Kaapstad, Kapstad. SW South Africa
Cape Verde 74 A 2 Port. Ilhas do Cabo Verde, Cabo Verde. Republic, W Africa
Official name: Republic of Cape Verde **Date of formation:** 1975 **Capital:** Praia **Population:** 400,000 **Total area:** 1,556 sq miles (4,030 sq km) **Languages:** Portuguese*, Creole **Religions:** Roman Catholic 98%, Protestant 2% **Ethnic mix:** Creole (mestiço) 71%, Black 28%, White 1% **Government:** Multiparty republic **Currency:** Escudo = 100 centavos
Cape Verde Basin 66 C 4 undersea basin, SW Atlantic Ocean
Cape Verde Plain 66 C 4 abyssal plain, E Atlantic Ocean
Cape York Peninsula 148 C 2 peninsula, N Australia
Cap-Haïtien 54 D 3 var. Le Cap. N Haiti
Capira 53 G 5 C Panama
Capitán Bado 64 D 2 E Paraguay
Capitán Pablo Lagerenza 64 D 1 var. Mayor Pablo Lagerenza. N Paraguay
Capri, Isola di 97 D 6 island, S Italy
Caprivi Strip 78 C 3 Ger. Caprivizipfel; prev. Caprivi Concession. Cultural region, NE Namibia
Caquetá 58 C 5 var. Rio Japurá, Yapurá. River, Brazil/Colombia
C A R see Central African Republic
Caracal 108 B 5 S Romania
Caracaraí 62 D 1 W Brazil
Caracas 58 D 1 country capital, N Venezuela
Caracollo 61 F 4 W Bolivia
Caralis see Cagliari
Caráquez 60 A 1 prev. Bahía de Caráquez. W Ecuador
Caráquez, Bahía de see Caráquez
Carasova 108 A 4 Hung. Krassóvár. SW Romania
Caratasca, Laguna de 53 E 2 lagoon, N Caribbean Sea
Carballiño 92 B 1 NW Spain
Carbondale 40 B 5 Illinois, N USA
Carbonia 97 A 6 var. Carbonia Centro. S Italy
Carbonia Centro see Carbonia
Carcaso see Carcassonne
Carcassonne 91 B 6 anc. Carcaso. S France
Cárdenas 54 B 2 W Cuba
Cardiff 89 C 7 Wel. Caerdydd. SE Wales, UK
Cardigan Bay 89 C 6 bay, SE Irish Sea
Carei 108 B 3 Ger. Gross-Karol, Karol, Hung. Nagykároly; prev. Careii-Mari. NW Romania
Carey, Lake 147 C 6 lake, Western Australia, SW Australia
Cariaco 59 E 1 NE Venezuela
Caribbean Sea 66 B 4 sea, W Atlantic Ocean
Caribou 37 F 4 Manitoba, C Canada
Carlisle 89 C 5 anc. Luguvallium, Luguvallum, Caer Luel. NW England, UK

Carlow 89 B 6 Ir. Ceatharlach. SE Ireland
Carlsbad 48 D 3 New Mexico, SW USA
Carlsberg Ridge 140 B 4 undersea ridge, NW Indian Ocean
Carlsruhe see Karlsruhe
Carmarthen 89 C 6 SW Wales, UK
Carmaux 91 C 6 S France
Carmel 40 C 4 Indiana, N USA
Carmelita 52 B 1 N Guatemala
Carmen 51 G 4 var. Ciudad del Carmen. SE Mexico
Carmona 92 D 4 S Spain
Carnarvon 147 A 5 Western Australia, W Australia
Carnegie, Lake 147 C 5 salt lake, Western Australia, W Australia
Car Nicobar 133 F 3 island, SW India
Caroço, Ilha 76 E 1 island, E Atlantic Ocean
Carolina 63 F 2 E Brazil
Caroline Island 145 H 3 prev. Thornton Island. Island, E Kiribati
Caroline Islands 144 B 2 island group, S Micronesia
Caroline Peak 151 A 7 mountain, South Island, S New Zealand
Caroní 59 E 3 river, E Venezuela
Carora 58 C 2 N Venezuela
Carpathian Mountains 81 E 4 var. Carpathians, Cz./Pol. Karpaty, Ger. Karpaten. Mountain range, E Europe
Carpaţii Meridionali 108 B 4 var. Alpi Transilvaniei, Carpaţii Sudici, Eng. South Carpathians, Transylvanian Alps, Ger. Südkarpaten, Transsylvanische Alpen, Hung. Déli-Kárpátok, Erdélyi-Havasok. Mountain Range, C Romania
Carpaţii Occidentali 108 B 4 Eng. Western Carpathians. Mountain range, W Romania
Carpentaria, Gulf of 148 B 2 gulf, N Arafura Sea
Carpi 96 B 2 N Italy
Carrara 96 B 3 C Italy
Carr Boyd Range 146 D 3 mountain range, N Australia
Čarsk see Charsk
Carson City 47 C 5 state capital, Nevada, W USA
Carson Sink 47 C 5 salt flat, Nevada, W USA
Cartagena 93 F 4 anc. Carthago Nova. SE Spain
Cartagena 58 B 1 var. Cartagena de los Indes. NW Colombia
Cartagena de los Indes see Cartagena
Cartago 53 E 4 C Costa Rica
Carthage 45 F 5 Missouri, C USA
Carthago Nova see Cartagena
Cartwright 39 G 2 Newfoundland and Labrador, E Canada
Carúpano 59 E 1 NE Venezuela
Carusbur see Cherbourg
Caruthersville 45 H 5 Missouri, C USA
Casablanca 70 C 2 Ar. Dar-el-Beida. NW Morocco
Casa Grande 48 B 2 Arizona, SW USA
Cascade Range 46 B 4 mountain range, NW USA
Cascadia Basin 153 E 1 undersea basin, NE Pacific Ocean

Cascais 92 B 4 Portugal
Caserta 97 D 5 S Italy
Casey 154 D 4 research station, Antarctica
Casino 149 E 5 New South Wales, SE Australia
Čáslav 99 B 5 Ger. Tschaslau. C Czech Republic
Casper 44 C 3 Wyoming, C USA
Caspian Sea 114 A 4 Az. Xäzär Dänizi, Kaz. Kaspiy Tengizi, Per. Daryā-ye Khazar, Baḩr-e Khazar, Rus. Kaspiyskoye More Inland sea, Asia/Europe
Cassel see Kassel
Casteggio 96 B 2 N Italy
Castelló de la Plana 93 F 3 var. Castellón. E Spain
Castellón see Castelló de la Plana
Castelnaudary 91 C 6 S France
Castelo Branco 92 B 3 C Portugal
Castelsarrasin 91 B 6 S France
Castelvetrano 97 C 7 SW Italy
Castilla-La Mancha 93 E 3 cultural region, NE Spain
Castilla-León 92 C 2 cultural region, NW Spain
Castlebar 89 A 5 Ir. Caisleán an Bharraigh. W Ireland
Castleford 89 D 5 W England, UK
Castle Harbour 42 B 5 harbour, E Bermuda
Castricum 86 C 3 W Netherlands
Castries 55 F 1 country capital, N Saint Lucia
Castro 65 B 6 W Chile
Castrovillari 97 D 6 SW Italy
Castuera 92 C 4 W Spain
Caswell Sound 151 A 7 sound, S Tasman Sea
Catacamas 52 D 2 C Honduras
Catacaos 60 B 3 NW Peru
Catalan Bay 93 H 4 var. Caleta. W Mediterranean Sea
Catalan Bay 93 H 4 E Gibraltar
Catalina 64 B 2 N Chile
Cataluña 93 G 2 cultural region, N Spain
Catamarca see San Fernando del Valle de Catamarca
Catania 97 D 7 SW Italy
Catanzaro 97 E 6 SW Italy
Catarroja 93 F 3 E Spain
Cat Island 54 C 1 island, C Bahamas
Catskill Mountains 41 F 3 mountain range, New York, NE USA
Cattaro see Kotor
Cauca 58 B 2 river, N Colombia
Caucasia 58 B 2 NW Colombia
Caucasus 117 F 1 Rus. Kavkaz. Mountain range, Georgia/Russian Federation
Caura 59 E 3 river, E Venezuela
Cavalla 74 D 5 var. Cavalla, Cavally Fleuve. River, Ivory Coast/Liberia
Cave Hill 55 G 2 W Barbados
Caviana de Fora, Ilha 63 F 1 var. Ilha Caviana. Island, N Brazil
Caviana, Ilha see Caviana de Fora, Ilha
Cawnpore see Kānpur
Caxamarca see Cajamarca
Caxias do Sul 57 D 5 S Brazil
Caxito 78 B 1 NW Angola
Cayenne 59 H 3 dependent territory capital, NE French Guiana
Cayman Brac 54 B 3 island, E Cayman Islands

man Islands 54 B 3 UK
ependent territory,
W Cayman Islands
Sal 54 B 2 island, SW Bahamas
in 100 B 3
W Bosnia & Herzegovina
orla 93 E 4 S Spain
rá 63 G 2 off. Estado do Ceará.
ate, C Brazil
rá see Fortaleza
ra Abyssal Plain see Ceará Plain
á, Estado do see Ceará
rá Plain 67 C 5 var. Ceara
byssal Plain. Abyssal plain,
W Atlantic Ocean
harlach see Carlow
aco, Isla 53 F 5 island,
W Panama
u 139 E 2 off. Cebu City. Cebu,
Philippines
u City see Cebu
ina 96 B 3 Italy
ar City 44 A 5 Utah, W USA
ar Falls 45 G 3 Iowa, C USA
ar Rapids 45 G 3 Iowa, C USA
ar River 45 E 4 river,
ebraska, C USA
ros, Isla 50 A 2 island, W Mexico
una 149 A 6 South Australia,
Australia
alù 97 C 7 anc. Cephaloedium.
W Italy
ebes Sea 152 A 3 Ind. Laut
ulawesi. Sea, W Pacific Ocean
ca 60 B 2 SW Ecuador
e 95 E 7 Ger. Cilli. C Slovenia
kar see Chelkar
dömölk 99 C 7 W Hungary
e 94 B 3 var. Zelle. N Germany
ovec see Klagenfurt
ic Sea 89 B 7 Ir. An Mhuir
heilteach. Sea, NE Atlantic Ocean
derawasih, Teluk 139 G 4
ar. Teluk Cendrawasih. Bay,
W Pacific Ocean
on 91 B 5 SW France

tral African Republic
6 C 4 var. République
entrafricaine, abbrev. CAR; prev.
ubangui-Chari, Territoire de
Oubangui-Chari, Ubangi-Shari.
Republic, C Africa

icial name: Central African
ublic Date of formation: 1960
ital: Bangui Population: 3.3
ion Total area: 240,530 sq miles
,980 sq km) Languages: French*,
gho, Banda Religions: Christian
, traditional beliefs 27%, Muslim
, other 8%
ic mix: Baya 34%, Banda 27%,
adjia 21%, other 18%
ernment: Multiparty republic
rency: CFA franc = 100 centimes

tral Group see Inner Islands
tralia 46 B 2
Vashington, NW USA
tral Indian Ridge see
Mid-Indian Ridge
tral Makrān Range 134 A 3
nountain range, W Pakistan
tral Pacific Basin 152 D 3
ndersea basin, C Pacific Ocean
tral Provinces and Berar see
Madhya Pradesh
tral Range 144 B 3 mountain
nge, New Guinea,
W Papua New Guinea
tral Russian Upland see
entral Russian Upland

Central Siberian Plateau see
Srednesibirskoye Ploskogor'ye
Central, Sistema 92 D 3 mountain
range, C Spain
Čepelare see Chepelare
Cephaloedium see Cefalù
Ceram Sea see Seram, Laut
Cereté 58 B 2 NW Colombia
Cerignola 97 D 5 SE Italy
Cernay 90 E 4 NE France
Cerro Chirripó see
Chirripó Grande, Cerro
Cerro de Pasco 60 C 3 C Peru
Cervera 93 F 2 NE Spain
Cesena 96 C 3 anc. Caesena. N Italy
Cēsis 106 D 3 Ger. Wenden. C Latvia
Česká Republika see
Czech Republic
České Budějovice 99 B 5
Ger. Budweis. SW Czech Republic
Český Krumlov 99 A 6
var. Böhmisch-Krumau, Ger.
Krummau. SW Czech Republic
Cetinje 101 C 5
It. Cettigne. SW Yugoslavia
Cette see Sète
Cettigne see Cetinje
Ceuta 92 D 5 enclave, Spain
N Africa
Cévennes 91 C 6 mountain range,
S France
Ceyhan 116 D 4 S Turkey
Ceylon Plain 140 C 4 abyssal plain,
N Indian Ocean
Ceyre to the Caribs see
Marie-Galante
Chabjuwardoo Bay 146 A 4 bay,
E Indian Ocean
Chachapoyas 60 C 3 NW Peru
Chachevichy 107 D 6
Rus. Chechevichi. E Belarus
Chachoengsao 137 C 5
var. Chaxerngsao. C Thailand
Chaco see Gran Chaco
Chaco Mesa 48 C 1 mountain,
New Mexico, SW USA

Chad
76 C 2 Fr. Tchad. Republic,
C Africa

Official name: Republic of Chad
Date of formation: 1960 Capital:
N'Djamena Population: 6 million
Total area: 495,752 sq miles
(1,284,000 sq km) Languages:
French*, Sara, Maba
Religions: Muslim 44%, Christian
33%, traditional beliefs 23% Ethnic
mix: Bagirmi, Sara and Kreish 31%,
Sudanic Arab 26%, Teda 7%, other
36% Government: Transitional
Currency: CFA franc = 100 centimes

Chad, Lake 76 B 3 Fr. Lac Tchad.
Lake, C Africa
Chadron 43 D 3
Nebraska, C USA
Chāgai Hills 134 A 2 var. Chāh Gay.
Mountain range, Afghanistan/
Pakistan
Chagos Islands see British Indian
Ocean Territory
Chagos-Laccadive Plateau 140 C 4
undersea plateau, C Indian Ocean
Chagos Trench 140 C 4 trench,
C Indian Ocean
Chāh Gay see Chāgai Hills
Chaillu, Massif du 77 B 6
mountain range, C Gabon
Chaîne Côtière see Coast Mountains
Chajul 52 B 2 W Guatemala
Chala 60 D 4 SW Peru

Chalatenango 52 C 3
N El Salvador
Chálki 105 E 7 island, Dodekánisos,
SE Greece
Chalkidikí 104 C 4
var. Khalkidhikí; anc. Chalcidice.
Peninsula, NE Greece
Challans 90 A 4 NW France
Challapata 61 F 4 SW Bolivia
Challenger Deep see Mariana Trench
Challenger Fracture Zone 153 F 4
fracture zone, SE Pacific Ocean
Châlons-en-Champagne 90 D 3
prev. Châlons-sur-Marne,
hist. Arcae Remorum,
anc. Carolopois. NE France
Chalon-sur-Saône 90 D 4
anc. Cabillonum. C France
Cha Mai see Thung Song
Chaman 134 B 2 SW Pakistan
Chambéry 91 D 5
anc. Cambería. E France
Champagne 90 D 3
cultural region, N France
Champaign 40 B 4 Illinois, N USA
Champasak 137 D 5 S Laos
Champlain, Lake 41 F 2 lake,
Canada/USA
Champotón 51 G 4 SE Mexico
Chañaral 64 B 3 N Chile
Chanco 64 B 4 C Chile
Chandeleur Islands 42 C 3
island, S USA
Chandīgarh 134 D 2 state capital,
N India
Chandler 48 B 2 Arizona, SW USA
Changane, Rio 78 D 3 river,
S Mozambique
Changchun 128 E 3
var. Ch'ang-ch'un, Ch'angch'un;
prev. Hsinking. Province capital,
NE China
Changi 138 B 1 E Singapore
Chang Jiang 129 C 5 var. Yangtze
Kiang, Eng. Yangtze. River,
C China
Chang, Ko 137 C 6 island,
C Thailand
Changsha 129 C 5 var. Ch'angsha,
Ch'ang-sha. Province capital,
S China
Changzhi 128 C 4 C China
Chaniá 105 C 7 var. Khaniá, Eng.
Canea; anc. Cydonia. SE Greece
Chañi, Nevado de 64 C 2
mountain, N Argentina
Channel Islands 89 C 8 Fr. Iles
Normandes. British dependency,
S England, UK
Channel Islands 46 C 4 island
group, California, W USA
Channel-Port aux Basques 39 G 4
Newfoundland and Labrador,
SE Canada
Channel Tunnel 89 E 7 tunnel,
France/United Kingdom
Chantada 92 C 1 NW Spain
Chanthaburi 137 C 6
var. Chantabun, Chantaburi.
Chanute 45 F 5 Kansas, C USA
Chaoyang 128 D 3 NE China
Chapais 38 D 4 Québec, SE Canada
Chapala 50 D 4 SW Mexico
Chapala, Lago de 50 D 4 lake,
C Mexico
Chapayevsk 111 C 6
W Russian Federation
Chaplynka 109 F 4 S Ukraine
Chapra see Chhapra
Chardzhev 122 D 3 prev.
Chardzhou, Chardzhui, Leninsk-
Turkmenski, Turkm. Chärjew.
E Turkmenistan

Charente 91 B 5 cultural region,
W France
Charhär Borjak 122 D 5
SW Afghanistan
Chari 76 B 3 var. Shari. River,
Central African Republic/Chad
Chārīkār 123 E 4 NE Afghanistan
Charity 59 F 2 NW Guyana
Charleroi 87 C 7 S Belgium
Charlesbourg 39 E 4 Québec,
SE Canada
Charles Island 38 D 1 island,
Northwest Territories, NE Canada
Charleston 43 F 2
South Carolina, SE USA
Charleston 40 B 4 Illinois, N USA
Charleston 40 D 5 state capital,
West Virginia, NE USA
Charleville 149 C 5 Queensland,
E Australia
Charleville-Mézières 90 D 3
N France
Charlotte 43 E 1
North Carolina, SE USA
Charlotte Amalie 55 F 3
prev. Saint Thomas. Dependent
territory capital,
N Virgin Islands (US)
Charlottenhof see Aegviidu
Charlottesville 41 E 5
Virginia, NE USA
Charlotte Town see Roseau
Charlottetown 39 F 4
Prince Edward Island,
SE Canada
Charsk 114 D 5 E Kazakhstan
Charters Towers 148 C 3
Queensland, NE Australia
Chartres 90 C 3 anc. Autricum,
Civitas Carnutum. C France
Chashniki 107 D 5 N Belarus
Chashniki see Chashniki
Châteaubriant 90 B 4 NW France
Châteaudun 90 C 4 C France
Châteauroux 90 B 4 prev.
Indreville. C France
Château-Thierry 90 D 3 N France
Châtelet 87 C 7 S Belgium
Châtelherault see Châtellerault
Châtellerault 90 B 4
Eng. Châtelherault. W France
Chatham 38 C 5
New Brunswick, SE Canada
Chatham Island see
San Cristóbal, Isla
Chatham Island Rise see
Chatham Rise
Chatham Islands 152 D 5 island
group, New Zealand
Chatham Rise 152 C 4
var. Chatham Island Rise.
Undersea rise, SW Pacific Ocean
Chatkal Range 123 F 2 Rus.
Chatkal'skiy Khrebet. Mountain
range, Kyrgyzstan/Uzbekistan
Chatkal'skiy Khrebet see
Chatkal Range
Chättagäm see Chittagong
Chattanooga 42 D 1
Tennessee, S USA
Chatyr-Tash 123 G 2
C Kyrgyzstan
Châu Ðôc 137 D 6 var. Chau Phu,
Chauphu. SW Vietnam
Chauk 136 A 3 W Myanmar
Chaumont 90 D 4 prev. Chaumont-
en-Bassigny. N France
Chausy see Chavusy
Chaves 92 C 2 anc. Aquae Flaviae.
N Portugal

Chavusy 107 E 6 *Rus.* Chausy.
E Belarus
Chaxerngsao *see* Chachoengsao
Chaykovskiy 111 D 5 *var.* Čajovskij
NW Russian Federation
Cheb 99 A 5 *Ger.* Eger.
W Czech Republic
Cheboksary 111 C 5
W Russian Federation
Cheboygan 40 C 2 Michigan, N USA
Chech, Erg 68 B 3 desert,
Algeria/Mali
Checker Hall 55 G 1 N Barbados
Cheduba Island 136 A 4 island,
W Myanmar
Chefchaouen 70 C 2 *var.* Chaouén,
Chaouèn, Chechaouén,
Chechaouèn, Chechaouen,
Chefchaouèn, *Sp.* Xauen.
N Morocco
Chehel Abdālān, Kūh-e 122 D 4
var. Chalap Dalam, *Pash.* Chalap
Dalan. Mountain range,
C Afghanistan
Cheju-do 128 E 4 *Jap.* Saishū; *prev.*
Quelpart. Island, S South Korea
Cheju Strait 128 E 4 strait,
Yellow Sea/Pacific Ocean
Chek Chue 128 B 2 *var.* Stanley.
S Hong Kong
Cheleken 122 B 2 W Turkmenistan
Chelkar 114 B 4 W Kazakhstan
Chełm 98 E 4 *Rus.* Kholm.
SE Poland
Chełmno 98 C 3 *Ger.* Culm, Kulm.
N Poland
Cheltenham 89 D 6 S England, UK
Chelyabinsk 114 C 3
C Russian Federation
Chemnitz 94 D 4
prev. Karl-Marx-Stadt. E Germany
Chengde 128 D 3 *var.* Jehol.
SE China
Chengdu 129 B 5 *var.* Ch'eng-tu,
Chengtu. Province capital,
SW China
Chenzhou 129 C 6 SE China
Chepelare 104 C 3 *var.* Čepelare.
S Bulgaria
Chepo 53 G 4 C Panama
Cher 90 C 4 river, C France
Cherbourg 90 B 3 *anc.* Carusbur.
N France
Cherepovets 110 B 4
var. Cerepoveo, Cerepovec.
NW Russian Federation
Chergui, Chott ech 70 D 2 salt lake,
N Algeria
Cherikov *see* Cherykaw
Cherkassy *see* Cherkasy
Cherkasy 109 E 2 *Rus.* Cherkassy.
C Ukraine
Cherkessk 111 B 7
SW Russian Federation
Chernigov *see* Chernihiv
Chernihiv 109 E 1 *Rus.* Chernigov.
NE Ukraine
Chernivtsi 108 C 3 *Ger.* Czernowitz,
Rom. Cernăuţi, *Rus.* Chernovtsy.
W Ukraine
Chernomorskoye *see*
Chornomors'ke
Chernyakhovsk 106 A 4 *Ger.*
Insterburg. W Russian Federation
Cherry Hill 41 F 4
New Jersey, NE USA
Cherski *see* Cherskogo, Khrebet
Cherskogo, Khrebet 115 F 3
var. Cherski. Mountain range,
NE Russian Federation
Cherson *see* Kherson
Chervyen' 107 D 6 C Belarus

Chervonograd *see* Chervonohrad
Chervonohrad 108 C 2 *Rus.*
Chervonograd. NW Ukraine
Cherykaw 107 E 7 *Rus.* Cherikov.
E Belarus
Chesapeake Bay 41 F 5 bay,
W Atlantic Ocean
Chester 89 C 6 *Wel.* Caerleon;
hist. Legaceaster, *Lat.* Deva,
Devana Castra. W England, UK
Chetumal 51 H 4 *var.* Payo Obispo.
SE Mexico
Cheviot Hills 88 D 4 hill range,
England/Scotland, UK
Cheyenne 44 D 4 state capital,
Wyoming, C USA
Cheyenne River 44 D 3 river,
South Dakota, N USA
Chhapra 135 F 3 *prev.* Chapra.
N India
Chiai 129 D 6 *var.* Chiayi, Kiayi,
Jap. Kagi. W Taiwan
Chiang Mai 136 C 4
var. Chiangmai, Chiengmai,
Kiangmai. NW Thailand
Chiang Rai 136 C 3 *var.* Chianpai,
Chienrai, Muang Chiang Rai.
N Thailand
Chiapa *see* Chiapa de Cerzo
Chiapa de Cerzo 51 G 5
var. Chiapa. SE Mexico
Chiba 131 D 5 *var.* Tiba. Honshū,
S Japan
Chibougamau 38 D 4 Québec,
SE Canada
Chicago 40 B 3 Illinois, N USA
Chicago Heights 40 B 3
Illinois, N USA
Chichester Range 146 B 4 mountain
range, W Australia
Chickasha 49 G 2 Oklahoma,C USA
Chiclayo 60 B 3 NW Peru
Chico 65 B 6 river, SE Argentina
Chico 47 B 5 California, W USA
Chicoutimi 39 E 4 Québec,
SE Canada
Chiemsee 95 C 6 lake, SE Germany
Chiesanuova 96 D 2 SW San Marino
Chieti 96 D 4 *var.* Teate. C Italy
Chifeng 127 G 2 *var.* Ulanhad.
N China
Chigirin *see* Chyhyryn
Chihli, Gulf of *see* Bo Hai
Chihuahua 50 C 2 NW Mexico
Childress 49 F 2 Texas, S USA
Chile
64-65 B 6 Republic,
S South America

Official name: Republic of Chile
Date of formation: 1818/1929
Capital: Santiago **Population:** 13.8
million **Total area:** 292,258 sq miles
(756,950 sq km) **Languages:**
Spanish*, Indian languages
Religions: Roman Catholic 89%,
Protestant 11% **Ethnic mix:** White
and *mestizo* 92%, Indian 6%, other 2%
Government: Multiparty system
Currency: Peso = 100 centavos

Chilean Antarctic Territory 154 B 3
Chilean territorial claim,
Antarctica
Chile Basin 67 A 5 undersea basin,
E Pacific Ocean
Chile Chico 65 B 6 W Chile
Chile, Republic of *see* Chile
Chile Rise 67 A 6 undersea rise,
SE Pacific Ocean
Chilia-Nouă *see* Kiliya

Chillán 65 B 5 C Chile
Chillicothe 40 D 4 Ohio, N USA
Chiloé, Isla de 65 A 6
var. Isla Grande de Chiloé. Island,
W Chile
Chiloé, Isla Grande de *see*
Chiloé, Isla de
Chilpancingo 51 E 5
var. Chilpancingo de los Bravos.
S Mexico
Chilpancingo de los Bravos *see*
Chilpancingo
Chilung 129 D 6 *var.* Keelung,
Jap. Kirun, Kirun'; *prev. Sp.*
Santissima Trinidad. N Taiwan
Chimán 53 G 5 E Panama
Chimbay *see* Chimboy
Chimborazo 60 B 1 mountain,
C Ecuador
Chimbote 60 C 3 W Peru
Chimboy 122 D 1 *Rus.* Chimbay.
NW Uzbekistan
Chimoio 79 E 3 C Mozambique

China
124 D 2 *Chin.* Chung-hua Jen-min
Kung-ho-kuo, Zhonghua Renmin
Gonghe Guo; *prev.* Chinese
Empire. Republic, E Asia

Official name: People's Republic of
China **Date of formation:** 1949/1950
Capital: Beijing **Population:**
1,234.3 million **Total area:**
3,628,166 sq miles (9,396,960 sq km)
Languages: Mandarin* **Religions:**
Confucianist 20%, Buddhist 6%,
Taoist 2%, other 72% **Ethnic mix:**
Han 93%, Zhaung 1%, Hui 1%,
other 5% **Government:** Single-party
republic **Currency:** Yuan = 10 jiao =
100 fen

Chinandega 52 C 3 NW Nicaragua
Chincha Alta 60 D 4 W Peru
Chindwin 136 B 2 river, NW Myanmar
Chingola 78 D 2 C Zambia
Chinguetti 74 C 2 *var.* Chinguetti.
C Mauritania
Chinguetti *see* Chinguetti
Chin Hills 136 A 3 mountain range,
W Myanmar
Chinook Trough 152 D 2 trough,
N Pacific Ocean
Chioggia 96 C 2
anc. Fossa Claudia. NE Italy
Chíos 105 D 5 *var.* Hios, Khíos,
It. Scio, *Turk.* Sakiz-Adasi. Chíos,
E Greece
Chíos 105 D 5
var. Khíos. Island, E Greece
Chipata 78 D 2
prev. Fort Jameson. E Zambia
Chippewa Falls 40 A 2
Wisconsin, N USA
Chiquimula 52 B 2 SE Guatemala
Chīrāla 132 D 1 E India
Chirchik *see* Chirchiq
Chirchiq 123 F 2
Rus. Chirchik. E Uzbekistan
Chiriquí, Golfo de 53 F 5
Eng. Chiriquí Gulf. Inlet,
E Pacific Ocean
Chiriquí Gulf *see* Chiriquí, Golfo de
Chiriquí, Laguna de 53 F 5 inlet,
E Pacific Ocean
Chiriquí, Volcán de *see* Barú, Volcán
Chirripó Grande, Cerro 53 E 4
var. Cerro Chirripó. Mountain,
SE Costa Rica
Chisec 52 B 2 C Guatemala
Chisholm 45 F 1
Minnesota, N USA

Chişinău 108 D 4 *Rus.* Kishinev
C Moldova
Chita 115 F 4 C Russian Federation
Chitangwiza *see* Chitungwiza
Chitina 36 D 3 Alaska, NW US
Chitose 130 D 2 *var.* Titose.
Hokkaidō, NE Japan
Chitré 53 F 5 S Panama
Chittagong 135 G 4 *Ben.*
Châttagām. SE Bangladesh
Chitungwiza 78 D 3 *prev.*
Chitangwiza. NE Zimbabwe
Chkalov *see* Orenburg
Chlef 70 D 2 *var.* Ech Cheleff,
Ech Cheliff; *prev.* Al-Asnam,
El Asnam, Orléansville.
NW Algeria
Choa Chu Kang 138 A 1
W Singapore
Chocolate Mountains 47 D 8
mountain range, California, W USA
Chodzież 98 C 3 NW Poland
Choele Choel 65 C 5 C Argenti
Choiseul 55 F 2 SW Saint Lucia
Choiseul 144 C 3 *var.* Lauru. Is
NW Solomon Islands
Ch'ok'ē 72 C 4 *var.* Choke
Mountains. Mountain range,
NW Ethiopia
Choke Mountains *see* Ch'ok'ē
Cholet 90 B 4 NW France
Choluteca 52 C 3 S Honduras
Choma 78 D 2 S Zambia
Chomutov 98 A 4 *Ger.* Komotau
NW Czech Republic
Chon Buri 137 C 5 *prev.*
Bang Pla Soi. C Thailand
Chone 60 A 1 W Ecuador
Ch'ŏngjin 128 E 3 NE North Ko
Chongqing 129 B 5 *var.* Ch'ang
ching, Ch'ung-ch'ing, Chung
Pahsien, Tchongking, Yuzhou
SW China
Chonos, Archipiélago de los 65
island group, S Chile
Chornomors'ke 109 E 5
Rus. Chernomorskoye. S Ukra
Chortkiv 108 C 2 *Rus.* Chortkov
W Ukraine
Chortkov *see* Chortkiv
Chorum *see* Çorum
Chorzów 99 C 5 *Ger.* Königshüt
prev. Królewska Huta. S Polan
Chōshi 131 D 5 *var.* Tyôsi. Hons
S Japan
Choszczno 98 B 3 *Ger.* Arnswal
W Poland
Chota Nagpur Plateau 135 E 4
plateau, C India
Choybalsan 127 F 2 E Mongolia
Christchurch 151 C 6 South Isla
C New Zealand
Christiana 54 B 5 C Jamaica
Christiansand *see* Kristiansand
Christmas Creek 146 C 3
NW Australia
Christmas Island 141 D 5
Australian external territory,
E Indian Ocean
Christmas Island *see* Kiritimati
Chu 114 C 5 *Kaz.* Shū. SE Kazakh
Chubut 65 B 6 river, SE Argent
Chūgoku-sanchi 131 B 6 moun
range, Honshū, SW Japan
Chuí 64 E 4 *var.* Chuy E Urugu
Chukchi Plain 155 F 2 abyssal
plain, Arctic Ocean
Chukchi Plateau 155 F 2 under
plateau, Arctic Ocean
Chukchi Sea 36 C 1
Rus. Chukotskoye More. Sea,
Arctic Ocean

kotskoye More *see* Chukchi Sea
la Vista 47 C 8
lifornia, W USA
lucanas 60 B 2 NW Peru
ym 114 D 4 *river*,
   Russian Federation
mphon 137 C 6 *var.* Jumporn.
   Thailand
nch'ŏn 128 E 4 *Jap.* Shunsen
   South Korea
nya 115 E 3 *river*,
   Russian Federation
or Phnum Dângrêk 137 D 5
r. Phanom Dang Raek, Phanom
ong Rak, *Fr.* Chaîne des
angrek. Mountain range,
ambodia/Thailand
quicamata 64 B 2 N Chile
r 95 B 7 *Fr.* Coire, *It.* Coira,
nsch. Cuera, Quera; *anc.* Curia
naetorum. E Switzerland
rchill 37 G 4 Manitoba,
Canada
rchill 39 F 2 *river*, E Canada
ska Mountains 48 C 1
ountain range, SW USA
sovoy 111 D 5 *var.* Čusovoj
W Russian Federation
uk 144 B 2 *var.* Hogoley
lands. Island group,
Micronesia
hyryn 109 E 3 *Rus.* Chigirin.
Ukraine
îr-Lunga 108 D 4 *var.* Ceadâr-
unga, *Rus.* Chadyr-Lunga.
Moldova
e 116 C 2 N Turkey
hanów 98 D 3 *prev.* Zichenau.
Poland
o de Ávila 54 C 2 C Cuba
aga 58 B 1 N Colombia
fuegos 54 B 2 C Cuba
a 93 E 4 SE Spain
anbeyli 116 C 3 C Turkey
bia 145 E 4 *prev.* Thikombia.
land, N Fiji
cap 138 C 5 *prev.* Tjilatjap. Jawa,
Indonesia
Airne *see* Killarney
Chainnigh *see* Kilkenny
i *see* Celje
pina *see* Câmpina
innati 40 C 4 Ohio, N USA
ty 87 C 7 SE Belgium
ra *see* Sintra
olletti 65 B 5 C Argentina
bon 138 C 4 *prev.* Tjirebon.
wa, C Indonesia
i Marina 97 E 6 Italy
ădie 108 B 4 *Ger.* Heltau,
ung. Nagydisznód. SW Romania
arista *see* la Ciotat
altépetl 35 C 7 mountain,
Mexico
us Heights 47 B 5
alifornia, W USA
i of Manila *see* Manila
dad Acuña 50 D 2 *var.* Villa
cuña. NE Mexico
dad Bolívar 59 E 2
ev. Angostura. C Venezuela
dad Camargo 50 D 2 N Mexico
dad Cortés *see* Cortés
dad Darío 52 D 3 *var.* Dario.
i Nicaragua
dad de Dolores Hidalgo *see*
olores Hidalgo
dad del Carmen *see* Carmen
dad del Este 64 E 2 *prev.* Ciudad
residente Stroessner, Presidente
roessner, Puerto Presidente
roessner. SE Paraguay

Ciudad Delicias *see* Delicias
Ciudad Guayana 59 E 2
   prev. San Tomé de Guayana, Santo
   Tomé de Guayana. NE Venezuela
Ciudad Guzmán 50 D 4 SW Mexico
Ciudad Hidalgo 51 G 5 SE Mexico
Ciudad Juárez 50 C 1 N Mexico
Ciudad Lerdo 50 D 3 C Mexico
Ciudad Madero 51 E 3
   var. Villa Cecilia. C Mexico
Ciudad Mante 51 E 3 C Mexico
Ciudad Miguel Alemán 51 E 2
   C Mexico
Ciudad Obregón 50 B 2 NW Mexico
Ciudad Ojeda 58 C 1
   NW Venezuela
Ciudad Porfirio Díaz *see*
   Piedras Negras
Ciudad Real 92 D 4 C Spain
Ciudad-Rodrigo 92 C 3 N Spain
Ciudad Trujillo *see* Santo Domingo
Ciudad Valles 51 E 4 C Mexico
Ciudad Victoria 51 E 3 C Mexico
Ciutadella *see*
   Ciutadella de Menorca
Ciutadella de Menorca 93 G 3
   var. Ciutadella. E Spain
Civitanova Marche 96 D 4 C Italy
Civitas Eburovicum *see* Évreux
Civitavecchia 96 C 4 *anc.* Centum
   Cellae, Trajani Portus. C Italy
Claremore 49 G 1 Oklahoma, C USA
Clarence 151 C 5 *river*,
   South Island, C New Zealand
Clarence Town 54 D 2 C Bahamas
Clarinda 45 F 4 Iowa, C USA
Clarion Fracture Zone 153 E 2
   fracture zone, NE Pacific Ocean
Clarión, Isla 50 A 5 *island*,
   W Mexico
Clark Fork 44 A 1 *river*, NW USA
Clark Hill Lake 43 E 2
   var. Storm Thurmond Reservoir.
   Reservoir, SE USA
Clarksburg 40 D 4
   West Virginia, NE USA
Clarksdale 42 B 2 Mississippi, S USA
Clarksville 42 C 1 Tennessee, S USA
Clearwater 43 E 4 Florida, SE USA
Clearwater Mountains 46 D 2
   mountain range, Idaho, NW USA
Clearwater River 46 D 2 *river*,
   Idaho, NW USA
Cleburne 49 G 3 Texas, S USA
Clermont 148 D 4 Queensland,
   E Australia
Clermont-Ferrand 91 C 5 C France
Cleveland 42 D 1 Tennessee, S USA
Cleveland 42 B 2 Mississippi, S USA
Cleveland 40 D 3 Ohio, N USA
Clifton 48 C 2 Arizona, SW USA
Clinton 42 B 2 Mississippi, S USA
Clinton 49 F 1 Oklahoma, C USA
Clipperton Fracture Zone 153 E 3
   fracture zone, E Pacific Ocean
Clipperton Island 153 F 3 *island*,
   E Pacific Ocean
Cloncurry 148 B 3 Queensland,
   NE Australia
Clonmel 89 A 6 *Ir.* Cluain Meala.
   S Ireland
Cloppenburg 94 B 3 NW Germany
Cloquet 45 G 2 Minnesota, N USA
Cloud Peak 44 C 3 mountain,
   Wyoming, C USA
Clovis 49 E 2 New Mexico, SW USA
Clovis 47 C 6 California, W USA
Cluain Meala *see* Clonmel
Cluj-Napoca 108 B 3 *Ger.*
   Klausenburg, *Hung.* Kolozsvár;
   prev. Cluj. NW Romania

Clutha 151 B 7 *river*, South Island,
   SW New Zealand
Clyde 88 C 4 *river*, C Scotland, UK
Coari 62 D 2 N Brazil
Coast Mountains 36 D 4 *Fr.* Chaîne
   Côtière. Mountain range,
   Canada/USA
Coast Ranges 46 A 4
   mountain range, W USA
Coats Island 38 C 1 *island*,
   Northwest Territories, NE Canada
Coats Land 154 B 2 physical region,
   Antarctica
Coatzacoalcos 51 F 4
   var. Quetzalcoalco; *prev.* Puerto
   México. SE Mexico
Cobán 52 B 2 C Guatemala
Cobar 57 C 6 New South Wales,
   SE Australia
Cobija 61 E 3 NW Bolivia
Coburg 95 C 5 SE Germany
Coca *see*
   Puerto Francisco de Orellana
Cocanada *see* Kākināda
Cochabamba 61 F 4 *hist.* Oropeza.
   C Bolivia
Cochin 132 C 3 *var.* Kochi. SW India
Cochrane 65 B 7 S Chile
Cochrane 38 C 4 Ontario, S Canada
Cockburn Town 55 E 2 dependent
   territory capital,
   E Turks & Caicos Islands
Cockpit Country, The 54 A 4
   physical region, NW Jamaica
Coco 52 D 2 *var.* Río Wanki,
   Segoviao Wangki. River,
   Honduras/Nicaragua
Cocobeach 77 A 5 NW Gabon
Coconino Plateau 48 B 1 plain,
   Arizona, SW USA
Cocos (Keeling) Islands 141 D 5
   Australian external territory,
   E Indian Ocean
Cocos Basin 140 D 4 undersea
   basin, E Indian Ocean
Cocos Island Ridge *see* Cocos Ridge
Cocos Ridge 153 G 3 *var.* Cocos
   Island Ridge. Undersea ridge,
   E Pacific Ocean
Cod, Cape 41 G 3 headland,
   Massachusetts, NE USA
Codfish Island 151 A 8 *island*,
   South Island, SW New Zealand
Cod Island 39 F 1 *island*,
   Newfoundland and Labrador,
   E Canada
Codlea 108 C 4 *Ger.* Zeiden,
   Hung. Feketehalom. C Romania
Cody 44 C 2 Wyoming, C USA
Coen 148 C 2 Queensland,
   NE Australia
Coetivy Island *see* Coëtivy
Coevorden 86 E 2 NE Netherlands
Coffin Bay 149 A 6 South Australia,
   S Australia
Coffs Harbour 149 E 6
   New South Wales, SE Australia
Cognac 91 B 5 *anc.* Compniacum.
   W France
Coiba, Isla de 53 F 5 *island*,
   SW Panama
Coihaique 65 B 7 *var.* Coyhaique.
   S Chile
Coimbatore 132 C 3 S India
Coimbra 92 B 3 *anc.* Conimbria,
   Conímbriga. N Portugal
Coín 92 D 5 S Spain
Coirib, Loch *see* Corrib, Lough
Colac 149 B 7 Victoria,
   SE Australia

Colchester 89 E 6 *hist.* Colneceaster,
   anc. Camulodunum.
   SE England, UK
Coleman 49 F 3 Texas, S USA
Coleraine 88 B 4 *Ir.* Cúil Raithin.
   N Northern Ireland, UK
Colesberg 78 C 5 C South Africa
Coles, Punta 61 E 5 headland,
   S Peru
Colima 50 D 4 S Mexico
Coll 88 B 3 *island*, W Scotland, UK
College Station 49 G 3 Texas, S USA
Collie 147 B 7
   Western Australia, W Australia
Collinsville 148 D 3 Queensland,
   E Australia
Collinsville 40 B 4 Illinois, N USA
Collipo *see* Leiria
Colmar 90 E 4 *Ger.* Kolmar.
   NE France
Colomb-Béchar *see* Béchar

Colombia
   58 B 3 . Republic,
   N South America

Official name: Republic of Colombia
Date of formation: 1819/1922
Capital: Bogotá **Population:** 34
   million **Total area:** 439,733 sq miles
   (1,138,910 sq km) **Languages:**
   Spanish*, Indian languages, English
   Creole **Religions:** Roman Catholic
   95%, other 5% **Ethnic mix:** *mestizo*
   58%, White 20%, mixed 14%,
   other 8% **Government:** Multiparty
   republic **Currency:** Peso = 100 centavos

Colombian Basin 66 A 4 undersea
   basin, W Atlantic Ocean
Colombie-Britannique *see*
   British Columbia
Colombo 132 C 4 country capital,
   W Sri Lanka
Colón 53 G 4
   prev. Aspinwall. C Panama
Colón, Archipiélago de *see*
   Galapagos Islands
Colonia *see* Kolonia
Colorado 65 B 5 *river*, E Argentina
Colorado 48 C 4 *var.* Río Colorado.
   River, Mexico/USA
Colorado 44 C 4 *off.* State of
   Colorado; *nicknames* Centennial
   State, Silver State. State, C USA
Colorado City 49 F 3 Texas, S USA
Colorado, Río *see* Colorado
Colorado Springs 44 D 5
   Colorado, C USA
Columbia 43 E 2 state capital,
   South Carolina, SE USA
Columbia 42 C 1 Tennessee, S USA
Columbia 41 F 4
   Maryland, NE USA
Columbia 45 G 4 Missouri, C USA
Columbia Plateau 46 C 3 plateau,
   NW USA
Columbine 44 C 4 Colorado, C USA
Columbus 42 D 2
   Georgia, SE USA
Columbus 42 C 2 Mississippi, S USA
Columbus 40 D 4 state capital,
   Ohio, N USA
Columbus 44 E 4 Nebraska, C USA
Colville Channel 150 D 2 channel,
   Bay of Plenty/Hauraki Gulf
Comacchio 96 C 3 *var.* Commachium.
   anc. Comactium. N Italy
Comalcalco 51 G 4 SE Mexico
Coma Pedrosa, Pic Alt de la *see*
   Coma Pedrosa, Pic de

Coma Pedrosa, Pic de 91 A 7
var. Pic Alt de la Coma Pedrosa.
Mountain, NW Andorra
Comarapa 61 G 4 C Bolivia
Comarnic 108 C 4 SE Romania
Comayagua 52 C 2 W Honduras
Combermere Bay 136 A 4 bay,
Bay of Bengal / Indian Ocean
Comilla 135 G 4 *Ben.* Kumillā.
E Bangladesh
Comino *see* Comino
Comitán 51 G 5 *var.* Comitán de
Domínguez. SE Mexico
Comitán de Domínguez *see*
Comitán
Commissioner's Point 42 A 5
headland, W Bermuda
Como 96 B 2
anc. Comum. N Italy
Comodoro Rivadavia 65 B 6
SE Argentina
Como, Lago di 96 B 2 *var.* Lario,
Eng. Lake Como, *Ger.* Comer
See. Lake, N Italy

Comoros
79 F 2 *Fr.* République Fédérale
Islamique des Comores.
Republic, Indian Ocean

Official name: Federal Islamic
Republic of the Comoros
Date of formation: 1975 **Capital:**
Moroni **Population:** 600,000
Total area: 861 sq miles
(2,230 sq km) **Languages:** Arabic*,
French* **Religions:** Muslim 86%,
Roman Catholic 14% **Ethnic mix:**
Comorian 96%, Makua 2%, other 2%
Government: Islamic republic
Currency: Franc = 100 centimes

Compiègne 90 C 3 N France
Compniacum *see* Cognac
Comrat 108 D 4 *Rus.* Komrat.
S Moldova
Comum *see* Como
Conakry 74 C 4 country capital,
SW Guinea
Conca *see* Cuenca
Concarneau 90 A 3 NW France
Concepción 65 B 5 C Chile
Concepción 64 D 2 *var.* Villa
Concepción. C Paraguay
Concepción 61 G 3 E Bolivia
Concepción *see* La Concepción
Concepción de la Vega *see*
La Vega
Conchos, Río 50 C 2 river,
NW Mexico
Concord 41 G 3 state capital,
New Hampshire, NE USA
Concordia 64 D 4 E Argentina
Concordia 45 E 4 Kansas USA
Condate *see* St-Claude
Condega 52 D 3 NW Nicaragua

Congo
77 B 5 *Fr.* Moyen-Congo; *prev.*
Middle Congo. Republic, C Africa

Official name: The Republic of the
Congo **Date of formation:** 1960
Capital: Brazzaville **Population:**
2.4 million **Total area:**
132,040 sq miles (342,000 sq km)
Languages: French*, Kongo
Religions: Roman Catholic 50%,
traditional beliefs 48%, other 2%
Ethnic mix: Bakongo 48%, Teke 17%,
Mboshi 17%, other 18%
Government: Multiparty republic
Currency: CFA franc = 100 centimes

Congo (Zaire)
77 D 6 *prev.* Zaire, Belgian Congo,
Congo (Kinshasa). Republic,
C Africa

Official name: Democratic Republic
of the Congo **Date of formation:**
1960 **Capital:** Kinshasa **Population:**
41.2 million **Total area:** 905,563 sq
miles (2,345,410 sq km) **Languages:**
French*, Kiswahili, Tshiluba
Religions: Christian 70%, traditional
beliefs 20%, Muslim 10% **Ethnic
mix:** Bantu 23%, Hamitic 23%, other
54% **Government:** Transitional
Currency: Congolese franc

Congo 77 C 6 *var.* Kongo, *Fr.* Zaire.
River, C Africa
Congo *see* Zaire
Congo Basin 77 C 6 basin,
W Congo (Zaire)
Congo Cone *see* Congo Fan
Coni *see* Cuneo
Conjeeveram *see* Kānchīpuram
Connaught 89 A 5 cultural region,
W Ireland
Connecticut 41 G 3 *off.* State of
Connecticut; *nicknames* Blue Law
State, Constitution State, Land of
Steady Habits, Nutmeg State.
State, NE USA
Connersville 40 C 4 Indiana, N USA
Conrad Rise 141 B 7 undersea rise,
SW Indian Ocean
Conroe 49 H 3 Texas, S USA
Consentia *see* Cosenza
Consolación del Sur 54 A 2 W Cuba
Con Son *see* Côn Đao
Con Son Island 137 E 7 Island,
S Vietnam
Constance, Lake 95 B 6 *Ger.* Bodensee.
Lake, Germany / Switzerland
Constanţa 108 D 5 *var.* Küstendje,
Eng. Constanza, *Ger.* Konstanza,
Turk. Küstence. SE Romania
Constantia *see* Coutances
Constantine 71 E 2 *var.* Qacentina,
Ar. Qoussantina. NE Algeria
Conway 43 F 2
South Carolina, SE USA
Coober Pedy 149 A 5
South Australia, S Australia
Cook Islands 145 F 4 territory
in free association with
New Zealand (defence, UN),
S Pacific Ocean
Cook, Mount 151 B 6 *prev.* Aoraki,
Aorangi. Mountain, South Island,
SW New Zealand
Cook Strait 151 D 5 *var.* Raukawa.
Channel, Pacific Ocean /
Tasman Sea
Cooktown 148 D 2 Queensland,
NE Australia
Coolgardie 147 C 6 Western
Australia, W Australia
Cooma 149 D 7 New South Wales,
SE Australia
Coomassie *see* Kumasi
Coon Rapids 45 F 2
Minnesota, N USA
Cooper Creek 149 B 5 *var.* Barcoo,
Cooper's Creek. River, S Australia
Coos Bay 46 A 3 Oregon, NW USA
Cootamundra 149 C 6
New South Wales, SE Australia
Copacabana 61 E 4 W Bolivia
Copenhagen *see* København
Copiapó 64 B 3 *hist.* San Francisco
de Selva . N Chile
Copiapó 57 B 5 N Chile
Copperas Cove 49 G 3 Texas, S USA

Coppermine 37 E 3 *var.*
Qurlurtuuq. Northwest
Territories, NW Canada
Coquilhatville *see* Mbandaka
Coquimbo 64 B 3 N Chile
Corabia 108 B 5 S Romania
Coral Harbour 37 G 3
Southampton Island, NE Canada
Coral Sea 144 B 4 sea,
W Pacific Ocean
Coral Sea Islands 148 E 3
Australian external territory.
NE Australia
Corcaigh *see* Cork
Corcovado, Golfo 65 B 6 gulf,
SE Pacific Ocean
Cordele 42 D 3 Georgia, SE USA
Cordillera Central 55 E 3 mountain
range, C Dominican Republic
Cordillera Central 58 B 3
mountain range, W Colombia
Cordillera Central 139 E 1
mountain range, Luzon,
N Philippines
Cordillera Occidental 58 B 3
mountain range, W Colombia
Cordillera Occidental 61 F 5
mountain range, Bolivia / Chile
Cordillera Occidental 60 D 4
mountain range, W Peru
Córdoba 92 D 4 *var.* Cordoba, *Eng.*
Cordova; *anc.* Corduba. SW Spain
Córdoba 64 C 4 C Argentina
Córdoba 51 F 4 E Mexico
Cordova 36 C 3 Alaska, NW USA
Córdova 60 D 4 SW Peru
Corfu *see* Kérkyra
Coria 92 C 3 W Spain
Corinth 42 C 1 Mississippi, S USA
Corinto 52 C 3 NW Nicaragua
Cork 89 A 6 *Ir.* Corcaigh. S Ireland
Corner Brook 39 G 3
Newfoundland and Labrador,
E Canada
Corn Islands *see* Maíz, Islas del
Cornwallis Island 37 F 2 island,
N Canada
Coro 58 C 1 *prev.* Santa Ana de
Coro. NW Venezuela
Corocoro 61 F 4 W Bolivia
Coromandel 150 D 2 North Island,
N New Zealand
Coromandel Coast 132 D 2 physical
region, E India
Coromandel Peninsula 150 D 2
peninsula, North Island,
N New Zealand
Coronado, Bahía de 53 E 5 inlet,
E Pacific Ocean
Coronel Dorrego 65 C 5 E Argentina
Coronel Oviedo 64 D 2 SE Paraguay
Corozal 52 C 1 N Belize
Corozo Pando 58 D 2 C Venezuela
Corpus Christi 49 G 5
Texas, S USA
Corpus Christi Bay 49 G 5 bay,
NW Gulf of Mexico
Corrib, Lough 89 A 5 *Ir.* Loch
Coirib. Lake, W Ireland
Corrientes 64 D 3 NE Argentina
Corse 91 E 7 *Eng.* Corsica. Island,
SE France
Corsica *see* Corse
Corsicana 49 G 3 Texas, S USA
Cortegana 92 C 4 S Spain
Cortés 53 E 5 *var.* Ciudad Cortés.
SE Costa Rica
Cortina d'Ampezzo 96 C 1 NE Italy
Coruche 92 B 3 C Portugal
Çorum 116 D 3 *var.* Chorum.
N Turkey

Çorun Çayı 117 E 3 river,
NE Turkey
Corvallis 46 B 3 Oregon, NW U[...]
Corvo 92 A 5 *var.* Ilha do Corvo[...]
Island, W Portugal
Corvo, Ilha do *see* Corvo
Cosenza 97 D 6 *anc.* Consentia.
SW Italy
Cosne-Cours-sur-Loire 90 C 4 *v[...]*
Cosne-sur-Loire; *anc.* Condate[...]
C France
Costa Dorada *see* Daurada, Cost[...]

Costa Rica
53 E 4 Republic,
C Central America

Official name: Republic of Cost[...]
Rica **Date of formation:** 1821 / 18[...]
Capital: San José **Population:** 3.3[...]
million **Total area:** 19,730 sq mil[...]
(51,100 sq km) **Languages:** Spani[...]
English Creole, Bribri, Cabecar
Religions: Catholic 95%, other 5[...]
Ethnic mix: White / *mestizo* (Euro[...]
Indian) 96%, Black 2%, Indian 2[...]
Government: Multiparty republi[...]
Currency: Colón = 100 centimos

Costermansville *see* Bukavu
Cotagaita 61 G 5 S Bolivia
Côte d'Ivoire *see* Ivory Coast
Cotonou 75 F 5 *var.* Kotonu. S B[...]
Cotswold Hills 89 D 6
var. Cotswolds. Hill range,
S England, UK
Cotswolds *see* Cotswold Hills
Cottbus 94 D 4 *prev.* Kottbus.
E Germany
Cottica 59 H 3 E Suriname
Cotyora *see* Ordu
Couentrey *see* Coventry
Couëron 90 B 4 NW France
Council Bluffs 45 F 4 Iowa, C U[...]
Courantyne River 59 G 4
var. Corantijn Rivier, Corentyr[...]
River. River, Guyana / Surinam[...]
Courland Lagoon 106 A 4
Ger. Kurisches Haff, *Rus.* Kurs[...]
Zaliv. Lagoon, SE Baltic Sea
Courtrai *see* Kortrijk
Coutances 90 B 3 *anc.* Constantia[...]
N France
Couvin 87 C 7 S Belgium
Coventry 89 D 6 *anc.* Couentrey.
C England, UK
Covilhã 92 C 3 E Portugal
Cowan, Lake 147 C 6 lake,
Western Australia, SW Austra[...]
Coyhaique *see* Coihaique
Cozumel, Isla 51 H 3 island,
SE Mexico
Cradock 78 C 5 S South Africa
Craig 44 C 4 Colorado, C USA
Craiova 108 B 5 SW Romania
Cranbrook 37 E 5 Alberta,
SW Canada
Crawley 89 E 7 SE England, UK
Cremona 96 B 2 N Italy
Cres 100 A 3 *It.* Cherso;
anc. Crexa. Island, W Croatia
Creston 45 F 4 Iowa, C USA
Crestview 42 D 3 Florida, SE US[...]
Crete *see* Kriti
Créteil 90 C 3 N France
Creuse 90 B 4 river, C France
Crewe 89 C 6 W England, UK
Crikvenica 100 A 2 *It.* Cirquenia[...]
prev. Cirkvenica, Crjkvenica.
NW Croatia
Crimea *see* Krym

óbal 53 G 4 C Panama
óbal Colón, Pico 58 B 1
ountain, N Colombia
uru Secuiesc 108 C 4 Ger.
eutz, Hung. Székelykeresztúr;
ev. Cristur, Cristuru Săcuiesc,
as Cristuru Szitás-Keresztúr,
itás-Keresztúr. C Romania
a Gora see Montenegro
 Reka 101 E 6 river, S Macedonia

tia
0 B 2 Ger. Kroatien, SCr.
vatska. Republic, SE Europe

cial name: Republic of Croatia
 of formation: 1991 Capital:
eb Population: 4.9 million Total
21,830 sq miles (56,540 sq km)
guages: Croatian*, Serbian
gions: Roman Catholic 77%,
odox Catholic 11%, Protestant
Muslim 1%, other 10%
ic mix: Croat 80%, Serb 12%,
garian, Slovenian, other 8%
ernment: Multiparty republic
ency: Kuna = 100 para

ker, Banjaran 138 D 3
r. Crocker Range. Mountain
nge, Borneo, E Malaysia
ker Range see Crocker, Banjaran
odile see Limpopo
er Island 146 E 2 island,
Australia
nwell 151 B 7 South Island,
V New Zealand
oked Island 54 D 2 island,
 Bahamas
oked Island Passage 54 D 2
annel, N Caribbean Sea
okston 45 F 1 Minnesota, N USA
one 97 E 6 var. Cotrone;
c. Crotona, Croton. SW Italy
ydon 89 E 7 SE England, UK
zet Basin 141 B 6 undersea
asin, S Indian Ocean
zet Islands 141 B 7 island
oup, W French Southern
Antarctic Territories
zet Plateau 141 B 6 var. Crozet
ateaus. Undersea plateau,
V Plateau
zet Plateaus see Crozet Plateau
stal Brook 149 B 6 South
ustralia, S Australia
a see Čadca
rna 99 C 6 NW Hungary
gó 99 C 7 SW Hungary
mba 79 E 2 prev. Nova Freixo.
Mozambique
ndo see Kwando
ngo 77 C 7 NW Angola
ngo see Kwango
nza 69 C 5 var. Kwanza. River,
Angola
ahtémoc 50 C 2 N Mexico
utla 51 E 4 S Mexico

a
 B 2 Republic, N Caribbean Sea

cial name: Republic of Cuba
e of formation: 1902
ital: Havana Population:
million Total area:
03 sq miles (110,860 sq km)
guages: Spanish*, English,
ch, Chinese Religions: Roman
olic 85%, other 15% Ethnic mix:
te 66%, Afro-European 22%,
r 12% Government: Socialist
blic Currency: Peso =
centavos

Cubal 78 B 2 W Angola
Cubango 78 B 2 var. Kuvango,
Port. Vila Artur de Paiva,
Vila da Ponte. C Angola
Cubango 78 B 2 var. Kavango,
Kavengo, Kubango, Okavanggo,
Okavango. River, S Africa
Cúcuta 58 C 2 var. San José de
Cúcuta. N Colombia
Cuddapah 132 C 2 S India
Cue 147 B 5 Western Australia,
W Australia
Cuenca 93 E 3 anc. Conca.
C Spain
Cuenca 60 B 2 S Ecuador
Cuernavaca 51 E 4 S Mexico
Cuiabá 63 E 3 prev. Cuyabá. State
capital, SW Brazil
Cuijck 86 D 4 SE Netherlands
Cúil Raithin see Coleraine
Cuito 78 B 2 var. Kwito. River,
SE Angola
Cukai 138 B 3 var. Chukai,
Kemaman. W Malaysia
Culiacán 50 C 3 var. Culiacán Rosales,
Culiacán-Rosales. C Mexico
Cullera 93 F 3 E Spain
Cullman 42 C 2
Alabama, S USA
Culpepper Island see Darwin, Isla
Cumaná 59 E 1 NE Venezuela
Cumbal, Nevada de 58 A 4
mountain, SW Colombia
Cumberland 41 E 4
Maryland, NE USA
Cumberland Plateau 42 D 1 hill
range, Alabama, S USA
Cumberland River 43 E 1 river,
S USA
Cunene 78 A 3 var. Kunene. River,
Angola/Namibia
Cuneo 96 A 2 Fr. Coni. NW Italy
Cunnamulla 149 C 5 Queensland,
E Australia
Cuprija 100 D 4 C Yugoslavia
Curaçao 55 E 5 island,
C Netherlands Antilles
Curicó 64 B 4 C Chile
Curitiba 63 F 4 prev. Curytiba.
State capital, S Brazil
Curtea de Argeş 108 B 4 var.
Curtea-de-Arges. S Romania
Curtea-de-Arges see
Curtea de Argeş
Curtici 108 A 4 Ger. Kurtitsch,
Hung. Kürtös. W Romania
Curtis Island 148 E 4 island,
Queensland, SE Australia
Curuguaty 64 E 2 E Paraguay
Curytiba see Curitiba
Cusco 60 D 4 var. Cuzco. C Peru
Čusovoj see Chusovoy
Cusset 91 C 5 C France
Cutch, Rann of 134 B 4
var. Rann of Kachh, Rann
of Kutch. Wetland,
India/Pakistan
Cuttack 135 F 5 E India
Cuvier Plateau 141 E 5 undersea
plateau, E Indian Ocean
Cuxhaven 94 B 2 NW Germany
Cuyabá see Cuiabá
Cuyuni 59 F 2 var. Río Cuyuni.
River, Guyana/Venezuela
Cuyuni, Río see Cuyuni River
Cuzco see Cusco
Čvrsnica 100 C 4 mountain range,
SW Bosnia & Herzegovina
Cyclades see Kykládes
Cymru see Wales

Cyprus
103 H4 Gk. Kypros, Turk. Kibris,
Kibris Cumhuriyeti. Republic,
SW Asia

Official name: Republic of Cyprus
Date of formation: 1960/1983
Capital: Nicosia Population: 700,000
Total area: 3,572 sq miles
(9,251 sq km) Languages: Greek*,
Turkish, other Religions: Greek
Orthodox 77%, Muslim 18%, other
5% Ethnic mix: Greek 77%, Turkish
18%, other (mainly British) 5%
Government: Multiparty republic
Currency: Cypriot £/Turkish lira

Cyprus
103 H4 Gk. Kypros,
Turk. Kibris, Kibris. Island,
NE Mediterranean Sea

Czech Republic
99 B 5 Cz. Česká Republika.
Republic, C Europe

Official name: Czech Republic Date
of formation: 1993 Capital: Prague
Population: 10.4 million Total area:
30,260 sq miles (78,370 sq km)
Languages: Czech*, Slovak, Romany
Religions: Roman Catholic 39%,
Protestant 2%, other Christian 12%,
other 38% Ethnic mix: Czech 85%,
Moravian 13%, other 2%
Government: Multiparty republic
Currency: Koruna = 100 halura

Częstochowa 98 C 4 Ger.
Czenstochau, Tschenstochau,
Rus. Chenstokhov. S Poland
Człuchów 98 C 3 Ger. Schlochau.
NW Poland

D

Dabajuro 58 C 1 NW Venezuela
Dabeiba 58 B 2 NW Colombia
Dąbrowa Tarnowska 99 D 5
SE Poland
Dabryn' 107 C 8 Rus. Dobryn'.
SE Belarus
Dacca see Dhākā
Dadanawa 59 F 4 SW Guyana
Dafang 129 B 5 E China
Dagana 74 B 3 N Senegal
Dagda 106 D 4 SE Latvia
Dagupan 139 E 1 off. Dagupan City.
Luzon, N Philippines
Dagupan City see Dagupan
Da Hinggan Ling 127 G 1
Eng. Great Khingan Range.
Mountain range, NE China
Dahm, Ramlat 121 B 6 desert,
NW Yemen
Daimiel 92 D 3 C Spain
Daimoniá 105 B 7 S Greece
Daingin, Bá an see Dingle Bay
Dakar 74 B 3 country capital,
W Senegal
Dakhla Oasis 72 B 2 var. Wāhat el
Dākhla. Oasis, C Egypt
Dakoro 75 G 3 S Niger
Dakovica 101 D 5 var. Djakovica,
Alb. Gjakovë. SW Yugoslavia
Dakovo 100 C 3 var. Djakovo,
Hung. Diakovár. E Croatia
Dakshin see Deccan
Dalaman 116 A 4 SW Turkey
Dalandzadgad 127 E 3 S Mongolia
Dalarna 85 C 5 prev. Eng.
Dalecarlia. Cultural region,
C Sweden

Da Lat 137 E 6 S Vietnam
Dalby 149 D 5 Queensland,
E Australia
Dalecarlia see Dalarna
Dale City 41 E 4 Virginia, NE USA
Dalhart 49 E 1
New Mexico, SW USA
Dalian 128 D 4 var. Dairen,
Dalien, Jay Dairen, Lüda,Ta-lien,
Rus. Dalny. NE China
Dallas 49 G 3 Texas, S USA
Dalmacija 100 B 4 Eng. Dalmatia,
Ger. Dalmatien, It. Dalmazia.
Cultural region S Croatia
Dalton 42 D 1 Georgia, SE USA
Daly Waters 148 A 2 Northern
Territory, N Australia
Damachava 107 A 6 var.
Damachova, Pol. Domaczewo,
Rus. Domachëvo. SW Belarus
Damān 134 C 5 Port. Damão.
W India
Damão see Damān
Damara 76 C 4
S Central African Republic
Damascus see Dimashq
Damietta see Dumyāt
Dammām 120 C 4 var. Ad
Dammān. NE Saudi Arabia
Damoûr 119 A 5 var. Ad Dāmūr.
W Lebanon
Dampier 146 B 4 Western Australia,
W Australia
Dampier, Selat 139 G 4 strait,
W Pacific Ocean
Damqawt 121 D 6 var. Damqut.
E Yemen
Damqut see Damqawt
Damxung 126 C 5 W China
Danané 74 D 5 W Ivory Coast
Đà Năng 137 E 5 prev. Tourane.
C Vietnam
Danborg see Daneborg
Danbury 41 F 3 Connecticut, NE USA
Dandong 128 D 4 var. Tan-tung;
prev. An-tung. NE China
Daneborg 83 E 3 var. Danborg.
E Greenland
Dangara see Danghara
Danghara 123 E 3 Rus. Dangara.
SW Tajikistan
Dangriga 52 C 1 prev. Stann Creek.
E Belize
Danlí 52 D 3 S Honduras
Danmark Havn 83 E 2 E Greenland
Danmarksstraedet see Denmark Strait
Dannenberg 94 C 3 N Germany
Dannevirke 150 D 4 North Island,
C New Zealand
Danube 81 E 4 Bul. Dunav, Cz.
Dunaj, Ger. Donau, Hung. Duna,
Rom. Dunărea. River, C Europe
Danube, Mouths of the 108 D 5
Delta, Romania/Ukraine
Danubian Plain see
Dunavska Ravnina
Danville see Doncaster
Danville 41 E 5 Illinois, N USA
Danville 40 B 4 Illinois, N USA
Dan Xian 129 C 7 var. Danxian,
Nada. Hainan Dao, S China
Danzig, Gulf of 98 C 2 var. Gulf of
Gdańsk, Ger. Danziger Bucht, Pol.
Zakota Gdańska, Rus. Gdan'skaya
Bukhta. Gulf, S Baltic Sea
Daqm see Duqm
Dar'ā 119 B 5 var. Dara, Fr. Déraa.
S Syria
Darabani 108 C 3 NW Romania
Daraut-Kurgan see Daroot-Korgon
Darbénai 106 B 3 NW Lithuania

Dardanelles see Çanakkale Boğazı
Dar-el-Beida see Casablanca
Dar es Salaam 73 D 7 E Tanzania
Darfield 151 C 6 South Island,
  C New Zealand
Darfur 72 A 4 var. Darfur Massif.
  Mountain range, W Sudan
Darfur Massif see Darfur
Dargaville 150 D 2 North Island,
  N New Zealand
Darhan 127 E 2 N Mongolia
Darién, Golfo del see Darien, Gulf of
Darien, Gulf of 53 H 4 Sp. Golfo
  del Darién. Gulf, SE Caribbean Sea
Darién, Serranía del 53 H 5
  mountain range,
  Colombia/Panama
Dario see Ciudad Darío
Dariorigum see Vannes
Darjeeling see Darjiling
Darjiling 135 F 3 prev. Darjeeling.
  NE India
Darling 149 C 6 river,
  New South Wales, SE Australia
Darling Downs 149 D 5 hill range,
  Queensland, SE Australia
Darlington 89 D 5 N England, UK
Darmiān 120 E 3 E Iran
Darmstadt 95 B 5 SW Germany
Darnah 71 G 2 var. Dérna. N Libya
Darnley, Cape 154 D 3 headland,
  Antarctica
Daroca 93 E 2 NE Spain
Daroot-Korgon 123 F 3 var. Daraut-
  Kurgan. SW Kyrgyzstan
Dartmoor 89 C 7 heathland,
  SW England, UK
Dartmouth 39 F 4 Nova Scotia,
  SE Canada
Darvaza 122 C 2 Turkm. Derweze.
  C Turkmenistan
Darwin 148 A 2 prev. Palmerston,
  Port Darwin. Territory capital,
  Northern Territory, N Australia
Darwin, Isla 60 A 4 var. Culpepper
  Island. Island, Galapagos Islands,
  E Pacific Ocean
Dashkawka 107 D 6
  Rus. Dashkovka. E Belarus
Dashkhovuz 122 C 2
  Turkm. Dashhowuz; prev. Tashauz.
  N Turkmenistan
Dashkovka see Dashkawka
Dasht 120 D 2 N Iran
Datong 128 C 3 var. Tatung,
  Ta-t'ung. N China
Daugavpils 106 D 4 Ger. Dünaburg;
  prev. Rus. Dvinsk. SE Latvia
Daung Kyun 137 B 6 island,
  S Myanmar
Dauphiné 91 D 5 cultural region,
  E France
Daurada, Costa 93 G 2 var. Costa
  Dorada. Coastal region, E Spain
Dāvangere 132 C 2 W India
Davao 139 F 2 off. Davao City.
  Mindanao, S Philippines
Davao City see Davao
Davao Gulf 139 F 3 gulf,
  W Pacific Ocean
Davenport 45 G 3 Iowa, C USA
David 53 F 5 W Panama
Davie Ridge 141 A 5 undersea
  ridge, W Indian Ocean
Davis 154 D 3 research station,
  Antarctica
Davis 47 B 6 California, W USA
Davis Mountains 48 D 3 mountain
  range, Texas, S USA
Davis Sea 154 D 3 sea, S Indian Ocean
Davis Strait 82 B 3 strait,
  Baffin Bay/Labrador Sea

Davlekanovo 111 D 6
  W Russian Federation
Dawei see Tavoy
Dawra 70 B 3 var. Daora,
  Daoura. NW Western Sahara
Dax 91 B 6 var. Ax; anc. Aquae
  Augustae, Aquae Tarbelicae.
  SW France
Dayr az Zawr 118 D 3
  var. Deir ez Zor. E Syria
Dayton 40 C 4 Ohio, N USA
Daytona Beach 43 E 4 Florida, SE USA
De Aar 78 C 5 C South Africa
Dead Sea 119 E 7 var. Bahret Lut,
  Lacus Asphaltites, Ar. Al Baḥr al
  Mayyit, Baḥrat Lūt, Heb. Yam
  HaMelaḥ. Salt lake, Israel/Jordan
Deán Funes 64 C 3 C Argentina
Death Valley 47 D 6 valley,
  California, W USA
Debar 101 D 6 Ger. Dibra,
  Turk. Debre. W Macedonia
De Bildt see De Bilt
De Bilt 86 C 3 var. De Bildt.
  C Netherlands
Debrecen 99 D 6 Ger. Debreczin,
  Rom. Debreţin; prev. Debreczen.
  E Hungary
Decatur 42 C 2 Alabama, S USA
Decatur 40 B 4 Illinois, N USA
Deccan 132 C 1 Hind. Dakshin.
  Plateau, C India
Děčín 98 A 4 Ger. Tetschen.
  NW Czech Republic
Dedeagaç see Alexandroúpoli
Dedemsvaart 86 E 3 E Netherlands
Dee 88 C 3 river, E Scotland, UK
Deering 36 C 2 Alaska, NW USA
De Funiak Springs 42 D 3
  Florida, SE USA
Deggendorf 95 D 6 SE Germany
Deh Bīd 120 D 4 C Iran
Deinze 87 B 6 NW Belgium
Deir ez Zor see Dayr az Zawr
Deirgeirt, Loch see Derg, Lough
Dej 108 B 3 Hung. Dés;
  prev. Deés. NW Romania
De Jouwer see Joure
Dékoa 76 C 4
  C Central African Republic
De Land 43 E 4 Florida, SE USA
Delano 47 C 7 California, W USA
Delārām 122 D 5 SW Afghanistan
Delaware 41 F 4 off. State of
  Delaware; nicknames Blue Hen
  State, Diamond State, First State.
  State, E USA
Delaware 40 D 4 Ohio, N USA
Delaware Bay 41 F 5 bay,
  W Atlantic Ocean
Delft 86 C 4 W Netherlands
Delfzijl 86 E 1 NE Netherlands
Delgo 72 B 3 N Sudan
Delhi 134 D 3 var. Dehli, Hind. Dilli;
  hist. Shahjahanabad. N India
Delicias 50 C 2 var. Ciudad
  Delicias. N Mexico
Delmenhorst 94 B 3 NW Germany
Del Rio 49 F 4 Texas, S USA
Demba 77 D 6 S Congo (Zaire)
Dembia 76 D 4
  SE Central African Republic
Demchok 126 A 4 var. Dêmqog.
  Disputed region, China/India
Deming 48 C 3 New Mexico, SW USA
Demmin 94 D 2 NE Germany
Dêmqog 126 A 4 var. Demchok.
  Disputed region, China/India
Denali see McKinley, Mount
Denau see Denow
Dender 87 B 6 Fr. Dendre. River,
  W Belgium

Dendre see Dender
Denekamp 86 E 3 E Netherlands
Den Ham 86 E 3 E Netherlands
Den Helder 86 C 2
  NW Netherlands
Denia 93 F 4 E Spain
Deniliquin 149 C 7
  New South Wales, SE Australia
Denison 49 G 2 Texas, S USA
Denison 45 F 3 Iowa, C USA
Denizli 116 B 4 SW Turkey

Denmark
  85 A 7 Dan. Danmark,
  anc. Hafnia. Monarchy, N Europe

Official name: Kingdom of
Denmark **Date of formation:**
AD 960/1953 **Capital:** Copenhagen
Population: 5.2 million
Total area: 16,629 sq miles
(43,069 sq km) **Languages:** Danish*
Religions: Evangelical Lutheran 91%
other Christian 9% **Ethnic mix:**
Danish 96%, Faeroese and
Inuit 1%, other 3% **Government:**
Constitutional monarchy
Currency: Krone = 100 øre

Denmark Strait 82 D 4
  var. Danmarksstraedet. Strait,
  N Atlantic Ocean
Dennery 55 F 1 E Saint Lucia
Denow 123 E 3 Rus. Denau.
  S Uzbekistan
Denpasar 138 D 5 prev. Paloe. Bali,
  C Indonesia
Denton 49 G 2 Texas, S USA
Denver 44 D 4 state capital,
  Colorado, C USA
Dera Ghāzi Khān 134 C 2
  var. Dera Ghāzikhān. C Pakistan
Dera Ghāzikhān see Dera Ghāzi Khān
Đeravica 101 D 5 mountain,
  SW Yugoslavia
Derby 89 D 6 C England, UK
Dergachi see Derhachi
Derg, Lough 89 A 6 Ir. Loch
  Deirgeirt. Lake, W Ireland
Derhachi 109 G 2 Rus. Dergachi.
  E Ukraine
De Ridder 42 A 3
  Louisiana, S USA
Dérna see Darnah
Dertosa see Tortosa
Derventa 100 C 3
  N Bosnia & Herzegovina
Derweze see Darvaza
Deschutes River 46 B 3 river,
  Oregon, NW USA
Desē 72 D 4 var. Dese,
  It. Dessie. N Ethiopia
Deseado 65 B 7 river, S Argentina
Desertas, Ilhas 70 A 2 island group,
  Madeira, E Atlantic Ocean
Des Moines 45 F 4 state capital,
  Iowa, C USA
Desna 109 E 1 river, Russian
  Federation/Ukraine
Dessau 94 C 4 E Germany
Dessie see Desē
Destêrro see Florianópolis
Detroit 40 D 3 Michigan, N USA
Detroit Lakes 45 F 2
  Minnesota, N USA
Deurne 87 D 5 SE Netherlands
Deutsch-Eylau see Iława
Deutsch Krone see Wałcz
Devana see Aberdeen
Deventer 86 D 3 E Netherlands

Devils Lake 45 E 1
  Missouri, C USA
Devoll see Devollit, Lumi i
Devollit, Lumi i 101 D 6
  var. Devoll. River, SE Albania
Devon Island 37 F 2 prev. North
  Devon Island. Island, NE Cana
Devonport 149 C 8 Tasmania,
  SE Australia
Devrek 116 C 2 N Turkey
Dexter 45 G 5 Missouri, C USA
Deynau 122 D 3 var. Dyanev,
  Turkm. Dänew. NE Turkmenist
Dezfūl 120 C 3 var. Dizful. SW I
Dezhou 128 D 4 NE China
Dhahran see Aẓ Ẓahrān
Dhākā 135 G 4 prev. Dacca. C
  capital, C Bangladesh
Dhanbād 135 F 4 NE India
Dhārwād 132 B 1
  prev. Dharwar. SW India
Dhíkti Ori see Díkti
Dhomokós see Domokós
Dhráma see Dráma
Dhrepanon, Akra see Drépano, A
Dhún na nGall, Bá see Donegal I
Diamantina, Chapada 63 F 3
  mountain range, E Brazil
Diamantina Fracture Zone 141 E
  fracture zone, E Indian Ocean
D'Iberville 42 C 3 Mississippi, S U
Dibio see Dijon
Dibrugarh 135 H 3 NE India
Dickinson 44 D 2
  North Dakota, N USA
Didymóteicho 104 D 3
  var. Dhidhimótikhon,
  Didimotiho. NE Greece
Diedenhofen see Thionville
Diekirch 87 D 8 C Luxembourg
Điện Biên 136 D 3 var. Bien Bien
  Dien Bien Phu. NW Vietnam
Diepenbeek 87 D 6 NE Belgium
Diepholz 94 B 3 NW Germany
Dieppe 90 C 2 N France
Dieren 86 D 4 E Netherlands
Differdange 87 D 8
  SW Luxembourg
Digby 39 F 5
  Nova Scotia, SE Canada
Digne 91 D 6
  var. Digne-les-Bains. SE France
Digne-les-Bains see Digne
Digoel see Digul, Sungai
Digoin 90 C 4 C France
Digul 139 H 5 prev. Digoel. River
  New Guinea, E Indonesia
Dijon 90 D 4 anc. Dibio. C Franc
Dikhil 72 D 4 SW Djibouti
Dikson 114 D 2
  N Russian Federation
Diktí 105 D 8 var. Dhíkti Ori.
  Mountain range, Kríti,
  SE Greece
Dili 139 F 5 var. Dilli,
  It. Dilli. E Indonesia
Dili see Delhi
Dilia 75 G 3
  var. Dillia. River, SE Niger
Dilijan 117 G 2 Rus. Dilizhan.
  NE Armenia
Di Linh 137 E 6 S Vietnam
Dilizhan see Dilijan
Dillia see Dilia
Dilling 72 B 4 var. Ad Dalanj.
  C Sudan
Dilolo 77 D 8 S Congo (Zaire)
Dimashq 119 B 5 var. Ash Shām,
  Esh Sham, Eng. Damascus,
  Fr. Damas, It. Damasco.
  Country capital, SW Syria

trovgrad 111 C 6
Russian Federation
itrovgrad 104 D 3 S Bulgaria
itrovo *see* Pernik
lang 75 G 4 *var.* Vogel Peak.
ountain, E Nigeria
ona 119 A 7 S Israel
ovo 104 B 1 NW Bulgaria
ijpur 135 G 3 NW Bangladesh
an 90 A 3 NW France
int 87 C 7 S Belgium
ir 116 B 4 SW Turkey
ira *see* Dinaric Alps
iric Alps 100 C 4 *var.* Dinara.
ountain range, Bosnia &
erzegovina/Croatia
ligul 132 C 3 SE India
gle Bay 89 A 6 *Ir.* Bá an
aingín. Inlet, NE Atlantic Ocean
guiraye 74 C 4 N Guinea
irbel 74 B 3 W Senegal
iction, Cape 148 C 2 headland,
eensland, NE Australia
Dawa 73 D 5 E Ethiopia
Hartog Island 147 A 5 island,
Australia
a 72 A 4 Sudan
chau *see* Tczew
ippointment, Lake 146 C 4
lt lake, Western Australia,
Australia
overy Bay 128 A 1 *Cant.*
ii Pak Wan. W Hong Kong
our 135 G 3 NE India
inópolis 63 F 4 SE Brazil
> 74 D 5 S Ivory Coast
irbakır 117 E 4 *var.* Diarbekr;
ic. Amida. SE Turkey
ful *see* Dezful
nbala 77 B 6 C Congo
nbi *see* Hari, Batang
net 71 E 4 *prev.* Fort Charlet.
E Algeria
fa 70 D 2 *var.* El Djelfa.
Algeria
na 76 D 4
Central African Republic
nber *see* Jember
rem 75 H 5 river, C Cameroon
ouri 72 D 4 *var.* Jibuti. Country
ipital, E Djibouti

outi
2 D 4 *var.* Jibuti; *prev.* French
omaliland, French Territory of
e Afars and Issas, *Fr.* Côte
rançaise des Somalis, Territoire
rançais des Afars et des Issas.
epublic, NE Africa

cial name: Republic of Djibouti
e of formation: 1977
ital: Djibouti Population:
000 Total area: 8,958 sq miles
200 sq km) Languages:
bic*, French*, Somali :
inic mix: Issa 35%, Afar 20%,
aboursis and Isaaks 28%,
er 17% Government:
le-party republic
rency: Franc = 100 centimes

guéni 74 D 3 SE Mauritania
ir el Choghour *see*
isr ash Shughūr
iurab, Erg du 76 C 2 desert,
l Chad
pivogur 83 E 5 SE Iceland
eprodzerzhinskoye
odokhranilishche *see*
iniprodzerzhyns'ke
odoskhovyshche

Dneprorudnoye *see* Dniprorudne
Dnieper 81 F 4 *Bel.* Dnyapro,
Rus. Dnepr, *Ukr.* Dnipro. River,
W Europe
Dnieper Lowland 109 F 2
Bel. Prydnyaprowskaya Nizina,
Ukr. Prydniprovs'ka Nyzovyna.
Lowlands, Belarus/Ukraine
Dniester 108 D 3 *var.* Tyras,
Rom. Nistru, *Rus.* Dnestr,
Ukr. Dnister. River,
Moldova/Ukraine
Dniprodzerzhyns'k 109 F 3
Rus. Dneprodzerzhinsk;
prev. Kamenskoye. C Ukraine
Dniprodzerzhyns'ke
Vodoskhovyshche 109 F 3
Rus. Dneprodzerzhinskoye
Vodokhranilishche. Reservoir,
NE Ukraine
Dnipropetrovs'k 109 F 3
Rus. Dnepropetrovsk;
prev. Yekaterinoslav. E Ukraine
Dniprorudne 109 F 3
Rus. Dneprorudnoye.
SE Ukraine
Doba 76 C 4 S Chad
Döbeln 94 D 4 E Germany
Doboj 100 C 3
N Bosnia & Herzegovina
Dobre Miasto 98 D 2
Ger. Guttstadt. N Poland
Dobrich 104 E 2 *var.* Dobrič,
Rom. Bazargic; *prev.* Tolbukhin.
NE Bulgaria
Dobrush 107 D 8 SE Belarus
Dobryn' *see* Dabryn'
Dodecanese *see* Dodekánisos
Dodekánisos 105 D 6 *var.* Nóties
Sporádes, *Eng.* Dodecanese; *prev.*
Dhodhekánisos. Island group,
SE Greece
Dodge City 45 E 5 Kansas, C USA
Dodoma 73 C 7 country capital,
C Tanzania
Dogana 96 E 1 NE San Marino
Dōgo 131 B 6 island, Oki-shotō,
W Japan
Dogondoutchi 75 F 3 SW Niger
Dogrular *see* Pravda
Doğu Karadeniz Dağları 117 E 3
var. Anadolu Daĕlari.
Mountain range, NE Turkey
Doha *see* Ad Dawhah
Dokkum 86 D 1 N Netherlands
Dokuchayevs'k 109 G 3 *var.*
Dokuchayevsk. SE Ukraine
Dokuchayevsk *see* Dokuchayevs'k
Doldrums Fracture Zone 66 C 4
fracture zone, W Atlantic Ocean
Dôle 90 D 4 E France
Dolina *see* Dolyna
Dolinskaya *see* Dolyns'ka
Dolisie 77 B 6 *prev.* Loubomo.
S Congo
Dolomitiche, Alpi 96 C 1
var. Dolomiti, *Eng.* Dolomites.
Mountain range, NE Italy
Dolores 64 D 4 W Uruguay
Dolores 64 D 4 E Argentina
Dolores 52 B 1 N Guatemala
Dolores Hidalgo 51 E 4 *var.*
Ciudad de Dolores Hidalgo.
C Mexico
Dolyna 108 B 2 *Rus.* Dolina.
W Ukraine
Dolyns'ka 109 F 3 *Rus.* Dolinskaya.
S Ukraine
Dombås 85 B 5 S Norway
Domesnes, Cape *see* Kolkasrags
Domeyko 64 B 3 N Chile

Dominica
55 H 4 Republic, E Caribbean Sea

Official name: Commonwealth of
Dominica Date of formation: 1978
Capital: Roseau Population: 72,000
Total area: 290 sq miles (750 sq km)
Languages: English*, French Creole,
Carib, Cocoy Religions: Roman
Catholic 77%, Protestant 15%, other
8% Ethnic mix: Black 98%, Indian 2%
Government: Multiparty republic
Currency: E. Caribbean $ = 100 cents

Dominican Republic
55 E 3 Republic, N Caribbean Sea

Official name: Dominican Republic
Date of formation: 1865 Capital:
Santo Domingo Population:
7.6 million Total area:
18,815 sq miles (48,730 sq km)
Languages: Spanish*, French Creole
Religions: Roman Catholic 95%,
other 5% Ethnic mix: Afro-European
73%, White 16%, Black 11%
Government: Multiparty republic
Currency: Peso = 100 centavos

Domokós 105 B 5 *var.* Dhomokós.
C Greece
Don 81 F 3 *var.* Duna, Tanais. River,
SW Russian Federation
Donauwörth 95 C 6 S Germany
Don Benito 92 C 4 W Spain
Doncaster 89 D 5 *anc.* Danum.
NE England, UK
Dondo 78 B 1 NW Angola
Donegal 89 A 5 *Ir.* Dún na nGall.
NW Ireland
Donegal Bay 89 A 5 *Ir.* Bá Dhún na
nGall. Bay, E Atlantic Ocean
Donets 109 G 2 river, Russian
Federation/Ukraine
Donets'k 109 G 3 *Rus.* Donetsk;
prev. Stalino. E Ukraine
Dongfang 129 B 7 *var.* Hainan Dao,
S China
Dongguan 129 C 6 SW China
Đông Ha 136 E 4 C Vietnam
Dong Hai *see* East China Sea
Đông Hoi 136 E 4 C Vietnam
Dongola 72 B 3 *var.* Donqola,
Dunqula. N Sudan
Dongou 77 C 5 NE Congo
Dongting Hu 129 C 5 *var.* Tung-
Tung-t'ing Hu. Lake, SE China
Dongxing 128 B 7 SW Australia
Donostia-San Sebastián 93 E 1
N Spain
Door Peninsula 40 C 2 peninsula,
Wisconsin, N USA
Dooxo Nugaaleed 73 E 5 *var.* Nogal
Valley. Valley, E Somalia
Dordogne 91 B 5 cultural region,
SW France
Dordogne 91 B 5 river, W France
Dordrecht 86 C 4 *var.* Dordt, Dort.
SW Netherlands
Doré Lake 37 F 5 Saskatchewan,
C Canada
Dorohoi 108 C 3 NE Romania
Dorotea 84 C 4 N Sweden
Dorre Island 147 A 5 island,
W Australia
Dortmund 94 D 4 W Germany
Dos Hermanas 92 C 5 S Spain
Dospat 104 C 3 SW Bulgaria
Dothan 42 D 3 Alabama, S USA
Dotnuva 106 B 4 C Lithuania
Douai 90 C 2 *prev.* Douay,
anc. Duacum. N France

Douala 77 A 5 *var.* Duala.
W Cameroon
Doubtful Island Bay 147 C 7 bay,
SE Indian Ocean
Douglas 89 C 5 dependent territory
capital, E Isle of Man, British Isles
Douglas 43 E 3 Georgia, SE USA
Douglas 48 C 3 Arizona, SW USA
Douglas 44 C 3 Wyoming, C USA
Douma *see* Dūmā
Douro 92 B 2 *Sp.* Duero. River,
Portugal/Spain
Douro, Rio *see* Duero
Dover 89 E 7 *Fr.* Douvres; *Lat.*
Dubris Portus. SE England, UK
Dover 129 C 8 Tasmania,
SE Australia
Dover 41 G 3
New Hampshire, NE USA
Dover 41 F 4 state capital,
Delaware, NE USA
Dover, Strait of 90 C 2 *var.* Straits of
Dover, *Fr.* Pas de Calais. Channel,
NE Atlantic Ocean
Dovrefjell 85 B 5 mountain range,
S Norway
Downpatrick 89 C 5 *Ir.* Dún
Pádraig. SE Northern Ireland, UK
Dōzen 131 B 6 island, Oki-shotō,
W Japan
Drachten 86 D 2 N Netherlands
Drăgăşani 108 B 5 SW Romania
Dragoman 104 B 2 W Bulgaria
Dragon's Mouth, The 59 F 1 strait,
A Atlantic Ocean
Dra, Hamada du 70 C 3 *var.*
Hammada du Drâa, Haut Plateau
du Dra. Plateau, W Algeria
Drahichyn 107 B 6 *Pol.* Drohiczyn
Poleski, *Rus.* Drogichin.
SW Belarus
Drakensberg 78 D 5 mountain
range, Lesotho/South Africa
Drake Passage 153 F 5 passage,
Atlantic Ocean/Pacific Ocean
Dralfa 104 D 2 N Bulgaria
Dráma 104 C 3 *var.* Dhráma.
NE Greece
Drammen 85 B 6 S Norway
Drava 100 C 3 *var.*
Eng. Drave, *Hung.* Dráva. River,
C Europe
Drawsko Pomorskie 98 B 3
Ger. Dramburg. NW Poland
Drépano, Akra 104 C 4 *var.* Akra
Dhrepanon. Headland, N Greece
Drepanum *see* Trapani
Dresden 94 D 4 E Germany
Drina 100 D 4 river, Bosnia &
Herzegovina/Yugoslavia
Drini i Zi 101 D 5 *var.* Black Drin,
Alb. Lumi i Drinit të Zi, *SCr.* Crni
Drim. River, Albania/Macedonia
Drissa 107 D 5 *Bel.* Drysa. River,
Belarus/Russian Federation
Droichead Átha *see* Drogheda
Drogheda 89 B 5 *Ir.* Droichead
Átha. NE Ireland
Drohobych 108 B 2 *Pol.* Drohobycz,
Rus. Drogobych. NW Ukraine
Droichead Átha *see* Drogheda
Drôme 91 D 6 cultural region,
E France
Dronning Maud Land *see*
Queen Maud Land
Drug *see* Durg
Drummond Island 40 D 2 island,
Michigan, N USA
Drummondville 39 E 4 Québec,
SE Canada

Druskienniki *see* Druskininkai
Druskininkai 107 B 5
Pol. Druskiennki. S Lithuania
Dryden 38 B 3 Ontario, C Canada
Drysa *see* Drissa
Drysdale 146 D 3 river, N Australia
Duala *see* Douala
Dubai *see* Dubayy
Dubăsari 108 D 3 *Rus.* Dubossary.
NE Moldova
Dubawnt 37 F 4 river, Northwest
Territories, C Canada
Dubayy 120 D 4 *Eng.* Dubai.
NE United Arab Emirates
Dubbo 149 D 6 New South Wales,
SE Australia
Dublin 89 B 6 *Ir.* Baile Átha Cliath;
anc. Eblana. Country capital,
E Ireland
Dublin 43 E 2 Georgia, SE USA
Dubno 108 C 2 NW Ukraine
Dubossary *see* Dubăsari
Dubrovnik 101 A 8
It. Ragusa. SE Croatia
Dubuque 45 G 3 Iowa, C USA
Dudelange 87 D 8 *var.* Forge du
Sud, *Ger.* Dudelingen.
S Luxembourg
D-U-D Municipality *see* Majuro
Duero 92 D 2 *Port.* Rio Douro.
River, Portugal/Spain
Duero *see* Douro
Duesseldorf *see* Düsseldorf
Duffel 87 C 5 C Belgium
Dufour Spitze 95 A 8 *var.* Punta
Dufour, *It.* Pizzo Dufour.
Mountain, Italy/Switzerland
Dugi Otok 100 A 3 *var.* Isola
Grossa, *It.* Isola Lunga. Island,
W Croatia
Duisburg 94 A 4 *prev.* Duisburg-
Hamborn. W Germany
Duisburg-Hamborn *see* Duisburg
Duitama 58 B 3 C Colombia
Duiven 86 D 4 E Netherlands
Duk Faiwil 73 B 5 Sudan
Dulan Xian 126 D 4 C China
Dulce, Golfo 53 E 5 gulf,
E Pacific Ocean
Dulce, Golfo *see* Izabal, Lago de
Dülmen 94 A 4 W Germany
Dulovo 104 E 1 NE Bulgaria
Duluth 45 G 2 Minnesota, N USA
Dūmā 119 B 5 *Fr.* Douma. SW Syria
Dumas 49 E 1 Texas, S USA
Dumfries 88 C 4 S Scotland, UK
Dumont d'Urville 154 D 4 research
station, Antarctica
Dumyât 72 B 1 *Eng.* Damietta.
N Egypt
Dunării, Delta *see* Danube,
Mouths of the
Dunaújváros 99 C 7
prev. Dunapentele, Sztálinváros.
C Hungary
Dunavska Ravnina 104 C 2 *Eng.*
Danubian Plain. Plain, N Bulgaria
Duncan 49 G 2 Oklahoma, C USA
Dundalk 89 B 5 *Ir.* Dún Dealgan.
NE Ireland
Dundalk 41 F 4 Maryland, NE USA
Dún Dealgan *see* Dundalk
Dundee 88 C 4 E Scotland, UK
Dundee 78 D 4 E South Africa
Dunedin 151 B 7 South Island,
SW New Zealand
Dunfermline 88 C 4 C Scotland, UK
Dungu 77 E 5 NE Congo (Zaire)
Dungun 138 B 3 *var.* Kuala
Dungun. W Malaysia
Dunholme *see* Durham

Dunkerque 90 C 2 *Eng.* Dunkirk,
Flem. Duinekerke;
prev. Dunquerque. N France
Dún Laoghaire 89 B 6 *Eng.* Dunleary;
prev. Kingstown. E Ireland
Dún na nGall *see* Donegal
Dún Pádraig *see* Downpatrick
Dupnitsa 104 C 2 *prev.* Stanke
Dimitrov, Marek. W Bulgaria
Duqm 121 E 5 *var.* Daqm. E Oman
Durance 91 D 6 river, SE France
Durango 50 D 3 *var.* Victoria de
Durango. W Mexico
Durango 44 C 5 Colorado, C USA
Durankulak 104 E 1 *Rom.* Răcari;
prev. Blatnitsa, Duranulac.
NE Bulgaria
Durant 49 G 2 Oklahoma, C USA
Durban 78 D 5 *var.* Port Natal.
E South Africa
Durbe 106 B 3 *Ger.* Durben. W Latvia
Durben *see* Durbe
Durg 135 E 4 *prev.* Drug. C India
Durham 89 D 5 *hist.* Dunholme.
N England, UK
Durham 43 F 1 North Carolina, SE USA
Durrës 101 C 6 *var.* Durrësi, Dursi,
It. Durazzo, *SCr.* Drač, *Turk.* Draç,
W Albania
Durūz, Jabal ad 119 C 5
mountain , SW Syria
Dushanbe 123 E 3 *var.* Dyushambe,
Taj. Stalinobod; *prev.* Stalinabad.
Country capital, W Tajikistan
Düsseldorf 94 A 4 *var.* Duesseldorf.
W Germany
Dusti *see* Düsti
Düsti 123 E 3 *Rus.* Dusti. SW Tajikistan
Dutch Harbor 36 B 3 Unalaska
Island, Alaska, USA
Dutch West Indies *see*
Netherlands Antilles
Dyersburg 42 C 1 Tennessee, S USA
Dzerzhinsk 111 C 5
W Russian Federation
Dzhalal-Abad 123 F 2
Kir. Jalal-Abad. W Kyrgyzstan
Dzhanak 122 C 2 physical region,
W Turkmenistan
Dzhankoy 109 F 4 S Ukraine
Dzharkurgan *see* Jarqŭrghon
Dzhelandy 123 F 3 SE Tajikistan
Dzhergalan 123 H 2 *Kir.* Jyrgalan.
NE Kyrgyzstan
Dzhetygara 114 B 4
Kaz. Zhetiqara. NW Kazakhstan
Dzhizak *see* Jizzakh
Dzhugdzhur, Khrebet 115 G 3
mountain range, E Russian
Federation
Dzhusaly 114 B 4 *Kaz.* Zholsaly.
SW Kazakhstan
Działdowo 98 D 3 C Poland
Dzungaria 126 C 2 *var.* Sungaria,
Zungaria. Physical region, W China
Dzüünbayan 127 E 2 SE Mongolia
Dzüünharaa 127 E 2 N Mongolia
Dzuunmod 127 E 2 C Mongolia

E

Eagle Lake 47 B 5 lake,
California, W USA
Eagle Pass 49 F 4 Texas, S USA
Easley 43 E 1 South Carolina, SE USA
East Antarctica *see* Greater Antarctica
East Australian Basin *see*
Tasman Basin
Eastbourne 89 E 7 SE England, UK
East Cape 150 E 3 region,
North Island, New Zealand

East Caroline Basin 152 B 3
undersea basin, SW Pacific Ocean
East Caroline Islands 144 C 2
island group, E Micronesia
East China Sea 152 B 2 *Chin.* Dong
Hai. Sea, NW Pacific Ocean
Easter Fracture Zone 153 F 4
fracture zone, E Pacific Ocean
Easter Island 153 F 4 island,
E Pacific Ocean
Eastern Ghats 124 B 3 mountain
range, SE India
Eastern Sayans 115 E 4
Mong. Dzüün Soyonï Nuruu,
Rus. Vostochnyy Sayan.
Mountain range, Mongolia/
Russian Federation
Eastern Sierra Madre *see* Madre
Oriental, Sierra
East Falkland 65 D 8 *var.* Soledad.
Island, E Falkland Islands
East Frisian Islands *see*
Ostfriesische Inseln
East Grand Forks 45 F 1
Minnesota, N USA
East Indiaman Ridge 141 D 5
undersea ridge, E Indian Ocean
East Kilbride 88 C 4 S Scotland, UK
East Korea Bay 128 E 3 bay,
Sea of Japan/Pacific Ocean
Eastleigh 89 D 7 S England, UK
East London 78 D 5 *Afr.* Oos-
Londen; *prev.* EMonti, Port Rex.
S South Africa
Eastmain 38 D 3 river, Québec,
C Canada
East Novaya Zemlya Trough 155
H 4 *var.* Novaya Zemlya Trough.
Trough, Arctic Ocean
East Pacific Rise 153 F 4 undersea
rise, E Pacific Ocean
East Saint Louis 40 B 4
Illinois, N USA
East Siberian Sea *see* Vostochno-
Sibirskoye More
Eau Claire 40 A 2 Wisconsin, N USA
Ébano 51 E 3 C Mexico
Ebensee 95 D 6 N Austria
Eberswalde-Finow 94 D 3 E Germany
Ebetsu 130 D 2 *var.* Ebetu.
Hokkaidō, NE Japan
Ebetu *see* Ebetsu
Ebeye 144 D 1 island,
C Marshall Islands
Ebolowa 77 A 5 S Cameroon
Ebon Atoll 144 D 2 *var.* Epoon.
Island, S Marshall Islands
Ébrié, Lagune 74 D 5 lake,
SW Ivory Coast
Ebro 93 E 2 river, NE Spain
Ecbatana *see* Hamadān
Echo Bay 37 E 3 Northwest
Territories, C Canada
Echt 87 D 5 SE Netherlands
Ecija 92 D 4 *anc.* Astigi. SW Spain
Eckengraf *see* Viesīte

Ecuador
60 A 2 Republic,
NW South America

Official name: Republic of Ecuador
Date of formation: 1830/1942
Capital: Quito **Population:** 11.3
million **Total area:** 109,483 sq miles
(283,560 sq km) **Languages:**
Spanish*, Quechua*, eight other
Indian languages **Religions:** Roman
Catholic 95%, other 5% **Ethnic mix:**
mestizo (Euro-Indian) 55%, Indian
25%, Black 10%, White 10%
Government: Multiparty republic
Currency: Sucre = 100 centavos

Edd *see* Ed
Ed Da'ein 72 A 4 W Sudan
Ed Damazin 72 C 4 *var.* Ad
Damazīn. E Sudan
Ed Damer 72 C 3 *var.* Ad Dama
Ad Dāmir. NE Sudan
Ed Debba 72 B 3 N Sudan
Ede 75 F 5 SW Nigeria
Ede 86 D 4 C Netherlands
Edéa 77 A 5 SW Cameroon
Edel Land 147 A 5 headland,
Western Australia, W Austral
Eden 43 F 1 North Carolina, SE
Eden 149 D 7 New South Wales
SE Australia
Edfu *see* Idfu
Edgeoya 83 G 2 island, S Svalba
Edinburg 49 G 5 Texas, S USA
Edinburgh 88 C 4 SE Scotland,
Edingen *see* Enghien
Edirne 116 A 2 *var.* Adrianopl
Hadrianopolis. NW Turkey
Edmonds 46 B 2 Washington, NW
Edmonton 37 E 5 province capi
Alberta, SW Canada
Edmundston 39 E 4
New Brunswick, SE Canada
Edna 49 G 4 Texas, S USA
Edolo 96 B 1 N Italy
Edremit 116 A 3 NW Turkey
Edward, Lake 77 E 6 *var.* Alber
Edward Nyanza, Edward Nya
Lac Idi Amin, Lake Rutanzige.
Lake, Congo (Zaire)/Uganda
Eeklo 87 B 5 *var.* Eekloo. NW Belg
Eekloo *see* Eeklo
Eems *see* Ems
Eersel 87 D 5 S Netherlands
Éfaté 144 D 4 *Fr.* Vaté; *prev.* Sand
Islands. Island group, C Vanua
Effingham 40 B 4 Illinois, N US
Eforie Sud 108 D 5 E Romania
Efstrátios, Ágios 104 D 4 *var.* Ay
Evstratios. Island, E Greece
Egadi, Isole 97 B 7 island group
S Italy
Eger 99 D 6 *Ger.* Erlau. NE Hung
Eger *see* Cheb
Eghezèe 87 C 6 C Belgium
Egiyn Gol 126 D 2 *var.* Egiyn G
River, N Mongolia
Egiyn Gul *see* Egiyn Gol
Egmont *see* Taranaki, Mount
Egmont, Cape 150 C 4 headlan
North Island, C New Zealand

Egypt
72 B 2 *Ar.* Jumhūrīyah Misr a
'Arabīyah; *prev.* United Arab
Republic, *anc.* Aegyptus.
Republic, NE Africa

Official name: Arab Republic of
Egypt **Date of formation:** 1936/
Capital: Cairo **Population:** 64.2
million **Total area:** 386,660 sq mil
(1,001,450 sq km) **Languages:**
Arabic*, French, English **Religio**
Muslim 94%, other 6% **Ethnic m**
Eastern Hamitic 90%, other 10%
Government: Multiparty republi
Currency: Pound = 100 piastres

Eibar 93 E 1 N Spain
Eibergen 86 E 3 E Netherlands
Eidfjord 85 A 5 S Norway
Eifel 95 A 5 plateau, W German
Eigg 88 B 3 island, W Scotland,
Eight Degree Channel 132 B 3
channel, N Indian Ocean
Eighty Miles Beach 146 B 3 bea
Western Australia, W Australi

den 87 D 6 SE Netherlands
dhoven 87 D 5 S Netherlands
enhüttenstadt 94 D 4 E Germany
eben 94 C 4 C Germany
issa 93 G 3 *var.* Iviza, *Cast.* Ibiza;
nc. Ebusus. Island, E Spain
ssa 93 G 4 *var.* Iviza, *Cast.* Ibiza;
nc. Ebusus. E Spain
a de los Caballeros 93 F 2
JE Spain
atapskiy Khrebet 115 G 1
nountain range,
JE Russian Federation
Alamein 72 B 1 *var.*
l 'Alamayn. N Egypt
t 119 B 8 *var.* Eilat, Elath. S Israel
zığ 117 E 3 *var.* Elâziz. E Turkey
ziz *see* Elâzığ
a, Isola d' 96 B 4 island, C Italy
asan 101 C 6 *var.* Elbasani.
: Albania
asani *see* Elbasan
e 94 C 3 *Cz.* Labe.
zech Republic/Germany
ert, Mount 44 C 4 mountain,
'olorado, C USA
lag 98 D 2 *var.* Elblag,
ier. Elbing. N Poland
rus 111 B 8 *var.* Gora El'brus.
Mountain, SW Russian Federation
rus, Gora *see* El'brus
Burgo de Osma 93 E 2 C Spain
urz Mountains *see* Alborz,
eshteh-ye Kūhhā-ye
Calafate 65 B 7 *var.* Calafate.
Argentina
Callao 59 F 2 E Venezuela
Campo 49 C 4 S USA
Carmen de Bolívar 58 B 2
NW Colombia
Centro 47 D 8
California, W USA
he 93 F 4 *var.* Elx- Elche;
nc. Ilici, *Lat.* Illicis. E Spain
a 93 F 4 E Spain
Djelfa *see* Djelfa
Dorado 50 C 3 C Mexico
Dorado 45 F 5 Kansas, C USA
Dorado 59 F 2 E Venezuela
orado 64 E 3 NE Argentina
oret 73 C 6 W Kenya
ctrostal' 111 B 5
W Russian Federation
ohant Butte Reservoir 48 C 2
eservoir, New Mexico, SW USA
sd *see* Aleşd
uthera Island 54 C 1 island,
J Bahamas
'asher 72 A 4 *var.* Al Fāshir.
V Sudan
in 88 C 3 UK
in 40 B 3 Illinois, N USA
iza 72 B 1 *var.* Al Jīzah, Gîza,
izeh. N Egypt
Goléa 70 D 3 *var.* Al Golea.
: Algeria
lank 68 A 3 desert ,
Mali/Mauritania
lank 74 D 1 cliff, S Mauritania
Hasaheisa 72 C 4 *var.*
al Hasahisa, Al Ḩuşayḩişah,
Hasaheisa. C Sudan
sabethville *see* Lubumbashi
ta 111 B 7
W Russian Federation
zabeth 149 B 6
South Australia, S Australia
zabeth City 43 G 1
North Carolina, NE USA
zabethtown 40 C 5
Kentucky, E USA

El-Jadida 70 C 2 *prev.* Mazagan.
W Morocco
Ełk 98 E 2 *Ger.* Lyck. NE Poland
Elk City 49 F 1 Oklahoma, C USA
Elkford 37 E 5 Alberta, SW Canada
El Khârga 72 B 2 *var.* Al Khārijah.
C Egypt
Elkhart 40 C 3 Indiana, N USA
Elk River 45 F 2 Minnesota, N USA
Ellef Ringnes Island 37 F 1 island,
N Canada
Ellen, Mount 44 B 5 mountain,
Utah, W USA
Ellensburg 46 B 2
Washington, NW USA
Ellesmere Island 37 F 1 island,
N Canada
Ellice Islands, The *see* Tuvalu
Elliston 149 A 6 South Australia,
S Australia
Ellsworth Land 154 A 3 physical
region, Antarctica
El Mina 118 B 4 *var.* Al Mīnā'.
N Lebanon
El Minya 72 B 2 *var.* Al Minyā,
Minya. C Egypt
Elmira 41 E 3 New York, NE USA
El Mreyyé 74 D 2 desert, E Mauritania
Elmshorn 94 B 3 N Germany
El Muglad 72 B 4 C Sudan
El Obeid 72 B 4 *var.* Al Obayyid,
Al Ubayyiḑ. C Sudan
El Oued 71 E 2 *var.* Al Oued,
El Ouâdi, El Wad. NE Algeria
Eloy 48 B 3 Arizona, SW USA
El Paso 48 D 3 Texas, S USA
El Porvenir 53 G 4 N Panama
El Progreso 52 C 2 NW Honduras
El Puerto de Santa María 92 B 5
S Spain
El Quweira *see* Al Quwayrah
El Rama 53 E 3 SE Nicaragua
El Real 53 H 5 *var.* El Real de Santa
María. SE Panama
El Real de Santa María *see* El Real
El Reno 49 F 1
Oklahoma, C USA

El Salvador
52 B 3 Republic,
W Central America

Official name: Republic of
El Salvador **Date of formation:**
1856/1838 **Capital:** San Salvador
Population: 6.4 million **Total area:**
8,124 sq miles (21,040 sq km)
Languages: Spanish*, Nahua
Religions: Roman Catholic 75%,
other 25% **Ethnic mix:** *mestizo* (Euro-
Indian) 89%, Indian 10%, White 1%
Government: Multiparty republic
Currency: Colón = 100 centavos

El Serrat 91 A 7 N Andorra
Elst 86 D 4 E Netherlands
Eltanin Fracture Zone 153 fracture
zone E 5 SE Pacific Ocean
El Tigre 59 E 2 NE Colombia
Elva 106 D 3
Ger. Elwa. SE Estonia
Elvas 92 C 4 C Portugal
El Vendrell 93 G 2 NE Spain
El Vigía 58 C 2 NW Venezuela
Elwa *see* Elva
Elwell, Lake 44 B 1 reservoir,
Montana, NW USA
El Yopal *see* Yopal
Emajõgi 106 D 3 *Ger.* Embach.
River, SE Estonia
Emámrúd 120 D 2 *prev.* Shāhrūd.
N Iran

Emba 114 B 4 *Kaz.* Embi.
W Kazakhstan
Embach *see* Emajõgi
Embi *see* Emba
Emden 94 A 3 NW Germany
Emerald 148 D 4 Queensland,
E Australia
Emerald Isle *see* Montserrat
Emi Koussi 68 C 3 mountain,
N Chad
Emmaste 106 C 2 Hiiumaa,
W Estonia
Emmeloord 86 D 2 N Netherlands
Emmen 86 E 2 NE Netherlands
Emmendingen 95 A 6
SW Germany
Empalme 50 B 2 NW Mexico
Emperor Seamounts 152 C 1
seamount range,
NW Pacific Ocean
Emporia 45 F 5 Kansas, C USA
Ems 94 A 3 *Dut.* Eems. River,
Germany
Encamp 91 A 8 C Andorra
Encarnación 64 D 3 S Paraguay
Encinitas 47 C 8 California, W USA
Encs 99 D 6 NE Hungary
Endeavour 55 G 1 NW Barbados
Endeavour Strait 148 C 1 strait,
Arafura Sea/Coral Sea
Enderbury Island 145 F 3 island,
C Kiribati
Enderby Land 154 D 2 physical
region, Antarctica
Enderby Plain 154 D 1 abyssal
plain, S Indian Ocean
Endersdorf *see* Jędrzejów
Enewetak Atoll 144 C 1
var. Änewetak, Eniwetok. Island,
W Marshall Islands
Enghien 87 B 6 *Dut.* Edingen.
SW Belgium
England 89 D 6 *Lat.* Anglia.
National region, UK
Englewood 44 D 4
Colorado, C USA
English Channel 90 B 2
var. The Channel, *Fr.* la Manche.
Channel, NE Atlantic Ocean
Engure 106 C 3 W Latvia
Engures Ezers 106 C 3 lake,
NW Latvia
Enguri 117 F 1 *Rus.* Inguri. River,
NW Georgia
En Hazeva 119 B 7 S Israel
Enid 47 F 1 Oklahoma, C USA
En Nâqoûra 119 A 5 *var.*
An Nāqūrah. SW Lebanon
Ennedi 76 D 2 plateau, E Chad
Ennis 118 B 4 *Ir.* Inis. W Ireland
Ennis 49 G 3 Texas, S USA
Enniskillen 89 A 5 *var.*
Inniskilling, *Ir.* Inis Ceithleann.
S Northern Ireland, UK
Enns 95 D 6 river, C Austria
Enschede 86 E 3 E Netherlands
Ensenada 50 A 1 NW Mexico
Ensley 42 C 3 Florida, SE USA
Entebbe 73 B 6 S Uganda
Entre Vientos 65 B 8 Chile
Entroncamento 92 B 3 C Portugal
Enugu 75 G 5 S Nigeria
Eolie, Isole 97 D 6 *var.* Isole Lipari,
Eng. Lipari Islands, Aeolian
Islands. Island group, S Italy
Epanomí 104 B 4 N Greece
Épéna 77 C 5 NE Congo
Épi 144 D 4 island, C Vanuatu
Épinal 90 D 4 NE France
Epoon *see* Ebon Atoll

Equatorial Guinea
77 A 5 Guinea. Republic,
C Africa

Official name: Republic of
Equatorial Guinea **Date of
formation:** 1968 **Capital:** Malabo
Population: 400,000 **Total area:**
10,830 sq miles (28,050 sq km)
Languages: Spanish*, Fang
Religions: Christian 89%, other 11%
Ethnic mix: Fang 72%, Bubi 14%,
Duala 3%, other 11% **Government:**
Multiparty republic **Currency:**
CFA franc = 100 centimes

Eravur 132 D 3 E Sri Lanka
Erciş 117 F 3 E Turkey
Erdenet 127 F 2 SE Mongolia
Erdenet 127 E 2 C Mongolia
Erdi 76 D 2 plateau, NE Chad
Erdi Ma 76 D 2 desert, NE Chad
Erebus, Mount 154 C 4 mountain,
Antarctica
Ereğli 116 B 2 NW Turkey
Ereğli 116 C 4 S Turkey
Erenhot 127 F 2 *var.* Erlian. NE China
Erfurt 94 C 4 C Germany
Ergene 116 A 2 *var.* Ergene Irmaêı.
River, NW Turkey
Ergene Irmağı *see* Ergene
Erg Iguîdi 70 C 3 *var.* Erg Iguîdi.
Desert , Algeria/ Mauritania
Erg Iguîdi *see* Erg Iguîdi
Erguig, Bahr 76 C 3 river, SW Chad
Ergun 127 F 1 river, N China
Ergun Zuoqi 127 F 1 N China
Erie 41 E 3 Pennsylvania, NE USA
Érié, Lac *see* Erie, Lake
Erie, Lake 40 D 3 *Fr.* Lac Érié. Lake,
Canada/USA

Eritrea
72 C 4 Transitional government,
NE Africa

Official name: State of Eritrea **Date
of formation:** 1993 **Capital:** Asmara
Population: 3.5 million **Total area:**
36,170 sq miles (93,679 sq km)
Languages: Tigrinya*, Arabic*, Tigre
Religions: Coptic Christian 45%,
Muslim 45%, other 10% **Ethnic mix:**
Nine main Ethnic groups
Government: Provisional military
government **Currency:**
Ethiopian birr = 100 cents

Erivan *see* Yerevan
Erlangen 95 C 5 S Germany
Erlau *see* Eger
Erlian *see* Erenhot
Ermelo 86 D 3 C Netherlands
Ermióni 105 C 6 S Greece
Ermoúpoli 105 D 6
var. Hermoupolis; *prev.*
Ermoúpolis. Kykládes, SE Greece
Ernākulam 132 C 3 SW India
Erode 132 C 3 SE India
Erquelinnes 87 B 7 S Belgium
Er-Rachidia 70 C 2 *var.* al Raudia,
Rashîdîya, Ksar al Soule. E Morocco
Er Rahad 72 B 4 *var.* Ar Rahad.
C Sudan
Erromango 144 D 4 island,
S Vanuatu
Erzerum *see* Erzurum
Erzgebirge 95 D 5 *var.* Krušné Hory,
Eng. Ore Mountains. Mountain
range, Czech Republic/Germany
Erzincan 117 E 3 *var.* Erzinjan.
E Turkey
Erzinjan *see* Erzincan

Erzurum 117 E 3 *prev.* Erzurum.
NE Turkey
Esbjerg 85 A 7 W Denmark
Esbo *see* Espoo
Escaldes 91 A 8 C Andorra
Escanabar 40 C 2 Michigan, N USA
Escárcega 51 G 4 SE Mexico
Esch-sur-Alzette 87 D 8 S Luxembourg
Escondido 47 C 8 California, W USA
Escuinapa 50 C 4 *var.* Escuinapa de
Hidalgo. C Mexico
Escuinapa de Hidalgo *see* Escuinapa
Escuintla 51 G 5 SE Mexico
Escuintla 52 B 3 S Guatemala
Eşfahān 120 D 3 *Eng.* Isfahan;
anc. Aspadana. C Iran
Esil *see* Ishim
Eskimo Point *see* Arviat
Eskişehir 116 B 3 *var.* Eskishehr.
W Turkey
Eskishehr *see* Eskişehir
Esla, Embalse de 92 C 2 *var.* Embalse
de Elsa. Reservoir, NW Spain
Eslāmābād 120 C 3 *var.* Eslāmābād-
e Gharb; *prev.* Shāhābād,
Harunabad. W Iran
Esmeraldas 60 A 1 N Ecuador
Esna *see* Isna
Espanola 48 D 1 New Mexico, SW USA
Esperance 147 C 7
Western Australia, SW Australia
Esperanza 50 B 2 NW Mexico
Esperanza 154 A 2 research station,
Antarctica
Esperanza 60 D 3 E Peru
Espinal 58 B 3 C Colombia
Espinhaço, Serra do 63 F 3
mountain range, SE Brazil
Espírito Santo 63 G 4 *off.* Estado do
Espírito Santo. State, SE Brazil
Espírito Santo, Estado do *see*
Espírito Santo
Espiritu Santo 144 C 4 *var.* Santo.
Island, W Vanuatu
Espoo 85 D 6 *Swe.* Esbo. S Finland
Esquel 65 B 6 SW Argentina
Essaouira 70 B 2 *prev.* Mogador.
W Morocco
Es Semara *see* Smara
Essen 94 A 4 *var.* Essen an der
Ruhr. W Germany
Essen 87 C 5 N Belgium
Essen an der Ruhr *see* Essen
Essequibo 56 C 2 river, C Guyana
Estacado, Llano 49 E 2 plain, SW USA
Estados, Isla de los 65 C 8
prev *Eng.* Staten Island. Island,
S Argentina
Estância 63 G 3 E Brazil
Estelí 52 D 3 NW Nicaragua
Estella 93 E 1 N Spain
Estepona 92 D 5 S Spain
Estevan 37 F 5 Saskatchewan,
S Canada

Estonia
106 D 2 *Est.* Eesti Vabariik,
Ger. Estland, *Latv.* Igaunija; *prev.*
Estonian SSR, *Rus.* Estonskaya
SSR. Republic, E Europe

Official name: Republic of Estonia
Date of formation: 1991 **Capital:**
Tallinn **Population:** 1.6 million **Total
area:** 17,423 sq miles (45,125 sq km)
Languages: Estonian*, Russian
Religions: Evangelical Lutheran
98%, Eastern Orthodox, Baptist 2%
Ethnic mix: Estonian 62%, Russian
30%, Ukrainian 3%, other 5%
Government: Multiparty republic
Currency: Kroon = 100 cents

Estrela, Serra da 92 C 3 mountain
range, C Portugal
Estremoz 92 B 4 C Portugal
Esztergom 99 C 6 *Ger.* Gran;
anc. Strigonium. N Hungary
Etāwa 134 D 3 N India

Ethiopia
73 C 5 *var.* Abyssinia; *prev.*
People's Democratic Republic of
Ethiopia. Republic, NE Africa

Official name: Undetermined **Date
of formation:** 1903/1993 **Capital:**
Addis Ababa **Population:** 56.7
million **Total area:** 435,605 sq miles
(1,128,221 sq km) **Languages:**
Amharic*, English, Arabic
Religions: Muslim 43%, Christian
37%, traditional beliefs, other 20%,
Ethnic mix: Oromo 40%, Amhara
and Tigrean 32%, other 28%
Government: Multiparty republic
Currency: Birr = 100 cents

Ethiopian Highlands *see*
Ethiopian Plateau
Ethiopian Plateau 73 C 5
var. Ethiopian Highlands. Plateau,
N Ethiopia
Etna, Monte 97 C 7 *Eng.* Mount
Etna. Volcano, SW Italy
Etna, Mount *see* Etna, Monte
Etosha Pan 78 B 3 salt lake,
N Namibia
Etoumbi 77 B 5 NW Congo
Etsch *see* Adige
Ettelbrück 87 D 8 C Luxembourg
'Eua 145 E 5 *prev.* Middleburg
Island. Island, S Tonga
Euboea *see* Évvoia
Eucla 147 D 6 Western Australia,
S Australia
Euclid 40 D 3 Ohio, N USA
Eufaula 42 D 3 Alabama, S USA
Eufaula Lake 49 G 1 *var.* Eufaula
Reservoir. Reservoir, Oklahoma,
C USA
Eufaula Reservoir *see* Eufaula Lake
Eugene 46 B 3 Oregon, NW USA
Eunice 42 B 3 Louisiana, S USA
Eupen 87 D 6 E Belgium
Euphrates 120 C 3 *var.* Firat Nehri,
Al-Furat. River, SW Asia
Eureka 37 F 1 Ellesmere Island,
Canada
Eureka 47 A 5 California, W USA
Eureka 44 A 1 Montana, NW USA
Europa Point 93 H 5 headland,
S Gibraltar
Europe 66 E 3 continent
Euskirchen 95 A 5 W Germany
Eutin 94 C 2 N Germany
Evansdale 45 G 3 Iowa, C USA
Evanston 40 B 3 Illinois, N USA
Evanston 44 B 4 Wyoming, C USA
Evansville 40 B 5 Indiana, N USA
Eveleth 45 G 1 Minnesota, N USA
Everard, Lake 149 A 6 salt lake,
S Australia
Everest, Mount 124 C 3
Chin. Qomolangma Feng,
Nep. Sagarmatha. Mountain,
China/Nepal
Everett 46 B 2
Washington, NW USA
Everglades, The 43 E 5 wetland,
Florida, SE USA
Evje 85 A 6 S Norway
Évora 92 B 4 *Lat.* Liberalitas Julia,
anc. Ebora. C Portugal
Évreux 90 C 3 *anc.* Civitas
Eburovicum. N France

Évry 90 C 3 N France
Evstratios, Ayios *see* Efstrátios, Ágios
Évvoia 105 C 5 *Lat.* Euboea. Island,
Kykládes, C Greece
Ewarton 54 B 5 C Jamaica
Excelsior Springs 45 F 4
Missouri, C USA
Exe 89 C 7 river, SW England, UK
Exeter 89 C 7 *anc.* Isca
Damnoniorum. SW England, UK
Exmoor 89 C 7 heathland,
SW England, UK
Exmouth 89 C 7 SW England, UK
Exmouth 146 A 4 Western
Australia, W Australia
Exmouth Gulf 146 A 4 gulf,
W Indian Ocean
Exmouth Plateau 141 E 5 undersea
plateau, E Indian Ocean
Extremadura 92 C 3 cultural region,
W Spain
Exuma Cayes 54 C 1 island group,
C Bahamas
Eyre 147 D 6 Western Australia,
W Australia
Eyre Mountains 151 A 7 mountain
range, South Island,
SW New Zealand
Eyre North, Lake 149 B 5
salt lake, S Australia
Eyre Peninsula 149 A 6
peninsula, S Australia
Eyre South, Lake 149 B 5
salt lake, S Australia
Ezequiel Ramos Mexía, Embalse 65
B 5 lake, C Argentina

F

Faadhippolhu Atoll 132 B 4
var. Fadiffolu, Lhaviyani Atoll.
Island, N Maldives
Fabens 48 D 3 Texas, S USA
Fada 76 C 2 E Chad
Fada-Ngourma 75 E 4 E Burkina
Fadghāmī *see* Tall Fadghāmī
Faenza 96 C 3 *anc.* Faventia. N Italy
Faeroe-Iceland Ridge 80 C 1
undersea ridge,
NW Norwegian Sea
Faeroe Islands 83 F 5 *Dan.*
Færøerne, *Faer.* Føroyar. Danish
external territory,
N Atlantic Ocean
Faeroe Islands 66 D 2 island group,
NE Atlantic Ocean
Faetano 96 E 2 E San Marino
Făgăraş 108 C 4 *Ger.* Fogarasch,
Hung. Fogaras. C Romania
Fagibina, Lake *see* Faguibine, Lac
Fagne 87 C 7 hill range, S Belgium
Faguibine, Lac 75 E 3 *var.* Lake
Fagibina. Lake, NW Mali
Fahlun *see* Falun
Fahraj 120 E 4 SE Iran
Faial 92 A 5 *var.* Ilha do Faial.
Island, W Portugal
Faial, Ilha do *see* Faial
Faifo *see* Hôi An
Fairbanks 36 C 3 Alaska, NW USA
Fairfield 47 B 6 California, W USA
Fair Isle 88 D 2 island,
NE Scotland, UK
Fairlie 151 B 6 South Island,
SW New Zealand
Fairmont 45 F 3 Minnesota, N USA
Faisalābād 134 C 2 *prev.* Lyallpur.
NE Pakistan
Faizābād 135 E 3 N India
Fakaofo Atoll 145 F 3 island,
SE Tokelau

Falam 136 A 3 NW Myanmar
Falconara Marittima 96 C 3 C It
Falkland Islands 65 C 7 island
group, SW Atlantic Ocean
Falkland Plateau 57 D 7 *var.*
Argentine Rise. Undersea plat
SW Atlantic Ocean
Fallbrook 47 C 8 California, W U
Falmouth 89 C 8 SW England, L
Falmouth 54 A 4 W Jamaica
Fălticeni 108 C 3 *Hung.* Falticsér
NE Romania
Falticsén *see* Fălticeni
Falun 85 C 5 *var.* Fahlun. C Swe
Famenne 87 C 7 physical region
SE Belgium
Fang 136 C 3 N Thailand
Fanling 128 A 1 N Hong Kong
Fanning Island *see* Tabuaeran
Fano 96 C 3 *anc.* Fanum Fortuna
Colonia Julia Fanestris. C Italy
Farafangana 79 G 4 SE Madagas
Farafra Oasis 72 B 2 *var.* Wāhat
Farāfra. Oasis, C Egypt
Farāfra, Wāhat el *see* Farafra Oas
Farāh 122 D 4 *var.* Farah, Fararu
W Afghanistan
Faranah 74 C 4 S Guinea
Farewell, Cape 150 C 4 headlan
South Island, C New Zealand
Farghona 123 F 2 *Rus.* Fergana;
prev. Novyy Margilan .
E Uzbekistan
Fargo 45 F 2 North Dakota, N U
Faribault 45 F 3 Minnesota, N U
Farīdābād 134 D 3 N India
Farkhor 123 E 3 *Rus.* Parkhar.
SW Tajikistan
Farmington 48 C 1
New Mexico, SW USA
Farmington 45 G 5
Missouri, C USA
Faro 92 B 5 S Portugal
Farquhar Group 79 G 2 island
group, S Seychelles
Fastiv 109 E 2 *Rus.* Fastov.
NW Ukraine
Fastov *see* Fastiv
Fauske 84 C 3 C Norway
Faventia *see* Faenza
Faxa Bay *see* Faxaflói
Faxaflói 83 E 5 *Eng.* Faxa Bay. Ba
N Atlantic Ocean
Faya 76 C 2 *prev.* Faya-Largeau,
Largeau. N Chad
Fayetteville 42 A 1
Arkansas, SE USA
Fayetteville 43 F 1
North Carolina, SE USA
Fazzān 71 F 4 *Eng.* Fezzan.
Cultural region, W Libya
Færingehavn 82 B 4 *var.*
Kangerluarsoruseq. S Greenla
Fdérik 74 C 2 *var.* Fdérick, Fdér
Fr. Fort Gouraud. NW Maurit
Fear, Cape 43 F 2 headland,
North Carolina, SE USA
Fécamp 90 B 3 N France
Fédala *see* Mohammedia
Federal Capital Territory *see*
Australian Capital Territory
Fehérgyarmat 99 E 6 E Hungary
Fehmarn 94 C 2 island, N Germ
Feijó 62 C 2 W Brazil
Feilding 150 D 4 North Island,
C New Zealand
Feira *see* Feira de Santana
Feira de Santana 63 G 3 *var.* Fei
E Brazil
Felanitx 93 H 3 *anc.* Canati,
Felaniche. E Spain

kirchen in Kärnten 95 D 7
vn. Trg.
gyháza *see* Kiskunfélegyháza
lhu Atoll 132 B 4 island,
  Maldives
pe Carrillo Puerto 51 H 4
  Mexico
kstowe 89 E 6 E England, UK
n *see* Viljandi
erbælt 94 C 2 *Dan.* Femer Bælt,
er. Fehmarnbelt.
Channel,
N Baltic Sea
unden 85 B 5 lake, S Norway
érive *see* Fenoarivo Atsinanana
gcheng 128 D 3 *var.* Feng-cheng,
p. Fenghwangcheng. NE China
parivo Atsinanana 79 G 3
ev. Fénérive. NE Madagascar
s, The 89 E 6 wetland,
  England, UK
losiya 109 G 5 *var.* Kefe,
  Kaffa; *anc.* Theodosia.
  Ukraine
s 104 D 3 NE Greece
us Falls 45 F 2
linnesota, N USA
aj see Uroševac
aandina, Isla 60 A 5
r. Narborough Island. Island,
alapagos Islands,
Pacific Ocean
aando de la Mora 64 D 2
Paraguay
aando de Noronha 63 H 2
and, E Brazil
ara 96 C 2 *anc.* Forum Alieni.
  Italy
ol 92 B 1 *var.* El Ferrol; *prev.*
  Ferrol del Caudillo. NW Spain
5 *see* Neusiedler See
70 C 2 *Eng.* Fez. N Morocco
iye 116 B 4 SW Turkey
ar 88 D 1 island,
E Scotland, UK
zābād 123 F 3 *var.* Faizabad,
aizābād, Feyzābād, Fyzabad.
E Afghanistan
see Fès
an *see* Fazzān
arantsoa 79 F 3 C Madagascar
ga 76 B 4 SW Chad
101 C 6 *var.* Fieri, SW Albania
see Fier
ac 91 C 5 S France
g *see* Figuig
eira da Foz 92 B 3 W Portugal
eres 93 G 2 E Spain
ig 70 D 2 *var.* Figig. E Morocco

5 E 5 *Fij.* Viti. Republic,
N Pacific Ocean

cial name: Sovereign
ocratic Republic of Fiji Date of
ation: 1970 Capital: Suva
lation: 700,000 Total Area:
 sq miles (18,270 sq km)
guages: English*, Fijian, Hindu,
a, Tamil, Telugu Religions:
stian 52%, Hindu 8%, Muslim
 49%, Indo-Fijian 46%, other
ther 2% Ethnic mix: Native
Government: Multiparty
blic Currency: Fiji $ = 100 cents

lelfia 52 D 4 W Costa Rica
și 108 B 5 SW Romania
istad 85 B 6 C Sweden
e Ligure 96 A 3 Italy
lay 40 D 4 Ohio, N USA
ke 116 B 4 SW Turkey

Finland
84 D 4 *Fin.* Suomen Tasavalta,
Suomi. Republic, N Europe

Official name: Republic of Finland
Date of formation: 1917/1920
Capital: Helsinki **Population:** 5
million **Total Area:** 130,552 sq miles
(338,130 sq km) **Languages:**
Finnish*, Swedish, Lappish
Religions: Evangelical Lutheran
89%, Greek Orthodox 1%, other 10%
Ethnic mix: Finnish 93%, Swedish
6%, other (inc. Sami)1%
Government: Multiparty republic
Currency: Markka = 100 pennia

Finland, Gulf of 85 E 6 *Est.* Soome
Laht, *Fin.* Suomenlahti,
Ger. Finnischer Meerbusen,
Rus. Finskiy Zaliv, *Swe.* Finska
Viken. Gulf, Atlantic Ocean/
Baltic Sea
Finnmarksvidda 84 D 2 physical
region, N Norway
Finsterwalde 94 D 4 E Germany
Fiorina 96 E 1 NE San Marino
Firenze 96 C 4 *Eng.* Florence;
anc. Florentia. C Italy
Fischbacher Alpen 95 E 7 mountain
range, E Austria
Fischhausen *see* Primorsk
Fish 78 B 4 *var.* Vis. River, S Namibia
Fishguard 89 B 6 *Wel.* Abergwaun.
SW Wales, UK
Fiskenæsset *see* Qeqertarsuatsiaat
Fisterra, Cabo 92 B 1 headland,
NW Spain
Fitzgerald 43 E 3 Georgia, SE USA
Fitzroy 146 C 3 river, Western
Australia, N Australia
Fitzroy Crossing 146 C 3
Western Australia, NW Australia
Flagstaff 48 B 2 Arizona, SW USA
Flanders 87 A 6 *Dut.* Vlaanderen,
Fr. Flandre. Cultural region,
Belgium/France
Flathead Lake 44 B 1 lake,
Montana, NW USA
Flatts Village 42 B 5 *var.* The Flatts
Village. C Bermuda
Flensburg 94 B 2 N Germany
Flinders 148 C 3 river, N Australia
Flinders Bay 147 A 7 bay,
SE Indian Ocean
Flinders Island 149 C 8 island,
Tasmania, SE Australia
Flinders Island 149 A 6 island,
South Australia, S Australia
Flinders Ranges 149 B 6 mountain
range, S Australia
Flinders Reefs 148 D 3 reef,
W Coral Sea
Flin Flon 37 F 5 Manitoba, C Canada
Flint 40 D 3 Michigan, N USA
Flint 145 H 4 island,
E Kiribati
Florence 43 F 2
South Carolina, SE USA
Florencia 58 B 4 S Colombia
Flores 92 A 5 island, W Portugal
Flores 52 B 1 N Guatemala
Flores 139 E 5 island, Nusa
Tenggara, C Indonesia
Flores, Laut 139 E 5 *Eng.* Flores Sea.
Sea, W Pacific Ocean
Flores Sea *see* Flores, Laut
Floriano 63 F 2 E Brazil
Florianópolis 63 F 5 *prev.* Destêrro.
State capital, S Brazil
Florida 33 E 4 *off.* State of Florida;
nicknames Peninsular State,
Sunshine State. State, SE USA

Florida 64 D 4 S Uruguay
Florida Bay 43 E 5 bay,
E Gulf of Mexico
Florida Keys 43 E 5 island,
Florida, SE USA
Florida Negra 65 C 7 SE Argentina
Florida, Straits of 43 F 5 strait,
W Atlantic Ocean
Flórina 104 B 4 *var.* Phlórina.
N Greece
Florissant 45 C 4 Missouri, C USA
Flóuda, Ákra 105 D 7 Headland,
Astypálaia, SE Greece
Flylân *see* Vlieland
Foča 100 C 4
SE Bosnia & Herzegovina
Focșani 108 C 4 E Romania
Foggia 97 D 5 SE Italy
Fogi 139 F 4 E Indonesia
Fogo 74 A 3 island, SW Cape Verde
Foix 91 B 6 S France
Folégandros 105 C 7 island,
Kykládes, SE Greece
Foleyet 38 C 4 Ontario, S Canada
Foligno 96 C 4 C Italy
Folkestone 89 E 7 SE England, UK
Folsom 47 B 5 California, W USA
Fond-du-Lac 37 F 4 Saskatchewan,
C Canada
Fongafale 145 E 3 *var.* Funafuti.
Country capital, Funafuti,
C Tuvalu
Fonseca, Golfo de *see* Fonseca,
Gulf of
Fonseca, Gulf of 52 C 3 *Sp.* Golfo
de Fonseca. Gulf, E Pacific Ocean
Fontainebleau 90 C 3 N France
Fontenay-le-Comte 90 A 4
NW France
Fonyód 99 C 7 W Hungary
Forchheim 95 C 5 SE Germany
Forel, Mount 82 D 4 mountain,
SE Greenland
Forfar 88 C 3 NE Scotland, UK
Forlì 96 C 3 *var.* Forum Livii.
N Italy
Formentera 93 G 4 *anc.* Ophiusa,
Lat. Frumentum. Island, E Spain
Formosa 64 D 3 NE Argentina
Formosa Bay 73 D 7 *var.* Ungama
Bay. Bay, NW Indian Ocean
Formosa, Serra 63 E 3 mountain
range, C Brazil
Fort Albany 38 C 3 Ontario,
C Canada
Fort-Archambault *see* Sarh
Fortaleza 63 G 2 *prev.* Ceará. State
capital, NE Brazil
Fortaleza 61 F 2 N Bolivia
Fort-Charlet *see* Djanet
Fort-Chimo *see* Kuujjuaq
Fort Collins 44 D 4 Colorado, C USA
Fort-Crampel *see* Kaga Bandoro
Fort-de-France 55 H 4 *prev.* Fort-
Royal. Dependent territory
capital, W Martinique
Fort Dodge 45 F 3 Iowa, C USA
Fortescue 146 B 4 river,
W Australia
Fort-Foureau *see* Kousséri
Fort Frances 38 B 4 Ontario,
S Canada
Fort Good Hope 37 E 4 *var.* Good
Hope. Northwest Territories,
NW Canada
Forth 88 C 4 river, S Scotland, UK
Forth, Firth of 88 D 4 estuary,
E Scotland, UK
Fortín General Diaz 64 D 2
W Paraguay
Fort Jameson *see* Chipata

Fort Lauderdale 43 F 5
Florida, SE USA
Fort Liard 37 E 4 *var.* Liard.
Northwest Territories, W Canada
Fort Madison 45 G 4 Iowa, C USA
Fort McMurray 37 F 4 Alberta,
C Canada
Fort McPherson 36 D 3
var. McPherson. Northwest
Territories, NW Canada
Fort Morgan 44 D 4 Colorado, C USA
Fort Myers 43 E 5 Florida, SE USA
Fort Nelson 37 E 4 British
Columbia, W Canada
Fort Peck Lake 44 C 1 reservoir,
Montana, NW USA
Fort Pierce 43 F 4 Florida, SE USA
Fort Providence 37 E 4 *var.*
Providence. Northwest
Territories, W Canada
Fort-Repoux *see* Akjoujt
Fort Rosebery *see* Mansa
Fort-Rousset *see* Owando
Fort-Royal *see* Fort-de-France
Fort St.John 37 E 5 British
Columbia, W Canada
Fort Scott 45 F 5 Kansas, C USA
Fort Severn 38 C 2 Ontario,
C Canada
Fort-Shevchenko 114 A 4
W Kazakhstan
Fort-Sibut *see* Sibut
Fort Simpson 37 E 4 *var.* Simpson.
Northwest Territories, W Canada
Fort Smith 37 F 4 Northwest
Territories, W Canada
Fort Smith 42 A 1 Arkansas, C USA
Fort Stockton 49 E 3 Texas, S USA
Fort Vermilion 37 E 4 Alberta,
W Canada
Fort Walton Beach 42 D 3
Florida, SE USA
Fort Wayne 40 C 4 Indiana, N USA
Fort William 88 B 3 W Scotland, UK
Fort Worth 49 G 3 Texas, S USA
Fort Yukon 36 D 3 Alaska, NW USA
Forum Alieni *see* Ferrara
Forum Livii *see* Forlì
Fossa Claudia *see* Chioggia
Fougamou 77 A 6 C Gabon
Fougères 90 B 3 NW France
Foulwind, Cape 151 B 5 headland,
South Island, C New Zealand
Foumban 76 A 4 NW Cameroon
Fouta Djallon 68 A 4 *var.* Futa Jallon.
Mountain range, W Guinea
Foveaux Strait 151 A 8 strait,
S Pacific Ocean
Fowlers Bay 147 E 6 bay, Great
Australian Bight/Indian Ocean
Foxe Basin 82 B 2 sea area basin,
NE Hudson Bay
Fox Mine 37 F 4 Manitoba, C Canada
Fraga 93 F 2 NE Spain

France
90 A 4 *It./Sp.* Francia; *prev.* Gaul,
Gaule, *Lat.* Gallia. Republic,
W Europe

Official name: The French Republic
Date of formation: 1685/1920
Capital: Paris **Population:** 57.4
million **Total Area:** 212,930 sq miles
(551,500 sq km) **Languages:** French*,
Provençal, Breton, German, Basque
Religions: Roman Catholic 90%,
Protestant 2%, Jewish 1%, other 7%
Ethnic mix: French 92%, North
African 3%, other 5% **Government:**
Multiparty republic **Currency:**
Franc = 100 cents

Franceville 77 B 6 *var.* Massoukou, Masuku. E Gabon
Franche-Comté 90 D 4 cultural region, E France
Francis Case, Lake 45 E 3 reservoir, South Dakota, N USA
Francisco Beltrão 63 E 5 S Brazil
Francistown 78 D 3 NE Botswana
Frankfort 40 C 5 state capital, Kentucky, E USA
Frankfurt *see* Słubice
Frankfurt am Main 95 B 5 *var.* Frankfurt, *Fr.* Francfort; *prev. Eng.* Frankfort on the Main. SW Germany
Frankfurt an der Oder 94 D 3 E Germany
Fränkische Alb 95 C 6 *var.* Frankenalb, *Eng.* Franconian Jura. Mountain range, S Germany
Franklin 42 C 1 Tennessee, S USA
Franklin D.Roosevelt Lake 46 C 1 reservoir, Washington, NW USA
Frantsa-Iosifa, Zemlya 114 D 1 *Eng.* Franz Josef Land. Island group, N Russian Federation
Franz Josef Land *see* Frantsa-Iosifa, Zemlya
Fraserburgh 88 D 3 NE Scotland, UK
Fraser Island 148 E 4 *var.* Great Sandy Island island, E Australia
Frauenburg *see* Saldus
Frederick Reef 148 E 4 reef, W Coral Sea
Fredericksburg 41 E 5 Virginia, NE USA
Fredericton 39 F 4 New Brunswick, SE Canada
Frederiksdal *see* Narsaq Kujalleq
Fredrikshald *see* Halden
Fredrikstad 85 B 6 S Norway
Freeport 54 C 1 N Bahamas
Freeport 49 H 4 Texas, S USA
Freetown 74 C 4 country capital, W Sierra Leone
Freiburg im Breisgau 95 A 6 *var.* Freiburg, *Fr.* Fribourg-en-Brisgau. SW Germany
Fremantle 147 B 6 Western Australia, SW Australia
Fremont 47 B 6 California, W USA
Fremont 45 F 4 Nebraska, C USA
French Guiana 59 H 3 *var.* Guiana, Guyane. French overseas department, NE South America
French Polynesia 145 G 5 French overseas territory, S Pacific Ocean
French Southern & Antarctic Territories 141 C 6 *Fr.* Terres Australes et Antarctiques Françaises. French overseas territory, S Indian Ocean
Fresnillo 50 D 3 *var.* Fresnillo de Gonzales Echeverria, Fresnillo de González Echeverría. C Mexico
Fresno 47 C 6 California, W USA
Freyming-Merlebach 90 E 3 NE France
Frías 64 C 3 N Argentina
Friedek-Mistek *see* Frýdek-Místek
Friedrichshafen 95 B 7 S Germany
Frobisher Bay *see* Iqaluit
Frohavet 84 B 4 sound, SE Norwegian Sea
Frolovo 111 B 6 SW Russian Federation
Frome, Lake 149 B 6 salt lake, S Australia
Frontera 51 G 4 SE Mexico
Frontignan 91 C 6 S France
Frostviken *see* Kvarnbergsvattnet

Frøya 84 A 4 island, W Norway
Frutal 63 F 4 SE Brazil
Frýdek-Místek 99 C 5 *Ger.* Friedek-Mistek. SE Czech Republic
Fuengirola 92 D 5 S Spain
Fuerte Olimpo 64 D 2 *var.* Olimpo. NE Paraguay
Fuerteventura 70 B 3 island, Islas Canarias, SW Spain
Fuji 131 D 6 *var.* Huzi. Honshū, S Japan
Fujian 129 D 6 *var.* Fu-chien, Fuhkien, Fukien, Min. Province, SE China
Fuji-san 131 D 6 *var.* Fujiyama, Mount Fuji. Mountain, Honshū, SE Japan
Fukang 126 C 2 W China
Fukui 131 C 6 *var.* Hukui. Honshū, SW Japan
Fukuoka 131 A 7 *var.* Hukuoka; *hist.* Najima. Kyūshū, SW Japan
Fukushima 130 D 4 *var.* Hukusima. Honshū, C Japan
Fulda 95 B 5 C Germany
Funafuti 145 E 3 island, C Tuvalu
Funafuti *see* Fongafale
Funchal 70 A 2 Madeira, SW Portugal
Fundy, Bay of 39 F 5 inlet, NW Atlantic Ocean
Fünen *see* Fyn
Fung Wong Shan *see* Lantau Peak
Furnes *see* Veurne
Fürth 95 C 5 S Germany
Furukawa 130 D 4 *var.* Hurukawa. Honshū, C Japan
Fushun 128 D 3 *var.* Fou-shan, Fu-shun. NE China
Füssen 95 C 7 S Germany
Futa Jallon *see* Fouta Djallon
Futog 100 D 3 N Yugoslavia
Futuna, Île 145 E 4 island, N Wallis & Futuna
Fuxin 128 D 3 *var.* Fou-hsin, Fu-hsin, Fusin. NE China
Fuzhou 129 D 6 *var.* Foochow, Fu-chou. Province capital, SE China
Fyn 85 B 8 *Ger.* Fünen. Island, C Denmark

G

Gaafu Alifu Atoll *see* North Huvadhu Atoll
Gaafu Dhaalu Atoll *see* South Huvadhu Atoll
Gaalkacyo 73 E 5 *var.* Galka'yo', *It.* Galcaio. C Somalia
Gabela 78 B 2 W Angola
Gaberones *see* Gaborone
Gabès 71 E 2 *var.* Qābis. E Tunisia
Gabès, Golfe de 71 F 2 *Ar.* Khalīj Qābis. Gulf, S Mediterranean Sea

Gabon
77 B 6 Republic, C Africa

Official name: The Gabonese Republic **Date of formation:** 1960 **Capital:** Libreville **Population:** 1.3 million **Total area:** 103,347 sq miles (267,670 sq km) **Languages:** French*, Fang **Religions:** Roman Catholic, other Christian 96%, Muslim 2%, other 2% **Ethnic mix:** Fang 36%, Mpongwe 15%, Mbete 14%, other 35% **Government:** Multiparty republic **Currency:** CFA franc = 100 centimes

Gaborone 78 C 4 *prev.* Gaberones. Country capital, SE Botswana

Gabrovo 104 D 2 C Bulgaria
Gadsden 42 D 2 Alabama, S USA
Gaeta 97 C 5 Italy
Gaeta, Golfo di 97 C 5 *var.* Gulf of Gaeta Gulf, E Tyrrhenian Sea
Gaeta, Gulf of *see* Gaeta, Golfo di
Gafsa 71 E 2 *var.* Qafṣah. W Tunisia
Gagnoa 74 D 5 C Ivory Coast
Gagra 117 E 1 NW Georgia
Gaillac 91 C 6 *var.* Gaillac-sur-Tarn. S France
Gaillac-sur-Tarn *see* Gaillac
Gaillimh *see* Galway
Gaillimhe, Cuan na *see* Galway Bay
Gailtaler Alpen 95 D 7 mountain range, S Austria
Gainesville 42 D 2 Georgia, SE USA
Gainesville 43 E 3 Florida, SE USA
Gainesville 49 G 2 Texas, S USA
Gairdner, Lake 149 A 6 salt lake, S Australia
Gaizin *see* Gaizina Kalns
Gaizina Kalns 106 D 4 *var.* Gaiziņ. Mountain, E Latvia
Galán, Cerro 64 B 2 mountain, N Argentina
Galanta 99 C 6 *Hung.* Galánta. SW Slovakia
Galánta *see* Galanta
Galapagos Fracture Zone 153 E 3 fracture zone, C Pacific Ocean
Galapagos Islands 153 G 3 *var.* Archipiélago de Colón. island group, E Pacific Ocean
Galapagos Rise 153 F 3 undersea rise, E Pacific Ocean
Galashiels 88 D 4 SE Scotland, UK
Galaţi 108 D 5 *Ger.* Galatz. E Romania
Galatz *see* Galaţi
Galesburg 40 B 4 Illinois, N USA
Galibi 59 H 3 NE Suriname
Galicia 92 B 1 cultural region, NW Spain
Galiuro Mountains 48 B 3 mountain range, Arizona, SW USA
Gallatin 42 D 1 Tennessee, S USA
Galle 132 D 4 *prev.* Point de Galle. SW Sri Lanka
Gallego Rise 153 F 3 undersea rise, E Pacific Ocean
Gallipoli 97 E 6 SW Italy
Gällivare 84 D 3 N Sweden
Gallup 48 C 1 New Mexico, SW USA
Galveston 49 H 4 Texas, S USA
Galveston Bay 49 H 4 bay, N Gulf of Mexico
Galway 89 A 6 *Ir.* Gaillimh. W Ireland
Galway Bay 89 A 6 *Ir.* Cuan na Gaillimhe. Bay, NE Atlantic Ocean
Gámas *see* Kaamanen
Gambell 36 B 2 Saint Lawrence Island, Alaska, USA
Gambia 74 C 3 river, Gambia/Senegal

Gambia
74 B 3 Republic, W Africa

Official name: Republic of The Gambia **Date of formation:** 1965 **Capital:** Banjul **Population:** 900,000 **Total area:** 4,363 sq miles (11,300 sq km) **Languages:** English* **Religions:** Muslim 85%, Christian 9%, traditional beliefs 6% **Ethnic mix:** Mandinka 41%, Fulani 14%, Wolof 13%, other 32% **Government:** Military regime **Currency:** Dalasi = 100 butut

Gambier, Îles 153 E 4 island grou E French Polynesia
Gamboma 77 B 6 E Congo
Gan 132 B 5 C Maldives
Gäncä 117 G 2 *Rus.* Gyandzha; *prev.* Kirovabad, Yelisavetpol. W Azerbaijan
Gandajika 77 D 7 S Congo (Zaire
Gander 39 G 3 Newfoundland and Labrador, SE Canada
Gandía 93 F 4 E Spain
Ganges 135 G 4 *Ben.* Padma. Riv Bangladesh/India
Ganges Cone *see* Ganges Fan
Ganges Fan 140 D 3 *var.* Ganges Cone. Undersea fan, N Indian Ocean
Ganges, Mouths of the 135 G 4 delta, Bangladesh/India
Ganges Plain 124 C 3 plain, India/Pakistan
Gangtok 135 G 3 NE India
Gansu 128 B 4 *var.* Gan,Kansu. Province, N China
Ganzhou 129 C 6 S China
Gao 75 E 3 E Mali
Gaoligong Shan 136 B 1 mounta range, Myanmar/China
Gaoual 74 C 4 N Guinea
Gap 91 D 6 *var.* Vapincum. SE Fra
Garabogazköl Bogazy *see* Kara-Bogaz-Gol, Proliv
Garachiné 53 G 5 SE Panama
Garagum Kanaly *see* Karakumskiy Kanal
Garagumy 122 C 3 *var.* Black Sanc Desert, Qara Qum, *Eng.* Kara Kum, *Turkm.* Garagum; *prev.* Pe Karakumy. Desert, C Turkmenis
Gara Khitrino 104 D 2 NE Bulga
Gárassavon *see* Kaaresuvanto
Garbsen 94 B 3 N Germany
Garda, Lago di 96 C 2 *var.* Benac *Eng.* Lake Garda, *Ger.* Gardase Lake, NE Italy
Garden City 45 E 5 Kansas, C U
Gardēz 123 E 4 *var.* Gardez, Gardez, Gordiaz. E Afghanista
Garegegasnjárga *see* Karigasnien
Gargždai 106 B 3 W Lithuania
Garissa 73 D 6 E Kenya
Garland 49 G 2 Texas, S USA
Garmo, Qullai 123 F 3 *Eng.* Communism Peak, *Rus.* Kommunizma Pik; *prev.* Stalin Peak. Mountain, E Tajikistan
Garoe *see* Garoowe
Garonne 91 B 5 *anc.* Garumna. River, S France
Garoowe 73 E 5 *var.* Garoe. N Som
Garoua 76 B 4 *var.* Garua. N Camer
Garrygala *see* Kara-Kala
Garsen 73 D 6 SE Kenya
Garua *see* Garoua
Garumna *see* Garonne
Garwolin 98 D 4 E Poland
Gar Xincun 126 A 4 *var.* Gar. W Ch
Gary 40 B 3 Indiana, N USA
Garzón 58 B 4 S Colombia
Gascogne 91 B 6 *Eng.* Gascony. Cultural region, S France
Gascogne, Golfe de *see* Gascony, Gulf of
Gascony *see* Gascogne
Gascony, Gulf of 91 A 6 *var.* Golfe Gascogne, *Sp.* Golfo de Vizcaya. Gulf, SW France
Gascoyne 147 B 5 river, W Austr
Gaspé 39 F 4 Québec, SE Canad
Gaspé, Péninsule de 39 F 4 *var.* Péninsule de la Gaspésie. Peninsula, Québec, SE Canada

pésie, Péninsule de la see
 aspé, Péninsule de
 oúni 105 B 6 S Greece
 hina 110 B 4 var. Gatčina
 W Russian Federation
 ina see Gatchina
 neau 38 D 4 Québec, SE Canada
 oma see Kadoma
 n, Lago 53 F 5 reservoir,
 Panama
 häti see Guwāhāti
 ja 106 D 3 Ger. Aa. River,
 atvia/Estonia
 bandī 120 D 4 S Iran
 ere 87 B 6 NW Belgium
 e 85 C 5 var. Gäfle; prev. Gefle.
 Sweden
 ler 149 B 6 South Australia,
 Australia
 a 135 F 4 N India
 a see Kyjov
 sin see Haysyn
 119 A 6 Ar. Ghazzah,
 b. 'Azza. NE Gaza Strip
 Achak 122 D 2 Turkm. Gazojak.
 E Turkmenistan
 lkent see Ghazalkent
 ndzhyk 122 B 2 Turkm.
 azanjyk; prev. Kazandzhik.
 Turkmenistan
 Strip 119 A 7 Ar. Qita Ghazzah.
 sputed region, SW Asia
 antep 116 D 4 var. Gazi Antep;
 v. Aintab, Antep. S Turkey
 paşa 116 C 5 Turkey
 i 122 D 2 C Uzbekistan
 jak see Gaz-Achak
 isk 98 C 2 Fr. Dantzig,
 r. Danzig.
 gen see Gdynia
 nia 98 C 2 Ger. Gdingen.
 Poland
 aref 72 C 4 var. Al Qaḍārif,
 Gedaref. E Sudan
 iz 116 A 3 river, W Turkey
 iz 116 B 3 W Turkey
 87 C 5 var. Gheel. N Belgium
 long 149 C 7 Victoria,
 E Australia
 o 85 A 5 S Norway
 u 129 B 6 var. Kochiu. S China
 97 C 7 prev. Terranova
 Sicilia. SW Italy
 dermalsen 86 C 4 C Netherlands
 en 87 D 6 SE Netherlands
 b see Jilib
 nsoor see Gellinsoor
 insoor 73 E 5 var. Gelinsoor.
 Somalia
 bloux 87 C 6 C Belgium
 ena 77 C 5 NW Congo (Zaire)
 erek 116 D 3 Turkey
 ona del Friuli 96 D 2 NE Italy
 ck see Genk
 eral Alvear 64 B 4 W Argentina
 eral Carrera, Lago see
 uenos Aires, Lago
 eral Eugenio A.Garay 64 C 1
 W Paraguay
 eral José F.Uriburu see Zárate
 eral Santos 139 F 3 off. General
 antos City. Mindanao,
 Philippines
 eral Santos City see
 eneral Santos
 eva, Lake 95 A 7 var. le Léman,
 . Lac Léman, Lac de Genève,
 r. Genfer See. Lake,
 rance/Switzerland
 ève 95 A 8 Eng. Geneva, Ger.
 enf, It. Ginevra. SW Switzerland

Genichesk see Heniches'k
Genk 87 D 6 var. Genck.
Gennep 86 D 4 SE Netherlands
Genoa see Genova
Genoa, Gulf of see Genova, Golfo di
Genova 96 A 2 Eng. Genoa,
 Fr. Gênes, anc. Genua. NW Italy
Genova, Golfo di 96 A 3 Eng. Gulf
 of Genoa. Gulf, N Ligurian Sea
Genovesa, Isla 60 B 5 var. Tower
 Island. Island, Galapagos Islands,
 E Pacific Ocean
Gent 87 B 5 Eng. Ghent, Fr. Gand.
 NW Belgium
Geographe Bay 147 A 7 bay,
 E Indian Ocean
Geok-Tepe 122 C 3 var. Gëkdepe,
 Turkm. Gökdepe. C Turkmenistan
George 78 C 5 S South Africa
George, Lake 43 E 4 lake,
 Florida, SE USA
Georges Bank 35 D 5 undersea
 bank, W Atlantic Ocean
George Sound 151 A 7 sound,
 S Tasman Sea
George Town 54 C 2 C Bahamas
George Town 54 B 3 var.
 Georgetown. Dependent territory
 capital, SW Cayman Islands
George Town 138 B 3 var. Penang,
 Pinang. Pulau Pinang, W Malaysia
Georgetown 43 F 2
 South Carolina, SE USA
Georgetown 59 G 2 country capital,
 N Guyana
Georgetown see George Town
Georgia 42 D 2 off. State of Georgia;
 nicknames Empire State of the
 South, Peach State. State, SE USA

Georgia
117 H 2 Geor. Sak'art'velo, Rus.
 Gruzinskaya SSR, Gruziya; prev.
 Georgian SSR. Republic, SW Asia
Official name: Republic of Georgia
Date of formation: 1991 Capital:
 Tbilisi Population: 5.6 million Total
 area: 26,911 sq miles (69,700 sq km)
Languages: Georgian*, Russian
Religions: Georgian Orthodox 70%,
 Russian Orthodox 10%, other 20%
Ethnic mix: Georgian 69%, Armenian
 9%, Russian 6%, Azerbaijani 5%,
 other 11% Government: Republic
Currency: Coupons

Georgian Bay 38 C 5 lake bay,
 Ontario, S Canada
Georgina 148 B 4 river, C Australia
Georgiu-Dezh see Liski
Georgiyevsk 111 B 7
 SW Russian Federation
Georg von Neumayer 154 B 2
 research station, Antarctica
Gera 94 C 4 E Germany
Geráki 105 B 6 S Greece
Geral de Goiás, Serra 63 F 3
 mountain range, E Brazil
Geraldine 151 B 6 South Island,
 SW New Zealand
Geraldton 147 A 6 Western
 Australia, W Australia
Gerdauen see Zheleznodorozhnyy
Gerede 116 C 3 N Turkey
Gereshk 123 D 5 SW Afghanistan
Gering 44 D 2 Nebraska, C USA
Gerlachovský Štít 99 D 5 var.
 Gerlachovka, Ger. Gerlsdorfer
 Spitze, Hung. Gerlachfalvi Csúcs;
 prev. Stalinov Štít, Ger. Franz-Josef
 Spitze, Hung. Ferencz-Jósef Csúcs.
 Mountain, N Slovakia

Germany
94 B 4 Ger. Deutschland. Federal
 republic, W Europe
Official name: Federal Republic of
 Germany Date of formation:
 1871/1990 Capital: Berlin
Population: 80.6 million Total area:
 137,800 sq miles (356,910 sq km)
Languages: German*, Sorbian
Religions: Protestant 45%, Roman
 Catholic 37%, other 18% Ethnic mix:
 German 92%, other 8%
Government: Multiparty republic
Currency: Deutsche Mark = 100
 pfennigs

Geroliménas 105 B 7 S Greece
Gerpinnes 87 C 7 S Belgium
Gerze 116 D 2 N Turkey
Getafe 92 D 3 C Spain
Gevaş 117 F 4 SE Turkey
Gevgelija 101 E 6 var. Devđelija,
 Djevdjelija, Turk. Gevgeli.
 SE Macedonia

Ghana
75 E 5 Republic, W Africa
Official name: Republic of Ghana
Date of formation: 1957 Capital:
 Accra Population: 16.4 million Total
 area: 92,100 sq miles (238,540 sq km)
Languages: English,* Akan, Mossi
Religions: Traditional beliefs 38%,
 Muslim 30%, Christian 24%, other
 8% Ethnic mix: Akan 52%, Mossi
 15%, Ewe 12%, Ga 8%, other 13%
Government: Multiparty republic
Currency: Cedi = 100 pesewas

Ghanzi 78 C 4 var. Khanzi.
 W Botswana
Gharandal 119 B 7 SW Jordan
Gharvān see Gharyān
Gharyān 71 F 2 var. Gharvān.
 NW Libya
Ghawdex 97 C 8 var. Gozo. Island,
 NW Malta
Ghazalkent 123 F 2 Rus. Gazalkent.
 E Uzbekistan
Ghaznī 123 E 4 var. Ghazni.
 E Afghanistan
Ghazni see Ghaznī
Gheel see Geel
Gheorgheni 108 C 4 var.
 Ger. Niklasmarkt,
 Hung. Gyergyószentmiklós;
 prev. Gheorghieni, Sîn-Miclăuş.
 C Romania
Gherla 108 B 3 var. Neuschloss,
 Hung. Szamosújvár;
 prev. Ger. Armenierstadt.
 NW Romania
Ghijduwon 122 D 2
 Rus. Gizhduvan. C Uzbekistan
Ghūdara 123 F 3 var. Gudara,
 Rus. Kudara. SE Tajikistan
Ghūrīān 122 D 4 W Afghanistan
Giannitsá 104 B 4 var. Yiannitsá.
 N Greece
Gibeon 78 B 4 S Namibia
Gibraltar 93 G 4 UK dependent
 territory, SW Gibraltar
Gibraltar, Bay of 93 G 5 var. Bahía de
 Algeciras. Bay, NE Atlantic Ocean
Gibraltar Harbour 93 H 4
 W Gibraltar
Gibraltar, Strait of 92 C 5 Fr.
 Détroit de Gibraltar, Sp. Estrecho
 de Gibraltar, Atlantic
 Ocean/Mediterranean Sea
Gibson Desert 147 C 5 desert,
 Western Australia, W Australia

Giedraičiai 107 C 5 E Lithuania
Giessen 95 B 5 W Germany
Gifu 131 C 6 var. Gihu. Honshū,
 SW Japan
Giganta, Sierra de la 50 B 3
 mountain range, W Mexico
Gihu see Gifu
Gijón 92 D 1 NW Spain
Gila River 48 A 2 river,
 Arizona, SW USA
Gilbert Islands 145 E 2 island
 group, W Kiribati
Gilf Kebir Plateau 72 A 2
 Ar. Haḍabat al Jilf al Kabīr.
 Plateau, SW Egypt
Gillette 44 D 3 Wyoming, C USA
Gilroy 47 B 6 California, W USA
Gimie, Mount 55 F 1 mountain,
 C Saint Lucia
Gingin 147 B 6 Western Australia,
 SW Australia
Gipeswic see Ipswich
Girardot 58 B 3 C Colombia
Giresun 117 E 2 var. Kerasunt;
 anc. Cerasus, Pharnacia.
 NE Turkey
Girona 93 G 2 var. Gerona;
 anc. Gerunda. E Spain
Gisborne 150 E 3 North Island,
 NE New Zealand
Gissar Range 123 E 3 Rus.
 Gissarskiy Khrebet. Mountain
 range, Tajikistan/Uzbekistan
Gissarskiy Khrebet see
 Gissar Range
Giulianova 96 D 4 C Italy
Giurgiu 108 C 5 S Romania
Gizhduvan see Ghijduwon
Gjirokastër 101 C 7 var. Gjirokastra,
 It. Argirocastro, Gk.
 Argyrokastron; prev. Gjinokastër,
 Gjirokastra. S Albania
Gjoa Haven 37 F 3
 King William Island, Canada
Gjøvik 85 B 5 S Norway
Glace Bay 39 G 4 Nova Scotia,
 SE Canada
Gladstone 148 E 4 Queensland,
 E Australia
Glåma 85 B 5 river, E Norway
Glasgow 88 C 4 C Scotland, UK
Glass Mountains 49 E 4 mountain
 range, Texas, SW USA
Glazov 111 D 5
 NW Russian Federation
Gleiwitz see Gliwice
Glendale 48 B 2 Arizona, SW USA
Glendale 47 C 7 California, W USA
Glendive 44 D 2 Montana, NW USA
Glen Innes 149 D 5
 New South Wales, SE Australia
Glina 100 B 3 NE Croatia
Glittertind 85 A 5 mountain,
 S Norway
Głogów 98 B 4 var. Glogau,
 Glogow. W Poland
Globino see Hlobyne
Głogów see Głogów
Glommen see Glomma
Gloucester 89 C 6 hist. Caer Glou,
 Lat. Glevum. W England, UK
Gloversville 41 F 4 New York,
 NE USA
Głowno 98 D 4 var. Główno.
 C Poland
Główno see Głowno
Glubokiy 111 B 6
 SW Russian Federation
Glubokoye see Hlybokaye
Glukhov see Hlukhiv

Gnesen *see* Gniezno
Gniezno 98 C 3 *Ger.* Gnesen.
C Poland
Gnjilane 101 E 5 *var.* Gilani,
Alb. Gjilan. S Yugoslavia
Goa 132 B 2 *var.* Old Goa,
Port. Goa Velha. State, India
Gobabis 78 B 3 E Namibia
Gobi 124 D 1 desert,
China/Mongolia
Gobō 131 C 7 Honshū, SW Japan
Godavari 135 E 5 river, S India
Godhra 134 C 4 W India
Göding *see* Hodonín
Godoy Cruz 64 B 4 W Argentina
Goeree 86 B 4 island, SW Netherlands
Goettingen *see* Göttingen
Gogebic Range 40 B 1 hill range,
N USA
Goiânia 63 F 3 *prev.* Goyania. State
capital, C Brazil
Goiás 63 E 3 *off.* Estado de Goiás;
prev. Goiaz or Goyaz. State,
C Brazil
Gojōme 130 D 4 Honshū, NW Japan
Göksun 116 D 4 C Turkey
Gol 85 A 5 S Norway
Golan Heights 119 B 5
Ar. Al Jawlān, *Heb.* HaGolan.
Mountain range, SW Syria
Golaya Pristan *see* Hola Prystan'
Goldap 98 E 2 *Ger.* Goldap.
NE Poland
Goldap *see* Goldap
Gold Coast 75 E 5 coastal region,
S Ghana
Gold Coast 149 E 5 Queensland,
E Australia
Golden Bay 150 C 4 bay,
South Island, E Tasman Sea
Goldingen *see* Kuldīga
Goldsboro 43 F 1
North Carolina, SE USA
Goleniów 98 B 3 *Ger.* Gollnow.
NW Poland
Gollnow *see* Goleniów
Golmud 126 D 4 *var.* Ge'e'mu,
Golmo, *Chin.* Ko-erh-mu. C China
Golovanevsk *see* Holovanivs'k
Goma 77 E 6 NE Congo (Zaire)
Gomel' *see* Homyel'
Gomera 70 A 3 island, Islas
Canarias, SW Spain
Gómez Palacio 50 D 3 C Mexico
Gonaïves 54 D 3 *var.* Les Gonaïves.
N Haiti
Gonâve, Île de la 54 D 3 island,
C Haiti
Gondar *see* Gonder
Gonder 72 C 4 *var.* Gondar.
NW Ethiopia
Gondia 135 E 4 C India
Gonggar X 126 C 5 W China
Gongola 75 G 4 river, E Nigeria
Gónnoi 104 B 4 *var.* Gónnos; *prev.*
Derelí. C Greece
Good Hope *see* Fort Good Hope
Good Hope, Cape of 78 C 5
Afr. Kaap die Goeie Hoop; *var.*
Kaap de Goede Hoop. Headland,
SW South Africa
Goodland 44 D 4 Kansas, C USA
Goondiwindi 149 D 5 Queensland,
E Australia
Goor 86 E 3 E Netherlands
Goose Creek 43 F 2
South Carolina, SE USA
Goose Green 65 D 7 E Falkland Islands
Goose Lake 46 B 4 *var.* Lago dos
Gansos. Lake, W USA
Göppingen 95 B 6 SW Germany

Gorakhpur 135 E 3 N India
Gorany *see* Harany
Goražde 101 A 8
SE Bosnia & Herzegovina
Gorbovichi *see* Harbavichy
Gore 151 B 7 South Island,
SW New Zealand
Gorē 73 C 5 W Ethiopia
Goré 76 C 4 S Chad
Gorgān 120 D 2 *var.* Astarabad,
Astrabad, Gurgan; *prev.*
Asterābād, *anc.* Hyrcania. N Iran
Gori 117 F 2 C Georgia
Gorinchem 86 C 4 *var.* Gorkum.
C Netherlands
Goris 117 G 3 SE Armenia
Gorki *see* Horki
Gor'kiy *see* Nizhniy Novgorod
Gorkum *see* Gorinchem
Görlitz 94 D 4 E Germany
Görlitz *see* Zgorzelec
Gorna Dzhumaya *see* Blagoevgrad
Gornji Milanovac 100 D 4
C Yugoslavia
Gorodets *see* Haradzyets
Gorodishche *see* Horodyshche
Gorodnya *see* Horodnya
Gorodok *see* Haradok
Gorontalo 139 E 4 Celebes,
C Indonesia
Gorssel 86 D 3 E Netherlands
Gorzów Wielkopolski 98 B 3
Ger. Landsberg, Landsberg an der
Warthe. W Poland
Gosford 149 D 6 New South Wales,
SE Australia
Goshogawara 130 D 3 *var.*
Gosyogawara. Honshū, C Japan
Gospić 100 A 3 C Croatia
Gostivar 101 D 6 W Macedonia
Gosyogawara *see* Goshogawara
Götaland 85 B 6 cultural region,
S Sweden
Göteborg 85 B 7 *Eng.* Gothenburg.
S Sweden
Gotel Mountains 75 G 5
mountain range, E Nigeria
Gotha 94 C 4 C Germany
Gothenburg *see* Göteborg
Gotland 85 C 6 island, SE Sweden
Gotō-rettō 131 A 7 island group,
Japan
Gotska Sandön 85 C 6 island,
SE Sweden
Gōtsu 131 B 6 *var.* Gōtu. Honshū,
SW Japan
Göttingen 94 B 4 *var.* Goettingen.
C Germany
Gottschee *see* Kočevje
Gottwaldov *see* Zlín
Gōtu *see* Gōtsu
Gouda 86 C 4 C Netherlands
Gough Fracture Zone 67 C 6
fracture zone, S Atlantic Ocean
Gough Island 69 B 8 island,
S Atlantic Ocean
Gouin, Réservoir 38 D 4 reservoir,
Québec, SE Canada
Goulburn 149 D 7 New South
Wales, SE Australia
Goulburn Islands 148 A 1 island
group, Northern Territory,
N Australia
Goundam 75 E 3 NW Mali
Gouré 75 G 3 SE Niger
Goverla, Gora *see* Hoverla, Hora
Governador Valadares 63 F 4 SE Brazil
Goya 64 D 3 NE Argentina
Goyania *see* Goiânia

Goz Beïda 76 D 3 SE Chad
Gozo *see* Gozo
Gračanica 100 C 3
NE Bosnia & Herzegovina
Graciosa 92 A 5 *var.* Ilha Graciosa.
Island, W Portugal
Graciosa, Ilha *see* Graciosa
Gradačac 100 C 3
N Bosnia & Herzegovina
Gradaús, Serra dos 63 E 3
mountain range, C Brazil
Grafton 149 E 6 New South Wales,
SE Australia
Grafton 45 E 1 North Dakota, N USA
Graham Land 154 A 2 physical
region, Antarctica
Grain Coast 74 C 5 coastal region,
S Liberia
Grajewo 98 E 2 NE Poland
Grampian Mountains 88 C 3
mountain range, C Scotland, UK
Grampians, The 149 B 7 mountain
range, Victoria, SE Australia
Granada 92 D 5 S Spain
Granada 52 D 3 SW Nicaragua
Gran Canaria 70 A 3 *var.* Grand
Canary. Island, Islas Canarias,
SW Spain
Gran Chaco 61 G 4 *var.* Chaco.
Physical region, SW South America
Grand Bahama Island 54 C 1
island, N Bahamas
Grand Banks of Newfoundland
66 B 3 undersea basin,
NW Atlantic Ocean
Grand Bassa *see* Buchanan
Grand Canary *see* Gran Canaria
Grand Canyon 48 B 1 valley,
Arizona, SW USA
Grand Cayman 54 B 3 island,
SW Cayman Islands
Grande, Bahía 65 C 7 bay,
SW Atlantic Ocean
Grand Comore 79 F 2 *var.*
Njazidja, Great Comoro. Island,
NW Comoros
Grande Deux, Réservoir la 38 D 3
reservoir, Québec, E Canada
Grande Prairie 37 E 5 Alberta,
W Canada
Grand Erg de Bilma 75 H 3 desert,
NE Niger
Grand Erg Occidental 70 D 3
desert, W Algeria
Grand Erg Oriental 71 E 3 desert,
Algeria/Tunisia
Grande, Rio 49 F 5 *var.* Río Bravo,
Río Bravo del Norte. River,
Mexico/USA
Grande Rivière 55 F 1 C Saint Lucia
Grande Terre 55 G 3 island,
E Guadeloupe
Grand Falls 39 G 3
New Brunswick, SE Canada
Grand Forks 45 E 1
North Dakota, N USA
Grandichi *see* Hrandzichy
Grand Island 45 E 4 Nebraska, C USA
Grand Junction 44 C 4
Colorado, C USA
Grand Lac de l'Ours *see*
Great Bear Lake
Grand Lac des Esclaves *see*
Great Slave Lake
Grand Paradis *see* Gran Paradiso
Grand Rapids 40 C 3 Michigan, N USA
Grand Rapids 45 F 1
Minnesota, N USA
Grand Ronde River 46 C 3 river,
NW USA
Grand-Santi 59 H 3
W French Guiana

Gran Malvina *see* West Falkland
Granollers 93 G 2 *var.* Granollé
NE Spain
Granollérs *see* Granollers
Gran Paradiso 96 A 2 *Fr.* Gran
Paradis. Mountain, NW Italy
Gran Santiago *see* Santiago
Grantley Adams 55 H 2
international airport, SE Barb
Grants 48 C 2 New Mexico, SW U
Grants Pass 46 B 4 Oregon, NW
Granville 90 B 3 N France
Gratz *see* Graz
Graulhet 91 C 6 S France
Grave 86 D 4 SE Netherlands
Grayling 36 C 2 Alaska, NW U
Graz 95 E 7 *prev.* Gratz. SE Aus
Great Abaco 54 C 1 *var.* Abaco
Island. Island, N Bahamas
Great Australian Bight 152 B 4
bight, E Indian Ocean
Great Barrier Island 150 D 2 is
North Island, N New Zealand
Great Barrier Reef 148 D 2 reef
W Pacific Ocean
Great Basin 47 C 5 basin,
Nevada, W USA
Great Bear Lake 37 E 3 *Fr.* Gran
Lac de l'Ours. Lake, Northwe
Territories, NW Canada
Great Bend 45 E 5 Kansas, C U
Great Dividing Range 148 C 2
mountain range, E Australia
Greater Antarctica 154 C 3 *var.*
East Antarctica. Physical regi
Antarctica
Greater Antilles 54 D 3 island
group, NW Caribbean Sea
Greater Caucasus 117 G 2 *Az.* E
Qafqaz Silsiläsi, *Geor.* Kavka
Rus. Bol'shoy Kavkaz. Moun
range, N Azerbaijan/Georgia
Russian Federation
Great Exhibition Bay 150 C 1 in
S Pacific Ocean
Great Exuma Island 54 C 2 isla
C Bahamas
Great Falls 44 B 1 Montana, NW
Great Grimsby *see* Grimsby
Great Hungarian Plain 99 D 7 *
Great Alfold, Plain of Hungar
Hung. Alföld. Plain, SE Europe
Great Inagua 54 D 2 *var.* Inagua
Islands. Island, S Bahamas
Great Karoo 78 C 5 *var.* Great
Karroo, High Veld, *Afr.* Grootc
Karoo, Hoë Karoo. Physical
region, S South Africa
Great Khingan Range *see*
Da Hinggan Ling
Great Lake *see* Tônlé Sap
Great Nicobar 133 G 3 island,
SE India
Great Plains 45 E 3 physical reg
C Canada/USA
Great Rift Valley 69 D 5 *var.* Ri
Valley, Depression, Africa/As
Great Ruaha 73 C 7 river,
S Tanzania
Great Saint Bernard Pass 95 A 8
Fr. Col du Grand-Saint-Bernar
It. Passo di Gran San Bernarde
Pass, Italy/Switzerland
Great Salt Desert *see* Kavir, Das
Great Salt Lake 44 B 3 salt lake,
Utah, W USA
Great Salt Lake Desert 44 A 4
plain, Utah, W USA
Great Sand Sea 72 A 2 desert,
Egypt/Libya
Great Sandy Desert 146 C 4 dese
Western Australia, W Austral

at Sandy Desert 112 B 5 desert,
W Asia
at Sandy Island see Fraser Island
at Slave Lake 37 E 4 Fr. Grand
ac des Esclaves. Lake, Northwest
rritories, NW Canada
at Sound 42 A 5 bay,
Atlantic Ocean
at Victoria Desert 142 A 4
esert, SW Australia
at Wall of China 127 E 4
ncient monument, C China
at Yarmouth 89 E 6
r. Yarmouth. E England, UK
penka see Hrebinka
dos, Sierra de 92 D 3 mountain
nge, C Spain

ece
05 A 5 Gk. Ellás; anc. Hellas.
epublic, SE Europe

cial name: Hellenic Republic
e of formation: 1830/1947
ital: Athens Population: 10.2
ion Total area: 50,961 sq miles
,990 sq km) Languages: Greek*,
kish, Albanian, Macedonian
gions: Greek Orthodox 98%,
slim 1%, other 1% Ethnic mix:
ek 98%, other 2%
ernment: Multiparty republic
rency: Drachma = 100 lepta

eley 44 D 4 Colorado, C USA
en Bay 40 B 2 N USA
en Bay 40 B 2 lake bay,
/isconsin, N USA
eneville 43 E 1 Tennessee, S USA
enland 82 D 3 Dan. Grønland,
nuit Kalaallit Nunaat. Danish
xternal territory, Arctic
Ocean/Atlantic Ocean
enland Sea 83 F 2 sea,
rctic Ocean
en Mountains 41 G 3 mountain
nge, Vermont, NE USA
enock 88 C 4 SW Scotland, UK
en River 40 C 5 river,
entucky, E USA
en River 44 B 4 river, C USA
ensboro 43 F 1
lorth Carolina, SE USA
enville 43 F 1
lorth Carolina, SE USA
enville 42 B 2 Arkansas, C USA
enville 42 D 3 Alabama, S USA
enville 43 E 1
outh Carolina, SE USA
enville 49 G 2 Texas, S USA
enwood 42 B 2 Mississippi, S USA
enwood 43 E 2
outh Carolina, SE USA
gory Range 148 C 3 mountain
nge, Queensland, E Australia
ifswald 94 D 2 NE Germany
nada 42 C 2 Mississippi, S USA

nada
5 G 5 Commonwealth republic,
Caribbean Sea

icial name: Grenada
e of formation: 1974 Capital:
George's Population: 91,000
al area: 131 sq miles (340 sq km)
guages: English*, English Creole
igions: Roman Catholic 68%,
testant 32% Ethnic mix: Black
, Afro-European 13%,
th Asian 3% Government:
iamentary democracy
rency: E. Caribbean $ = 100 cents

Grenadines, The 55 H 5 island
group, E Caribbean Sea
Grenoble 91 D 5 anc. Cularo,
Gratianopolis. E France
Grenville, Cape 148 C 2 headland,
Queensland, NE Australia
Gresham 46 B 3 Oregon, NW USA
Grevelingen 86 B 4 estuary,
S North Sea
Grevená 104 B 4 N Greece
Greymouth 151 B 5 South Island,
C New Zealand
Grey Range 149 C 5 mountain
range, E Australia
Greytown see San Juan del Norte
Grimari 76 C 4
C Central African Republic
Grimsby 89 E 5 prev. Great
Grimsby. NE England, UK
Grise Fiord 37 F 2 var. Ausuittoq.
Ellesmere Island, N Canada
Grobin see Grobiņa
Grobiņa 106 B 3 Ger. Grobin.
W Latvia
Grodno see Hrodna
Groesbeek 86 D 4
SE Netherlands
Grójec 98 D 4 C Poland
Groningen 86 E 1 NE Netherlands
Groote Eylandt 148 B 2 island,
N Australia
Grootfontein 78 B 3 N Namibia
Groot Karasberge 78 B 4 mountain
range, S Namibia
Gros Islet 55 F 1 N Saint Lucia
Grosser Sund see Suur Väin
Grosseto 96 B 4 NW Italy
Grossglockner 95 D 7 mountain,
N Austria
Grosskanizsa see Nagykanizsa
Groznyy 111 B 8
SW Russian Federation
Grudziądz 98 C 3 var. Grudziàdz,
Ger. Graudenz. N Poland
Grums 85 B 6 C Sweden
Grünau 78 B 4 S Namibia
Gryazi 111 B 6
W Russian Federation
Gryfice 98 B 2 Ger. Greifenberg,
Greifenberg in Pommern.
NW Poland
Guabito 53 E 4 NW Panama
Guadalajara 93 E 3 Ar. Wad Al-
Hajarah; anc. Arriaca. C Spain
Guadalajara 50 D 4 C Mexico
Guadalcanal 144 C 3 island,
C Solomon Islands
Guadalquivir 92 D 4 river, W Spain
Guadalupe 50 D 3 C Mexico
Guadalupe Mountains 48 D 3
mountain range, SW USA
Guadeloupe 55 H 3 French overseas
department, E Caribbean Sea
Guadiana 92 C 4 river,
Portugal/Spain
Guadix 93 E 5 S Spain
Guaico 55 H 5 C Trinidad & Tobago
Guaimaca 52 C 2 C Honduras
Guajira, Península de la 58 C 1
peninsula, N Colombia
Gualaco 52 D 2 C Honduras
Gualán 52 B 2 C Guatemala
Gualaquiza 60 B 2 SE Ecuador
Gualdicciolo 96 D 1 NW San Marino
Gualeguaychú 64 D 4 E Argentina
Guam 144 A 1 US unincorporated
territory, W Pacific Ocean
Guamúchil 50 C 3 C Mexico
Guanabacoa 54 B 2 W Cuba
Guanare 58 C 2 N Venezuela
Guanare 58 D 2 river, NW Venezuela

Guangdong 129 C 6 var.
Kuang-tung, Kwangtung,
Yue. Province, SE China
Guangxi Zhuangzu Zizhiqu 129 B 6
var. Guangxi, Gui, Kuang-hsi,
Kwangsi, Eng. Kwangsi Chuang
Autonomous Region.
Autonomous region, S China
Guangyuan 129 B 5 var. Kuang-
yuan, Kwangyuan. SW China
Guangzhou 129 C 6 var. Kuang-
chou, Kwangchow, Eng. Canton.
Province capital, SE China
Guantánamo 54 D 3 SE Cuba
Guantanamo Bay 54 D 3 US
military base, E Cuba
Guaporé 61 F 3 var. Río Iténez.
River, Bolivia/Brazil
Guarda 92 C 3 E Portugal
Guarumal 53 F 5 S Panama
Guasave 50 C 3 C Mexico

Guatemala
52 A 2 Republic,
NW Central America

Official name: Republic of
Guatemala Date of formation: 1838
Capital: Guatemala City
Population: 10 million Total area:
42,043 sq miles (108,890 sq km)
Languages: Spanish*, Quiché, Kekchi,
Kekchí Religions: Christian 99%,
other 1% Ethnic mix: Indian 55%,
ladino (Euro-Indian, White) 45%
Government: Multiparty republic
Currency: Quetzal = 100 centavos

Guatemala Basin 153 F 3 undersea
basin, E Pacific Ocean
Guatemala City see
Guatemala, Ciudad de
Guatemala, Ciudad de 52 B 2
see Guatemala City; prev.
Santiago de los Caballeros.
Country capital, C Guatemala
Guatemala, Republic of see
Guatemala
Guaviare 58 C 3 river, E Colombia
Guayana, Macizo de las see
Guiana Highlands
Guayaquil 60 B 2 var. Santiago de
Guayaquil. SW Ecuador
Guayaquil, Gulf of 60 A 2 gulf,
E Pacific Ocean
Guayaramerín 61 F 2 N Bolivia
Guaymas 50 B 2 NW Mexico
Gubadag 122 D 2 Turkm. Tel'man;
prev. Tel'mansk. N Turkmenistan
Gubkha 111 D 5
var. Gubachaj, Gubaha.
NW Russian Federation
Guben 94 D 4 var. Wilhelm-Pieck-
Stadt. E Germany
Gubkin 111 B 6
W Russian Federation
Gudaut'a 117 E 1 NW Georgia
Guelta Zemmur 70 B 3
E Western Sahara
Guéret 91 C 5 C France
Guerguerat 70 A 4
SW Western Sahara
Guernsey 89 D 8 island,
W Channel Islands
Guerrero Negro 50 A 2 NW Mexico
Guiana Basin 66 B 4 undersea
basin, W Atlantic Ocean
Guiana Highlands 56 C 2
var. Macizo de las Guayana.
Mountain range,
N South America
Guidder see Guider
Guider 76 B 4 var. Guidder.
N Cameroon

Guidimouni 75 G 3 S Niger
Guildford 89 D 7 SE England, UK
Guilin 129 C 6 var. Kuei-lin,
Kweilin. E China
Guimarães see Guimarães
Guimarães 92 B 2 var. Guimaráes.
N Portugal

Guinea
74 C 4 var. Guinée; prev. French
Guinea, People's Revolutionary
Republic of Guinea. Republic,
W Africa

Official name: Republic of Guinea
Date of formation: 1958 Capital:
Conakry Population: 6.3 million
Total area: 94,926 sq miles
(245,860 sq km) Languages: French*,
Fulani, Malinke, Susu Religions:
Muslim 85%, Christian 8%, traditional
beliefs 7% Ethnic mix: Fulani 40%,
Malinke 25%, Susu 12%, other 23%
Government: Multiparty republic
Currency: Franc = 100 centimes

Guinea Basin 67 D 5 undersea
basin, E Atlantic Ocean

Guinea-Bissau
74 B 4 Fr. Guinée-Bissau, Port.
Guiné-Bissau; prev. Portuguese
Guinea. Republic, W Africa

Official name: Republic of Guinea-
Bissau Date of formation: 1974
Capital: Bissau Population:
1 million Total area: 13,940 sq miles
(36,120 sq km) Languages:
Portuguese*, local languages
Religions: Traditional beliefs 54%,
Muslim 38%, Christian 8%
Ethnic mix: Balante 27%, Fulani
22%, Malinke 12%, other 39%
Government: Multiparty republic
Currency: Peso = 100 centavos

Guinea, Gulf of 69 B 5 Fr. Golfe de
Guinée. Inlet, E Atlantic Ocean
Guinée, Golfe de see
Guinea, Gulf of
Güiria 59 E 1 NE Venezuela
Guiyang
129 B 6 var. Kuei-Yang,
Kuei-yang, Kueyang, Kweiyang;
prev. Kweichu. Province capital,
S China
Guizhou 129 B 6 var. Kuei-chou,
Kweichow, Qian. Province,
S China
Gujarāt 134 C 4 var. Gujarat. State,
W India
Gujerat see Gujarāt
Gujrānwāla 134 D 2 NE Pakistan
Gujrāt 134 C 2 E Pakistan
Gulbarga 132 C 1 C India
Gulbene 106 D 3 Ger. Alt-
Schwanenburg. NE Latvia
Gulf, The see Persian Gulf
Gulistan see Guliston
Guliston 123 E 2 Rus. Gulistan.
E Uzbekistan
Gulkana 36 D 3 Alaska, NW USA
Gulu 73 B 6 N Uganda
Gulyantsi 104 C 1 NW Bulgaria
Guma see Pishan
Gumbinnen see Gusev
Gümüşhane 117 E 3
var. Gumushkhane, Gümüşane.
NE Turkey
Güney Doğu Toroslar 117 F 4
mountain range, SE Turkey
Gunnedah 149 D 6 New South
Wales, SE Australia
Gunnison 44 C 5 Colorado, C USA

Gurbantünggüt Shamo 126 C 2 desert, NW China
Guri, Embalse de 59 E 2 reservoir, E Venezuela
Gurktaler Alpen 95 D 7 mountain range, S Austria
Gürün 116 D 3 C Turkey
Gur'yev *see* Atyrau
Gusau 75 G 4 N Nigeria
Gusev 106 B 4 *Ger.* Gumbinnen. W Russian Federation
Gushgy 122 D 4 *prev.* Kushka. S Turkmenistan
Gustavus 36 D 4 Alaska, NW USA
Güstrow 94 C 3 NE Germany
Gütersloh 94 B 4 W Germany
Guthrie 49 G 1 Oklahoma, C USA
Gutland 87 D 8 physical region, S Luxembourg
Guttstadt *see* Dobre Miasto
Guwāhāti 135 G 3 *prev.* Gauhāti. NE India

Guyana 59 F 3 *prev.* British Guiana. Republic, N South America

Official name: Cooperative Republic of Guyana **Date of formation:** 1966 **Capital:** Georgetown **Population:** 800,000 **Total area:** 83,000 sq miles (214,970 sq km) **Languages:** English*, English Creole, other **Religions:** Christian 57%, Hindu 33%, Muslim 9%, other 1% **Ethnic mix:** South Asian 51%, Black and mixed 43%, other 6% **Government:** Multiparty republic **Currency:** Guyana $ =100 cents

Guymon 49 E 1 Oklahoma, C USA
Gvardeysk 106 A 4 *Ger.* Tapaiu. W Russian Federation
Gwādar 134 A 3 *var.* Gwadur. SW Pakistan
Gwadur *see* Gwādar
Gwalior 134 D 3 C India
Gwanda 78 D 3 SW Zimbabwe
Gwy *see* Wye
Gyangzê 126 C 5 W China
Gyaring Hu 126 C 5 lake, C China
Gympie 149 E 5 Queensland, E Australia
Gyomaendrőd 99 D 7 SE Hungary
Gyöngyös 99 D 6 NE Hungary
Győr 99 C 6 *Ger.* Raab; *Lat.* Arrabona. NW Hungary
Gýtheio 105 B 6 *prev.* Yíthion. S Greece
Gyumri 117 F 2 *var.* Giumri, *Rus.* Kumayri; *prev.* Leninakan, Aleksandropol'. W Armenia
Gyzylarbat 122 C 2 *prev.* Kizyl-Arvat. W Turkmenistan

H

Haabai *see* Ha'apai Group
Haacht 87 C 6 C Belgium
Haaksbergen 86 E 3 E Netherlands
Ha'apai Group 145 E 5 *var.* Haabai. Island group, C Tonga
Haapsalu 106 D 2 *Ger.* Hapsal. W Estonia
Haarlem 86 C 3 *prev.* Harlem. W Netherlands
Haast 151 B 6 South Island, SW New Zealand
Habomai Islands 130 E 2 island group, SE Russian Federation
Hachijō-jima 131 E 6 *var.* Hatizyô Zima. Island, Izu-shotô, E Japan

Hachinohe 130 D 3 Honshū, C Japan
Hadejia 75 G 4 N Nigeria
Hadejia 75 G 4 river, N Nigeria
Hadera 119 A 6 C Israel
Hadhdhunmati Atoll 132 A 5 *var.* Haddummati Atoll, Laamu Atoll. Island, S Maldives
Hadhramaut *see* Ḥaḍramawt
Ha Đông 136 D 3 *var.* Hadong. N Vietnam
Hadong *see* Ha Đông
Ḥaḍramawt 121 C 6 *Eng.* Hadhramaut. Mountain range, S Yemen
Hafren *see* Severn
Hagerstown 41 E 4 Maryland, NE USA
Ha Giang 136 D 3 NW Vietnam
Hagondange 90 D 3 NE France
Haguenau 90 E 3 NE France
Haicheng 128 D 3 NE China
Haidarabad *see* Hyderābād
Haifa, Bay of *see* Ḥefa, Mifraz
Haikang 129 C 7 *var.* Leizhou. S China
Haikou 129 C 7 *var.* Hai-k'ou, Hoihow, *Fr.* Hoï-Hao. Hainan Dao, S China
Ḥā'il 120 B 4 NW Saudi Arabia
Hailar 127 F 1 *var.* Hai-la-erh; *prev.* Hulun. N China
Hailuoto 84 D 4 *Swe.* Karlö. Island, W Finland
Hainan 129 B 7 *var.* Qiong. Province, S China
Hainan Dao 129 C 7 island, S China
Haines 36 D 4 Alaska, NW USA
Hainichen 94 D 4 E Germany
Hai Phong 136 E 3 *var.* Haifong, Haiphong. N Vietnam

Haiti 54 D 3 Republic, N Haiti

Official name: Republic of Haiti **Date of formation:** 1804 **Capital:** Port-au-Prince **Population:** 6.9 million **Total area:** 10,714 sq miles (27,750 sq km) **Languages:** French*, French Creole, English **Religions:** Roman Catholic 80%, Protestant 16%, Voodoo 4% **Ethnic mix:** Black 95%, Afro-European 5% **Government:** Multiparty republic **Currency:** Gourde = 100 centimes

Hajdúhadház 99 E 6 E Hungary
Hakodate 130 D 3 Hokkaidô, NE Japan
Hakosberge 78 B 4 mountain range, C Namibia
Ha Kwai Chung 128 A 1 W Hong Kong
Hal *see* Halle
Ḥalab 118 B 2 *Eng.* Aleppo, *Fr.* Alep; *anc.* Beroea. NW Syria
Ḥalāniyāt, Juzur al 121 D 6 *var.* Jazā'ir Bin Ghalfān, *Eng.* Kuria Muria Islands. Island group, S Oman
Halberstadt 94 C 4 C Germany
Halden 85 B 6 *prev.* Fredrikshald. S Norway
Halfmoon Bay 151 A 8 *var.* Oban. South Island, SW New Zealand
Halifax 39 F 4 Nova Scotia, SE Canada
Halifax Bay 148 D 3 bay, W Pacific Ocean
Halle 94 C 4 *var.* Halle an der Saale. C Germany
Halle 87 B 6 *Fr.* Hal. C Belgium
Halle an der Saale *see* Halle

Halle-Neustadt 94 C 4 C Germany
Halley 154 B 2 research station, Antarctica
Hall Islands 144 B 1 island group, C Micronesia
Halls Creek 146 D 3 Western Australia, NW Australia
Halmahera 139 F 3 *prev.* Djailolo, Gilolo, Jailolo. Island, E Indonesia
Halmahera, Laut 139 F 4 sea, W Pacific Ocean
Halmstad 85 B 7 S Sweden
Hälsingborg *see* Helsingborg
Hamada 131 B 6 Honshū, SW Japan
Hamadān 120 C 3 *anc.* Ecbatana. W Iran
Ḥamāh 118 B 3 *var.* Hama; *anc.* Epiphania, *Bibl.* Hamath. W Syria
Hamamatsu 131 D 6 *var.* Hamamatu. Honshū, S Japan
Hamamatu *see* Hamamatsu
Hamar 85 B 5 *prev.* Storhammer. S Norway
Hamburg 94 B 3 N Germany
Ḥamḍ, Wādī al 120 A 4 dry watercourse, W Saudi Arabia
Hämeenlinna 85 D 5 *Swe.* Tavastehus. SW Finland
Hamersley Range 146 B 4 mountain range, Western Australia, W Australia
Hamhŭng 128 E 3 C North Korea
Hami 126 C 3 *var.* Ha-mi, *Uigh.* Kumul, Qomul. NW China
Hamilton 88 C 4 S Scotland, UK
Hamilton 42 A 5 dependent territory capital, C Bermuda
Hamilton 150 D 3 North Island, N New Zealand
Hamilton 38 D 5 Ontario, S Canada
Hamm 94 B 3 *var.* Hamm in Westfalen. W Germany
Hamm in Westfalen *see* Hamm
Hampden 151 B 7 South Island, SW New Zealand
Hampton 41 F 5 Virginia, NE USA
Handan 128 C 4 *var.* Han-tan. NE China
HaNegev 119 A 7 *Eng.* Negev. Desert, S Israel
Hanford 47 C 7 California, W USA
Hangayn Nuruu 126 D 2 mountain range, W Mongolia
Hangö *see* Hanko
Hangzhou 129 D 5 *var.* Hang-chou, Hangchow. Province capital, E China
Hanhöhiy Uul 126 C 2 mountain range, NW Mongolia
Hanko 85 D 6 *Swe.* Hangö. SW Finland
Hanmer Springs 151 C 5 South Island, C New Zealand
Hanna 37 E 5 Alberta, SW Canada
Hannibal 45 G 4 Missouri, C USA
Hannover 94 B 3 *Eng.* Hanover. NW Germany
Hanöbukten 85 B 7 bay, SW Baltic Sea
Ha Nôi 136 D 3 *var.* Ha Noi, Ha noi, *Eng.* Hanoi, *Fr.* Ha noï. Country capital, N Vietnam
Hanover *see* Hannover
Han-tan *see* Handan
Hantsavichy 107 B 6 *Pol.* Hancewicze, *Rus.* Gantsevichi. SW Belarus
Hanzhong 129 B 5 C China

Hāora 135 G 4 *prev.* Howrah. NE India
Haparanda 84 D 3 N Sweden
Hapsal *see* Haapsalu
Haradok 107 E 5 *Rus.* Gorodok, N Belarus
Haradzyets 107 B 6 *Rus.* Gorodets. SW Belarus
Haramachi 131 D 5 Honshū, E Japan
Harany 107 D 5 *Rus.* Gorany. N Belarus
Härar 73 D 5 Ethiopia
Harare 78 D 3 *prev.* Salisbury. Country capital, NE Zimbabwe
Harbavichy 107 E 6 *Rus.* Gorbovichi. E Belarus
Harbel 74 C 5 W Liberia
Harbin 128 E 2 *var.* Haerbin, Ha-erh-pin, Kharbin; *prev.* Haerhpin, Pinkiang, Pingkiang. Province capital, NE China
Hardanger-fjorden 85 A 5 fjord, E Norwegian Sea
Hardangervidda 85 A 6 mountain range, S Norway
Hardenberg 86 E 3 E Netherlands
Hardy 42 B 1 Arkansas, C USA
Harelbeke 87 A 6 *var.* Harlebek. W Belgium
Harem *see* Ḥārim
Haren 86 E 2 NE Netherlands
Hargeisa *see* Hargeysa
Hargeysa 73 D 5 *var.* Hargeisa. NW Somalia
Hariana *see* Haryāna
Hari, Batang 138 B 4 *prev.* Djam River, Sumatera, W Indonesia
Ḥārim 118 B 2 *var.* Harem. W S
Harima-nada 131 B 6 sea, NW Pacific Ocean
Harīrūd 123 E 4 river, C Asia
Harlan 45 F 3 Iowa, C USA
Harlebeke *see* Harelbeke
Harlem *see* Haarlem
Harlingen 49 G 5 Texas, S USA
Harlingen 86 D 2 *Fris.* Harns. N Netherlands
Harlow 89 E 6 SE England, UK
Harmanli *see* Kharmanli
Harney Lake 46 C 4 lake, Oregon, NW USA
Härnösand 85 C 5 *var.* Hernösa C Sweden
Harns *see* Harlingen
Har Nuur 126 C 2 lake, NW Mongolia
Harper 74 D 5 *var.* Cape Palma NE Liberia
Ḥarrat Rahaṭ 121 B 5 lavaflow, W Saudi Arabia
Harris 88 B 3 physical region, NW Scotland, UK
Harrisburg 41 E 4 state capital, Pennsylvania, NE USA
Harrison 42 B 1 Arkansas, C US
Harrisonburg 41 E 5 Virginia, NE USA
Harrison, Cape 39 F 2 headland Newfoundland and Labrador E Canada
Harrogate 89 D 5 N England, UK
Hârşova 108 D 5 *prev.* Hîrsova. SE Romania
Harstad 84 C 2 N Norway
Hartford 41 G 3 state capital, Connecticut, C USA
Hartlepool 89 D 5 N England, l
Har Us Nuur 126 C 2 lake, NW Mongolia
Harwich 89 E 6 E England, UK

ryāna 134 D 2 *var.* Hariana.
tate, N India
skovo *see* Khaskovo
sselt 87 D 6 NE Belgium
tings 89 E 7 SE England, UK
tings 55 G 2 SW Barbados
tings 150 E 4 North Island,
NE New Zealand
tings 45 E 4 Nebraska, C USA
eg 108 B 4 *Ger.* Wallenthal,
lung. Hátszeg; *prev. Ger.* Hatzeg,
lötzing.
SW Romania
tem 86 D 3 E Netherlands
teras, Cape 43 G 1 headland,
North Carolina, SE USA
tiesburg 42 C 3 Mississippi, S USA
Yai 137 C 7 *var.* Ban Hat Yai.
Thailand
gesund 85 A 6 S Norway
Hoi Wan 128 A 1 bay,
NW Hong Kong
keligrend 85 A 6 S Norway
kivesi 85 E 5 lake, SE Finland
raki Gulf 150 D 2 gulf,
Pacific Ocean
t Atlas 70 C 3 *Eng.* High Atlas.
Mountain range, C Morocco
tes Fagnes 87 D 6 *Ger.* Hohes
Venn. Mountain range, E Belgium
ts Plateaux 70 D 2
ar. Hauts-Plateaux. Plateau,
Algeria/Morocco
ts-Plateaux *see* Hauts Plateaux
zenberg 95 D 6 SE Germany
vana 35 D 6 country capital,
NW Cuba
vana *see* La Habana
vant 89 D 7 S England, UK
velock 43 F 1
North Carolina, SE USA
velock North 150 E 4
North Island, NE New Zealand
verfordwest 89 B 6 SW Wales, UK
viřov 99 C 5 E Czech Republic
vre 44 C 1 Montana, C USA
vre-St-Pierre 39 F 3 Québec,
Canada
yza 116 D 2 N Turkey
waii 47 A 8 *off.* state of Hawaii;
icknames Aloha State, Paradise of
the Pacific. State, W USA
waii 47 B 8
law. Hawai'i. Island, W USA
waiian Islands 152 D 2
waiian Islands 152 D 2
ar. The Hawaiian Islands;
rev. The Sandwich Islands.
sland group, C Pacific Ocean
waiian Ridge 152 D 2 undersea
idge, N Pacific Ocean
wea, Lake 151 B 6 lake,
South Island, SW New Zealand
wera 150 D 4 North Island,
C New Zealand
wick 88 D 4 S Scotland, UK
wke Bay 150 E 4 bay,
Pacific Ocean
wke's Bay 150 E 4 cultural
region, North Island,
N New Zealand
y 149 C 6 New South Wales,
SE Australia
y River 37 E 4 Northwest
Territories, W Canada
vs 45 E 5 Kansas, C USA
ysyn 108 D 3 *Rus.* Gaysin.
Ukraine
ard & McDonald Islands 141 C 7
Australian external territory,
Indian Ocean
rst 38 C 4 Ontario, S Canada
bei 128 C 4 *var.* Hopeh, Hopei, Ji;
rev. Chihli. Province, NE China

Hebron 39 F 1 Newfoundland
and Labrador, NE Canada
Hebron 119 E 7 *var.* Al Khalīl,
El Khalil, *Heb.* Hevron;
anc. Kiriath-Arba. S West Bank
Heemskerk 86 C 3 W Netherlands
Heerde 86 D 3 E Netherlands
Heerenveen 86 D 2 *Fris.*
It Hearrenfean. N Netherlands
Heerhugowaard 86 C 2
NW Netherlands
Heerlen 87 D 6 SE Netherlands
Hefa 119 A 5 *var.* Haifa; *hist.* Caiffa,
Caiphas, *anc.* Sycaminum.
N Israel
Hefa, Mifraz 119 A 5 *Eng.* Bay of
Haifa. Bay, E Mediterranean Sea
Hefei 129 D 5 *var.* Hofei;
hist. Luchow. E China
Heide 94 B 2 N Germany
Heidelberg 95 B 5 SW Germany
Heidenheim *see* Heidenheim
an der Brenz
Heidenheim an der Brenz 95 B 6
var. Heidenheim. S Germany
Heilbronn 95 B 6 SW Germany
Heiligenbeil *see* Mamonovo
Heilong Jiang *see* Amur
Heilongjiang 128 D 2 *var.* Hei,
Hei-lung-chiang, Heilungkiang.
Province, NE China
Heiloo 86 C 3 NW Netherlands
Heilsberg *see* Lidzbark Warmiński
Heimdal 84 B 4 S Norway
Helan Shan 127 E 3 mountain
range, N China
Helena 44 B 4 state capital,
Montana, NW USA
Helensville 150 D 2 North Island,
N New Zealand
Helgoländer Bucht 94 A 2 *var.*
Helgoland Bay, Heligoland Bight.
Bay, SE North Sea
Hellevoetsluis 86 B 4
SW Netherlands
Hellín 93 E 4 C Spain
Helmand, Daryā-ye 122 D 5
var. Hīrmand Rūd-e. River,
Afghanistan/Iran
Helmond 87 D 5 S Netherlands
Helsingborg 85 B 7
prev. Hälsingborg. S Sweden
Helsingfors *see* Helsinki
Helsinki 85 D 5 *Swe.* Helsingfors.
Country capital, S Finland
Henan 129 C 5 *var.* Honan, Yu.
Province, C China
Henderson 43 F 1
North Carolina, SE USA
Henderson 49 H 3 Texas, S USA
Henderson 40 B 5 Kentucky, E USA
Henderson 47 D 7 Nevada, W USA
Hendersonville 43 E 1
North Carolina, SE USA
Hendū Kosh *see* Hindu Kush
Hengduan Shan 126 D 5 mountain
range, SW China
Hengelo 86 E 3 E Netherlands
Hengyang 129 C 6 *var.* Hengnan,
Heng-yang; *prev.* Hengchow.
S China
Heniches'k 109 F 4 *Rus.* Genichesk.
S Ukraine
Hennebont 90 A 3 NW France
Hentiesbaai 78 B 3 W Namibia
Henzada 136 B 4 SW Myanmar
Herald Cays 148 D 3 island,
E Australia
Herāt 122 D 4 *var.* Herat; *anc.* Aria.
W Afghanistan
Herchmer 37 G 4 Manitoba,
C Canada

Heredia 53 E 4 C Costa Rica
Hereford 49 E 2 Texas, S USA
Herford 94 B 4 NW Germany
Héristal *see* Herstal
Herk-de-Stad 87 C 6 NE Belgium
Hermansverk 85 A 5 S Norway
Hermiston 46 C 2 Oregon, NW USA
Hermon, Mount 119 B 5 *Ar.* Jabal
ash Shaykh. Mountain, SW Syria
Hermosillo 50 B 2 NW Mexico
Hernösand *see* Härnösand
Herrera del Duque 92 D 3 W Spain
Herrick 149 C 8 Tasmania,
SE Australia
Herselt 87 C 5 C Belgium
Herstal 87 D 6 *Fr.* Héristal. E Belgium
Hervey Bay 148 E 4 bay, SE Coral Sea
Herzliyya 119 A 6 *var.* Hertseliya,
Herzeliyya. C Israel
Hessen 95 B 5 cultural region,
C Germany
Heydekrug *see* Šilutė
Hialeah 43 F 5 Florida, SE USA
Hibbing 45 F 1 Minnesota, N USA
Hidalgo del Parral 50 C 2
var. Parral. N Mexico
Hida-sanmyaku 131 C 5 mountain
range, Honshū, S Japan
Hierro 70 A 3 *var.* Ferro. Island,
Islas Canarias, SW Spain
High Atlas *see* Haut Atlas
High Point 43 F 1
North Carolina, SE USA
Hiiumaa 106 C 2 *Ger.* Dagden,
Swe. Dagö. Island, W Estonia
Hikurangi 150 D 2 North Island,
N New Zealand
Hildesheim 94 B 4 N Germany
Hilla *see* Al Hillah
Hillaby, Mount 55 G 1 mountain,
N Barbados
Hill Bank 52 C 1 N Belize
Hillegom 86 C 3 W Netherlands
Hilo 47 B 8 Hawaii, W USA
Hilton Head Island 43 E 2
South Carolina, SE USA
Hilversum 86 C 3 C Netherlands
Himalayas 124 C 2 *var.* Himalaya,
Chin. Himalaya Shan. Mountain
range, S Asia
Himeji 131 C 6 *var.* Himezi.
Honshū, SW Japan
Himezi *see* Himeji
Hims 118 B 4 *var.* Homs;
anc. Emesa. C Syria
Hînceşti 108 D 4 *var.* Hânceşti;
prev. Kotovsk. C Moldova
Hinds 151 C 6 South Island,
SW New Zealand
Hindu Kush 123 F 4 *Per.* Hendū
Kosh. Mountain range,
Afghanistan/Pakistan
Hinesville 43 E 3 Georgia, SE USA
Hinson Bay 42 A 5 bay,
W Atlantic Ocean
Hīrmand Rūd-e *see*
Helmand, Daryā-ye
Hirosaki 130 D 3 Honshū, C Japan
Hiroshima 131 B 7 *var.* Hirosima.
Honshū, SW Japan
Hirosima *see* Hiroshima
Hirson 90 D 3 N France
Hîrşova *see* Hârşova
Hitachi 131 D 5 *var.* Hitati.
Honshū, S Japan
Hitati *see* Hitachi
Hitchinbrook Island 148 D 3
island, Queensland, NE Australia
Hitra 84 A 4 *prev.* Hitteren. Island,
S Norway
Hitteren *see* Hitra

Hjälmaren 85 C 6 *Eng.* Lake
Hjalmar. Lake, C Sweden
Hjalmar, Lake *see* Hjälmaren
Hjørring 85 B 7 N Denmark
Hkakabo Razi 136 B 1 mountain,
Myanmar/China
Hlobyne 109 F 2 *Rus.* Globino.
NE Ukraine
Hlukhiv 109 F 1 *Rus.* Glukhov.
NE Ukraine
Hlybokaye 107 D 5
Rus. Glubokoye, N Belarus
Hoa Binh 136 D 3 N Vietnam
Hoang Liên Sơn 136 D 3 mountain
range, N Vietnam
Hobart 149 C 8 *prev.* Hobart Town,
Hobarton. State capital, Tasmania,
SE Australia
Hobbs 49 E 3 New Mexico, SW USA
Hobro 85 A 7 N Denmark
Hồ Chi Minh 137 E 6 *var.* Ho Chi
Minh, Ho Chi Minh City, Thanh
Pho-Ho Chi Minh, Thanh Pho Ho
Chi Minh, *prev.* Saigon, Sai Gon.
S Vietnam
Hodeida *see* Al Hudaydah
Hódmezővásárhely 99 D 7
SE Hungary
Hodonín 99 B 6 *Ger.* Göding.
SE Czech Republic
Hof 95 C 5 SE Germany
Höfu 131 B 7 Honshū, SW Japan
Hofuf *see* Al Hufūf
Hohenems 95 B 7 W Austria
Hohenstadt *see* Zábřeh
Hohes Venn *see* Hautes Fagnes
Hohe Tauern 95 C 7 mountain
range, W Austria
Hohhot 127 F 3 *var.* Huhehot,
Huhohaot'e, Mongg. Kukukhoto;
prev. Kweisui, Kwesui. N China
Hôi An 137 E 5 *prev.* Faifo.
C Vietnam
Hokianga Harbour 150 C 2
harbour, North Island,
N New Zealand
Hokitika 151 B 5 South Island,
SW New Zealand
Hokkaidō 130 C 2 territory,
Hokkaidō, NE Japan
Hola Prystan' 109 E 4 *Rus.* Golaya
Pristan. S Ukraine
Holbrook 48 B 2 Arizona, SW USA
Holetown 55 G 1 *prev.* Jamestown.
W Barbados
Holguín 54 C 2 SE Cuba
Hollabrunn 95 E 6 NE Austria
Holland 40 C 3 Michigan, N USA
Hollywood 43 F 5 Florida, SE USA
Holman 37 E 3 Victoria Island,
Canada
Holmes Reef 148 D 3 Reef,
W Coral Sea
Holmsund 84 D 4 N Sweden
Holon 119 A 6 C Israel
Holovanivs'k 109 E 3
Rus. Golovanevsk. C Ukraine
Holstebro 85 F 1 Minnesota, N USA
Holyhead 89 C 6 *Wel.* Caer Gybi.
NW Wales, UK
Holyoke 41 G 3
Massachusetts, NE USA
Hombori Tondo 75 E 3 mountain,
E Mali
Homestead 43 F 5 Florida, SE USA
Homonsова, Khrebet *see*
Lomonsov Ridge
Homr, Dar el 72 B 4 physical
region, C Sudan
Homyel' 107 D 7 *Rus.* Gomel'.
SE Belarus
Hondo 49 F 4 Texas, S USA

Honduras
52 C 2 Republic,
N Central America

Official name: Republic of
Honduras **Date of formation:** 1838
Capital: Tegucigalpa **Population:** 5.6
million **Total area:** 43,278 sq miles
(112,090 sq km) **Languages:**
Spanish*, English Creole, Garifuna,
Indian languages **Religions:** Roman
Catholic 97%, other 3% **Ethnic mix:**
mestizo 90%, Indian 7%, Garifuna
(Black Carib) 2%, White 1%
Government: Multiparty republic
Currency: Lempira = 100 centavos

Honduras, Gulf of 52 C 2
Sp. Golfo de Honduras. Gulf,
W Caribbean Sea
Honduras, Republic of *see*
Honduras
Hønefoss 85 B 6 S Norway
Hông Gai 136 E 3 *var.* Hon Gai,
Hongay. N Vietnam
Hong Kong 129 C 6 (official name
Xianggang) former UK dependent
territory, S. China
Hong Kong Island 128 B 2 island,
S Hong Kong
Honiara 144 C 3 country capital,
C Solomon Islands
Honjō 130 D 4 *var.* Honzyô.
Honshū, C Japan
Honolulu 47 A 8 state capital,
Hawaii, W USA
Honshū, 131 E 5 *var.* Hondo,
Honsyû. Island, Japan
Honzyô *see* Honjō
Hood Point 147 B 7 headland,
Western Australia, W Australia
Hoogeveen 86 E 2 NE Netherlands
Hoogezand-Sappemeer 86 E 2
NE Netherlands
Hoorn 86 E 2 NW Netherlands
Hopa 117 F 2 NE Turkey
Hope 36 C 3 Alaska, NW USA
Hopedale 39 F 2 Newfoundland
and Labrador, NE Canada
Hopewell 41 E 5 Virginia, NE USA
Hopkinsville 40 B 5
Kentucky, E USA
Horasan 117 F 3 NE Turkey
Horki 107 E 6 *Rus.* Gorki. E Belarus
Horlivka 109 G 3 *Rom.* Adâncata,
Rus. Gorlovka. E Ukraine
Hormuz, Strait of 120 D 4 *var.*
Strait of Ormuz; *Per.* Tangeh-ye
Hormoz. Strait, Arabian
Sea/Persian Gulf
Hornepayne 38 C 4 Ontario,
S Canada
Hornos, Cabo de 65 C 8 *Eng.* Cape
Horn. Headland, S Chile
Horodnya 109 E 1 *Rus.* Gorodnya.
NE Ukraine
Horodok 108 B 2 *Pol.* Gródek
Jagielloński, *Rus.* Gorodok,
Gorodok Yagellonski. NW Ukraine
Horodyshche 109 E 2
Rus. Gorodishche. C Ukraine
Horoshiri-dake 130 D 2
var. Horosiri Dake. Mountain,
Hokkaidō, NE Japan
Horosiri Dake *see* Horoshiri-dake
Horsburgh Atoll 132 B 4 island,
N Maldives
Horseshoe Bay 42 A 5 bay,
W Atlantic Ocean
Horsham 149 B 7 Victoria,
SE Australia
Horst 87 D 5 SE Netherlands
Horten 85 B 6 S Norway

Hospitalet *see* L'Hospitalet
de Llobregat
Hotan 126 B 4 *var.* Khotan,
Chin. Ho-t'ien. NW China
Hoting 84 C 4 C Sweden
Hot Springs 42 B 1 Arkansas, C USA
Hougang New Town 138 A 1
N Singapore
Houilles 91 B 6 France
Houston 49 H 4 Texas, S USA
Hovd 126 C 2 *var.* Khovd.
W Mongolia
Hove 89 D 7 S England, UK
Hoverla, Hora 108 B 3 *Rus.* Gora
Goverla. Mountain, W Ukraine
Hovsgol, Lake *see* Hövsgöl Nuur
Hövsgöl Nuur 126 D 1 *var.* Lake
Hovsgol. Lake, N Mongolia
Howe, Cape 149 D 7 headland,
SE Australia
Howrah *see* Hāora
Hoy 88 C 2 island, N Scotland, UK
Hoyerswerda 94 D 4 E Germany
Hradec Králové 99 B 5 *Ger.*
Königgrätz. NE Czech Republic
Hrandzichy 107 B 5 *Rus.* Grandichi.
W Belarus
Hranice 99 C 5 *Ger.* Mährisch-
Weisskirchen. E Czech Republic
Hrasnica 100 C 4
SE Bosnia & Herzegovina
Hrebinka 109 E 2 *Rus.* Grebenka.
NE Ukraine
Hrodna 107 B 5 *Pol.* Grodno.
W Belarus
Huacho 60 C 4 W Peru
Hua Hin *see* Ban Hua Hin
Huaihua 129 C 6 C China
Huailai 128 C 3 NE China
Huainan 129 D 5 *var.* Huai-nan,
Hwainan. E China
Huajuapan 51 E 5 *var.* Huajuapan
de León. SE Mexico
Huajuapan de León *see* Huajuapan
Hualapai Mountains 48 A 2
mountain range,
Arizona, SW USA
Huallaga 60 C 2 river, N Peru
Huambo 78 B 2 *Port.* Nova Lisboa.
C Angola
Huancavelica 60 D 4 SW Peru
Huancayo 60 D 4 C Peru
Huang He (Yellow River) 128 C 4
var. Yellow River. River, C China
Huangshi 129 C 5 *var.* Huang-shih,
Hwangshih. E China
Huanta 60 D 4 C Peru
Huánuco 60 C 3 C Peru
Huanuni 61 F 4 W Bolivia
Huaral 60 C 4 W Peru
Huarás *see* Huaraz
Huaraz 60 C 3 *var.* Huarás. W Peru
Huarmey 60 C 3 W Peru
Huatabampo 50 B 2 NW Mexico
Hubei 129 C 5 *var.* E, Hupei.
Province, C China
Hubli 132 B 2 SW India
Huddersfield 89 D 5 N England, UK
Hudiksvall 85 C 5 C Sweden
Hudson 38 C 1 inlet,
NW Atlantic Ocean
Hudson, Détroit d' *see* Hudson Strait
Hudson Strait 38 D 1 *Fr.* Détroit
d'Hudson. Strait, Atlantic
Ocean/Hudson Bay
Huê 136 E 4 C Vietnam
Huehuetenango 52 A 2 W Guatemala
Huelva 92 C 5 *anc.* Onuba. SW Spain
Huesca 93 F 2 *anc.* Osca. NE Spain
Huéscar 93 E 4 S Spain
Hughenden 148 C 3 NE Australia

Hugo 49 G 2 Oklahoma, C USA
Huíla Plateau 78 B 2 plateau,
S Angola
Huixtla 51 G 5 SE Mexico
Hukui *see* Fukui
Hukusima *see* Fukushima
Hull 38 D 4 Québec, SE Canada
Hull *see* Kingston upon Hull
Hull Island *see* Orona
Hulst 87 B 5 SW Netherlands
Hulun Nur 127 F 1 *var.* Hu-lun
Ch'ih; *prev.* Dalai Nor. Lake,
NE China
Humaitá 62 D 2 N Brazil
Humboldt 42 C 1 Tennessee, S USA
Humboldt River 47 C 5 river,
Nevada, W USA
Humpolec 99 B 5 *Ger.* Gumpolds,
Humpoletz. C Czech Republic
Hunan 129 C 5 *var.* Xiang. Province,
S China
Hunedoara 108 B 4 *Ger.* Eisenmarkt,
Hung. Vajdahunyad. SW Romania
Hünfeld 95 B 5 C Germany

Hungary
99 D 6 *Ger.* Ungarn, *Hung.*
Magyarország, *Rom.* Ungaria,
SCr. Madarska, *Ukr.* Uhorshchyna;
prev. Hungarian People's
Republic. Republic, C Europe

Official name: Republic of Hungary
Date of formation: 1918/1945
Capital: Budapest **Population:** 10.5
million **Total area:** 35,919 sq miles
(93,030 sq km) **Languages:**
Hungarian (Magyar)*, German,
Slovak **Religions:** Roman Catholic
68%, Protestant 25%, other 7%
Ethnic mix: Hungarian (Magyar)
90%, German 2%, other 8%
Government: Multiparty republic
Currency: Forint = 100 filler

Hunjiang 128 E 3 NE China
Hunter Islands 149 B 8 island
group, Tasmania, SW Australia
Huntington 40 D 5
West Virginia, NE USA
Huntington Beach 47 C 8
California, W USA
Huntly 150 D 3 North Island,
N New Zealand
Huntsville 42 D 1 Alabama, S USA
Huntsville 38 D 5 Ontario, S Canada
Huntsville 49 G 3 Texas, S USA
Huolin Gol He 127 F 2 NE China
Hurghada 72 C 2 *var.* Al
Ghurdaqah, Ghurdaqah. E Egypt
Huri Hills 73 C 5 mountain range,
NW Kenya
Huron 45 E 3 South Dakota, N USA
Huron, Lake 40 D 2 lake,
Canada/USA
Hurukawa *see* Furukawa
Húsavík 83 E 4 NE Iceland
Husum 94 B 2 N Germany
Hutchinson 45 E 5 Kansas, C USA
Huy 87 C 6 *Dut.* Hoei, Hoey.
E Belgium
Hvannadalshnúkur 83 E 5
mountain, S Iceland
Hvar 100 B 4 *It.* Lesina; *anc.* Pharus.
Island, S Croatia
Hwange 78 D 3 *prev.* Wankie.
W Zimbabwe
Hyargas Nuur 126 D 2 lake,
W Mongolia
Hyderābād 134 D 5
var. Haidarabad. C India
Hyderābād 134 B 3
var. Haidarabad. SE Pakistan

Hyères 91 D 6 SE France
Hyères, Îles d' 91 D 6 island gro
S France
Hyvinge *see* Hyvinkää
Hyvinkää 85 D 5 *Swe.* Hyvinge.
S Finland

I

Ialomita 108 C 5 river, SE Roma
Iaşi 108 D 4 *Ger.* Jassy.
NE Romania
Ibadan 75 F 5 SW Nigeria
Ibagué 58 B 3 C Colombia
Ibar 100 D 4 *Alb.* Ibër. River,
C Yugoslavia
Ibarra 60 B 1 *var.* San Miguel de
Ibarra. N Ecuador
Ibër *see* Ibar
Iberian Basin 66 C 3 undersea
basin, E Atlantic Ocean
Iberian Peninsula 68 B 2 physica
region, Portugal/Spain
Ibérico, Sistema 93 E 2 *var.*
Cordillera Ibérica, *Eng.* Iberian
Mountains. Mountain range,
NE Spain
Ibiza *see* Eivissa
Ibusuki 130 B 2 Kyūshū, SW Jap
Ica 60 D 4 SW Peru
Içá *see* Putumayo

Iceland
83 E 4 *Dan.* Island, *Icel.* Ísland
Republic, NW Europe

Official name: Republic of Icelan
Date of formation: 1944 **Capital:**
Reykjavik **Population:** 300,000 **To**
area: 39,770 sq miles (103,000 sq k
Languages: Icelandic*, English
Religions: Evangelical Lutheran
96%, other Christian 3%, other 1%
Ethnic mix: Icelandic (Norwegian
Celtic descent) 98%, other 2%
Government: Constitutional repu
Currency: Krona = 100 aurar

Iceland Basin 66 C 2 undersea
basin, N Atlantic Ocean
Icelandic Plateau 155 F 5
var. Iceland Plateau. Undersea
plateau, Arctic Ocean/
Atlantic Ocean
Iculisma *see* Angoulême
Idabel 49 H 2 Oklahoma, C USA
Idaho 46 D 3 *off.* State of Idaho;
nicknames Gem State, Gem of t
Mountains. State, NW USA
Idaho Falls 46 E 3 Idaho, NW US
Idensalmi *see* Iisalmi
Idfu 72 B 2 *var.* Edfu. SE Egypt
Idlib 118 B 3 NW Syria
Idre 85 B 5 C Sweden
Iecava 106 C 3 S Latvia
Ieper 87 A 6 *Fr.* Ypres. W Belgiur
Ierápetra 105 D 8 Kríti, SE Greece
Ierisós 104 C 4 *var.* Ierisós.
N Greece
Iferouâne 75 G 2 N Niger
Ifôghas, Adrar des 75 F 2 *var.* Ad
des Iforas. Mountain range,
NE Mali
Iforas, Adrar des *see*
Adrar des Ifôghas
Igarka 114 D 3
N Russian Federation
Iglesias 97 A 5 W Italy
Igloolik 37 G 3 Northwest
Territories, N Canada
Ignace 38 B 4 Ontario, S Canada
Igoumenítsa 104 A 4 W Greece

ala 51 E 5 var. Iguala de la
ndependencia.
S Mexico
ala de la Independencia see Iguala
vandiffulu Atoll see
navandippolhu Atoll
vandippolhu Atoll 132 B 4
ar. Ihavandiffulu Atoll. Island,
J Maldives
sy 79 F 4 S Madagascar
mi 84 E 4 var. Idensalmi. C Finland
ne 74 D 2 desert, Mauritania
el 86 D 3 var. Yssel. River,
Germany/Netherlands
elmeer 86 C 2 prev. Zuider Zee.
ake, N Netherlands
elmuiden 86 D 3
Netherlands
r 87 A 6 river, W Belgium
ria 105 D 6 var. Kariot, Nicaria,
Nikaria; anc. Icaria. Island,
E Greece
131 A 7 island, Japan
gan 139 E 1 Luzon,
J Philippines
va 98 D 3 Ger. Deutsch-Eylau.
J Poland
o 77 C 6 prev. Port-Francqui.
N Congo (Zaire)
de-France 90 C 3 cultural
egion, N France
acombe 89 C 7 SW England, UK
z 116 C 2 Turkey
avo 92 B 3 W Portugal
nna Lake 36 C 3 lake,
Alaska, NW USA
chevsk see Illichivs'k
an 139 F 2 off. Iligan City.
Mindanao, S Philippines
an City see Iligan
pel 64 B 4 C Chile
chivs'k 109 E 4 Rus. Il'ichevsk.
W Ukraine
nois 40 B 4 off. State of Illinois;
nicknames Prairie State, Sucker
tate. State, C USA
nois River 40 B 4 river,
Illinois, N USA
ro see Mataró
61 E 4 SW Peru
lo 139 E 2 off. Iloilo City. Panay
sland, C Philippines
lo City see Iloilo
in 75 F 4 W Nigeria
n see Batman
issat 82 C 3 Dan. Jakobshavn.
W Greenland
aly 122 C 2 var. Ylylanly.
N Turkmenistan
atra 85 E 5 SE Finland
shli see Imişli
şli 117 H 3 Rus. Imishli.
Azerbaijan
ola 96 C 3 N Italy
peratriz 63 F 2 NE Brazil
peria 96 A 3 NW Italy
pfondo 77 C 5 NE Congo
phäl 135 H 3 NE India
gua Islands see Great
nagua/Little Inagua
Amenas 71 E 3 var. In Aménas,
n Amnas. E Algeria
rijärvi 84 D 2 Lapp. Aanaarjävri,
Sive. Enareträsk. Lake, N Finland
washiro-ko 131 D 5 var.
nawasiro Ko. Lake, Honshū,
Japan
wasiro Ko see Inawashiro-ko
esu 116 D 3 C Turkey
h'ŏn 128 E 4 off. Inch'ŏn-
kwangyŏksi, Jap. Jinsen; prev.
Chemulpo. NW South Korea

Independence 45 F 4
Missouri, C USA
Independence Fjord 83 E 1 fjord,
W Wandell Sea
Independence Island see
Malden Island
Independence Mountains 46 D 4
mountain range, Nevada, W USA
India
124 B 3 var. Indian Union, Union
of India, Hind. Bhārat. Republic,
S Asia
Official name: Republic of India
Date of formation: 1947/1961
Capital: New Delhi Population: 953
million Total Area:
1,269,338 sq miles (3,287,590 sq km)
Languages: Hindi*, English*
Religions: Hindu 83%, Muslim 11%,
Christian 2%, Sikh 2%, other 2%
Ethnic mix: Indo-Aryan 72%,
Dravidian 25%, Mongoloid and
other 3% Government: Multiparty
republic Currency: Rupee =
100 paisa

Indiana 40 B 4 off. State of Indiana;
nickname Hoosier State. State,
C USA
Indianapolis 40 C 4 state captal,
Indiana, N USA
Indian Church 52 C 1 N Belize
Indian Ocean 141 C 5 ocean,
Indianola 45 F 4 Iowa, C USA
Indigirka 115 G 2 river,
NE Russian Federation
Indija 100 D 3 var. Indhja,
Hung. India. N Yugoslavia
Indio 47 D 8 California, W USA
Indomed Fracture Zone 141 A 6
fracture zone, SW Indian Ocean
Indonesia
138 C 4 Ind. Republik Indonesia;
prev. Dutch East Indies,
Netherlands East Indies, United
States of Indonesia. Republic,
SE Asia
Official name: Republic of Indonesia
Date of formation: 1949/1963
Capital: Jakarta Population: 200.6
million Total Area: 735,555 sq miles
(1,904,570 sq km) Languages: Bahasa
Indonesia*, 250 (est.) languages or
dialects Religions: Muslim 87%,
Christian 10%, Hindu 2%, Buddhist
1% Ethnic mix: Javanese 45%,
Sundanese 14%, Madurese 8%, other
33% Government: Multiparty
republic Currency: Rupiah = 100 sen

Indonesian Borneo see
Kalimantan
Indore 134 D 4 C India
Indreville see Châteauroux
Indus 135 C 4 Chin. Yindu He;
prev. Yin-tu Ho. River, S Asia
Indus Cone see Indus Fan
Indus Fan 140 B 3 var. Indus Cone.
Undersea fan, N Indian Ocean
Indus, Mouths of the 134 B 4 delta,
S Pakistan
İnebolu 116 C 2 N Turkey
Ineu 108 A 4 Hung. Borosjenő;
prev. Inău. W Romania
Infiernillo, Presa del 51 E 4
reservoir, S Mexico
Inglefield Land 82 D 1 physical
region, NW Greenland
Ingolstadt 95 C 6 S Germany
Ingulets see Inhulets'
Inguri see Enguri
Inhambane 79 E 4 SE Mozambique

Inhulets' 109 F 3 Rus. Ingulets.
E Ukraine
Inis see Ennis
Inn 95 C 6 river, C Europe
Inner Hebrides 88 B 4 island
group, W Scotland, UK
Inner Islands 79 H 1 var. Central
Group. Island group, Seychelles
Innisfail 148 D 3 Queensland,
NE Australia
Innsbruch see Innsbruck
Innsbruck 95 C 7 var. Innsbruch.
W Austria
Inowrocław 98 C 3
Ger. Hohensalza; prev.
Inowrazlaw. C Poland
I-n-Salah 70 D 3 var. In Salah.
C Algeria
In Salah see I-n-Salah
Insterburg see Chernyakhovsk
Inta 110 E 3
NW Russian Federation
Interamna see Terni
Interamna Nahars see Terni
International Falls 45 F 1
Minnesota, N USA
Inukjuak 38 D 2 var. Inoucdjouac;
prev. Port Harrison. Québec,
NE Canada
Inuuvik see Inuvik
Inuvik 37 E 3 var. Inuuvik.
Northwest Territories, NW Canada
Invercargill 151 A 7 South Island,
SW New Zealand
Inverell 149 D 6 New South Wales,
SE Australia
Inverness 88 C 3 N Scotland, UK
Investigator Ridge 140 D 4
undersea ridge, E Indian Ocean
Investigator Strait 149 A 7 strait,
SE Indian Ocean
Inyangani 78 D 3 mountain,
NE Zimbabwe
Ioánnina 104 A 4 var. Janina,
Yannina. W Greece
Iola 45 F 5 Kansas, C USA
Ionia Basin see Ionian Basin
Ionian Basin 80 D 5 var. Ionia
Basin. Undersea basin,
C Mediterranean Sea
Ionian Islands see Iónioi Nísoi
Ionian Sea 103 E 3 Gk. Iónio
Pélagos, It. Mar Ionio. Sea,
C Mediterranean Sea
Iónioi Nísoi 105 A 5 Eng. Ionian
Islands. Island group, W Greece
Íos 105 D 7 Íos, SE Greece
Íos 105 D 7 var. Nio. Island,
Kykládes, SE Greece
Iowa 45 F 3 off. State of Iowa; nickname
Hawkeye State. State, C USA
Iowa City 45 G 3 Iowa, C USA
Iowa Falls 45 G 3 Iowa, C USA
Ipel' 99 C 6 var. Ipoly, Ger. Eipel.
River, Hungary/Slovakia
Ipiales 51 A 4 SW Colombia
Ipirá 63 G 3 E Brazil
Ipoh 138 B 3 W Malaysia
Ippy 76 C 4
C Central African Republic
Ipswich 89 E 6 hist. Gipeswic.
E England, UK
Ipswich 149 E 5 Queensland,
E Australia
Iqaluit 37 H 3 prev. Frobisher Bay.
Baffin Island, NE Canada
Iquique 64 B 1 N Chile
Iquitos 60 C 1 N Peru
Irákleio 105 D 8 var. Herakleion,
Eng. Candia; prev. Iráklion. Kríti,
SE Greece

Iran
120 C 3 prev. Persia. Republic,
SW Asia
Official name: Islamic Republic of
Iran Date of formation: 1906
Capital: Tehran Population: 68.7
million Total area: 636,293 sq miles
(1,648,000 sq km) Languages: Farsi
(Persian)*, Azerbaijani, Kurdish
Religions: Shi'a Muslim 95%, Sunni
Muslim 4%, other 1% Ethnic mix:
Persian 52%, Azerbaijani 24%,
Kurdish 9%, other 15%
Government: Islamic Republic
Currency: Rial = 100 dinars

Iranian Plateau 120 D 3 var. Plateau
of Iran. Plateau, C Iran
Iran, Plateau of see Iranian Plateau
Irapuato 51 E 4 C Mexico
Iraq
120 B 3 Ar. 'Irāq. Republic,
SW Asia
Official name: Republic of Iraq
Date of formation: 1932/1981
Capital: Baghdad Population: 21
million Total area: 169,235 sq miles
(438,320 sq km) Languages:
Arabic*, Kurdish, Turkish, Farsi
(Persian) Religions: Shi'a Muslim
63%, Sunni Muslim 34%, other 3%
Ethnic mix: Arab 79%, Kurdish 16%,
Persian 3%, Turkish 2%
Government: Single-party republic
Currency: Dinar = 1,000 fils

Irbid 119 B 5 NW Jordan
Ireland, Republic of
89 B 5 var. Ireland, Ir. Éire.
Republic, NW Europe
Official name: Republic of Ireland
Date of formation: 1921/1922
Capital: Dublin Population: 3.5
million Total area: 27,155 sq miles
(70,280 sq km) Languages: English*,
Irish Gaelic* Religions: Roman
Catholic 93%, Protestant 5%, other
2% Ethnic mix: Irish 95%, other 5%
Government: Multiparty republic
Currency: Irish pound = 100 pence

Irian Jaya 139 H 4 cultural region,
E Indonesia
Iringa 73 C 7 C Tanzania
Iriomote-jima 130 A 4 var.
Sakishima-shotō, SW Japan
Iriona 52 D 2 NE Honduras
Irish Sea 89 C 5 Ir. Muir Éireann.
Sea, NE Atlantic Ocean
Irkutsk 115 E 4 C Russian Federation
Iroise 90 A 3 NW France
Irrawaddy 136 B 2 var.
Ayeyarwady. River, C Myanmar
Irrawaddy, Mouths of the 137 A 5
delta area, SW Myanmar
Irtysh 114 C 3 var. Irtish, Kaz. Ertis.
River, C Asia
Irún 93 E 1 N Spain
Irving 49 G 2 Texas, S USA
Isabela, Isla 60 A 5 var. Albemarle
Island. Island, W Ecuador
Isaccea 108 D 5 E Romania
Isachsen 37 F 1
Ellef Ringnes Island, N Canada
Isbarta see Isparta
Isca Damnoniorum see Exeter
Ischia, Isola d' 97 C 5 island, S Italy
Ise 131 C 6 Honshū, SW Japan
Iseghem see Izegem
Isère 91 D 5 river, E France

Isernia 97 D 5 *var.* Æsernia.
S Italy
Ise-wan 131 C 6 bay, NW Pacific Ocean
Isfahan *see* Isfahan
Isherton 59 F 4 S Guyana
Ishigaki-jima 130 A 4 *var.* Isigaki
Zima. Island, Sakishima-shotō,
SW Japan
Ishikari-wan 130 C 2 bay,
NE Sea of Japan
Ishim 114 C 4 C Russian Federation
Ishim 114 C 4 *Kaz.* Esil.
River,
Kazakhstan/Russian Federation
Ishimbay 111 D 6
W Russian Federation
Ishinomaki 130 D 4 *var.* Isinomaki.
Honshū, C Japan
Ishkashim *see* Ishkoshim
Ishkoshim 123 F 3 *Rus.* Ishkashim.
S Tajikistan
Isinomaki *see* Ishinomaki
Isiro 77 E 5 NE Congo (Zaire)
Iskår *see* Iskūr
İskenderun 116 D 4 *Eng.*
Alexandretta. S Turkey
Iskŭr 104 C 2 *var.* Iskår. River,
NW Bulgaria
Iskŭr, Yazovir 104 C 2 *prev.* Stalin,
Yazovir. Reservoir, W Bulgaria
Isla Cristina 92 C 5 S Spain
Isla de León *see* San Fernando
Islāmābād 134 C 1 country capital,
NE Pakistan
Island Lagoon 149 B 6 lake,
South Australia, S Australia
Islay 88 B 4 island, SW Scotland, UK
Isle 91 B 5 river, W France
Ismailia *see* Ismā'īliya
Ismā'īliya 72 B 1 *var.* Ismailia.
N Egypt
Isna 72 B 2 *var.* Esna. SE Egypt
Isoka 78 D 1 NE Zambia
İsparta 116 B 4 *var.* Isbarta.
SW Turkey
İspir 117 E 3 NE Turkey

Israel
119 A 7 *var.* Medinat Israel,
Heb. Yisrael, Yisra'el. Republic,
SW Asia

Official name: State of Israel
Date of formation: 1948/1982
Capital: Jerusalem **Population**
5.4 million **Total area:** 7,992 sq miles
(20,700 sq km) **Languages:** Hebrew*,
Arabic, Yiddish
Religions: Jewish 83%, Muslim 13%,
Christian 2%, other 2% **Ethnic mix:**
Jewish 83%, Arab 17%
Government: Multiparty republic
Currency: New shekel = 100 agorat

Issoire 91 C 5 C France
Issyk-Kul', Ozero 123 G 2 *var.* Issiq
Köl, *Kir.* Ysyk-Köl. Lake,
E Kyrgyzstan
İstanbul 116 B 2 *Bul.* Tsarigrad,
Eng. Istanbul; *prev.* Constantinople,
anc. Byzantium. NW Turkey
Istanbul *see* Istanbul
İstanbul Boğazı 116 B 2
var. Bosporus Thracius,
Eng. Bosporus, *Turk.* Karadeniz
Boëazi. Strait, Sea of
Marmara/Black Sea
Istra 96 D 2 *Eng.* Istria. Peninsula,
Slovenia/Yugoslavia
Istra 100 A 2 *Eng.* Istria, *Ger.* Istrien.
Cultural region, NW Croatia
Istria *see* Istra
Itabuna 63 G 3 E Brazil
Itagüí 58 B 3 W Colombia
Itaituba 63 E 2 NE Brazil

Italy
96 C 3 *It.* Italia, Republica
Italiana. Republic, S Europe

Official name: Italian Republic
Date of formation: 1871/1954
Capital: Rome **Population:** 57.8
million **Total area:** 116,320 sq miles
(301,270 sq km) **Languages:** Italian*,
French, Rhaeto-Romanic, Sardinian
Religions: Roman Catholic 99%,
other 1% **Ethnic mix:** Italian 98%,
other 2% **Government:** Multiparty
republic **Currency:** Lira =
100 centesimi

It Amelân *see* Ameland
Iténez, Río *see* Guaporé
Ithaca 41 F 3 New York, NE USA
It Hearrenfean *see* Heerenveen
Itoigawa 131 C 5 Honshū, C Japan
Ittoqqortoormiit 83 E 4
var. Itseqqortoormiit,
Dan. Scoresbysund, *Eng.* Scoresby
Sound. SE Greenland
Iturup, Ostrov 115 H 4 island,
Kuril'skiye Ostrova,
SE Russian Federation
Itzehoe 94 B 2 N Germany
Ivalo 84 D 2 *Lapp.* Avvil, Avveel.
N Finland
Ivanava 107 B 7 *var.* Janów Poleski,
Pol. Janów, *Rus.* Ivanovo.
SW Belarus
Ivangrad 101 D 5 *var.* Berane
C Yugoslavia
Ivanhoe 149 C 6 New South Wales,
SE Australia
Ivano-Frankivs'k 108 C 2
Ger. Stanislau, *Pol.* Stanisĵawów,
Rus. Ivano-Frankovsk; *prev.*
Stanislav. W Ukraine
Ivanovo 111 C 5
W Russian Federation
Ivatsevichy 107 B 6 *Pol.*
Iwacewicze, *Rus.* Ivantsevichi,
Ivatsevichi. SW Belarus
Ivigtut *see* Ivittuut
Ivittuut 82 B 4 *var.* Ivigtut.
SW Greenland
Ivory Coast 74 D 5 *Fr.* Côte
d'Ivoire. Coastal region,
S Ivory Coast

Ivory Coast
74 D 4 *Fr.* République de la Côte
d'Ivoire, Côte d'Ivoire. Republic,
NW Africa

Official name: Republic of the Ivory
Coast **Date of formation:** 1960
Capital: Yamoussoukro **Population:**
13.4 million **Total area:** 124,503 sq
miles (322,463 sq km) **Languages:**
French*, Akran **Religions:**
Traditional beliefs 63%, Muslim
25%, Christian 12% **Ethnic mix:**
Baoule 23%, Bété 18%, Kru 17%,
Malinke 15%, other 27%
Government: Multiparty republic
Currency: CFA franc = 100 centimes

Ivujivik 38 D 1 Québec, NE Canada
Iwaki 131 D 5 Honshū, N Japan
Iwakuni 131 B 7 Honshū, SW Japan
Iwanai 130 C 2 Hokkaidō,
NE Japan
Iwate 130 D 4 Honshū, N Japan
Ixtapa 51 F 5 S Mexico
Ixtepec 51 F 5 SE Mexico
Iyo-nada 131 B 7 sea,
NW Pacific Ocean
Izabal, Lago de 52 B 2 *prev.* Golfo
Dulce. Lake, E Guatemala

Izberbash 111 B 8
SW Russian Federation
Izegem 87 A 6 *prev.* Iseghem.
W Belgium
Izhevsk 111 D 5 *prev.* Ustinov.
NW Russian Federation
Izmail *see* Izmayil
Izmayil 108 D 4 *Rus.* Izmail.
SW Ukraine
İzmir 116 A 3 *prev.* Smyrna. W Turkey
İzmit 116 B 3 *var.* Ismid;
anc. Astacus. NW Turkey
İznik Gölü 116 B 3 lake, NW Turkey
Izúcar de Matamoros *see*
Matamoros
Izu-hantō 131 D 6 peninsula,
Honshū, S Japan
Izu-shotō 131 D 6 island group,
Japan
Izvor 104 B 2 W Bulgaria
Izyaslav 108 C 2 W Ukraine
Izyum 109 G 2 E Ukraine

J

Jabalpur 135 E 4 *prev.* Jubbulpore.
C India
Jabbūl, Sabkhat al 118 C 2 salt flat,
NW Syria
Jablah 118 B 3 *var.* Jeble, *Fr.* Djéblé.
W Syria
Jaca 93 F 1 NE Spain
Jacaltenango 52 A 2 W Guatemala
Jackson 42 B 2 Mississippi, S USA
Jackson 42 C 1 Alabama, S USA
Jackson 42 C 3 Tennessee, S USA
Jackson 45 H 5 Missouri, C USA
Jackson Head 151 A 6 headland,
South Island, SW New Zealand
Jacksonville 43 E 3 Florida, SE USA
Jacksonville 43 F 1
North Carolina, SE USA
Jacksonville 42 B 1
Arkansas, SE USA
Jacksonville 49 H 3 Texas, S USA
Jacksonville 40 B 4 Illinois, N USA
Jacksonville Beach 43 E 3
Florida, SE USA
Jacmel 54 D 3 *var.* Jaquemel. S Haiti
Jacob *see* Nkayi
Jacobābād 134 B 3 SE Pakistan
Jadotville *see* Likasi
Jādū 71 F 2 NW Libya
Jaén 92 D 4 SW Spain
Jaén 62 B 3 N Peru
Jaffna 132 D 3 N Sri Lanka
Jagdalpur 135 E 5 C India
Jagodina *see* Svetozarevo
Jaipur 134 D 3 *prev.* Jeypore.
State capital, N India
Jajce 100 B 3
W Bosnia & Herzegovina
Jakarta 138 C 5 *Dut.* Batavia;
prev. Djakarta. Country capital,
Jawa, C Indonesia
Jakobshavn *see* Ilulissat
Jakobstad 84 D 4 *Fin.* Pietarsaari.
W Finland
Jakobstadt *see* Jēkabpils
Jalal-Abad *see* Dzhalal-Abad
Jalālābād 123 F 4 *var.* Jalalabad,
Jelalabad. E Afghanistan
Jalandhar 134 D 2 *prev.* Jullundur.
N India
Jalapa 52 D 3 NW Nicaragua
Jalpa 50 D 4 C Mexico
Jaluit Atoll 144 D 2 *var.* Jalwoj.
Island, S Marshall Islands
Jālwōj *see* Jaluit Atoll
Jamaame 73 D 6 *It.* Giamame;
prev. Margherita. S Somalia

Jamaica
54 A 4 Commonwealth republ
N Caribbean Sea

Official name: Jamaica **Date of**
formation: 1962 **Capital:** Kingsto
Population: 2.5 million **Total area**
4,243 sq miles (10,990 sq km)
Languages: English*, English
Creole, other **Religions:** Christiar
60%, other 40% **Ethnic mix:** Black
75%, mixed 15%, South Asian 5%
other 5% **Government:**
Parliamentary democracy **Current**
Jamaican $ = 100 cents

Jamaica Channel 54 D 3 channel,
N Caribbean Sea
Jamālpur 135 G 3 N Bangladesh
Jambi 138 B 4 *var.* Telanaipura;
prev. Djambi. Sumatera,
W Indonesia
Jamdena *see* Yamdena, Pulau
James Bay 38 C 3 bay, S Hudson
James River 45 E 3 river, N USA
Jamestown 41 E 3
New York, NE USA
Jamestown 45 E 2
North Dakota, N USA
Jamestown *see* Holetown
Jammerbugten 85 A 7 bay,
E North Sea
Jammu 134 D 2 *prev.* Jummoo.
State capital, NW India
Jammu and Kashmir 134 D 1
var. Jammu-Kashmir, Kashmir.
State, NW India
Jammu and Kashmir *see* Kashmir
Jāmnagar 134 C 4 *prev.* Navanaga
W India
Jamshedpur 135 F 4 NE India
Janaúba 63 F 3 SE Brazil
Janesville 40 B 3 Wisconsin, N U
Janischken *see* Joniškis
Jankovac *see* Jánoshalma
Jan Mayen 83 F 4 Norwegian
territory, N Norwegian Sea
Jánoshalma 99 D 7 *SCr.* Jankovac
S Hungary

Japan
130 C 4 *var.* Nippon, *Jap.* Nihor
Monarchy, E Asia

Official name: Japan **Date of**
formation: 1868/1945 **Capital:**
Tokyo **Population:** 125 million **To**
Area: 145,869 sq miles (800 sq km
Languages: Japanese*, Korean,
Chinese **Religions:** Shinto and
Buddhist 76%, Buddhist 16%, othe
8% **Ethnic mix:** Japanese 99.4%,
other 0.6% **Government:**
Constitutional monarchy
Currency: Yen = 100 sen

Japan, Sea of 130 B 4
Rus. Yapanskoye More. Sea,
SW Pacific Ocean
Japan Trench 152 B 2 trench,
NW Pacific Ocean
Japen *see* Yapen, Pulau
Japiim 62 C 2 *var.* Máncio Lima.
W Brazil
Japurá, Río 62 C 1 *var.* Río Caque
Yapurá. River, Brazil/Colombia
Jaqué 53 G 5 SE Panama
Jaquemel *see* Jacmel
Jarābulus 118 C 2 *var.* Jarablos,
Jerablus, *Fr.* Djérablous. N Syria
Jaransk *see* Yaransk
Jardines de la Reina, Archipiéla
de los 54 B 2 island, group
C Cuba

ega *see* Yarega
id, Shaṭṭ al *see* Jerid, Chott el
ocin 98 C 4 C Poland
oslavl *see* Yaroslavl'
osław 99 E 5 *Ger.* Jaroslau,
Rus. Yaroslav. SE Poland
qŭrghon 123 E 3 *Rus.*
Dzharkurgan. S Uzbekistan
vis Island 145 F 2 US
unincorporated territory,
C Pacific Ocean
do 99 D 5 SE Poland
per 42 C 2 Alabama, S USA
sy *see* Iaşi
rzębie-Zdrój 99 C 5 *var.*
astrzebie Zdrój, Jastrzebie-Zdrój.
S Poland
naí 63 E 3 C Brazil
f *see* Al Jawf
npiebalga 106 D 3 NE Latvia
npur 135 E 3 N India
a *see* Jawa
ari 60 D 2 *var.* Yavari. River,
Brazil/ Peru
ari *see* Yavari
a Sea *see* Jawa, Laut
a Trench 141 E 5 trench,
E Indian Ocean
va 138 C 5 *Eng.* Java; *prev.* Djawa.
Island, C Indonesia
va, Laut 138 D 4 *Eng.* Java Sea.
Sea, W Pacific Ocean
whar 73 D 6 *var.* Jowhar,
It. Giohar. S Somalia
a, Puncak 139 G 4 *prev.* Puntjak
Carstensz, Puntjak Sukarno.
Mountain, New Guinea,
E Indonesia
apura 139 H 4 *var.* Djajapura,
Dut. Hollandia; *prev.* Kotabaru,
Sukarnapura. New Guinea,
E Indonesia
Murian, Hamun-e 120 E 4 lake,
SE Iran
oba 75 F 4 W Nigeria
el ash Shifā 120 A 4 desert,
NW Saudi Arabia
lda *see* Jiddah
lrzejów 98 D 4 *Ger.* Endersdorf.
S Poland
ferson City 45 G 5 state capital,
Missouri, C USA
ga 75 F 4 NW Nigeria
ol *see* Chengde
abpils 106 D 4 *Ger.* Jakobstadt.
S Latvia
enia Góra 98 B 4 *Ger.* Hirschberg,
Hirschberg im Riesengebirge,
Hirschberg in Riesengebirge,
Hirschberg in Schlesien. SW Poland
gava 106 C 3 *Ger.* Mitau. C Latvia
nappes 87 B 7 S Belgium
nber 138 D 5 *prev.* Djember. Jawa,
C Indonesia
na 94 C 4 C Germany
ain 119 E 6 N Israel
quitinhonha 56 E 4 river, E Brazil
ada 70 D 2 NE Morocco
ba, Île de 71 F 2 *var.* Djerba,
Jazirat Jarbah. Island, E Tunisia
émie 54 D 3 SW Haiti
éz de la Frontera 92 C 5
var. Jerez; *prev.* Xeres. SW Spain
éz de los Caballeros 92 C 4
W Spain
richo 119 E 7 *Ar.* Arīḥā,
Heb. Yeriho. E West Bank
rid, Chott el 71 E 2 lake, N Tunisia
rsey 89 D 8 island,
S Channel Islands
rsey City 41 F 4
New Jersey, NE USA

Jerusalem 119 B 6 *var.* Al Quds ash
Sharīf, *Ar.* Al Quds, *Heb.*
Yerushalayim; *anc.* Hierosolyma.
Country capital, NE Israel
Jesenice 95 D 7 *Ger.* Assling.
NW Slovenia
Jesselton *see* Kota Kinabalu
Jessore 135 G 4 W Bangladesh
Jesús María 64 C 3 C Argentina
Jeypore *see* Jaipur
Jhānsi 134 D 3 N India
Jhelum 134 C 2 NE Pakistan
Jiangmen 129 C 6 SE China
Jiangsu 128 D 4 *var.* Chiang-su,
Kiangsu, Su. Province, E China
Jiangxi 129 C 5 *var.*Chiang-hsi,
Gan, Kiangsi. Province,
SE China
Jiaxing 129 D 5 E China
Jibuti *see* Djibouti
Jiddah 121 A 5 *Eng.* Jedda.
W Saudi Arabia
Jiftlik Post 119 E 7 E West Bank
Jīgān 121 B 6 *var.* Qīzān.
SW Saudi Arabia
Jihlava 99 B 5 *Ger.* Iglau,
Pol. Iglawa. S Czech Republic
Jilf al Kabīr, Haḍabat al *see*
Gilf Kebir Plateau
Jilib 73 D 6 *It.* Gelib. S Somalia
Jilin 128 E 3 *var.* Chi-lin, Girin,
Kirin; *prev.* Yunki, Yungki.
NE China
Jilin 128 E 3 *var.* Chi-lin, Girin,
Kirin, Ji. Province, NE China
Jill, Kediet ej 74 C 2 *var.* Kédia
d'Idjil, Kediet Ijill. Mountain,
NW Mauritania
Jīma 73 C 5 *var.* Jimma, *It.* Gimma.
SW Ethiopia
Jimbolia 108 A 4 *Ger.* Hatzfeld,
Hung. Zsombolya. W Romania
Jiménez 50 D 2 N Mexico
Jimsar 126 C 3 W China
Jinan 128 D 4 *var.* Chinan, Chi-nan,
Tsinan. Province capital, E China
Jingdezhen 129 D 5 E China
Jinghong 129 A 7 SW China
Jinhua 129 D 5 E China
Jining 127 F 3 NW China
Jinja 73 C 6 S Uganda
Jinotega 52 D 3 NW Nicaragua
Jinotepe 52 D 3 SW Nicaragua
Jinsha 129 A 5 river, SW China
Jinzhou 128 D 3 *var.* Chin-chou,
Chinchow; *prev.* Chinhsien.
NE China
Ji-Paraná 62 D 3 W Brazil
Jisr ash Shughūr 118 B 3
Fr. Djisr el Choghour. NW Syria
Jiu 108 B 5 *Ger.* Schil, Schyl, *Hung.*
Zsil, Zsily. River, S Romania
Jiujiang 129 D 5 E China
Jiulong *see* Kowloon
Jizl, Wādī al 120 A 4 dry
watercourse, W Saudi Arabia
Jizzakh 123 E 2 *Rus.* Dzhizak.
C Uzbekistan
João Pessoa 63 G 2 *prev.* Paraíba.
State capital, E Brazil
Joazeiro *see* Juazeiro
Jodhpur 134 C 3 NW India
Joensuu 84 E 4 SE Finland
Jõetsu 131 C 5 *var.* Zyôetu.
Honshū, C Japan
Johannesburg 78 D 4 *var.* Egoli,
Erautini, Gauteng, *abbrev.* Jo'burg.
NE South Africa
Johannisburg *see* Pisz
John Day River 46 B 3 river,
Oregon, NW USA

John H.Kerr Reservoir 43 F 1
var. Buggs Island Lake, Kerr Lake.
Reservoir, SE USA
Johnson City 41 F 3 New York,
NE USA
Johor Bahru 138 B 3 *var.* Johor
Baharu, Johore Bahru.
W Malaysia
Johore Strait 138 A 1 *Mal.* Selat
Johor. Strait, Indian Ocean/
Pacific Ocean
Joinvile *see* Joinville
Joinville 63 F 5 *var.* Joinvile.
S Brazil
Jojutla 51 E 4 *var.* Jojutla de Juárez.
S Mexico
Jojutla de Juárez *see* Jojutla
Jokkmokk 84 C 3 N Sweden
Joliet 40 B 3 Illinois, N USA
Jonava 106 B 4 *Ger.* Janow,
Pol. Janów. C Lithuania
Jonesboro 42 B 1 Louisiana, S USA
Joniškis 106 C 4 *Ger.* Janischken.
N Lithuania
Jönköping 85 B 7 S Sweden
Jonquière 39 E 4 Québec,
SE Canada
Joplin 45 F 5 Missouri, C USA

Jordan
119 B 6 *Ar.* Al Mamlaka al
Urduniya al Hashemiyah,
Al Urdunn; *prev.* Transjordan.
Monarchy, SW Asia

Official name: Hashemite Kingdom
of Jordan Date of formation:
1946/1976 Capital: Amman
Population: 4.4 million Total area:
34,440 sq miles (89,210 sq km)
Languages: Arabic*, Armenian
Religions: Muslim 95%, Christian
5% Ethnic mix: Arab 98%,
(Palestinian 49%), Armenian 1%,
Circassian 1% Government:
Constitutional monarchy
Currency: Dinar = 1,000 fils

Jorhāt 135 H 3 NE India
Jos 75 G 4 C Nigeria
Joseph Bonaparte Gulf 146 D 2
gulf, S Timor Sea
Jos Plateau 75 G 4 plateau,
C Nigeria
Jotunheimen 85 A 5 mountain
range, S Norway
Joûnié 118 A 4 *var.* Junīyah.
W Lebanon
Joure 86 D 2 *Fris.* De Jouwer.
N Netherlands
Joutseno 85 E 5 SE Finland
J. Storm Thurmond Reservoir *see*
Clark Hill Lake
Juan Aldama 50 D 3 C Mexico
Juan de Fuca, Strait of 46 A 1 strait,
Canada/USA
Juan Fernández Islands 153 G 4
Eng. Juan Fernandez Islands.
Island group, SE Pacific Ocean
Juazeiro 63 G 2 *prev.* Joazeiro.
E Brazil
Juazeiro do Norte 63 G 2 E Brazil
Juba 73 B 5 *var.* Jubā. S Sudan
Jūbā *see* Juba
Jubbulpore *see* Jabalpur
Jucar *see* Júcar
Júcar 93 F 3 *var.* Jucar. River, C Spain
Juchitán de Zaragosa *see* Juchitán
Judayyidat Hāmir 120 B 3 S Iraq
Judenburg 95 C 7 C Austria
Juigalpa 52 D 3 S Nicaragua

Juiz de Fora 63 F 4 SE Brazil
Jujuy *see* San Salvador de Jujuy
Juliaca 61 E 4 SE Peru
Juliana Top 59 G 3 mountain,
C Suriname
Julianehåb *see* Qaqortoq
Juliomagus *see* Angers
Jullundur *see* Jalandhar
Jumba 73 D 6 S Somalia
Jumilla 93 F 4 SE Spain
Jummoo *see* Jammu
Jumna *see* Yamuna
Jumporn *see* Chumphon
Junction City 45 F 4 Kansas, C USA
Juneau 36 D 4 state capital,
Alaska, NW USA
Jungfrau 95 A 7 mountain,
S Switzerland
Junín 64 C 4 E Argentina
Junīyah *see* Joûnié
Jura 88 B 4 island, SW Scotland, UK
Jura 95 A 7 *var.* Jura Mountains.
Mountain range,
France/Switzerland
Jura Mountains *see* Jura
Jurbarkas 106 B 4 *Ger.*
Georgenburg, Jurburg.
W Lithuania
Jūrmala 106 C 3 C Latvia
Juruá 62 C 2 *var.* Río Yuruá.
River, Brazil/Peru
Jutiapa 52 B 2 S Guatemala
Juticalpa 52 D 2 C Honduras
Jutland *see* Jylland
Juvavum *see* Salzburg
Juventud, Isla de la 54 A 2 *var.*
Isla de Pinos, *Eng.* Isle of Youth;
prev. The Isle of the Pines.
Island, W Cuba
Jwaneng 78 C 4 SE Botswana
Jylland 85 A 7 *Eng.* Jutland.
Peninsula, W Denmark
Jyrgalan *see* Dzhergalan
Jyväskylä 85 D 5 C Finland

K

K2 134 D 1 *Chin.* Qogir Feng,
Eng. Mount Godwin Austen.
Mountain, China/Pakistan
Kaafu Atoll *see* Male' Atoll
Kaaimanston 59 G 3 N Suriname
Kaakhka 122 C 3 *var.* Kaka.
S Turkmenistan
Kaamanen 84 D 2 *Lapp.* Gámas.
N Finland
Kaambooni 73 D 6 S Somalia
Kaaresuvanto 84 D 2 *Lapp.*
Gárassavon. N Finland
Kabale 73 B 6 SW Uganda
Kabinda 77 D 7 SE Congo (Zaire)
Kabinda *see* Cabinda
Kabul 123 F 4 *var.* Darya-ye
Kābul. River, Afghanistan/
Pakistan
Kabul 123 E 4 *var.* Kabul,
Kābol. Capital, province,
E Afghanistan
Kābul, Daryā-ye *see* Kabul
Kabwe 78 D 2 C Zambia
Kachchh, Gulf of 134 B 4 *var.*
Gulf of Cutch, Gulf of Kutch.
Gulf, N Arabian Sea
Kadan Kyun 137 B 6 *prev.*
King Island, S Myanmar
Kadavu 145 E 4 *prev.* Kandavu.
Island, S Fiji
Kadoma 78 D 3 *prev.* Gatooma.
C Zimbabwe
Kadugli 72 B 4 S Sudan
Kaduna 75 G 4 C Nigeria

Kadzhi-Say 123 G 2 *Kir.* Kajisay.
NE Kyrgyzstan
Kaédi 74 C 3 S Mauritania
Käfar Jar Ghar 123 E 5 mountain
range, C Afghanistan
Kafue 78 C 2 river, C Zambia
Kafue 78 D 2 SE Zambia
Kaga Bandoro 76 C 4
prev. Fort-Crampel.
C Central African Republic
Kagan *see* Kogon
Kägithane 116 B 2 Turkey
Kagoshima 131 A 8 *var.* Kagosima.
Kyūshū, SW Japan
Kagoshima-wan 131 A 8 bay,
NW Pacific Ocean
Kagosima *see* Kagoshima
Kagul *see* Cahul
Kahramanmaraş 116 D 4 *var.*
Kahraman Maraş, Maraş, Marash.
S Turkey
Kaiapoi 151 C 6 South Island,
C New Zealand
Kaifeng 128 C 4 C China
Kai, Kepulauan 139 G 4 *prev.* Kei
Islands. Island group, Maluka,
E Indonesia
Kaikohe 150 C 2 North Island,
N New Zealand
Kaikoura 151 C 5 South Island,
C New Zealand
Kaikoura Peninsula 151 C 5
peninsula, South Island,
C New Zealand
Kainji Lake *see* Kainji Reservoir
Kainji Reservoir 75 F 4 *var.* Kainji
Lake. Reservoir, W Nigeria
Kaipara Harbour 150 C 2 harbour,
North Island, N New Zealand
Kairouan 71 E 2 *var.* Al Qayrawān.
E Tunisia
Kaiserslautern 95 A 5 SW Germany
Kaišiadorys 107 B 5 S Lithuania
Kaitaia 150 C 2 North Island,
N New Zealand
Kajaani 84 E 4 *Swe.* Kajana.
C Finland
Kajan *see* Kayan, Sungai
Kajana *see* Kajaani
Kajisay *see* Kadzhi-Say
Kaka *see* Kaahka
Kake 36 D 4 Alaska, NW USA
Kakhovka 109 F 4 S Ukraine
Kakhovs'ka Vodoskhovyshche 109
F 4 *Rus.* Kakhovskoye
Vodokhranilishche. Reservoir,
SE Ukraine
Kakhovskoye Vodokhranilishche
see Kakhovs'ka Vodoskhovyshche
Kākināda 132 D 1 *prev.* Cocanada.
E India
Ka-Krem *see* Malyy Yenisey
Kakshaal-Too, Khrebet *see*
Kokshaal-Tau
Kaktovik 36 D 2 Alaska, NW USA
Kalach 111 B 6
W Russian Federation
Kalach-na-Donu 111 B 6
SW Russian Federation
Kalahari Desert 78 C 4 desert,
S Africa
Kalaikhum *see* Qal'aikhum
Kalámai *see* Kalámata
Kalamariá 104 C 4 N Greece
Kalámata 105 B 6 *prev.* Kalámai.
S Greece
Kalamazoo 40 C 3 Michigan, N USA
Kalambaka *see* Kalampáka
Kálamos 105 C 5 C Greece
Kalampáka 104 B 4 C Greece
Kalanchak 109 F 4 S Ukraine

Kalasin 136 D 4 *var.* Muang
Kalasin. NE Thailand
Kalāt 134 B 2 *var.* Kelat, Khelat.
SW Pakistan
Kalāt 123 E 5 *Per.* Qalāt. S Afghanistan
Kalbarri 147 A 5 Western Australia,
W Australia
Kalecik 116 C 3 N Turkey
Kalemie 77 E 7 *prev.* Albertville.
SE Congo (Zaire)
Kalgoorlie 147 C 6 SW Australia
Kalima 77 D 6 E Congo (Zaire)
Kalimantan 138 D 4 *Eng.*
Indonesian Borneo. Geopolitical
region, Borneo, C Indonesia
Kálimnos 105 D 6 island, W Greece
Kalinin *see* Tver'
Kaliningrad 106 A 4
Russian Federation
Kaliningrad 106 A 4 enclave,
W Russian Federation
Kalinkavichy 107 C 7
Rus. Kalinkovichi. SE Belarus
Kalinkovichi *see* Kalinkavichy
Kalispell 44 B 1 Montana, NW USA
Kalisz 98 C 4 *Ger.* Kalisch,
Rus. Kalish; *anc.* Calisia. C Poland
Kalix 84 D 4 N Sweden
Kalixälven 84 D 3 river, N Sweden
Kallaste 106 E 3 *Ger.* Krasnogor.
SE Estonia
Kallavesi 85 E 5 lake, SE Finland
Kalloní 105 D 5 Lésvos, E Greece
Kalmar 85 C 7 *var.* Calmar. S Sweden
Kalmthout 87 C 5 N Belgium
Kalpáki 104 A 4 W Greece
Kalpeni Island 132 B 3 island,
Lakshadweep, SW India
Kaltdorf *see* Pruszków
Kaluga 111 B 5
W Russian Federation
Kalush 108 C 2 *Pol.* Kałusz.
W Ukraine
Kałusz *see* Kalush
Kalutara 132 D 4 SW Sri Lanka
Kalvarija 107 B 5 *Pol.* Kalwaria.
S Lithuania
Kalwaria *see* Kalvarija
Kalyān 134 C 5 W India
Kama 110 D 4 river,
Russian Federation
Kamarang 59 F 3 W Guyana
Kamchatka *see*
Kamchatka, Poluostrov
Kamchatka, Poluostrov 115 H 2
Eng. Kamchatka. Peninsula,
NE Russian Federation
Kamchiya 104 D 2 river, E Bulgaria
Kamenets-Podol'skiy *see*
Kam"yanets'-Podil's'kyy
Kamenka Dneprovskaya *see*
Kam"yanka-Dniprovs'ka
Kamensk-Shakhtinskiy 111 B 6
SW Russian Federation
Kamina 77 D 7 S Congo (Zaire)
Kamloops 37 E 5 British Columbia,
SW Canada
Kampala 73 B 6 country capital,
S Uganda
Kampar 138 B 3 W Malaysia
Kâmpóng Cham 137 D 6 *prev.*
Kompong Cham. S Cambodia
Kâmpóng Chhnǎng 137 D 6
prev. Kompong. C Cambodia
Kâmpóng Saôm 137 D 6 *prev.*
Kompong Som, Sihanoukville.
SW Cambodia
Kâmpóng Spoe 137 D 6
prev. Kompong Speu. S Cambodia
Kâmpóng Thum 137 D 6 *prev.*
Kompong Thom. C Cambodia

Kâmpôt 137 D 6 S Cambodia
Kam"yanets'-Podil's'kyy 108 C 3
Rus. Kamenets-Podol'skiy.
W Ukraine
Kam"yanka-Dniprovs'ka 109 F 3
Rus. Kamenka Dneprovskaya.
SE Ukraine
Kamyshin 111 C 6
SW Russian Federation
Kananga 77 D 7 *prev.* Luluabourg.
S Congo (Zaire)
Kanash 111 C 5
W Russian Federation
Kanazawa 131 C 5 Honshū,
SW Japan
Kānchipuram 132 C 2
prev. Conjeeveram. SE India
Kandahār 123 E 5 *var.* Qandahār.
S Afghanistan
Kandalaksha 110 C 2
var. Kandalak3a, *Fin.* Kantalahti.
NW Russian Federation
Kandangan 138 D 4 Borneo,
C Indonesia
Kandau *see* Kandava
Kandava 106 C 3 *Ger.* Kandau.
W Latvia
Kandavu *see* Kadavu
Kandla 134 C 4 W India
Kandy 132 D 3 C Sri Lanka
Kane Fracture Zone 66 B 4 fracture
zone, NW Atlantic Ocean
Kaneohe 47 A 8 *Haw.* Kāne'ohe.
Hawaii, W USA
Kāne'ohe *see* Kaneohe
Kanestron, Akra *see* Palioúri, Ákra
Kanëv *see* Kaniv
Kanevskoye Vodokhranilishche *see*
Kanivs'ke Vodoskhovyshche
Kangaatsiaq 82 C 3 *var.* Kangatsiak,
Kángâtsiaq. W Greenland
Kangān 120 D 4 S Iran
Kangaroo Island 149 A 7 island,
S Australia
Kangerluarsoruseq *see* Færingehavn
Kangerlussuaq 82 C 3 *Dan.* Søndre
Strømfjord. SW Greenland
Kangertittivaq 83 E 4 *Dan.* Scoresby
Sund. Inlet, N Atlantic Ocean
Kaniv 109 E 2 *Rus.* Kanëv.
C Ukraine
Kanivs'ke Vodoskhovyshche 109
E 2 *Rus.* Kanevskoye
Vodokhranilishche. Reservoir,
C Ukraine
Kanjiža 100 D 2 *Ger.* Altkanischa,
Hung. Magyarkanizsa, Ókanizsa;
prev. Stara Kanjiža. N Yugoslavia
Kankaanpää 85 D 5 SW Finland
Kankakee 40 B 4 Illinois, N USA
Kankan 74 D 4 E Guinea
Kano 75 G 4 N Nigeria
Kānpur 135 E 3 *Eng.* Cawnpore.
N India
Kansas 45 E 5 off. State of Kansas;
nicknames Jayhawker State,
Sunflower State. State, C USA
Kansas City 45 F 4 Kansas, C USA
Kansas City 45 F 4 Missouri, C USA
Kansas River 45 F 5 River,
Kansas, C USA
Kansk 115 E 4 S Russian Federation
Kántanos 105 C 8 Kríti, SE Greece
Kantemirovka 111 B 6
W Russian Federation
Kantipur *see* Kathmandu
Kanton 145 F 3 *var.* Abariringa,
Canton Island; *prev.* Mary Island.
Island, C Kiribati
Kaohsiung 129 D 6 *var.* Gaoxiong,
Jap. Takao, Takow. SW Taiwan

Kaolack 74 B 3 *var.* Kaolak.
W Senegal
Kaolak *see* Kaolack
Kaoma 78 C 2 W Zambia
Kapelle 87 B 5 SW Netherlands
Kapellen 87 C 5 N Belgium
Kapka, Massif du 76 D 2 mounta᷍
range, E Chad
Kapoeas *see* Kapuas, Sungai
Kaposvár 99 C 7 SW Hungary
Kappeln 94 B 2 N Germany
Kaptsevichy 107 C 7
Rus. Koptsevichi. SE Belarus
Kapuas 138 C 4 *prev.* Kapoeas.
River, Borneo, C Indonesia
Kapuskasing 38 C 4 Ontario,
S Canada
Kapyl' 107 C 6 *Rus.* Kopyl'.
C Belarus
Kara-Balta 123 F 2 N Kyrgyzstan
Karabil', Vozvyshennost' 122 D 3᷍
mountain range, S Turkmenista᷍
Kara-Bogaz-Gol, Proliv 122 B 2
Turkm. Garabogazköl Bogazy.
Strait, E Caspian Sea
Kara-Bogaz-Gol, Zaliv 122 B 2 ba᷍
E Caspian Sea
Karabük 116 C 2 N Turkey
Karachev 111 B 5
W Russian Federation
Karāchi 134 B 3 province capital,
SE Pakistan
Karácsonkő *see* Piṭra-Neamt
Karaganda 114 C 4 *Kaz.*
Qaraghandy. C Kazakhstan
Karaginskiy, Ostrov 115 H 2 isla᷍
E Russian Federation
Karaginskiy Zaliv 115 H 2 bay,
W Bering Sea
Karaj 120 C 3 N Iran
Kara-Kala 122 C 3 *var.* Garrygala
W Turkmenistan
Karakax *see* Moyu
Karakol 123 G 2 *var.* Karakolka.
NE Kyrgyzstan
Karakol 123 G 2 *prev.* Przheval'sk᷍
NE Kyrgyzstan
Karakolka *see* Karakol
Karakoram Range 134 D 1
mountain range, India/Pakista᷍
Karaköse 117 F 3 Turkey
Karakul' *see* Qarokül
Kara Kum *see* Garagumy
Karakumskiy Kanal 122 D 3
Turkm. Garagum Kanaly. Canal᷍
C Turkmenistan
Karaman 116 C 4 S Turkey
Karamay 126 B 2 *var.* Karamai,
Kelamayi, *Chin.* K'o-la-ma-i.
NW China
Karamea Bight 151 C 5 bight,
South Island, E Tasman Sea
Karapelit 104 E 1 *Rom.* Stejarul.
NE Bulgaria
Kara-Say 123 G 2 NE Kyrgyzstan
Karasburg 78 B 4 S Namibia
Kara Sea *see* Karskoye More
Karatau 114 C 5 *Kaz.* Qarataū.
S Kazakhstan
Karavanke *see* Karawanken
Karavás 105 B 7 Kýthira, S Greece
Karbalā' 120 B 3 *var.* Kerbala,
Kerbela. S Iraq
Kardhítsa *see* Kardítsa
Karditsa 105 B 5 *var.* Kardhítsa.
C Greece
Kärdla 106 C 2 *Ger.* Kertel.
Hiiumaa, W Estonia
Kargı 116 C 2 N Turkey
Kargilik *see* Yecheng
Kariba 78 D 2 N Zimbabwe

riba, Lake 78 D 3 reservoir,
ambia/Zimbabwe
ibib 78 B 3 C Namibia
ies *see* Karyés
rigasniemi 84 D 2 *Lapp.*
Jaregegasnjárga. N Finland
rimata, Selat 138 C 4 strait,
ava Sea/South China Sea
rimnagar 135 E 5 C India
rin 72 D 4 N Somalia
ristos *see* Kárystos
rkinits'ka Zatoka 109 F 4
Rus. Karkinitskiy Zaliv. Gulf,
N Black Sea
rkinitskiy Zaliv *see*
Karkinits'ka Zatoka
rl-Marx-Stadt *see* Chemnitz
rlö *see* Hailuoto
rlovac 100 B 2 *Ger.* Karlstadt,
Hung. Károlyváros. C Croatia
rlovy Vary 99 A 5 *Ger.* Karlsbad;
prev. Eng. Carlsbad.
N Czech Republic
rlskrona 85 C 7 S Sweden
rlsruhe 95 B 6 *var.* Carlsruhe.
SW Germany
rlstad 85 B 6 C Sweden
rnäl 134 D 2 N India
rnátaka 132 C 1 *var.* Kanara; *prev.*
Maisur, Mysore. State, W India
rnobat 104 E 2 E Bulgaria
rnul *see* Kurnool
rpathos 105 E 7 Kárpathos,
SE Greece
rpathos 105 E 7 *It.* Scarpanto;
anc. Carpathos, Carpathus. Island,
Dodekánisos, SE Greece
rpenísi 105 B 5
prev. Karpenísion. C Greece
rpenísion *see* Karpenísi
rs 117 F 3 *var.* Qars. NE Turkey
rsava 106 D 4 *Ger.* Karsau;
prev. Rus. Korsovka. E Latvia
rskoye More 114 D 2 *Eng.* Kara
Sea. Sea, Arctic Ocean
rün 120 C 3 *var.* Rûd-e Kárún.
River, SW Iran
rün, Rûd-e *see* Kärün
ryés 104 C 4 *var.* Karíes. N Greece
rystos 105 C 6 *var.* Káristos.
Évvoia, C Greece
s 116 B 5 SW Turkey
sai 77 C 6 *var.* Cassai, Kassai.
River, Angola/Congo (Zaire)
sama 78 D 1 N Zambia
sane *see* Koson
sane 78 C 3 NE Botswana
saragod 132 B 2 SW India
shân 120 C 3 C Iran
shi 126 A 3 *Chin.* Kaxgar,
K'o-shih, *Uigh.* Kashgar.
NW China
shmir 134 D 1 cultural region,
N India
skaskia River 40 B 5 river,
Illinois, N USA
songo 77 D 6 E Congo (Zaire)
sos 105 E 7 island, S Greece
spiysk 111 B 8
SW Russian Federation
ssala 72 C 4 E Sudan
ssel 94 B 4 *prev.* Cassel.
C Germany
sserine 71 E 2 *var.* Al Qaşrayn.
W Tunisia
stamonu 116 C 2 *var.* Castamoni,
Kastamuni. N Turkey
staneá 104 B 4 N Greece
stélli 105 C 7 Kríti, SE Greece
storía 104 B 4 N Greece

Kástro 105 C 6 Sífnos, SE Greece
Kastsyukovichy 107 E 7
Rus. Kostyukovichi. E Belarus
Kastsyukowka 107 D 7 *Rus.*
Kostyukovka. SE Belarus
Kasulu 73 B 7 W Tanzania
Kasumiga-ura 131 D 5 lake,
Honshū, S Japan
Katalla 36 C 3 Alaska, NW USA
Katana *see* Qaţanā
Katanning 147 B 7 Western
Australia, W Australia
Katchall Island 133 F 3 island,
SW India
Kateríni 104 B 4 N Greece
Katha 136 B 2 N Myanmar
Katherina, Gebel 72 C 2 *var.* Jabal
Katrînah, *Eng.* Mount Catherine.
Mountain, NE Egypt
Katherine 148 A 2 Northern
Territory, N Australia
Kathmandu 135 F 3 *prev.* Kantipur.
Country capital, C Nepal
Katikati 150 D 3 North Island,
NE New Zealand
Katima Mulilo 78 C 3 NE Namibia
Katiola 74 D 4 C Ivory Coast
Káto Achaïa 105 B 6 *var.* Káto
Akhaía. S Greece
Kat O Chau 128 B 1 island,
NE Hong Kong
Katoúna 105 B 5 C Greece
Katowice 99 C 5 *Ger.* Kattowitz.
S Poland
Katsina 75 G 4 N Nigeria
Kattakurgan *see* Kattaqürghon
Kattaqürghon 123 E 2
Rus. Kattakurgan. C Uzbekistan
Kattavía 105 E 7 Ródos, SE Greece
Kattegat 85 B 7 *Dan.* Kattegat.
Strait, E North Sea
Kattegat *see* Kattegat
Kattowitz *see* Katowice
Kauai 47 A 7 *Haw.* Kaua'i.
Island, Hawaii, W USA
Kaua'i *see* Kauai
Kaufbeuren 95 C 6 S Germany
Kaunas 106 B 4 *Ger.* Kauen,
Pol. Kowno; *prev. Rus.* Kovno.
C Lithuania
Kauno Marios 106 B 4 reservoir,
S Lithuania
Kau-Ye Kyun 137 B 6 *var.*
Sir Charles Forbes Island. Island,
S Myanmar
Kavadar *see* Kavadarci
Kavadarci 101 E 6 *Turk.* Kavadar.
C Macedonia
Kavajë 101 C 6 *It.* Cavaia, Kavaja.
W Albania
Kavakli *see* Topolovgrad
Kavála 104 C 3 *prev.* Kaválla.
NE Greece
Kāvali 132 D 2 E India
Kaválla *see* Kavála
Kavaratti Island 132 B 3 island,
Lakshadweep, SW India
Kavarna 104 E 2 NE Bulgaria
Kavīr, Dasht-e 120 D 3 *var.*
Dasht-e-Kavir. Salt lake, N Iran
Kavkaz *see* Caucasus
Kawagoe 131 D 5 Honshū, S Japan
Kawasaki 131 D 5 Honshū,
S Japan
Kawerau 150 E 3 North Island,
NE New Zealand
Kaya 75 E 4 C Burkina
Kayan 136 B 4 S Myanmar
Kayan 138 D 3 *prev.* Kajan. River,
Borneo, C Indonesia
Kayes 74 C 3 W Mali

Kayseri 116 D 3 *var.* Kaisaria;
anc. Caesarea Mazaca, Mazaca.
C Turkey
Kazach'ye 115 F 2
N Russian Federation
Kazakhskiy Melkosopochnik
114 B 4 *Eng.* Kazakh Uplands,
Kirghiz Steppe, *Kaz.* Saryarqa.
Physical region, C Kazakhstan

Kazakhstan
114 B 4 Qazaqstan Respublikasy,
var. Kazakstan, *Kaz.* Qazaqstan;
prev. Kazakh Soviet Socialist
Republic, *Rus.* Kazakhskaya SSR.
Republic, C Asia

Official name: Republic of
Kazakhstan **Date of formation:** 1991
Capital: Astana **Population:** 17.2
million **Total area:** 1,049,150 sq
miles (2,717,300 sq km)
Languages: Kazakh*, Russian
Religions: Muslim 47%, other 53%
(mostly Russian Orthodox,
Lutheran) **Ethnic mix:** Kazakh 40%,
Russian 38%, Ukrainian 6%, other
16% **Government:** Multiparty
republic **Currency:** Tenge = 100 tein

Kazakh Uplands *see*
Kazakhskiy Melkosopochnik
Kazan' 111 D 5
W Russian Federation
Kazan' 111 D 5 international
airport, W Russian Federation
Kazanlâk 104 D 2 *var.* Kazanlák;
prev. Kazanlik. C Bulgaria
Kazanlik *see* Kozyatyn
Kazbek 117 F 2 *Geor.* Mqinvartsveri.
Mountain, Armenia/Georgia
Käzerün 120 D 4 S Iran
Kazi Magomed *see* Qazimämmäd
Kazvin *see* Qazvīn
Kéa 105 C 6 Kéa, SE Greece
Kéa 105 C 6 *prev.* Kéos, *anc.* Ceos.
Island, Kykládes, SE Greece
Kearney 45 E 4 Nebraska, C USA
Keban 117 E 3 C Turkey
Keban, Baraji 117 E 3 lake,
C Turkey
Kebkabiya 72 A 4 W Sudan
Kebnekaise 84 C 3 mountain,
N Sweden
Kecskemét 99 D 7 C Hungary
Kedainiai 106 B 4 C Lithuania
Kediri 138 D 5 Jawa, C Indonesia
Keetmanshoop 78 B 4 S Namibia
Keewatin 38 A 3 Ontario, S Canada
Kefallinía 105 A 5 *var.* Kefalloniá.
Island, Iónioi Nísoi, W Greece
Kefalloniá *see* Kefallinía
Kefar Tappuaḥ 119 E 7 C West Bank
Kegel *see* Keila
Kehl 95 A 6 SW Germany
Kei Islands *see* Kai, Kepulauan
Keila 106 D 2 *Ger.* Kegel.
N Estonia
Keith 149 B 7 South Australia,
S Australia
Keizer 46 B 3 Oregon, NW USA
Këk-Art 123 G 2 *prev.* Alay-Kel',
Alay-Kuu. SW Kyrgyzstan
Kelang 138 B 3 *var.* Kelang; *prev.*
Port Swettenham. W Malaysia
Kelifskiy Uzboy 122 D 3 wetland,
E Turkmenistan
Kélo 76 B 4 SW Chad
Kelowna 37 E 5 British Columbia,
SW Canada

Kelso 46 B 2 Washington, NW USA
Keltsy *see* Kielce
Keluang 138 B 3 *var.* Kluang.
W Malaysia
Kem' 110 B 3
NW Russian Federation
Kemah 117 E 3 E Turkey
Kemerovo 114 D 4
prev. Shcheglovsk.
C Russian Federation
Kemi 84 D 3 NW Finland
Kemijärvi 84 D 3 *Swe.* Kemiträsk.
N Finland
Kemijoki 84 D 3 river, NW Finland
Kemiö *see* Kimito
Kemiräsk *see* Kemijärvi
Kempele 84 D 4 C Finland
Kempten 95 C 7 S Germany
Kempton 149 C 8 Tasmania,
SE Australia
Kendal 89 C 5 NW England, UK
Kendall 43 F 5 Florida, SE USA
Kendari 139 E 4 Celebes,
C Indonesia
Kenedy 49 G 4 Texas, S USA
Kenema 74 C 4 SE Sierra Leone
Këneurgench 122 C 2
Turkm. Köneürgench; *prev.*
Kunya-Urgench. N Turkmenistan
Kenge 77 C 6 SW Congo (Zaire)
Keng Tung 136 C 3 *var.* Kentung.
SE Myanmar
Kénitra 70 C 2 *prev.* Port-Lyautey.
NW Morocco
Kennebec River 41 G 2 river,
Maine, NE USA
Kenner 42 B 3 Louisiana, S USA
Kennett 45 H 5 Missouri, C USA
Kennewick 46 C 2
Washington, NW USA
Kenora 38 A 3 Ontario, S Canada
Kenosha 40 B 3 Wisconsin, N USA
Kent 46 B 2 Washington, NW USA
Kentau 114 B 5 S Kazakhstan
Kentucky 40 C 5 off.
Commonwealth of Kentucky;
nickname Bluegrass State.
State, C USA
Kentucky Lake 40 B 5
reservoir, C USA
Kentung *see* Keng Tung

Kenya
73 C 6 Republic, NE Africa

Official name: Republic of Kenya
Date of formation: 1963
Capital: Nairobi **Population:** 29.1
million **Total area:** 224,081 sq miles
(580,370 sq km) **Languages:**
Swahili*, English, Kikuyu, Luo,
Kamba **Religions:** Christian 66%,
traditional beliefs 26%, other 8%
Ethnic mix: Kikuyu 21%, Luhya
14%, Kamba 11%, other 54%
Government: Multiparty republic
Currency: Shilling = 100 cents

Kenya, Mount *see* Kirinyaga
Keokuk 45 G 4 Iowa, C USA
Kepno 98 C 4 C Poland
Kerala 132 C 2 state, S India
Keratea *see* Keratéa
Keratéa 105 C 6 *var.* Keratea.
C Greece
Kerch 109 G 5 *Rus.* Kerch'. SE Ukraine
Kerch' *see* Kerch
Kerch Strait 109 G 4 *var.* Bosporus
Cimmerius, Enikale Strait,
Rus. Kerchenskiy Proliv,
Ukr. Kerchens'ka Protska. Strait,
Sea of Azov/Black Sea
Kerchevskiy *see* Lyulyakovo

199

Kerguelen 141 C 7 island, C French Southern & Antarctic Territories
Kerguelen Plateau 141 C 7 undersea plateau, S Indian Ocean
Kerí 105 A 6 Zákynthos, W Greece
Kerikeri 150 D 2 North Island, N New Zealand
Kerki 123 E 3 E Turkmenistan
Kerkrade 87 D 6 SE Netherlands
Kérkyra 104 A 4 *var.* Kérkira, *Eng.* Corfu. Island, Iónioi Nísoi, W Greece
Kérkyra 104 A 4 *var.* Kérkira, *Eng.* Corfu. Kérkyra, W Greece
Kermadec Islands 152 C 4 island group, NE New Zealand
Kermadec Trench 152 D 4 trench, S Pacific Ocean
Kermān 120 D 4 *var.* Kirman; *anc.* Carmana. C Iran
Kerrville 49 F 4 Texas, S USA
Kertel *see* Kärdla
Kerulen 127 E 2 *Chin.* Herlen He, *Mong.* Herlen Gol. River, China/Mongolia
Kessennuma 130 D 4 Honshū, C Japan
Keszthely 99 C 7 SW Hungary
Ketchikan 36 D 4 Alaska, NW USA
Kettering 89 D 6 C England, UK
Kettering 40 C 4 Ohio, N USA
Keupriya *see* Primorsko
Keuruu 85 D 5 C Finland
Keweenaw Peninsula 40 B 1 headland, Michigan, N USA
Key Largo 54 B 2 island, W Cuba
Key West 43 E 5 Florida, SE USA
Khabarovsk 115 G 4 SE Russian Federation
Khachmas *see* Xaçmaz
Khairpur 134 B 3 SE Pakistan
Khambhāt, Gulf of 134 C 4 *Eng.* Gulf of Cambay. Gulf, NE Arabian Sea
Khānābād 123 E 3 NE Afghanistan
Khān al Baghdādī *see* Al Baghdādī
Khandwa 134 D 4 C India
Khanh Hung *see* Soc Trăng
Khanka, Lake 128 E 2 *var.* Hsing-K'ai Hu, Lake Hanka, *Chin.* Xingkai Hu, *Rus.* Ozero Khanka. Lake, China/ Russian Federation
Khanty-Mansiysk 114 C 3 *prev.* Ostyako-Voguls'k. C Russian Federation
Khan Yums 119 A 7 S Israel
Khanzi *see* Ghanzi
Kharagpur 135 F 4 NE India
Kharkiv 109 G 2 *Rus.* Khar'kov. NE Ukraine
Khar'kov *see* Kharkiv
Kharmanli 104 D 3 *var.* Harmanli. S Bulgaria
Kharovsk 110 C 4 *var.* Charovsk, Harovsk. NW Russian Federation
Khartoum 72 B 4 *var.* El Khartûm, Khartum. Country capital, C Sudan
Khasavyurt 111 B 8 SW Russian Federation
Khashm el Girba 72 C 4 E Sudan
Khaskovo 104 D 3 *var.* Haskovo. S Bulgaria
Khaybar, Kowtal-e *see* Khyber Pass
Khaydarkan 123 F 2 *var.* Khaydarken. SW Kyrgyzstan
Khaydarken *see* Khaydarkan
Kherson 109 E 4 *var.* Cherson. S Ukraine
Kheta 115 E 2 river, N Russian Federation

Khíos *see* Chíos
Khiva *see* Khiwa
Khiwa 122 D 2 *Rus.* Khiva. W Uzbekistan
Khmel'nyts'kyy 108 C 2 *Rus.* Khmel'nitskiy; *prev.* Proskurov. W Ukraine
Khodasy 107 E 7 *Rus.* Khodosy. E Belarus
Khodoriv 108 C 2 *Pol.* Chodorów, *Rus.* Khodorov. NW Ukraine
Khodosy *see* Khodasy
Kholm 123 E 3 *var.* Tashqurghan, *Pash.* Khulm. N Afghanistan
Kholm *see* Chełm
Khong Sedone *see* Muang Khôngxédôn
Khon Kaen 136 D 4 *var.* Muang Khon Kaen. N Thailand
Khor 115 G 4 SE Russian Federation
Khorugh 123 F 3 *var.* Horog, *Rus.* Khorog. S Tajikistan
Kho Sawai Plateau *see* Korat Plateau
Khosf 120 E 3 E Iran
Khouribga 70 C 2 C Morocco
Khovd *see* Hovd
Khowst 123 F 4 E Afghanistan
Khoyniki 107 D 8 SE Belarus
Khujand 123 F 2 *var.* Khodzhent, Khojend, *Rus.* Khudzhand, *Taj.* Leninobod; *prev.* Leninabad. N Tajikistan
Khulna 135 G 4 SW Bangladesh
Khust 108 B 3 *var.* Husté, *Cz.* Chust, *Hung.* Huszt. W Ukraine
Khvalynsk 111 C 6 W Russian Federation
Khvoy 120 C 2 *var.* Khoi, Khoy. NW Iran
Khyber Pass 123 F 4 *var.* Kowtal-e Khaybar. Pass, Afghanistan/Pakistan
Kiáto 105 B 6 *prev.* Kiáton. S Greece
Kiáton *see* Kiáto
Kibangou 77 B 6 SW Congo
Kibombo 77 D 6 E Congo (Zaire)
Kičevo 101 D 6 SW Macedonia
Kidderminster 89 C 6 W England, UK
Kiel 94 B 2 N Germany
Kielce 98 D 4 *Rus.* Keltsy. SE Poland
Kieler Bucht 94 C 2 bay, W Baltic Sea
Kiev *see* Kyyiv
Kiffa 74 C 3 S Mauritania
Kigali 73 B 6 country capital, C Rwanda
Kigoma 73 B 7 W Tanzania
Kihnu 106 C 2 *var.* Kihnu Saar, *Ger.* Kühnö. Island, SW Estonia
Kihti *see* Skiftet
Kii-saidō 131 C 7 strait, NW Pacific Ocean
Kikinda 100 D 3 *Ger.* Grosskikinda, *Hung.* Nagykikinda; *prev.* Velika Kikinda. NE Yugoslavia
Kikwit 77 C 6 W Congo (Zaire)
Kili 144 D 2 Island, S Marshall Islands
Kilien Mountains *see* Qilian Shan
Kilimanjaro 73 C 7 *var.* Vhuru Peak. Mountain, NE Tanzania
Kilingi-Nõmme 106 D 3 *Ger.* Kurkund. SW Estonia
Kilis 116 D 4 S Turkey
Kiliya 108 D 4 *Rom.* Chilia-Nouă. SW Ukraine
Kilkenny 89 B 6 *Ir.* Cill Chainnigh. S Ireland

Kilkís 104 B 3 N Greece
Killarney 89 A 6 *Ir.* Cill Airne. SW Ireland
Killeen 49 G 3 Texas, S USA
Kilmarnock 88 C 4 SW Scotland, UK
Kimberley 78 C 4 C South Africa
Kimberley Plateau 146 D 3 plateau, Western Australia, NW Australia
Kimch'aek 128 E 3 *prev.* Sŏngjin. E North Korea
Kími *see* Kými
Kimito 85 D 6 *Swe.* Kemiö. Island, SW Finland
Kimovsk 111 B 5 W Russian Federation
Kindersley 37 F 5 Saskatchewan, S Canada
Kindia 74 C 4 SW Guinea
Kindley Field Airport 42 B 5 international airport, E Bermuda
Kindu 77 D 6 *prev.* Kindu-Port-Empain. C Congo (Zaire)
Kindu-Port-Empain *see* Kindu
Kineshma 111 C 5 *var.* Kinešma. W Russian Federation
Kinešma *see* Kineshma
King Charles Islands *see* Kong Karls Land
King Christian IX Land *see* Kong Christian IX Land
King Christian X Land *see* Kong Christian X Land
King Frederik VI Coast *see* Kong Frederik VI Kyst
King Frederik VIII Land *see* Kong Frederik VIII Land
King Frederik IX Land *see* Kong Frederik IX Land
King I *see* Kadan Kyun
King Island 149 B 8 island, Tasmania, SE Australia
Kingman 48 A 2 Arizona, SW USA
Kingman Reef 145 G 2 reef, NE Australia
King's Lynn 89 E 6 *var.* Bishop's Lynn, Kings Lynn, Lynn, Lynn Regis. E England, UK
King Sound 146 C 3 inlet, Indian Ocean/Timor Sea
Kingsport 43 E 1 Tennessee, S USA
Kingston 54 B 5 country capital, SE Jamaica
Kingston 38 D 5 Ontario, SE Canada
Kingston 41 F 3 New York, NE USA
Kingston upon Hull 89 E 5 *var.* Hull. NE England, UK
Kingstown 55 H 4 country capital, N Saint Vincent and the Grenadines
Kingsville 49 G 5 Texas, S USA
King William Island 37 F 3 island, N Canada
Kinrooi 87 D 5 NE Belgium
Kinshasa 77 B 6 *prev.* Léopoldville. Country capital, W Congo (Zaire)
Kinston 43 F 1 North Carolina, SE USA
Kintyre 88 B 4 peninsula, NE Scotland, UK
Kinyeti 73 B 5 mountain, S Sudan
Kiparissía *see* Kyparissía
Kipili 73 B 7 W Tanzania
Kipushi 77 E 8 SE Congo (Zaire)
Kirghiz Range 114 C 5 *Rus.* Kirgizskiy Khrebet; *prev.* Alexander Range. Mountain range, Kazakhstan/Kyrgyzstan
Kirghiz Steppe *see* Kazakhskiy Melkosopochnik

Kiribati
145 F 2 Republic, C Pacific Oce[an]
Official name: Republic of Kiriba[ti]
Date of formation: 1979 **Capital:**
Bairiki **Population:** 7,500 **Total Ar[ea]**
274 sq miles (710 sq km) **Languag[es]**
English*, Kiribati **Religions:** Rom[an]
Catholic 53%, Protestant 40%, othe[r]
3% **Ethnic mix**
I-Kiribati 98%, other 2% **Ethnic mix**
Government: Multiparty republic
Currency: Australian $ = 100 cents

Kiribati, Republic of *see* Kiribati
Kirinyaga 73 C 6 *prev.* Mount Kenya. Volcano, C Kenya
Kirishi 110 B 4 *var.* Kirisi. NW Russian Federation
Kirisi *see* Kirishi
Kiritimati 145 G 2 *prev.* Christmas Island. Island, E Kiribati
Kiriwina Islands 144 C 3 *var.* Trobriand Islands. Island group, S Papua New Guinea
Kirkenes 84 E 2 *var.* Kirkkoniemi. N Norway
Kirk-Kilissa *see* Kırklareli
Kirkkoniemi *see* Kirkenes
Kirkland Lake 38 D 4 Ontario, S Canada
Kırklareli 116 A 2 *prev.* Kirk-Kilis[sa] NW Turkey
Kirkpatrick, Mount 154 C 3 mountain, Antarctica
Kirksville 45 G 4 Missouri, C US[A]
Kirkūk 120 B 3 *var.* Karkūk, Kerkuk. N Iraq
Kirkwall 88 C 2 island authority area capital, NE Scotland, UK
Kirkwood 45 C 5 Missouri, C US[A]
Kirov 110 C 4 *prev.* Vyatka. NW Russian Federation
Kirovakan *see* Vanadzor
Kirovo-Cepeck *see* Kirovo-Chepets[k]
Kirovo-Chepetsk 111 D 5 *var.* Kirovo-Čepeck. NW Russian Federation
Kirovohrad 109 E 3 *Rus.* Kirovograd; *prev.* Kirovo,Yelizavetgrad, Zinov'yevsk. C Ukraine
Kirsanov 111 B 6 W Russian Federation
Kīrthar Range 134 A 3 mountain range, S Pakistan
Kiruna 84 C 3 N Sweden
Kisangani 77 D 5 *prev.* Stanleyville. NE Congo (Zaire)
Kishinev *see* Chişinău
Kiskörei-víztároló 99 D 6 reservoir, E Hungary
Kiskunfélegyháza 99 D 7 *var.* Félegyháza. C Hungary
Kislovodsk 111 B 7 SW Russian Federation
Kismaayo 73 D 6 *var.* Chisimayu, Kismayu, *It.* Chisimaio. S Somalia
Kissidougou 74 C 4 S Guinea
Kissimmee 43 E 4 Florida, SE USA[/]
Kistna *see* Krishna
Kisumu 73 C 6 *prev.* Port Florence. W Kenya
Kisvárda 99 E 6 *Ger.* Kleinwardein. E Hungary
Kita 74 D 3 W Mali
Kitab *see* Kitob
Kitakyūshū 131 A 7 *var.* Kitakyūsyū. Kyūshū, SW Japan
Kitakyūsyû *see* Kitakyūshū
Kitami 130 D 2 Hokkaidō, NE Japa[n]

:hener 38 C 5 Ontario, S Canada
mat 36 D 5 British Columbia,
W Canada
nen 84 D 3 river, N Finland
ob 123 E 3 Rus. Kitab.
Uzbekistan
ve 78 D 2 var. Kitwe-Nkana.
Zambia
ve-Nkana see Kitwe
zbühler Alpen 95 D 7 mountain
ange, W Austria
alina 36 C 2 Alaska, NW USA
alo 84 D 3 ridge, C Finland
ertsi 108 C 1 Pol. Kiwerce,
us. Kivertsy. NW Ukraine
u, Lac see Kivu, Lake
u, Lake 77 E 6 Fr. Lac Kivu.
ake, Congo (Zaire)/Rwanda
evskoye Vodokhranilishche see
yyivs'ke Vodoskhovyshche
el 111 D 5
W Russian Federation
l Irmak 116 C 3 river, C Turkey
lyurt 111 B 8
W Russian Federation
yl-Arvat see Gyzylarbat
len see Kölen
dno 99 A 5 NW Czech Republic
genfurt 95 D 7 Slvn. Celovec.
Austria
pėda 106 B 3 Ger. Memel.
W Lithuania
nath Falls 46 B 4
rregon, NW USA
nath Mountains 46 B 4
aountain range, W USA
älven 85 B 6 river,
lorway/Sweden
ovy 99 A 5 Ger. Klattau.
W Czech Republic
ttau see Klatovy
rienaveen 86 E 2
E Netherlands
nwardein see Kisvárda
soúra 105 A 5 W Greece
rksdorp 78 D 4 N South Africa
navichy 107 E 7
us. Klimovichi. E Belarus
novichi see Klimavichy
ntsy 111 A 5
/ Russian Federation
ura 104 C 2 C Bulgaria
aė 100 B 3
W Bosnia & Herzegovina
buck 98 C 4 S Poland
ndike 36 D 3 river, Yukon
erritory, W Canada
ang see Keluang
czbork 98 C 4 Ger. Kreuzburg,
reuzburg in Oberschlesien.
/ Poland
n 100 B 4 S Croatia
aževac 100 E 4 E Yugoslavia
kke-Heist 87 A 5 NW Belgium
xville 42 D 1 Tennessee, S USA
d Rasmussen Land 82 D 1
hysical region, N Greenland
e 131 C 6 Honshū, SW Japan
enhavn 85 B 7 Eng.
openhagen; anc. Hafnia.
ountry capital, E Denmark
enni 74 D 3 S Mauritania
lenz 95 A 5 Fr. Coblence;
ev. Coblenz, anc. Confluentes.
/ Germany
ryn 107 A 6 Pol. Kobryn,
us. Kobrin. SW Belarus
pulet'i 117 F 2 W Georgia
ani 101 E 6 NE Macedonia
evje 95 E 8 Ger. Gottschee.
Slovenia

Koch Bihār 135 G 3 NE India
Kōchi 131 B 7 var. Kôti.
SW Japan
Kochi see Cochin
Kochiu see Gejiu
Kodiak 36 C 3 Kodiak Island,
Alaska, USA
Kodiak Island 36 C 3 island,
Alaska, NW USA
Koedoes see Kudus
Koepang see Kupang
Kofa Mountains 48 A 2 mountain
range, Arizona, SW USA
Kōfu 131 D 5 var. Kôhu. Honshū,
S Japan
Kogon 122 D 2 Rus. Kagan .
C Uzbekistan
Kohīma 135 H 3 var. Kohima.
NE India
Kohima see Kohīma
Kohtla-Järve 106 E 2 NE Estonia
Kokkola 84 D 4 Swe. Karleby; prev.
Swe. Gamlakarleby. W Finland
Kokrines 36 C 3 Alaska, NW USA
Kokshaal-Tau 123 G 2 Rus. Khrebet
Kakshaal-Too. Mountain range,
China/Kyrgyzstan
Kokshetau 114 C 4 Kaz.
Kökshetaū; prev. Kokchetav.
N Kazakhstan
Koksijde 87 A 5 W Belgium
Kokstad 78 D 5 E South Africa
Kolaka 139 E 4 Celebes,
C Indonesia
Kola Peninsula see Kol'skiy
Poluostrov
Kolari 84 D 3 NW Finland
Kolárovo 99 C 6 Ger. Gutta, Hung.
Gúta; prev. Guta. SW Slovakia
Kolberg see Kołobrzeg
Kolda 74 B 3 S Senegal
Kolding 85 A 7 C Denmark
Kōle see Kili Island
Kolguyev, Ostrov 110 D 2 island,
NW Russian Federation
Kolhāpur 132 B 1 SW India
Kolhumadulu Atoll 132 B 5
var. Kolumadulu Atoll,
Thaa Atoll. Island, S Maldives
Kolín see Kolín
Kolín 99 B 5 Ger. Kolin.
C Czech Republic
Kolka 106 C 2 NW Latvia
Kolkasrags 106 C 2 prev. Eng.
Cape Domesnes. Headland,
NW Latvia
Kolmar see Colmar
Köln 94 A 4 var. Koeln, Eng./Fr.
Cologne; prev. Cöln, anc. Colonia
Agrippina, Oppidum Ubiorum.
W Germany
Koło 98 C 3 C Poland
Kołobrzeg 98 B 2 Ger. Kolberg.
NW Poland
Kolokani 74 D 3 W Mali
Kolomea see Kolomyya
Kolomna 111 B 5
W Russian Federation
Kolomyya 108 B 3 Ger. Kolomea.
W Ukraine
Kolpa 100 A 2 var. Kulpa, SCr.
Kupa. River, Croatia/Slovenia
Kolpino 110 B 4
NW Russian Federation
Kol'skiy Poluostrov 110 C 2
Eng. Kola Peninsula. Peninsula,
NW Russian Federation
Kolwezi 77 D 7 S Congo (Zaire)
Kolyma 115 G 2 river,
NE Russian Federation
Kolyma Range 113 G 2 mountain
range, NE Russian Federation

Kolymskoye Nagor'ye 115 G 2 var.
Khrebet Kolymskiy, Eng. Kolyma
Range. Mountain range,
NE Russian Federation
Komatsu 131 C 5 var. Komatu.
Honshū, SW Japan
Komatu see Komatsu
Komoé 75 E 4 var. Komoé Fleuve.
River, E Ivory Coast
Komoé Fleuve see Komoé
Komotau see Chomutov
Komotiní 104 D 3 var. Gümüljina,
Turk. Gümülcine. NE Greece
Kompong see Kâmpóng
Kompong Chhnang see Kâmpóng Chhnăng
Kompong Cham see Kâmpóng Cham
Kompong Speu see Kâmpóng Spoe
Kompong Thom see Kâmpóng Thum
Komrat see Comrat
Komsomolets, Ostrov 115 E 1
island, Severnaya Zemlya,
N Russian Federation
Komsomol'sk-na-Amure 115 G 4
SE Russian Federation
Kondolovo 104 E 3 SE Bulgaria
Kondopoga 110 B 3
NW Russian Federation
Kong Christian IX Land 82 D 4
Eng. King Christian IX Land.
Physical region, SE Greenland
Kong Christian X Land 83 E 3
Eng. King Christian X Land.
Physical region, E Greenland
Kong Frederik VI Kyst 82 C 4
Eng. King Frederik VI Coast.
Physical region, SE Greenland
Kong Frederik VIII Land 83 E 2
Eng. King Frederik VIII Land.
Physical region, NE Greenland
Kong Frederik IX Land 82 C 3
Eng. King Frederik IX Land.
Physical region, SW Greenland
Kong Karls Land 83 G 2 Eng. King
Charles Island. Island group,
SE Svalbard
Kongor 73 B 5 SE Sudan
Kongsberg 85 B 6 S Norway
Königgrätz see Hradec Králové
Konin 98 C 3 Ger. Kuhnau.
C Poland
Konispol 101 C 7 var. Konispoli.
S Albania
Konispoli see Konispol
Konjic 100 C 4
S Bosnia & Herzegovina
Konosha 110 C 4 var. Konoša.
NW Russian Federation
Konotop 109 F 1 NE Ukraine
Konstantinovka see Kostyantynivka
Konstanz 95 B 7 var. Constanz,
Eng. Constance; hist. Kostnitz,
anc. Constantia. S Germany
Konya 116 C 4 var. Konieh; prev.
Konia, anc. Iconium. C Turkey
Kóohu see Kōfu
Kōootió see Kōōchi
Kopaonik 101 D 5 mountain range,
C Yugoslavia
Koper 100 A 2 It. Capodistria;
prev. Kopar. SW Slovenia
Kopetdag, Khrebet 122 C 3
Turkm. Köpetdag Gershi,
Per. Koppeh Dāgh. Mountain
range, Iran/Turkmenistan
Koprivnica 100 C 2 Ger. Kopreinitz,
Hung. Kaproncza. N Croatia
Köprülü see Veles
Kopyl' see Kapyl'
Korat Plateau 137 D 5 plateau,
NE Thailand

Korba 135 E 4 N India
Korçë 101 D 7 var. Korça,
Gk. Korytsa, It. Corriza;
prev. Koritsa. SE Albania
Korčula 100 B 4 It. Curzola; anc.
Corcyra Nigra. Island, S Croatia
Korea Strait 131 A 7 Jap. Chōsen-
kaikyō, Kor. Taehan-haehyŏp .
Strait, East China Sea/Sea of Japan
Korhogo 74 D 4 N Ivory Coast
Korinthiakós Kólpos 105 B 5 Eng.
Gulf of Corinth; anc. Corinthiacus
Sinus. Gulf, E Ionian Sea
Kórinthos 105 B 6 Eng. Corinth;
anc. Corinthus. S Greece
Kōriyama 131 D 5 Honshū, C Japan
Korjazma see Koryazhma
Korla 126 B 3 Chin. K'u-erh-lo.
NW China
Körmend 99 B 7 W Hungary
Koróni 105 B 6 S Greece
Koror 144 A 2 country capital,
Babelthuap, C Palau
Korosten' 108 D 1 NW Ukraine
Koro Toro 76 C 2 N Chad
Kortrijk 87 A 6 Fr. Courtrai.
W Belgium
Koryak Range see Koryakskoye
Nagor'ye
Koryakskoye Nagor'ye 115 H 2 var.
Koryakskiy Khrebet, Eng. Koryak
Range. Mountain range,
NE Russian Federation
Koryazhma 110 C 4 var. Korjazma.
NW Russian Federation
Kos 105 E 6 Kos, SE Greece
Kos 105 E 6 It. Coo; anc. Cos.
Island, Dodekánisos, SE Greece
Kō-saki 131 A 7 headland,
Tsushima, SW Japan
Kościerzyna 98 C 2 NW Poland
Kosciusko, Mount 149 C 7
mountain, New South Wales,
SE Australia
Košice 99 D 6 Ger. Kaschau,
Hung. Kassa. E Slovakia
Kosikizima Rettō see
Kōshikijima-rettō
Kōshikijima-rettō 131 A 8 var.
Kosikizima Rettō. Island group,
Japan
Koslin see Koszalin
Koson 123 E 3 Rus. Kasan.
S Uzbekistan
Kosovo 101 D 5 prev. Autonomous
Province of Kosovo and Metohija.
Cultural region, S Yugoslavia
Kosovo Polje 101 D 5 S Yugoslavia
Kosovska Mitrovica 101 D 5
Mitrović; prev. Mitrovica,
Titova Mitrovica. S Yugoslavia
Kosrae 144 D 2 prev. Kusaie. Island,
E Micronesia
Kostenets 101 C 5 prev. Kostenec;
prev. Georgi Dimitrov. W Bulgaria
Kostroma 110 C 4
NW Russian Federation
Kostyantynivka 109 G 3
Rus. Konstantinovka. SE Ukraine
Kostyukovichi see Kastsyukovichy
Kostyukovka see Kastsyukowka
Koszalin 98 B 2 Ger. Köslin.
NW Poland
Kota 134 D 3 var. Kotah.
Kota Bharu 138 B 3 var. Kota
Baharu, Kota Bahru. W Malaysia
Kotaboemi see Kotabumi
Kotabumi 138 B 4 prev. Kotaboemi.
C Indonesia
Kota see Kota
Kota Kinabalu 138 D 3
prev. Jesselton. Borneo, E Malaysia

Kota Kota *see* Nkhotakota
Kotelnič *see* Kotel'nich
Kotel'nich 114 B 3 *var.* Kotelnič.
 NW Russian Federation
Kotel'nyy, Ostrov 115 F 2 island,
 Novosibirskiye Ostrova,
 N Russian Federation
Kotka 85 E 5 S Finland
Kotlas 110 C 4
 NW Russian Federation
Kotonu *see* Cotonou
Kotor 101 C 5 *It.* Cattaro.
 SW Yugoslavia
Kotovs'k 108 D 3 *Rus.* Kotovsk.
 SW Ukraine
Kotovsk *see* Kotovs'k
Kottbus *see* Cottbus
Kotto 76 D 4 river, Central African
 Republic/Congo (Zaire)
Kotuy 115 E 2 river,
 N Russian Federation
Koudougou 75 E 4 C Burkina
Koulamoutou 77 B 6 C Gabon
Koulikoro 74 D 4 SW Mali
Koumra 76 C 4 S Chad
Kourou 59 H 3 N French Guiana
Kousséri 76 B 3 *prev.* Fort-Foureau.
 NE Cameroon
Kouvola 85 E 5 S Finland
Kovel' 108 C 1 *Pol.* Kowel.
 NW Russian Federation
Kowel *see* Kovel'
Kowloon 128 A 1 *Chin.* Jiulong.
 SW Hong Kong
Kowt-e 'Ashrow 123 E 4
 E Afghanistan
Kozáni 104 B 4 N Greece
Kozara 100 B 3 mountain range,
 NW Bosnia & Herzegovina
Kozhikode *see* Calicut
Koz'modem'yansk 111 C 5
 W Russian Federation
Kōzu-shima 131 D 6 island,
 Izu-shotō, E Japan
Kozyatyn 108 D 2 *Rus.* Kazatin.
 C Ukraine
Kpalimé 75 E 5 *var.* Palimé.
 SW Togo
Kráchéh 137 D 6 *prev.* Kratie.
 E Cambodia
Kragujevac 100 D 4 C Yugoslavia
Krainburg *see* Kranj
Kra, Isthmus of 137 B 6 isthmus,
 Malaysia/Thailand
Krakatau 124 D 5 volcano,
 C Indonesia
Kraków 99 D 5 *Eng.* Cracow,
 Ger. Krakau; *anc.* Cracovia.
 S Poland
Králánh 137 D 5 NW Cambodia
Kraljevo 100 D 4 *prev.*
 Rankovićevo. C Yugoslavia
Kramators'k 109 G 3
 Rus. Kramatorsk. SE Ukraine
Kramatorsk *see* Kramators'k
Kramfors 85 C 5 C Sweden
Kranéa 104 B 4 N Greece
Kranj 95 D 7 *Ger.* Krainburg.
 NW Slovenia
Kráslava 106 D 4 SE Latvia
Krasnaye 107 C 5 *Rus.* Krasnoye.
 C Belarus
Krasnoarmeysk 111 C 6
 W Russian Federation
Krasnodar 111 A 7
 prev. Yekaterinodar. Kray capital,
 SW Russian Federation
Krasnodon 109 H 3 E Ukraine
Krasnogor *see* Kallaste
Krasnogvardeyskoye *see*
 Krasnohvardiys'ke

Krasnohvardiys'ke 109 F 4
 Rus. Krasnogvardeyskoye.
 S Ukraine
Krasnokamsk 111 D 5
 W Russian Federation
Krasnoperekops'k 109 F 4
 Rus. Krasnoperekopsk.
 S Ukraine
Krasnoperekopsk *see*
 Krasnoperekops'k
Krasnostav *see* Krasnystaw
Krasnovodsk *see* Turkmenbashi
Krasnovodskiy Zaliv 122 B 2
 Turkm. Krasnowodsk Aylagy.
 Gulf, E Caspian Sea
Krasnowodsk Aylagy *see*
 Krasnovodskiy Zaliv
Krasnoyarsk 114 D 4
 C Russian Federation
Krasnoye *see* Krasnaye
Krasnozatonskiy 110 D 4 *var.*
 Krasnozatonski, Krasnozatonskij.
 NW Russian Federation
Krasnystaw 98 E 4 *Rus.* Krasnostav.
 SE Poland
Krasnyy Luch 109 H 3
 prev. Krindachevka. E Ukraine
Krassóvár *see* Caraşova
Kratie *see* Kráchéh
Krâvanh, Chuŏr Phnum 137 D 6
 Eng. Cardamom Mountains,
 Fr. Chaîne des Cardamomes.
 Mountain range, SW Cambodia
Krefeld 94 A 4 W Germany
Kremenchug *see* Kremenchuk
Kremenchuk 109 F 3
 Rus. Kremenchug. C Ukraine
Kremenchuts'ke Vodoskhovyshche
 109 F 2 *Eng.* Kremenchuk
 Reservoir, *Rus.* Kremenchugskoye
 Vodokhranilishche. Reservoir,
 C Ukraine
Kremenets' 108 C 2
 Pol. Krzemieniec, *Rus.* Kremenets.
 W Ukraine
Kremennaya *see* Kreminna
Kreminna 109 H 2
 Rus. Kremennaya. E Ukraine
Kresena *see* Kresna
Kresna 104 C 3 *var.* Kresena.
 SW Bulgaria
Kretinga 106 B 3 *Ger.* Krottingen.
 NW Lithuania
Kreuz *see* Risti
Krichëv *see* Krychaw
Krindachevka *see* Krasnyy Luch
Krishna 132 C 1 *prev.* Kistna. River,
 C India
Krishnagiri 132 C 2 SE India
Kristiansand 85 A 6
 var. Christiansand. S Norway
Kristianstad 85 B 7 S Sweden
Kristiansund 84 A 4
 var. Christiansund. S Norway
Kríti 105 D 8 *Eng.* Crete. Island,
 SE Greece
Krivoy Rog *see* Kryvyy Rih
Krivyie Ozero *see* Kryve Ozero
Križevci 100 B 2 *Ger.* Kreuz,
 Hung. Körös. NE Croatia
Krk 100 A 2 *It.* Veglia; *anc.* Curieta.
 Island, NW Croatia
Krolevets' 109 F 1 *Rus.* Krolevets.
 NE Ukraine
Krolevets *see* Krolevets'
Kronach 95 C 5 E Germany
Kronshtadt 110 B 4 *var.* Kronštadt
 NW Russian Federation
Kronštadt *see* Kronshtadt
Kroonstad 78 D 4 C South Africa
Kropotkin 111 B 7
 SW Russian Federation

Krosno 99 E 5 *Ger.* Krossen.
 SE Poland
Krosno Odrzańskie 98 B 3 *Ger.*
 Crossen, Kreisstadt. W Poland
Krossen *see* Krosno
Krottingen *see* Kretinga
Krško 95 E 8 *Ger.* Gurkfeld;
 prev. Videm-Krško. E Slovenia
Krugloye *see* Kruhlaye
Kruhlaye 107 D 6 *Rus.* Krugloye.
 E Belarus
Krujë 101 D 6 *var.* Kruja, *It.* Croia.
 C Albania
Krung Thep 137 C 5 *var.* Krung
 Thep Mahanakhon, *Eng.*
 Bangkok. Country capital,
 C Thailand
Krung Thep, Ao 137 C 5 bay,
 South China Sea/Pacific Ocean
Krupki 107 D 6 C Belarus
Kruševac 100 D 4 C Yugoslavia
Krychaw 107 E 7 *Rus.* Krichëv.
 E Belarus
Krym 109 F 5 *var.* Crimea.
 Cultural region, S Ukraine
Kryms'ki Hory 109 F 5 mountain
 range, S Ukraine
Kryve Ozero 109 E 3 *Rus.* Krivyje
 Ozero. SW Ukraine
Kryvyy Rih 109 F 3 *Rus.* Krivoy
 Rog. SE Ukraine
Ksar-el-Kebir 70 C 2 *var.* Alcázar,
 Ksar al Kabir, Ksar el Kebir,
 Ksar-el-Kébir, Al-Kasr
 al-Kebir, Al-Qsar al-Kbir,
 Sp. Alcazarquivir. NW Morocco
Kstovo 111 C 5
 W Russian Federation
Kuala Dungun *see* Dungun
Kuala Lumpur 138 B 3 country
 capital, W Malaysia
Kuala Terengganu 138 B 3 *var.*
 Kuala Trengganu. W Malaysia
Kuala Trengganu *see*
 Kuala Terengganu
Kualatungkai 138 B 4 W Indonesia
Kuantan 138 B 3 W Malaysia
Kuba *see* Quba
Kuching 138 C 3 *prev.* Sarawak.
 Borneo, E Malaysia
Kúchnay Darvīshān 122 D 5
 S Afghanistan
Kuçovë 101 C 6 *var.* Kuçova;
 prev. Qyteti Stalin. C Albania
Kudus 125 C 5 *prev.* Koedoes. Jawa,
 C Indonesia
K'u-erh-lo *see* Korla
Kufra Oasis *see* Al Kufrah
Kuhmo 84 E 4 E Finland
Kuhnau *see* Konin
Kuito 78 B 2 *Port.* Silva Porto.
 C Angola
Kuji 130 D 3 *var.* Kuzi. Japan
Kula Kangri 135 G 3 mountain,
 Bhutan/China
Kuldīga 106 B 3 *Ger.* Goldingen.
 W Latvia
Kullorsuaq 82 C 2
 var. Kuvdlorssuak, Kuvdlorssuaq.
 N Greenland
Kulob 123 F 3 *Rus.* Kulyab.
 SW Tajikistan
Kulu 116 C 3 W Turkey
Kulundinskaya Step' 114 D 4
 physical region,
 S Russian Federation
Kulyab *see* Kulob
Kuma 111 B 7 river,
 SW Russian Federation
Kumaka 59 F 3 SE Guyana
Kumamoto 131 A 7 Kyūshū,
 SW Japan

Kumanova *see* Kumanovo
Kumanovo 101 E 5 *Turk.*
 Kumanova. N Macedonia
Kumasi 75 E 5 *prev.* Coomassie.
 C Ghana
Kumba 77 A 5 W Cameroon
Kumertau 111 D 6
 W Russian Federation
Kumillā *see* Comilla
Kumo 75 G 4 E Nigeria
Kumon Range 136 B 2 mountain
 range, N Myanmar
Kunashir, Ostrov 130 E 1 *var.*
 Kunashiri. Island, Kurile Island
 SE Russian Federation
Kunda 106 E 2 NE Estonia
Kunduz 123 E 3 *var.* Kondoz,
 Kundūz, Qondūz, *Per.* Kondūz
 NE Afghanistan
Kunene *see* Cunene
Kungsbacka 85 B 7 S Sweden
Kungur 111 D 5
 NW Russian Federation
Kunlun Mountains *see* Kunlun Sh
Kunlun Shan 126 B 4 *var.* Kunlu
 Mountains. Mountain range,
 China/India
Kunming 129 B 6 *var.* K'un-min
 prev. Yunnan. Province capital,
 SW China
Kununurra 146 D 3 Western
 Australia, N Australia
Kuopio 84 E 4 C Finland
Kupang 139 E 5 *prev.* Koepang.
 Timor, C Indonesia
Kup"yans'k 109 G 2
 Rus. Kupyansk. E Ukraine
Kupyansk *see* Kup"yans'k
Kura 117 G 2 *Az.* Kür, Geor.
 Mtkvari, *Turk.* Kura Nehri. Riv
 SW Asia
Kurashiki 131 B 6 *var.* Kurasiki.
 Honshū, SW Japan
Kurasiki *see* Kurashiki
Kürdzhali 104 D 3 *var.* Kårdžali,
 Kirdzhali. S Bulgaria
Kure 131 B 7 Honshū, SW Japar
Küre 116 C 2 Turkey
Küre Dağları 116 C 2 mountain
 range, N Turkey
Kuressaare 106 C 2 *Ger.* Arensbu
 prev. Kingissepp. Saaremaa,
 W Estonia
Kureyka 115 E 3 river,
 C Russian Federation
Kurgan-Tyube *see* Qŭrghonteppa
Kuria Muria Bay *see* Ḩalānīyāt,
 Khal'ij al
Kurile Islands *see* Kuril'skiye
 Ostrova
Kurile-Kamchatka Depression *s*
 Kurile Trench
Kurile Trench 152 C 1 *var.* Kuril
 Kamchatka Depression. Trenc
 NW Pacific Ocean
Kuril'sk 115 H 4 Kuril'skiye
 Ostrova, SE Russian Federation
Kuril'skiye Ostrova 115 H 4
 Eng. Kurile Islands. Island gro
 E Russian Federation
Kurkund *see* Kilingi-Nõmme
Kurnool 132 C 1 *var.* Karnul. S I
Kursk 111 B 6
 W Russian Federation
Kuršumlija 101 D 5 SE Yugosla
Kuruktag 126 C 3 mountain rang
 NW China
Kurume 131 A 7 Kyūshū, SW Ja
Kurupukari 59 F 3 C Guyana
Kurzeme 106 B 3 *Eng.* Courland
 Ger. Kurland. Cultural region,
 W Latvia

aie *see* Kosrae
hiro 130 D 2 *var.* Kusiro.
okkaidō, NE Japan
hka *see* Gushgy
iro *see* Kushiro
kokwim Mountains 36 C 3
ountain range, Alaska, NW USA
tanay 114 C 4 *Kaz.* Qostanay.
Kazakhstan
ahya 116 B 3 *prev.* Kutaia.
/ Turkey
aia *see* Kütahya
t'aisi 117 F 2 W Georgia
na 100 B 3 NE Croatia
no 98 D 3 C Poland
jjuaq 39 E 2 *prev.* Fort-Chimo.
uébec, E Canada
jjuarapik 38 D 2 Québec,
Canada
samo 84 E 3 E Finland

ait
20 C 4 *var.* Dawlat al Kuwait,
oweit, Kuweit. Monarchy,
N Asia

cial name: State of Kuwait Date
ormation: 1961/1981 Capital:
rait City Population: 1.8 million
l area: 6,880 sq miles
820 sq km) Languages: Arabic*,
ish Religions: Muslim 92%,
istian 6%, other 2%
nic mix: Arab 85%, South Asian
Persian 4%, other 2%
ernment: Constitutional monarchy
rency: Dinar = 1,000 fils

vajleen *see* Kwajalein Atoll
vayt 120 C 3 E Iraq
byshev *see* Samara
byshevskoye
odokhranilishche 111 C 5
ır. Kuibyshev, *Eng.* Kuybyshev
eservoir. Reservoir,
/ Russian Federation
tun 126 B 3 NW China
tun 126 B 2 NW China
i *see* Kuji
netsk 111 C 6
/ Russian Federation
loya 84 C 2 island, N Norway
rnbergs-vattnet 84 B 4 *var.*
ostviken. Lake, N Sweden
rner 100 A 3 *var.* Carnaro,
Quarnero. Gulf, Adriatic
ea/Mediterranean Sea
oya 83 G 1 island, NE Svalbard
ai Chung 128 A 1 C Hong Kong
ajalein Atoll 144 D 1
ır. Kuwajleen. Island,
Marshall Islands
ando *see* Cuando
ando 78 C 2 *var.* Cuando. River,
Africa
angju 128 E 4 *off.* Kwangju-
wangyōksi, *var.* Kwangchu,
p. Kōshū. SW South Korea
ango 77 C 7 *Port.* Cuango. River,
ngola/Congo (Zaire)
ango *see* Cuango
anza *see* Cuanza
ekwe 78 D 3 *prev.* Que Que.
Zimbabwe
idzyń 98 C 2 *Ger.* Marienwerder.
Poland
gillingok 36 B 3 Alaska, NW USA
ilu 78 B 1 river, W Congo (Zaire)
ito *see* Cuito
un Tong 128 B 1 SE Hong Kong
bé 76 C 4 S Chad
ikkami 137 B 5 *prev.* Amherst.
E Myanmar

Kyaiklat 136 B 4 S Myanmar
Kyaikto 136 B 4 S Myanmar
Kyakhta 115 E 5
S Russian Federation
Kyaukse 136 B 3 C Myanmar
Kyjov 99 C 5 *Ger.* Gaya.
SE Czech Republic
Kykládes 105 D 6 *var.* Kikládhes,
Eng. Cyclades. Island group,
SE Greece
Kými 105 C 5 *prev.* Kími.
C Greece
Kyōto 131 C 6 Honshū, SW Japan
Kyparissía 105 B 6 *var.* Kiparissía.
S Greece
Kyrá Panagía 105 C 5 island,
Vóreioi Sporádes, E Greece

Kyrgyzstan
123 F 2 *var.* Kirghizia; *prev.*
Kirghiz SSR, Kirgizskaya SSR,
Republic of Kyrgyzstan. Republic,
C Asia

Official name: Kyrgyz Republic
Date of formation: 1991 Capital:
Bishkek Population: 4.6 million
Total Area: 76,640 sq miles
(198,500 sq km) Languages:
Kirghiz*, Russian, Uzbek Religions:
Muslim 65%, other (mostly Russian
Orthodox) 35% Ethnic mix: Kirghiz
52%, Russian 21%, Uzbek 13%, other
(mostly Kazakh and Tajik) 14%
Government: Multiparty republic
Currency: Som = 100 teen

Kýthira 105 B 7 *var.* Kíthira,
It. Cerigo; *Lat.* Cytheria. Kýthira,
S Greece
Kýthira 105 C 7 *var.* Kíthira,
It. Cerigo; *Lat.* Cytheria. Island,
S Greece
Kýthnos 105 C 6 Kýthnos, SE Greece
Kýthnos 105 C 6 *var.* Kíthnos,
Thermiá, *It.* Termia; *anc.* Cythnos.
Island, Kykládes, SE Greece
Kythréa *see* Degirmenlik
Kyūshū 131 B 8
var. Kyûshyû. Island, Japan
Kyustendil 104 B 2 *var.* Kjustendil;
anc. Pautalia. W Bulgaria
Kyusyu-Palau Ridge *see*
Kyushu-Palau Ridge
Kyyiv 109 E 2 *Eng.* Kiev, *Rus.* Kiyev.
Country capital, N Ukraine
Kyyiv's'ke Vodoskhovyshche 109
E 1 *Rus.* Kiyevskoye
Vodokhranilishche. Reservoir,
N Ukraine
Kyzyl-Kiya 123 F 2 *Kir.* Kyzyl-
Kyya. SW Kyrgyzstan
Kyzyl Kum 122 D 2 *var.* Kizil Kum,
Qizil Qum, *Uzb.* Qizilqum.
Desert, Kazakhstan/Uzbekistan
Kyzyl-Kyya *see* Kyzyl-Kiya
Kyzylrabot *see* Qizilrabot
Kyzyl-Suu 123 G 2 *prev.* Pokrovka.
NE Kyrkazakhstan/
Kizilstanrgyzstan
Ky`usy`u *see* Kyūshū
Kzyl-Orda 114 B 5 *var.* Qizil Orda,
Kaz. Qyzylorda; *prev.* Perovsk.
S Kazakhstan

L

Laaland *see* Lolland
La Algaba 92 C 4 S Spain
Laarne 87 B 5 NW Belgium
La Asunción 59 E 1 NE Venezuela
Laâyoune 70 A 3 *var.* Aaiún.
Country capital,
NW Western Sahara

La Baie 39 E 4 Québec, SE Canada
la Baule-Escoublac 90 A 4
NW France
Labe *see* Elbe
Labé 74 C 4 NW Guinea
La Blanquilla *see* Blanquilla, Isla
Laborca *see* Laborec
Laborec 99 E 5 *Hung.* Laborca.
River, E Slovakia
Labrador 39 F 2 physical region,
Newfoundland and Labrador,
SW Canada
Labrador Basin 66 B 2 undersea
basin, NW Atlantic Ocean
Labrador Sea 39 G 1 sea,
NW Atlantic Ocean
Labutta 137 A 5 SW Myanmar
Laç 101 C 6 *var.* Laci. C Albania
La Calera 64 B 4 C Chile
La Carolina 92 D 4 S Spain
La Ceiba 52 D 2 N Honduras
Lacepede Bay 149 B 7 bay,
E Indian Ocean
Lacey 46 B 2 Washington, NW USA
Lachanás 104 C 3 N Greece
La Chaux-de-Fonds 95 A 7
W Switzerland
Lachlan 149 C 6 river, SE Australia
Laci *see* Laç
la Ciotat 91 D 6 *anc.* Citharista.
SE France
Lacobriga *see* Lagos
La Concepción 53 E 5 *var.*
Concepción. W Panama
La Concepción 58 C 1
NW Venezuela
Laconia 41 G 2
New Hampshire, NE USA
La Croix Maingot 55 F 1
NW Saint Lucia
La Cruz 52 D 4 NW Costa Rica
Ladozhskoye Ozero 110 B 3 *var.*
Laa Tokka, *Eng.* Lake Ladoga,
Fin. Laatokka. Lake,
NW Russian Federation
Lae 144 B 3 New Guinea,
W Papua New Guinea
La Esperanza 52 C 2 SW Honduras
Lafayette 42 B 3 Louisiana, S USA
Lafayette 40 C 4 Indiana, N USA
La Fé 54 A 2 W Cuba
Lafia 75 G 4 C Nigeria
la Flèche 90 B 4 NW France
Laghouat 70 D 2 N Algeria
Lagos 75 F 5 SW Nigeria
Lagos 92 B 5 *anc.* Lacobriga.
S Portugal
Lagos 75 F 5 SW Nigeria
Lagos de Moreno 50 D 4 SW Mexico
La Grande 46 C 3 Oregon, NW USA
La Grange 43 F 2 Georgia, SE USA
Lagunas 64 B 1 N Chile
Lagunillas 61 G 4 SE Bolivia
La Habana 54 B 2 *var.* Havana.
Country capital, W Cuba
Lahat 138 B 4 Sumatera,
W Indonesia
Laholm 85 B 7 S Sweden
Lahore 134 D 2 province capital,
NE Pakistan
Lahr 95 A 6 SW Germany
Lahti 85 E 5 *Swe.* Lahtis. S Finland
Lahtis *see* Lahti
Laï 76 B 4 *prev.* Behagle,
SW Chad
Lai Châu 136 D 3 NW Vietnam
Laila *see* Laylā
La Junta 44 D 5 Colorado, C USA
Lake Charles 42 A 3
Louisiana, S USA

Lake City 43 E 3
South Carolina, SE USA
Lake District 89 C 5 physical
region, NW England, UK
Lake Havasu City 48 A 2
Arizona, SW USA
Lake Jackson 49 H 4 Texas, S USA
Lakeland 43 E 4 Florida, SE USA
Lakes Entrance 149 D 7 inlet,
W Tasman Sea
Lakeside 47 D 8 California, W USA
Lakewood 44 C 4 Colorado, C USA
Lake Worth 43 F 5 Florida, SE USA
Lakhnau *see* Lucknow
Lakonikós Kólpos 105 B 7 gulf,
C Mediterranean Sea
Lakselv 84 D 2 N Norway
Lakshadweep 132 A 3 *prev.* the
Laccadive, Minicoy and Amindivi
Islands. Union territory,
SW India
Lala 139 E 2 SW Philippines
La Laguna 70 A 3 Tenerife,
SW Spain
La Libertad 52 B 1 N Guatemala
La Libertad 60 A 2 W Ecuador
La Ligua 64 B 4 C Chile
Lalín 92 C 1 NW Spain
Lalitpur 135 F 3 C Nepal
La Louvière 87 B 6 S Belgium
La Maçana *see* La Massana
La Maddalena 96 A 4 W Italy
Lamar 44 D 5 Iowa, C USA
La Massana 91 A 8 *var.* la Maçana.
W Andorra
Lambaré 64 D 2 S Paraguay
Lambaréné 77 A 6 W Gabon
Lamego 92 C 2 N Portugal
Lamesa 49 E 3 Texas, S USA
Lamezia 97 D 6 SE Italy
Lamía 105 B 5 C Greece
Lamma Island 128 A 2 *Cant.* Pok
Liu Chau. Island, S Hong Kong
Lamon Bay 139 E 1 bay,
SW Philippine Sea
Lamoni 45 F 4 Wyoming, C USA
La Mosquitia 53 E 3 *var.* Miskito
Coast, *Eng.* Mosquito Coast.
Coastal region, E Nicaragua
Lampang 136 C 4 *var.* Muang
Lampang. NW Thailand
Lámpeia 105 B 6 S Greece
Lanbi Kyun 137 B 6 *prev.* Sullivan
Island. Island, S Myanmar
Lancaster 89 C 5 NW England, UK
Lancaster 40 D 4 Ohio, N USA
Lancaster 47 C 7 California, W USA
Lancaster Sound 37 F 2 channel,
Arctic Ocean/Baffin Bay
Landen 87 C 6 C Belgium
Lander 44 C 3 Wyoming, C USA
Landerneau 90 A 3 NW France
Landes 91 B 5 cultural region,
SW France
Landsberg am Lech 95 C 6
S Germany
Land's End 89 B 8 headland,
SW England, UK
Landshut 95 C 6 SE Germany
Langar 123 E 2 *Rus.* Lyangar.
C Uzbekistan
Langfang 128 D 4 NE China
Langres 90 D 4 N France
Lang Son 136 D 3
N Vietnam
Langson *see* Lang Son
Lang Suan 137 C 6 Thailand
Languedoc 91 C 6 cultural region,
S France

Länkäran 117 H 3 *Rus.* Lenkoran'.
S Azerbaijan
Lansing 40 C 3 state capital,
Michigan, N USA
Lanta, Ko 137 B 7 island, S Thailand
Lantau Island 128 A 2 *Cant.* Tai Yue
Shan. Island, SW Hong Kong
Lantau Peak 128 A 1 *Cant.* Fung
Wong Shan. Mountain, Lantau
Island, W Hong Kong
Lantung, Gulf of *see* Liaodong Wan
Lanzarote 70 B 3 island, Islas
Canarias, SW Spain
Lanzhou 128 B 4 *var.* Lan-chou,
Lanchow, Lan-chow; *prev.* Kaolan.
Province capital, C China
Lao Cai 136 D 3 NW Vietnam
Laoet *see* Laut, Pulau
Laoha He 127 F 2 river, NE China
Laon 90 D 3 *var.* la Laon;
anc. Laudunum. N France
Lao People's Democratic Republic
see Laos
La Orchila, Isla 58 D 1 island,
N Venezuela
La Oroya 60 C 3 C Peru

Laos
136 C 4 . Republic, SE Asia

Official name: Lao People's
Democratic Republic **Date of
formation:** 1953 **Capital:** Vientiane
Population: 4.6 million **Total Area:**
91,428 sq miles (236,800 sq km)
Languages: Lao*, Miao, Yao
Religions: Buddhist 85%,
Christian 2%, other 13% **Ethnic mix:**
Lao Loum 56%, Lao Theung 34%,
Lao Soung 10% **Government:**
Single-party republic
Currency: Kip = 100 cents

La Palma 53 G 5 SE Panama
La Palma 70 A 3 island, Islas
Canarias, SW Spain
La Paz 50 B 3 NW Mexico
La Paz 61 F 4 *var.* La Paz de
Ayacucho. Country capital,
W Bolivia
La Paz, Bahía de 50 B 3 bay, Golfo
de California / Pacific Ocean
La Paz de Ayacucho *see* La Paz
La Perouse Strait 130 C 1 *Jap.* Sōya-
kaikyō, *Rus.* Proliv Laperuza.
Strait, Sea of Japan/Sea of Okhotsk
Lápithos *see* Lapta
Lapland 84 D 2 *Fin.* Lappi,
Swe. Lappland. Cultural region,
N Europe
La Plata 64 D 4 E Argentina
Lappeenranta 85 E 5
Swe. Villmanstrand. SE Finland
Lappo *see* Lapua
Laptev Sea *see* Laptevykh, More
Laptevykh, More 115 F 2 *Eng.*
Laptev Sea. Sea, Arctic Ocean
Lapua 85 D 5 *Swe.* Lappo. W Finland
La Puebla *see* Sa Pobla
Lapurdum *see* Bayonne
Łapy 98 E 3 E Poland
La Quiaca 64 C 2 N Argentina
L'Aquila 96 C 4 *var.* Aquila, Aquila
degli Abruzzi. C Italy
Laracha 92 B 1 NW Spain
Larache 70 C 2 *var.* al Araïch,
El Araïch, *Ar.* Al-Araish; *prev.*
El Araïche, *anc.* Lixus. NW Morocco
Laramie 44 C 4 Wyoming, C USA
Laramie Mountains 44 C 3
mountain range, Wyoming, C USA
Laredo 93 E 1 N Spain

Laredo 49 F 5 Texas, S USA
La Réunion *see* Réunion
Largo 43 E 4 Florida, SE USA
La Rioja 93 E 2 cultural region,
N Spain
La Rioja 64 C 3 NW Argentina
Lárisa 104 B 4 *var.* Larissa. C Greece
Larissa *see* Lárisa
Lārkāna 134 B 3 *var.* Larkhana.
SE Pakistan
Larkhana *see* Lārkāna
la Rochelle 90 A 4 *anc.* Rupella.
W France
la Roche-sur-Yon 90 A 4
prev. Bourbon Vendée, Napoléon-
Vendée. NW France
La Roda 93 E 3 C Spain
La Romana 55 E 3
E Dominican Republic
La Sarre 38 D 4 Québec, SE Canada
Las Cabezas de San Juan 92 C 5
S Spain
Las Cruces 48 D 3 New Mexico,
SW USA
La See d'Urgel 93 F 2 *var.* La Seu
d'Urgell, Seo de Urgel. NE Spain
La Serena 64 B 3 N Chile
la Seyne-sur-Mer 91 D 6 SE France
Lashio 136 B 3 NE Myanmar
Lashkar Gāh 122 D 5 *var.* Lashkar
Gah, Lash-Kar-Gar'. S Afghanistan
La Sila 97 E 6 mountain range,
SW Italy
La Sirena 52 D 3 E Nicaragua
Łask 98 C 4 C Poland
Las Lomitas 64 D 2 N Argentina
La Solana 93 E 4 C Spain
Las Palmas 70 A 3 *var.* Las Palmas
de Gran Canaria. Regional
capital, Gran Canaria, SW Spain
Las Petas 61 H 3 NE Bolivia
La Spezia 96 B 3 NW Italy
Las Piedras 61 E 3 E Peru
Las Tablas 53 G 5 S Panama
Las Tunas 54 C 2 *var.* Victoria de las
Tunas. E Cuba
Las Vegas 47 D 7 Nevada, W USA
Las Yaras 61 E 4 S Peru
Latacunga 60 B 1 C Ecuador
la Teste 91 A 5 SW France
Latgale 106 D 4 *Eng.* Latgallia.
Cultural region, SE Latvia
Latgallia *see* Latgale
Latina 97 C 5 *prev.* Littoria. C Italy
La Tortuga, Isla 59 E 1 *var.* Isla
Tortuga. Island, N Venezuela
La Tuque 39 E 4 Québec, SE Canada

Latvia
106 C 3 *Ger.* Lettland, *Latv.*
Latvija, Latvijas Republika, *Rus.*
Latviyskaya SSR; *prev.* Latvian
SSR. Republic, NE Europe

Official name: Republic of Latvia
Date of formation: 1991 **Capital:**
Riga **Population:** 2.7 million **Total
area:** 24,938 sq miles (64,589 sq km)
Languages: Latvian*, Russian
Religions: Evangelical Lutheran
85%, other Christian 15% **Ethnic
mix:** Latvian 52%, Russian 34%,
Belarussian 5%, other 9%
Government: Multiparty republic
Currency: Lats = 100 santimi

Lau Group 145 E 4 island group,
E Fiji
Launceston 149 C 8 Tasmania,
SE Australia
La Unión 93 F 4 SE Spain
La Unión 65 B 5 C Chile

La Unión 52 C 2 C Honduras
La Unión 60 C 3 C Peru
Laurel 42 C 3 Mississippi, S USA
Laurel 44 C 2 Montana, NW USA
Laurentian Highlands 39 E 3
var. Laurentian Mountains,
Fr. Les Laurentides. Plateau,
Canada/USA
Lauria 97 D 6 S Italy
Laurinburg 43 F 1
North Carolina, SE USA
Lauru *see* Choiseul
Lausanne 95 A 7 *It.* Losanna
SW Switzerland
Laut, Pulau 138 D 4 *prev.* Laoet.
Island, C Indonesia
Laval 90 B 3 NW France
Laval 38 D 4 Québec, SE Canada
La Vega 55 E 3 *var.* Concepción de
la Vega. C Dominican Republic
La Vila Jojosa *see* Villajoyosa
Lávrio 105 C 6 *prev.* Lávrion.
C Greece
Lávrion *see* Lávrio
Lawrence 41 G 3
Massachusetts, NE USA
Lawrenceburg 42 C 1 Tennessee, S USA
Lawton 49 F 2 Oklahoma, C USA
Laylá 121 C 5 *var.* Laila.
C Saudi Arabia
Lazarev Sea 154 B 1 sea,
S Atlantic Ocean
Lázaro Cárdenas 50 D 5 SW Mexico
Læsø 85 B 7 island, N Denmark
League City 49 H 4 Texas, S USA
Leal *see* Lihula
Leamhcán *see* Lucan
Leamington 38 C 5 Ontario,
S Canada
Lebak 139 E 3 Mindanao, S Philippines
Lebanon 42 D 1 Tennessee, S USA
Lebanon 41 G 2 Kentucky, NE USA
Lebanon 46 B 3 Oregon, NW USA
Lebanon 45 G 5 Missouri, C USA

Lebanon
118 A 4 *Ar.* Al Lubnān, *Fr.* Liban.
Republic, SW Asia

Official name: Republic of Lebanon
Date of formation: 1944 **Capital:**
Beirut **Population:** 2.9 million **Total
area:** 4,015 sq miles (10,400 sq km)
Languages: Arabic*, French,
Armenian, Assyrian **Religions:**
Muslim (mainly Sunni) 57%,
Christian (mainly Maronite) 43%
Ethnic mix: Arab 93% (Lebanese
83%, Palestinian 10%), other 7%
Government: Multiparty republic
Currency: Pound = 100 piastres

Lebap 122 D 2 NE Turkmenistan
Lebedin *see* Lebedyn
Lebedyn 109 F 2 *Rus.* Lebedin.
NE Ukraine
Lebel-sur-Quévillon 38 D 4
Québec, SE Canada
Lębork 98 C 2 *var.* Lębórk,
Ger. Lauenburg, Lauenburg in
Pommern. NW Poland
Lebrija 92 C 5 S Spain
Lebu 65 A 5 C Chile
le Cannet 91 D 6 SE France
Le Cap *see* Cap-Haïtien
Lecce 97 E 6 SE Italy
Lechainá 105 B 6 *var.* Lekhainá.
S Greece
Ledo Salinarius *see* Lons-le-Saunier
Leduc 37 E 5 Alberta, SW Canada
Leech Lake 45 F 2 lake,
Minnesota, N USA

Leeds 89 D 5 N England, UK
Leek 86 E 2 NE Netherlands
Leer 94 A 3 NW Germany
Leesburg 43 E 4 Florida, SE USA⁄
Leeuwarden 86 D 1 *Fris.* Ljouwe
N Netherlands
Leeuwin, Cape 142 A 5 headlan
Western Australia, SW Austra
Leeward Islands 55 G 3 *var.* Soci
Islands. Island group,
E Caribbean Sea
Leeward Islands *see* Sotavento,
Ilhas de
Lefkáda 105 A 5 *prev.* Levkás.
Lefkáda, W Greece
Lefkáda 105 A 5 *It.* Santa Maura
prev. Levkás, *anc.* Leucas. Islar
Iónioi Nísoi, W Greece
Lefká Óri 105 C 7 mountain ran
Kriti, SE Greece
Lefkímmi 105 A 5 *var.* Levkímm
Kérkyra, W Greece
Legaspi 139 E 2 *off.* Legaspi City
Luzon, N Philippines
Legaspi City *see* Legaspi
Leghorn *see* Livorno
Legnica 98 B 4 *Ger.* Liegnitz. W Pol
le Havre 90 B 3 *Eng.* Havre; *prev.*
le Havre-de-Grâce. N France
Lehčevo *see* Lekhchevo
Leicester 89 D 6 *Lat.* Batae
Coritanorum. C England, UK
Leichhardt Range 148 D 4
mountain range, Queensland,
NE Australia
Leiden 86 C 3 *prev.* Leyden,
anc. Lugdunum Batavorum.
W Netherlands
Leie 87 B 6 *Fr.* Lys. River,
Belgium/France
Leigh Creek 149 B 6
South Australia, S Australia
Leinster 89 B 6 cultural region,
E Ireland
Leipsoi 105 E 6 island,
Dodekánisos, SE Greece
Leipzig 94 C 4 *Pol.* Lipsk; hist. E
Leipsic, *anc.* Lipsia. E German
Leiria 92 B 3 *anc.* Collipo.
W Portugal
Leirvik 85 A 6 S Norway
Leizhou *see* Haikang
Lek 86 C 4 river, SW Netherland
Lekhchevo 104 C 2 *var.* Lehčevo
NW Bulgaria
Leksand 85 C 5 C Sweden
Lel'chitsy *see* Lyel'chytsy
Lelystad 86 D 3 C Netherlands
le Mans 90 B 3 NW France
le Maroni Fleuve *see*
Marowijne Rivier
Lemnos *see* Límnos
Lena 115 F 3 river,
E Russian Federation
Lengshuitan 129 C 6 E China
Lenine 109 G 5 *Rus.* Lenino.
S Ukraine
Leningradskaya 154 C 4 researc
station, Antarctica
Lenino *see* Lenine
Leningorsk 114 D 5 *Kaz.* Lenīn
E Kazakhstan
Leninpol' 123 F 2 NW Kyrgyzst
Lenkoran' *see* Lenkeran
Lenti 99 B 7 SW Hungary
Lentia *see* Linz
Lenya 137 B 6 S Myanmar
Leoben 95 E 7 C Austria
León 92 D 1 NW Spain
León 51 E 4 *var.* León de los
Aldamas. C Mexico

52 C 3 NW Nicaragua
de los Aldamas *see* León
ídi 105 B 6 S Greece
old II, Lac *see* Mai-Ndombe, Lac
oldville *see* Kinshasa
92 C 4 S Spain
ıl' *see* Lyepyel'
ıntine Alps 95 B 7 *Fr.* Alpes
ıpontiennes, *It.* Alpi
ıpontine. Mountain range,
ıly/Switzerland
ırtel 90 C 2 N France
ıy 91 C 5 *prev.* le Puy-en-
ılay, *hist.* Anicium, Podium
ıicensis. C France
76 B 4 SW Chad
da *see* Lleida
ıa 92 D 2 N Spain
ıs 105 D 6 island, Dodekánisos,
Greece
ıvick 88 D 1 island authority
ıea capital, NE Scotland, UK
ıos *see* Lésvos
Cayes 54 D 3 *var.* Cayes. SW Haiti
Gonaïves *see* Gonaïves
ıan 129 B 5 C China
Herbiers 90 B 4 NW France
ovac 101 E 5 SE Yugoslavia

tho
D 4 *prev.* Basutoland.
onarchy, S Africa

cial name: Kingdom of Lesotho
e of formation: 1966 Capital:
eru Population: 1.9 million
al area: 11,718 sq miles
50 sq km) Languages: English*,
tho*, Zulu Religions:
stian 93%, other 7%
ıic mix: Basotho 80%, other 1%
ernment: Constitutional
archy Currency: Loti = 100 lisente

ables-d'Olonne 90 A 4
W France
er Antarctica 154 B 3 *var.*
est Antarctica. Physical region,
ntarctica
er Antilles 55 E 5 island group,
Caribbean Sea
er Caucasus 117 F 2 *Rus.* Malyy
ıvkaz. Mountain range, SW Asia
er Khingan Range *see*
ao Hinggan Ling
er Sunda Islands *see*
ausa Tenggara
os 105 D 5 *anc.* Lesbos. Island,
Greece
ıno 98 B 4 *Ger.* Lissa. W Poland
bridge 37 E 3 Alberta, SW Canada
em 59 F 3 S Guyana
tia 58 C 3 S Colombia
Kepuluan 139 F 5 island
oup, E Indonesia
adan 136 B 4 W Myanmar
5k-aw Kyun 137 B 6
r. Letsutan Island; *prev.* Domel
'and. Island, S Myanmar
ven 87 C 6 *Fr.* Louvain,
rr. Löwen. C Belgium
ze *see* Leuze-en-Hainaut
ze-en-Hainaut 87 B 6
r. Leuze. SW Belgium
anger 84 C 4 N Norway
'lland 49 E 2 Texas, S USA
que, Cape 146 C 3 headland,
estern Australia, W Australia
rkusen 94 A 4 W Germany
ce 99 C 6 *var.* Lewenz, *Ger.*
ewenz, *Hung.* Léva. SW Slovakia
n 150 D 4 North Island,
New Zealand

Levkás *see* Lefkáda
Levkímmi *see* Lefkímmi
Lewis, Isle of 88 B 3 island,
NW Scotland, UK
Lewis Range 44 B 1 mountain
range, NW USA
Lewis Smith Lake 42 C 2 reservoir,
Alabama, S USA
Lewiston 41 G 2 Maine, NE USA
Lewiston 46 C 2 Idaho, NW USA
Lewistown 44 C 1 Montana, NW USA
Lexington 40 C 5 Kentucky, E USA
Lexington 45 E 4 Nebraska, C USA
Leyte 139 F 2 island, Visayan
Islands, C Philippines
Leżajsk 99 E 5 SE Poland
Lezhë 101 C 6 *var.* Lezha; *prev.* Lesh,
Leshi. NW Albania
Lhasa 126 C 5 *var.* La-sa, Lassa.
W China
Lhazê 126 C 5 SW China
L'Hospitalet de Llobregat 93 G 2
var. Hospitalet. NE Spain
Liancourt Rocks 131 A 5 island
group, Japan/South Korea
Lianyungang 128 D 4 *var.* Xinpu.
E China
Liaoning 128 D 3 *var.* Liao,
Shengking; *hist.* Fengtien,
Shenking. Province, NE China
Liao-yang *see* Liaoyang
Liaoyang 128 E 3 *var.* Shuang-liao,
Jap. Chengchiatun. NE China
Liard *see* Fort Liard
Liban, Jebel 118 B 4 *var.* Jabal al
Gharbt, *Ar.* Jabal Lubnán,
Eng. Mount Lebanon. Mountain
range, C Lebanon
Libau *see* Liepāja
Libby 44 A 1 Montana, NW USA
Liberal 45 E 5 Kansas, C USA
Liberec 98 B 4 *Ger.* Reichenberg.
N Czech Republic

Liberia
75 D 5 Republic, W Africa

Official name: Republic of Liberia
Date of formation: 1847/1907
Capital: Monrovia Population: 2.8
million Total area: 43,000 sq miles
(111,370 sq km) Languages:
English*, Kpelle, Bassa Vai
Religions: Traditional beliefs 70%,
Muslim 20%, Christian 10% Ethnic
mix: Kpelle 20%, Bassa 14%,
Americo-Liberians 5%, other 61%
Government: Transitional
Currency: Liberian $ = 100 cents

Liberia 52 D 4 NW Costa Rica
Libourne 91 B 5 SW France
Libreville 77 A 5 country capital,
NW Gabon

Libya
71 F 3 *Ar.* Al Jamāhīrīyah al
'Arabīyah al Lībīyah ash
Sha'bīyah al Ishtirākīyah; *prev.*
Libyan Arab Republic. Islamic
state, N Africa

Official name: The Great Socialist
People's Libyan Arab Jamahiriya
Date of formation: 1951 Capital:
Tripoli Population: 5.5 million
Total area: 679,358 sq miles
(1,759,540 sq km) Languages:
Arabic*, Tuareg Religions: Muslim
97%, other 3% Ethnic mix: Arab
and Berber 97%, other 3%
Government: Socialist *jamahiriya*
(state of the masses)
Currency: Dinar = 1,000 dirhams

Libyan Desert 68 C 3 *var.* Libian
Desert, *Ar.* Aş Şahrā' al Lībīyah.
Desert, NE Africa
Libyan Plateau 68 C 2 plateau,
Egypt/Libya
Lichtenfels 95 C 5 SE Germany
Lichtenvoorde 86 E 4
E Netherlands
Lichuan 129 C 5 C China
Lida 107 B 5 W Belarus
Lidköping 85 B 6 S Sweden
Lidoríki 105 B 5 *prev.* Lidhorikíon,
Lidokhorikíon. C Greece
Lidzbark Warmiński 98 D 2
Ger. Heilsberg. N Poland
Liechtenstein
94 D 1 Monarchy, C Europe

Official name: Principality of
Liechtenstein Date of formation:
1719 Capital: Vaduz Population:
29,000 Total area: 62 sq miles
(160 sq km) Languages: German*,
Alemannish Religions: Roman
Catholic 87%, Protestant 8%,
other 5% Ethnic mix:
Liechtensteiner 63%, Swiss 15%,
German 9%, other 13% Government:
Constitutional monarchy
Currency: Swiss franc =
100 centimes

Liechtenstein, Principality of *see*
Liechtenstein
Liège 87 D 6 *Dut.* Luik, *Ger.* Lüttich.
E Belgium
Liegnitz *see* Legnica
Lienz 95 D 7 W Austria
Liepāja 106 B 3 *Ger.* Libau. W Latvia
Lievenhof *see* Līvāni
Liezen 95 D 7 C Austria
Liffey 89 B 6 river, E Ireland
Lifou 144 D 5 island,
E New Caledonia
Liger *see* Loire
Ligure, Appennino 96 A 2
Eng. Ligurian Mountains.
Mountain range, NW Italy
Ligurian Mountains *see*
Ligure, Appennino
Ligurian Sea 102 D 2 *Fr.* Mer
Ligurienne, *It.* Mar Ligure. Sea,
N Mediterranean Sea
Lihou Reef & Cays 148 E 3 reef,
C Coral Sea
Lihue 47 A 8 *Haw.* Lihu'e.
Hawaii, W USA
Līhu'e *see* Lihue
Lihula 106 D 2 *Ger.* Leal. W Estonia
Likasi 77 D 8 *prev.* Jadotville.
SE Congo (Zaire)
Liknes 85 A 6 S Norway
Lille 90 C 2 *var.* l'Isle, *Dut.* Rijssel,
Flem. Ryssel; *prev.* Lisle,
anc. Insula. N France
Lillehammer 85 B 5 S Norway
Lillestrøm 85 B 6 S Norway
Lilongwe 79 E 2 country capital,
W Malawi
Lilybaeum *see* Marsala
Lima 60 C 4 country capital, W Peru
Limanowa 99 D 5 S Poland
Limassol *see* Lemesós
Lim Chu Kang 138 A 1 NW Singapore
SW Ireland
Limín Vathéos *see* Sámos
Límnos 104 D 4 *anc.* Lemnos.
E Greece
Limoges 91 C 5 *anc.* Augustoritum
Lemovicensium, Lemovices.
C France

Limón 53 E 4 *var.* Puerto Limón.
E Costa Rica
Limón 52 D 2 NE Honduras
Limousin 91 C 5 cultural region,
C France
Limoux 91 C 6 S France
Limpopo 78 D 3
var. Crocodile. River, S Africa
Linares 92 D 4 S Spain
Linares 64 B 4 C Chile
Linares 51 E 3 NE Mexico
Linchuan 129 D 5 E China
Lincoln 89 D 6 *anc.* Lindum,
Lindum Colonia. E England, UK
Lincoln 45 F 4 state capital,
Nebraska, C USA
Lincoln Sea 83 E 1 sea, Arctic Ocean
Linden 59 G 3 E Guyana
Líndhos *see* Líndos
Lindi 73 D 8 SE Tanzania
Líndos 105 E 7 *var.* Líndhos. Ródos,
SE Greece
Line Islands 145 H 3 island group,
E Kiribati
Lingen 94 A 3 *var.* Lingen an der
Ems. NW Germany
Lingen an der Ems *see* Lingen
Lingga, Kepulauan 138 B 4 island
group, W Indonesia
Linköping 85 C 6 S Sweden
Linz 95 D 6 *anc.* Lentia. N Austria
Lion, Golfe du 91 C 7
Eng. Gulf of Lion, Gulf of Lions;
anc. Sinus Gallicus. Inlet,
NW Mediterranean Sea
Liozno *see* Lyozna
Lípari, Isola 97 D 7 island, S Italy
Lipetsk 111 B 5 W Russian Federation
Lipova 108 A 4 *Hung.* Lippa.
W Romania
Lipovets *see* Lypovets'
Lippa *see* Lipova
Lippstadt 94 B 4 W Germany
Lira 73 B 6 N Uganda
Lisala 77 C 5 N Congo (Zaire)
Lisboa *see* Lisbon
Lisbon 92 B 4 country capital,
var. Felicitas Julia, Olisipo.
C Portugal
Lisbon *see* Lisboa
Lisichansk *see* Lysychans'k
Lisieux 90 B 3 *anc.* Noviomagus.
N France
Liski 111 B 6 *prev.* Georgiu-Dezh.
W Russian Federation
Lismore 149 E 5 New South Wales,
SE Australia
Lissa *see* Leszno
Lisse 86 C 3 W Netherlands
Litang 129 A 5 C China
Litani, Nahrel 119 B 5 *var.* Nahr al
Lītāni. River, C Lebanon
Litant, Nahr al *see* Litani, Nahrel
Lithgow 149 D 6 New South Wales,
SE Australia

Lithuania
106 B 4 *Ger.* Litauen, *Lith.*
Lietuva, *Pol.* Litwa, *Rus.* Litva,
Litovskaya SSR; *prev.* Lithuanian
SSR. Republic, NE Europe

Official name: Republic of Lithuania
Date of formation: 1991 Capital:
Vilnius Population: 3.8 million Total
area: 625,174 sq miles (5,200 sq km)
Languages: Lithuanian*,
Russian: Religions: Roman Catholic
87%, Russian Orthodox 10%, other
3% Ethnic mix: Lithuanian 80%,
Russian 9%, Polish 8%, other 3%
Government: Multiparty republic
Currency: Litas = 100 centas

Litóchoro 104 B 4 var. Litókhoron.
N Greece
Little Alföld 99 C 6 Ger. Kleines
Ungarisches Tiefland, Hung.
Kisalföld, Slvk. Podunajská
Rovina. Plain, Hungary/Slovakia
Little Andaman 133 F 2 island,
SW India
Little Barrier Island 150 D 2 island,
North Island, N New Zealand
Little Bay 93 H 5 bay,
NE Atlantic Ocean
Little Cayman 54 B 3 island,
E Cayman Islands
Little Falls 45 F 2 Minnesota, N USA
Littlefield 49 E 2 Texas, S USA
Little Fort 37 E 5 British Columbia,
SW Canada
Little Inagua 54 D 2 var. Inagua
Islands. Island, S Bahamas
Little Minch, The 88 B 3 strait,
NE Atlantic Ocean
Little Missouri River 44 D 2 river,
NW USA
Little Nicobar 133 G 3 island,
SW India
Little Rock 42 B 1 state capital,
Arkansas, C USA
Little St.Bernard Pass 96 A 2
Fr. Col du Petit St-Bernard,
It. Colle di Piccolo San Bernardo.
Pass, France/Italy
Little Sound 42 A 5 bay,
W Atlantic Ocean
Littleton 44 C 4 Colorado, C USA
Littoria see Latina
Liuzhou 129 C 6 var. Liu-chou,
Liuchow. S China
Livanátai see Livanátes
Livanátes 105 C 5 prev. Livanátai.
C Greece
Līvāni 106 D 4 Ger. Lievenhof.
SE Latvia
Liverpool 89 C 5 NW England, UK
Liverpool 39 F 5 Nova Scotia,
SE Canada
Livingston 44 B 2 Montana, NW USA
Livingstone 78 C 3 var. Maramba.
S Zambia
Livingstone Mountains 151 A 7
mountain range, South Island,
SW New Zealand
Livingston, Lake 49 H 3 reservoir,
Texas, SW USA
Livno 100 B 4
SW Bosnia & Herzegovina
Livojoki 84 D 4 river, C Finland
Livonia 40 D 3 Michigan, N USA
Livonia see Vidzeme
Livorno 96 B 3 Eng. Leghorn. C Italy
Lixoúri 105 A 5 prev. Lixoúrion.
Iónioi Nísoi, W Greece
Lixoúrion see Lixoúri
Ljouwert see Leeuwarden
Ljubljana 95 D 8 Ger. Laibach,
It. Lubiana; anc. Aemona, Emona.
Country capital, C Slovenia
Ljungby 85 B 7 S Sweden
Ljusdal 85 C 5 C Sweden
Ljusnan 85 C 5 river, C Sweden
Llallagua 61 F 4 SW Bolivia
Llanelli 89 C 7 prev. Llanelly.
S Wales, UK
Llanelly see Llanelli
Llanes 92 D 1 N Spain
Llanos 58 D 2 physical region,
Colombia/Venezuela
Lleida 93 F 2 var. Lérida; anc. Ilerda.
NE Spain
Lluchmayor see Llucmajor
Llucmajor 93 G 3 var. Lluchmayor.
E Spain

Lobatse 78 C 4 var. Lobatsi.
SE Botswana
Lobatsi see Lobatse
Löbau 94 D 4 E Germany
Lobito 78 B 2 W Angola
Lobositz see Lovosice
Loburi see Lop Buri
Lochem 86 E 3 E Netherlands
Loch Garman see Wexford
Lockport 41 E 3 New York, NE USA
Lodeynoye Pole 110 B 4 var.
Lodejnoje Pole, Lodeinoje
Polje. NW Russian Federation
Lodi 47 B 6 California, W USA
Lodja 77 D 6 C Congo (Zaire)
Lodz see Łódź
Łódź 98 D 4 Rus. Lodz. C Poland
Loei 136 C 4 var. Loey, Muang Loei.
N Thailand
Lofoten 84 B 3 var. Lofoten Islands.
Island group, C Norway
Lofoten Islands see Lofoten
Logan 44 B 3 Utah, W USA
Logan, Mount 36 D 3 mountain,
Yukon Territory, W Canada
Logansport 40 C 4 Indiana, N USA
Logroño 93 E 2 anc. Vareia,
Lat. Juliobriga. N Spain
Loibl Pass 95 D 7 Ger. Loiblpass,
Slvn. Ljubelj. Pass,
Austria/Slovenia
Loi-Kaw 136 B 4 E Myanmar
Loire 90 B 4 var. Liger. River, C France
Loita Hills 73 C 6 hill range,
SW Kenya
Loja 60 B 2 S Ecuador
Lokitaung 73 C 5 NW Kenya
Lokoja 75 G 5 C Nigeria
Loksa 106 E 2 Ger. Loxa. NW Estonia
Lolland 85 A 8 prev. Laaland.
Island, S Denmark
Lom 75 H 5 river, Cameroon/
Central African Republic
Lom 104 C 4 prev. Lom-Palanka.
NW Bulgaria
Loma Mansa see Bintimani
Lomami 77 D 6 river,
C Congo (Zaire)
Lomas de Zamora 64 D 4
E Argentina
Lombok, Pulau 138 D 5 island,
C Indonesia
Lomé 75 F 5 country capital, S Togo
Lommel 87 D 5 N Belgium
Lomond, Loch 88 C 4 lake,
W Scotland, UK
Lomonsov Ridge 155 F 3 var.
Harris Ridge, Rus. Khrebet
Lomonsova. Undersea ridge,
Arctic Ocean
Lom-Palanka see Lom
Lompoc 47 B 7 California, W USA
Lom Sak 136 C 4 var. Muang Lom
Sak. N Thailand
Łomża 98 D 3 Rus. Lomzha.
NE Poland
Lomzha see Łomża
Loncoche 65 B 5 C Chile
London 89 E 7 anc. Augusta,
Lat. Londinium. Country capital,
SE England, UK
London 38 C 5 Ontario, S Canada
Londonderry 88 A 4 var. Derry,
Ir. Doire. N Northern Ireland, UK
Londonderry, Cape 146 C 2
headland, Western Australia,
W Australia
Londrina 63 E 4 S Brazil
Longa, Proliv 115 G 1 Eng. Long
Strait. Strait, Chukchi Sea/
East Siberian Sea

Long Bay 43 F 2 bay,
NW Atlantic Ocean
Long Beach 47 C 8
California, W USA
Longford 89 B 5 Ir. An Longfort.
C Ireland
Long Island 54 D 2 island,
C Bahamas
Long Island 148 D 4 island,
Queensland, E Australia
Long Island 41 G 4 island,
New York, NE USA
Long Island Sound 41 G 3 sound,
W Atlantic Ocean
Longlac 38 C 4 Ontario, S Canada
Longmont 44 C 4 Colorado, C USA
Longreach 148 C 4 Queensland,
E Australia
Long Strait see Longa, Proliv
Longview 49 H 3 Texas, S USA
Longview 46 B 2
Washington, NW USA
Long Xuyên 137 D 6
var. Longxuyen. SW Vietnam
Longxuyen see Long Xuyên
Longyan 129 D 6 SE China
Longyearbyen 83 G 2 dependent
territory capital, W Svalbard
Lons-le-Saunier 90 D 4
anc. Ledo Salinarius. E France
Lop Buri 137 C 5 var. Loburi.
C Thailand
Lop Nur 126 C 3 var. Lob Nor, Lop
Nor, Lo-pu Po. Lake,
NW China
Loppersum 86 E 1
NE Netherlands
Lorain 40 D 3 Ohio, N USA
Lorca 93 E 4 S Spain
Eliocroca, Lat. Illur co. S Spain
Lord Howe Island 142 C 4 island,
E Australia
Lord Howe Rise 152 C 4 undersea
rise, SW Pacific Ocean
Loreto 50 B 3 W Mexico
Lorient 90 A 4 prev. l'Orient.
NW France
l'Orient see Lorient
Lorn, Firth of 88 B 4 inlet,
NE Atlantic Ocean
Lörrach 95 A 7 S Germany
Lorraine 90 D 3 cultural region,
NE France
Los Alamos 48 D 1
New Mexico, SW USA
Los Amates 52 B 2 E Guatemala
Los Angeles 47 C 8
California, W USA
Los Ángeles 65 B 5 C Chile
Losanna see Lausanne
Los Banos 47 B 6 California, W USA
Losinj 100 A 3 var. Lošinj,
Ger. Lussin, It. Lussino. Island,
W Croatia
Los Mochis 50 C 3 C Mexico
Los Roques, Islas 58 D 1 island
group, N Venezuela
Los Testigos 59 E 1 island,
NE Venezuela
Lost River Range 46 D 3 mountain
range, Idaho, NW USA
Lot 91 B 5 cultural region,
SW France
Lot 91 B 5 river, S France
Lotagipi Swamp 73 C 5 wetland,
Kenya/Sudan
Loualaba see Lualaba
Louangnamtha 136 C 3
var. Luong Nam Tha. N Laos

Louangphabang 136 C 3
var. Louangphrabang, Luang
Prabang. C Laos
Loubomo see Dolisie
Loudéac 90 A 3 NW France
Loudi 129 C 6 E China
Louga 74 B 3 NW Senegal
Louisiade Archipelago 144 C 4
island group,
SE Papua New Guinea
Louisiana 42 A 2 off. State of
Louisiana; nicknames Creole St[...]
Pelican State. State, S USA
Louisville 40 C 5 Kentucky, E U[...]
Louisville Ridge 152 D 4 under[...]
ridge, SW Pacific Ocean
Lourdes 91 B 6 S France
Lourenço Marques see Maputo
Louth 89 E 5 E England, UK
Loutrá 104 C 4 N Greece
Louvain-la-Neuve 87 C 6
C Belgium
Louviers 90 C 3 N France
Loveč see Lovech
Lovech 104 C 2 var. Loveč.
NW Bulgaria
Loveland 44 C 4 Colorado, C US[...]
Lovosice 99 E 5 Ger. Lobositz.
NW Czech Republic
Lóvua 78 C 1 NE Angola
Lowell 41 G 3
Massachusetts, NE USA
Lower California see Baja Califo[...]
Lower Hutt 151 D 5 North Islan[...]
C New Zealand
Lower Lough Erne 89 A 5 lake,
SW Northern Ireland, UK
Lower Red Lake 45 F 1 lake,
Minnesota, USA
Lower Tunguska see
Nizhnyaya Tunguska
Lowestoft 89 E 6 E England, UK
Loxa see Loksa
Loyauté, Îles 144 D 5 island gro[...]
S New Caledonia
Loyev see Loyew
Loyew 107 D 8 Rus. Loyev.
SE Belarus
Loznica 100 D 3 W Yugoslavia
Lualaba 78 D 7 Fr. Loualaba. Ri[...]
SE Congo (Zaire)
Luanda 78 A 1 var. Loanda,
Paulo de Loanda, Port. São.
Country capital, NW Angola
Luang, Thale 137 C 7 lagoon,
South China Sea/Pacific Ocean
Luanshya 78 D 2 C Zambia
Luarca 92 C 1 N Spain
Lubaczów 99 E 5 var. Lubaczów
SE Poland
Lubań 98 B 4 Ger. Kosten. SW Pola[...]
Lubānas Ezers see Lubāns
Lubango 78 B 2 Port. Sá da
Bandeira. SW Angola
Lubāns 106 D 4 var. Lubānas Ez[...]
Lake, E Latvia
Lubao 77 D 6 C Congo (Zaire)
Lübben 94 D 4 E Germany
Lübbenau 94 D 4 E Germany
Lubbock 49 E 2 Texas, S USA
Lübeck 94 C 2 N Germany
Lubelska, Wyżyna 98 E 4
plateau, SE Poland
Lüben see Lubin
Lubin 98 B 4 Ger. Lüben. W Pola[...]
Lublin 98 E 4 Rus. Lyublin.
E Poland
Lubliniec 98 C 4 S Poland
Lubny 109 F 2 NE Ukraine
Lubsko 98 B 4 Ger. Sommerfeld.
W Poland

umbashi 77 E 8 *prev.*
lisabethville. SE Congo (Zaire)
utu 77 D 6 E Congo (Zaire)
a 61 F 5 SW Bolivia
a *see* Lucca
an 89 B 5 *Ir.* Leamhcán.
  Ireland
anian Mountains *see* Lucano,
  ppennino
ano, Appennino 97 D 6
ng. Lucanian Mountains.
lountain range, S Italy
apa 78 C 1 *var.* Lukapa.
IE Angola
ca 96 B 3 *anc.* Luca. C Italy
ea 54 A 4 W Jamaica
edale 42 C 3 Mississippi, S USA
ena 92 D 4 S Spain
ena 139 E 1 *off.* Lucena City.
uzon, N Philippines
ena City *see* Lucena
enec 99 D 6 *Ger.* Losontz,
ung. Losonc. S Slovakia
erne, Lake of *see*
  ierwaldstätter See
know 135 E 3 *var.* Lakhnau.
tate capital, N India
eritz 78 B 4 *prev.* Angra
equena. SW Namibia
lsan *see* Ludza
luş 108 B 4 *Ger.* Ludasch,
ung. Marosludas. C Romania
vika 85 C 6 C Sweden
twiglust 94 C 3 N Germany
wigsburg 95 B 6 SW Germany
wigsfelde 94 D 4 NE Germany
wigshafen. 95 B 5 W Germany
za 106 D 4 *Ger.* Ludsan. E Latvia
bo 77 C 6 SW Congo (Zaire)
na 78 C 2 *var.* Lwena,
ort. Luso. E Angola
ra 77 E 7 river, SE Congo (Zaire)
kin 49 H 3 Texas, S USA
a 110 A 4
  W Russian Federation
enda, Rio 79 E 2 river,
  Mozambique
h Ganana *see* Luuq
o 92 C 1 *anc.* Lugus Augusti.
JW Spain
oj 108 A 4 *Ger.* Lugosch,
ung. Lugos. W Romania
us Augusti *see* Lugo
ans'k 109 H 3 *Rus.* Lugansk;
rev. Voroshilovgrad. E Ukraine
nneach *see* Limerick
apa *see* Lucapa
enie 77 D 6 river,
  Congo (Zaire)
ovit 104 C 2 NW Bulgaria
ów 98 E 4 *Ger.* Bogendorf.
  Poland
uga 77 E 7 river,
E Congo (Zaire)
eà 84 D 4 N Sweden
eälven 84 C 3 river, N Sweden
onga 77 C 5 river,
  W Congo (Zaire)
uabourg *see* Kananga
aberton 43 F 1
  orth Carolina, SE USA
abo 79 F 2 NE Mozambique
ai i Vjosës 104 A 4 *var.* Vijosa,
ujosë, *Gk.* Aóos. River,
  lbania/Greece
nsden 151 A 7 South Island,
  W New Zealand
d 85 B 7 S Sweden
eburg 94 B 3 N Germany
gué-Bungo *see* Lungwebungu

Lungwebungu 78 C 2 *var.* Lungué-
  Bungo. River, Angola/Zambia
Luninyets 107 B 7 *Pol.* Łuniniec,
  Rus. Luninets. SW Belarus
Lunteren 86 D 4 C Netherlands
Luong Nam Tha *see* Louangnamtha
Luoyang 128 C 4 *var.* Honan,
  Lo-yang. C China
Lupatia *see* Altamura
Lúrio 79 F 2 NE Mozambique
Lúrio, Rio 79 E 2 river,
  NE Mozambique
Lusaka 78 D 2 country capital,
  SE Zambia
Lushnja *see* Lushnjë
Lushnjë 101 C 6 *var.* Lushnja.
  C Albania
Lūt, Dasht-e 120 D 3 *var.* Kavīr-e
  Lūt. Desert, E Iran
Lūt, Kavīr-e *see* Lūt, Dasht-e
Luton 89 D 6 S England, UK
Łutselk'e 37 F 4 *prev.* Snowdrift.
  Northwest Territories, C Canada
Luts'k 108 C 1 *Pol.* Łuck,
  Rus. Lutsk. NW Ukraine
Lutzow-Holm Bay 154 C 2
  var. Lützow Holmbukta. Bay,
  Atlantic Ocean/Indian Ocean
Lützow Holmbukta *see*
  Lutzow-Holm Bay
Luuq 73 D 6 *It.* Lugh Ganana.
  SW Somalia
Luvua 77 E 7 river, SE Congo (Zaire)
Luxembourg 87 D 8 country
  capital, S Luxembourg

Luxembourg
87 D 8 *var.* Lëtzebuerg,
Luxemburg. Monarchy, W Europe

Official name: Grand Duchy of
Luxembourg **Date of formation:**
1890 **Capital:** Luxembourg
Population: 400,000 **Total area:**
998 sq miles (2,586 sq km)
Languages: Letzebúrgish*, French,
Portuguese, Italian **Religions:**
Roman Catholic 97%, other 3%
Ethnic mix: Luxembourger 72%,
Portuguese 9%, Italian 5%,
other 14% **Government:**
Constitutional monarchy
Currency: Franc = 100 centimes

Luxor 72 B 2 *Ar.* Al Uqşur. E Egypt
Luza 110 C 4
  NW Russian Federation
Luzern 95 B 7 *Fr.* Lucerne,
  It. Lucerna. C Switzerland
Luzon 139 E 1 island, N Philippines
Luzon Strait 139 E 1 strait,
  W Pacific Ocean
L'viv 108 B 2 *Ger.* Lemberg,
  Pol. Lwów, *Rus.* L'vov. W Ukraine
Lyakhavichy 107 D 6 *Rus.*
  Lyakhovichi. SW Belarus
Lyakhovichi *see* Lyakhavichy
Lyallpur *see* Faisalābād
Lyangar *see* Langar
Lyck *see* Ełk
Lycksele 84 C 4 N Sweden
Lyel'chytsy 107 C 7 *Rus.* Lel'chitsy.
  SE Belarus
Lyepyel' 107 D 5 *Rus.* Lepel'.
  N Belarus
Lyme Bay 89 D 7 bay, Atlantic
  Ocean/English Channel
Lynchburg 41 E 5 Virginia, NE USA
Lynn 41 G 3 Massachusetts, NE USA
Lyon 91 D 5 *Eng.* Lyons;
  anc. Lugdunum. E France
Lyozna 107 E 6 *Rus.* Liozno.
  NE Belarus

Lypovets' 108 D 2 *Rus.* Lipovets.
  C Ukraine
Lys *see* Leie
Lysychans'k 109 H 3
  Rus. Lisichansk. E Ukraine
Lyttelton 151 C 6 South Island,
  C New Zealand
Lyublin *see* Lublin
Lyubotin *see* Lyubotyn
Lyubotyn 109 G 2 *Rus.* Lyubotin.
  E Ukraine
Lyulyakovo 104 E 2
  prev. Keremitlik. E Bulgaria
Lyusina 107 C 6 *Rus.* Lyusino.
  SW Belarus
Lyusino *see* Lyusina

M

Ma'ān 119 B 7 SW Jordan
Maardu 106 D 2 *Ger.* Maart.
  NW Estonia
Maarmovilik 82 C 3 *var.*
  Mârmorilik. W Greenland
Ma'arrat an Nu'mān 118 B 3
  var. Ma'aret-en-Nu'man, *Fr.*
  Maarret enn Naamâne. NW Syria
Maart *see* Maardu
Maas *see* Meuse
Maaseik 87 D 5 *prev.* Maeseyck.
  NE Belgium
Maastricht 87 D 6 *var.* Maestricht;
  anc. Traiectum ad Mosam,
  Traiectum Tungorum.
  SE Netherlands
Macao 129 C 7 *var.* Macau,
  Chin. Aomen, *Port.* Mação.
  Portuguese territory, E Asia
Macao 129 C 6 *var.* Macau,
  Macará 60 B 2 S Ecuador
Macarov Basin 155 G 3 undersea
  basin, Arctic Ocean
Macarsca *see* Makarska
Macău *see* Makó
MacCluer Gulf *see* Berau, Teluk
Macdonnell Ranges 142 A 4
  mountain range, Northern
  Territory, C Australia

Macedonia
101 A 2 *abbrev.* FYR Macedonia,
Mac. Makedonija. Republic,
SE Europe

Official name: Former Yugoslav
Republic of Macedonia **Date of
formation:** 1991 **Capital:** Skopje
Population: 1.9 million **Total area:**
9,929 sq miles (25,715 sq km)
Languages: Macedonian, Albanian
Turkish (*no official language*)
Religions: Christian 80%, Muslim
20% **Ethnic mix:** Macedonian 67%,
Albanian 20%, Turkish 4%, other 9%
Government: Multiparty republic
Currency: Denar = 100 deni

Maceió 63 G 3 state capital, E Brazil
Macfarlane, Lake 149 B 6 *var.* Lake
  Mcfarlane. Lake, South Australia,
  S Australia
Machakos 73 C 6 S Kenya
Machala 60 B 2 SW Ecuador
Machanga 79 E 3 E Mozambique
Macheng 128 B 4 C China
Machilipatnam 132 D 1 *var.* Bandar,
  Masulipatnam. E India
Machiques 58 C 2 NW Venezuela
Măcin 108 D 5 SE Romania
Mackay 148 D 4 Queensland,
  NE Australia

Mackay, Lake 146 D 4 salt lake,
  C Australia
Mackenzie 37 E 3 river, Northwest
  Territories, NW Canada
Mackenzie Bay 154 D 3 bay,
  C Indian Ocean
Mackenzie Mountains 36 D 3
  mountain range, Northwest
  Territories, NW Canada
Macleod, Lake 146 A 4 lake,
  W Australia
Macomb 40 A 4 Illinois, N USA
Macomer 97 A 5 W Italy
Macon 42 D 2 Georgia, SE USA
Macon 45 G 4 Missouri, C USA
Mâcon 91 D 5 *anc.* Matisco, Matisco
  Ædourum. C France
Macquarie Ridge 154 C 5 undersea
  ridge, SW Pacific Ocean
Macuspana 51 G 4 SE Mexico
Ma'dabā 119 B 6 *var.* Mādabā,
  Madeba; *anc.* Medeba. NW Jordan

Madagascar
79 F 3 *Malg.* Madagasikara; *prev.*
Malagasy Republic. Republic,
E Africa

Official name: Democratic Republic
of Madagascar **Date of formation:**
1960 **Capital:** Antananarivo
Population: 13.3 million **Total area:**
226,660 sq miles (587,040 sq km)
Languages: Malagasy*, French*
Religions: Traditional beliefs 52%,
Christian 41%, Muslim 7% **Ethnic
mix:** Merina 26%, Betsimisaraka
15%, Betsileo 12%, other 47%
Government: Multiparty republic
Currency: Franc = 100 centimes

Madagascar Basin 141 B 5 undersea
  basin, W Indian Ocean
Madagascar Plateau 141 A 6 *var.*
  Madagascar Ridge, Madagascar
  Rise, Madagaskarskiy Khrebet.
  Undersea plateau,
  W Indian Ocean
Madang 144 B 3 New Guinea,
  N Papua New Guinea
Madanīyīn *see* Médenine
Made 86 C 4 S Netherlands
Madeira 62 D 2 *var.* Rio Madera.
  River, Bolivia/Brazil
Madeira 70 A 2 Portuguese
  autonomous region,
  E Atlantic Ocean
Madeira *see* Madera. Ilha da
  Madeira. Island, E Atlantic Ocean
Madeira, Ilha de *see* Madeira
Madeleine, Îles de la 39 F 4 *Eng.*
  Magdalen Islands. Island group,
  Québec, E Canada
Madera 47 C 6 California, W USA
Madera, Rio *see* Madeira
Madhya Pradesh 135 E 4
  prev. Central Provinces and Berar.
  State, C India
Madinat al Abyār *see* Al Abyār
Madīnat ath Thawrah 118 C 2
  var. Ath Thawrah. N Syria
Madioen *see* Madiun
Madison 40 B 3 state capital,
  Wisconsin, N USA
Madison 45 F 3 South Dakota, N USA
Madiun 138 D 5 *prev.* Madioen.
  Jawa, C Indonesia
Madoera *see* Madura, Pulau
Madona 106 D 4 *Ger.* Modohn.
  E Latvia
Madras 132 D 2 S India
Madras *see* Tamil Nādu
Madre de Dios 61 E 3 river,
  Bolivia/Peru

Madre del Sur, Sierra 51 E 5
mountain range, S Mexico
Madre, Laguna 49 G 5 lake,
Texas, S USA
Madre, Laguna 51 F 3 lagoon,
NW Gulf of Mexico
Madre Occidental, Sierra 50 C 2
var. Western Sierra Madre.
Mountain range, C Mexico
Madre Oriental, Sierra 51 E 3
var. Eastern Sierra Madre.
Mountain range, C Mexico
Madrid 92 D 3 country capital,
C Spain
Madura 138 D 5 *prev.* Madoera.
Island, C Indonesia
Madurai 132 C 3 *prev.* Madura,
Mathurai. S India
Maebashi 131 D 5 *var.* Maebasi,
Mayebashi. Honshū, S Japan
Maeikiai 106 B 3 NW Lithuania
Mae Nam Nan 136 C 4 river,
S Thailand
Mae Nam Yom 136 C 4 river,
S Thailand
Maeseyck *see* Maaseik
Maewo 144 D 4 *prev.* Aurora.
Island, C Vanuatu
Mafraq *see* Al Mafraq
Magadan 115 G 3
NE Russian Federation
Magallanes *see* Punta Arenas
Magallanes, Estrecho de *see*
Magellan, Strait of
Magangué 58 B 2 N Colombia
Magdalena 50 B 2 NW Mexico
Magdalena 61 F 3 N Bolivia
Magdalena, Isla 50 B 3 island,
W Mexico
Magdalen Islands *see* Madeleine,
Îles de la
Magdeburg 94 C 4 C Germany
Magdelena 58 B 2 river, C Colombia
Magelang 138 C 5 Jawa, C Indonesia
Magellan, Strait of 65 C 8
Sp. Estrecho de Magallanes. Strait,
Atlantic Ocean/Pacific Ocean
Magerøy *see* Magerøya
Magerøya 84 D 1 *var.* Magerøy.
Island, N Norway
Maggiore, Lago *see* Maggiore, Lake
Maggiore, Lake 96 B 1 *It.* Lago
Maggiore. Lake,
Italy/Switzerland
Maglaj 100 C 3
N Bosnia & Herzegovina
Maglie 97 E 6 SE Italy
Magna 44 B 4 Utah, W USA
Magnitogorsk 114 B 4
C Russian Federation
Magta' Lahjar 74 C 3 *var.* Magta'
Lahjar, Magtá Lahjar, Magta
Lahjar. SW Mauritania
Magway *see* Magwe
Magwe 136 A 3 *var.* Magway.
W Myanmar
Mahajanga 79 G 3 *var.* Majunga.
N Madagascar
Mahakam, 138 D 4 *var.* Koetai,
Kutai. River, Borneo, C Indonesia
Mahalapye 78 D 3 *var.* Mahalatswe.
SE Botswana
Mahalatswe *see* Mahalapye
Mahān 120 D 4 E Iran
Mahārāshtra 134 D 5 state, W India
Mahé 79 H 1 island, NE Seychelles
Mahia Peninsula 150 E 4 peninsula,
North Island, E New Zealand
Mahilyow 107 E 6 *Rus.* Mogilëv.
E Belarus
Maḥmūd-e 'Erāqī *see*
Maḥmūd-e Rāqī

Maḥmūd-e Rāqī 123 E 4 *var.*
Maḥmūd-e 'Erāqī. NE Afghanistan
Mahón 93 H 3 *Cat.* Maó, *Eng.* Port
Mahon; *anc.* Portus Magonis.
E Spain
Mährisch-Weisskirchen *see* Hranice
Maicao 58 C 1 N Colombia
Maidstone 89 E 7 SE England, UK
Maiduguri 75 H 4 NE Nigeria
Main 95 B 5 river, C Germany
Mai-Ndombe, Lac 77 C 6 *prev.* Lac
Léopold II. Lake, W Congo (Zaire)
Maine 90 B 3 cultural region,
NW France
Maine 41 G 2 *off.* State of Maine;
nicknames Lumber State,
Pine Tree State. State, NE USA
Maine, Gulf of 41 H 2 gulf,
NW Atlantic Ocean
Mainland 88 D 2 island,
NE Scotland, UK
Mainland 88 D 1 island
NE Scotland, UK
Mainz 95 B 5 *Fr.* Mayence.
SW Germany
Maio 74 A 3 *var.* Mayo. Island,
SE Cape Verde
Maisur *see* Mysore
Maitland 149 D 6
New South Wales, SE Australia
Maizhokunggar X 126 C 5 W China
Maíz, Islas del 53 E 3
var. Corn Islands. Island group,
SE Nicaragua
Majunga *see* Mahajanga
Majuro 142 D 2 *var.* D-U-D
Municipality. Country capital,
SE Marshall Islands
Makale *see* Mek'elē
Makarikari Pans *see* Makgadikgadi
Makarska 100 B 4 *It.* Macarsca.
SE Croatia
Makasar, Selat 138 D 4
Eng. Makassar Strait. Strait,
Celebes Sea/Java Sea
Makassar Strait *see* Makasar, Selat
Makeni 74 C 4 C Sierra Leone
Makgadikgadi 78 C 3 *var.*
Makarikari Pans. Salt lake,
NE Botswana
Makhachkala 111 B 8 *prev.*
Petrovsk-Port.
SW Russian Federation
Makin Atoll 144 D 2 *prev.* Pitt
Island. Island, W Kiribati
Makira *see* San Cristobal
Makiyivka 109 G 3 *Rus.*
Makeyevka; *prev.* Dmitriyevsk.
E Ukraine
Makkah 121 A 5 *Eng.* Mecca.
W Saudi Arabia
Makkovik 39 F 2 Newfoundland
and Labrador, NE Canada
Makó 99 D 7 *Rom.* Macău.
SE Hungary
Makoua 77 B 5 C Congo
Makran Coast 120 E 4 physical
region, SE Iran
Makrany 107 A 6 *Rus.* Mokrany.
SW Belarus
Mākū 120 B 2 NW Iran
Makurdi 75 G 5 C Nigeria
Mala *see* Malaita
Malabār Coast 132 B 3 physical
region, SW India
Malabo 77 A 5 *prev.* Santa Isabel.
Country capital,
NW Equatorial Guinea
Malaca *see* Málaga
Malacca *see* Melaka
Malacca, Strait of 138 A 3 strait,
Indian Ocean/Pacific Ocean

Malacka *see* Malacky
Malacky 99 C 6 *Hung.* Malacka.
W Slovakia
Maladzyechna 107 C 5 *Pol.*
Molodeczno, *Rus.* Molodechno.
C Belarus
Málaga 92 D 5 *anc.* Malaca.
S Spain
Malagarasi River 73 B 7 river,
SW Tanzania
Malaita 144 C 3 *var.* Mala. Island,
N Solomon Islands
Malakal 73 B 5 S Sudan
Malambo 58 B 1 N Colombia
Malang 138 D 5 Jawa, C Indonesia
Malange *see* Malanje
Malanje 78 B 1 *var.* Malange.
NW Angola
Mälaren 85 C 6 lake, C Sweden
Malatya 117 E 4 *anc.* Melitene.
SE Turkey
Mala Vyska 109 E 3 *Rus.* Malaya
Viska. S Ukraine

Malawi
79 E 1 *prev.* Nyasaland,
Nyasaland Protectorate. Republic,
S Africa

Official name: Republic of Malawi
Date of formation: 1964 Capital:
Lilongwe Population: 10.7 million
Total area: 45,745 sq miles
(118,480 sq km) Languages: English*
Chewa Religions: Christian 66%,
traditional beliefs 18%, other 16%
Ethnic mix: Maravi 55%, Lomwe
17%, Yao 13%, other 15%
Government: Multiparty republic
Currency: Kwacha = 100 tambala

Malaya Viska *see* Mala Vyska

Malaysia
138 B 3 *var.* Federation of
Malaysia; *prev.* the separate
territories of Federation of
Malaya, Sarawak and Sabah
(NorthBorneo) and Singapore.
Monarchy, SE Asia

Official name: Malaysia Date of
formation: 1957/1965 Capital:
Kuala Lumpur Population: 20.6
million Total Area: 127,317 sq miles
(329,750 sq km) Languages: Malay*,
Chinese, Tamil Religions: Muslim
53%, Buddhist and Confucianist
30%, other 17% Ethnic mix: Malay
and aborigine 60%, Chinese 30%,
Indian 8%, other 2% Government:
Federal constitutional monarchy
Currency: Ringgit = 100 cents

Malbork 98 C 2 *Ger.* Marienburg,
Marienburg in Westpreussen.
N Poland
Malchin 94 C 3 N Germany
Malden 45 H 5 Missouri, C USA
Malden Island 145 G 3 *prev.*
Independence Island. Island,
E Kiribati

Maldives
132 A 4 Republic, Indian Ocean

Official name: Republic of Maldives
Date of formation: 1965
Capital: Male' Population: 200,000
Total Area: 116 sq miles (300 sq km)
Languages: Dhivehi (Maldivian)*,
Sinhala, Tamil Religions: Sunni
Muslim 100% Ethnic mix: Maldivian
99%, Sinhalese and other South
Asian 1% Government: Republic
Currency: Rufiyaa - 100 laari

Male' 132 B 4 country capital,
C Maldives
Male' Atoll 132 B 4 *var.* Kaafu
Atoll. Island, C Maldives
Malekula 144 D 4 *var.* Malakula;
prev. Mallicolo. Island, W Vanu
Malesína 105 C 5 E Greece
Malheur Lake 46 C 3 lake,
Oregon, NW USA
Malheur River 46 C 4 river,
Oregon, NW USA

Mali
75 E 2 . *Fr.* République du Ma
prev. Sudanese Republic, Frenc
Sudan. Republic, W Africa

Official name: Republic of Mali
Date of formation: 1960 Capital:
Bamako Population: 10.1 million
Total area: 478,837 sq miles
(1,240,190 sq km) Languages:
French*, Bambara, Fulani, Senuf
Religions: Muslim 80%, tradition
beliefs 18%, Christian 2% Ethnic
mix: Bambara 31%, Fulani 13%,
Senufo 12%, other 44%
Government: Multiparty republic
Currency: CFA franc = 100 centi

Malik, Wadi al *see* Milk, Wadi el
Mali Kyun 137 B 5 *var.* Tavoy
Island. Island, S Myanmar
Malin *see* Malyn
Malindi 73 D 7 SE Kenya
Malko Tŭrnovo 104 E 3 SE Bulg
Mallaig 88 C 3 W Scotland, UK
Mallawi 72 B 2 C Egypt
Mallorca 93 H 3 *Eng.* Majorca; *a*
Baleares Major. Island, E Spai
Malmberget 84 C 3 N Sweden
Malmédy 87 D 7 E Belgium
Malmö 85 B 7 S Sweden
Malmyž *see* Malmyzh
Maloelap 144 D 1 *var.* Maoeap.
Island, E Marshall Islands
MaloeJap *see* Maloelap Atoll
Małopolska 98 D 4 plateau,
S Poland
Malozemel'skaja Tundra *see*
Malozemel'skaya Tundra
Malozemel'skaya Tundra 110 D
var. Malozemel'skaja Tundra.
Physical region,
NW Russian Federation

Malta
97 C 8 Republic, Mediterrane

Official name: Republic of Malt
Date of formation: 1964 Capital
Valletta Population: 400,000
Total area: 124 sq miles (320 sq k
Languages: Maltese*, English
Religions: Roman Catholic 98%,
other (mostly Anglican) 2%
Ethnic mix: Maltese (mixed Ara
Sicilian, Norman, Spanish, Italia
English) 98%, other 2%
Government: Multiparty republi
Currency: Lira = 100 cents

Malta 97 C 8 island, S Europe
Malta 106 D 4 SE Latvia
Malta 44 C 1 Montana, NW US
Malta, Canale di *see* Malta Chan
Malta. Channel,
C Mediterranean Sea
Malta, Republic of *see* Malta
Maluka 139 F 4 *Eng.* Moluccas,
Dut. Molukken; *prev.* Spice
Islands. Island group, E Indonesia
Maluku, Laut 139 F 4 *Eng.* Mol
Sea. Sea, W Pacific Ocean

alung 85 B 5 C Sweden
alyn 108 D 2 *Rus.* Malin.
  N Ukraine
alyy Kavkaz *see* Lesser Caucasus
amberamo 139 H 4 river,
  New Guinea, E Indonesia
amonovo 106 A 4 *Ger.*
Heiligenbeil.
  W Russian Federation
amoré 61 F 3 river, Bolivia/Brazil
amou 74 C 4 W Guinea
amoudzou 79 F 2 dependent
  territory capital, N Mayotte
amuno 78 C 3 W Botswana
anacor 93 H 3 E Spain
anado 139 F 3 *prev.* Menado.
  Celebes, C Indonesia
anagua 52 D 3 country capital,
  W Nicaragua
anagua, Lago de 52 C 3
  var. Xolotlán.
  Lake, W Nicaragua
anahiki Plateau 152 D 3 undersea
  plateau, SW Pacific Ocean
anakara 79 G 4 SE Madagascar
anama *see* Al Manāmah
ananjary 79 G 3 SE Madagascar
anáos *see* Manaus
anapouri, Lake 151 A 7 lake,
  South Island, SW New Zealand
anar *see* Mannar
anas, Gora 123 F 2 mountain,
  Kyrgyzstan/Uzbekistan
anaus 62 D 2 *prev.* Manáos. State
  capital, NW Brazil
anavgat 116 B 4 SW Turkey
anbij 118 C 2 *var.* Mambij,
  Fr. Membidj. N Syria
anchester 89 D 5
  Lat. Mancunium. N England, UK
anchester 41 G 3
  New Hampshire, NE USA
an-chou-li *see* Manzhouli
anchuria 128 D 2 cultural region,
  NE China
áncio Lima *see* Japiim
áncora 60 B 2 NE Peru
ancunium *see* Manchester
and 120 D 4 *var.* Rüd-e Mand.
  River, S Iran
andalay 136 B 3 N Myanmar
andan 45 E 2
  North Dakota, N USA
andara Mountains 75 H 4
  mountain range, E Nigeria
andaue 139 E 2 *off.* Mandaue City.
  Cebu, C Philippines
andaue City *see* Mandaue
andeville 54 B 5 C Jamaica
ándra 105 C 6 C Greece
and, Rüd-e *see* Mand
andurah 147 B 6 Western
  Australia, SW Australia
andya 132 C 2 C India
anfredonia 97 D 5 SE Italy
angai 77 C 6 W Congo (Zaire)
angaia 145 G 5 island group,
  S Cook Islands
angalia 108 D 5 *anc.* Callatis.
  SE Romania
angalmé 76 C 3 SE Chad
angalore 132 B 2 W India
angaung *see* Bloemfontein
angin Range 136 B 2 mountain
  range, C Myanmar
ango *see* Sansanné-Mango
angoky 79 F 3 river,
  SW Madagascar
anhattan 45 F 4 Kansas, C USA
anicouagan, Réservoir 39 E 3
  lake, Québec, E Canada
anihiki 145 G 4 island,
  N Cook Islands

Maniitsoq 82 C 3 *var.* Manîtsoq,
  Dan. Sukkertoppen. SW Greenland
Manila 139 E 1 *off.* City of Manila.
  Country capital, Luzon,
  N Philippines
Manisa 116 A 3 *var.* Manissa;
  prev. Saruhan, *anc.* Magnesia.
  W Turkey
Man, Isle of 89 C 5 British
  dependency, W England, UK
Manistee River 40 C 2 river,
  Michigan, N USA
Manitoba 37 F 5 province,
  S Canada
Manitoulin Island 38 C 5 island,
  Ontario, S Canada
Manitowoc 40 B 2 Wisconsin, N USA
Manizales 58 B 3 W Colombia
Manjimup 147 B 7
  Western Australia, SW Australia
Mankato 45 F 3 Minnesota, N USA
Manlleu 93 G 2 NE Spain
Manmād 134 C 5 W India
Mannar 132 C 3 *var.* Manar.
  NW Sri Lanka
Mannar, Gulf of 132 C 3 gulf,
  N Indian Ocean
Mannheim 95 B 5 SW Germany
Manono 77 E 7 SE Congo (Zaire)
Manosque 91 D 6 SE France
Manra 145 F 3 *prev.* Sydney Island.
  Island, C Kiribati
Mansa 78 D 2 *prev.* Fort Rosebery.
  N Zambia
Mansel Island 38 C 1 island,
  Northwest Territories,
  NE Canada
Mansfield 40 D 4 Ohio, N USA
Manta 60 A 2 W Ecuador
Manteca 47 B 6 California, W USA
Mantova 96 B 2 *Eng.* Mantua,
  Fr. Mantoue. NW Italy
Manuae 145 G 5 island,
  S Cook Islands
Manukau *see* Manurewa
Manurewa 150 D 3 *var.* Manukau.
  North Island, N New Zealand
Manzanares 93 E 4 C Spain
Manzanillo 54 C 3 E Cuba
Manzanillo 50 D 4 SW Mexico
Manzano Mountains 48 D 2
  mountain range, New Mexico,
  SW USA
Manzhouli 127 F 1 *var.*
  Man-chou-li. N China
Manzil 119 B 7 W Jordan
Mao 76 B 3 W Chad
Maoke, Pegunungan 139 H 4
  Dut. Sneeuw-gebergte, *Eng.* Snow
  Mountains. Mountain range,
  New Guinea, E Indonesia
Maoming 129 C 6 S China
Maputo 78 D 4 *prev.* Lourenço
  Marques. Country capital,
  S Mozambique
Maputo, Baía de 79 E 4 *var.* Baía de
  Lourenço Marques, *Eng.* Delagoa
  Bay. Bay, W Indian Ocean
Marabá 63 F 2 NE Brazil
Maracaibo 58 C 1 NW Venezuela
Maracaibo, Lago de 58 C 2 *var.*
  Lake Maracaibo. Lagoon,
  NW Venezuela
Maracaibo, Lake *see*
  Maracaibo, Lago de
Maracay 58 D 1 N Venezuela
Maradi 75 G 3 S Niger
Maragha *see* Marāgheh
Marāgheh 120 C 2
  var. Maragha. NW Iran
Marajó, Baía de 63 F 1 bay,
  W Atlantic Ocean

Marajó, Ilha de 63 E 1 island,
  N Brazil
Maramba *see* Livingstone
Maranhão 63 F 2 *off.* Estado do
  Maranhão. State, E Brazil
Maranhão, Estado do *see* Maranhão
Marañón 60 C 2 river, N Peru
Marathon 38 C 4 Ontario,
  S Canada
Marathón *see* Marathónas
Marathónas 105 C 5
  prev. Marathón. C Greece
Marbella 92 D 5 S Spain
Marble Bar 146 B 4 Western
  Australia, W Australia
Marburg an der Lahn
Marburg *see* Maribor
Marburg an der Lahn 94 B 4
  hist. Eng. Marburg . W Germany
March *see* Morava
Marche 91 C 5 cultural region,
  C France
Marche-en-Famenne 87 D 7
  SE Belgium
Marchena, Isla 60 B 5 *var.* Bindloe
  Island. Island, Galapagos Islands,
  E Pacific Ocean
Marchfield 55 H 2 SE Barbados
Mar Chiquita, Laguna 64 C 3 lake,
  C Argentina
Marcona 60 D 4 SW Peru
Marcounda *see* Markounda
Mardān 134 C 1 N Pakistan
Mar del Plata 65 D 5 E Argentina
Mardin 117 E 4 SE Turkey
Maré 144 D 5 island,
  E New Caledonia
Mareeba 148 C 3 Queensland,
  NE Australia
Marganets *see* Marhanets'
Margarita, Isla de 59 E 1 island,
  N Venezuela
Margate 89 E 7 *prev.* Mergate.
  SE England, UK
Marghita 108 B 3 *Hung.* Margitta.
  NW Romania
Margitta *see* Marghita
Mārgow, Dasht-e 122 D 5 desert,
  SW Afghanistan
Marhanets' 109 F 3 *Rus.* Marganets.
  E Ukraine
Maria Cleofas, Isla 50 C 4 island,
  C Mexico
Maria Island 149 C 8 island,
  Tasmania, SE Australia
Maria Island 148 B 2 island,
  Northern Territory, NE Australia
Maria Madre, Isla 50 C 4 island,
  C Mexico
Maria Magdalena, Isla 50 C 4
  island, C Mexico
Marianao 54 B 2 NW Cuba
Mariana Trench 152 B 2 *var.*
  Challenger Deep. Trench,
  W Pacific Ocean
Mariánské Lázně 99 A 5 *Ger.*
  Marienbad. W Czech Republic
Marías, Islas 50 C 4 island group,
  C Mexico
Marias River 44 C 1 river,
  Montana, NW USA
Maribor 95 E 7 *Ger.* Marburg.
  NE Slovenia
Maridi 73 B 5 SW Sudan
Marie Byrd Land 154 B 3 physical
  region, Antarctica
Marie Celeste Fracture Zone 141
  C 5 fracture zone,
  C Indian Ocean
Marie Galante 55 H 4 *var.* Ceyre to
  the Caribs. Island, SE Guadeloupe
Marienbad *see* Mariánské Lázně

Marienburg *see* Alūksne
Marienhausen *see* Viš|aka
Mariental 78 B 4 SW Namibia
Marienwerder *see* Kwidzyń
Mariestad 85 B 6 S Sweden
Marília 63 E 4 S Brazil
Marín 92 B 2 NW Spain
Marina 47 B 6 California, W USA
Mar"ina Horka *see* Mar"ina Horka
Mar"ina Horka 107 C 6 *Rus.*
  Mar'ina Gorka. C Belarus
Maringá 63 E 4 S Brazil
Marion 40 C 4 Indiana, N USA
Marion 40 D 4 Ohio, N USA
Marion 45 G 3 Iowa, C USA
Marion, Lake 43 E 2 reservoir,
  South Carolina, SE USA
Marion Reef 148 E 3 reef,
  C Coral Sea
Mariscal Estigarribia 64 D 2
  NW Paraguay
Marisule Estate 55 F 1
  N Saint Lucia
Maritsa 104 D 3 *var.* Marica, *Gk.*
  Évros, *Turk.* Meriç; *anc.* Hebrus.
  River, SE Europe
Maritzburg *see* Pietermaritzburg
Mariupol' 109 G 4 *prev.* Zhdanov.
  SE Ukraine
Marka 73 D 6 *var.* Merca. S Somalia
Markham, Mount 154 C 4
  mountain, Antarctica
Markounda 76 C 4 *var.* Marcounda.
  NW Central African Republic
Marktredwitz 95 C 5 E Germany
Marla 109 A 5 South Australia,
  S Australia
Marmande 91 B 5 *anc.* Marmanda.
  SW France
Marmara Denizi 116 A 2
  Eng. Sea of Marmara. Sea,
  NE Mediterranean Sea
Marmara, Sea of *see*
  Marmara Denizi
Marmaris 116 A 4 SW Turkey
Mârmorilik *see* Maarmorilik
Marne 90 D 3 river, N France
Marne 90 D 3 cultural region,
  N France
Maro 76 C 4 S Chad
Maroantsetra 79 G 3 NE Madagascar
Maromme 90 C 3 N France
Maroni 79 H 3 *Dut.* Marowijne.
  River, French Guiana/Suriname
Marotiri 145 H 5 *var.* Îlots de Bass.
  Island group, SE French Polynesia
Maroua 76 B 3 N Cameroon
Marowijne 59 G 3 *var.* le Maroni
  Fleuve. River, French Guiana/
  Suriname
Marqādah 118 E 2 NE Syria
Marquesas Fracture Zone 153 E 3
  fracture zone, E Pacific Ocean
Marquesas Islands *see*
  Marquises, Îles
Marquesas Keys 43 E 5 island,
  Florida, SE USA
Marquette 40 C 1 Michigan, N USA
Marquises, Îles 145 H 4 *Eng.*
  Marquesas Islands. Island group,
  N French Polynesia
Marrakech 70 C 2 *var.* Marakesh,
  Eng. Marrakesh, *prev.* Morocco.
  W Morocco
Marrawah 149 B 8 Tasmania,
  SE Australia
Marree 149 B 5 South Australia,
  S Australia
Marsala 97 B 7 *anc.* Lilybaeum.
  SW Italy

Marsberg 94 B 4 W Germany
Marseille 91 D 6 *Eng.* Marseilles;
  anc. Massilia. SE France
Marshall 49 H 3 Texas, S USA
Marshall 45 F 2 Minnesota, N USA

Marshall Islands
  144 D 1. Republic, C Pacific Ocean

Official name: Republic of the
Marshall Islands **Date of formation:**
1986 **Capital:** Majuro **Population:**
48,000 **Total Area:** 70 sq miles
(181 sq km) **Languages:** English*,
Marshallese* **Religions:** Protestant
80%, Roman Catholic 15%, other 5%
Ethnic mix: Marshallese 90%, other
Pacific Islanders 10% **Government:**
Republic **Currency:** US $ = 100 cents

Marsh Harbour 54 C 1 W Bahamas
Marsh Island 42 A 3 island, S USA
Martaban 136 B 4 *var.* Moktama.
  SE Myanmar
Martigues 91 D 6 SE France
Martin 99 C 5 *Ger.* Sankt Martin,
  Hung. Turócszentmárton;
  prev. Svätý Martin, Turčiansky.
  NW Slovakia
Martinique 55 G 4 French overseas
  department, E Caribbean Sea
Martinique Passage 55 G 4 *var.*
  Dominica Channel, Martinique
  Channel. Channel, Atlantic
  Ocean/Caribbean Sea
Martinsville 41 E 5 Virginia, NE USA
Marton 150 D 4 North Island,
  C New Zealand
Martos 92 D 4 S Spain
Marungu 77 E 7 mountain range,
  SE Congo (Zaire)
Mary 122 D 3 *prev.* Merv.
  S Turkmenistan
Maryborough 149 E 5 Queensland,
  E Australia
Maryland 41 F 5 *off.* State of
  Maryland; *nicknames* America in
  Miniature, Cockade State, Free
  State, Old Line State. State, E USA
Maryville 42 D 1 Tennessee, S USA
Maryville 45 F 4 Missouri, C USA
Masai Steppe 73 C 8 grassland,
  NW Tanzania
Masaka 73 B 6 SW Uganda
Masasi 73 C 8 SE Tanzania
Masaya 52 D 3 W Nicaragua
Mascarene Basin 141 B 5 undersea
  basin, W Indian Ocean
Mascarene Islands 79 H 4 island
  group, W Madagascar
Mascarene Plain 141 B 5 abyssal
  plain, W Indian Ocean
Mascarene Plateau 140 B 4 undersea
  plateau, W Indian Ocean
Maseru 78 D 4 country capital,
  W Lesotho
Mas-ha 119 D 7 W West Bank
Mashhad 120 E 2 *var.* Meshed. NE Iran
Maṣīrah, Jazīrat 121 E 5 *var.* Masira.
  Island, E Oman
Maṣīrah, Khalīj 121 E 5 *var.*
  Gulf of Masira. Gulf, E Oman
Masindi 73 B 6 W Uganda
Masira Gulf of *see* Maṣīrah, Khalīj
Mason City 45 G 3 Iowa, C USA
Masqaṭ 121 E 5 *var.* Maskat, *Eng.*
  Muscat. Country capital, NE Oman
Massa 96 B 3 C Italy
Massachusetts 41 G 3
  off. Commonwealth of
  Massachusetts; *nicknames* Bay
  State, Old Bay State, Old Colony
  State. State, NE USA

Massawa 72 C 4 *Amh.* Mits'iwa.
  E Eritrea
Massenya 76 B 3 SW Chad
Massif Central 91 C 5 plateau,
  C France
Mastanli *see* Momchilgrad
Masterton 151 D 5 North Island,
  C New Zealand
Masty 107 B 5 *Rus.* Mosty.
  W Belarus
Masuda 131 B 6 Honshū, SW Japan
Masvingo 78 D 3 *prev.* Victoria, Fort
  Victoria, Nyanda. SE Zimbabwe
Maṣyāf 118 B 3 *Fr.* Misiaf. W Syria
Matadi 77 B 7 W Congo (Zaire)
Matagalpa 52 D 3 C Nicaragua
Matagorda Bay 49 H 4 bay, Texas,
  S Gulf of Mexico
Matale 132 D 4 C Sri Lanka
Matam 74 C 3 NE Senegal
Matamata 150 D 3 North Island,
  N New Zealand
Matamoros 51 E 2 *var.* Izúcar de
  Matamoros. S Mexico
Matamoros 50 D 3 NE Mexico
Matane 39 E 4 Québec, SE Canada
Matanzas 54 B 2 NW Cuba
Matara 132 D 4 S Sri Lanka
Mataró 93 G 2 *anc.* Illuro. E Spain
Mataura 151 B 7 South Island,
  SW New Zealand
Mata Uta *see* Matā'utu
Matā'utu 145 E 4 *var.* Mata Uta.
  Dependent territory capital,
  S Wallis & Futuna
Matera 97 E 5 S Italy
Matías Romero 51 G 5 SE Mexico
Mato Grosso 63 E 3 *off.* Estado de
  Mato Grosso; *prev.* Matto Grosso.
  State, W Brazil
Mato Grosso do Sul 63 E 4 *off.*
  Estado de Mato Grosso do Sul.
  State, S Brazil
Mato Grosso do Sul, Estado de *see*
  Mato Grosso do Sul
Matosinhos 92 B 2 *prev.*
  Matozinhos. NW Portugal
Matozinhos *see* Matosinhos
Mătrăşeşti 108 C 4 E Romania
Matsue 131 B 6 *var.* Matsuye,
  Matue. Honshū, SW Japan
Matsumoto 131 C 5 *var.* Matumoto.
  Honshū, S Japan
Matsuyama 131 B 7 *var.* Matuyama.
  Shikoku, SW Japan
Matthews Ridge 59 F 2 N Guyana
Matthew Town 54 D 2 S Bahamas
Matumoto *see* Matsumoto
Maturín 59 E 2 NE Venezuela
Matuyama *see* Matsuyama
Mau 135 E 3 *var.* Maunāth Bhanjan.
  N India
Maui 47 B 8 island, Hawaii, W USA
Maun 78 C 3 C Botswana
Maunāth Bhanjan *see* Mau
Mauren 94 E 1 NE Liechtenstein

Mauritania
  74 C 2 *Ar.* Mūrītānīyah. Republic,
  W Africa

Official name: Islamic Republic of
Mauritania **Date of formation:** 1960
Capital: Nouakchott **Population:**
2.2 million **Total area:**
395,953 sq miles (1,025,520 sq km)
Language: French*, Hassaniyah
Arabic, Wolof **Religions:** Muslim
100% Ethnic mix: Maure 80%, Wolof
7%, Tukulor 5%, other 8%
Government: Multiparty republic
Currency: Ouguiya = 5 khoums

Mauritius
  79 H 3 *Fr.* Maurice. Republic,
  E Africa

Official name: Mauritius **Date of
formation:** 1968 **Capital:** Port Louis
Population: 1.1 million **Total area:**
718 sq miles (1,860 sq km)
Languages: English*, French Creole,
Hindi **Religions:** Hindu 52%, Roman
Catholic, 26%, Muslim 17%,
other 5% **Ethnic mix:** Creole 55%,
South Asian 40%, Chinese 3%,
other 2% **Government:** Multiparty
republic **Currency:** Rupee = 100 cents

Mauritius Ridge 141 B 5 undersea
  ridge, W Indian Ocean
Mawson 154 D 2 research station,
  Antarctica
Maya 115 G 3 river,
  E Russian Federation
Mayaguana 54 D 2 island,
  SE Bahamas
Mayaguana Passage 54 D 2
  channel, N Caribbean Sea
Mayagüez 55 F 3 W Puerto Rico
Mayamey 120 D 2 N Iran
Maya Mountains 52 B 1
  Sp. Montañas Mayas. Mountain
  range, Belize/Guatemala
Maych'ew 72 D 4 *var.* Mai Chio,
  It. Mai Ceu. N Ethiopia
Mayence *see* Mainz
Mayfield 151 C 6 South Island,
  SW New Zealand
Maykop 111 B 7
  SW Russian Federation
Maymyo 136 B 3 N Myanmar
Mayo *see* Maio
Mayor Pablo Lagerenza *see*
  Capitán Pablo Lagerenza
Mayotte 79 F 2 French territorial
  collectivity, E Africa
May Pen 54 B 5 C Jamaica
Mazabuka 78 D 2 S Zambia
Mazagan *see* El-Jadida
Mazar *see* Al Mazār al Janūbī
Mazār-e Sharīf 123 E 3 *var.* Mazar-i-
  Sharif, Mazâr-i Sharif.
  N Afghanistan
Mazatlán 50 C 3 C Mexico
Mazirbe 106 C 2 NW Latvia
Mazury 98 D 3 physical region,
  NE Poland
Mazyr 107 C 7 *Rus.* Mozyr'.
  SE Belarus
Mbabane 78 D 4 country capital,
  NW Swaziland
M'Baiki *see* Mbaïki
Mbaïki 77 C 5 *var.* M'Baiki.
  SW Central African Republic
Mbala 78 D 1 *prev.* Abercorn.
  NE Zambia
Mbale 73 C 6 E Uganda
Mbandaka 77 C 5 *prev.*
  Coquilhatville. NW Congo (Zaire)
M'Banza Congo 78 B 1 *var.* Mbanza
  Congo; *prev.* São Salvador do
  Congo, São Salvador. NW Angola
Mbanza-Ngungu 77 B 6
  W Congo (Zaire)
Mbarara 73 B 6 SW Uganda
Mbé 76 B 4 N Cameroon
Mbeya 73 C 8 SW Tanzania
Mbomou 77 C 5 *var.* Bomu,
  M'Bomu, Mbomu. River, Central
  African Republic/Congo (Zaire)
Mbour 74 B 3 W Senegal
Mbuji-Mayi 77 D 7 *prev.*
  Bakwanga. S Congo (Zaire)
McAdam 39 F 4 New Brunswick,
  SE Canada

McAlester 49 G 2 Oklahoma, C US
McAllen 49 G 5 Texas, S USA
McClintock Channel 37 F 2
  channel, Arctic Ocean
McComb 42 B 3 Mississippi, S US
McCook 45 E 4 Nebraska, C USA
Mcfarlane, Lake *see*
  Macfarlane, Lake
McKean Island 145 E 3 island,
  C Kiribati
McKinley, Mount 36 C 3 *var.*
  Denali. Mountain, Alaska,
  NW USA
McKinley Park 36 D 3
  Alaska, NW USA
McMinnville 46 B 3
  Oregon, NW USA
McMurdo Base 154 C 4 research
  station, Antarctica
McPherson 45 F 5 Kansas, C USA
McPherson *see* Fort McPherson
Mead, Lake 48 A 1 reservoir,
  W USA
Meander River 37 E 4 Alberta,
  W Canada
Mecca *see* Makkah
Mechelen 87 C 5 *Eng.* Mechlin,
  Fr. Malines. C Belgium
Mecheria 70 D 2 *var.* Mechriyya.
  NW Algeria
Mechlin *see* Mechelen
Mechriyya *see* Mecheria
Mecklenburg 94 C 3 cultural
  region, N Germany
Mecklenburger Bucht 94 C 2 bay,
  SW Baltic Sea
Mecsek 99 C 7 mountain range,
  SW Hungary
Medan 138 B 3 Sumatera,
  E Indonesia
Medellín 58 B 3 NW Colombia
Médenine 71 F 2 *var.* Madanīyīn.
  SE Tunisia
Medeshamstede *see* Peterborough
Medford 46 B 4
  Oregon, NW USA
Medgidia 108 D 5 SE Romania
Mediaş 108 B 4 *Ger.* Mediasch,
  Hung. Medgyes. C Romania
Medicine Hat 37 F 5 Alberta,
  SW Canada
Medina *see* Al Madīnah
Medinaceli 93 E 2 N Spain
Medina del Campo 92 C 2 N Spai
Mediolanum *see* Saintes
Mediterranean Sea 102 D 3
  Fr. Mer Méditerranée. Sea,
  E Atlantic Ocean
Méditerranée, Mer *see*
  Mediterranean Sea
Médoc 91 B 5 cultural region,
  SW France
Medvezh'yegorsk 110 B 3 *var.*
  Medvejegorsk, Medvezjegorsk.
  NW Russian Federation
Meekatharra 147 B 5 Western
  Australia, W Australia
Meemu Atoll *see* Mulaku Atoll
Meerssen 87 D 6 *var.* Mersen.
  SE Netherlands
Meerut 134 D 2 N India
Mehrīz 120 D 3 C Iran
Mehtarlām 123 F 4 *var.* Mehtar
  Lām, Meterlam, Metharjam,
  Metharlam. E Afghanistan
Meiktila 136 B 3 C Myanmar
Mejerda *see* Medjerda
Mejerda *see* Oued
  Medjerda, Wādī Majardah.
  River, Algeria/Tunisia
Mejillones 64 B 2 N Chile
Mek'elē 72 C 4 *var.* Makale.
  N Ethiopia
Mékhé 74 B 3 NW Senegal

ekong 124 D 3 var. Lan-ts'ang
Chiang, Cam. Mékôngk,
Chin. Lancang Jiang, Lao. Mènam
Khong, Th. Mae Nam Khong,
Tib. Dza Chu, Vtn. Sông Tiên
Giang. River, E Asia
ekong, Mouths of the 137 E 7
delta, S Vietnam
elaka 138 B 3 var. Malacca.
W Malaysia
elanesia 144 D 3 island group,
SW Pacific Ocean
elanesian Basin 152 C 3 undersea
basin, W Pacific Ocean
elbourne 43 E 4 Florida, SE USA
elbourne 149 C 7 state capital,
Victoria, SE Australia
elchor, Isla 65 A 6 island, S Chile
elghir, Chott 71 E 2 var. Chott
Melrhir. Salt lake, E Algeria
elilla 68 B 2 anc. Rusaddir,
Russadir. Spain, N Africa
elilla 70 C 2 enclave, Spain,
N Africa
elita 37 F 5 Manitoba, S Canada
elitene see Malatya
elitopol' 109 G 4 SE Ukraine
elle 87 B 5 NW Belgium
ellerud 85 B 6 S Sweden
ellizno Sur, Cerro 65 B 7
mountain, S Chile
elo 64 E 4 E Uruguay
elodunum see Melun
elun 90 C 3 anc. Melodunum.
N France
elville, Cape 148 C 2 headland,
Queensland, NE Australia
elville Fracture Zone 141 B 6
fracture zone, C Indian Ocean
elville Island 37 F 2 island,
NW Canada
elville Island 146 D 2 island,
N Australia
elville, Lake 39 F 2 lake,
Newfoundland and Labrador,
E Canada
elville Peninsula 37 G 3
peninsula, Northwest Territories,
NE Canada
elville Sound see Viscount
Melville Sound
emel see Klaipėda
emmingen 95 B 6 S Germany
emphis 42 C 1 Tennessee, S USA
enaam see Menaldum
enado see Manado
enaka 75 F 3 E Mali
enaldum 86 D 1 Fris. Menaam.
N Netherlands
endaña Fracture Zone 153 F 4
fracture zone, E Pacific Ocean
ende 91 C 6 anc. Mimatum. S France
endeleyev Ridge 155 F 2
undersea ridge, Arctic Ocean
endocino Fracture Zone 152 D 2
fracture zone, NE Pacific Ocean
endoza 64 B 4 W Argentina
enemen 116 A 3 W Turkey
enengiyn Tal 127 F 2 plain,
E Mongolia
enomonie 40 A 2 Wisconsin, N USA
enongue 78 B 2 var. Vila Serpa
Pinto, Port. Serpa Pinto. C Angola
enorca 93 H 3 Eng. Minorca; anc.
Balearis Minor. Island, E Spain
entawai, Kepulauan 138 B 4
island group, W Indonesia
eppel 86 D 2 NE Netherlands
eran see Merano
erano 96 C 1 Ger. Meran. N Italy
erca see Marka
ercedes 64 D 3 E Argentina

Mercedes 64 D 4 W Uruguay
Mercedes 64 C 4 NE Argentina
Meredith, Lake 49 E 1 reservoir,
Texas, S USA
Merefa 109 G 2 E Ukraine
Mergate see Margate
Mergui 137 B 6 SE Myanmar
Mergui Archipelago 137 B 6 island
group, S Myanmar
Mérida 92 C 4 anc. Augusta
Emerita. W Spain
Mérida 51 H 3 SW Mexico
Mérida 58 C 2 W Venezuela
Mérida, Cordillera de 58 C 2
var. Sierra Nevada de Mérida.
Mountain range, W Venezuela
Meridian 42 C 2 Mississippi, S USA
Mérignac 91 A 5 SW France
Merkinė 107 B 5 S Lithuania
Merkulovichi see Myerkulavichy
Merredin 147 B 6 Western
Australia, SW Australia
Mersen see Merssen
Mersey 89 D 6 river, NW England, UK
Mersin 116 C 4 S Turkey
Mērsrags 106 C 3 NW Latvia
Meru 73 C 6 C Kenya
Merv see Mary
Merzig 95 A 5 SW Germany
Mesa 48 B 2 Arizona, SW USA
Meseritz see Międzyrzecz
Meshed see Mashhad
Messalo, Rio 79 E 2 var. Mualo.
River, NE Mozambique
Messina 97 D 7 var. Messana,
Messene; anc. Zancle. SW Italy
Messina 78 D 3 NE South Africa
Messina, Strait of see
Messina, Stretto di
Messina, Stretto di 97 D 7
Eng. Strait of Messina. Strait,
C Mediterranean Sea
Messíni 105 B 6 S Greece
Mestghanem see Mostaganem
Mestre 96 C 2 NE Italy
Meta 58 C 3 river,
Colombia/Venezuela
Metairie 42 B 3 Louisiana USA
Metan 64 C 2 N Argentina
Metapán 52 B 2 NW El Salvador
Metković 100 B 4 SE Croatia
Métsovo 104 B 4 prev. Métsovon.
C Greece
Métsovon see Métsovo
Metz 90 D 3 anc. Divodurum
Mediomatricum, Mediomatrica,
Metis. NE France
Meuse 86 D 4 Dut. Maas. River,
W Europe
Mexcala, Río see Balsas, Río
Mexicali 50 A 1 NW Mexico
Mexicana, Altiplanicie 49 E 5
Eng. Mexican Plateau, Plateau of
Mexico. Plateau, N Mexico

Mexico
50 C 3 var. Méjico, México,
Sp. Estados Unidos Mexicanos.
Federal republic,
S North America

Official name: United Mexican States
Date of formation: 1836/1867
Capital: Mexico City Population:
95.5 million Total area: 756,061 sq
miles (1,958,200 sq km) Languages:
Spanish*, Mayan dialects Religions:
Roman Catholic 89%, Protestant 6%,
other 5% Ethnic mix: mestizo 55%,
Indian 30%, White 6%, other 9%
Government: Multiparty republic
Currency: Peso = 100 centavos

Mexico 45 G 3 Missouri, C USA
México 51 E 4 var. Ciudad de
México, Eng. Mexico City.
Country capital, C Mexico
Mexico Basin 35 C 6 var. Sigsbee
Deep. Undersea basin,
N Gulf of Mexico
Mexico City see Mexico
México, Golfo de see Mexico,Gulf of
Mexico, Gulf of 66 A 4 Sp. Golfo de
México. Gulf, W Atlantic Ocean
Mezen' 110 D 3 river,
NW Russian Federation
Mezőtúr 99 D 7 E Hungary
Miahuatlán 51 F 5 var. Miahuatlán
de Porfirio Díaz. SE Mexico
Miahuatlán de Porfirio Díaz see
Miahuatlán
Miami 43 F 5 Florida, SE USA
Miami 49 G 1 Oklahoma, C USA
Miami Beach 43 F 5 Florida, SE USA
Mīāneh 120 C 2 var. Miyáneh.
NW Iran
Mianyang 129 B 5 C China
Miastko 98 C 2 Ger. Rummelsburg
in Pommern. NW Poland
Michalovce 99 E 6 Ger.
Grossmichel, Hung. Nagymihály.
E Slovakia
Michigan 40 C 2 off. State of
Michigan; nicknames Great Lakes
State, Lake State, Wolverine State.
State, N USA
Michigan, Lake 40 C 3 lake, N USA
Michurinsk 111 B 5
W Russian Federation
Micoud 55 F 2 SE Saint Lucia
Micronesia 144 C 1 island group,
W Pacific Ocean

Micronesia
144 B 1 Federation,
W Pacific Ocean

Official name: Federated States of
Micronesia Date of formation: 1986
Capital: Kolonia Population:
101,000 Total Area: 1,120 sq miles
(2,900 sq km) Languages: English*,
Trukese, Pohnpeian, Mortlockese
Religions: Catholic 50%, Protestant
48%, other 2% Ethnic mix:
Micronesian 99%, other 1%
Government: Republic
Currency: US $ = 100 cents

Micronesia, Federated States of see
Micronesia
Mid-Atlantic Ridge 67 C 5 var.
Mid-Atlantic Cordillera, Mid-
Atlantic Rise, Mid-Atlantic Swell.
Undersea ridge, C Atlantic Ocean
Middelburg 87 B 5 SW Netherlands
Middelharnis 86 B 4
SW Netherlands
Middelkerke 87 A 5 W Belgium
Middle America Trench 153 F 3
trench, E Pacific Ocean
Middle Andaman 133 G 2 island,
SE India
Middle Atlas see Moyen Atlas
Middlesboro 40 C 5 Kentucky, E USA
Middlesbrough 89 D 5
N England, UK
Middletown 41 F 4
New Jersey, NE USA
Middletown 41 F 3
Connecticut, NE USA
Mid-Indian Basin 140 C 4 undersea
basin, C Indian Ocean
Mid-Indian Ridge 141 C 5 var.
Central Indian Ridge. Undersea
ridge, C Indian Ocean

Midland 38 D 5 Ontario, S Canada
Midland 49 E 3 Texas, S USA
Midland 40 C 3 Michigan, N USA
Mid-Pacific Mountains 152 C 2 var.
Mid-Pacific Seamounts. Seamount
range, NW Pacific Ocean
Mid-Pacific Seamounts see
Mid-Pacific Mountains
Miechów 99 D 5 S Poland
Międzyrzec Podlaski 98 E 3
E Poland
Międzyrzecz 98 B 3 Ger. Meseritz.
W Poland
Mielec 99 D 5 SE Poland
Miercurea-Ciuc 108 C 4 Ger.
Szeklerburg, Hung. Csíkszereda.
C Romania
Mieres 92 D 1 NW Spain
Mi'ēso 73 D 5 var. Meheso, Miesso.
E Ethiopia
Miguel Asua 50 D 3 var. Miguel
Auza. C Mexico
Miguel Auza see Miguel Asua
Mijdrecht 86 C 3 C Netherlands
Mikashevichy 107 C 7 Pol.
Mikaszewicze, Rus. Mikashevichi.
SW Belarus
Mikhaylovka 111 B 6
SW Russian Federation
Mikonos see Mýkonos
Mikre 104 C 2 C Bulgaria
Mikun' 110 D 4
NW Russian Federation
Mikuni-sanmyaku 131 D 5
mountain range, Honshū, N Japan
Mikura-jima 131 D 6 island,
Izu-shotō, E Japan
Milagro 60 B 2 SW Ecuador
Milan see Milano
Milange 79 E 2 NE Mozambique
Milano 96 B 2 Eng. Milan,
Ger. Mailand; anc. Mediolanum.
N Italy
Milas 116 A 4 SW Turkey
Milashavichy 107 C 7 Rus.
Milashevichi. SE Belarus
Milashevichi see Milashavichy
Mildura 149 B 6 Victoria,
SE Australia
Mile see Mili Atoll
Miles 149 D 5 Queensland,
E Australia
Miles City 44 C 2 Montana, NW USA
Milford see Milford Haven
Milford Haven 89 B 7 prev. Milford.
SW Wales, UK
Milford Sound 151 A 7
South Island, SW New Zealand
Milford Sound 151 A 7 sound,
E Tasman Sea
Mili Atoll 144 D 2 var. Mile.
SE Marshall Islands
Mil'kovo 115 H 3
E Russian Federation
Milk River 37 E 5 Alberta,
SW Canada
Milk River 44 C 1 river, NW USA
Milk, Wadi el 72 B 4 var. Wadi al
Malik. River, C Sudan
Milledgeville 43 E 2 Georgia, SE USA
Mille Lacs Lake 45 F 2 lake,
Minnesota, N USA
Millerovo 111 B 6
SW Russian Federation
Millet 55 F 1 C Saint Lucia
Millicent 149 B 7 South Australia,
S Australia
Millwood Lake 42 A 3 reservoir,
Arkansas, C USA
Milo 74 D 4 river, E Guinea
Mílos 105 C 6 Mílos, SE Greece

Mílos 105 C 7 island, Kykládes, SE Greece
Milparinka 149 C 5 New South Wales, SE Australia
Milton 151 B 7 South Island, SW New Zealand
Milton Keynes 89 D 6 SE England, UK
Milwaukee 40 B 3 Wisconsin, N USA
Mimatum *see* Mende
Mīnā' Sa'ūd 120 C 4 *var.* Minā' Su'ūd. SE Kuwait
Minas Gerais 63 F 3 *off.* Estado de Minas Gerais. State, SE Brazil
Minas Gerais, Estado de *see* Minas Gerais
Minatitlán 51 F 4 E Mexico
Minbu 136 A 3 W Myanmar
Minch, The 88 B 3 *var.* North Minch. Strait, NE Atlantic Ocean
Mindanao 139 F 2 island, S Philippines
Mindanao Sea *see* Bohol Sea
Mindelheim 95 C 6 S Germany
Mindelo 74 A 2 *var.* Mindello; *prev.* Porto Grande. N Cape Verde
Minden 94 B 4 *anc.* Minthun. NW Germany
Mindoro 139 E 2 island, N Philippines
Mindoro Strait 139 E 2 strait, South China Sea/Sulu Sea
Mineral Wells 49 G 3 Texas, S USA
Mingäçevir 117 G 2 *Rus.* Mingechaur, Mingechevir C Azerbaijan
Mingan 39 F 3 Québec, E Canada
Mingāora 134 C 1 *var.* Mingora, Mongora. N Pakistan
Mingenew 147 B 6 W Australia
Minho 92 B 2 *Sp.* Miño. River, Portugal/Spain
Minho *see* Miño
Minicoy Island 132 A 3 island, Lakshadweep, SW India
Minigwal, Lake 147 C 6 lake, C Australia
Minneapolis 45 F 2 Minnesota, N USA
Minnesota 45 F 2 *off.* State of Minnesota; *nicknames* Gopher State, New England of the West, North Star State. State, N USA
Miño 92 B 2 *var.* Mino, Minius, *Port.* Minho. River, Portugal/Spain
Minot 44 D 1 North Dakota, N USA
Minsk 107 C 6 country capital, C Belarus
Minskaya Wzvyshsha 107 C 6 mountain range, E Belarus
Minthun *see* Minden
Minto, Lac 38 D 2 lake, Québec, C Canada
Miranda de Ebro 93 E 1 N Spain
Mirgorod *see* Myrhorod
Miri 138 D 3 Borneo, E Malaysia
Mirim Lagoon 63 E 5 *var.* Lake Mirim, *Port.* Lagoa Mirim, *Sp.* Laguna Merín. Lagoon, SW Atlantic Ocean
Mírina *see* Mýrina
Mīrjāveh 120 E 4 SE Iran
Mirnyy 115 F 3 C Russian Federation
Mirnyy 154 D 3 research station, Antarctica
Mirs Bay 128 B 1 bay, NE Hong Kong
Mirtóo Pelagos 105 C 6 *Eng.* Mirtoan Sea; *anc.* Myrtoum Mare. Sea, SW Aegean Sea
Misiaf *see* Maşyāf

Miskitos, Cayos 53 E 2 island group, NE Nicaragua
Miskolc 99 D 6 NE Hungary
Misool, Pulau 139 G 4 island, E Indonesia
Mişrātah 71 F 2 *var.* Misurata. NW Libya
Mission 49 G 5 Texas, S USA
Mississippi 42 B 2 *off.* State of Mississippi; *nicknames* Bayou State, Magnolia State. State, SE USA
Mississippi Delta 35 C 6 delta, Mississippi, S USA
Mississippi River 35 C 6 river, C USA
Mississippi River Delta 42 C 4 river delta, Louisiana, S USA
Missoula 44 A 1 Montana, NW USA
Missouri 45 G 5 *off.* State of Missouri; *nicknames* Bullion State, Show Me State. State, C USA
Missouri City 49 H 4 Texas, S USA
Missouri River 45 F 4 river, N USA
Mistassini, Lac 38 D 3 lake, Québec, SE Canada
Mistelbach an der Zaya 95 E 6 NE Austria
Misti, Volcán 61 E 4 mountain, S Peru
Misurata *see* Mişrātah
Mitau *see* Jelgava
Mitchell 148 C 2 river, NE Australia
Mitchell 149 D 5 Queensland, E Australia
Mitchell 45 E 3 South Dakota, N USA
Mi Tho *see* My Tho
Mito 131 D 5 Honshū, S Japan
Mitú 58 C 4 SE Colombia
Mitumba, Monts 77 E 7 *var.* Chaîne des Mitumba, Mitumba Range. Mountain range, E Congo (Zaire)
Miyake-jima 131 D 6 island, Sakishima-shotō, SW Japan
Miyako 130 D 4 Honshū, C Japan
Miyakonojō 131 B 8 *var.* Miyakonzyô. Kyūshū, SW Japan
Miyakonzyô *see* Miyakonojō
Miyāneh *see* Miāneh
Miyazaki 131 B 8 Kyūshū, SW Japan
Mizija 104 C 1 NW Bulgaria
Mizil 108 C 5 SE Romania
Mizpé Ramon 119 A 7 S Israel
Mjosa 85 B 5 *var.* Mjøsen. Lake, S Norway
Mjøsen *see* Mjøsa
Mladenovac 100 D 4 Yugoslavia
Mława 98 D 3 C Poland
Mljet 101 B 5 *It.* Meleda; *anc.* Melita. Island, S Croatia
Mmabatho 78 C 4 N South Africa
Moab 44 B 5 Utah, W USA
Moa Island 148 C 1 island, Queensland, NW Australia
Moanda 77 B 6 *var.* Mouanda SE Gabon
Moba 77 E 7 E Congo (Zaire)
Mobay *see* Montego Bay
Mobaye 77 C 5 S Central African Republic
Moberly 45 G 4 Missouri, C USA
Mobile 42 C 3 Alabama, S USA
Mobile Bay 42 C 3 bay, N Gulf of Mexico
Moçambique 79 F 2 NE Mozambique
Mochudi 78 C 4 SE Botswana
Mocímboa da Praia 79 F 2 *var.* Vila de Mocímboa da Praia. N Mozambique

Môco 78 B 2 *var.* Morro de Môco. Mountain, W Angola
Mocoa 58 A 4 SW Colombia
Môco, Morro de *see* Môco
Mocuba 79 E 3 NE Mozambique
Modena 96 B 3 *anc.* Mutina. N Italy
Modesto 47 B 6 California, W USA
Modica 97 C 8 *anc.* Motyca. SW Italy
Modohn *see* Madona
Modriča 100 C 3 N Bosnia & Herzegovina
Moe 149 C 7 Victoria, SE Australia
Möen *see* Møn
Moena *see* Muna, Pulau
Moerewa 150 D 2 North Island, N New Zealand
Moero, Lac *see* Mweru, Lake
Moeskroen *see* Mouscron
Mogadishu *see* Muqdisho
Mogador *see* Essaouira
Mogilëv *see* Mahilyow
Mogilev-Podol'skiy *see* Mohyliv-Podil's'kyy
Mogilno 98 C 3 C Poland
Moguer 92 C 4 S Spain
Mohammedia 70 C 2 *prev.* Fédala. NW Morocco
Mohave, Lake 47 D 7 lake, W USA
Mohawk Mountains 48 A 3 mountain range, Arizona, SW USA
Mohéli 79 F 2 island, S Comoros
Mohns Ridge 155 F 5 undersea ridge, Arctic Ocean
Moho 61 E 4 SW Peru
Mohoro 73 C 7 E Tanzania
Mohyliv-Podil's'kyy 108 C 3 *Rus.* Mogilev-Podol'skiy. C Ukraine
Moi 85 A 6 S Norway
Moincêr 126 B 4 W China
Moíres 105 D 8 Kríti, SE Greece
Mõisaküla 106 D 3 *Ger.* Moiseküll. S Estonia
Moiseküll *see* Mõisaküla
Mo i Rana 84 C 3 C Norway
Moissac 91 B 6 S France
Mojácar 93 E 5 S Spain
Mojave Desert 47 D 7 plain, California, W USA
Mokrany *see* Makrany
Moktama *see* Martaban
Mol 87 C 5 *prev.* Moll. N Belgium
Moldava *see* Moldova
Molde 85 A 5 S Norway
Moldotau, Khrebet *see* Moldo-Too, Khrebet
Moldo-Too, Khrebet 123 G 2 *prev.* Khrebet Moldotau. Mountain range, C Kyrgyzstan

Moldova 108 D 3 *var.* Moldavia, *Rus.* Moldavskaya SSR; *prev.* Moldavian SSR. Republic, E Europe

Official name: Republic of Moldova Date of formation: 1991 Capital: Chişinău Population: 4.4 million Total area: 13,000 sq miles (33,700 sq km) Languages: Moldovan*, Ukrainian Religions: Romanian Orthodox 98%, Jewish 2%, other 1% Ethnic mix: Moldovan (Romanian) 65%, Ukrainian 14%, Russian 13%, other 8% Government: Multiparty republic Currency: Leu = 100 bani

Moldova Nouă 108 A 4 *Ger.* Neumoldowa, *Hung.* Újmoldova. W Romania

Molfetta 97 E 5 SE Italy
Moline 40 B 3 Illinois, N USA
Moll *see* Mol
Mollendo 61 E 4 S Peru
Mölndal 85 B 7 S Sweden
Molochans'k 108 C 3 *Rus.* Molochansk. SE Ukraine
Molochansk *see* Molochans'k
Molodezhnaya 154 D 2 research station, Antarctica
Molokai 47 B 8 *Haw.* Moloka'i. Island, Hawaii, W USA
Moloka'i *see* Molokai
Molokai Fracture Zone 153 E 2 fracture zone, NE Pacific Ocean
Molopo 78 D 4 *var.* Molopo River, Botswana/South Africa
Mólos 105 B 5 C Greece
Molotov *see* Perm'
Moluccas *see* Maluccas
Molucca Sea *see* Maluku, Laut
Mombasa 73 D 7 SE Kenya
Momchilgrad 104 D 3 *prev.* Mastanli. S Bulgaria
Mon 85 B 8 *prev.* Möen. Island, SE Denmark
Monaco 91 B 7 *var.* Monaco-Ville; *anc.* Monoecus. Country capital, C Monaco

Monaco 91 B 7 Monarchy, W Europe

Official name: Principality of Monaco Date of formation: 1861 Capital: Monaco Population: 28,000 Total area: 0.75 sq miles (1.95 sq km) Languages: French*, Italian Religions: Roman Catholic 95%, other 5% Ethnic mix: French 47%, Monégasque 17%, Italian 16%, other 20% Government: Constitutional monarchy Currency: French franc = 100 centimes

Monaco, Principality of *see* Monaco
Monahans 49 E 3 Texas, S USA
Mona, Isla 55 F 3 island, W Puerto Rico
Mona Passage 55 F 3 channel, N Caribbean Sea
Monastir 71 F 2 *var.* Al Munastīr. NE Tunisia
Monbetsu 130 D 2 *var.* Mombetsu, Monbetu. Hokkaidō, NE Japan
Moncalieri 96 A 2 NW Italy
Moncêgorsk *see* Monchegorsk
Monchegorsk 110 C 2 *var.* Mončegorsk. NW Russian Federation
Monclova 50 D 2 NE Mexico
Moncton 39 F 4 New Brunswick, SE Canada
Mondovì 96 A 2 NW Italy
Mondsee 95 D 6 lake, N Austria
Monfalcone 96 D 2 NE Italy
Monforte 92 C 1 NW Spain
Mongo 76 C 3 C Chad

Mongolia 126 C 2 *Mong.* Mongol Uls. Republic, Mongolia

Official name: Mongolia Date of formation: 1921 Capital: Ulan Bator Population: 2.4 million Total area: 604,245 sq miles (1,565,000 sq km) Languages: Khalkha Mongol*, Turkic, Russian, Chinese Religions: Predominantly Tibetan Buddhist, with a Muslim minority Ethnic mix: Khalkha Mongol 90%, Kazakh 4%, Chinese 2%, other 4% Government: Multiparty republic Currency: Tughrik = 100 möngös

ongos, Chaîne des *see*
Bongo, Massif des
ongu 78 C 2 W Zambia
onkey Bay 79 E 2 SE Malawi
onkey River *see*
Monkey River Town
onkey River Town 52 C 2
var. Monkey River.
ono Lake 47 C 6 lake,
California, W USA
onóvar 93 F 4 E Spain
onroe 42 B 2 Louisiana, S USA
onroe 43 E 1
North Carolina, SE USA
onrovia 74 C 5 country capital,
W Liberia
ons 87 B 6 *Dut.* Bergen.
S Belgium
onselice 96 C 2 Italy
ontana 104 C 2 *prev.* Ferdinand,
Mikhaylovgrad. NW Bulgaria
ontana 44 B 1 *off.* State of
Montana; *nicknames* Mountain
State, Treasure State. State,
NW USA
ontañas Mayas *see* Maya
Mountains
ontargis 90 C 4 C France
ontauban 91 B 6 S France
ontbéliard 90 D 4 E France
ontcalm, Lake *see* Dogai Coring
ont Cenis, Col du 91 E 5 pass,
E France
ont-de-Marsan 91 A 6 SW France
onteagudo 61 G 4 S Bolivia
onte Alegre 63 E 2 N Brazil
onte-Carlo 91 C 8 *var.* Monte
Carlo. NE Monaco
onte Carlo *see* Monte-Carlo
onte Caseros 64 D 3 E Argentina
onte Cristi 55 E 3 *var.* San
Fernando de Monte Cristi.
NW Dominican Republic
ontegiardino 91 E 2 SE San Marino
ontego Bay 54 A 4 *var.* Mobay.
W Jamaica
ontélimar 91 C 6 *anc.* Acunum
Acusio, Montilium Adhemari.
E France
ontemorelos 51 E 3 NE Mexico
ontenegro 101 C 5 *Serb.* Crna
Gora. Constituent republic of
Yugoslavia, Yugoslavia.
See also Yugoslavia
onte Patria 64 B 3 N Chile
onterey 47 B 6
California, W USA
onterey *see* Monterrey
onterey Bay 47 A 6 bay,
E Pacific Ocean
ontería 58 B 2 NW Colombia
ontero 61 G 4 C Bolivia
onterrey 51 E 3 *var.* Monterey.
NE Mexico
ontes Claros 63 F 3 SE Brazil
ontevideo 64 D 4 country capital,
S Uruguay
ontevideo 45 F 2 Minnesota, N USA
ontgenèvre, Col de 91 E 5 pass,
France/Italy
ontgomery 42 D 2 state capital,
Alabama, S USA
ontgomery *see* Sāhīwāl
onthey 95 A 8 SW Switzerland
ontluçon 90 C 4 C France
ontmagny 39 E 4 Québec,
SE Canada
onto 148 D 4 Queensland,
E Australia
ontoro 92 D 4 S Spain
ontpelier 41 G 2 state capital,
Vermont, NE USA

Montpellier 91 C 6 S France
Montreal *see* Montréal
Montréal 39 E 4 *Eng.* Montreal.
Québec, SE Canada
Montrose 88 D 3 E Scotland, UK
Montrose 44 C 5
Colorado, C USA
Montserrat 55 G 3 *var.*
Emerald Isle. UK dependent
territory, E Caribbean Sea
Monturaqui 64 B 2 NE Chile
Monywa 136 B 3 NW Myanmar
Monza 96 B 2 N Italy
Monze 78 D 2 S Zambia
Monzón 93 F 2 NE Spain
Moora 147 B 6 Western Australia,
SW Australia
Moore 49 G 1 Oklahoma, C USA
Moore, Lake 147 B 6 lake, Western
Australia, W Australia
Moorhead 45 F 2
North Dakota, N USA
Moosehead Lake 41 G 1 lake,
Maine, NE USA
Moosonee 38 C 3
Ontario, SE Canada
Mopti 75 E 3 C Mali
Moqor 123 E 4 SE Afghanistan
Moquegua 61 E 4 SE Peru
Mora 85 C 5 C Sweden
Morales 52 C 2 E Guatemala
Morant Bay 54 B 5 E Jamaica
Moratalla 93 E 4 SE Spain
Moratuwa 132 D 4 SW Sri Lanka
Morava 99 C 5 *var.* March. River,
C Europe
Morava 101 E 5 *var.* March.
C Europe
Moravia 99 B 5 *Cz.* Morava,
Ger. Mähren. Cultural region,
E Czech Republic
Morawhanna 59 F 2 N Guyana
Moray Firth 88 C 3 inlet,
NW North Sea
Moreau River 44 D 2 river,
South Dakota, N USA
Moree 149 D 5 New South Wales,
SE Australia
Morelia 51 E 4 S Mexico
Morena, Sierra 92 C 4 mountain
range, SW Spain
Moreni 108 C 5 S Romania
Moreno 61 E 4 N Bolivia
Moreton Island 149 E 5 island,
Queensland, SE Australia
Morgan City 42 B 3
Louisiana, S USA
Morghāb, Daryā-ye 122 D 4 *var.*
Murgap Deryasy, *Rus.* Murgab.
River, Afghanistan/Turkmenistan
Morioka 130 D 4 Honshū, C Japan
Morlaix 90 A 3 NW France
Mornington Abyssal Plain 153 F 5
abyssal plain, SE Pacific Ocean
Mornington Island 148 B 2 island,
Queensland, NW Australia

Morocco
70 C 2 *Ar.* Al Mamlakah.
Monarchy, NW Africa

Official name: Kingdom of Morocco
Date of formation: 1956
Capital: Rabat Population: 27 million
Total area: 269,757 sq miles
(698,670 sq km) Languages: Arabic*,
Berber, French Religions: Muslim
99%, other 1%
Ethnic mix: Arab and Berber 99%,
European 1% Government:
Constitutional monarchy
Currency: Dirham =100 centimes

Morococha 60 C 4 W Peru
Morogoro 73 C 7 E Tanzania
Moro Gulf 139 E 3 gulf,
N Celebes Sea
Morón 54 C 2 C Cuba
Morón 64 D 4 E Argentina
Mörön 126 D 2 N Mongolia
Morondava 79 F 3 W Madagascar
Moroni 79 F 2 country capital,
N Comoros
Morotai, Pulau 139 F 3 island,
E Indonesia
Morrinsville 150 D 3 North Island,
N New Zealand
Morris 45 F 2 Minnesota, N USA
Morristown 43 E 1 Tennessee, S USA
Mors 85 A 7 island, NW Denmark
Morvan 90 D 4 physical region,
C France
Morwell 149 C 7 Victoria,
SE Australia
Moscow 46 D 2 Idaho, NW USA
Moscow *see* Moskva
Mosel 95 A 5 *Fr.* Moselle. River,
W Europe
Moselle *see* Mosel
Mosgiel 151 B 7 South Island,
SW New Zealand
Moshi 73 C 7 NE Tanzania
Mosjøen 84 B 3 C Norway
Moskva 111 B 5 *Eng.* Moscow.
Country capital,
W Russian Federation
Moskva 123 E 3 *Rus.* Moskovskiy;
prev. Chubek. SW Tajikistan
Mosonmagyaróvár 99 C 6 *Ger.*
Wieselburg-Ungarisch-Altenburg;
prev. Moson and Magyaróvár, *Ger.*
Wieselburg and Ungarisch-
Altenburg. NW Hungary
Mosquito Coast *see* La Mosquitia
Mosquito Gulf *see* Mosquitos,
Golfo de los
Mosquitos, Golfo de los 53 F 5
Eng. Mosquito Gulf. Gulf,
S Caribbean Sea
Moss 85 B 6 S Norway
Mosselbaai 78 C 5 *var.* Mosselbai,
Eng. Mossel Bay. SW South Africa
Mossendjo 77 B 6 SW Congo
Mossoró 63 G 2 NE Brazil
Most 99 A 4 *Ger.* Brüx.
NW Czech Republic
Mostaganem 70 D 2 *var.*
Mestghanem. NW Algeria
Mostar 100 C 4
S Bosnia & Herzegovina
Mosty *see* Masty
Mosul *see* Al Mawṣil
Mota del Cuervo 93 E 3 C Spain
Motril 92 D 5 S Spain
Motru 108 B 5 SW Romania
Motueka 151 C 5 South Island,
C New Zealand
Motul 51 H 3 *var.* Motul de Felipe
Carrillo Puerto. SE Mexico
Motul de Felipe Carrillo Puerto *see*
Motul
Motyca *see* Modica
Mouanda *see* Moanda
Mouila 77 A 6 C Gabon
Mould Bay 37 E 2 Prince Patrick
Island, N Canada
Moulins 90 C 4 C France
Moulmein 136 B 4 *var.* Maulmain,
Mawlamyine. SE Myanmar
Moultrie, Lake 43 F 2 reservoir,
South Carolina, SE USA
Moundou 76 B 4 SW Chad
Moŭng Roeesei 137 D 5
W Cambodia

Mount Cavenagh 147 E 5
C Australia
Mount Cook 151 B 6 South Island,
SW New Zealand
Mount Desert Island 41 H 2 island,
Maine, NE USA
Mount Friendship 55 G 2
SW Barbados
Mount Gambier 149 B 7
South Australia, S Australia
Mount Isa 148 B 3 Queensland,
C Australia
Mount Magnet 147 B 5
Western Australia, W Australia
Mount Pleasant 40 C 3
Michigan, N USA
Mount Pleasant 45 G 4
Iowa, C USA
Mount Vernon 40 B 5 Illinois, N USA
Mount Vernon 46 B 1
Washington, NW USA
Mouscron 87 A 6
Dut. Moeskroen. W Belgium
Moussoro 76 C 3 W Chad
Moyen Atlas 70 C 2 *Eng.* Middle
Atlas. Mountain range,
N Morocco
Moyobamba 60 C 2 NW Peru
Moyu 126 B 4 *var.* Karakax.
NW China
Moyynqum *see* Muyunkum, Peski

Mozambique
79 E 3 *off.* Republic of
Mozambique; *prev.* People's
Republic of Mozambique,
Portuguese East Africa.
Republic, S Africa

Official name: Republic of
Mozambique Date of formation:
1975 Capital: Maputo
Population: 15.3 million Total area:
309,493 sq miles (801,590 sq km)
Languages: Portuguese* Religions:
Traditional beliefs 60%, Christian
30%, Muslim 10% Ethnic mix:
Makua-Lomwe 47%, Tsonga 23%,
Malawi 12%, other 18%
Government: Multiparty republic
Currency: Metical = 100 centavos

Mozambique Basin *see* Natal Basin
Mozambique Channel 69 E 6
Fr. Canal de Mozambique,
Mal. Lakandranon' i Mozambika,
Port. Canal de Moçambique.
Channel, W Indian Ocean
Mozambique Plateau 67 E 6
var. Mozambique Rise. Undersea
plateau, SW Indian Ocean
Mozambique Rise *see*
Mozambique Plateau
Mozambique Scarp *see*
Mozambique Escarpment
Mozyr' *see* Mazyr
Mpama 87 B 6 river, C Congo
Mpika 78 D 2 NE Zambia
Mqinvartsveri *see* Kazbek
Mragowo 98 D 2 *var.* Mragowo,
Ger. Sensburg. NE Poland
M'Sila 71 E 2 *var.* Msila. N Algeria
Msila *see* M'Sila
Mtwara 73 D 8 SE Tanzania
Mualo *see* Messalo, Rio
Muang Kalasin *see* Kalasin
Muang Khammouan 136 D 4
var. Thakhek. S Laos
Muang Khanthabuli *see*
Khanthabouli
Muang Không 137 D 5 S Laos
Muang Khôngxédôn 137 D 5 *var.*
Khong Sedone. S Laos

Muang Khon Kaen *see* Khon Kaen
Muang Lampang *see* Lampang
Muang Lom Sak *see* Lom Sak
Muang Namo 136 C 3 N Laos
Muang Nan *see* Nan
Muang Pakxan 136 D 4
  var. Pak Sane. C Laos
Muang Phalan 136 D 4
  var. Muang Phalane.
Muang Phalane *see* Muang Phalan
Muang Phayao *see* Phayao
Muang Sing 136 C 3 NW Laos
Muang Xaignabouri 136 C 4
  var. Sayaboury. W Laos
Muar 138 B 3 *var.* Bandar Maharani.
  W Malaysia
Muarabungo 138 B 4 Sumatera,
  W Indonesia
Muchinga Escarpment 78 D 2
  mountain range, NE Zambia
Mucojo 79 F 2 N Mozambique
Mudanjiang 128 E 3
  var. Mu-tan-chiang.
Mudon 137 B 5 SE Myanmar
Mufulira 78 D 2 C Zambia
Mughla *see* Muğla
Muğla 116 A 4 *var.* Mughla.
  SW Turkey
Mūh, Sabkhat al 118 C 3 lake,
  C Syria
Muir Éireann *see* Irish Sea
Muisne 60 A 1 NW Ecuador
Mukachene 108 B 3 *Cz.* Mukačevo,
  Hung. Munkács, *Rus.* Mukachevo.
  W Ukraine
Mukalla *see* Al Mukallā
Mula 93 E 4 SE Spain
Mulaku Atoll 132 B 4 *var.* Meemu
  Atoll. Island, C Maldives
Muleshoe 49 E 2 Texas, S USA
Mulhacén 93 E 5 mountain, S Spain
Mülhausen *see* Mulhouse
Mulhouse 90 E 4 *Ger.* Mülhausen.
  NE France
Müller-gerbergte *see* Muller,
  Pegunungan
Muller, Pegununga 138 D 4
  Dut. Müller-gerbergte. Mountain
  range, Borneo, Indonesia
Mullewa 147 B 6 W Australia
Müllheim 95 A 6 SW Germany
Mull, Isle of 88 B 4 island,
  W Scotland, UK
Mulongo 77 D 7 SE Congo (Zaire)
Multān 134 C 2 E Pakistan
Mumbai *see* Bombay
Mumbwa 78 D 2 C Zambia
Muna, Pulau 139 E 5 *prev.* Moena.
  Island, C Indonesia
Münchberg 95 C 5 E Germany
München 95 C 6 *var.* Muenchen,
  Eng. Munich, *It.* Monaco.
  SE Germany
Muncie 40 C 4 Indiana, N USA
Mu Nggava *see* Rennell
Munich *see* München
Munster 89 A 6 cultural region,
  S Ireland
Munster 94 A 4 NW Germany
Muong Xiang Ngeun 136 C 4
  var. Xiang Ngeun. C Laos
Muonio 84 D 3 N Finland
Muonionjoki 84 D 3 *var.*
  Muoniojoki, *Swe.* Muonioälv.
  River, Finland/Sweden
Muqdisho 73 D 6 *Eng.* Mogadishu,
  It. Mogadiscio. Country capital,
  S Somalia
Mur 95 E 7 *SCr.* Mura. River,
  C Europe
Mura *see* Mur

Muradiye 117 F 3 E Turkey
Murapara *see* Murupara
Murata 96 E 2 S San Marino
Murchison 147 B 5 river, Western
  Australia, W Australia
Murcia 93 E 4 cultural region,
  SE Spain
Murcia 93 F 4 SE Spain
Mureş 108 A 4 *var.* Maros, Mureşul,
  Ger. Marosch, Mieresch. River,
  Hungary/Romania
Murfreesboro 42 D 1
  Tennessee, S USA
Murgab 122 D 3 *var.* Murghab,
  Pash. Daryā-ye Morghāb,
  Turkm. Murgap Deryasy. River,
  Afghanistan/Turkmenistan
Murgab *see* Murghob
Murghob 123 G 3 *Rus.* Murgab.
  SE Tajikistan
Murgon 149 D 5 Queensland,
  E Australia
Müritz 94 C 3 *var.* Müritzee. Lake,
  NE Germany
Müritzee *see* Müritz
Murmansk 110 C 2
  NW Russian Federation
Murmashi 110 C 2 *var.* Murmaši.
  NW Russian Federation
Murmaši *see* Murmashi
Murom 111 B 5
  W Russian Federation
Muroran 130 D 3 Hokkaidō,
  NE Japan
Muros 92 B 1 NW Spain
Murray 149 C 7 river, SE Australia
Murray Bridge 149 B 7
  South Australia, SE Australia
Murray Fracture Zone 153 E 2
  fracture zone, NE Pacific Ocean
Murray, Lake 43 E 2 reservoir,
  South Carolina, SE USA
Murray Range *see* Murray Ridge
Murray Ridge 140 B 3 *var.* Murray
  Range. Undersea ridge,
  N Indian Ocean
Murrumbidgee 149 C 6 river,
  SE Australia
Murska Sobota 95 E 7 *Ger.* Olsnitz.
  NE Slovenia
Murupara 150 E 3 *var.* Murapara.
  North Island, NE New Zealand
Murwāra 135 E 4 N India
Murwillumbah 149 E 5
  New South Wales, SE Australia
Mürzzuschlag 95 E 7 E Austria
Muş 117 F 3 *var.* Mush. E Turkey
Musala 104 C 3 mountain,
  W Bulgaria
Muscat *see* Masqaţ
Muscatine 45 G 4 Iowa, C USA
Musgrave Ranges 147 D 5
  mountain range,
  South Australia, S Australia
Mush *see* Muş
Muskegon 40 C 3 Michigan, N USA
Muskogean *see* Tallahassee
Muskogee 49 G 1 Oklahoma, C USA
Musoma 73 C 6 N Tanzania
Mussau Island 144 B 3 island,
  NE Papua New Guinea
Mustafa-Pasha *see* Svilengrad
Musters, Lago 65 B 6 lake,
  S Argentina
Mut 116 C 4 S Turkey
Mu-tan-chiang *see* Mudanjiang
Mutare 78 D 3 *var.* Mutari;
  prev. Umtali. E Zimbabwe
Mutina *see* Modena
Mutsu-wan 130 D 3 bay,
  NW Pacific Ocean

Muttonbird Islands 151 A 8 island
  group, South Island,
  SW New Zealand
Mu Us Shamo *see* Ordos Desert
Muy Muy 52 D 3 C Nicaragua
Muynak *see* Mŭynoq
Mŭynoq 122 C 1 *Rus.* Muynak.
  NW Uzbekistan
Mužlja 100 D 3 *Hung.*
  Felsőmuzslya; *prev.* Gornja
  Mužlja. NE Yugoslavia
Mvolo 73 B 5 Sudan
Mwanza 73 C 7 NW Tanzania
Mweka 77 C 6 C Congo (Zaire)
Mwene-Ditu 77 D 7 S Congo (Zaire)
Mweru, Lake 78 D 1 *var.* Lac
  Moero. Lake, Congo
  (Zaire)/Zambia
Myadzel 107 C 5 *Pol.* Miadzioł
  Nowy, *Rus.* Myadel'. N Belarus
Myanaung 136 B 4 SW Myanmar
Myanmar
  136 B 3 *var.* Myanmar. Military
  dictatorship, SE Asia

  Official name: Union of Myanmar
  Date of formation: 1948 **Capital:**
  Rangoon (Yangon) **Population:**
  47.5 million **Total Area:**
  261,200 sq miles (676,550 sq km)
  Languages: Burmese*, Karen, Mon
  Religions: Buddhist 89%, Muslim
  4%, other 7% **Ethnic mix:** Burman
  68%, Shan 9%, Karen 6%,
  Rakhine 4%, other 13%
  Government: Military regime
  Currency: Kyat = 100 pyas

Myaungmya 136 A 4 SW Myanmar
Myerkulavichy 107 D 7
  Rus. Merkulovichi. SE Belarus
Myingyan 136 B 3 C Myanmar
Myitkyina 136 B 2 N Myanmar
Mykolayiv 109 E 4 *Rus.* Nikolayev.
  S Ukraine
Mýkonos 105 D 6 *var.* Mikonos.
  Island, Kykládes, SE Greece
Myrhorod 109 F 2 *Rus.* Mirgorod.
  NE Ukraine
Mýrina 104 D 4 *var.* Mírina.
  Límnos, SE Greece
Myrtle Beach 43 F 2
  South Carolina, SE USA
Mýrtos 105 D 8 Kríti, SE Greece
Mysore 132 C 2 *var.* Maisur W India
My Tho 137 E 6 *var.* Mi Tho.
  S Vietnam
Mytilíni 105 D 5 *var.* Mitilíni;
  anc. Mytilene. Lésvos, E Greece
Mytishchi 111 B 5
  W Russian Federation
Mzuzu 79 E 2 N Malawi

N

Naberezhnyye Chelny 111 D 5 *prev.*
  Brezhnev. W Russian Federation
Nablus 119 E 7 *var.* Nābulus,
  Heb. Shekhem; *anc.* Neapolis,
  Bibl. Shechem. N West Bank
Nacala 79 F 2 NE Mozambique
Nacogdoches 49 H 3 Texas, S USA
Nadi 145 E 4 *prev.* Nandi. Viti Levu,
  W Fiji
Nadvirna 108 B 3 *Pol.* Nadwóma,
  Rus. Nadvornaya. W Ukraine
Nadvoicy *see* Nadvoitsy
Nadvoitsy 110 B 3 *var.* Nadvoicy.
  NW Russian Federation
Nadym 114 D 3

Nadym 114 D 3 river,
  C Russian Federation
Náfpaktos 105 B 5
  var. Návpaktos. C Greece
Náfplio 105 B 6
  prev. Návplion. S Greece
Naga 139 E 1 *off.* Naga City;
  prev. Nueva Caceres. Luzon,
  N Philippines
Nagano 131 D 5 Honshū, S Japan
Nagaoka 131 D 5 Honshū, C Japan
Nagasaki 131 A 7 Kyūshū,
  SW Japan
Nagato 131 A 7 Honshū, SW Japan
Nāgercoil 132 C 3 SE India
Nagornyy Karabakh 117 G 3 *var.*
  Avtonomnaya Oblast Nagorno-
  Karabakhskaya, *Arm.* Lerrnayin
  Gharabakh, *Az.* Dağlïq Quarabağ.
  Former autonomous region,
  SW Azerbaijan
Nagoya 131 C 6 Honshū, SW Japan
Nāgpur 134 D 4 C India
Nagqu 126 C 5 *Chin.* Na-Ch'ii;
  prev. Hei-ho. W China
Nagykálló 99 E 6 E Hungary
Nagykanizsa 99 B 7
  Ger. Grosskanizsa. SW Hungary
Nagykőrös 99 D 7 C Hungary
Nagysurány *see* Šurany
Nagyszalonta *see* Salonta
Nagytapolcsány *see* Topoľčany
Naḩal Elisha 119 E 7 E West Bank
Nahariya *see* Nahariyya
Nahariyya 119 A 5 *var.* Nahariya.
  N Israel
Nahuel Huapí, Lago 65 B 5 lake,
  W Argentina
Nain 39 F 2 Newfoundland and
  Labrador, NE Canada
Na'īn 120 D 3 C Iran
Nairobi 73 C 6 country capital,
  S Kenya
Najaf *see* An Najaf
Najin 128 E 3 NE North Korea
Najrān 121 B 6 *var.* Abā as Su'ūd.
  S Saudi Arabia
Nakamura 131 B 7 Shikoku,
  SW Japan
Nakatsugawa 131 C 6 *var.*
  Nakatugawa. Honshū, SW Japan
Nakatugawa *see* Nakatsugawa
Nakhichevan' *see* Naxçıvan
Nakhodka 115 G 5
  SE Russian Federation
Nakhon Pathom 137 C 5 *var.*
  Nagara Pathom, Nakorn Pathom.
  C Thailand
Nakhon Ratchasima 137 C 5 *var.*
  Khorat, Korat. E Thailand
Nakhon Sawan 137 C 5 *var.* Muang
  Nakhon Sawan, Nagara Svarga.
  W Thailand
Nakhon Si Thammarat 137 C 7
  var. Nagara Sridharmaraj,
  Nakhon Sithamnaraj. S Thailand
Nakina 38 C 3 British Columbia,
  W Canada
Nalayh 127 E 2 C Mongolia
Nal'chik 111 B 8
  SW Russian Federation
Namangan 123 F 2 E Uzbekistan
Nam Co 126 C 5 *var.* W China
Nam Đinh 136 D 3 N Vietnam
Namen *see* Namur
Namibe 78 A 2 *Port.* Moçâmedes,
  Mossâmedes. SW Angola

amibia
78 B 3 *Afr.* Suidwes-Afrika, *Eng.*
South West Africa, *Ger.* Deutsch-
Südwestafrika; *prev.* German
Southwest Africa, South-West
Africa. Republic, S Africa

fficial name: Republic of Namibia
ate of formation: 1990/1994
apital: Windhoek **Population:**
 million **Total area:** 318,260 sq miles
24,290 sq km) **Languages:**
glish*, Afrikaans, Ovambo
ligions: Christian 90%, other 10%
hnic mix: Ovambo 50%, Kavango
%, Herero 7%, Damara 7%,
her 27% **Government:** Multiparty
public **Currency:** Rand = 100 cents

am Ngum 136 D 4 river, C Laos
amo *see* Namu Atoll
am Ou 136 C 3 river, N Laos
ampa 46 D 3 Idaho, NW USA
ampula 79 E 2 NE Mozambique
amrole 139 F 4 E Indonesia
amsos 84 B 4 C Norway
amu 36 D 5 British Columbia,
SW Canada
amu 144 D 2 island,
C Marshall Islands
amur 87 C 6 *Dut.* Namen.
SE Belgium
an 136 C 4 *var.* Muang Nan.
N Thailand
anaimo 36 D 5 Vancouver Island,
SW Canada
anchang 129 C 5 *var.* Nan-ch'ang,
Nanch'ang-hsien. Province
capital, SE China
ancy 90 D 3 NE France
andaime 52 D 4 SW Nicaragua
inded 134 D 5 C India
andi *see* Nadi
andyāl 132 C 2 E India
aniwa *see* Ōsaka
anjing 129 D 5 *var.* Nan-ching,
Nanking; *prev.* Chian-ning,
Chianning, Kiang-ning.
Province capital, E China
anning 129 B 6 *var.* Nan-ning;
prev. Yung-ning. Autonomous
region capital, S China
anortalik 82 C 5 S Greenland
anping 129 D 6 *var.* Nan-p'ing;
prev. Yenping. E China
ansei-shotō 130 A 2 *var.* Ryukyu
Islands. Island group, Japan
ansei Syotō Trench *see*
Ryukyu Trench
ansen Basin 155 G 4 undersea
basin, Arctic Ocean
ansen Cordillera 155 G 3
seamount range, Arctic Ocean
ansha Qundao *see* Spratly Islands
anterre 90 C 3 N France
antes 90 A 4 *Bret.* Naoned; *anc.*
Condivincum, Namnetes.
NW France
antucket Island 41 G 3 island,
Massachusetts, NE USA
anumaga 145 E 3 *var.*
Nanumanga. Island, NW Tuvalu
anumanga *see* Nanumaga
anumea 145 E 3 island, NW Tuvalu
anyang 129 C 5 *var.* Nan-yang.
C China
an-yang *see* Nanyang
iapa 47 B 6 California, W USA
iapier 150 E 4 North Island,
N New Zealand
iaples 43 E 5 Florida, SE USA
iaples *see* Napoli

Napo 60 C 1 river, Ecuador/Peru
Napoli 97 D 5 *Eng.* Naples,
Ger. Neapel; *anc.* Neapolis.
S Italy
Naracoorte 149 B 7 South Australia,
S Australia
Naradhivas *see* Narathiwat
Narathiwat 137 C 7 *var.*
Naradhivas. S Thailand
Narbo Martius *see* Narbonne
Narbonne 91 C 6 *anc.* Narbo
Martius. S France
Narborough Island *see*
Fernandina, Isla
Nares Abyssal Plain *see* Nares Plain
Nares Plain 35 E 6 *var.* Nares
Abyssal Plain. Abyssal plain,
NW Atlantic Ocean
Nares Strait 82 D 1 *Dan.* Nares
Stræde. Strait, S Lincoln Sea
Nares Stræde *see* Nares Strait
Narew 98 E 3 river, E Poland
Narova *see* Narva
Narovlya *see* Narowlya
Narowlya 107 C 8 *Rus.* Narovlya.
SE Belarus
Närpes 85 D 5 *Fin.* Närpiö.
W Finland
Närpiö *see* Närpes
Narrogin 147 B 7 SW Australia
Narsaq 82 C 4 *var.* Narssaq.
SW Greenland
Narsaq Kujallea 82 C 5
Dan. Frederiksdal. S Greenland
Narssaq *see* Narsaq
Narva 106 E 2 NE Estonia
Narva 106 E 2 *prev.* Narova. River,
Estonia/Russian Federation
Narva Bay 106 E 2 *Est.* Narva Laht,
Ger. Narwa-Bucht. *Rus.* Narvskiy
Zaliv. Bay, E Baltic Sea
Narva Reservoir 106 E 2 *Est.* Narva
Veehoidla, *Rus.* Narvskoye
Vodokhranilishche. Reservoir,
Estonia/Russian Federation
Narvik 84 C 3 N Norway
Nar'yan-Mar 110 D 3 *var.* Narjan-
Mar, Nar'jan-Mar; *prev.*
Dzerzhinskiy, Beloshchel'ye.
NW Russian Federation
Naryn 123 G 2 C Kyrgyzstan
Năsăud 108 B 3 *Ger.* Nussdorf,
Hung. Naszód. N Romania
Nāshik 134 C 5 *prev.* Nāsik. W India
Nashua 41 G 3 New Hampshire,
NE USA
Nashville 42 C 1 state capital,
Tennessee, S USA
Näsijärvi 85 D 5 lake, SW Finland
Nāsik *see* Nāshik
Nasiriya *see* An Nāşirīyah
Nassau 54 C 1 country capital,
C Bahamas
Nasser, Lake 68 D 3 lake,
Egypt/Sudan
Nata 78 C 3 NE Botswana
Natal 63 G 2 state capital, E Brazil
Natal Basin 141 A 6 *var.*
Mozambique Basin. Undersea
basin, SW Indian Ocean
Natchitoches 42 A 3
Louisiana, S USA
National City 47 C 8
California, W USA
Natitingou 75 F 4 NW Benin
Natuna, Kepulauan 138 C 3 island
group, W Indonesia
Naturaliste Plateau 141 E 6
undersea plateau, E Indian Ocean
Naujamiestis 106 C 4 C Lithuania
Nauru 144 D 2 island,
W Pacific Ocean

Nauru
144 D 3 *prev.* Pleasant Island.
Republic, W Pacific Ocean

Official name: Republic of Nauru
Date of formation: 1968
Capital: No offical Capital
Population: 10,000 **Total Area:**
8.2 sq miles (21.2 sq km)
Languages: Nauruan*, English
Religions: Christian 95%, other 5%
Ethnic mix: Nauruan 58%, other
Pacific Islanders 26%, Chinese 8%,
European 8% **Government:**
Parliamentary democracy
Currency: Australian $ = 100 cents

Nauta 60 C 2 N Peru
Navahrudak 107 C 6 *Pol.*
Nowogródek, *Rus.* Novogrudok.
W Belarus
Navanagar *see* Jāmnagar
Navapolatsk 107 D 5
Rus. Novopolotsk. N Belarus
Navarra 93 E 2 cultural region,
N Spain
Navassa Island 54 D 3
US unincorporated territory,
N Caribbean Sea
Navoi *see* Nawoiy
Navojoa 50 B 2 NW Mexico
Navolat 50 C 3 *var.* Navolato.
C Mexico
Navolato *see* Navolat
Návpaktos *see* Náfpaktos
Návplion *see* Náfplio
Nawabashah *see* Nawābshāh
Nawābshāh 134 B 3 *var.*
Nawabashah. S Pakistan
Nawoiy 123 E 2 *Rus.* Navoi.
C Uzbekistan
Naxçıvan 117 G 3 *Rus.*
Nakhichevan'. SW Azerbaijan
Náxos *see* Náxos
Náxos 105 D 6 *var.* Naxos. Náxos,
SE Greece
Náxos 105 D 6 island, Kykládes,
SE Greece
Nayoro 130 D 2 Hokkaidō, NE Japan
Nazca 60 D 4 S Peru
Nazca Ridge 57 A 5 undersea ridge,
E Pacific Ocean
Naze 130 B 3 Nansei-shotō, S Japan
Nazerat 119 A 5 *Ar.* En Nazira,
Heb. Nazareth. N Israel
Nazilli 116 A 4 SW Turkey
Nazrēt 73 C 5 *var.* Adama, Hadama.
C Ethiopia
N'Dalatando 78 B 1 *var.* Salazar,
Port. Vila Salazar. NW Angola
Ndélé 76 C 4
N Central African Republic
Ndendé 77 A 6 S Gabon
Ndindi 77 A 6 S Gabon
Ndjamena 76 B 3 *var.* N'Djamena,
prev. Fort-Lamy. Country capital,
W Chad
Ndjolé 77 A 5 C Gabon
Ndola 78 D 2 C Zambia
Neagh, Lough 89 B 5 lake,
E Northern Ireland, UK
Néa Moudhaniá 104 C 4 *var.* Néa
Moudhaniá. N Greece
Néa Moudhaniá *see* Néa Moudaniá
Neápoli 104 B 4 *prev.* Neápolis.
N Greece
Neápoli 105 C 7 SE Greece
Neápoli 105 D 8 Kríti, SE Greece
Neápolis *see* Neápoli
Néa Zíchni 104 C 3 *var.* Néa Zíkhni;
prev. Néa Zíkhna. NE Greece
Nebaj 52 B 2 W Guatemala

Nebitdag 122 B 2 W Turkmenistan
Neblina, Pico da 62 D 1 mountain,
NW Brazil
Nebraska 44 D 4 *off.* State of
Nebraska; *nicknames* Blackwater
State, Cornhusker State, Tree
Planters State. State, C USA
Nebraska City 45 F 4
Nebraska, C USA
Neches River 49 H 3 river,
Texas, S USA
Neckar 95 B 6 river,
SW Germany
Necochea 65 D 5 E Argentina
Necocli 58 A 2 NW Colombia
Nederland 49 H 4 Texas, S USA
Nederweert 87 D 5
SE Netherlands
Neede 86 E 3 E Netherlands
Neerpelt 87 D 5 NE Belgium
Neftekamsk 111 D 5
W Russian Federation
Neftezavodsk *see* Seydi
Negēlē 73 D 5 *var.* Negelli,
It. Neghelli. S Ethiopia
Negev *see* HaNegev
Negomane 79 E 2 *var.* Negomano.
N Mozambique
Negomano *see* Negomane
Negombo 132 C 3 SW Sri Lanka
Negotin 100 E 4 E Yugoslavia
Negra, Punta 60 A 3 headland,
NW Peru
Negreşti-Oaş 108 B 3
Hung. Avasfelsőfalu;
prev. Negreşti. NE Romania
Negro, Río 65 C 5 river,
Brazil/Uruguay
Negro, Río 62 D 1 river,
N South America
Negros 139 E 2 island, Visayan
Islands, C Philippines
Nehbandān 120 E 3 E Iran
Neijiang 129 B 5 C China
Nei Mongol Zizhiqu 127 F 3
var. Nei Mongol, *Eng.* Inner
Mongolian Autonomous
Region, Inner Mongolia;
prev. Nei Monggol Zizhiqu.
Autonomous region,
N China
Neiva 58 B 3 S Colombia
Nellore 132 D 2 E India
Nelson 151 C 5 South Island,
C New Zealand
Neman 106 B 4 *Bel.* Nyoman,
Ger. Memel, *Lith.* Nemunas,
Pol. Niemen. River, NE Europe
Neman 106 B 4 *Ger.* Ragnit.
W Russian Federation
Neméa 105 B 6 S Greece
Nemetocenna *see* Arras
Nemours 90 C 4 N France
Nemuro 130 E 2 Hokkaidō,
NE Japan
Neochóri 105 B 5 C Greece

Nepal
135 E 3 . Monarchy, S Asia

Official name: Kingdom of Nepal
Date of formation: 1769 Capital:
Kathmandu **Population:** 21.1 million
Total Area: 54,363 sq miles
(140,800 sq km) **Languages:**
Nepali*, Maithili **Religions:** Hindu
90%, Buddhist 5%, Muslim 3%,
other 17% **Ethnic mix:** Nepalese 58%,
Bihari 19%, Tamang 6%,
other 17% **Government:**
Constitutional monarchy
Currency: Rupee = 100 paisa

Nepean 38 D 5 Ontario, SE Canada
Nereta 106 C 4 S Latvia
Neretava 100 C 4 river,
Bosnia & Herzegovina/Croatia
Neringa 106 A 3 *Ger.* Nidden;
prev. Nida. SW Lithuania
Neris 107 C 5 *Bel.* Viliya,
Pol. Wilia; *prev. Pol.* Wilja.
River, Belarus/Lithuania
Nerva 92 C 4 S Spain
Neskaupstadhur 83 E 5 E Iceland
Ness, Loch 88 C 3 lake, N Scotland, UK
Néstos 104 C 3 *Bul.* Mesta, *Turk.*
Kara Su. River, Bulgaria/Greece
Netanya 119 A 6 *var.* Natanya,
Nathanya. C Israel

Netherlands
86 C 3 *var.* Holland, *Dut.*
Koninkrijk der Nederlanden,
Nederland. Monarchy, W Europe

Official name: Kingdom of the
Netherlands **Date of formation:**
1815/1890 **Capitals:** Amsterdam,
The Hague **Population:** 15.3 million
Total area: 14,410 sq miles
(37,330 sq km) **Languages:** Dutch*,
Frisian **Religions:** Roman Catholic
36%, Protestant 27%, other 37%
Ethnic mix: Dutch 96%, other 4%
Government: Constitutional monarchy
Currency: Guilder = 100 cents

Netherlands Antilles 55 F 5
prev. Dutch West Indies.
Autonomous region of
Netherlands, S Caribbean Sea
Nettilling Lake 82 A 2 lake, N Canada
Netze see Noteć
Neu Amerika see Puławy
Neubrandenburg 94 D 3 NE Germany
Neuchâtel, Lac de 95 A 7
Ger. Neuenburger See. Lake,
W Switzerland
Neuenburger See see Neuchâtel,
Lac de
Neufchâteau 87 D 8 SE Belgium
Neukuhren see Pionerskiy
Neumünster 94 B 2 N Germany
Neunkirchen 95 A 5 SW Germany
Neunkirchen 95 E 6 *var.*
Neunkirchen am Steinfeld E Austria
Neunkirchen am Steinfeld see
Neunkirchen
Neuquén 65 B 5 SE Argentina
Neuruppin 94 C 3 NE Germany
Neu Sandec see Nowy Sącz
Neusiedler See 95 E 6 *Hung.* Fertő.
Lake, Austria/Hungary
Neustadt an der Weinstrasse 95 B 5
prev. Neustadt an der Haardt;
hist. Niewenstat, *anc.* Nova
Civitas. SW Germany
Neustettin see Szczecinek
Neustrelitz 94 D 3 NE Germany
Neu-Ulm 95 B 6 S Germany
Neuwied 95 A 5 W Germany
Neuzen see Terneuzen
Nevada 47 C 5 *off.* State of Nevada;
nicknames Battle Born State,
Sagebrush State, Silver State.
State, W USA
Nevada, Sierra 92 D 5 mountain
range, S Spain
Nevers 90 C 4 *anc.* Noviodunum.
C France
Nevinnomyssk 111 B 7
SW Russian Federation
Nevşehir 116 C 3 *var.* Nevsehir.
C Turkey
Nevsehir see Nevşehir
Newala 73 D 8 SE Tanzania

New Albany 42 C 2 Mississippi, S USA
New Albany 40 C 5 Indiana, N USA
New Amsterdam 59 G 3 E Guyana
Newark 41 F 4 New Jersey, N USA
Newark 40 D 4 Ohio, NE USA
New Bedford 41 G 3
Massachusetts, NE USA
Newberg 46 B 3 Oregon, NW USA
New Bern 43 F 1
North Carolina, SE USA
New Braunfels 49 G 4 Texas, S USA
Newbridge 89 B 6 *Ir.* An Droichead
Nua. C Ireland
New Britain 41 G 3
Connecticut, NE USA
New Britain 144 B 3 island,
E Papua New Guinea
New Brunswick 39 F 4
Fr. Nouveau-Brunswick.
Province, SE Canada
New Caledonia 144 C 4 *var.*
Kanaky, *Fr.* Nouvelle-Calédonie.
French overseas territory,
S Pacific Ocean
New Caledonia 144 C 5 island,
S New Caledonia
New Caledonia Basin 152 C 4
undersea basin, W Pacific Ocean
Newcastle 149 D 6 New South
Wales, SE Australia
Newcastle upon Tyne 88 D 4
var. Newcastle; *hist.* Monkchester,
Lat. Pons Aelii. N England, UK
New Delhi 134 D 3 country capital,
N India
Newfoundland 39 G 3 *Fr.* Terre-
Neuve. Island, Newfoundland
and Labrador, SE Canada
Newfoundland & Labrador 39 F 2
Fr. Terre Neuve. Province, E Canada
Newfoundland Basin 66 B 3
undersea basin, NW Atlantic Ocean
New Georgia Islands 144 C 3
island group, NW Solomon Islands
New Glasgow 39 F 4 Nova Scotia,
SE Canada
New Guinea 144 A 3 *Dut.* Nieuw
Guinea, *Ind.* Irian. Island,
Indonesia/Papua New Guinea
New Hampshire 41 F 2 *off.* State of
New Hampshire; *nickname*
Granite State. State, NE USA
New Haven 41 G 3
Connecticut, NE USA
New Iberia 42 B 3 Louisiana, S USA
New Ireland 144 C 3 island,
NE Papua New Guinea
New Jersey 41 F 4 *off.* State of New
Jersey; *nickname* Garden State.
State, E USA
Newman 146 B 4 Western
Australia, W Australia
Newmarket 89 E 6 E England, UK
New Mexico 48 C 2 *off.* State of
New Mexico; *nicknames* Land of
Enchantment, Sunshine State.
State, SW USA
New Orleans 42 B 3 Louisiana, S USA
New Plymouth 150 D 4
North Island, C New Zealand
Newport 89 D 7 S England, UK
Newport 89 D 7 SE Wales, UK
Newport 42 B 1 Arkansas, C USA
Newport 40 C 4 Kentucky, E USA
Newport 41 G 2 Maine, NE USA
Newport News 41 F 5
Virginia, NE USA
New Providence 54 C 1 island,
N Bahamas
Newquay 89 B 7 SW England, UK
Newry 89 B 5 *Ir.* An tIúr.
SE Northern Ireland, UK

Newry 146 D 3 N Australia
New Sarum see Salisbury
New Siberian Islands see
Novosibirskiye Ostrova
New Smyrna Beach 43 E 4
Florida, SE USA
New South Wales 149 C 6 state,
SE Australia
New Territories 128 A 1
geopolitical region, N Hong Kong
Newton 45 F 5 Iowa, C USA
Newton 45 G 3 Kansas, C USA
Newtownabbey 89 B 5
Ir. Baile na Mainistreach.
E Northern Ireland, UK
New Ulm 45 F 3 Minnesota, N USA
New York 41 F 3 New York, NE USA
New York 41 E 3 state, NE USA

New Zealand
150 A 4 Commonwealth republic,
SW Pacific Ocean

Official name: The Dominion of
New Zealand **Date of formation:**
1947 **Capital:** Wellington
Population: 3.5 million **Total Area:**
103,730 sq miles (268,680 sq km)
Languages: English*, Maori
Religions: Protestant 62%, Roman
Catholic 18%, other 20% **Ethnic mix:**
European 88%, Maori 9%, other 3%
Government: Constitutional
monarchy **Currency:** NZ $ = 100 cents

Neyveli 132 C 2 SE India
Nezhin see Nizhyn
Ngabang 138 C 4 Borneo,
C Indonesia
Ngangzê Co 126 B 5 lake, W China
N'Gaoundéré see Ngaoundéré
Ngaoundéré 76 B 4
var. Ngaoundéré. N Cameroon
N'Giva 78 B 3 *var.* Ondjiva,
Port. Vila Pereira de Eça.
S Angola
Ngo 77 B 6 SE Congo
Ngoko 77 B 5 river,
Cameroon/Congo
Ngorongoro Crater 69 D 5 crater,
N Tanzania
Ngourti 75 H 3 E Niger
N'Guigmi see Nguigmi
Nguigmi 75 H 3 *var.* N'Guigmi.
SE Niger
Nguru 75 G 4 NE Nigeria
Nha Trang 137 E 6 SE Vietnam
Niagara Falls 38 D 5 Ontario,
S Canada
Niagara Falls 41 E 3 New York,
NE USA
Niagara Falls 35 D 5 waterfall,
Canada/USA
Niamey 75 F 3 country capital,
SW Niger
Niangay, Lac 75 E 3 lake, E Mali
Nia-Nia 77 D 5 NE Congo (Zaire)
Nias, Pulau 138 A 3 island,
W Indonesia

Nicaragua
52 D 3 Republic, C Central America

Official name: Republic of
Nicaragua **Date of formation:** 1838
Capital: Managua **Population:** 4.1
million **Total area:** 50,193 sq miles
(130,000 sq km) **Languages:**
Spanish*, English Creole, Miskito
Religions: Roman Catholic 95%,
other 5% **Ethnic mix:** *mestizo* 69%,
White 17%, Black 9%, Indian 5%
Government: Multiparty republic
Currency: Córdoba = 100 pence

Nicaragua, Lago de 52 D 4
var. Cocibolca, Gran Lago,
Eng. Lake Nicaragua. Lake,
S Nicaragua
Nicaragua, Lake see
Nicaragua, Lago de
Nicaragua, Republic of see
Nicaragua
Nice 91 D 6 *It.* Nizza; *anc.* Nicaea.
SE France
Nicholas II Land see
Severnaya Zemlya
Nicholls Town 54 C 1 NW Baham
Nicholson Range 147 B 5 mounta
range, W Australia
Nicobar Islands 133 F 3 island
group, SE India
Nicoya 52 D 4 W Costa Rica
Nicoya, Golfo de 52 D 5 gulf,
E Pacific Ocean
Nicoya, Península de 52 D 4
peninsula, NW Costa Rica
Nidzica 98 D 3 *Ger.* Niedenburg.
N Poland
Niedenburg see Nidzica
Niedere Tauern 95 D 7 mountain
range, C Austria
Nieuw Amsterdam 59 G 3
NE Suriname
Nieuw-Bergen 86 D 4
SE Netherlands
Nieuwegein 86 C 4 C Netherland
Nieuw Nickerie 59 G 3
NW Suriname
Niğde 116 C 4 S Turkey
Niger 75 F 4 river, W Africa

Niger
75 F 3 Republic, W Africa

Official name: Republic of Niger
Date of formation: 1960 **Capital:**
Niamey **Population:** 8.5 million
Total area: 489,188 sq miles
(1,267,000 sq km) **Languages:**
French*, Hausa, Djerma, Fulani
Religions: Muslim 85%, traditional
beliefs 14%, Christian 1% **Ethnic mi**
Hausa 56%, Djerma 22%, Fulani 9%
other 13% **Government:** Multiparty
republic **Currency:** CFA franc =
100 centimes

Nigeria
75 F 4 Nigeria. Federal republic,
W Africa

Official name: Federal Republic of
Nigeria **Date of formation:** 1960
Capital: Abuja **Population:** 115
million **Total area:** 356,668 sq miles
(923,770 sq km) **Languages:**
English*, Hausa, Yoruba, Ibo
Religions: Muslim 50%, Christian
40%, traditional beliefs 10%
Ethnic mix: Hausa 21%, Yoruba
20%, Ibo 17%, Fulani 9%, other 33%
Government: Military regime
Currency: Naira = 100 kobo

Niger, Mouths of the 75 G 5 delta,
S Nigeria
Niigata 131 D 5 Honshū, C Japan
Niihama 131 B 7 Japan
Niihau 47 A 7 island, Hawaii, W US,
Nii-jima 131 D 6 island, Izu-shotō,
E Japan
Nijkerk 86 D 3 C Netherlands
Nijlen 87 C 5 N Belgium
Nijmegen 86 D 4 *Ger.* Nimwegen;
anc. Noviomagus. SE Netherland
Nikel' 110 C 2
NW Russian Federation
Nikiniki 139 E 5 Timor,
S Indonesia

kólaos, Áyios *see* Ágios Nikólaos
kolayev *see* Mykolayiv
kopol' 109 F 3 SE Ukraine
kšić 101 C 5 SW Yugoslavia
kumaroro 145 F 3 *prev.* Gardner
 sland, Kemins Island. Island,
 C Kiribati
kunau 145 E 3 *var.* Nukunau;
 prev. Byron Island. Island,
 W Kiribati
 e 72 B 3 *Ar.* Nahr an Nīl. River,
 NE Africa
 e Delta 72 B 1 delta, N Egypt
 l, Nahr an *see* Nile
 mba, Mount 74 D 4 mountain,
 W Africa
 nes 91 C 6 *anc.* Nemausus,
 Nismes. S France
 nawé 117 F 5 N Iraq
 ne Degree Channel 132 B 3
 hannel, N Indian Ocean
 netyeast Ridge 141 D 5 undersea
 idge, E Indian Ocean
 igbo 129 D 5 *var.* Ning-po, Yin-
 sien; *prev.* Ninghsien. E China
 ngxia Huizu Zizhiqu 128 B 4
 autonomous region, N China
 o *see* Íos
 obrara River 45 E 3 river, C USA
 oro 74 D 3 *var.* Nioro du Sahel.
 W Mali
 oro du Sahel *see* Nioro
 ort 90 B 4 W France
 oigon 38 B 4 Ontario, S Canada
 oigon, Lake 38 B 3 lake, Ontario,
 S Canada
 š 101 E 5 *Eng.* Nish, *Ger.* Nisch;
 anc. Naissus. SE Yugoslavia
 jab 120 B 4 N Saudi Arabia
 sibin *see* Nusaybin
 siros *see* Nísyros
 sko 98 E 4 SE Poland
 syros 105 E 7 *var.* Nisiros. Island,
 Dodekánisos, SE Greece
 ra 99 C 6 *Ger.* Neutra,
 Hung. Nyitra. River, W Slovakia
 ra 99 C 6 *Ger.* Neutra,
 Hung. Nyitra. SW Slovakia
 aatoputapu 145 E 4
 var. Niuatobutabu; *prev.* Keppel
 sland. Island, N Tonga
 ue 145 F 4 self-governing
 erritory, S Pacific Ocean
 alakita 145 E 3 *var.* Nurakita.
 sland, S Tuvalu
 atao 145 E 3 island, NW Tuvalu
 vernais 90 C 4 cultural region,
 C France
 zāmābād 134 D 5 C India
 zhnegorskiy *see* Nyzhn'ohirs'kyy
 zhnekamsk 111 C 5
 W Russian Federation
 zhnevartovsk 114 D 3
 C Russian Federation
 zhniy Novgorod 111 C 5 *prev.*
 Gor'kiy. W Russian Federation
 zhniy Odes 110 D 4 *var.*
 Nižni Odes, Nižnij Odes.
 NW Russian Federation
 zhnyaya Tunguska 115 E 3
 Eng. Lower Tunguska. River,
 C Russian Federation
 zhyn 109 E 1 *Rus.* Nezhin.
 NE Ukraine
 ombe 73 C 8 S Tanzania
 ayi 77 B 6 *prev.* Jacob. S Congo
 hotakosi 79 E 2 *var.* Kota Kota.
 C Malawi
 Kongsamba *see* Nkongsamba

Nkongsamba 76 A 4 *var.*
 N'Kongsamba. W Cameroon
Nobeoka 131 B 7 Kyūshū, SW Japan
Noboribetsu 130 D 3 *var.*
 Noboribetu. Hokkaidō, NE Japan
Noboribetu *see* Noboribetsu
Nogales 48 B 3 Arizona, SW USA
Nogales 50 B 1 NW Mexico
Nogal Valley *see* Dooxo Nugaaleed
Nokia 85 D 5 SW Finland
Nokou 76 B 3 SW Chad
Nola 77 B 5
 SW Central African Republic
Nolinsk 111 D 5
 NW Russian Federation
Nong Chang 137 C 5 W Thailand
Nong Khai 136 D 4 *var.* Mi Chai,
 Nongkaya. NE Thailand
Nonouti 145 E 2 *prev.* Sydenham
 Island. Island, W Kiribati
Noord-Beveland *see* Noord-Beveland
Noordoewer 78 B 4 S Namibia
Noordwijk aan Zee 86 C 3
 W Netherlands
Nora 85 C 6 C Sweden
Norak 123 E 3 *Rus.* Nurek.
 W Tajikistan
Nord 83 F 1 N Greenland
Nordaustlandet 83 G 1 island,
 NE Svalbard
Norden 94 A 3 NW Germany
Norderstedt 94 B 3 N Germany
Nordfriesische Inseln 94 B 2
 var. North Frisian Islands. Island
 group, N Germany
Nordhausen 94 C 4 C Germany
Nordhorn 94 A 3 NW Germany
Nordkapp 84 D 1 *Eng.* North Cape.
 Headland, N Norway
Nord-Ouest, Territoires du *see*
 Northwest Territories
Norfolk 45 F 3 Virginia, NE USA
Norfolk 45 F 3 Nebraska, C USA
Norfolk Ridge 142 D 4 undersea
 ridge, W Pacific Ocean
Noril'sk 114 D 3
 N Russian Federation
Normal 40 B 4 Illinois, N USA
Norman 49 G 2 Oklahoma, C USA
Normandes, Iles *see* Channel Islands
Normandie 90 B 3 *Eng.* Normandy.
 Cultural region, N France
Normandy *see* Normandie
Normanton 148 C 3 Queensland,
 NE Australia
Norquay 37 F 5
 Saskatchewan, S Canada
Norrköping 85 C 6 S Sweden
Norrtälje 85 C 6 C Sweden
Norseman 147 C 6 Western
 Australia, SW Australia
North Albanian Alps 101 D 5
 Alb. Bjeshkët e Namuna,
 SCr. Prokletije. Mountain range,
 Albania/Yugoslavia
Northallerton 89 D 5 N England, UK
Northam 147 B 6 Western Australia,
 SW Australia
North America 66 A 3 continent
North American Basin 66 B 3
 undersea basin, W Atlantic Ocean
Northampton 89 D 6 C England, UK
Northampton 147 A 6 W Australia
North Andaman 133 F 2 island,
 E India
North Australian Basin 152 A 3
 Fr. Bassin Nord de l' Australie.
 Undersea basin, E Indian Ocean
North Bay 38 D 4 Ontario,
 S Canada

North Beveland *see* Noord-Beveland
North Cape 150 C 1 headland,
 North Island, N New Zealand
North Cape *see* Nordkapp
North Carolina 43 E 1 *off.* State of
 North Carolina; *nicknames* Old
 North State, Tar Heel State,
 Turpentine State. State, SE USA
North Charleston 43 F 2
 South Carolina, SE USA
North Dakota 45 E 1 *off.* State of
 North Dakota; *nicknames*
 Flickertail State, Peace Garden
 State, Sioux State. State, N USA
North Devon Island *see*
 Devon Island
Northeim 94 B 4 C Germany
Northern Cook Islands 145 G 4
 island group, N Cook Islands
Northern Dvina *see*
 Severnaya Dvina
Northern Ireland 88 B 4 *var.* the Six
 Counties. Political division, UK
Northern Mariana Islands 144 C 1
 US commonwealth territory,
 W Pacific Ocean
Northern Territory 148 A 3
 territory, N Australia
Northfield 45 G 2 Minnesota, N USA
North Fiji Basin 152 C 3 undersea
 basin, SW Pacific Ocean
North Frisian Islands *see*
 Nordfriesische Inseln
North German Plain *see*
 Norddeutsches Tiefland
North Huvadhu Atoll 132 B 5
 var. Gaafu Alifu Atoll. Island,
 S Maldives
North Island 150 B 2 island,
 North Island, N New Zealand

North Korea
128 E 3 *Kor.* Chosŏn-minjujuŭi-
 inmin-kanghwaguk. Republic,
 E Asia

Official name: Democratic People's
 Republic of Korea **Date of
 formation:** 1948 **Capital:** Pyongyang
 Population: 23.1 million **Total Area:**
 46,540 sq miles (120,540 sq km)
 Languages: Korean*, Chinese
 Religions: Traditional beliefs 16%,
 Ch'ondogyo 14%, Buddhist 2%,
 non-religious 68% **Ethnic mix:**
 Korean 99%, other 1% **Government:**
 Single-party republic
 Currency: Won = 100 chon

North Las Vegas 47 D 7
 Nevada, W USA
North Little Rock 42 B 1
 Arkansas, C USA
North Minch *see* Minch, The
North Mole 93 H 4
 harbour wall, N Gibraltar
North Platte 45 E 4
 Nebraska, C USA
North Platte River 44 D 4
 river, N USA
North Pole 155 F 3 pole,
 Arctic Ocean
North Saskatchewan 37 F 5 river,
 S Canada
North Scotia Ridge *see*
 South Georgia Ridge
North Sea 66 D 2 *var.* Mare
 Germanicum, *Dan.* Nordsøen,
 Dut. Noordzee, *Fr.* Mer du Nord,
 prev. German Ocean, Sea,
 NE Atlantic Ocean
North Siberian Plain 112 D 2 plain,
 N Russian Federation

North Taranaki Bight 150 D 3
 bight, E Tasman Sea
North Uist 88 B 3 island,
 NW Scotland, UK
Northwest Atlantic Mid-Ocean
 Canyon 66 B 2 trough,
 NW Atlantic Ocean
North West Highlands 88 C 3
 mountain range, NW Scotland, UK
Northwest Pacific Basin 152 C 2
 undersea basin, NW Pacific Ocean
Northwest Providence 54 C 1
 channel, N Caribbean Sea
Northwest Territories 37 E 3
 Fr. Territoires du Nord-Ouest.
 Territory, NW Canada
Northwind Plain 155 F 2 abyssal
 plain, Arctic Ocean
Norton Sound 36 C 2 inlet,
 N Bering Sea

Norway
85 A 5 *Nor.* Norge. Monarchy,
 N Europe

Official name: Kingdom of Norway
 Date of formation: 1905/1930
 Capital: Oslo **Population:** 4.3
 million **Total area:** 125,060 sq miles
 (323,900 sq km) **Languages:**
 Norwegian (*Bokmål* and *Nynorsk*)*,
 Lappish, Finnish **Religions:**
 Evangelical Lutheran 88%,
 other Christian 12%
 Ethnic mix: Norwegian 95%, Lapp
 1%,other 4% **Government:**
 Constitutional monarchy
 Currency: Krone = 100 øre

Norwegian Basin 66 D 2 undersea
 basin, NE Atlantic Ocean
Norwegian Sea 66 D 2 *var.* Norske
 Havet, Norskehavet. Sea,
 NE Atlantic Ocean
Norwich 89 E 6 E England, UK
Noshiro 130 D 4 *var.* Nosiro; *prev.*
 Noshiromination. Honshū, C Japan
Nosivka 109 E 1 *Rus.* Nosovka.
 NE Ukraine
Nosop 78 C 4 *var.* Nossob, Nossop.
 River, Botswana/Namibia
Nosovka *see* Nosivka
Noşratābād 120 E 3 E Iran
Notabile *see* Mdina
Noteć 98 C 3 *Ger.* Netze. River,
 NW Poland
Nottingham 89 D 6 C England, UK
Nouâdhibou 74 B 2 *prev.* Port-
 Étienne. W Mauritania
Nouakchott 74 B 2 country capital,
 SW Mauritania
Nouméa 144 D 5 dependent
 territory capital, S New Caledonia
Nouveau-Brunswick *see*
 New Brunswick
Nouvelle Écosse *see* Nova Scotia
Nova Freixo *see* Cuamba
Nova Gorica 95 D 8 W Slovenia
Nova Gradiška 100 C 3 *var.*
 Neugradiska, *Hung.* Újgradiska.
 NE Croatia
Nova Iguaçu 63 F 4 SE Brazil
Nova Kakhovka 109 F 4 *Rus.*
 Novaya Kakhovka. SE Ukraine
Nova Lisboa *see* Huambo
Novara 96 A 2 *anc.* Novaria. NW Italy
Novaria *see* Novara
Nova Scotia 39 F 4 *Fr.* Nouvelle
 Écosse. Province, SE Canada
Nova Scotia 35 E 5 physical region,
 E Canada
Novaya Kakhovka *see*
 Nova Kakhovka

Novaya Sibir', Ostrov 115 F 1 island, Novosibirskiye Ostrova, N Russian Federation
Novaya Zemlya 110 D 1 island group, N Russian Federation
Novgorod 110 B 4 W Russian Federation
Novi Iskŭr *see* Novi Iskŭr
Novi Iskŭr 104 C 2 *var.* Novi Iskŭr. W Bulgaria
Noviodunum *see* Nevers
Noviomagus *see* Lisieux
Novi Pazar 101 D 5 *Turk.* Yenipazar. C Yugoslavia
Novi Sad 100 D 3 *Ger.* Neusatz, *Hung.* Újvidék. N Yugoslavia
Novoaleksejevka *see* Novoalekseyevka
Novoazovs'k 109 H 4 *Rus.* Novoazovsk. E Ukraine
Novoazovsk *see* Novoazovs'k
Novocherkassk 111 B 6 SW Russian Federation
Novodvinsk 110 C 3 NW Russian Federation
Novograd-Volynskiy *see* Novohrad-Volyns'kyy
Novohrad-Volyns'kyy 108 D 2 *Rus.* Novograd-Volynskiy. N Ukraine
Novokazalinsk 114 B 4 *Kaz.* Zhangaqazaly. SW Kazakhstan
Novokuznetsk 114 D 4 *prev.* Stalinsk. C Russian Federation
Novolazarevskaya 154 C 2 research station, Antarctica
Novo Mesto 95 E 8 *Ger.* Rudolfswert; *prev. Ger.* Neustadtl. SE Slovenia
Novomoskovsk 111 B 5 W Russian Federation
Novomoskovs'k 109 F 3 *Rus.* Novomoskovsk. C Ukraine
Novomoskovsk *see* Novomoskovs'k
Novopolotsk *see* Navapolatsk
Novoradomsk *see* Radomsko
Novorossiysk 111 A 7 SW Russian Federation
Novoshakhtinsk 111 B 7 SW Russian Federation
Novosibirsk 114 D 4 C Russian Federation
Novosibirskiye Ostrova 115 F 1 *Eng.* New Siberian Islands. Island group, N Russian Federation
Novosokol'niki 110 A 4 W Russian Federation
Novotroitsk 111 D 6 W Russian Federation
Novotroitskoye *see* Novotroyits'ke
Novotroyits'ke 109 F 4 *Rus.* Novotroitskoye. S Ukraine
Novovolyns'k 108 C 1 *Rus.* Novovolynsk. NW Ukraine
Novovolynsk *see* Novovolyns'k
Novy Dvor 107 B 6 *Rus.* Novyy Dvor. W Belarus
Novyy Bug *see* Novyy Buh
Novyy Buh 109 E 3 *Rus.* Novyy Bug. S Ukraine
Novyy Dvor *see* Novy Dvor
Novyy Uzen' 114 A 4 *Kaz.* Zhangaözen. W Kazakhstan
Nowogard 98 B 3 *var.* Nowógard, *Ger.* Naugard. NW Poland
Nowy Dwór Mazowiecki 98 D 3 C Poland
Nowy Sącz 99 D 5 *Ger.* Neu Sandec. S Poland
Nowy Tomyśl 98 B 3 *var.* Nowy Tomysl. W Poland
Nowy Tomysl *see* Nowy Tomyśl
Noyon 90 C 3 N France

Nsanje 79 E 3 S Malawi
Nsawam 75 E 5 SE Ghana
Ntomba, Lac 77 C 6 *var.* Lac Tumba. Lake, NW Congo (Zaire)
Nubian Desert 72 C 3 desert, NE Sudan
Nu'eima 119 E 7 E West Bank
Nueva Gerona 54 B 2 S Cuba
Nueva Rosita 50 D 2 NE Mexico
Nuevitas 54 C 2 E Cuba
Nuevo, Bajo 53 F 1 reef, NW Colombia
Nuevo Casas Grandes 50 C 1 N Mexico
Nuevo, Golfo 65 C 6 gulf, SW Atlantic Ocean
Nuevo Laredo 51 E 2 NE Mexico
Nûgâtsiaq *see* Nuugaatsiaq
Nui 145 E 3 island, W Tuvalu
Nuku' alofa 145 E 5 country capital, Tongatapu, S Tonga
Nukufetau 145 E 3 island, C Tuvalu
Nukulaelae 145 E 3 *var.* Nukulailai. Island, E Tuvalu
Nukulailai *see* Nukulaelae Atoll
Nukunonu Atoll 145 F 3 island, C Tokelau
Nukus 122 C 2 W Uzbekistan
Nullarbor 147 E 6 South Australia, S Australia
Nullarbor Plain 147 D 6 plateau, S Australia
Nuneaton 89 D 6 C England, UK
Nunivak Island 36 B 2 island, Alaska, NW USA
Nunspeet 86 D 3 E Netherlands
Nuoro 97 A 5 W Italy
Nuquí 58 A 3 W Colombia
Nurakita *see* Niulakita
Nurata *see* Nurota
Nurek *see* Norak
Nuremberg *see* Nürnberg
Nurlat 111 C 6 W Russian Federation
Nurmes 84 E 4 E Finland
Nürnberg 95 C 5 *Eng.* Nuremberg. S Germany
Nurota 123 E 2 *Rus.* Nurata. C Uzbekistan
Nusa Tenggara 139 E 5 *Eng.* Lesser Sunda Islands. Island group, C Indonesia
Nusaybin 117 F 4 *var.* Nisibin. SE Turkey
Nuşayrīyah, Jabal an 118 B 3 mountain range, W Syria
Nuugaatsiaq 82 C 3 *var.* Nûgâtsiaq. W Greenland
Nuuk 82 B 4 *var.* Nûk, *Dan.* Godthåb, Godthaab. Dependent territory capital, SW Greenland
Nuussuaq 82 C 2 *var.* Nûgssuaq, *Dan.* Kraulshavn. W Greenland
Nyainqêntanglha Shan 126 C 5 mountain range, W China
Nyala 72 A 4 W Sudan
Nyamapanda 78 D 3 NE Zimbabwe
Nyamlell 73 B 5 SW Sudan
Nyamtumbo 73 C 8 S Tanzania
Nyandoma 110 C 4 *var.* Njandoma, N'andoma. NW Russian Federation
Nyantakara 73 B 7 NW Tanzania
Nyasa, Lake 79 E 2 *var.* Lake Malawi, *Port.* Lago Niassa; *prev.* Lago Nyassa. Lake, S Africa
Nyasvizh 107 C 6 *Pol.* Nieśwież, *Rus.* Nesvizh. C Belarus
Nyaunglebin 136 B 4 S Myanmar
Nyeboe Land 83 E 1 physical region, NW Greenland
Nyeri 73 C 6 C Kenya

Nyima 126 C 5 W China
Nyíregyháza 99 E 6 NE Hungary
Nykobing 85 B 8 SE Denmark
Nyköping 85 C 6 S Sweden
Nylstroom 78 D 4 NE South Africa
Nyngan 149 C 6 New South Wales, SE Australia
Nyurba 115 F 3 E Russian Federation
Nyzhn'ohirs'kyy 109 F 5 *Rus.* Nizhnegorskiy. S Ukraine
Nzega 73 C 7 NW Tanzania
Nzérékoré 74 C 5 SE Guinea

O

Oahu 47 A 8 *Haw.* O'ahu. Island, Hawaii, W USA
O'ahu *see* Oahu
Oak Harbor 46 B 1 Washington, NW USA
Oakland 47 B 6 California, W USA
Oamaru 151 B 7 South Island, SW New Zealand
Oaxaca 51 F 5 *var.* Oaxaca de Juárez; *prev.* Antequera. SE Mexico
Ob' 114 C 3 river, C Russian Federation
Obal' 107 D 5 *Rus.* Obol'. N Belarus
Oban 88 B 4 W Scotland, UK
Oban *see* Halfmoon Bay
Obando *see* Puerto Inírida
Oban Hills 75 G 5 hill range, Cameroon/Nigeria
Obdorsk *see* Salekhard
Obeliai 106 C 4 NE Lithuania
Oberhollabrunn *see* Tulln
Ob, Gulf of *see* Obskaya Guba
Obidovichi *see* Abidavichy
Obihiro 130 D 2 Hokkaidō, NE Japan
Obo 76 D 4 C Central African Republic
Obock 72 D 4 E Djibouti
Obol' *see* Obal'
Oborniki 98 B 3 W Poland
Obrovo *see* Abrova
Obskaya Guba 114 D 2 *Eng.* Gulf of Ob. Gulf, N Kara Sea
Ocala 43 E 4 Florida, SE USA
Ocaña 92 D 3 C Spain
Ocaña 58 B 2 N Colombia
Ocean Falls 36 D 5 British Columbia, SW Canada
Ocean Island *see* Banaba
Oceanside 47 C 8 California, W USA
Ochakiv 109 E 4 *Rus.* Ochakov. S Ukraine
Ochakov *see* Ochakiv
Ochamchira *see* Och'amch'ire
Och'amch'ire 117 E 2 *Rus.* Ochamchira W Georgia
Ocho Rios 54 B 4 C Jamaica
Ocozocuautla 51 G 5 SE Mexico
October Revolution Island *see* Oktyabr'skoy Revolyutsii, Ostrov
Ocú 53 F 5 S Panama
Ödate 130 D 3 Honshū, C Japan
Ödenburg *see* Sopron
Odenpäh *see* Otepää
Odense 85 B 7 C Denmark
Oder 80 D 3 *Cz./Pol.* Odra. River, C Europe
Oderhaff 94 D 4 *var.* Stettiner Haff, Zalew Szczeciński. Bay, S Baltic Sea
Odesa 109 E 4 *Rus.* Odessa. SW Ukraine
Odessa 49 E 3 Texas, S USA
Odessa *see* Odesa

Odienné 74 D 4 NW Ivory Coast
Ôdôngk 137 D 6 S Cambodia
Odoorn 86 E 2 NE Netherlands
Odra *see* Oder
Oeiras 92 B 4 W Portugal
Of 117 E 2 NE Turkey
Ofanto 97 D 5 river, S Italy
Offenbach 95 B 5 *var.* Offenbach Main. W Germany
Offenbach am Main *see* Offenbach
Offenburg 95 B 6 SW Germany
Ôgaki 131 C 6 Honshū, SW Japan
Ogallala 44 D 4 Nebraska, C USA
Ogbomosho 75 F 4 W Nigeria
Ogden 44 B 4 Utah, W USA
Ogulin 100 B 3 NW Croatia
Ohio 40 C 4 *off.* State of Ohio; nickname Buckeye State. State, NE USA
Ohio River 40 C 4 river, N USA
Ohlau *see* Oława
Ohrid 101 D 6 *Turk.* Ochrida, Ohri SW Macedonia
Ohrid, Lake 101 D 6 *var.* Lake Ochrida, *Alb.* Liqeni i Ohrit, *Mac.* Ohridsko Ezero. Lake, Albania/Macedonia
Ohura 150 D 3 North Island, C New Zealand
Oildale 47 C 7 California, W USA
Oirschot 87 C 5 S Netherlands
Oise 90 C 3 river, N France
Oistins 55 G 2 S Barbados
Ôita 131 B 7 Kyūshū, SW Japan
Ojinaga 50 D 2 N Mexico
Ojos del Salado, Nevado 64 B 3 mountain, N Chile
Okaihau 150 C 2 North Island, N New Zealand
Okāra 134 C 2 E Pakistan
Okavango 78 C 3 *var.* Cubango, Kavango, Kavengo, Kubango, Okavanggo. River, S Africa
Okavango Delta 78 C 3 wetland, N Botswana
Okayama 131 B 6 Honshū, SW Jap
Okazaki 131 C 6 Honshū, C Japa
Okeechobee, Lake 43 E 4 lake, Florida, SE USA
Okhotsk 115 G 3 SE Russian Federation
Okhotsk, Sea of 152 C 1 sea, NW Pacific Ocean
Okhtyrka 109 F 2 *Rus.* Akhtyrka. NE Ukraine
Okinawa 130 A 3 island, Japan
Okinawa-shotō 130 A 3 island group, Nansei-shotō, S Japan
Oki-shotō 131 B 6 *var.* Oki-guntô. W Japan
Oklahoma 49 G 2 *off.* State of Oklahoma; nickname Sooner State. State, C USA
Oklahoma City 49 G 1 state capi Oklahoma, C USA
Okmulgee 49 G 1 Oklahoma, C US
Oktyabr'skiy 111 D 6 W Russian Federation
Oktyabr'skoy Revolyutsii, Ostro 115 E 2 *Eng.* October Revolutic Island, Severnaya Zeml, N Russian Federation
Okulovka *see* Uglovka
Okushiri-tō 130 C 3 *var.* Okusiri Island, Japan
Okusiri-tō *see* Okushiri-tō
Öland 85 C 7 island, S Sweden
Olavarría 65 D 5 E Argentina
Oława 98 C 4 *Ger.* Ohlau. SW Poland
Olbia 97 A 5 *prev.* Terranova Pausania. W Italy

lebroek 86 D 3 E Netherlands
lenburg 94 C 2 N Germany
lenburg 94 B 3 N Germany
lenzaal 86 E 3 E Netherlands
l Harbour 54 B 5 C Jamaica
ean 41 E 3 New York, NE USA
ékminsk 115 F 3
C Russian Federation
eksandrivka 109 E 3
Rus. Aleksandrovka. C Ukraine
eksandriya 109 F 3
Rus. Aleksandriya.
enegorsk 114 C 2
NW Russian Federation
enëk 115 F 3 river,
C Russian Federation
enyok *see* Olenëk
ron, Île d' 91 A 5 island, W France
evs'k 108 D 1 *Rus.* Olevsk.
N Ukraine
evsk *see* Olevs'k
giy 126 C 2 W Mongolia
não 92 B 5 S Portugal
mpo *see* Fuerte Olimpo
ta *see* Alytus
va 93 F 4 E Spain
vet 90 C 4 C France
naliq 123 F 2 *Rus.* Almalyk.
E Uzbekistan
mouc 99 C 5 *Ger.* Olmütz,
Pol. Olomuniec. E Czech Republic
onec *see* Olonets
onets 110 B 3 *var.* Olonec.
NW Russian Federation
ovyannaya 115 F 4
S Russian Federation
oe 94 B 4 W Germany
shanka *see* Vil'shanka
snitz *see* Murska Sobota
sztyn 98 D 2 *Ger.* Allenstein.
N Poland
l 108 B 5 *var.* Oltul,
Ger. Alt.
enita 108 C 5 S Romania
vera 92 C 5 S Spain
viopol' *see* Pervomays'k
ympia 46 B 2 state capital,
Washington, NW USA
ympic Mountains 46 B 2
mountain range, Washington,
NW USA
ympos 104 B 4 *var.* Ólimbos,
Eng. Mount Olympus. Mountain,
N Greece
aagh 89 B 5 *Ir.* An Ómaigh.
C Northern Ireland, UK
aaha 45 F 4 Nebraska, C USA

an
21 D 6 *Ar.* Salţanat 'Umān; *prev.*
Muscat and Oman, Sultanat
Masqat wah Oman. Monarchy,
SW Asia
ficial name: Sultanate of Oman
e of formation: 1650/1951
pital: Muscat
lion Total area: 82,030 sq miles
2,460 sq km) Languages: Arab*,
uchi Religions: Ibadi Muslim
%, other Muslim 11%, Hindu 14%
nic mix: Arab 75%, Baluchi 15%
vernment: Monarchy with
nsultative Council
rency: Rial = 1,000 baizas

an, Gulf of 120 E 4 *Ar.* Khalīj
Umān. Gulf, W Arabian Sea
boué 77 A 6 W Gabon
durman 72 B 4 *var.* Umm
Durmān. C Sudan
etepe, Isla de 52 D 4 island,
Nicaragua

Ōmiya 131 D 5 Honshū, SE Japan
Ommen 86 E 3 E Netherlands
Omsk 114 C 4 C Russian Federation
Ōmuta 131 A 7 Kyūshū, SW Japan
Onda 93 F 3 E Spain
Ondangua *see* Ondangwa
Ondangwa 78 B 3 *var.* Ondangua.
N Namibia
Öndörhaan 127 E 2 E Mongolia
Onega 110 C 3
NW Russian Federation
Onega 110 C 4 river,
NW Russian Federation
Onega, Lake *see* Onezhskoye Ozero
Onex 95 A 8 SW Switzerland
Onezhskoye Ozero 110 B 3
Eng. Lake Onega. Lake,
NW Russian Federation
Ongole 132 D 2 E India
Onitsha 75 G 5 S Nigeria
Onon 127 E 2 river, N Mongolia
Onslow 146 A 4 Western Australia,
W Australia
Onslow Bay 43 G 2 bay,
NW Atlantic Ocean
Ontario 38 B 3 province, S Canada
Ontario, Lake 41 E 3 lake,
Canada/USA
Ontenente *see* Ontinyent
Ontinyent 93 F 4 *var.* Onteniente.
E Spain
Ontong Java Rise 152 C 3 undersea
rise, W Pacific Ocean
Onuba *see* Huelva
Oodeypore *see* Udaipur
Oostakker 87 B 5 NW Belgium
Oostburg 87 B 5 SW Netherlands
Oostende 87 A 5 *Eng.* Ostend,
Fr. Ostende. NW Belgium
Oosterbeek 86 D 4 SE Netherlands
Oosterhout 86 C 4 S Netherlands
Opatija 100 A 2 *It.* Abbazia.
NW Croatia
Opava 99 C 5 *Ger.* Troppau.
E Czech Republic
Opelousas 42 B 3 Louisiana, S USA
Opmeer 86 C 2 NW Netherlands
Opochka 110 A 4 *var.* Opočka.
W Russian Federation
Opočka *see* Opochka
Opole 98 C 4 *Ger.* Oppeln. SW Poland
Opotiki 150 E 3 North Island,
NE New Zealand
Oppeln *see* Opole
Oqtosh 123 E 2 *Rus.* Aktash.
C Uzbekistan
Oradea 108 A 3 *prev.* Oradea Mare,
Ger. Grosswardein, *Hung.*
Nagyvárad. NW Romania
Orahovac 101 D 5 *Alb.* Rahovec.
S Yugoslavia
Oral *see* Ural'sk
Oran 70 D 2 *var.* Ouahran, Wahran.
NW Algeria
Orange 91 D 6 *anc.* Arausio.
SE France
Orange 49 H 4 Texas, S USA
Orange 149 D 6 New South Wales,
SE Australia
Orangeburg 43 E 2
South Carolina, SE USA
Orange Cone *see* Orange Fan
Orange Fan 67 D 6 *var.* Orange Cone.
Undersea fan, SW Indian Ocean
Orange River 78 B 4
Afr. Oranjerivier. River, S Africa
Orange Walk 52 C 1 N Belize
Oranienburg 94 D 3 NE Germany
Oranjemund 78 B 4 *var.*
Orangemund; *prev.* Orange
Mouth. SW Namibia

Oranjerivier *see* Orange River
Oranjestad 55 E 5 dependent
territory capital, W Aruba
Orantes 118 B 3 *var.* Ononte,
Orontes, *Ar.* Nahr al 'Aşī, Nahr al
'Āsī Oronte, Nahr el Aassi. River,
SW Asia
Orany *see* Varėna
Orašje 100 C 3
N Bosnia & Herzegovina
Oravita 108 A 4 *Ger.* Orawitsa,
Hung. Oravicabanyá. W Romania
Orbetello 96 B 4 W Italy
Orcadas 154 A 2 research station,
Antarctica
Orchard Homes 44 B 1
Montana, NW USA
Ord 146 D 3 river, N Australia
Ordino 91 A 8 NW Andorra
Ordos Desert 127 E 3 *Chin.* Mu Us
Shamo. Desert, N China
Ordu 116 D 2 *anc.* Cotyora. N Turkey
Ordzhonikidze 109 F 3 E Ukraine
Orealla 59 G 3 E Guyana
Örebro 85 C 6 C Sweden
Oregon 40 D 3 Ohio, N USA
Oregon 46 B 3 *off.* State of Oregon;
nicknames Beaver State, Sunset
State, Valentine State, Webfoot
State. State, NW USA
Oregon City 46 B 3 Oregon, NW USA
Orekhov *see* Orikhiv
Orël 111 B 5 W Russian Federation
Orem 44 B 4 Utah, W USA
Orenburg 111 D 6 *prev.* Chkalov.
W Russian Federation
Orestiáda 104 D 3 *prev.* Orestiás
NE Greece
Orestiás *see* Orestiáda
Orhei 108 D 3 *var.* Orheiu,
Rus. Orgeyev. N Moldova
Orhon Gol 127 E 2 river,
N Mongolia
Oriental, Cordillera 58 B 3
mountain range, C Colombia
Oriental, Cordillera 61 F 4
mountain range, C Bolivia
Oriental, Cordillera 60 D 3
mountain range, C Peru
Orihuela 93 F 4 E Spain
Orikhiv 109 G 3 *Rus.* Orekhov.
E Ukraine
Orillia 38 D 5 Ontario, S Canada
Orinoco 58 D 3 river,
Colombia/Venezuela
Orissa 135 F 5 state, NE India
Orissaar *see* Orissaare
Orissaare 106 C 2 *Ger.* Orissaar.
Saaremaa, W Estonia
Oristano 97 A 5 W Italy
Orito 58 A 4 SW Colombia
Orizaba 51 F 4 *prev.* Orizaba
Orkney Islands 88 C 2 *var.*
Orkneys, Orkney. Island group,
NE Scotland, UK
Orlando 43 E 4 Florida, SE USA
Orléanais 90 C 4 cultural region,
C France
Orléans 90 C 4 *anc.* Aurelianum.
C France
Orlya 107 B 6 W Belarus
Örnsköldsvik 84 C 4 C Sweden
Oroluk Atoll 144 C 2 island,
C Micronesia
Oromocto 39 F 4 New Brunswick,
SE Canada
Orona 145 F 3 *prev.* Hull Island.
Island, C Kiribati
Oropeza *see* Cochabamba
Oroqen Zizhiqi 127 G 1 N China
Orsha 107 E 6 NE Belarus
Orsk 111 D 6 W Russian Federation

Orşova 108 A 5 *Ger.* Orschowa,
Hung. Orsova. W Romania
Ortelsburg *see* Szczytno
Orthez 91 B 6 SW France
Ortona 96 D 4 C Italy
Oruba *see* Aruba
Orümïyeh, Daryācheh-ye 120 B 2
var. Matianus, Sha Hī, Urumi Yeh,
Eng. Lake Urmia; *prev.*
Daryācheh-ye Rezā'īyeh. Lake,
NW Iran
Oruro 61 F 4 W Bolivia
Ōsaka 131 C 6 *hist.* Naniwa.
Honshū, SW Japan
Osa, Península de 53 E 5 peninsula,
S Costa Rica
Osborn Plateau 141 D 5 undersea
plateau, E Indian Ocean
Osca *see* Huesca
Osh 123 F 2 SW Kyrgyzstan
Oshawa 38 D 5 Ontario, SE Canada
Oshikango 78 B 3 N Namibia
Ō-shima 131 D 6 island, E Japan
Oshmyany *see* Ashmyany
Osijek 100 C 3 *Ger.* Esseg, *Hung.*
Eszék; *prev.* Osiek, Osjek. E Croatia
Oskaloosa 45 G 4 Iowa, C USA
Oskarshamn 85 C 7 S Sweden
Öskemen *see* Ust'-Kamenogorsk
Oskil *see* Oskol
Oskol 109 G 2 *Ukr.* Oskil. River,
Russian Federation/Ukraine
Oslo 85 B 6 *prev.* Christiania,
Kristiania. Country capital,
S Norway
Osmaniye 116 D 4 S Turkey
Osnabrück 94 B 3 NW Germany
Osogovski Planini 104 B 3
var. Osogovske Planine,
Mac. Osogovski Planini.
Mountain range, Bulgaria/
Macedonia
Osorno 65 B 5 C Chile
Osprey Reef 148 D 2 reef,
NW Coral Sea
Oss 86 D 4 S Netherlands
Ossabaw Island 43 E 3
island, SE USA
Ossa, Serra d' 92 C 4 mountain
range, SE Portugal
Ossora 115 H 2
E Russian Federation
Oster 109 E 1 N Ukraine
Östermyra *see* Seinäjoki
Östersund 84 C 4 C Sweden
Ostfriesische Inseln 94 A 3 *Eng.*
East Frisian Islands. Island group,
NW Germany
Ostiglia 96 C 2 N Italy
Ostrava 99 C 5 N Czech Republic
Ostróda 98 D 3 *var. Ger.* Osterode,
Osterode in Ostpreussen.
N Poland
Ostrołęka 98 D 3 *var.* Wiesenhof,
Rus. Ostrolenka. NE Poland
Ostrov 110 A 4 *Latv.* Austrava.
W Russian Federation
Ostrowiec Świętokrzyski 98 D 4
var. Ostrowiec; *prev.*
Ostrowiec Świętokrzyski
Świętokrzyskie. E Poland
Ostrów Mazowiecka 98 D 3 *var.*
Ostrów Mazowiecki. NE Poland
Ostrów Mazowiecki *see*
Ostrów Mazowiecka
Ostrów Wielkopolski 98 C 4 *var.*
Ostrów; *Ger.* Ostrowo. C Poland
Ostyako-Voguls'k *see*
Khanty-Mansiysk
Osum *see* Osumi; Lumi i
Ōsumi-shotō 131 A 8 island group,
Nansei-shotō, SW Japan

Osumit, Lumi i 101 D 7 *var.* Osum.
River, SE Albania
Osuna 92 D 5 S Spain
Oswego 41 F 3 New York, NE USA
Otago Peninsula 151 B 7 peninsula,
South Island, SW New Zealand
Otaki 150 D 4 North Island,
C New Zealand
Otaru 130 C 2 Hokkaidō, NE Japan
Otavalo 60 B 1 N Ecuador
Otavi 78 B 3 N Namibia
Otelu Roşu 108 A 4
Ger. Ferdinandsberg,
Hung. Nándorhgy. SW Romania
Otepää 106 D 3 *Ger.* Odenpäh.
SE Estonia
Otira 151 C 6 South Island,
C New Zealand
Otjiwarongo 78 B 3 N Namibia
Otorohanga 150 D 3 North Island,
N New Zealand
Otra 85 A 6 river, S Norway
Otranto, Canale d' *see*
Otranto, Strait of
Otranto, Strait of 103 E 3
It. Canale d'Otranto. Strait,
Adriatic Sea/Ionian Sea
Otrokovice 99 C 5 *Ger.* Otrokowitz.
SE Czech Republic
Otrokowitz *see* Otrokovice
Ōtsu 131 C 6 *var.* Ôtu. Honshū,
SW Japan
Ottawa 38 D 5 country capital,
Ontario, SE Canada
Ottawa 40 B 3 Illinois, N USA
Ottawa 45 F 5 Kansas, C USA
Ottawa Islands 38 C 1 island
group, Northwest Territories,
C Canada
Ottignies 87 C 6 C Belgium
Ottobrunn 95 C 6 SE Germany
Ottumwa 45 G 4 Iowa, C USA
Otu *see* Ōtsu
Ouachita Mountains 42 A 1
mountain range, C USA
Ouachita River 42 B 2 river,
Arkansas, C USA
Ouâd Nâga 74 B 2 SW Mauritania
Ouagadougou 75 E 4 *var.*
Wagadugu. Country capital,
C Burkina
Ouahigouya 75 E 3 NW Burkina
Oualata *see* Oualâta
Oualâta 74 D 3 *var.* Oualata.
SE Mauritania
Ouanary 59 H 3 E French Guiana
Ouanda Djallé 76 D 4
NE Central African Republic
Ouarâne 74 D 2 physical region,
C Mauritania
Ouargla 71 E 2 *var.* Wargla.
NE Algeria
Ouarzazate 70 C 3 S Morocco
Oubangui *see* Ubangi
Oudenaarde 87 B 6 *Fr.* Audenarde.
SW Belgium
Ouessant, Île d' 90 A 3 *Eng.*
Ushant. Island, NW France
Ouésso 77 B 5 NW Congo
Oujda 70 D 2 *Ar.* Ujda, Oudjda.
NE Morocco
Oujeft 74 C 2 C Mauritania
Ouled Djellal 71 E 2 *var.* Awled
Djellal. N Algeria
Oulu 84 D 4 *Swe.* Uleåborg. C Finland
Oulujärvi 84 D 4 *Swe.* Uleträsk.
Lake, C Finland
Oulujoki 84 D 4 *Swe.* Uleälv. River,
C Finland
Ounasjoki 84 D 3 river, N Finland
Ounianga Kébir 76 C 2 N Chad

Oup *see* Auob
Oupeye 87 D 6 E Belgium
Our 87 D 7 river, W Europe
Ourense 92 C 2 *Cast.* Orense;
Lat. Aurium. NW Spain
Ourique 92 B 4 S Portugal
Ourthe 87 D 7 river, E Belgium
Ouse 89 D 5 river, N England, UK
Outaouais *see* Ottawa
Outer Hebrides 88 B 2
var. Western Isles. Island group,
NW Scotland, UK
Outer Islands 79 G 1 island group,
SW Seychelles
Outes 92 B 1 NW Spain
Outreau 90 C 2 N France
Ouvéa 144 D 5 island,
NE New Caledonia
Ouyen 149 B 6 Victoria, SE Australia
Ovalle 64 B 3 N Chile
Ovar 92 B 2 W Portugal
Overflakkee 86 B 4 island,
SW Netherlands
Overijse 87 C 6 C Belgium
Oviedo 92 D 1 *anc.* Asturias.
NW Spain
Ovilava *see* Wels
Ovruch 108 D 1 N Ukraine
Owando 77 B 6 *prev.* Fort-Rousset.
C Congo
Owase 131 C 6 Honshū, SW Japan
Owatonna 45 F 3 Minnesota, N USA
Owen Fracture Zone 140 B 4
fracture zone, NW Indian Ocean
Owen, Mount 151 C 5 mountain,
South Island, C New Zealand
Owensboro 40 B 5 Kentucky, E USA
Owen Stanley Range 144 B 3
mountain range,
S Papua New Guinea
Owerri 75 G 5 S Nigeria
Owo 75 F 5 SW Nigeria
Owyhee River 46 C 4 river, NW USA
Oxford 89 D 6 *Lat.* Oxonia.
S England, UK
Oxford 151 C 6 South Island,
C New Zealand
Oxford 40 C 4 Ohio, N USA
Oxkutzcab 51 H 4 SE Mexico
Oxnard 47 C 7 California, W USA
Oxonia *see* Oxford
Oyama 131 D 5 Honshū, S Japan
Oyem 77 B 5 N Gabon
Oyo 75 F 5 W Nigeria
Oyo 77 B 6 C Congo
Ozark 42 D 3 Alabama, S USA
Ozark Plateau 45 G 5 plain,
Missouri, C USA
Ozarks, Lake of the 45 G 5
Fr. Lac des Bois. Reservoir,
Missouri, C USA
Ózd 99 D 6 NE Hungary
Ozieri 97 A 5 W Italy

P

Paamiut 82 B 4 *var.* Pâmiut,
Dan. Frederikshåb. SW Greenland
Pa-an 136 B 4 SE Myanmar
Pābna 135 G 4 W Bangladesh
Pacaraima, Serra 59 F 3 *var.*
Pakaraima Mountains. Mountain
range, N South America
Pachuca 51 E 4 *var.* Pachuca de
Soto. C Mexico
Pachuca de Soto *see* Pachuca
Pacific-Antarctic Ridge 152 D 5
undersea ridge, S Pacific Ocean
Pacific Ocean 152 D 3 ocean
Padang 138 B 4 Sumatera,
W Indonesia

Paderborn 94 B 4 NW Germany
Padma *see* Ganges
Padova 96 C 2 *Eng.* Padua;
anc. Patavium. NE Italy
Padre Island 49 G 5 island,
Texas, S USA
Paducah 40 B 5
Kentucky, E USA
Paeroa 150 D 3 North Island,
N New Zealand
Pag 100 A 3 *It.* Pago. Island,
C Croatia
Page 48 B 1 Arizona, SW USA
Pago *see* Pag
Pago Pago 145 F 4 dependent territory
capital, W American Samoa
Pahiatua 150 D 4 North Island,
C New Zealand
Paide 106 D 2 *Ger.* Weissenstein.
N Estonia
Paihia 150 D 2 North Island,
N New Zealand
Päijänne 85 E 5 lake, S Finland
Paine, Cerro 65 B 7 mountain,
S Chile
Painted Desert 48 B 1 plain,
Arizona, SW USA
Paisley 88 C 4 W Scotland, UK
País Valenciano 93 F 3 cultural
region, NE Spain
País Vasco 93 E 1 cultural region,
N Spain
Paita 60 B 3 NW Peru
Pakanbaru *see* Pekanbaru

Pakistan
134 A 2 *var.* Islami Jamhuriya e
Pakistan. Republic, S Asia

Official name: Islamic Republic
of Pakistan **Date of formation:**
1947/1972 **Capital:** Islamabad
Population: 144.5 million **Total Area:**
307,374 sq miles (796,100 sq km)
Languages: Urdu*, Punjabi
Religions: Sunni Muslim 77%, Shi'a
Muslim 20%, Hindu 2%, Christian
1% **Ethnic mix:** Punjabi 56%, Sindhi
13%, Pashtun 8%, other 23%
Government: Multiparty republic
Currency: Rupee = 100 paisa

Pakokku 136 A 3 W Myanmar
Pak Phanang 137 C 7
var. Ban Pak Phanang. S Thailand
Pakruojis 106 C 4 N Lithuania
Paks 99 C 7 S Hungary
Paksé *see* Pakxé
Pakxé 137 D 5 *var.* Paksé. S Laos
Palafrugell 93 G 2 NE Spain
Palagruža 101 B 5 *It.* Pelagosa.
Island, SW Croatia
Palaiá Epídavros 105 C 6 S Greece
Palamós 93 G 2 NE Spain
Palamuse 106 E 2 *Ger.* Sankt-
Bartholomäi. E Estonia
Palanka *see* Bačka Palanka
Palapye 78 D 3 SE Botswana
Palatka 43 E 3 Florida, SE USA

Palau
144 A 2 *var.* Belau. Republic,
W Pacific Ocean

Official name: Republic of Palau
Date of formation: 1994 **Capital:**
Koror **Population:** 16,000 **Total
Area:** 192 sq miles (497 sq km)
Languages: Palauan*, English
Religions: Christian 70%, traditional
beliefs 30% **Ethnic mix:** Palaun 99%,
other 1% **Government:** Multiparty
republic **Currency:** US $ = 100 cents

Palawan 139 E 2 island, W Philippin
Palawan Passage 139 E 2 passage
SE South China Sea
Paldiski 106 D 2 *prev.* Baltiski,
Ger. Baltischport; *prev. Eng.* Balt
Port. NW Estonia
Palembang 138 B 4 Sumatera,
W Indonesia
Palencia 92 D 2 *anc.* Palantia,
Pallantia. NW Spain
Palermo 97 C 7 *Fr.* Palerme; *anc.*
Panormus, Panhormus. SW Ital
Palestine 49 G 3 Texas, S USA
Päli 134 C 3 N India
Palikir 144 C 2 Country capital,
Pohnpei, E Micronesia
Palimé *see* Kpalimé
Palioúri, Ákra 104 C 4 *var.* Akra
Kanestron. Headland, N Greece
Palk Strait 132 D 3 strait,
N Indian Ocean
Palliser, Cape 151 D 5 headland,
North Island, C New Zealand
Palma 93 G 3 *var.* Palma de
Mallorca. E Spain
Palma del Río 92 D 4 S Spain
Palma de Mallorca *see* Palma
Palmar Sur 53 E 5 SE Costa Rica
Palma Soriano 54 C 3 E Cuba
Palmdale 47 C 7 California, W U
Palmer 154 A 2 research station,
Antarctica
Palmer Land 154 A 3 physical
region, Antarctica
Palmerston 145 G 4 island,
S Cook Islands
Palmerston North 150 D 4
North Island, C New Zealand
Palmi 97 D 7 SW Italy
Palmira 58 B 3 W Colombia
Palm Springs 47 D 8 California, W U
Palmyra Atoll 145 G 2 US
unincorporated territory,
C Pacific Ocean
Palo Alto 47 B 6 California, W US
Paloe *see* Denpasar
Paloe *see* Palu
Palu 139 E 4 *prev.* Paloe. Celebes,
C Indonesia
Pamiers 91 B 6 S France
Pamir 123 F 3 *var.* Daryā-ye Pāmi
River, Afghanistan/Tajikistan
Pāmīr, Daryā-ye *see* Pamir
Pamirs 123 F 3 *Pash.* Daryā-ye
Pāmīr, *Rus.* Pamir, *Taj.* Daryoi
Pomir. Mountain range, C Asia
Pamlico Sound 43 G 1 bay,
NW Atlantic Ocean
Pampa 49 F 1 Texas, S USA
Pampa Aullagas, Lago *see* Poopó, La
Pampas 64 C 4 plain, C Argentin
Pamplona 93 E 1 *Basq.* Iruñea; *prev.*
Pampeluna, *anc.* Pompaelo. N Sp
Pamplona 58 C 2 N Colombia
Panaji 132 B 1 *var.* New Goa, Pang
Panjim. State capital, W India

Panama
53 G 5 Republic,
SE Central America

Official name: Republic of Panam
Date of formation: 1903 **Capital:**
Panama City **Population:** 2.6 mill
Total area: 29,761 sq miles
(77,080 sq km) **Languages:** Spanis
English Creole, Indian languages
Religions: Roman Catholic 93%,
other 7% **Ethnic mix:** *mestizo* 70%
Black 14%, White 10%, Indian 6%
Government: Multiparty republi
Currency: Balboa = 100 centesim

amá 53 G 5 *var.* Ciudad de
anamá, *Eng.* Panama City.
ountry capital, C Panama
amá, Bahía de 53 G 5 bay,
W Pacific Ocean
ama Basin 56 A 2 undersea
asin, E Pacific Ocean
ama Canal 53 F 4 canal,
Panama
ama City 42 D 3 Florida, SE USA
ama City 35 D 7 country
apital, C Panama
ama City *see* Panamá
amá, Golfo de 53 G 5 *var.* Gulf
'f Panama.
Gulf, E Pacific Ocean
ama, Gulf of *see* Panamá, Golfo de
ama, Isthmus of *see*
anama, Isthmus of
amá, Istmo de 53 G 4 *Eng.*
sthmus of Panama; *prev.* Isthmus
f Darien.
Isthmus, E Panama
ama, Republic of *see* Panama
ay Island 139 E 2 island,
Philippines
čevo 100 D 3 *Ger.* Pantschowa,
Hung. Pancsova. NE Yugoslavia
dan, Selat 138 A 2 strait, Indian
cean/Pacific Ocean
evėžys 106 C 4 C Lithuania
gkalpinang 138 C 4 Bangka,
W Indonesia
ong Jiang *see* Lô, Sông
opolis *see* Akhmîm
ormos 105 C 7 Kríti, SE Greece
tanal 63 E 4 *var.* Pantanalmato-
Grossense. Wetland, SW Brazil
tanalmato-Grossense *see*
antanal
ttelleria, Isola di 97 B 7 island,
W Italy
uco 51 E 3 E Mexico
shan *see* Baoshan
agayo, Golfo de 52 D 4 gulf,
Pacific Ocean
akura 150 D 3 North Island,
New Zealand
antla 51 F 4 *var.* Papantla de
larte.
E Mexico
antla de Olarte *see* Papantla
atoetoe 150 D 3 North Island,
New Zealand
eete 145 H 4 dependent
erritory capital, Tahiti,
W French Polynesia
hos *see* Páfos
ilė 106 B 3 NW Lithuania
illion 45 F 4 Nebraska, C USA
ua, Gulf of 144 B 3 gulf,
Papua New Guinea

ua New Guinea
44 B 2 *prev.* Territory of
apua and New Guinea.
ommonwealth republic,
dian Ocean/Pacific Ocean
icial name: The Independent
e of Papua New Guinea **Date of**
nation: 1975 **Capital:** Port
esby **Population:** 4.1 million
al **Area:** 178,700 sq miles
, 840 sq km) **Languages:** Pidgin
lish*, Motu*, 750 (est.) native
guages **Religions:** Christian 66%,
er 34% **Ethnic mix:** Papuan 85%,
er 15% **Government:**
iamentary democracy
rrency: Kina = 100 toea

uk 100 C 3 mountain range,
NE Croatia
á 63 E 2 *off.* Estado do Pará.
tate, NE Brazil

Pará *see* Belém
Paracas, Bahía de 60 C 4 bay,
E Pacific Ocean
Paracel Islands 138 D 1 disputed
territory, N South China Sea
Paraćin 100 E 4 C Yugoslavia
Pará, Estado do *see* Pará
Paragua 59 E 3 river, SE Venezuela

Paraguay
64 D 2 country, S South America
Official name: Republic of
Paraguay **Date of formation:**
1811/1935 **Capital:** Asunción
Population: 4.5 million **Total area:**
157,046 sq miles (406,750 sq km)
density: 11 people per sq km
Languages: Spanish*, Guaraní
Religions: Roman Catholic 90%,
other 10% **Ethnic mix:** *mestizo* (Euro-
Indian) 95%, White 3%, Indian 2%
Government: Multiparty republic
Currency: Guaraní = 100 céntimos

Paraguay 64 D 2 *Port.* Rio Paraguai.
River, S South America
Paraíba 63 G 2 *off.* Estado da
Paraíba; *prev.* Parahiba, Parahyba.
State, E Brazil
Paraíba *see* João Pessoa
Parakou 75 F 4 C Benin
Paramaribo 59 G 3 country capital,
N Suriname
Paramushir, Ostrov 115 H 3 island,
E Russian Federation
Paraná 64 E 3 *var.* Alto Paraná.
River, S South America
Paraná 64 D 4 E Argentina
Paraná 63 G 4 *off.* Estado do Paraná.
State, S Brazil
Paraná, Estado do *see* Paraná
Paranéstio 104 C 3 NE Greece
Paraparaumu 151 D 5 North Island,
C New Zealand
Parchim 94 C 3 N Germany
Parczew 98 E 4 E Poland
Pardubice 99 B 5 *Ger.* Pardubitz.
C Czech Republic
Pardubitz *see* Pardubice
Parechcha 107 B 5 *Pol.* Porzecze,
Rus. Porech'ye. W Belarus
Parecis, Chapada dos 62 D 3 *var.*
Serra dos Parecis. Mountain
range, W Brazil
Parecis, Serra dos *see*
Parecis, Chapada dos
Parenzo *see* Poreč
Parepare 139 E 4 C Indonesia
Párga 105 A 5 W Greece
Paria, Golfo de *see* Paria, Gulf of
Paria, Gulf of 59 E 1 *var.* Golfo de
Paria. Gulf, W Atlantic Ocean
Parika 59 F 2 NE Guyana
Paris 90 C 3 *anc.* Lutetia, Lutetia
Parisiorum, Parisii. Country
capital, N France
Paris 42 C 1 Tennessee, S USA
Paris 49 G 2 Texas, S USA
Parkent 123 F 2 E Uzbekistan
Parkersburg 40 D 4
West Virginia, NE USA
Parkes 149 C 6
New South Wales, SE Australia
Parkhar *see* Farkhor
Parma 96 B 2 N Italy
Parnahyba *see* Parnaíba
Parnaíba 63 G 2 *var.* Parnahyba.
E Brazil
Pärnu 106 D 2 *Ger.* Pernau, *Latv.*
Pērnava; *prev. Rus.* Pernov.
SW Estonia

Pärnu 106 D 2 *var.* Parnu Jõgi,
Ger. Pernau. River, SW Estonia
Pärnu-Jaagupi 106 D 2 *Ger.* Sankt-
Jakobi. SW Estonia
Pärnu Laht 106 D 2 *Ger.* Pernauer
Bucht. Bay, Baltic Sea/
Gulf of Riga
Páros 105 D 6 Páros, SE Greece
Páros 105 D 6 island, Kykládes,
SE Greece
Parral 64 B 4 C Chile
Parral *see* Hidalgo del Parral
Parramatta 149 D 6 New South
Wales, SE Australia
Parras 50 D 3 *var.* Parras de la
Fuente. NE Mexico
Parras de la Fuente *see* Parras
Parsons 45 F 5 Kansas, C USA
Pasadena 49 H 4 Texas, S USA
Pasadena 47 C 7 California, W USA
Paşcani 108 C 3 *Hung.* Páskán.
NE Romania
Pasco 46 C 2 Washington, NW USA
Pasewalk 94 D 3 NE Germany
Pashkeni *see* Bolyarovo
Pasłęk 98 C 2 *Ger.* Preußisch
Holland. N Poland
Pasinler 117 F 3 NE Turkey
Pasni 134 A 3 SW Pakistan
Paso de Indios 65 B 6 S Argentina
Paso de los Vientos *see*
Windward Passage
Passarowitz *see* Požarevac
Passau 95 D 6 SE Germany
Passo Fundo 63 E 5 S Brazil
Pastavy 107 C 5 *Pol.* Postawy,
Rus. Postavy. NW Belarus
Pastaza 60 B 2 river, Ecuador/Peru
Pasto 58 A 4 SW Colombia
Pasvalys 106 C 4 N Lithuania
Patagonia 65 B 7 physical region,
Argentina/Chile
Patani *see* Pattani
Patea 150 D 4 North Island,
C New Zealand
Pátmos 105 D 6 island,
Dodekánisos, SE Greece
Patna 135 F 3 *var.* Azimabad.
NE India
Patnos 117 F 3 E Turkey
Patos, Lagoa dos 63 E 5 lagoon,
SW Atlantic Ocean
Pátra 105 B 5 *Eng.* Patras;
prev. Pátrai. S Greece
Patras *see* Pátra
Pattani 137 C 7 *var.* Patani.
S Thailand
Pattaya 137 C 5 C Thailand
Patuca 52 D 2 river, E Honduras
Pau 91 B 6 SW France
Paulatuk 37 E 3 Northwest
Territories, NW Canada
Paungde 136 B 4 SW Myanmar
Pavia 96 B 2 *anc.* Ticinum. N Italy
Pavlikeni 104 D 2 N Bulgaria
Pavlodar 114 C 4 NE Kazakhstan
Pavlograd *see* Pavlohrad
Pavlohrad 109 G 3 *Rus.* Pavlograd.
E Ukraine
Pavlovsk 111 B 6
W Russian Federation
Pavlovskaya 111 A 7
SW Russian Federation
Pawai, Pulau 138 A 2 island,
SW Singapore
Pawn 136 B 3 river, C Myanmar
Pax Augusta *see* Badajoz

Paxí 105 A 5 island, Iónioi Nísoi,
W Greece
Pax Julia *see* Beja
Payakumbuh 138 B 4 Sumatera,
W Indonesia
Paynes Find 147 B 6 W Australia
Payo Obispo *see* Chetumal
Paysandú 64 D 4 NW Uruguay
Pazar 117 E 2 NE Turkey
Pazardzhik 104 C 3 *var.* Pazardžik;
prev. Tatar Pazardzhik. SW Bulgaria
Pearl Islands *see*
Perlas, Archipiélago de las
Pearl Lagoon *see* Perlas, Laguna de
Pearl River 42 B 3 river, S USA
Pearsall 49 F 4 Texas, S USA
Peary Land 83 E 1 physical region,
Greenland
Peć 101 D 5 *Alb.* Pejë, *Turk.* Ipek.
C Yugoslavia
Pechora 110 E 3 *var.* Pečora.
NW Russian Federation
Pechora 110 D 3 *var.* Pečora. River,
NW Russian Federation
Pechorskoye More 110 D 2 sea,
Arctic Ocean/Barents Sea
Pečora *see* Pechora
Pecos 49 E 3 Texas, S USA
Pecos Plains 49 E 3 plain,
Texas, S USA
Pecos River 49 E 3 river, SW USA
Pécs 99 C 7 *Ger.* Fünfkirchen;
Lat. Sopianae. SW Hungary
Pedra Lume 74 A 3 NE Cape Verde
Pedro Cays 54 C 3 island group,
S Jamaica
Pedro Juan Caballero 64 D 2
E Paraguay
Peer 87 D 5 NE Belgium
Pegasus Bay 151 C 6 bay,
S South Island
Pegu 136 B 4 *var.* Bago. S Myanmar
Pehuajó 64 C 4 E Argentina
Peihai *see* Beihai
Peine 94 B 4 N Germany
Peiraías 105 C 6 *prev.* Piraiévs,
Eng. Piraeus. C Greece
Pekalongan 138 C 5 Jawa,
C Indonesia
Pekanbaru 138 B 4 *var.* Pakanbaru.
Sumatera, W Indonesia
Pekin 40 B 4 Illinois, N USA
Peking *see* Beijing
Pelagie, Isole 97 B 8 island group,
SW Italy
Pelagosa *see* Palagruža
Pelly Bay 37 F 3 Northwest
Territories, N Canada
Pelopónnisos 105 B 6 *var.* Morea,
Eng. Peloponnese; *anc.*
Peloponnesus. Peninsula,
S Greece
Pematangsiantar 138 B 3 Sumatera,
W Indonesia
Pemba 73 D 7 *var.* E Tanzania
Pemba 79 F 2 *var.* Port Amelia,
Porto Amélia. NE Mozambique
Pembroke 38 D 4 Ontario,
SE Canada
Penderma *see* Bandırma
Pendleton 46 C 3 Oregon, NW USA
Pend Oreille, Lake 46 D 1 lake,
Idaho, NW USA
Peng-pu *see* Bengbu
Peniche 92 B 3 W Portugal
Penn Hills 41 E 4 Pennsylvania,
NE USA
Pennine Alps 95 A 8 *Fr.* Alpes
Pennines, *It.* Alpi Pennine; *Lat.*
Alpes Penninae. Mountain range,
Italy/Switzerland

Pennine Chain *see* Pennines
Pennines 89 D 5 *var.* Pennine Chain. Mountain range, NW England, UK
Pennsylvania 41 E 4 *off.* Commonwealth of Pennsylvania; nickname Keystone State. State, NE USA
Penobscot River 41 H 1 river, Maine, NE USA
Penong 147 E 6 South Australia, S Australia
Penonomé 53 F 5 C Panama
Penrhyn 145 G 3 island, N Cook Islands
Penrhyn Basin 152 D 3 undersea basin, C Pacific Ocean
Penrith 89 D 5 NW England, UK
Pensacola 42 C 3 Florida, SE USA
Pentecost 144 D 4 *Fr.* Pentecôte. Island, C Vanuatu
Pentecôte *see* Pentecost
Penza 111 C 6 W Russian Federation
Penzance 89 B 8 SW England, UK
Peoria 40 B 4 Illinois, N USA
Perchtoldsdorf 95 E 6 NE Austria
Percival Lakes 146 C 4 lake, Western Australia, NW Australia
Pereira 58 B 3 W Colombia
Peremyshl *see* Przemyśl
Pergamino 64 D 4 E Argentina
Périgueux 91 B 5 *anc.* Vesuna. SW France
Perito Moreno 65 B 6 S Argentina
Perlas, Archipiélago de las 53 G 5 *Eng.* Pearl Islands. Island group, SE Panama
Perlas, Laguna de 53 E 3 *var.* Pearl Lagoon. Lagoon, W Caribbean Sea
Perleberg 94 C 3 N Germany
Perlepe *see* Prilep
Perm' 111 D 5 *prev.* Molotov. NW Russian Federation
Pernambuco 63 G 2 *off.* Estado de Pernambuco. State, E Brazil
Pernambuco *see* Recife
Pernambuco Abyssal Plain *see* Pernambuco Plain
Pernambuco, Estado de *see* Pernambuco
Pernambuco Plain 67 C 5 *var.* Pernambuco Abyssal Plain. Abyssal plain, E Atlantic Ocean
Pernauer Bucht *see* Pärnu Laht
Pernik 104 C 2 *prev.* Dimitrovo. W Bulgaria
Perote 51 F 4 E Mexico
Perpignan 91 C 7 S France
Perryton 49 F 1 Texas, S USA
Perryville 45 H 5 Missouri, C USA
Persian Gulf 120 C 4 *var.* The Gulf, *Ar.* Khalīj al 'Arabī, *Per.* Khalīj-e Fars. Gulf, W Arabian Sea
Perth 88 C 4 E Scotland, UK
Perth 38 D 5 Ontario, SE Canada
Perth 149 C 8 Tasmania, SE Australia
Perth 147 B 6 state capital, Western Australia, SW Australia
Perth Basin 141 E 6 undersea basin, SE Indian Ocean
Peru *see* Beru

Peru
60 C 3 Republic, W South America

Official name: Republic of Peru
Date of formation: 1824/1942
Capital: Lima **Population:** 22.9 million **Total area:** 496,223 sq miles (1,285,220 sq km) **Languages:**

Spanish*, Quechua*, Aymará*
Religions: Roman Catholic 95%, other 5% **Ethnic mix:** Indian 45%, *mestizo* 37%, White 15%, other 3% **Government:** Multiparty republic **Currency:** New sol = 100 centimos

Peru Basin 56 A 4 undersea basin, E Pacific Ocean
Peru-Chile Trench 56 A 4 trench, E Pacific Ocean
Perugia 96 C 4 *Fr.* Pérouse; *anc.* Perusia. C Italy
Peru, Republic of *see* Peru
Péruwelz 87 B 6 SW Belgium
Pervomays'k 109 E 3 *prev.* Ol'viopol'. S Ukraine
Pervyy Kuril'skiy Proliv 115 H 3 strait, Pacific Ocean/Sea of Okhotsk
Pesaro 96 C 3 *anc.* Pisaurum C Italy
Pescara 96 D 4 *anc.* Aternum, Ostia Aterni. C Italy
Peshāwar 134 C 1 N Pakistan
Peshkopi 101 D 6 *var.* Peshkopia, Peshkopija. NE Albania
Pessac 91 B 5 SW France
Pétange 87 D 8 SW Luxembourg
Peta' Tiqwa 119 A 6 *var.* Petach-Tikva, Petah Tiqva. C Israel
Peterborough 89 E 6 *prev.* Medeshamstede. E England, UK
Peterborough 38 D 5 Ontario, SE Canada
Peterborough 149 B 6 South Australia, S Australia
Peterhead 88 D 3 NE Scotland, UK
Petersburg 41 E 5 Virginia, NE USA
Peters Mine 59 F 3 *var.* Peter's Mine. N Guyana
Peter's Mine *see* Peters Mine
Peto 51 H 4 SE Mexico
Petra *see* Wādī Mūsá
Petrich 104 C 3 SW Bulgaria
Petrikov *see* Pyetrykaw
Petrinja 100 B 3 C Croatia
Petropavl *see* Petropavlovsk
Petropavlovsk 114 C 4 *Kaz.* Petropavl. N Kazakhstan
Petropavlovsk-Kamchatskiy 115 H 3 NE Russian Federation
Petroşani 108 B 4 *var.* Petroşeni, *Ger.* Petroschen, *Hung.* Petrozsény. W Romania
Petroskoi *see* Petrozavodsk
Petrovsk 111 C 6 W Russian Federation
Petrovsk-Port *see* Makhachkala
Petrov Val 111 C 6 SW Russian Federation
Petrozavodsk 110 B 3 *Fin.* Petroskoi. NW Russian Federation
Pevek 115 G 1 NE Russian Federation
Pezinok 99 C 6 *Ger.* Bösing, *Hung.* Bazin. SW Slovakia
Pforzheim 95 B 6 SW Germany
Pfungstadt 95 B 5 W Germany
Phangan, Ko 137 C 6 island, S Thailand
Phan Rang-Thap Cham 137 E 6 *var.* Phan Rang, Phanrang, Phan Rang Thap Cham. SE Vietnam
Phan Thiêt 137 E 6 S Vietnam
Phatthalung 137 C 7 *var.* Padalung, Patalung. S Thailand
Phayao 136 C 4 *var.* Muang Phayao. N Thailand
Phenix City 42 D 2 Alabama, S USA
Phetchaburi 137 C 5 *var.* Bejraburi, Petchaburi, Phet Buri. C Thailand
Philadelphia 41 F 4 Pennsylvania, NE USA
Philippeville *see* Skikda

Philippine Basin 152 B 2 undersea basin, W Pacific Ocean

Philippines
139 F 1 *off.* Republic of the Philippines. Republic, SE Asia

Official name: Republic of the Philippines **Date of formation:** 1946 **Capital:** Manila **Population:** 66.5 million **Total Area:** 115,831 sq miles (300,000 sq km) **Languages:** Pilipino*, English **Religions:** Roman Catholic 83%, Protestant 9%, Muslim 5%, other 3% **Ethnic mix:** Filipino 96%, Chinese 2%, other 2% **Government:** Multiparty republic **Currency:** Peso = 100 centavos

Philippine Sea 152 B 3 sea, W Pacific Ocean
Philippines, Republic of the *see* Philippines
Philippine Trench 142 A 1 trench, W Pacific Ocean
Phitsanulok 136 C 4 *var.* Bisnulok, Muang Phitsanulok, Pitsanulok. N Thailand
Phlórina *see* Flórina
Phnom Penh *see* Phnum Penh
Phnum Penh 137 D 6 *var.* Phnom Penh. Country capital, S Cambodia
Phoenix 48 B 2 state capital, Arizona, SW USA
Phoenix Islands 145 F 3 island group, C Kiribati
Phôngsali 136 C 3 *var.* Phong Saly. N Laos
Phong Saly *see* Phôngsali
Phrae 136 C 4 *var.* Muang Phrae, Prae. N Thailand
Phra Nakhon Si Ayutthaya *see* Ayutthaya
Phra Thong, Ko 137 B 7 island, S Thailand
Phuket 137 B 7 *var.* Bhuket, Puket, *Mal.* Ujung Salang; *prev.* Junkseylon, Salang. S Thailand
Phuket, Ko 137 B 7 island, S Thailand
Phumĭ Kâmpóng Trâlach 137 D 5 C Cambodia
Phumĭ Sâmraông 137 D 5 NW Cambodia
Phu Vinh *see* Tra Vinh
Piacenza 96 B 2 *Fr.* Paisance; *anc.* Placentia. N Italy
Piatra-Neamţ 108 C 3 *Hung.* Karácsonkó. NE Romania
Piauí 63 F 2 *off.* Estado do Piauí; *prev.* Piauhy. State, E Brazil
Picardie 90 C 3 *Eng.* Picardy. Cultural region, N France
Picardy *see* Picardie
Picayune 42 C 3 Mississippi, S USA
Pichilemu 64 B 4 C Chile
Pichincha 60 B 1 NE Ecuador
Pico 92 A 5 *var.* Ilha do Pico. Island, W Portugal
Pico, Ilha do *see* Pico
Picos 63 G 2 E Brazil
Picsi 60 B 3 W Peru
Picton 151 C 5 South Island, C New Zealand
Piedras Negras 51 E 2 *var.* Ciudad Porfirio Díaz. NE Mexico
Pielinen 84 E 4 *var.* Pielisjärvi. Lake, E Finland
Pielisjärvi *see* Pielinen
Pierre 45 E 3 state capital, South Dakota, N USA
Piešt'any 99 C 6 *Ger.* Pistyan, *Hung.* Pöstyén. W Slovakia

Pietarsaari *see* Jakobstad
Pietermaritzburg 78 D 4 *var.* Maritzburg. E South Africa
Pietersburg 78 D 4 NE South A
Pigs, Bay of 54 B 2 *Sp.* Bahia de Cochinos. Bay, N Caribbean S
Pijijiápán 51 G 5 SE Mexico
Pikes Peak 44 C 5 mountain, Colorado, C USA
Pikine 74 B 3 *var.* Pikini Bougou W Senegal
Pikini Bougou *see* Pikine
Pikinni *see* Bikini Atoll
Piła 98 C 3 *Ger.* Schneidemühl. NW Poland
Pilar 64 D 3 *var.* Villa del Pilar. S Paraguay
Pilar 63 G 3 W Brazil
Pilcomayo 64 C 2 river, S South America
Pilos *see* Pýlos
Pinang, Pulau 138 B 3 *var.* Pena, Pinang; *prev.* Prince of Wales Island. Island, W Malaysia
Pinar del Río 54 A 2 W Cuba
Píndos 104 A 4 *var.* Píndhos Óro *Eng.* Pindus Mountains; *prev.* Pindhos. Mountain range, C Greece
Pindus Mountains *see* Píndos
Pine Bluff 42 B 2 Arkansas USA
Pine Creek 148 A 2 Northern Territory, N Australi
Pine Dock 37 G 5 Manitoba, S Canada
Pinega 110 C 3 river, NW Russian Federation
Pineiós 104 B 4 *var.* Piniós; *anc.* Peneius. River, C Greece
Pine Island Bay 154 A 3 bay, S Pacific Ocean
Pines, Lake O' the 49 H 2 reserv Texas, S USA
Pingdingshan 128 C 4 C China
Ping, Mae Nam 136 B 4 river, NW Thailand
Pingyang 128 D 4 E China
Pínnes, Ákra 104 C 4 headland, N Greece
Pinotepa Nacional 51 F 5 *var.* Santiago Pinotepa Nacional. SE Mexico
Pinsk 107 B 7 *Pol.* Pińsk. SW Bel
Pińsk *see* Pinsk
Pinta, Isla 60 A 5 *var.* Abingdon Island, Galapagos Islands, E Pacific Ocean
Piombino 96 B 3 C Italy
Pionerskiy 106 A 4 *Ger.* Neukuh W Russian Federation
Piotrków Trybunalski 98 D 4 *G* Petrikau, *Rus.* Petrokov. C Pola
Piraeus *see* Peiraías
Pírgos *see* Pýrgos
Piripiri 63 G 2 E Brazil
Pirot 101 E 5 E Yugoslavia
Piryatin *see* Pyryatyn
Pisa 96 B 3 *anc.* Pisae. C Italy
Pisae *see* Pisa
Pisaurum *see* Pesaro
Pisco 60 D 4 SW Peru
Písek 99 B 5 SW Czech Republic
Pishan 126 A 3 *var.* Guma. NW China
Pistoia 96 B 3 *anc.* Pistoria, Pisto C Italy
Pisz 98 D 3 *Ger.* Johannisburg. NE Poland
Pita 74 C 4 NW Guinea
Pitalito 58 B 4 S Colombia

airn Islands 143 H 4 UK
ependent territory, S Pacific Ocean
å 84 D 4 N Sweden
șsti 108 B 5 S Romania
Island see Makin
sburg 45 F 5 Kansas, C USA
sburgh 41 E 4
ennsylvania, NE USA
sfield 41 F 3 New York, NE USA
ffik 82 C 1 var. Uummannaq;
rev. Dundas. NW Greenland
ra 60 B 3 NW Peru
dennyy Buh 109 E 3 Rus.
uzhnyy Bug. River, S Ukraine
cetas 54 B 2 C Cuba
nview 49 E 2 Texas, S USA
heta Rica 58 B 2 NW Colombia
nken 94 E 1 C Liechtenstein
no 49 G 2 Texas, S USA
encia 92 C 3 W Spain
a, Rio de la 64 D 4 estuary,
W Atlantic Ocean
inum 36 B 3 Alaska, NW USA
te River 45 E 4 river,
Jebraska, C USA
tsburgh 41 F 2 Vermont, NE USA
uen 95 C 5 var. Plauen im
ogtland. E Germany
uen im Vogtland see Plauen
vinas 106 D 4
er. Stockmannshof. S Latvia
Cu 137 E 5 var. Pleiku. S Vietnam
ku see Plây Cu
nty, Bay of 150 E 3 inlet,
W Pacific Ocean
in 90 A 3 NW France
eck see Plesetsk
etsk 110 C 3 var. Pleseck.
W Russian Federation
hchenitsy see Plyeshchanitsy
zew 98 C 4 C Poland
ven 104 C 2 prev. Plevna.
Bulgaria
na see Pleven
vlja 100 C 4 prev. Plevlja,
evlje. N Yugoslavia
e 100 B 4 It. Plocce;
rev. Kardeljevo. SE Croatia
ck 98 D 3 Ger. Plozk. C Poland
ken Pass 95 C 7 Ger.
lockenpass, It. Passo di Monte
roce Carnico. Pass, SW Austria
k see Plock
ngě 106 B 3 W Lithuania
shchanitsy 107 D 6
us. Pleshchenitsy. N Belarus
nouth 89 C 7 SW England, UK
nouth 55 G 3 dependent
rritory capital, SW Montserrat
ñ 99 A 5 var. Pilsen, Pol. Pilzno.
Czech Republic
6 A 2 river, N Italy
edy, Pik 132 H 2 var. Pobeda
eak, Chin. Tomur Feng.
ountain, China/Kyrgyzstan
Bocche del see Po, Foci del
atello 36 E 4 Idaho, NW USA
ninok 111 A 5
Russian Federation
king 95 D 6 SE Germany

Poděbrady 99 B 5 Ger. Podiebrad.
C Czech Republic
Podgorica 101 C 5 prev. Titograd.
Country capital, SW Yugoslavia
Podiebrad see Poděbrady
Podil' s'ka Vysochyna 108 D 3
Rus. Podol'skaya Vozvyshennost'.
Mountain range, SW Ukraine
Podol'sk 111 B 5
W Russian Federation
Podol'skaya Vozvyshennost' see
Podil' s'ka Vysochyna
Podravska Slatina 100 C 2 Hung.
Szlatina; prev. Slatina. NE Croatia
Podujevo 101 D 5 C Yugoslavia
Po, Foci del 96 C 2 var. Bocche del
Po. River, Italy
Pogradec 101 D 6 var. Pogradeci.
SE Albania
Pogradeci see Pogradec
Pohnpei 144 C 2 prev. Ponape
Ascension Island. Island,
E Micronesia
Pohnpei 144 C 2 island group,
E Micronesia
Poinsett, Cape 154 D 4 headland,
Antarctica
Point Au Fer Island 42 B 4 island,
S USA
Point de Galle see Galle
Pointe-à-Pitre 55 G 3 C Guadeloupe
Pointe-Noire 77 A 6 S Congo
Point Lay 36 C 2 Alaska, NW USA
Poitiers 90 B 4 prev. Poictiers,
anc. Limonum. W France
Poitou 90 B 4 cultural region,
W France
Pokhara 135 F 3 C Nepal
Pok Liu Chau see Lamma Island
Pokrovka see Kyzyl-Suu
Pokrovs'ke 109 G 3 Rus.
Pokrovskoye. E Ukraine
Pokrovskoye see Pokrovs'ke
Pola de Lena 92 C 1 N Spain

Poland
98 C 4 var. Polish Republic,
Polska Rzeczpospolita Ludowa,
Rzeczpospolita Polska, Pol.
Polska; prev. The Polish People's
Republic. Republic, C Europe
Official name: Republic of Poland
Date of formation: 1918/1945
Capital: Warsaw Population: 38.5
million Total area: 120,720 sq miles
(312,680 sq km) Languages:
Polish*, German Religions: Roman
Catholic 95%, other Christian 5%
Ethnic mix: Polish 98%, other 2%
Government: Multiparty republic
Currency: Zloty = 100 groszy

Polatsk 107 D 5 Rus. Polotsk.
N Belarus
Pol-e Khomrī 123 E 4 var. Pul-i-
Khumri. NE Afghanistan
Polikraïshte see Polikrayshte
Polikrayshte 104 D 2 var.
Polikraište. N Bulgaria
Pollença 93 G 3 var. Pollensa. E Spain
Pollensa see Pollença
Pologi see Polohy
Polohy 109 G 3 Rus. Pologi.
SE Ukraine
Polonne 108 D 2 Rus. Polonnoye.
NW Ukraine
Polonnoye see Polonne
Polotsk see Polatsk
Polsko Kosovo 104 D 2 N Bulgaria
Poltava 109 F 2 NE Ukraine
Põlva 106 E 3 Ger. Pölwe.
SE Estonia

Pölwe see Põlva
Polyarnyy 110 C 2 var. Pol'arnyj,
Poljarny. NW Russian Federation
Polýkastro 104 B 3 prev.
Políkastron. N Greece
Polynesia 145 G 3 island group,
SW Pacific Ocean
Pomerania Bay 94 D 2 Ger.
Pommersche Bucht, Pol. Zatoka
Pomorska. Bay, S Baltic Sea
Pommern 94 D 2 cultural region,
NE Germany
Pompano Beach 43 F 5
Florida, SE USA
Ponape Ascension Island see
Pohnpei
Ponca City 49 G 1 Oklahoma, C USA
Ponce 55 F 3 S Puerto Rico
Pondicherry 132 D 2 var.
Puduchcheri. SE India
Ponferrada 92 C 1 NW Spain
Poniatowa 98 E 4 E Poland
Pons Vetus see Pontevedra
Ponta Delgada 92 A 5 W Portugal
Ponta Grossa 63 E 4 S Brazil
Pontarlier 90 D 4 E France
Pontchartrain, Lake 42 C 3 lake,
Louisiana USA
Ponteareas 92 B 2 NW Spain
Ponte da Barca 92 B 2 N Portugal
Pontevedra 92 B 1 anc. Pons Vetus.
NW Spain
Pontiac 40 D 3 Michigan, N USA
Pontianak 138 C 4 Borneo,
C Indonesia
Pontivy 90 A 3 NW France
Pontoise 90 C 3 anc. Briva Isarae,
Cergy-Pontoise, Pontisarae.
N France
Ponton 37 F 5 Manitoba, C Canada
Ponziane, Isole 97 C 5 island,
C Italy
Poole 89 D 7 S England, UK
Poona see Pune
Poopó, Lago 61 F 4 var. Lago
Pampa Aullagas. Lake, W Bolivia
Popayán 58 A 4 SW Colombia
Poperinge 87 A 6 W Belgium
Poplar Bluff 45 G 5 Missouri, C USA
Popocatépetl 51 E 4 volcano,
S Mexico
Poprad 99 D 5 Ger. Popper, Hung.
Poprád. River, Poland/Slovakia
Poprad 99 D 5 Ger. Deutschendorf,
Hung. Poprád. NE Slovakia
Porbandar 134 B 4 W India
Pordenone 96 C 2 anc. Portenau.
NE Italy
Poreč 100 A 3 Ital. Parenzo. NW Croatia
Pori 85 D 5 Swe. Björneborg.
SW Finland
Porirua 151 D 5 North Island,
C New Zealand
Porkhov 110 A 4
W Russian Federation
Porlamar 59 E 1 NE Venezuela
Póros 105 C 6 S Greece
Póros 105 A 5 Kefallinía, W Greece
Porsangen 84 D 2 fjord, NE Norway
Porsgrunn 85 B 6 S Norway
Portachuelo 61 G 4 C Bolivia
Portadown 89 B 5 Ir. Port An
Dúnáin. SE Northern Ireland, UK
Port Alexander 36 D 4
Alaska, NW USA
Port Alfred 78 D 5 S South Africa
Port An Dúnáin see Portadown
Port Angeles 46 B 1
Washington, NW USA

Port Antonio 54 B 5 NE Jamaica
Port Augusta 149 B 6
South Australia, S Australia
Port-au-Prince 54 D 3
country capital, C Haiti
Port Blair 133 F 2 SE India
Port d'Envalira 91 B 8 W Andorra
Port Elizabeth 78 C 5 S South Africa
Portenau see Pordenone
Porterville 47 C 7 California, W USA
Port-Étienne see Nouâdhibou
Port Florence see Kisumu
Port-Francqui see Ilebo
Port-Gentil 77 A 6 W Gabon
Port Harcourt 75 G 5 S Nigeria
Port Hardy 36 D 5 Vancouver
Island, SW Canada
Port Hedland 146 B 4 Western
Australia, W Australia
Port Huron 40 D 3 Michigan, N USA
Portimão 92 B 5 var. Vila Nova de
Portimão. S Portugal
Port Láirge see Waterford
Portland 49 G 5 Texas, S USA
Portland 149 B 7 Victoria,
SE Australia
Portland 41 G 2 Maine, NE USA
Portland 46 B 3 Oregon, NW USA
Portland Bight 54 B 5 bay,
N Caribbean Sea
Port Laoise 89 B 6 var. Portlaoise, Ir.
Portlaoighise; prev. Maryborough.
C Ireland
Port Lavaca 49 G 4 Texas, S USA
Port Lincoln 149 A 6 South
Australia, S Australia
Port Louis 79 H 3 country capital,
NW Mauritius
Port-Lyautey see Kénitra
Port Macquarie 149 E 6
New South Wales, SE Australia
Portmore 54 B 5 C Jamaica
Port Moresby 144 B 3 country
capital, New Guinea,
SW Papua New Guinea
Port Natal see Durban
Porto 92 B 2 Eng. Oporto;
anc. Portus Cale. NW Portugal
Porto Alegre 63 E 5 var. Pôrto
Alegre. State capital, S Brazil
Porto Alegre 76 E 2
S Sao Tome & Principe
Pôrto Alegre see Porto Alegre
Porto Alexandre see Tombua
Portobelo 53 G 4 var. Porto Bello,
Puerto Bello. N Panama
Portoferraio 96 B 4 W Italy
Port-of-Spain 55 H 5 country
capital, C Trinidad & Tobago
Portogruaro 96 C 2 NE Italy
Porto-Novo 75 F 5 country capital,
S Benin
Porto Santo 70 A 2 var. Ilha do
Porto Santo. Island, Madeira,
Portugal
Porto Torres 97 A 5 W Italy
Porto Velho 62 D 2 var. Velho.
W Brazil
Portoviejo 60 A 2 var. Puertoviejo.
W Ecuador
Port Phillip Bay 149 C 7 bay,
SW Tasman Sea
Port Pirie 149 B 6 South Australia,
S Australia
Port Said 72 B 1 Ar. Būr Sa'īd.
N Egypt
Portsmouth 89 D 7 S England, UK
Portsmouth 40 D 4 Ohio, N USA
Portsmouth 41 G 3
New Hampshire, NE USA
Port Stanley see Stanley

Port Sudan 72 C 3 NE Sudan
Port Talbot 89 C 7 S Wales, UK

Portugal
92 B 3 Republic, W Europe

Official name: Republic of Portugal
Date of formation: 1140/1640
Capital: Lisbon **Population:** 9.9
million **Total area:** 35,670 sq miles
(92,390 sq km) **Languages:**
Portuguese* **Religions:** Roman
Catholic 97%, Protestant 1%,
other 2% **Ethnic mix:** Portuguese
98%, African 1%, other 1%
Government: Multiparty republic
Currency: Escudo = 100 centavos

Port-Vila 144 D 4 *var.* Vila. Country
capital, Éfaté, C Vanuatu
Porvenir 65 B 8 S Chile
Porvenir 61 E 3 NW Bolivia
Porvoo 85 E 5 *Swe.* Borgå. S Finland
Posadas 64 D 3 NE Argentina
Posterholt 87 D 5 SE Netherlands
Postojna 95 D 8 *Ger.* Adelsberg,
It. Postumia. SW Slovenia
Potamós 105 C 7 Andikithira,
S Greece
Potentia *see* Potenza
Potenza 97 D 5 *anc.* Potentia. S Italy
P'ot'i 117 F 2 W Georgia
Potiskum 75 G 4 NE Nigeria
Po Toi Island 128 A 2 island,
S Hong Kong
Potosí 61 F 4 S Bolivia
Potsdam 94 D 3 NE Germany
Potwar Plateau 134 C 2 plateau,
NE Pakistan
Poŭthĭsăt 137 D 6 *prev.* Pursat.
W Cambodia
Po Valley 96 B 2 *It.* Valle del
Po. Valley, N Italy
Považská Bystrica 99 C 5 *Ger.*
Waagbistritz, *Hung.* Vágbeszterce.
NW Slovakia
Poverty Bay 150 E 4 bay,
SW Pacific Ocean
Póvoa de Varzim 92 B 2
NW Portugal
Povorino 111 B 6
W Russian Federation
Povungnituk *see* Puvirnituq
Poway 47 C 8 California, W USA
Powder River 44 D 2 river,
Montana, NW USA
Powell 44 C 2 Wyoming, C USA
Powell, Lake 44 B 5 lake,
Utah, W USA
Požarevac 100 E 4 *Ger.* Passarowitz.
E Yugoslavia
Poza Rica 51 F 4 *var.* Poza Rica de
Hidalgo. E Mexico
Poza Rica de Hidalgo *see* Poza Rica
Požega 100 D 4 C Yugoslavia
Poznań 98 B 3 *Ger.* Posen,
Posnania. W Poland
Pozoblanco 92 D 4 S Spain
Pozzallo 97 C 8 SW Italy
Prachatice 99 A 5 *Ger.* Prachatitz.
SW Czech Republic
Prachatitz *see* Prachatice
Prague *see* Praha
Praha 99 B 5 *Eng.* Prague, *Ger.* Prag,
Pol. Praga. Country capital,
NW Czech Republic
Praia 74 A 3 country capital,
S Cape Verde
Praslin 55 F 1 E Saint Lucia
Prato 96 B 3 C Italy
Pratt 45 E 5 Kansas, C USA
Prattville 42 D 2 Alabama, S USA
Pravia 92 C 1 N Spain

Preny *see* Prienai
Prenzlau 94 D 3 NE Germany
Prerau *see* Přerov
Přerov 99 C 5 *Ger.* Prerau.
E Czech Republic
Prescott 48 B 2 Arizona USA
Preševo 101 D 5 S Yugoslavia
Presidente Epitácio 63 E 4 S Brazil
Presidente Prudente 57 D 5 S Brazil
Prešov 99 D 5 *var.* Preschau,
Ger. Eperies, *Hung.* Eperjes.
NE Slovakia
Prespa, Lake 101 D 7 *var.* Limni
Prespa, Prespansko Jezero, *Alb.*
Liqen i Prespës, *Gk.* Límni Megáli
Préspa, *Mac.* Prespansko Ezero.
Lake, SE Europe
Preston 89 C 5 NW England, UK
Prestwick 88 C 4 SW Scotland, UK
Pretoria 78 D 4 *var.* Epitoli,
Tshwane. Country capital,
NE South Africa
Preussisch Eylau *see* Bagrationovsk
Preussisch-Stargard *see*
Starogard Gdański
Preußisch Holland *see* Pasłęk
Préveza 105 A 5 W Greece
Pribilof Islands 36 A 3 island
group, Alaska, NW USA
Priboj 100 D 4 W Yugoslavia
Price 44 B 4 Utah, W USA
Prichard 42 C 3 Alabama, S USA
Pridneprovskaya Vozvyshennost'
see Prydniprovs'ka Vysochyna
Priekulé 106 B 3 *Ger.* Prökuls.
W Lithuania
Prienai 107 B 5 *Pol.* Preny.
S Lithuania
Prieska 78 C 5 C South Africa
Prijedor 100 B 3
NW Bosnia & Herzegovina
Prijepolje 100 D 4 W Yugoslavia
Prilep 101 D 6 *Turk.* Perlepe.
S Macedonia
Priluki *see* Pryluky
Primorsk 106 A 4 *Ger.* Fischhausen.
W Russian Federation
Primorsko 104 E 2 *prev.* Keupriya.
SE Bulgaria
Prince Albert 37 F 5 Saskatchewan,
S Canada
Prince-Édouard, Île-du *see*
Prince Edward Island
Prince Edward Island 39 F 4 *Fr.* Île-
du Prince-Édouard. Province,
SE Canada
Prince Edward Islands 69 E 8
island group, S South Africa
Prince George 37 E 5 British
Columbia, SW Canada
Prince of Wales Island 37 F 2
island, NW Canada
Prince of Wales Island 148 B 1
island, Queensland, N Australia
Prince Patrick Island 37 E 2 island,
NW Canada
Prince Rupert 36 D 4 British
Columbia, SW Canada
Princess Charlotte Bay 148 C 2 bay,
W Coral Sea
Princess Elizabeth Land 154 D 3
physical region, Antarctica
Príncipe 76 E 1 *var.* Príncipe Island,
Eng. Prince's Island. Island,
N Sao Tome & Principe
Prinzapolka 53 E 3 NE Nicaragua
Pripet 107 C 7 *Bel.* Prypyats',
Ukr. Prypyat'. River,
Belarus/Ukraine
Pripet Marshes 107 B 7 wetland,
Belarus/Ukraine
Prishtinë *see* Priština

Priština 101 D 5 *Alb.* Prishtinë.
C Yugoslavia
Privas 91 C 5 E France
Prizren 101 D 5 *Alb.* Prizreni.
S Yugoslavia
Prizreni *see* Prizren
Probolinggo 138 D 5 Jawa,
C Indonesia
Probstberg *see* Wyszków
Progreso 51 H 3 SE Mexico
Prökuls *see* Priekulé
Prokuplje 101 E 5 C Yugoslavia
Prome 136 B 4 *var.* Pyè.
SW Myanmar
Promyshlennyy 110 E 3 *var.*
Promšlennyj, Promyšlenny.
NW Russian Federation
Prostějov 99 C 5 *Ger.* Prossnitz, *Pol.*
Prosciejów. SE Czech Republic
Provence 91 D 6 cultural region,
SE France
Providence 41 G 3 state capital,
Rhode Island, NE USA
Providence *see* Fort Providence
Providencia, Isla de 53 F 3 island,
Colombia
Provo 44 B 4 Utah, W USA
Provost 37 F 5 Alberta, SW Canada
Prudhoe Bay 36 D 2 Alaska,
NW USA
Pruszków 98 D 3 *Ger.* Kaltdorf.
C Poland
Prut 108 D 4 *Ger.* Pruth. River,
E Europe
Pruth *see* Prut
Pružana *see* Pruzhany
Pruzhany 107 B 6 *Pol.* Pruzana.
SW Belarus
Prychornomors'ka Nyzovyna 109
E 4 *Eng.* Black Sea Lowland.
Physical region, S Ukraine
Prydniprovs'ka Vysochyna 109 G 3
Rus. Pridneprovskaya
Vozvyshennost'. Mountain range,
NW Ukraine
Prydz Bay 154 D 3 bay,
S Indian Ocean
Pryluky 109 E 2 *Rus.* Priluki.
NE Ukraine
Prymors'k 109 G 4 *Rus.* Primorsk;
prev. Prymors'koye. SE Ukraine
Przemyśl 99 E 5 *Rus.* Peremyshl.
SE Poland
Przheval'sk *see* Karakol
Psará 105 D 5 island, E Greece
Pskov 110 A 4 *Ger.* Pleskau, *Latv.*
Pleskava. W Russian Federation
Pskov, Lake 106 E 3 *Est.* Pihkva
Järv, *Ger.* Pleskauer See,
Rus. Pskovskoye Ozero.
Lake, Estonia/Russian Federation
Ptich' *see* Ptsich
Ptsich 107 C 7 *Rus.* Ptich'. River,
SE Belarus
Ptsich 107 C 7 *Rus.* Ptich'. SE Belarus
Ptuj 95 E 7 *Ger.* Pettau;
anc. Poetovio. NE Slovenia
Pucallpa 60 C 3 C Peru
Puck 98 C 2 N Poland
Pudasjärvi 84 E 4 C Finland
Puduchcheri *see* Pondicherry
Puebla 51 F 4 *var.* Puebla de
Zaragoza. S Mexico
Puebla de Zaragoza *see* Puebla
Pueblo 44 D 5 Colorado, C USA
Puerto Acosta 61 E 4 W Bolivia
Puerto Aisén 65 B 6 S Chile
Puerto Arturo 61 G 3 N Bolivia
Puerto Ayacucho 58 D 3
SW Venezuela
Puerto Bahía Negra 64 D 1
N Paraguay

Puerto Baquerizo Moreno 60 B 5
var. Baquerizo Moreno. Galápa
Islands, E Pacific Ocean
Puerto Barrios 52 C 2 E Guatema
Puerto Berrío 58 B 2 C Colombia
Puerto Cabello 58 D 1 N Venezu
Puerto Cabezas 53 E 2 *var.* Bilwi
NE Nicaragua
Puerto Carreño 58 D 3 NE Colon
Puerto Casado 64 D 2 C Paragua
Puerto Cortés 52 C 2 NW Hondu
Puerto Cumarebo 58 C 1 N Venezu
Puerto Deseado 65 C 7 SE Argent
Puerto Escondido 51 F 5 W Mex
Puerto Francisco de Orellana 60
var. Coca. N Ecuador
Puerto Inírida 58 D 3 *var.* Oband
E Colombia
Puerto La Cruz 59 E 1 NE Venez
Puerto Lempira 53 E 2 E Hondu
Puerto Limón *see* Limón
Puertollano 92 D 4 SW Spain
Puerto López 58 C 1 N Colombi
Puerto Maldonado 61 E 3 E Peru
Puerto Montt 65 B 5 C Chile
Puerto Natales 65 B 7 S Chile
Puerto Nuevo 58 C 3 N Colomb
Puerto Obaldía 53 H 5 NE Pana
Puerto Plata 55 E 3 *var.*
San Felipe de Puerto Plata.
N Dominican Republic
Puerto Portillo 60 D 3 E Peru
Puerto Princesa 139 E 2 *off.* Puer
Princesa City. Palawan,
W Philippines
Puerto Princesa City *see*
Puerto Princesa
Puerto Príncipe *see* Camagüey
Puerto Rico 55 F 3 *off.*
Commonwealth of Puerto Ric
prev. Porto Rico. US
commonwealth territory,
N Caribbean Sea
Puerto Rico Trench 66 B 4 trenc
W Atlantic Ocean
Puerto San José *see* San José
Puerto San Julián 65 B 7
var. San Julián. SE Argentina
Puerto Suárez 61 H 4 E Bolivia
Puerto Supe 60 C 3 W Peru
Puerto Vallarta 50 D 4 SW Mexi
Puerto Varas 65 B 5 C Chile
Puerto Viejo 53 E 4 NE Costa Ri
Puertoviejo *see* Portoviejo
Puerto Williams 65 C 8 S Chile
Puget Sound 46 B 1 inlet,
E Pacific Ocean
Pukaki, Lake 151 B 6 lake,
South Island, SW New Zealan
Pukekohe 150 D 3 North Island
N New Zealand
Pukhavichy 107 D 6
Rus. Pukhovichi. C Belarus
Pukhovichi *see* Pukhavichy
Pula 100 A 3 *It.* Pola; *prev.* Pulj.
NW Croatia
Puławy 98 E 4 *Ger.* Neu Amerik
E Poland
Pul-i-Khumri *see* Pol-e Khomrī
Pullman 46 C 2
Washington, NW USA
Pułtusk 98 D 3 C Poland
Puná, Isla 60 A 2 island, SW Ecu
Pune 134 C 5 *prev.* Poona. W Indi
Punjab 134 C 2 *prev.* Western
Punjab, West Punjab. Province
E Pakistan
Puno 61 E 4 S Peru
Punta Alta 65 C 5 E Argentina
Punta Arenas 65 B 8 *prev.*
Magallanes . S Chile

ta Gorda 53 E 4 SE Nicaragua
ta Gorda 52 C 2 SE Belize
tarenas 52 D 4 W Costa Rica
to Fijo 58 C 1 N Venezuela
uya, Nevado 61 E 4 mountain,
W Bolivia
i 135 F 5 var. Jagannath.
E India
merend 86 C 3 C Netherlands
sat see Poŭthĭsăt
us 62 C 2 var. Río Purús.
River,
Brazil/Peru
ús, Río see Purus
an 128 E 4 off. Pusan-kwangyōksi,
var. Busan, Jap. Fusan.
E South Korea
spökladány 99 D 6 E Hungary
orana Mountains see
Putorana, Plato
orana, Plato 115 E 3 var.
Putorana Mountains. Mountain
range, N Russian Federation
talam 132 C 3 W Sri Lanka
tgarden 94 C 2 N Germany
umayo 58 B 5 var. Içá. River,
N South America
umayo, Río see Içá
armani 106 D 2 Ger. Talkhof.
E Estonia
yirnituq 38 D 1 prev.
Povungnituk. Québec, NE Canada
yallup 46 B 2 Washington,
NW USA
atigorsk 111 B 7
SW Russian Federation
atikhatki see P″yatykhatky
yatykhatky 109 F 3 Rus.
Pyatikhatki. C Ukraine
è see Prome
etrykaw 107 C 7 Rus. Petrikov.
SE Belarus
inmana 136 B 4 C Myanmar
los 105 B 6 S Greece
ôngyang 128 D 4 Eng.
Pyongyang. Country capital,
SW North Korea
ramiden 83 G 2 W Svalbard
ramid Lake 47 C 5 lake,
Nevada, W USA
renees 93 F 1 Fr. Pyrénées, Sp.
Pirineos; anc. Pyrenaei Montes.
Mountain range, SW Europe
rgos 105 B 6 var. Pírgos. S Greece
ritz see Pyrzyce
ryatyn 109 F 2 Rus. Piryatin.
NE Ukraine
rzyce 98 B 3 Ger. Pyritz.
NW Poland
u 136 B 4 S Myanmar
untaza 136 B 4 S Myanmar

Q

′ al Jafr 119 C 7 lake, S Jordan
aanaaq 82 D 1 var. Qânâq, Dan.
Thule. N Greenland
abatiya 119 E 6 N West Bank
ibis see Gabès
ibis, Khalīj see Gabès, Golfe de
afşah see Gafsa
aidam Pendi 126 C 4 basin,
C China
al'aikhum 123 F 3
Rus. Kalaikhum. S Tajikistan
alāt see Kalāt
al 'at Bīshah 121 B 5
SW Saudi Arabia
alqiliya 119 D 7 var. Qalqiliya.
W West Bank
amdo 126 D 5 S China
andahār see Kandahār
anix see Alazani

Qaqortoq 82 C 5 Dan.
Julianehåb. SW Greenland
Qaraghandy see Karaganda
Qarataū see Karatau
Qarokŭl 123 F 3 Rus. Karakul'.
E Tajikistan
Qars see Kars
Qarshi 123 E 3 Rus. Karshi;
prev. Bek-Budi. S Uzbekistan
Qasigiannguit 82 C 3 var.
Qasigianguit, Dan. Christianshåb.
W Greenland
Qaṭanā 119 B 5 var. Katana. SW Syria

Qatar
120 D 4 Ar. Dawlat Qaṭar.
Monarchy, Qatar

Official name: State of Qatar Date
of formation: 1971 Capital: Doha
Population: 500,000 Total area:
4,247 sq miles (11,000 sq km)
Languages: Arabic*, Farsi (Persian),
Urdu, Hindi, English
Religions: Sunni Muslim 86%,
Hindu 10%, Christian 4% Ethnic
mix: Arab 40%, South Asian 35%,
Persian 12%, other 13%
Government: Absolute monarchy
Currency: Riyal = 100 dirhams

Qattara Depression see
Qaṭṭâra, Monkhafad el
Qaṭṭâra, Monkhafad el 72 B 1
var. Munkhafaç al Qaḍḍârah,
Eng. Qattara Depression.
Desert, NW Egypt
Qazimämmäd 117 H 3 Rus. Kazi
Magomed. SE Azerbaijan
Qazris see Cáceres
Qazvīn 120 C 2 var. Kazvin.
NW Iran
Qena 72 B 2 var. Qinâ; anc. Caene,
Caenepolis. E Egypt
Qeqertarsuaq 82 C 3 var.
Qeqertarssuaq, Dan. Godhavn.
W Greenland
Qeqertarsuaq 82 C 3 island,
W Greenland
Qeqertarsuatsiaat 82 B 4
Dan. Fiskenæsset. S Greenland
Qeshm 120 D 4 var. Jazīreh-ye
Qeshm, Qeshm Island.
Island, S Iran
Qezi'ot 119 A 7 S Israel
Qilian Shan 128 A 3 var. Kilien
Mountains. Mountain range,
N China
Qimantag Shan 126 C 4 mountain
range, C China
Qimusseriarsuaq 82 C 2 Dan.
Melville Bugt, Eng. Melville Bay.
Bay, E Baffin Bay
Qingdao 128 D 4 var. Ching-Tao,
Ch'ing-tao, Tsingtao, Tsintao,
Ger. Tsingtau. E China
Qinghai 126 D 4 var. Chinghai,
Koko Nor, Qing, Tsinghai.
Province, C China
Qinghai Hu 126 D 4 var. Ch'ing
Hai, Tsing Hai, Mong. Koko
Nor. Lake, C China
Qinghai Nanshan 126 D 4
mountain range, N China
Qinhuangdao 128 D 3 NE China
Qinzhou 129 B 6 SE China
Qiong see Hainan
Qiqihar 125 E 1 var. Ch'i-ch'i-ha-
erh,Tsitsihar; prev. Lungkiaw.
NE China
Qira 126 B 4 NW China
Qita Ghazzah see Gaza Strip
Qitai 126 C 3 NW China
Qitaihe 128 E 2 NE China

Qīzān see Jīzān
Qizilrabat 123 G 3 Rus. Kyzylrabot.
SE Tajikistan
Qolleh-ye Damāvand 120 D 3
mountain, N Iran
Qom 120 C 3 var. Kum, Qum.
N Iran
Qondūz, Daryā-ye 123 E 4 river,
NE Afghanistan
Qornet es Saouda 118 B 4
mountain, NE Lebanon
Qorveh 120 C 3 var. Qerveh,
Qurveh. W Iran
Quang Ngai 137 E 5 var.
Quangngai, Quang Nghia.
E Vietnam
Quanzhou 129 C 6 S China
Quanzhou 129 D 6
var. Ch'uan-chou, Tsinkiang;
prev. Chin-chiang. SE China
Quarles, Pegunungan 139 E 4
mountain range, Celebes,
W Indonesia
Quartu Sant' Elena 97 A 6 W Italy
Quba 117 H 2 Rus. Kuba.
N Azerbaijan
Qubba see Ba'qūbah
Queanbeyan 149 D 7
New South Wales, SE Australia
Quebec see Québec
Québec 38 D 3 var. Quebec.
Province, Québec, SE Canada
Queen Charlotte 36 C 5 Queen
Charlotte Islands, SW Canada
Queen Charlotte Islands 36 D 5
Fr. Îles de la Reine-Charlotte.
Island group, SW Canada
Queen Charlotte Sound 36 D 5 bay,
NE Pacific Ocean
Queen Elizabeth Islands 37 F 2
Fr. Îles de la Reine-Élisabeth.
Island group, N Canada
Queen Maud Land 154 C 2
var. Dronning Maud Land.
Physical region, Antarctica
Queensland 148 B 4 state,
N Australia
Queenstown 151 B 7 South Island,
SW New Zealand
Queenstown 149 B 8 Tasmania,
SE Australia
Queenstown 78 D 5 S South Africa
Queenstown 138 A 1 S Singapore
Quelimane 79 E 3 var. Kilimane,
Kilmain, Quilimane.
NE Mozambique
Quepos 53 E 5 S Costa Rica
Que Que see Kwekwe
Querétaro 51 E 4 C Mexico
Quesada 53 E 4 var. Ciudad
Quesada, San Carlos. N Costa Rica
Quetta 134 B 2 province capital,
SW Pakistan
Quetzaltenango see Quezaltenango
Quezaltenango 52 A 2 var.
Quetzaltenango. W Guatemala
Quezon 139 F 2 off. Quezon City.
C Philippines
Quezon City see Quezon
Quibdó 58 B 3 W Colombia
Quilon 125 C 3 var. Kolam, Kollam.
SW India
Quimper 90 A 3 anc. Quimper
Corentin. NW France
Quimper Corentin see Quimper
Quimperlé 90 A 3 NW France
Quincy 40 A 4 Illinois, N USA
Quirós Fracture Zone 153 F 4
fracture zone, E Pacific Ocean
Quissico 79 E 4 S Mozambique
Quito 60 B 1 country capital,
N Ecuador

Qüqon 123 F 2 var. Khokand,
Rus. Kokand. E Uzbekistan
Qürghonteppa 123 E 3
Rus. Kurgan-Tyube. SW Tajikistan
Qurlurtuuq see Coppermine
Qŭs 72 B 2 anc. Apollinopolis
Parva. E Egypt
Quy Nhon 137 E 5 var. Qui Nhon,
Quinhon. SE Vietnam

R

Raab see Rába
Raahe 84 D 4 Swe. Brahestad.
W Finland
Raalte 86 D 3 E Netherlands
Raamsdonksveer 86 C 4
S Netherlands
Raasiku 106 D 2 Ger. Rasik.
NW Estonia
Raas Xaafuun 72 E 4 var. Ras
Hafun. Headland, NE Somalia
Rabat 70 C 2 var. al Dar al Baida.
Country capital, NW Morocco
Rabat see Victoria
Rabinal 52 B 2 C Guatemala
Rabka 99 D 5 S Poland
Rabyānah, Ramlat 71 G 3
var. Rebiana Sand Sea, Şaḩrā'
Rabyānah. Desert, SE Libya
Race, Cape 39 H 4 headland,
Newfoundland and Labrador,
E Canada
Rach Gia 137 D 6 SW Vietnam
Rach Gia, Vinh 137 D 6 bay,
South China Sea/Pacific Ocean
Racine 40 B 3 Wisconsin, N USA
Rădăuţi 108 C 3 Ger. Radautz,
Hung. Rádóc. N Romania
Radom 98 D 4 C Poland
Radomsko 98 C 4
Rus. Novoradomsk. C Poland
Radomyshl' 108 D 2 N Ukraine
Radoviš 101 E 6 prev. Radovište.
E Macedonia
Radoviš te see Radoviš
Radviliškis 106 C 4 N Lithuania
Radzyń Podlaski 98 E 4 E Poland
Rae-Edzo 37 E 4 Northwest
Territories, NW Canada
Raeside, Lake 147 C 5 lake,
C Australia
Raetihi 150 D 3 North Island,
C New Zealand
Rafaela 64 C 3 E Argentina
Rafah 119 A 7 S Israel
Rafḩā' 120 B 4 N Saudi Arabia
Ragged Island Range 54 C 2 island
group, S Bahamas
Ragnit see Neman
Ragusa 97 C 7 SW Italy
Ragusa see Dubrovnik
Rahachow 107 D 7
Rus. Rogachev. SE Belarus
Rahaeng see Tak
Rahīmyär Khän 134 C 3
SE Pakistan
Rahovec see Orahovac
Raiatea 145 G 4 island,
W French Polynesia
Rāichūr 132 C 1 C India
Rainy Lake 38 B 4 lake, Ontario,
C Canada
Raipur 135 E 4 C India
Rājahmundry 135 E 5 E India
Rajang see Rajang, Batang
Rajang, Batang 138 D 3 var. Rajang.
River, Borneo, E Malaysia
Rājapālaiyam 132 C 3 SE India
Rājasthān 134 C 3 state,
NW India

Rājkot 134 C 4 W India
Rāj Nāndgaon 135 E 4 C India
Rājshāhi 135 G 4 *prev.* Rampur
Boalia. W Bangladesh
Rakahanga 145 F 3 island,
N Cook Islands
Rakke 106 E 2 NE Estonia
Rakvere 106 E 2 *Ger.* Wesenberg.
N Estonia
Raleigh 43 F 1 state capital,
North Carolina, SE USA
Raleigh Bay 43 G 1 bay,
NW Atlantic Ocean
Ralik Chain 144 D 1 island group,
W Marshall Islands
Ram 119 B 8 SW Jordan
Ramallah 119 E 7 C West Bank
Ramat Gan 119 A 6 C Israel
Râmnicu Sărat 108 C 4 *prev.*
Râmnicul-Sărat, Rîmnicu-Sărat.
E Romania
Râmnicu Vîlcea 108 B 4
prev. Rîmnicu Vîlcea. C Romania
Ramotswa 78 C 4 SE Botswana
Rampur Boalia *see* Rājshāhi
Ramree Island 136 A 4 island,
W Myanmar
Ramtha *see* Ar Ramthā
Rancagua 64 B 4 C Chile
Rānchi 135 F 4 N India
Randers 85 B 7 C Denmark
Rangiora 151 C 6 South Island,
C New Zealand
Rangoon *see* Yangon
Rangpur 135 G 3 N Bangladesh
Rankin Inlet 37 G 3 Northwest
Territories, C Canada
Rankovićevo *see* Kraljevo
Ranong 137 B 6 SW Thailand
Rantoul 40 B 4 Illinois, N USA
Rapid City 44 D 3
South Dakota, N USA
Räpina 106 E 3 *Ger.* Rappin.
SE Estonia
Rapla 106 D 2 *Ger.* Rappel.
NW Estonia
Rappel *see* Rapla
Rappin *see* Räpina
Rarotonga 145 F 5 island,
S Cook Islands
Ras al'Ain *see* Ra's al 'Ayn
Ra's al 'Ayn 118 D 1 *var.* Ras al'Ain.
N Syria
Ra's an Naqb 119 B 8 S Jordan
Raseiniai 106 B 4 C Lithuania
Ras Hafun *see* Raas Xaafuun
Rasht 120 C 2 *var.* Resht. NW Iran
Rasik *see* Raasiku
Râşnov 108 C 4 *Hung.*
Barcarozsnyó; *prev.* Rişnov,
Hung. Rozsnyó. C Romania
Rason Lake 147 C 5 lake,
C Australia
Ratak Chain 144 D 1 island group,
E Marshall Islands
Ratan 85 C 5 C Sweden
Rat Buri *see* Ratchaburi
Ratchaburi 137 C 5 *var.* Rat Buri.
C Thailand
Ratlām 134 D 4 *prev.* Rutlam. C India
Ratnapura 132 D 4 S Sri Lanka
Raton 48 D 1 New Mexico, SW USA
Rättvik 85 C 5 C Sweden
Raudhatain *see* Ar Rawḍatayn
Raufarhöfn 83 E 4 NE Iceland
Raukawa *see* Cook Strait
Rauma 85 D 5 *Swe.* Raumo.
SW Finland
Raumo *see* Rauma
Raurkela 135 F 4 *prev.* Rourkela.
E India

Ravenna 96 C 3 N Italy
Rāvi 134 C 2 river, India/Pakistan
Rāwalpindi 134 C 1 NE Pakistan
Rawa Mazowiecka 98 D 4 C Poland
Rawicz 98 C 4 *Ger.* Rawitsch.
W Poland
Rawitsch *see* Rawicz
Rawlins 44 C 3 Wyoming, C USA
Rawson 65 C 6 SE Argentina
Rayak 118 B 4 *var.* Rayaq, Riyāq.
E Lebanon
Rayong 137 C 6 C Thailand
Razāzah, Buḥayrat ar 120 B 3
var. Baír al Mili. Lake, C Iraq
Razdolnoye *see* Rozdol'ne
Razelm, Lacul *see* Razim, Lacul
Razgrad 104 D 2 NE Bulgaria
Razim, Lacul 108 D 5 *prev.* Lacul
Razelm. Lagoon, W Black Sea
Răznas Ezers 106 D 4 lake,
SE Latvia
Reading 89 D 7 S England, UK
Reading 41 F 4 Pennsylvania,
NE USA
Realicó 64 C 4 C Argentina
Reâng Kesei 137 D 5 W Cambodia
Rebecca, Lake 147 C 6 lake,
Western Australia, C Australia
Rebun-tō 130 C 1 island, Japan
Recherche, Archipelago of the 147
C 7 island group, SW Australia
Rechitsa *see* Rechytsa
Rechytsa 107 D 7 *Rus.* Rechitsa.
SW Belarus
Recife 63 G 2 *prev.* Pernambuco.
State capital, E Brazil
Recklinghausen 94 A 4 W Germany
Recogne 87 D 7 SE Belgium
Reconquista 64 D 3 NE Argentina
Red Bluff Lake 49 E 3 lake, SW USA
Red Deer 37 E 5 Alberta, SW Canada
Redding 47 B 5 California, W USA
Redon 90 B 4 NW France
Red River 136 C 2 *var.* Yijan
Chiang. River, China/Vietnam
Red River 35 C 6 river, S USA
Red River 45 E 1 river,
Canada/USA
Red Sea 140 A 3 *var.* Sinus
Arabious. Sea, NW Indian Ocean
Red Sea Hills 72 C 3 hill range,
NE Sudan
Red Wing 45 G 2 Minnesota, N USA
Reedley 47 C 6 California, W USA
Reefton 151 C 5 South Island,
C New Zealand
Refahiye 117 E 3 C Turkey
Regensburg 95 C 6 *Eng.* Ratisbon,
Fr. Ratisbonne; *hist.* Ratisbona,
anc. Castra Regina, Reginum.
SE Germany
Regenstauf 95 C 6 SE Germany
Reggane 70 D 3 C Algeria
Reggio di Calabria 97 D 7
var. Reggio Calabria, *Gk.* Rhegion;
anc. Regium, Rhegium. SW Italy
Reggio nell' Emilia 96 B 2 *var.*
Reggio Emilia, *abbrev.* Reggio;
anc. Regium Lepidum. N Italy
Reghin 108 C 4 *Ger.* Sächsisch-
Reen, *Hung.* Szászrégen;
prev. Reghinul Săsesc,
Ger. Sächsisch-Regen. C Romania
Regina 37 F 5 province capital,
Saskatchewan, S Canada
Registan *see* Rīgestān
Rehoboth 78 B 4 C Namibia
Reichenau *see* Bogatynia
Reichenberg *see* Liberec

Reid 147 D 6 Western Australia,
S Australia
Reikjavik *see* Reykjavík
Ré, Île de 90 A 4 island, W France
Reims 90 D 3 *Eng.* Rheims; *anc.*
Durocortorum, Remi. N France
Reindeer Lake 34 C 4 lake,
C Canada
Reine-Charlotte, Îles de la *see*
Queen Charlotte Islands
Reine-Élisabeth, Îles de la *see*
Queen Elizabeth Islands
Reinosa 92 D 1 N Spain
Reliance 37 F 4 Northwest
Territories, C Canada
Rendina *see* Rentína
Rendsburg 94 B 2 N Germany
Rengat 138 B 4 Sumatera,
W Indonesia
Reni 108 D 4 SW Ukraine
Rennell 144 C 4 *var.* Mu Nggava.
Island, S Solomon Islands
Rennes 90 B 3 *Bret.* Roazon;
anc. Condate. NW France
Reno 47 C 5 Nevada, W USA
Renqiu 128 C 4 NE China
Rentína 105 B 5 *var.* Rendina.
C Greece
Repulse Bay 37 G 3 Northwest
Territories, NE Canada
Resht *see* Rasht
Resistencia 64 D 3 NE Argentina
Reşita 108 A 4 *Ger.* Reschitza,
Hung. Resicabánya. W Romania
Resolute 37 F 2 Cornwallis Island,
N Canada
Resolution Island 151 A 7 island,
South Island, SW New Zealand
Resolution Island 39 E 1 island,
Northwest Territories, NE Canada
Réunion 79 H 4 *off.* La Réunion.
French overseas department,
E Africa
Reus 93 F 2 E Spain
Reutlingen 95 B 6 S Germany
Reuver 87 D 5 SE Netherlands
Revillagigedo Islands *see*
Revillagigedo, Islas
Revillagigedo, Islas 50 B 5
Eng. Revillagigedo Islands. Island
group, SW Mexico
Rexburg 46 E 3 Idaho, NW USA
Reyes 61 F 3 NW Bolivia
Rey, Isla del 53 G 5 island,
SE Panama
Reykjanes Basin 66 C 2 undersea
basin, N Atlantic Ocean
Reykjavík 83 E 5 *var.* Reikjavik.
Country capital, W Iceland
Reynosa 51 E 2 C Mexico
Reza, Gora 122 C 3 *var.* Gora Riza.
Mountain, SW Turkmenistan
Rezé 90 B 4 NW France
Rēzekne 106 D 4 *Ger.* Rositten;
prev. Rus. Rezhitsa. SE Latvia
Rezovo 104 E 3 *Turk.* Rezve.
SE Bulgaria
Rezve *see* Rezovo
Rhätikon 95 B 7 mountain range,
C Europe
Rheine 94 A 4 *var.* Rheine in
Westfalen. NW Germany
Rheine in Westfalen *see* Rheine
Rheinisches Schiefergebirge 95 A 5
var. Rhine State Uplands,
Eng. Rhenish Slate Mountains.
Mountain range, W Germany
Rhine 80 D 4 *Dut.* Rijn, *Fr.* Rhin,
Ger. Rhein. River, W Europe
Rhinelander 40 B 2
Wisconsin, N USA
Rho 96 B 2 N Italy

Rhode Island 41 G 3 *off.* State of
Rhode Island and Providence
Plantations; *nicknames* Little
Rhody, Ocean State. State, NE U
Rhodes *see* Ródos
Rhodope Mountains 104 C 3
var. Rodhópi Óri, *Bul.* Rhodope
Planina, Rodopi, *Gk.* Orosirá
Rodhópis, *Turk.* Dospad Dagh.
Mountain range, Bulgaria/Gree
Rhondda 89 C 7 S Wales, UK
Rhône 80 C 4 river,
France/Switzerland
Rhum 88 B 3 *var.* Rum. Island,
W Scotland, UK
Ribble 89 D 5 river,
NW England, UK
Ribeira 92 B 1 NW Spain
Ribeirão Preto 63 F 4 S Brazil
Riberalta 61 E 2 N Bolivia
Ribniţa 108 D 3 *var.* Rābniţa,
Rus. Rybnitsa. NE Moldova
Richard Toll 74 B 3 N Senegal
Richfield 44 B 4 Utah, W USA
Richland 46 C 2
Washington, NW USA
Richmond 151 C 5 North Island,
C New Zealand
Richmond 41 E 5 state capital,
Virginia, NE USA
Richmond 40 C 5 Kentucky, E US
Richmond Range 151 C 5 mounta
range, North Island,
C New Zealand
Ricomagus *see* Riom
Ridgecrest 47 C 7 California, W US.
Ried *see* Ried im Innkreis
Ried im Innkreis 95 D 6 *var.* Ried
NW Austria
Riemst 87 D 6 NE Belgium
Riesa 94 D 4 E Germany
Rift Valley *see* Great Rift Valley
Riga *see* Rīga
Rīga 106 C 3 *var.* Riga, *Eng.* Riga.
Country capital, C Latvia
Riga, Gulf of 106 C 3 *Est.* Liivi
Laht, *Ger.* Rigaer Bucht, *Latv.*
Rīgas Jūras Līcis, *Rus.* Rizhskiy
Zaliv; *prev.* Riia Laht. Gulf,
E Baltic Sea
Rīgān 120 E 4 SE Iran
Rīgestān 122 D 5 *var.* Registan.
Physical region, S Afghanistan
Riihimäki 85 D 5 S Finland
Rijeka 100 A 2 *Ger.* Sankt Veit am
Flaum, *It.* Fiume, *Slvn.* Reka;
anc. Tarsatica. NW Croatia
Rijssen 86 E 3 E Netherlands
Rimah, Wādī ar 120 B 4 *var.* Wādí
ar Rummah. Dry watercourse,
C Saudi Arabia
Rimini 96 C 3 *anc.* Ariminum.
N Italy
Rîmnicu Vîlcea *see* Râmnicu Vâlce
Rimouski 39 E 4 Québec,
SE Canada
Rincón del Bonete, Lago Artificial
de *see* Río Negro, Embalse del
Ringebu 85 B 5 S Norway
Ringen *see* Rõngu
Ringkøbing Fjord 85 A 7 fjord,
E North Sea
Ringsaker 85 B 5 S Norway
Ringvassøy 84 C 2 island, N Norwa
Ringwood *see* Rio de Janeiro
Riobamba 60 B 1 C Ecuador
Río Bravo 51 E 2 C Mexico
Río Cuarto 64 C 4 C Argentina
Rio de Janeiro 63 F 4
var. Rio. State capital, SE Brazil
Río Gallegos 65 B 7 *var.* Gallegos,
Puerto Gallegos. S Argentina

o Grande 63 E 5 *var.* São Pedro
do Rio Grande do Sul. S Brazil
o Grande do Norte 63 G 2
off. Estado do Rio Grande do
Norte. State, E Brazil
o Grande do Norte, Estado do *see*
Rio Grande do Norte
o Grande do Sul 63 E 5
off. Estado do Rio Grande do Sul.
State, S Brazil
o Grande do Sul, Estado do *see*
Rio Grande do Sul
o Grande Plateau *see*
Rio Grande Rise
o Grande Rise 57 E 5 *var.*
Rio Grande Plateau. Undersea
plateau, SW Atlantic Ocean
ohacha 58 C 1 N Colombia
om 91 C 5 *anc.* Ricomagus.
C France
o Negro, Embalse del 64 D 4
var. Lago Artificial de Rincón del
Bonete. Reservoir, C Uruguay
o Rancho Estates 48 D 2
New Mexico, SW USA
o Santa Cruz 65 B 7 S Argentina
overde *see* Río Verde
o Verde 51 E 4 *var.* Rioverde.
C Mexico
poll 93 G 2 NE Spain
ishiri-tō 130 C 2 *var.* Risiri Tô.
Island, NE Japan
isiri Tô *see* Rishiri-tō
isti 106 D 2 *Ger.* Kreuz. W Estonia
ivas 52 D 4 SW Nicaragua
vera 64 D 3 N Uruguay
ver Falls 40 A 2 Wisconsin, N USA
verside 47 C 8 California, W USA
verton 151 A 7 South Island,
SW New Zealand
verton 44 C 3 Wyoming, C USA
iviera Beach 43 F 4
Florida, SE USA
ivière-du-Loup 39 E 4 Québec,
SE Canada
ivne 108 C 1 *Pol.* Równe,
Rus. Rovno. NW Ukraine
ivoli 96 A 2 NW Italy
ixheim 90 E 4 E France
iyadh *see* Ar Riyāḍ
iza, Gora *see* Reza, Gora
ize 117 E 2 NE Turkey
izhao 128 D 4 E China
kiz, Lac 74 B 3 lake,
SW Mauritania
oad Town 55 F 3 dependent
territory capital,
C British Virgin Islands
oanne 91 D 5 *anc.* Rodunma.
E France
oanoke 41 E 5 Virginia, NE USA
oanoke Rapids 43 F 1 North
Carolina, SE USA
oanoke River 43 F 1 river, E USA
oatán 52 C 2 *var.* Coxen Hole,
Coxin Hole. N Honduras
obinson Ranges 147 B 5 mountain
range, Western Australia,
W Australia
obson, Mount 37 E 5 mountain,
Alberta, SW Canada
obstown 49 G 5 Texas, S USA
oca Partida, Isla 50 B 5 island,
W Mexico
ocas, Atol das 63 H 2 island,
E Brazil
ochefort 91 B 5 *var.* Rochefort sur
Mer. W France
ochefort 87 C 7 SE Belgium
ochefort sur Mer *see* Rochefort
ochester 41 E 3
New York, NE USA

Rochester 41 G 2
New Hampshire, NE USA
Rochester 45 G 3
Minnesota, N USA
Rockall Bank 66 C 2 undersea
bank, N Atlantic Ocean
Rockford 40 B 3 Illinois, N USA
Rockhampton 148 D 4
Queensland, E Australia
Rock Hill 43 E 1
South Carolina, SE USA
Rockingham 147 B 6 Western
Australia, SW Australia
Rock Island 40 B 3 Illinois, N USA
Rock Sound 54 C 1 C Bahamas
Rock Springs 44 B 3
Wyoming, C USA
Rockstone 59 F 3 C Guyana
Rocky Mountains 34 B 4 *var.*
Rockies, *Fr.* Montagnes
Rocheuses. Mountain range,
NW USA
Roden 86 E 2 NE Netherlands
Rodez 91 C 6 *anc.* Segodunum.
S France
Ródos 105 E 7 *var.* Ródhos,
Eng. Rhodes, *It.* Rodi. Ródos,
SE Greece
Ródos 105 E 7 *var.* Ródhos,
Eng. Rhodes, *It.* Rodi;
anc. Rhodos. Island, Dodekánisos,
SE Greece
Rodunma *see* Roanne
Roebuck Bay 146 B 3 bay,
E Indian Ocean
Roermond 87 D 5 SE Netherlands
Roeselare 87 A 6 *Fr.* Roulers; *prev.*
Rousselaere. W Belgium
Rogačhëv *see* Rahachow
Rogers 42 A 1 Arkansas, C USA
Roggeveld Berge 78 C 5 mountain
range, S South Africa
Roi Et 137 D 5 *var.* Muang Roi Et,
Roi Ed. NE Thailand
Roja 106 D 4 NW Latvia
Rokiškis 106 C 4 NE Lithuania
Rokycany 99 A 5 *Ger.* Rokytzan.
W Czech Republic
Rokytzan *see* Rokycany
Rôlas, Ilha das 76 E 2 island, S Sao
Tome & Principe
Rolla 45 G 5 Missouri, C USA
Röm *see* Rømø
Roma 96 C 4 *Eng.* Rome. Country
capital, C Italy
Roma 149 D 5 Queensland,
E Australia
Roman 108 C 4 *Hung.* Románvásár.
NE Romania
Roman 104 C 2 NW Bulgaria
Romania
108 B 4 *Bul.* Rumŭniya,
Ger. Rumänien, *Hung.* Románia,
Rom. Romînia, *SCr.* Rumunjska,
Ukr. Romuniya; *prev.* Republica
Socialistă România, Roumania,
Rumania, Socialist Republic of
Romania, *Rom.* Romînia.
Republic, SE Europe

Official name: Romania **Date of
formation:** 1947 **Capital:** Bucharest
Population: 23.4 million **Total area:**
91,700 sea miles (237,500 sq km)
Languages: Romanian*, Hungarian
Religions: Romanian Orthodox 70%,
Roman Catholic 6%, Protestant 6%,
other 18% **Ethnic mix:** Romanian
89%, Hungarian 8%, other (inc.
Gypsy) 3% **Government:** Multiparty
republic **Currency:** Leu = 100 bani

Románvásár *see* Roman
Rome 42 D 2 Georgia, SE USA
Rome *see* Roma
Romny 109 F 2 NE Ukraine
Rømø 85 A 7 *Ger.* Röm. Island,
SW Denmark
Ronda 92 D 5 S Spain
Rondônia 62 D 3 *off.* Território de
Rondônia. State, W Brazil
Rondônia, State, W Brazil *see*
Rondônia
Rondonópolis 63 E 3 W Brazil
Rongelap Atoll 144 D 1 *var.* Rônlap.
Island, NW Marshall Islands
Rŏngu 106 D 3 *Ger.* Ringen.
SE Estonia
Rônlap *see* Rongelap Atoll
Rønne 85 B 8 E Denmark
Ronne Ice Shelf 154 B 3 ice shelf,
Antarctica
Roosendaal 87 C 5 S Netherlands
Roraima 62 D 1 *off.* Território de
Roraima; *prev.* Território do Rio
Branco. State, N Brazil
Roraima, Mount 59 F 3 mountain,
N South America
Røros 85 B 5 S Norway
Rosa, Lake 54 D 2 lake, S Bahamas
Rosario 64 D 4 E Argentina
Rosario 64 D 2 C Paraguay
Rosario *see* Rosarito
Rosarito 50 A 1 *var.* Rosario.
NW Mexico
Roscianum *see* Rossano
Roscommon 40 C 2
Michigan, N USA
Roseau 55 G 4 *prev.* Charlotte Town.
Country capital, SW Dominica
Roseburg 46 B 4 Oregon, NW USA
Rosenberg 49 G 4 Texas, S USA
Rosenheim 95 C 6 S Germany
Rosia 93 H 5 W Gibraltar
Rosia Bay 93 H 5 bay,
NE Atlantic Ocean
Roşiori de Vede 108 B 5 S Romania
Roslavl' 111 A 5
W Russian Federation
Rosmalen 86 D 4 S Netherlands
Ross 151 B 6 South Island,
SW New Zealand
Rossano 97 E 6
anc. Roscianum. SW Italy
Ross Dependency 154 B 4
dependent territory of
New Zealand, Antarctica
Ross Ice Shelf 154 B 4 ice shelf,
Antarctica
Rosso 74 B 3 SW Mauritania
Ross Sea 154 B 4 sea, S Pacific Ocean
Rostock 94 C 2 NE Germany
Rostov-na-Donu 111 B 7 *var.*
Rostov, *Eng.* Rostov-on-Don.
SW Russian Federation
Rostov-on-Don *see* Rostov-na-Donu
Roswell 48 D 2 New Mexico,
SW USA
Rota 144 B 1 island,
S Northern Mariana Islands
Rotcher Island *see* Tamana
Rothera 154 A 3 research station,
Antarctica
Rotomagus *see* Rouen
Rotorua 150 D 3 North Island,
NE New Zealand
Rotorua, Lake 150 E 3 lake,
North Island, NE New Zealand
Rotterdam 86 C 4 SW Netherlands
Rottweil 95 B 6 S Germany
Rotuma 147 E 4 island, NW Fiji
Roubaix 90 D 2 N France
Rouen 90 C 3 *anc.* Rotomagus.
N France

Round Rock 49 G 3 Texas, S USA
Rourkela *see* Raurkela
Roussillon 91 C 7 cultural region,
S France
Rouyn-Noranda 38 D 4 Québec,
SE Canada
Rovaniemen mlk 84 D 3 N Finland
Rovigno *see* Rovinj
Rovigo 96 C 2 NE Italy
Rovinj 100 A 2 *It.* Rovigno.
NW Croatia
Rovuma 69 D 5 *var.* Ruvuma. River,
Mozambique/Tanzania
Roxas 139 E 2 Panay Island,
C Philippines
Royale, Isle 40 B 1 island,
Michigan, N USA
Royan 91 B 5 W France
Rozdol'ne 109 F 4 *Rus.* Razdolnoye.
S Ukraine
Rožňava 99 D 6 *Ger.* Rosenau,
Hung. Rozsnyó. E Slovakia
Ruacana 78 B 3 NW Namibia
Ruapehu, Mount 150 D 4
mountain, North Island,
C New Zealand
Ruapuke Island 151 B 8 island,
South Island, SW New Zealand
Ruatoria 150 E 3 North Island,
NE New Zealand
Rub' al Khali 121 C 6 *Eng.*
Empty Quarter, Great Sandy
Desert. Desert, SW Asia
Rubezhnoye *see* Rubizhne
Rubizhne 109 H 2 *Rus.*
Rubezhnoye. E Ukraine
Ruby Mountains 47 D 5 mountain
range, Nevada, W USA
Rucava 106 B 3 SW Latvia
Rudensk *see* Rudzyensk
Rūdiškės 107 B 5 S Lithuania
Rudnik 104 E 2 E Bulgaria
Rudny *see* Rudnyy
Rudnyy 114 C 4 *var.* Rudny.
N Kazakhstan
Rudolf, Lake 68 D 4 *var.* Lake
Turkana. Lake, N Kenya
Rudzyensk 107 C 6 *Rus.* Rudensk.
C Belarus
Rufino 64 C 4 C Argentina
Rugāji 106 D 4 E Latvia
Ruggell 94 E 1 N Liechtenstein
Ruhnu 106 C 2 *var.* Ruhnu Saar,
Swe. Runö. Island, SW Estonia
Rūjiena 106 D 3 *Est.* Ruhja,
Ger. Rujen. N Latvia
Rukwa, Lake 73 B 7 lake,
SE Tanzania
Rum *see* Rhum
Ruma 100 D 3 N Yugoslavia
Rumbek 73 B 5 S Sudan
Rum Cay 54 D 2 island,
C Bahamas
Rumia 98 C 2 N Poland
Rummah, Wādī ar *see*
Rimah, Wādī ar
Rummelsburg in Pommern *see*
Miastko
Runanga 151 B 5 South Island,
C New Zealand
Runaway Bay 54 B 4 C Jamaica
Rundu 78 C 3 *var.* Runtu.
NE Namibia
Runtu *see* Rundu
Ruoqiang 126 C 3 *var.* Jo-ch'iang,
Ruoqiang, *Uigh.* Charkhlik,
Charkhliq, Qarkilik. NW China
Rupea 109 C 4 *Ger.* Reps, *Hung.*
Kőhalom; *prev.* Cohalm.
C Romania
Rupel 87 C 5 river, N Belgium

Rupella *see* la Rochelle
Rupert, Rivière de 38 D 3 river, Québec, C Canada
Ruse 104 D 1 *var.* Ruschuk, Rustchuk, *Turk.* Rusçuk. N Bulgaria

Russian Federation 110 B 4 *var.* Russia, *Latv.* Krievija, *Rus.* Rossiyskaya Federatsiya. Republic, Asia/Europe
Official name: Russian Federation **Date of formation:** 1991 **Capital:** Moscow **Population:** 149.2 million **Total area:** 6,592,800 sq miles (17,075,400 sq km) **Languages:** Russian* **Religions:** Russian Orthodox 80%, other (inc. Jewish, Muslim) 20% **Ethnic mix:** Russian 80%, Tartar 4%, Ukrainian 3%, other 13% **Government:** Multiparty republic **Currency:** Rouble = 100 kopeks

Rust'avi 117 G 2 SE Georgia
Rutba *see* Ar Ruṭbah
Rutlam *see* Ratlām
Rutland 41 G 2 Vermont, NE USA
Rutog 126 A 4 *var.* Rutok. W China
Rutok *see* Rutog
Ruvuma *see* Rovuma, Rio
Ruwenzori 77 E 5 mountain range, Congo (Zaire)/Uganda
Ruzhany 107 B 6 SW Belarus
Ružomberok 99 D 5 *Ger.* Rosenberg, *Hung.* Rózsahegy. N Slovakia

Rwanda 73 B 6 *prev.* Ruanda. Republic, NE Africa
Official name: Republic of Rwanda **Date of formation:** 1962 **Capital:** Kigali **Population:** 7.5 million **Total area:** 10,170 sq miles (26,340 sq km) **Languages:** Kinyarwanda*, French*, Kiswahili **Religions:** Christian 74%, traditional beliefs 25%, other 1% **Ethnic mix:** Hutu 90%, Tutsi 9%, Twa pygmy 1% **Government:** Multiparty republic **Currency:** Franc = 100 centimes

Ryazan' 111 B 5 W Russian Federation
Rybinsk 110 B 4 *prev.* Andropov.
Rybnik 99 C 5 S Poland
Ryki 98 E 4 E Poland
Rypin 98 D 3 C Poland
Rysy 99 D 5 mountain, S Poland
Ryukyu Islands *see* Nansei-shotō
Ryukyu Trench 152 B 2 *var.* Nansei Syotō Trench. Trench, NW Pacific Ocean
Rzeszów 99 E 5 SE Poland
Ržev *see* Rzhev
Rzhev 110 B 4 *var.* Ržev. W Russian Federation

S

Saalfeld 95 C 5 *var.* Saalfeld an der Saale. C Germany
Saalfeld an der Saale *see* Saalfeld
Saarbrücken 95 A 6 *Fr.* Sarrebruck. SW Germany
Sääre 106 C 2 *var.* Sjar. Saaremaa, W Estonia
Saaremaa 106 C 2 *Ger.* Oesel, Ösel; *prev.* Saare. Island, W Estonia
Saariselkä 84 D 2 *Lapp.* Suoločielgi. N Finland

Sab' Ābār 118 C 4 *var.* Sab'a Biyar, Sa'b Bi'ár. C Syria
Šabac 100 D 3 W Yugoslavia
Sabadell 93 G 2 E Spain
Sabah 138 D 3 cultural region, Borneo, E Malaysia
Sabanalarga 58 B 1 N Colombia
Sabaneta 58 C 1 N Venezuela
Sab'atayn, Ramlat as 121 C 6 desert, C Yemen
Sabaya 61 F 5 S Bolivia
Sabhā 71 F 3 C Libya
Sabi *see* Save, Rio
Sabinas 50 D 2 NE Mexico
Sabinas Hidalgo 51 E 2 NE Mexico
Sabine Lake 49 H 4 lake, SW USA
Sabine River 49 H 3 river, SW USA
Sabkha *see* As Sabkhah
Sable, Cape 39 F 5 headland, Newfoundland and Labrador, SE Canada
Sable Island 39 G 4 island, Nova Scotia, SE Canada
Şabyā 121 B 6 SW Saudi Arabia
Sabzawar *see* Sabzevār
Sabzevār 120 D 2 *var.* Sabzawar. NE Iran
Săcele 108 C 4 *Hung.* Négyfalu; *prev.* Sieben Dörfer, *Hung.* Hétfalu. C Romania
Sachsen 94 D 4 *Eng.* Saxony, *Fr.* Saxe. Cultural region, E Germany
Sachs Harbor 37 E 2 Banks Island, NW Canada
Sächsische Saale 94 C 4 river, C Germany
Sacramento 47 B 6 state capital, California, W USA
Sacramento Mountains 48 D 2 mountain range, New Mexico, SW USA
Sacramento River 47 B 5 river, California, W USA
Sacramento Valley 47 B 5 valley, California, W USA
Sá da Bandeira *see* Lubango
Şa'dah 121 B 6 NW Yemen
Sad Ishträgh 123 F 3 pass, Afghanistan/Pakistan
Sado 131 C 5 *var.* Sadoga-shima. Island, N Japan
Sadoga-shima *see* Sado
Şafāqis *see* Sfax
Säffle 85 B 6 C Sweden
Safford 48 C 3 Arizona, SW USA
Safi 70 B 2 W Morocco
Safīd Kūh, Selseleh-ye 122 D 4 mountain range, NW Afghanistan
Sagaing 136 B 3 C Myanmar
Sagami-nada 131 D 6 inlet, NW Pacific Ocean
Sāgar 134 D 4 *prev.* Saugor. C India
Saginaw 40 C 3 Michigan, N USA
Saginaw Bay 40 D 2 lake bay, Michigan, N USA
Sagua la Grande 54 B 2 C Cuba
Sagunto 93 F 3 *var.* Sagunt, *Ar.* Murviedro; *anc.* Saguntum. E Spain
Sahara 68 B 3 desert, Algeria/Libya
Sahara el Gharbīya 72 B 2 *var.* Aşṣaḥrā' al Gharbīyah, *Eng.* Western Desert. Desert, C Egypt
Saharan Atlas *see* Atlas Saharien
Sahel 74 D 3 physical region, N Africa
Sāhīwāl 134 C 2 *prev.* Montgomery. E Pakistan
Sahtinsk *see* Shakhtinsk
Saïda 119 A 5 *var.* Ṣaydā, Sayida; *anc.* Sidon. W Lebanon
Saidpur 135 G 3 *var.* Syedpur. NW Bangladesh

Sai Kung 128 B 1 E Hong Kong
Saimaa 85 E 5 lake, SE Finland
St Anthony 39 G 3 Newfoundland and Labrador, SE Canada
St Catharines 38 D 5 Ontario, S Canada
St George's 55 H 5 country Capital, SW Grenada
St John 39 F 4 New Brunswick, SE Canada
St John's 39 H 3 province capital, Newfoundland and Labrador, E Canada
St. Lawrence 39 E 4 *Fr.* Fleuve St-Laurent. River, Canada/USA
St Patricks 55 H 2 S Barbados
St Albans 89 E 7 *anc.* Verulamium. SE England, UK
Saint Albans 40 D 5 West Virginia, NE USA
St Andrews 88 D 4 E Scotland, UK
St Ann's Bay 54 B 4 C Jamaica
Saint Augustine 43 E 3 Florida, SE USA
St Austell 89 C 7 SW England, UK
St. Botolph's Town *see* Boston
Saint Catherines Island 43 E 3 island, SE USA
Saint Clair, Lake 40 D 3 lake, Canada/USA
St Cloud 45 F 2 Minnesota, N USA
St Croix 55 G 3 island, S Virgin Islands (US)
Saint Croix River 40 A 2 river, N USA
St David's Island 42 B 5 island, E Bermuda
Saintes 91 B 5 *anc.* Mediolanum. W France
St George 42 B 4 N Bermuda
St George 149 D 5 Queensland, E Australia
Saint George 44 A 5 Utah, W USA
Saint George's Channel 89 B 6 channel, Celtic Sea/Irish Sea
St George's Island 42 B 4 island, E Bermuda
St Helena 67 D 5 island, E Atlantic Ocean
St.Helena Bay 78 B 5 bay, SW South Africa
Saint Helena Sound 43 F 2 bay, SE USA
Saint Helens, Mount 34 B 4 volcano, Washington, NW USA
St Helier 89 D 8 dependent territory capital, S Jersey, Channel Islands
St.Iago de la Vega *see* Spanish Town
Saint Joe River 46 D 2 river, N USA
St John's 55 G 3 country capital, S Antigua & Barbuda
St Kilda 88 A 3 island, NW Scotland, UK

Saint Kitts & Nevis 55 G 3 *var.* Saint Christopher-Nevis. Commonwealth republic, E Caribbean Sea
Official name: Federation of Saint Christopher and Nevis **Date of formation:** 1983 **Capital:** Basseterre **Population:** 44,000 **Total area:** 139 sq miles (360 sq km) **Languages:** English*, English Creole **Religions:** Protestant 85%, Roman Catholic 10%, other Christian 5% **Ethnic mix:** Black 95%, mixed 5% **Government:** Parliamentary democracy **Currency:** E. Caribbean $ = 100 cents

St Lawrence, Gulf of 39 F 3 gulf, NW Atlantic Ocean
Saint Lawrence Island 36 C 2 island, Alaska, NW USA
St Lawrence Seaway 41 F 2 waterway, NW Atlantic Ocean
St Louis 45 G 5 Missouri, C USA

Saint Lucia 55 E 1 Commonwealth republic, E Caribbean Sea
Official name: Saint Lucia **Date of formation:** 1979 **Capital:** Castries **Population:** 156,000 **Total area:** 239 sq miles (620 sq km) **Languages:** English*, French Creole **Religions:** Roman Catholic 90%, other 10% **Ethnic mix:** Black 90%, Afro-European 6%, South Asian 4% **Government:** Parliamentary democracy **Currency:** E. Caribbean $ = 100 cents

St Lucia Channel 55 H 4 channel, E Caribbean Sea
St Margareth's Bay *see* St.Margareth's Bay
Saint Martin *see* Sint Maarten
St Matthew's Island *see* Zadetkyi Kyun
Saint Nicholas *see* São Nicolau
Saint-Nicolas *see* Sint-Niklaas
Saint Paul 45 F 2 state capital, Minnesota, N USA
St Paul Island *see* St-Paul, Île
St Peter Port 89 D 8 dependent territory capital, C Guernsey, Channel Islands
Saint Petersburg 43 E 4 Florida, SE USA
Saint Petersburg *see* Sankt-Peterburg
St. Pierre 39 G 4 dependent territory capital, Saint Pierre & Miquelon
St Simon Island 43 E 3 island, SE USA
Saint Thomas *see* Charlotte Amalie
Saint Thomas *see* São Tomé
Saint Vincent 55 G 4 island, N Saint Vincent & the Grenadines
Saint Vincent *see* São Vicente

Saint Vincent & the Grenadines 55 H 4 Commonwealth republic, E Caribbean Sea
Official name: St. Vincent and the Grenadines **Date of formation:** 1979 **Capital:** Kingstown **Population:** 109,000 **Total area:** 31 sq miles (340 sq km) **Languages:** English*, English Creole **Religions:** Protestant 62% Roman Catholic 19%, other 19% **Ethnic mix:** Black 82%, mixed 14%, White 3%, South Asian 1% **Government:** Parliamentary democracy **Currency:** E. Caribbean $ = 100 cents

Saint Vincent, Cape *see* São Vicente, Cabo de
Saint Vincent Passage 55 H 4 channel, E Caribbean Sea
Saipan 144 B 1 island, S Northern Mariana Islands
Saipan 144 B 1 capital of Northern Mariana Islands, Saipan, S Northern Mariana Islands
Sai Yok 137 B 5 C Thailand
Sajama, Nevado 61 F 4 mountain, W Bolivia
Sajószentpéter 99 D 6 NE Hungary
Sakākah 120 B 4 NW Saudi Arabia

kakawea, Lake 44 D 2 reservoir, North Dakota, N USA
kata 130 D 4 Honshū, C Japan
khalin see Sakhalin, Ostrov
khalin, Ostrov 115 H 4 var. Sakhalin. Island, SE Russian Federation
ki see Saky
prev. Nukha. NW Azerbaijan
kishima-shotō 130 A 3 var. Sakisima Syotō. Island group, Nansei-shotō, S Japan
kon Nakhon 136 D 4 var. Muang Sakon Nakhon, Sakhon Nakhon. NE Thailand
ky 109 F 5 Rus. Saki. S Ukraine
l 74 A 3 island, NE Cape Verde
la 85 C 6 C Sweden
lacgriva 106 C 3 Est. Salatsi. N Latvia
la Consilina 97 D 5 S Italy
lado 64 C 3 river, C Argentina
lālah 121 D 6 SW Oman
lamá 52 B 2 C Guatemala
lamanca 92 D 2 anc. Helmantica, Salmantica. NW Spain
lamanca 64 B 3 C Chile
lamīyah 118 B 3 var. As Salamīyah. W Syria
lantai 106 B 3 NW Lithuania
latsi see Salacgrīva
lavan 137 E 5 var. Saravan, Saravane. SE Laos
lavat 111 D 6 W Russian Federation
la y Gomez 153 F 4 island, E Pacific Ocean
lčininkai 107 C 5 SE Lithuania
ldus 106 B 3 Ger. Frauenburg. W Latvia
le 149 C 7 Victoria, SE Australia
lé 70 C 2 NW Morocco
lekhard 114 D 3 prev. Obdorsk. N Russian Federation
lem 46 B 3 state capital, Oregon, NW USA
lem 132 C 2 SE India
lentina, Penisola 97 E 6 peninsula, S Italy
lerno 97 D 5 anc. Salernum. S Italy
lerno, Golfo di 97 D 5 Eng. Gulf of Salerno. Gulf, E Tyrrhenian Sea
lerno, Gulf of see Salerno, Golfo di
lernum see Salerno
lihorsk 107 C 7 Rus. Soligorsk. S Belarus
lima 79 E 2 C Malawi
lina 45 E 5 Kansas, C USA
lina Cruz 51 F 5 SE Mexico
linas 47 B 6 California, W USA
linas de Santiago 61 G 4 E Bolivia
linas Grandes 64 C 3 wetland, C Argentina
lisbury 89 D 7 var. New Sarum. S England, UK
lisbury see Harare
llisaw 49 H 1 Oklahoma, C USA
llūm, Khalīj as see Salūm, Gulf of
llyana see Salyan
lmon Gums 147 C 7 SW Australia
lmon River 46 D 3 river, Idaho, NW USA
lmon River Mountains 46 D 3 mountain range, Idaho, NW USA
lo 85 D 6 SW Finland
lon-de-Provence 91 D 6 SE France

Salonta 108 A 3 Hung. Nagyszalonta. NW Romania
Sal'sk 111 B 7 SW Russian Federation
Salt see As Salt
Salta 64 C 2 NW Argentina
Saltash 89 C 7 SE England, UK
Saltillo 51 E 3 NE Mexico
Salt Lake City 44 B 4 state capital, Utah, W USA
Salto 64 D 4 NW Uruguay
Salton Sea 47 D 8 var. Mar de Salton. Lake, California, W USA
Salvador 63 G 3 prev. São Salvador. State capital, E Brazil
Salvador, Lake 42 B 3 lake, Louisiana, S USA
Salween 136 B 3 var. Nu Jiang, Bur. Thanlwin, Chin. Nu Chiang. River, SE Asia
Salyan 135 E 3 var. Sallyana. W Nepal
Salzburg 95 D 6 anc. Juvavum. N Austria
Salzgitter 94 B 4 prev. Watenstedt-Salzgitter. C Germany
Salzwedel 94 C 3 N Germany
Samar 139 F 2 island, Visayan Islands, C Philippines
Samara 111 C 6 prev. Kuybyshev. W Russian Federation
Samarang see Semarang
Samarinda 138 D 4 Borneo, C Indonesia
Samarkand see Samarqand
Samarqand 123 E 2 Rus. Samarkand. C Uzbekistan
Samawa see As Samāwah
Şamaxı 117 H 2 Rus. Shemakha. C Azerbaijan
Sambalpur 135 F 4 E India
Sambava 79 G 2 NE Madagascar
Sambir 108 B 3 Rus. Sambor. NW Ukraine
Sambor see Sambir
Sambre 87 B 7 river, Belgium/France
Samfya 78 D 2 N Zambia
Saminatal 94 E 2 valley, Austria/Liechtenstein
Samnān see Semnān
Sam Neua see Xam Nua
Samoa 145 F 4 Sam. Smoa-i-Sisifo; prev. Western Samoa. Monarchy, S Pacific Ocean

Official name: Independent State of Samoa Date of formation: 1962 Capital: Apia Population: 162,000 Total Area: 1,027 sq miles (2,840 sq km) Languages: Samoan*, English Religions: Protestant 74%, Roman Catholic 26% Ethnic mix: Samoan 93%, other 7% Government: Parliamentary state Currency: Tala = 100 sene

Samoa Basin 152 D 4 undersea basin, W Pacific Ocean
Samobor 100 B 2 N Croatia
Samos 105 E 6 prev. Limín Vathéos. Sámos, SE Greece
Sámos 105 D 6 island, SE Greece
Samothrace see Samothráki
Samothráki 104 D 4 Samothráki, NE Greece
Samothráki 104 D 4 anc. Samothrace. Island, Samothráki, NE Greece
Sampit 138 D 4 C Indonesia
Samsun 116 D 2 anc. Amisus. N Turkey

Samtredia 117 F 2 W Georgia
Samui, Ko 137 C 6 island, S Thailand
Samut Prakan 137 C 5 var. Muang Samut Prakan, Paknam. C Thailand
San 99 E 5 river, SE Poland
San 74 D 3 C Mali
Sana 100 B 3 river, NW Bosnia & Herzegovina
Şan'ā' 121 B 6 Eng. Sana. Country capital, W Yemen
Sana see Şan'ā'
Saña 60 B 3 NW Peru
Sanae 154 B 2 research station, Antarctica
San Ambrosio Island 153 G 4 var. Isla San Ambrosio. Island, SE Pacific Ocean
San Ambrosio, Isla see San Ambrosio Island
Sanandaj 120 C 3 prev. Sinneh. W Iran
San Andrés, Isla de 53 F 3 island, Colombia
San Andrés Tuxtla 51 F 4 var. Tuxtla. E Mexico
San Angelo 49 F 3 Texas, S USA
San Antonio 64 B 4 C Chile
San Antonio 49 F 4 Texas, S USA
San Antonio 52 B 2 S Belize
San Antonio Bay 49 H 4 bay, Texas, S Gulf of Mexico
San Antonio Oeste 65 C 5 E Argentina
San Antonio River 49 G 4 river, Texas, S USA
Sanāw 121 D 6 var. Sanaw. NE Yemen
Sanaw see Sanāw
San Benedicto, Isla 50 B 5 island, W Mexico
San Benito 49 G 5 Texas, S USA
San Benito 52 B 1 N Guatemala
San Bernardino 47 C 7 California, W USA
San Blas 50 C 3 C Mexico
San Blas, Cordillera de 53 G 4 mountain range, NE Panama
San Carlos de Ancud see Ancud
San Carlos de Bariloche 65 B 5 SW Argentina
San Carlos del Zulia 58 C 2 W Venezuela
San Carlos Reservoir 48 B 2 reservoir, Arizona, SW USA
San Clemente Island 47 C 8 island, California, W USA
San Cristobal 144 C 4 var. Makira. Island, SE Solomon Islands
San Cristóbal 58 C 2 W Venezuela
San Cristóbal see San Cristóbal de Las Casas
San Cristóbal de Las Casas 51 G 5 var. San Cristóbal. SE Mexico
San Cristóbal, Isla 60 B 5 var. Chatham Island. Island, Galapagos Islands, E Pacific Ocean
Sancti Spíritus 54 B 2 C Cuba
Sandakan 139 E 3 Borneo, E Malaysia
Sandanski 104 C 3 prev. Sveti Vrach. SW Bulgaria
Sand Hills 44 D 3 mountain range, Nebraska, C USA
Sandia 48 D 2 New Mexico, SW USA
San Diego 47 C 8 California, W USA
Sandnes 85 A 6 S Norway
Sandomierz 98 D 4 Rus. Sandomir. SE Poland
Sandomir see Sandomierz

Sandoway 136 A 4 W Myanmar
Sand Springs 49 G 1 Oklahoma, C USA
Sandvika 85 B 6 S Norway
Sandviken 85 C 5 C Sweden
Sandy Bay 93 H 5 bay, W Mediterranean Sea
Sandy City 44 B 4 Utah, W USA
Sandy Desert 134 A 2 physical region, W Pakistan
Sandy Lake 38 B 3 lake, Ontario, C Canada
Sandy Springs 42 D 2 Georgia, SE USA
San Esteban 52 D 2 C Honduras
San Felipe 58 D 1 NW Venezuela
San Felipe de Puerto Plata see Puerto Plata
San Félix Island 153 G 4 Eng. San Felix Island. Island, SE Pacific Ocean
San Fernando 92 C 5 prev. Isla de León. S Spain
San Fernando 55 H 5 S Trinidad & Tobago
San Fernando 64 B 4 C Chile
San Fernando 58 D 2 var. San Fernando de Apure see San Fernando
San Fernando de Apure see San Fernando
San Fernando del Valle de Catamarca 64 C 3 var. Catamarca. NW Argentina
San Fernando de Monte Cristi see Monte Cristi
San Francisco 64 C 4 C Argentina
San Francisco 47 A 6 California, W USA
San Francisco Bay 47 A 6 bay, California, W Pacific Ocean
San Francisco del Oro 50 C 2 N Mexico
San Francisco de Macorís 55 E 3 C Dominican Republic
San Francisco de Selva see Copiapó
San Fructuoso see Tacuarembó
Sanger 47 C 6 California, W USA
Sangihe, Kepulauan 139 F 3 island group, C Indonesia
Sāngli 132 B 1 W India
Sangmélima 77 B 5 S Cameroon
San Gottardo, Passo del 95 B 7 Eng. St.Gotthard Pass. Pass, C Switzerland
Sangre de Cristo Mountains 44 D 5 mountain range, C USA
San Ignacio 52 B 1 prev. Cayo, El Cayo. W Belize
San Ignacio 61 F 3 N Bolivia
San Joaquin Valley 47 B 6 valley, California, W USA
San Jorge, Golfo 65 C 6 var. Gulf of San Jorge, Golfo
San Jorge, Gulf of see San Jorge, Golfo
San Jose 47 B 6 Port. San José. C USA
San José 52 B 3 var. Puerto San José. S Guatemala
San José 53 E 4 country capital, C Costa Rica
San José 61 G 4 var. San José de Chiquitos. E Bolivia
San José de Chiquitos see San José
San José de Cúcuta see Cúcuta
San José del Guaviare 58 C 4 var. C Colombia
San Juan 55 F 3 dependent territory capital, NE Puerto Rico
San Juan 64 B 4 W Argentina

San Juan 53 E 4 river,
Costa Rica/Nicaragua
San Juan *see* San Juan de los Morros
San Juan Bautista 64 D 3
S Paraguay
San Juan Bautista *see* Villahermosa
San Juan Bautista Tuxtepec *see*
Tuxtepec
San Juan de Alicante 93 F 4 E Spain
San Juan del Norte 53 E 4
var. Greytown.
San Juan del Norte, Bahía de 53 E 4
bay, W Caribbean Sea
San Juan de los Morros 58 D 2
var. San Juan. N Venezuela
San Juan del Río 51 E 4 C Mexico
San Juanito, Isla 50 C 4 island,
C Mexico
San Juan Mountains 44 C 5
mountain range, Colorado, C USA
San Juan River 44 B 5 river, C USA
San Julián *see* Puerto San Julián
Sankt-Bartholomäi *see* Palamuse
Sankt Gallen 95 B 7 *var.* St.Gallen,
Eng. Saint Gall, *Fr.* St-Gall.
NE Switzerland
Sankt-Jakobi *see* Pärnu-Jaagupi
Sankt-Peterburg 110 B 4 *prev.*
Leningrad, Petrograd, *Eng.* Saint
Petersburg, *Fin.* Pietari.
NW Russian Federation
Sankt Pölten 95 E 6 N Austria
Sankuru 77 D 7 river,
C Congo (Zaire)
San Lázaro 64 D 2 NE Paraguay
Şanlurfa 117 E 4 *prev.* Sanli Urfa,
Urfa, *anc.* Edessa. S Turkey
San Lorenzo 61 G 5 S Bolivia
San Lorenzo 60 A 1 N Ecuador
San Lorenzo, Isla 60 C 4 island,
W Peru
Sanlúcar de Barrameda 92 C 5
S Spain
San Luis 64 C 4 C Argentina
San Luis 50 A 1 *var.* San Luis Río
Colorado. NW Mexico
San Luis 52 B 2 NE Guatemala
San Luis Obispo 47 B 7
California, W USA
San Luis Potosí 51 E 3 C Mexico
San Luis Río Colorado *see* San Luis
San Marcos 49 G 4 Texas, S USA
San Marcos 52 A 2 W Guatemala
San Marcos 60 C 3 W Peru
San Marcos de Arica *see* Arica
San Marino 96 E 1 country capital,
C San Marino

San Marino
96 D 1 Marino. Republic,
S Europe

Official name: Republic of San
Marino **Date of formation:** AD
301/1862 **Capital:** San Marino
Population: 23,000 **Total area:** 24 sq
miles (61 sq km) **Languages:** Italian*
Religions: Roman Catholic 96%,
Protestant 2%, other 2%
Ethnic mix: Sammarinese 95%,
Italian 4%, other 1% **Government:**
Multiparty republic
Currency: Italian lira = 100 centesimi

San Martín 154 A 3 research
station, Antarctica
San Mateo 47 B 6 California, W USA
San Mateo 59 E 2 NE Venezuela
San Matías 61 H 3 E Bolivia
San Matías, Golfo 65 C 6 gulf,
SW Atlantic Ocean
Sanmenxia 128 C 4 *var.* Shan Xian.
C China

San Miguel 52 C 3 SE El Salvador
San Miguel 61 G 3 river,
Colombia/Ecuador
San Miguel de Allende 51 E 4
C Mexico
San Miguel de Ibarra *see* Ibarra
San Miguel de Tucumán 64 C 3
var. Tucumán. N Argentina
San Miguelito 53 G 4 C Panama
Sannär *see* Sennar
San Nicolás, Bahía 60 D 4 bay,
E Pacific Ocean
San Nicolas Island 47 C 8 island,
California, W USA
Sânnicolau Mare 108 A 4
var. Sânnicolaul-Mare,
Hung. Nagyszentmiklós;
prev. Sânmiclăus Mare, Sînnicolau
Mare. W Romania
Sanok 99 E 5 SE Poland
San Pablo 61 F 5 S Bolivia
San Pedro 50 D 3 *var.* San Pedro de
las Colonias. NE Mexico
San Pedro 52 C 1 NE Belize
San-Pédro 74 D 5 S Ivory Coast
San Pedro de las Colonias *see*
San Pedro
San Pedro de Lloc 60 B 3 NW Peru
San Pedro Mártir, Sierra 50 A 1
mountain range, NW Mexico
San Pedro Sula 52 C 2 NW Honduras
San Rafael 64 B 4 W Argentina
San Rafael Mountains 47 B 7
mountain range, California, W USA
San Ramón de la Nueva Orán 64
C 2 N Argentina
San Remo 96 A 3 NW Italy
San Salvador 54 D 1 *prev.* Watlings
I. Island, E Bahamas
San Salvador 52 B 3 country
capital, SW El Salvador
San Salvador de Jujuy 64 C 2
var. Jujuy. N Argentina
Sansanné-Mango 75 E 4
var. Mango. N Togo
Sansepolcro 96 C 3, Italy
San Severo 97 D 5 SE Italy
Santa 60 C 3 W Peru
Santa Ana 52 B 3 NW El Salvador
Santa Ana 47 C 8 California, W USA
Santa Ana 61 F 3 N Bolivia
Santa Ana de Coro *see* Coro
Santa Barbara 50 C 2 N Mexico
Santa Barbara 47 C 7
California, W USA
Santa Catalina, Gulf of 47 B 8
gulf, W USA
Santa Catalina Island 47 C 8 island,
California, W USA
Santa Catarina 63 E 5 *off.* Estado de
Santa Catarina. State, S Brazil
Santa Catarina, Estado de *see*
Santa Catarina
Santa Clara 54 B 2 C Cuba
Santa Clara 47 B 6 California, W USA
Santa Comba 92 B 1 NW Spain
Santa Cruz 65 B 7 river,
S Argentina
Santa Cruz 47 B 6 California, W USA
Santa Cruz 76 E 2 *var.* São João. São
Tomé, SE Sao Tome & Principe
Santa Cruz 61 G 4 *var.* Santa Cruz
de la Sierra. C Bolivia
Santa Cruz Barillas *see* Barillas
Santa Cruz de la Sierra *see*
Santa Cruz
Santa Cruz del Quiché 52 B 2
W Guatemala
Santa Cruz de Tenerife 70 A 3
regional capital, Tenerife,
SW Spain

Santa Cruz, Isla 60 B 5 *var.*
Indefatigable Island, Isla Chávez.
Island, Galapagos Islands,
E Pacific Ocean
Santa Cruz Islands 144 D 4 island
group, E Solomon Islands
Santa Elena 64 D 3 NE Argentina
Santa Elena 52 B 1 W Belize
Santa Fe 64 D 4 NE Argentina
Santa Fe 48 D 1 state capital,
New Mexico, SW USA
Santa Inês 63 F 2 NE Brazil
Santa Isabel 144 C 3 *var.* Bughotu.
Island, N Solomon Islands
Santa Isabel *see* Malabo
Santa Lucia Range 47 B 6 mountain
range, California, W USA
Santa Margarita, Isla 50 B 3 island,
W Mexico
Santa Maria 92 A 5 island,
W Portugal
Santa Maria 63 E 5 S Brazil
Santa Maria 47 B 7 California, W USA
Santa Maria del Buen Aire *see*
Buenos Aires
Santa María del Orinoco 58 D 2
C Venezuela
Santa María, Isla 60 A 5 *var.*
Charles Island, Isla Floreana.
Island, Galapagos Islands,
E Pacific Ocean
Santa Marta 58 B 1 N Colombia
Santana 76 E 2 São Tomé,
C Sao Tome & Principe
Santander 92 D 1 N Spain
Santanilla, Islas 53 E 1 *Eng.* Swan
Islands. Island, NE Honduras
Santarém 92 B 3 *anc.* Scalabis.
W Portugal
Santarém 63 E 2 N Brazil
Santa Rosa 65 C 5 C Argentina
Santa Rosa 47 B 6 California, W USA
Santa Rosa *see* Santa Rosa de Copán
Santa Rosa de Copán 52 C 2 *var.*
Santa Rosa. W Honduras
Santa Rosa Island 47 B 8 island,
California, W USA
Sant Carles de la Rápida *see* Sant
Carles de la Ràpita
Sant Carles de la Ràpita 93 F 3
var. Sant Carles de la Rápida.
NE Spain
Santiago 92 B 1 *var.* Santiago de
Compostela, *Eng.* Compostella;
anc. Campus Stellae. NW Spain
Santiago 55 E 3 *var.* Santiago de los
Caballeros. N Dominican Republic
Santiago 64 B 4 *var.* Gran Santiago.
Country capital, C Chile
Santiago 74 A 3 *var.* São Tiago.
Island, S Cape Verde
Santiago 53 F 5 S Panama
Santiago 60 B 2 river, N Peru
Santiago *see* Santiago de Cuba
Santiago de Cuba 54 C 3
var. Santiago. E Cuba
Santiago de Guayaquil *see*
Guayaquil
Santiago del Estero 64 C 3
C Argentina
Santiago de los Caballeros *see*
Santiago
Santiago, Isla 60 A 5 *var.* Isla San
Salvador, James Island.
Island, Galapagos Islands,
E Pacific Ocean
Santiago Mountains 49 E 4
mountain range, Texas, S USA
Santiago Pinoteqa Nacional *see*
Pinoteqa Nacional

Santo *see* Espiritu Santo
Santo André 63 F 4 S Brazil
Santo Antão 74 A 2 island,
N Cape Verde
Santo António 76 E 1 *var.* São
António Príncipe,
N Sao Tome & Principe
Santo Domingo 55 E 3 *prev.* Ciuda
Trujillo. Country capital,
SE Dominican Republic
Santo Domingo de Los Colorados
60 B 1 NW Ecuador
Santo Domingo Tehuantepec *see*
Tehuantepec
San, Tônle 137 E 5 *var.* San, Sé.
River, Cambodia/Vietnam
Santos 63 F 4 S Brazil
Santos Plateau 57 D 5 undersea
plateau, SW Atlantic Ocean
Santo Tomé 64 D 3 NE Argentina
San Valentín, Cerro 65 B 7
mountain, S Chile
San Vicente 52 C 3 C El Salvador
São António *see* Santo António
São Francisco 63 F 3 river, E Brazil
São Hill 73 C 7 S Tanzania
São João *see* Santa Cruz
São João da Madeira 92 B 2
W Portugal
São Jorge 92 A 5 island, W Portuga
São Luís 63 F 2 state capital,
NE Brazil
São Marcos, Baía de 63 F 1 bay,
W Atlantic Ocean
Saona, Isla 55 E 3 island,
SE Dominican Republic
Saône 91 D 5 river, E France
São Nicolau 74 A 3 *Eng.* Saint
Nicholas. Island, N Cape Verde
São Paulo 63 F 4 state capital,
S Brazil
São Paulo 63 E 4 *off.* Estado de São
Paulo. State, S Brazil
São Paulo, Estado de *see* São Paulo
São Pedro do Rio Grande do Sul *see*
Rio Grande
São Salvador *see* Salvador
São Tiago *see* Santiago
São Tomé 76 E 2 *Eng.* Saint Thomas
Island, S Sao Tome & Principe
São Tomé 76 E 2 country capital,
São Tomé, S Sao Tome & Principe

Sao Tome & Principe
76 D 1 of Sao Tome and Principe
Port. São Tomé e Príncipe.
Republic, C Africa

Official name: Democratic Republic
of Sao Tome and Principe **Date of
formation:** 1975 **Capital:** São Tomé
Population: 121,000 **Total area:**
372 sq miles (964 sq km) **Languages:**
Portuguese*, Portuguese Creole
Religions: Roman Catholic 90%,
other Christian 10%
Ethnic mix: Black 90%, Portuguese
and Creole 10%
Government: Multiparty republic
Currency: Dobra = 100 centimos

São Tomé, Pico de 76 E 2 mountair
S Sao Tome & Principe
São Vicente 74 A 3 *Eng.* Saint
Vincent. Island, N Cape Verde
São Vicente, Cabo de 92 B 5 *Eng.*
Cape Saint Vincent. Headland,
SW Portugal
Sápai *see* Sápes
Sapele 75 F 5 S Nigeria
Sápes 104 D 3 *var.* Sápai. NE Greec
Sa Pobla 93 G 3 *var.* La Puebla.
E Spain

apporo 130 D 2 Hokkaidō, NE Japan
apri 97 D 6 Italy
apulpa 49 G 1 Oklahoma, C USA
aqqez 120 C 2 *var.* Saghez, Sakiz, Saqqiz. NW Iran
ara Buri 137 C 5 *var.* Saraburi. C Thailand
araburi *see* Sara Buri
aragt *see* Serakhs
araguro 60 B 2 S Ecuador
arajevo 101 A 8 country capital, SE Bosnia & Herzegovina
arakhs 120 E 2 NE Iran
araktash 111 D 6 W Russian Federation
aran' 114 C 4 *Kaz.* Saran. C Kazakhstan
aran *see* Saran'
arandë 101 C 7 *var.* Saranda, *It.* Porto Edda; *prev.* Santi Quaranta. S Albania
aransk 111 C 5 W Russian Federation
arasota 43 E 4 Florida, SE USA
aratov 111 C 6 W Russian Federation
arawak 138 D 3 cultural region, Borneo, E Malaysia
arawak *see* Kuching
ardegna 97 A 5 *Eng.* Sardinia. Island, W Italy
ardinia *see* Sardegna
ar-e Pol *see* Sar-e Pol-e Żahāb
argasso Sea 66 B 4 sea, N Atlantic Ocean
argodha 134 C 2 NE Pakistan
arh 76 C 4 *prev.* Fort-Archambault. S Chad
aría 105 E 7 island, Dodekánisos, SE Greece
arıkamış 117 F 3 NE Turkey
arikol Range 123 G 3 mountain range, China/Tajikistan
ark 89 D 8 *Fr.* Sercq. Island , C Channel Islands
arkışla 116 D 3 C Turkey
armiento 65 B 6 S Argentina
arnia 38 C 5 Ontario, S Canada
arny 108 C 1 NW Ukraine
arochyna 107 D 5 *Rus.* Sorochino. N Belarus
arpsborg 85 B 6 S Norway
arrebruck *see* Saarbrücken
artène 91 E 7 SE France
arthe 90 B 4 cultural region, NW France
árti 104 C 4 N Greece
ary-Tash 123 F 3 SW Kyrgyzstan
asebo 131 A 7 Kyūshū, SW Japan
askatchewan 37 F 5 province, SW Canada
askatchewan 37 F 5 river, C Canada
askatoon 37 F 5 Saskatchewan, S Canada
asovo 111 B 5 W Russian Federation
assandra 74 D 5 S Ivory Coast
assandra 74 D 5 *var.* Ibo, Sassandra Fleuve. River, S Ivory Coast
assari 97 A 5 W Italy
assenheim 86 C 3 W Netherlands
assnitz 94 D 2 NE Germany
átoraljaújhely 99 E 6 NE Hungary
ātpura Range 134 D 4 mountain range, C India
atsunan-shotō 130 A 3 *var.* Satunan Syotō. Island group, Nansei-shotō, S Japan

Sattanen 84 D 3 NE Finland
Satu Mare 108 B 3 *Ger.* Sathmar, *Hung.* Szatmárnémeti. NW Romania
Sauceda Mountains 48 B 3 mountain range, Arizona, SW USA

Saudi Arabia
121 B 5 *Ar.* Al 'Arabīyah as Su'ūdīyah, Al Mamlakah al 'Arabīyah as Su'ūdīyah. Monarchy, SW Asia
Official name: Kingdom of Saudi Arabia **Date of formation:** 1932/ 1981 **Capital:** Riyadh **Population:** 16.5 million **Total area:** 829,995 sq miles (2,149,690 sq km) **Languages:** Arabic* **Religions:** Sunni Muslim 85%, Shi'a Muslim 14%, Christian 1% **Ethnic mix:** Arab 90%, Yemeni 8%, other Arab 1%, other 1% **Government:** Absolute monarchy **Currency:** Riyal = 100 malalah

Sauer *see* Sûre
Saugor *see* Sāgar
Saulkrasti 106 C 3 C Latvia
Sault Ste.Marie 38 C 4 Ontario, S Canada
Sault Ste Marie 40 C 2 Michigan, N USA
Saumarez Reef 148 E 4 reef, S Coral Sea
Saumur 90 B 4 NW France
Saurimo 78 C 1 *var.* Henrique de Carvalho, *Port.* Vila Henrique de Carvalho. NE Angola
Sava 100 B 3 river, SE Europe
Sava 107 E 6 E Belarus
Savá 52 D 2 N Honduras
Savai'i 145 E 4 island, NW Samoa
Savannah 43 E 2 Georgia, SE USA
Savannah River 43 E 2 river, SE USA
Savannakhét 136 D 4 S Laos
Savanna-La-Mar 54 A 5 W Jamaica
Save, Rio 79 E 3 *var.* Sabi. River, Mozambique/Zimbabwe
Saverne 90 E 3 *var.* Zabern; *anc.* Tres Tabernae. NE France
Savigliano 96 A 2 NW Italy
Savissivik *see* Savissivik
Savinski *see* Savinskiy
Savinskiy 110 C 3 *var.* Savinski. NW Russian Federation
Savissivik 82 D 1 *var.* Savigsivik. NW Greenland
Savoie 91 D 5 cultural region, SE France
Savona 96 A 2 NW Italy
Sävsjö 85 B 7 S Sweden
Savu Sea *see* Sawu, Laut
Sawakin *see* Suakin
Şawqirah 121 E 6 *var.* Suqrah. S Oman
Sawu, Laut 139 E 5 *Eng.* Savu Sea. Sea, E Indian Ocean
Sayaboury *see* Xaignabouli
Sayat 122 D 3 E Turkmenistan
Sayaxché 52 B 2 N Guatemala
Sayḥūt 121 D 6 E Yemen
Saylac 72 D 4 *var.* Zeila. NW Somalia
Saynshand 127 E 2 S Mongolia
Say 'ün 121 C 6 *var.* Saywūn. C Yemen
Saywūn *see* Say 'ün
Scalabis *see* Santarém
Scandinavia 66 D 2 geophysical region, NW Europe
Scania *see* Skåne
Scarborough 89 D 5 NE England, UK

Scarborough 38 D 5 Ontario, S Canada
Schaan 94 E 1 W Liechtenstein
Schaerbeek 87 C 6 C Belgium
Schaffhausen 95 B 7 *Fr.* Schaffhouse. N Switzerland
Schaffhouse *see* Schaffhausen
Schagen 86 C 2 NW Netherlands
Schaulen *see* Šiauliai
Schaumburg 40 B 3 Illinois, N USA
Schebschi Mountains *see* Shebshi Mountains
Scheessel 94 B 3 NW Germany
Schefferville 39 E 2 Québec, E Canada
Scheldt 87 B 5 *Dut.* Schelde, *Fr.* Escaut. River, W Europe
Schell Creek Range 47 D 5 mountain range, Nevada, W USA
Schenectady 41 F 3 New York, NE USA
Scherrebek *see* Skærbæk
Schertz 49 G 4 Texas, S USA
Schiedam 86 C 4 SW Netherlands
Schiermonnikoog 86 D 1 *Fris.* Skiermûntseach. Island, N Netherlands
Schijndel 86 D 4 S Netherlands
Schivelbein *see* Świdwin
Schleswig 94 B 2 N Germany
Schleswig-Holstein 94 B 2 cultural region, N Germany
Schlettstadt *see* Sélestat
Schlochau *see* Człuchów
Schneekoppe *see* Sněžka
Schneidemühl *see* Piła
Schönebeck 94 C 4 C Germany
Schönlanke *see* Trzcianka
Schooten *see* Schoten
Schoten 87 C 5 *var.* Schooten. N Belgium
Schouwen 86 B 4 island, SW Netherlands
Schwäbische Alb 95 B 6 *var.* Schwabenalb, *Eng.* Swabian Jura. Mountain range, S Germany
Schwandorf 95 C 5 SE Germany
Schwarzwald 95 B 6 *Eng.* Black Forest. Mountain range, SW Germany
Schwaz 95 C 7 W Austria
Schweidnitz *see* Świdnica
Schweinfurt 95 B 5 SE Germany
Schwerin 94 C 3 N Germany
Schwertberg *see* Świecie
Schwiebus *see* Świebodzin
Scilly, Isles of 89 B 8 island group, SW England, UK
Scoresby Sund *see* Kangertittivaq
Scotia Ridge 54 A 1 undersea ridge, S Atlantic Ocean
Scotia Sea 67 B 7 sea, SW Atlantic Ocean
Scotland 88 C 3 national region, UK
Scott Base 154 C 4 research station, Antarctica
Scott Island 154 B 5 island, Antarctica
Scottsbluff 45 D 3 Nebraska, C USA
Scottsdale 48 B 2 Arizona, SW USA
Scranton 41 F 3 Pennsylvania, NE USA
Scrobesbyrig' *see* Shrewsbury
Scutari, Lake 101 C 5 *Alb.* Liqeni i Shkodrës; *SCr.* Skadarsko Jezero. Lake, Albania/Yugoslavia

Seabra 59 F 3 E Brazil
Seaford 42 F 4 Delaware, NE USA
Searcy 42 B 1 Arkansas, C USA

Sebastián Vizcaíno, Bahía 50 A 2 bay, E Pacific Ocean
Sebastopol *see* Sevastopol'
Sebenico *see* Šibenik
Sebta *see* Ceuta
Sechura, Bahía de 60 A 3 bay, W Pacific Ocean
Secunderābād 132 C 1 *var.* Sikandarabad. C India
Sedan 90 D 3 N France
Seddon 151 D 5 South Island, C New Zealand
Seddonville 151 C 5 South Island, C New Zealand
Sédhiou 74 B 4 SW Senegal
Sedona 48 B 2 Arizona, SW USA
Seesen 94 B 4 C Germany
Segeża *see* Segezha
Segezha 110 B 3 *var.* Segeža. NW Russian Federation
Segodunum *see* Rodez
Ségou 74 D 3 *var.* Segu. C Mali
Segovia 92 D 2 C Spain
Segu *see* Ségou
Séguédine 75 H 2 NE Niger
Seguin 49 G 4 Texas, S USA
Segura 93 E 4 river, S Spain
Seinäjoki 85 D 5 *Swe.* Östermyra. W Finland
Seine 90 C 3 river, N France
Seine, Baie de la 90 B 3 bay, E English Channel
Sekondi *see* Sekondi-Takoradi
Sekondi-Takoradi 75 E 5 *var.* Sekondi. S Ghana
Sélestat 90 E 4 *Ger.* Schlettstadt. NE France
Seleucia *see* Silifke
Selfoss 83 E 5 SW Iceland
Sélibaby *see* Sélibabi
Selibi Phikwe 78 D 3 E Botswana
Selima Oasis 72 B 3 oasis, N Sudan
Selma 42 C 6 California, W USA
Selway River 46 D 2 river, Idaho, NW USA
Selwyn Range 148 B 3 mountain range, Queensland, NW Australia
Selzaete *see* Zelzate
Semarang 138 C 5 *var.* Samarang. Jawa, C Indonesia
Sembé 77 B 5 NW Congo
Semendria *see* Smederevo
Semey *see* Semipalatinsk
Semezhevo *see* Syemyezhava
Seminole 49 E 3 Texas, S USA
Seminole, Lake 42 D 3 reservoir, SE USA
Semipalatinsk 114 D 4 *Kaz.* Semey. E Kazakhstan
Semna 72 B 3 N Sudan
Semnān 120 D 3 *var.* Samnān. N Iran
Semois 87 C 8 river, SE Belgium
Senatobia 42 C 2 Mississippi, S USA
Sendai 130 D 4 Honshū, C Japan
Sendai 131 A 8 Kyūshū, SW Japan
Sendai-wan 130 D 4 bay, NW Pacific Ocean
Senec 99 C 6 *Ger.* Wartberg, *Hung.* Szempcz. W Slovakia

Senegal
74 B 3 *Fr.* Sénégal. River, W Africa

Senegal
74 B 3 *Fr.* Sénégal. Republic, W Africa
Official name: Republic of Senegal **Date of formation:** 1960 **Capital:** Dakar **Population:** 7.9 million **Total area:** 75,950 sq miles (196,720 sq km) **Languages:** French*, Wolof, Fulani

Religions: Muslim 92%, traditional beliefs 6%, Christian 2% **Ethnic mix:** Wolof 46%, Fulani 25%, Serer 16%, other 13% **Government:** Multiparty republic **Currency:** CFA franc = 100 centimes

Senftenberg 94 D 4 E Germany
Sengkang 139 E 4 *var.* Singkang. Celebes, C Indonesia
Senica 99 C 6 *Ger.* Senitz, *Hung.* Szenice. W Slovakia
Seniça *see* Sjenica
Senj 100 A 3 *Ger.* Zengg, *It.* Segna; *anc.* Senia. NW Croatia
Senja 84 C 2 *prev.* Senjen. Island, N Norway
Senjen *see* Senja
Senkaku-shotō 130 A 3 island group, Nansei-shotō, S Japan
Senlis 90 C 3 N France
Sennar 72 C 4 *var.* Sannār. C Sudan
Sens 90 C 4 *anc.* Agendicum, Senones. C France
Sên, Stœng 137 D 5 river, N Cambodia
Senta 100 D 2 *Hung.* Zenta. N Yugoslavia
Sentosa 138 A 2 island, S Singapore
Sept-Îles 39 E 3 Québec, SE Canada
Seraing 87 D 6 E Belgium
Serakhs 122 D 3 *var.* Saragt. S Turkmenistan
Seram, Laut 139 F 4 *Eng.* Ceram Sea. Sea, W Pacific Ocean
Seram, Pulau 139 F 4 *var.* Serang, *Eng.* Ceram. Island, Maluku, E Indonesia
Serang 138 C 5 Jawa, C Indonesia
Serasan, Selat 138 C 3 strait, W Pacific Ocean
Serbia 100 D 4 *Ger.* Serbien, *Serb.* Srbija. Constituent republic of Yugoslavia, Yugoslavia. *See also* Yugoslavia
Sercq *see* Sark
Serdo 72 D 4 N Ethiopia
Seremban 138 B 3 W Malaysia
Serenje 78 D 2 E Zambia
Sérifos 105 C 6 *anc.* Seriphos. Island, Kykládes, SE Greece
Seriphos *see* Sérifos
Serov 114 C 3 C Russian Federation
Serowe 78 D 3 SE Botswana
Serpent's Mouth, The 59 F 2 *Sp.* Boca de la Serpiente. Strait, W Atlantic Ocean
Serpiente, Boca de la *see* Serpent's Mouth, The
Serpukhov 111 B 5 W Russian Federation
Serravalle 96 E 1 N San Marino
Sérres 104 C 3 *var.* Seres; *prev.* Sérrai. NE Greece
Sesto San Giovanni 96 B 2 N Italy
Sesvete 100 B 2 N Croatia
Sète 91 C 6 *prev.* Cette. S France
Sétif 71 E 2 *var.* Stif. N Algeria
Setté Cama 77 A 6 SW Gabon
Setúbal 92 B 4 *Eng.* Saint Ubes, Saint Yves. W Portugal
Setúbal, Baía de 92 B 4 bay, NE Atlantic Ocean
Seul, Lac 38 B 3 lake, Ontario, S Canada
Sevan 117 G 2 C Armenia
Sevana Lich 117 G 3 *Eng.* Lake Sevan, *Rus.* Ozero Sevan. Lake, E Armenia
Sevastopol' 109 F 5 *Eng.* Sebastopol. S Ukraine

Severn 89 D 7 *Wel.* Hafren. River, England/Wales, UK
Severn 38 B 2 river, Ontario, S Canada
Severnaya Dvina 110 C 4 *var.* Northern Dvina. River, NW Russian Federation
Severnaya Zemlya 115 E 2 *var.* Nicholas II Land, North Land. Island group, N Russian Federation
Severnyy 110 E 3 *var.* Severny, Severnyj. NW Russian Federation
Severodonetsk *see* Syeverodonets'k
Severodvinsk 110 C 3 *prev.* Molotov, Sudostroy. NW Russian Federation
Severomorsk 110 C 2 NW Russian Federation
Sevier Lake 44 A 4 lake, Utah, W USA
Sevier River 44 B 5 river, W USA
Sevilla 92 C 5 *Eng.* Seville; *anc.* Hispalis, SW Spain
Seville *see* Sevilla
Sevlievo 104 D 2 C Bulgaria

Seychelles
79 G 1 E Africa

Official name: Republic of the Seychelles **Date of formation:** 1976 **Capital:** Victoria **Population:** 69,000 **Total area:** 108 sq miles (280 sq km) **Languages:** Creole*, French, English **Religions:** Roman Catholic 90%, other 10% **Ethnic mix:** Seychellois (mixed African, South Asian and European) 94%, Chinese and South Asian 5% **Government:** Multiparty republic **Currency:** Rupee = 100 cent

Seydhisfjördhur 83 E 5 E Iceland
Seydi 122 D 2 *prev.* Neftezavodsk. E Turkmenistan
Seyhan Deresi 116 D 4 river, NW Turkey
Sfákia 105 C 8 Kríti, SE Greece
Sfântu Gheorghe 108 C 4 *Ger.* Sankt-Georgen, *Hung.* Sepsiszentgyörgy; *prev.* Sepsi-Sângeorz, Sfintu Gheorghe. C Romania
Sfax 71 F 2 *var.* Şafāqis. E Tunisia
's-Gravenhage 86 B 4 *var.* Den Haag, *Eng.* The Hague, *Fr.* La Haye. Seat of government, W Netherlands
's-Gravenzande 86 B 4 W Netherlands
Shaanxi 129 B 5 *var.* Shaan, Shan-hsi, Shenshi, Shensi. Province, C China
Shabani *see* Zvishavane
Shache 126 A 3 *var.* Yarkant. NW China
Shackleton Ice Shelf 154 D 3 ice shelf, Antarctica
Shafer, Mount 154 C 4 mountain, Antarctica
Shahr-e Kord 120 C 3 *var.* Shahr Kord. C Iran
Shahr Kord *see* Shahr-e Kord
Shakawe 78 C 3 NW Botswana
Shakhtinsk 114 C 4 C Kazakhstan
Shaluli Shan 129 A 5 mountain range, S China
Shandī *see* Shendi
Shandong 128 C 4 *var.* Lu, Shantung. Province, E China
Shanghai 129 D 5 *var.* Shang-hai. E China

Shang-hai *see* Shanghai
Shangrao 129 D 5 E China
Shannon 89 A 6 C Ireland
Shannon 89 A 6 *Ir.* An tSionainn. River, W Ireland
Shan Plateau 136 B 3 plateau, C Myanmar
Shantar Islands *see* Shantarskiye Ostrova
Shantarskiye Ostrova 115 G 3 *Eng.* Shantar Islands. Island group, SE Russian Federation
Shantou 129 D 6 *var.* Shan-t'ou, Swatow. SE China
Shanxi 128 C 4 *var.* Jin, Shan-hsi, Shansi. Province, NE China
Shan Xian *see* Sanmenxia
Shaoguan 129 C 6 *var.* Shao-kuan, *Cant.* Kukong; *prev.* Ch'u-chiang. S China
Shaqrā' 120 C 4 C Saudi Arabia
Shaqrā *see* Shuqrah
Shari *see* Chari
Shari 130 D 2 Hokkaidō, NE Japan
Sharif 135 F 3 N India
Sharīngol 127 E 2 N Mongolia
Shark Bay 147 A 5 bay, E Indian Ocean
Sharqī, Jazīrat ash *see* Chergui, Île
Shashe 78 D 3 *var.* Shashi. River, Botswana/Zimbabwe
Shashi *see* Shashe
Shasta Lake 47 B 5 reservoir, California, W USA
Shawnee 49 G 1 Oklahoma, C USA
Shaykh, Jabal ash *see* Hermon, Mount
Shchadryn 107 D 7 *Rus.* Shchedrin. SE Belarus
Shchedrin *see* Shchadryn
Shcheglovsk *see* Kemerovo
Shchekino 111 B 5 W Russian Federation
Shchigry 111 B 5 W Russian Federation
Shchors 109 E 1 N Ukraine
Shchuchinsk 114 C 4 *prev.* Shchuchye. N Kazakhstan
Shchuchyn 107 B 5 *Pol.* Szczuczyn Nowogródzki, *Rus.* Shchuchin. W Belarus
Shebekino 111 A 6 W Russian Federation
Shebeli 73 D 5 *Amh.* Wabē Shebelē Wenz, *It.* Scebeli, *Som.* Webi Shabeelle. River, Ethiopia/Somalia
Sheberghān 123 E 3 *var.* Shibarghan, Shibarghān, Shiberghan, Shiberghān. N Afghanistan
Sheboygan 40 B 3 Wisconsin, N USA
Shebshi Mountains 75 H 4 *var.* Schebschi Mountains. Mountain range, E Nigeria
Sheffield 89 D 6 N England, UK
Shelburne 39 F 5 Ontario, S Canada
Shelburne Bay 148 C 1 bay, NW Coral Sea
Shelby 44 B 7 Montana, NW USA
Shelbyville, Lake 40 B 4 reservoir, Illinois, N USA
Sheldon 45 F 3 Iowa, C USA
Shelekhov Gulf *see* Shelikhova, Zaliv
Shelikhova, Zaliv 115 H 2 *Eng.* Shelekhov Gulf. Gulf, N Sea of Okhotsk
Shemakha *see* Şamaxı
Shendi 72 C 3 *var.* Shandī. NE Sudan

Shenyang 128 D 3 *Chin.* Shen-yan *Eng.* Moukden, Mukden; *prev.* Fengtien. Province capital, NE China
Shepetivka 108 D 2 *Rus.* Shepetovka. NW Ukraine
Shepetovka *see* Shepetivka
Shepparton 149 C 7 Victoria, SE Australia
Sherbrooke 39 E 4 Québec, SE Canada
Shereik 72 C 3 N Sudan
Shergui, Shatt al- *see* Ech Chergui, Chott
Sheridan 44 C 2 Wyoming, C USA[?]
Sherman 49 G 2 Texas, S USA
's-Hertogenbosch 86 D 4 *Fr.* Bois-l Duc, *Ger.* Herzogenbusch. S Netherlands
Shetland Islands 88 D 1 island group, NE Scotland, UK
Shibushi-wan 131 B 8 bay, NW Pacific Ocean
Shihezi 126 C 2 NW China
Shiichi *see* Shyichy
Shijiazhuang 128 C 4 *var.* Shih-chia-chuang, Shihkiachwang; *prev.* Shihmen. NE China
Shikārpur 134 B 3 S Pakistan
Shikoku 131 C 7 *var.* Sikoku. Island, Japan
Shikoku Basin 152 B 2 *var.* Sikoku[?] Basin. Undersea basin, NE Pacific Ocean
Shiliguri 135 F 3 *prev.* Siliguri. NE India
Shilka 115 F 4 river, C Russian Federation
Shimbir Berris *see* Shimbiris
Shimbiris 72 E 4 *var.* Shimbir Berris. Mountain, N Somalia
Shimoga 132 C 2 W India
Shimonoseki 131 A 7 *var.* Simonoseki; *hist.* Akamagaseki, Bakan. Honshū, SW Japan
Shinano-gawa 131 C 5 *var.* Sinano Gawa. River, Honshū, C Japan
Shīndand 122 D 4 W Afghanistan
Shingū 131 C 7 *var.* Singū. Honshū SW Japan
Shinjō 130 D 4 *var.* Sinzyō. Honshū C Japan
Shinyanga 73 C 7 NW Tanzania
Shiprock 48 C 1 New Mexico, SW USA
Shiquanhe 126 A 4 W China
Shīrāz 120 D 4 *var.* Shīrāz. S Iran
Shīrāz *see* Shīrāz
Shishchitsy *see* Shyshchytsy
Shivpuri 134 D 3 C India
Shizugawa 130 D 4 Honshū, NE Japan
Shizuoka 131 D 6 *var.* Sizuoka. Honshū, S Japan
Shklov *see* Shklow
Shklow 107 E 6 *Rus.* Shklov. E Belarus
Shkodër 101 C 5 *var.* Shkodra, *It.* Scutari, *SCr.* Skadar. NW Albania
Shkumbinit, Lumi i 101 D 6 *var.* Shkumbi, Shkumbin. River, C Albania
Shoal Lake 37 F 5 Manitoba, S Canada
Sholāpur *see* Solapur
Shostka 109 F 1 NE Ukraine
Show Low 48 B 2 Arizona, SW US..[?]
Shpola 109 E 3 C Ukraine
Shreveport 42 A 2 Louisiana, S USA[?]
Shrewsbury 89 C 6 *hist.* Scrobesbyrig'. W England, UK

hūlgareh 123 E 3 N Afghanistan
humagin Islands 36 B 3 island
  group, Alaska, NW USA
humen 104 D 2 *var.* Šumen.
  NE Bulgaria
humerlya 111 C 5
  W Russian Federation
humilina 107 E 5 *Rus.* Shumilino.
  NE Belarus
humilino *see* Shumilina
hunsen *see* Ch'unch'ŏn
huqrah 121 C 7 *var.* Shaqrā.
  SW Yemen
hwebo 136 B 3 N Myanmar
hyichy 107 C 7 *Rus.* Shiichi.
  SE Belarus
hymkent 114 B 5 *var.* Čimkent;
  prev. Chimkent. S Kazakhstan
hyshchytsy 107 C 6 *Rus.*
  Shishchitsy. C Belarus
īāh Kūh 122 D 4 mountain range,
  Afghanistan/Iran
iauliai 106 B 4 *Ger.* Schaulen.
  N Lithuania
iazan' *see* Siyäzän
ibay 111 D 6
  W Russian Federation
ibenik 100 A 4 *It.* Sebenico.
  S Croatia
iberia 115 E 3 *var.* Sibir'. Physical
  region, C Russian Federation
iberoet *see* Siberut, Pulau
iberut, Pulau 138 A 4 *prev.*
  Siberoet. Island, Kepulauan
  Mentawai, W Indonesia
ibi 134 B 2 SW Pakistan
ibiu 108 B 4 *Ger.* Hermannstadt,
  Hung. Nagyszeben. C Romania
ibolga 138 B 3 Sumatera,
  N Indonesia
ibu 138 D 3 Borneo, E Malaysia
ibut 76 C 4 *prev.* Fort-Sibut.
  S Central African Republic
ibuyan Sea 139 E 2 sea,
  W Pacific Ocean
ichon 137 C 7 *var.* Ban Sichon.
  S Chon. S Thailand
ichuan 129 B 5 *var.* Chuan, Ssu-
  ch'uan, Szechuan, Szechwan.
  Province, C China
ichuan Pendi 129 B 5 depression,
  C China
icilia 97 C 7 *Eng.* Sicily;
  anc.Trinacria. Island, S Italy
icilian Channel *see* Sicily, Strait of
icily *see* Sicilia
icuani 61 E 4 S Peru
idári 104 A 4 Kérkyra, W Greece
iderno 97 D 7 SW Italy
idhirókastron *see* Sidirókastro
idi Barrâni 72 A 1 NW Egypt
idi Bel Abbès 70 D 2 *var.* Sidi bel
  Abbès, Sidi-Bel-Abbès.
  NW Algeria
idirókastro 104 C 3
  prev. Sidhirókastron. NE Greece
idley, Mount 154 B 4 mountain,
  Antarctica
idney 40 C 4 Ohio, N USA
idney 44 D 1 Nebraska, C USA
idney 44 A 4 Missouri, C USA
iedlce 98 E 3 *Ger.* Sedlez,
  Rus. Sedlets. E Poland
iegen 94 B 4 W Germany
iemiatycze 98 E 3 E Poland
iena 96 C 3 *Fr.* Sienne; anc. Saena
  Julia. C Italy
ieradz 98 C 4 C Poland
ierpc 98 D 3 C Poland
ierra de Soconusco *see*
  Sierra Madre

Sierra Leone
74 C 4 Leone. Republic, W Africa
Official name: Republic of Sierra
  Leone Date of formation: 1961
Capital: Freetown Population: 4.5
  million Total area: 27,699 sq miles
  (71,740 sq km) Languages: English*,
  Krio (Creole) Religions: Traditional
  beliefs 52%, Muslim 40%, Christian
  8% Ethnic mix: Mende 34%, Temne
  31%, Limba 9%, Kono 5%, other 21%
Government: Military regime
Currency: Leone = 100 cents

Sierra Leone Basin 66 C 4 undersea
  basin, E Atlantic Ocean
Sierra Leone Rise 66 C 4 *var.* Sierra
  Leone Ridge, Sierra Leone
  Schwelle. Undersea rise,
  E Atlantic Ocean
Sierra Madre 82 A 2 *var.*
  Sierra de Soconusco.
  Mountain range, Guatemala/
  Mexico
Sierra Nevada 47 C 6 mountain
  range, California, W USA
Sierra Nevada de Mérida *see*
  Mérida, Cordillera de
Sierra Vieja 48 D 4 mountain
  range, Texas, S USA
Sierra Vista 48 B 3
  Arizona, SW USA
Sífnos 105 C 6 anc. Siphnos. Island,
  Kykládes, SE Greece
Sigli 138 A 3 W Indonesia
Siglufjördhur 83 E 4 N Iceland
Signy 154 A 2 research station,
  Antarctica
Sigsbee Deep *see* Mexico Basin
Siguatepeque 52 C 2 W Honduras
Siguiri 74 D 4 NE Guinea
Siilinjärvi 84 E 4 C Finland
Siirt 117 F 4 *var.* Sert; anc.
  Tigranocerta. SE Turkey
Sikaianana *see* Stewart Island
Sikandarabad *see* Secunderābād
Sikasso 74 D 4 S Mali
Sikeston 45 H 5 Iowa, C USA
Sikhote-Alin', Khrebet 115 G 4
  mountain range,
  SE Russian Federation
Siklós 99 C 7 SW Hungary
Sikoku *see* Shikoku
Sikoku Basin *see* Shikoku Basin
Šilalė 106 B 4 W Lithuania
Silchar 135 G 3 NE India
Silifke 116 C 4 anc. Seleucia.
  S Turkey
Siliguri *see* Shiliguri
Siling Co 126 C 5 lake, W China
Silistra 104 E 1 *var.* Silistria;
  anc. Durostorum. NE Bulgaria
Sillamäe 106 E 2 *Ger.* Sillamäggi.
  NE Estonia
Sillamäggi *see* Sillamäe
Silsbee 49 H 3 Texas, S USA
Šilutė 106 B 4 *Ger.* Heydekrug.
  W Lithuania
Silvan 117 E 4 SE Turkey
Silva Porto *see* Kuito
Silverek 117 E 4 SE Turkey
Simanichy 107 C 7 *Rus.* Simonichi.
  SE Belarus
Simav 116 B 3 W Turkey
Simav 116 A 3 river, NW Turkey
Simbirsk *see* Ul'yanovsk
Simeto 97 C 7 river, SW Italy
Simeulue, Pulau 138 A 3 island,
  NW Indonesia
Simferopol' 109 F 5 S Ukraine
Simitli 104 C 3 SW Bulgaria

Simleu Silvaniei 108 B 3
  Hung. Szilágysomlyo; *prev.*
  Şimläul Silvaniei, Şimleul
  Silvaniei. NW Romania
Simonichi *see* Simanichy
Simpang 138 B 4 W Indonesia
Simpelveld 87 D 6 SE Netherlands
Simplon Pass 95 B 8 pass,
  S Switzerland
Simplon Tunnel 95 B 8 tunnel,
  Italy/Switzerland
Simpson *see* Fort Simpson
Simpson Desert 148 B 4 desert,
  C Australia
Sinä' *see* Sinai
Sinai 72 C 2 *Ar.* Shibh Jazīrat Sīnā',
  Sīnä'. Physical region, NE Egypt
Sinaia 108 C 4 SE Romania
Sinano Gawa *see* Shinano-gawa
Sincelejo 58 B 2 NW Colombia
Sind 134 B 3 *var.* Sindh. Province,
  SE Pakistan
Sindelfingen 95 B 6 SW Germany
Sindh *see* Sind
Sindi 106 D 2 *Ger.* Zintenhof.
  SW Estonia
Sinegorskiy 111 B 7
  SW Russian Federation
Sinel'nikovo *see* Synel'nykove
Sines 92 B 4 S Portugal

Singapore
138 A 1 Singapore. Republic,
  SE Asia
Official name: Republic of
  Singapore Date of formation: 1965
Capital: Singapore City Population:
  2.8 million Total Area: 239 sq miles
  (620 sq km) Languages:
  Malay*, Chinese Religions:
  Buddhist 30%, Christian 20%,
  Muslim 17%, other 33%
Ethnic mix: Chinese 76%, Malay
  15%, South Asian 7%, other 2%
Government: Multiparty democracy
Currency: Singapore $ = 100 cents

Singapore, Strait of 138 A 2 strait,
  W Pacific Ocean
Singen 95 B 7 S Germany
Singida 73 C 7 C Tanzania
Singkang *see* Sengkang
Singkawang 138 C 4 Borneo,
  C Indonesia
Singû *see* Shingū
Siniscola 97 A 5 W Italy
Sinj 100 B 4 SE Croatia
Sinnamarie *see* Sinnamary
Sinnamary 59 H 3 *var.* Sinnamarie.
  N French Guiana
Sinneh *see* Sanandaj
Sinoe, Lacul *see* Sinoie, Lacul
Sinoie, Lacul 108 D 5 *prev.* Lacul
  Sinoe. Lagoon, W Black Sea
Sinop 116 D 2 anc. Sinope. N Turkey
Sinope *see* Sinop
Sinsheim 95 B 6 SW Germany
Sint Maarten 55 G 3
  Eng: Saint Martin. Island,
  N Netherlands Antilles
Sint-Niklaas 87 B 5
  Fr. Saint-Nicolas. N Belgium
Sint-Pieters-Leeuw 87 B 6
  C Belgium
Sintra 92 B 4 *prev.* Cintra. W Portugal
Sinüjiif 73 E 5 NE Somalia
Sinus Arabious *see* Red Sea
Sinzyô *see* Shinjō
Siorapaluk 82 D 1 NW Greenland

Simleu Silvaniei 108 B 3
Sioux City 45 F 3
  South Dakota, N USA
Sioux Falls 45 F 3
  South Dakota, N USA
Siphnos *see* Sífnos
Siping 128 D 3 *var.* Ssu-p'ing,
  Szeping; *prev.* Ssu-p'ing-chieh
  NE China
Siple, Mount 154 A 4 mountain,
  Antarctica
Siquirres 53 E 4 E Costa Rica
Siracusa 97 D 7 *Eng.* Syracuse.
  SW Italy
Sir Charles Forbes Island *see*
  Kau-Ye Kyun
Sir Edward Pellew Islands 148 B 2
  island group, Northern Territory,
  NE Australia
Siret 108 C 3 *var.* Siretul,
  Ger. Sereth, *Rus.* Seret, *Ukr.* Siret.
  River, Romania/Ukraine
Sirikit Reservoir 136 C 4 lake,
  N Thailand
Sirna *see* Sýrna
Sirte, Gulf of 103 E 4 *var.* Khalīj
  Surt, *Eng.* Gulf of Sidra,
  Gulf of Sirti, Sidra. Gulf,
  E Mediterranean Sea
Sisak 100 B 3 *var.* Siscia, *Ger.* Sissek,
  Hung. Sziszek; anc. Segestica.
  C Croatia
Sisimiut 82 C 3 *var.* Holsteinborg,
  Holsteinsborg, Holstenborg,
  Holstensborg. W Greenland
Sīstān, Daryācheh-ye 122 D 5 *var.*
  Daryācheh-ye Hāmūn, Hāmūn-e
  flāberi. Lake, E Iran
Siteía 105 D 8 *var.* Sitía. Kríti,
  SE Greece
Sitges 93 G 2 NE Spain
Sitía *see* Siteía
Sittang 136 B 4 *var.* Sittoung. River,
  C Myanmar
Sittard 87 D 5 SE Netherlands
Sittoung *see* Sittang
Sittwe 136 A 3 *var.* Akyab.
  W Myanmar
Siuna 52 D 3 NE Nicaragua
Sivas 116 D 3 anc. Sebaste, Sebastia.
  C Turkey
Siwa Oasis 72 A 2 oasis, NW Egypt
Six Counties, The *see*
  Northern Ireland
Six-Fours-les-Plages 91 D 6
  SE France
Siyäzän 117 H 2 *Rus.* Siazan'.
  NE Azerbaijan
Sizuoka *see* Shizuoka
Sjar *see* Sääre
Sjælland 85 B 8 *Eng.* Zealand.
  Ger. Seeland. Island,
  E Denmark
Sjenica 101 D 5 SW Serbia.
  SW Yugoslavia
Skagerrak 85 A 6 *var.* Skagerak,
  Skag-e-rak. Channel,
  Baltic Sea/North Sea
Skagit River 46 B 1 river,
  Washington, NW USA
Skalka 84 C 3 lake, N Sweden
Skåne 85 B 7 *prev.* Eng. Scania.
  Cultural region, S Sweden
Skaudvilė 106 B 4 SW Lithuania
Skegness 89 E 6 E England, UK
Skeleton Coast 78 A 3 physical
  region, NW Namibia
Skellefteå 84 D 4 N Sweden
Skellefteälven 84 C 4 river,
  N Sweden
Ski 85 B 6 S Norway
Skíathos 105 C 5 Vóreioi Sporádes,
  E Greece

Skidal' 107 B 5 *Rus.* Skídel'.
Skídel' *see* Skidal'
Skiermûntseach *see*
  Schiermonnikoog
Skíros *see* Skýros
Skópelos 105 C 5 Vóreioi Sporádes,
  E Greece
Skopje 101 D 6 *var.* Üsküb, *Turk.*
  Usküp; *prev.* Skoplje, *anc.* Scupi.
  Country capital, N Macedonia
Skovorodino 115 F 4
  SE Russian Federation
Skrīveri 106 C 4 S Latvia
Skuodas 106 B 3 *Ger.* Schoden,
  Pol. Szkudy. NW Lithuania
Skye, Isle of 88 B 3 island,
  W Scotland, UK
Skylge *see* Terschelling
Skýros 105 C 5 *var.* Skíros. Skýros,
  E Greece
Skýros 105 C 5 *var.* Skíros; *anc.*
  Scyros. Island, Vóreioi Sporádes,
  E Greece
Slagelse 85 B 7 E Denmark
Slatina 108 B 4 S Romania
Slave Coast 75 F 5 coastal region,
  W Africa
Slavgorod *see* Slawharad
Slavonska Požega 100 C 3
  Ger. Poschega, *Hung.* Pozsega;
  prev. Požega. NE Croatia
Slavonski Brod 100 C 3 *Ger.* Brod,
  Hung. Bród; *prev.* Brod, Brod na
  savi. NE Croatia
Slavuta 108 C 2 NW Ukraine
Slavyansk *see* Slov"yans'k
Slawharad 107 E 7 *Rus.* Slavgorod.
  E Belarus
Sławno 98 B 2 NW Poland
Sléibhte Chill Mhantáin *see*
  Wicklow Mountains
Sligeach *see* Sligo
Sligo 89 A 5 *Ir.* Sligeach.
  NW Ireland
Sliven 104 D 2 *var.* Slivno. E Bulgaria
Slivnitsa 104 C 2 W Bulgaria
Slivno *see* Sliven
Slobozia 108 D 5 SE Romania
Slonim 107 B 6 *Pol.* Słonim,
  Rus. Slonim. W Belarus

Slovakia
99 D 6 *Ger.* Slowakei,
Hung. Szlovákia, *Slvk.* Slovensko.
Republic, C Europe

Official name: Slovak Republic
Date of formation: 1993 **Capital:**
Bratislava **Population:** 5.3 million
Total area: 19,100 sq miles
(49,500 sq km) **Languages:** Slovak*,
Hungarian (Magyar), Czech
Religions: Roman Catholic 80%,
Protestant 12%, other 8% **Ethnic
mix:** Slovak 85%, Hungarian 9%,
Czech 1%, other (inc. Gypsy) 5%
Government: Multiparty republic
Currency: Koruna = 100 halierov

Slovenia
95 D 8 *Ger.* Slowenien, *Slvn.*
Slovenija. Republic, C Europe

Official name: Republic of Slovenia
Date of formation: 1991 **Capital:**
Ljubljana **Population:** 2 million
Total area: 7,820 sq miles
(20,250 sq km) **Languages:** Slovene*,
Serbian, Croatian **Religions:** Roman
Catholic 96%, Muslim 1%, other 3%
Ethnic mix: Slovene 92%, Croat 3%,
Serb 1%, other 4%
Government: Multiparty republic
Currency: Tolar = 100 stotins

Slovenské Rudohorie 99 D 6
var. Ungarisches Erzgebirge,
Eng. Slovak Ore Mountains,
Ger. Slowakisches Erzgebirge.
Mountain range, C Slovakia
Slov"yans'k 109 G 3
Rus. Slavyansk. E Ukraine
Słubice 98 B 3 *Ger.* Frankfurt.
W Poland
Sluch 108 D 1 river, NW Ukraine
Słupsk 98 C 2 *Ger.* Stolp.
NW Poland
Slutsk 107 C 6 S Belarus
Småland 85 B 7 cultural region,
S Sweden
Smallwood Reservoir 39 F 2 lake,
Newfoundland and Labrador,
S Canada
Smara 70 B 3 N Western Sahara
Smarhon' 107 C 5 *Pol.* Smorgonie,
Rus. Smorgon'. NW Belarus
Smederevo 100 E 4 *Ger.* Semendria.
N Yugoslavia
Smela *see* Smila
Smila 109 E 2 *Rus.* Smela. C Ukraine
Smilten *see* Smiltene
Smiltene 106 D 3 *Ger.* Smilten.
N Latvia
Smithton 149 C 8 Tasmania,
SE Australia
Smoky Cape 149 E 6 headland,
New South Wales, SE Australia
Smøla 84 A 4 island, W Norway
Smolensk 111 A 5
W Russian Federation
Smyrna *see* İzmir
Snake River 46 C 3 river, NW USA
Snake River Plain 46 D 4 plain,
Idaho, NW USA
Sneek 86 D 2 N Netherlands
Snĕžka 98 B 4 *Ger.* Schneekoppe.
Mountain, N Czech Republic
Sniečkus *see* Visaginas
Snina 99 E 5 *Hung.* Szinna. E Slovakia
Snowdonia 89 C 6 mountain range,
N Wales, UK
Snowdrift *see* Łutselk'e
Snyder 49 F 3 Texas, S USA
Sobradinho, Barragem de *see*
  Sobradinho, Represa de
Sobradinho, Represa de 63 F 2
var. Barragem de Sobradinho.
Reservoir, E Brazil
Socabaya 61 E 4 SE Peru
Sochi 111 A 7
SW Russian Federation
Société, Archipel de la 145 G 4
var. Îles de la Société, *Eng.*
Society Islands. Island group,
W French Polynesia
Society Islands *see* Leeward Islands
Socorro, Isla 50 B 5 island,
W Mexico
Socotra 121 D 7 *var.* Sokotra. Island,
SE Yemen
Soc Trăng 137 D 6 *var.* Khanh
Hung. S Vietnam
Socuéllamos 93 E 3 C Spain
Sodankylä 84 D 3 N Finland
Söderhamn 85 C 5 C Sweden
Södertälje 85 C 6 C Sweden
Sodiri 72 B 4 *var.* Sawdirī, Sodari.
C Sudan
Soekaboemi *see* Sukabumi
Sofia *see* Sofiya
Sofiya 104 C 2 *var.* Sofija, Sophia,
Eng. Sofia; *Lat.* Serdica . Country
capital, W Bulgaria
Sogamoso 58 B 3 C Colombia
Sognefjorden 85 A 5 fjord,
NE North Sea

Sohâg 72 B 2 *var.* Sawhāj, Suliag.
C Egypt
Sohar *see* Şuḥār
Sokal' 108 C 2 *Rus.* Sokal. NW Ukraine
Sokal *see* Sokal'
Söke 116 A 4 SW Turkey
Sokhumi 117 E 1 *Rus.* Sukhumi.
NW Georgia
Sokodé 75 F 4 C Togo
Sokol 110 C 4 NW Russian Federation
Sokótka 98 E 3 W Hungary
Sokolov 99 A 5 *Ger.* Falkenau an
der Eger; *prev.* Falknov nad Ohří.
W Czech Republic
Sokoto 75 F 4 State capital
NW Nigeria
Sokotra *see* Socotra
Solapur 132 C 1 *prev.* Sholāpur.
SW India
Solca 108 C 3 *Ger.* Solka. N Romania
Sol, Costa del 92 D 5 coastal region,
S Spain
Soldeu 91 B 8 NE Andorra
Solec Kujawski 98 C 3 W Poland
Soledad 58 B 1 N Colombia
Soledad *see* East Falkland
Soligorsk *see* Salihorsk
Solikamsk 110 D 4
NW Russian Federation
Sol'-Iletsk 111 D 6
W Russian Federation
Solin 100 B 4 *It.* Salona;
anc. Salonae. S Croatia
Solingen 94 A 4 W Germany
Solka *see* Solca
Sollentuna 85 C 6 C Sweden
Solok 138 B 3 W Indonesia

Solomon Islands
144 D 3 *prev.* British Solomon
Islands Protectorate.
Commonwealth republic,
SW Pacific Ocean

Official name: Solomon Islands
Date of formation: 1978
Capital: Honiara **Population:**
400,000 **Total Area:** 111,583 sq miles
(289,000 sq km) **Languages:**
English*, 87 (est.) native languages
Religions: Christian 91%, other 9%
Ethnic mix: Melanesian 94%,
other 6% **Government:**
Parliamentary democracy
Currency: Solomon Is $ = 100 cents

Solomon Sea 144 B 3 sea,
SW Pacific Ocean
Soltau 94 B 3 NW Germany
Sol'tsy 110 A 4 *var.* Solcy,Sol'cy.
W Russian Federation
Solwezi 78 D 2 NW Zambia
Sōma 130 D 4 Honshū, C Japan

Somalia
73 E 5 *Som.* Jamuuriyada
Demuqraadiga Soomaaliyeed,
Soomaaliya; *prev.* Italian
Somaliland, Somaliland
Protectorate. Republic,
NE Africa

Official name: Somali Democratic
Republic **Date of formation:** 1960
Capital: Mogadishu **Population:** 9.5
million **Total area:** 246,200 sq miles
(637,660 sq km) **Languages:** Somali,*
Arabic **Religions:** Sunni Muslim 99%,
other (inc. Christian) 1% **Ethnic mix:**
Somali 98%, Bantu, Arab and other
2% **Government:** Transitional
Currency: Shilling = 100 cents

Somali Basin 140 B 4 undersea
basin, W Indian Ocean
Somali Peninsula 68 E 4 coastal
feature, NE Somalia
Sombor 100 D 3 *Hung.* Zombor.
NW Yugoslavia
Someren 87 D 5
SE Netherlands
Somerset 42 A 5 *var.* Somerset
Village. W Bermuda
Somerset 40 C 5
Massachusetts, NE USA
Somerset Island 37 F 2 island,
NW Canada
Somerset Island 42 A 5 island,
W Bermuda
Somerset Village *see* Somerset
Somerton 48 A 3
Arizona, SW USA
Somerville Lake 49 G 3 reservoir,
Texas, S USA
Someş 108 B 3 *var.* Someşul,
Szamos, *Ger.* Samosch,
Somesch. River, Hungary/
Romania
Somme 90 C 2 river, N France
Sommerfeld *see* Lubsko
Somotillo 52 C 3 NW Nicaragua
Somoto 52 D 3 NW Nicaragua
Sonaguera 52 D 2 N Honduras
Søndre Strømfjord *see*
  Kangerlussuaq
Songea 73 C 8 S Tanzania
Sŏngjin *see* Kimch'aek
Songkhla 137 C 7 *var.* Songkla,
Mal. Singora. S Thailand
Sŏng Srepok *see* Srêpôk, Tônle
Sonsonate 52 B 3
W El Salvador
Sop Hao 136 D 3 NE Laos
Sopot 98 C 2 *Ger.* Zoppot.
N Poland
Sopron 99 B 6 *Ger.* Ödenburg.
NW Hungary
Sorgues 91 D 6 SE France
Sorgun 116 D 3 C Turkey
Soria 93 E 2 N Spain
Soroca 108 D 3 *Rus.* Soroki.
N Moldova
Sorocaba 57 D 5 S Brazil
Sorochino *see* Sarochyna
Soroki *see* Soroca
Sorong 139 G 4 New Guinea,
E Indonesia
Sørøy *see* Sørøya
Sørøya 84 C 2 *var.* Sørøy. Island,
N Norway
Sortavala 110 B 3
NW Russian Federation
Sosnogorsk 110 D 4
NW Russian Federation
Sotavento, Ilhas de 74 A 3 *var.*
Leeward Islands. Island group,
S Cape Verde
Sotkamo 84 E 4 C Finland
Souanké 77 B 5 NW Congo
Souflí 104 D 3 *prev.* Souflíon.
NE Greece
Souflíon *see* Souflí
Soufrière 55 F 2 W Saint Lucia
Soûl 128 E 4 *off.* Sŏul-t'úkpyŏlsi,
Eng. Seoul, *Jap.* Keijō; *prev.*
Kyŏngsŏng; Country capital,
NW South Korea
Soûr 119 A 5 *var.* Şür; *anc.* Tyre.
SW Lebanon
Souris River 45 E 1 river,
Canada/USA
Sourpi 105 B 5 C Greece
Sousse 71 F 2 *var.* Süsah.
NE Tunisia

uth Africa
78 C 4 Africa, *Afr.* Suid-Afrika.
Republic, S Africa

fficial name: Republic of South
rica **Date of formation:** 1910/1934
apitals: Pretoria, Cape Town,
emfontein Population: 37.4
llion **Total area:** 471,443 sq miles
221,040 sq km) **Languages:**
rikaans*, English, 11 African
nguages **Religions:** Protestant
%, Roman Catholic 9%, Hindu
, Muslim 1%, other 34%
nnic mix: Black 75%, White 14%,
xed 9%, South Asian 2%
overnment: Multiparty republic
urrency: Rand = 100 cents

uth America 67 B 5 continent
uthampton 89 D 7 *hist.* Hamwih,
Lat. Clausentum.
S England, UK
uthampton Island 37 G 3 island,
NE Canada
uth Andaman 133 F 2 island,
SE India
uth Australia 149 A 5 state,
S Australia
uth Australian Basin 152 B 4
undersea basin, SW Indian Ocean
uth Bend 40 C 3 Indiana, N USA
uth Beveland *see* Zuid-Beveland
uth Carolina 43 E 2 *off.* State of
South Carolina; nickname
Palmetto State. State, SE USA
uth China Basin 152 A 3
undersea basin, E Pacific Ocean
uth China Sea 152 A 2 *Chin.* Nan
Hai, *Ind.* Laut Cina Selatan, *Vtn.*
Biên fông. Sea, E Pacific Ocean
uth Dakota 45 E 2 *off.* State of
South Dakota; nicknames Coyote
State, Sunshine State. State, N USA
uth East Cape 149 C 7 headland,
Victoria, SE Australia
utheast Indian Ridge 141 D 6
undersea ridge, S Indian Ocean
utheast Pacific Basin 153 F 5 *var.*
Bellany Hausen Mulde. Undersea
basin, SE Pacific Ocean
uthend-on-Sea 89 E 6
SE England, UK
uthern Alps 151 B 6 mountain
range, South Island,
SW New Zealand
uthern Cook Islands 145 F 5
island group, S Cook Islands
uthern Cross 147 B 6 Western
Australia, SW Australia
uthern Ocean 152 C 5 ocean
uthern Uplands 88 C 4 mountain
range, S Scotland, UK
uthesk Tablelands 146 D 3 plain,
NW Australia
uth Fiji Basin 152 C 4 undersea
basin, S Pacific Ocean
ut!: Georgia 154 A 1 island,
SW Atlantic Ocean
uth Georgia Ridge 57 C 8 *var.*
North Scotia Ridge. Undersea
ridge, SW Atlantic Ocean
uth Huvadhu Atoll 132 B 5
var. Gaafu Dhaalu Atoll. Island,
S Maldives
uth Indian Basin 141 D 7
undersea basin, S Indian Ocean
uth Indian Lake 37 F 4
Manitoba, C Canada
uth Indian Lake 38 A 2 lake,
Manitoba, C Canada
uth Island 151 C 6 island,
South Island, S New Zealand
uth Island *see* Auk Bok

South Korea
128 E 4 *Kor.* Taehan Min'guk.
Republic, E Asia

Official name: Republic of Korea
Date of formation: 1948 **Capital:**
Seoul **Population:** 44.5 million **Total
Area:** 38,232 sq miles (99,020 sq km)
Languages: Korean*, Chinese
Religions: Mahayana Buddhist 47%,
Protestant 38%, Roman Catholic
11%, Confucianist 3%, other 1%
Ethnic mix: Korean 99% other
0.1% **Government:** Multiparty
republic **Currency:** Won = 100 chon

South Lake Tahoe 47 C 5
California, W USA
South Magnetic Pole 154 D 5 pole,
Antarctica
South Orkney Islands 154 A 2
island group, Antarctica
South Ossetia 117 F 2 region,
C Georgia
South Pacific Basin *see* Southwest
Pacific Basin
South Platte River 44 D 4 river,
C USA
South Pole 154 B 3 pole, Antarctica
South Portland 41 G 2
Maine, NE USA
South Sandwich Islands 154 A 1
island group, S Atlantic Ocean
South Sandwich Trench 154 A 1
trench, SW Atlantic Ocean
South Shetland Islands 154 A 2
island group, Antarctica
South Shields 88 D 4 N England, UK
South Sioux City 45 F 3
Nebraska, C USA
South Taranaki Bight 150 C 4
bight, E Tasman Sea
South Tasmania Plateau *see*
Tasman Plateau
South Uist 88 B 3 island,
W Scotland, UK
South Wellesley Islands 148 B 3
island group, Northern Territory,
N Australia
Southwest Indian Ocean Ridge *see*
Southwest Indian Ridge
Southwest Indian Ridge 141 A 6
var. Southwest Indian Ocean
Ridge. Undersea ridge,
SW Indian Ocean
South West Island 148 D 3 island,
E Australia
Southwest Pacific Basin 152 D 4
var. Southwest Pacific Basin. Undersea
basin, SE Pacific Ocean
Soweto 78 D 4 NE South Africa

Spain
92-93 D 3 *Sp.* España; *anc.* Hispania,
Iberia, *Lat.* Hispana. Monarchy,
SW Europe

Official name: Kingdom of Spain
Date of formation: 1492/1713
Capital: Madrid **Population:** 39.2
million **Total area:** 194,900 sq miles
(504,780 sq km) **Languages:**
Castilian Spanish*, Catalan*,
Galician*, Basque*
Religions: Roman Catholic 99%,
other 1% **Ethnic mix:** Castilian
Spanish 72%, Catalan 16%, Galician
7%, other 5% **Government:**
Constitutional monarchy
Currency: Peseta = 100 céntimos

Spalato *see* Split
Spaldings 54 B 5 C Jamaica
Spanish Town 54 B 5 *hist.* St.Iago
de la Vega. C Jamaica

Spanish Wells 54 C 1 C Bahamas
Sparks 47 C 5 Nevada, W USA
Sparta *see* Spárti
Spartanburg 43 E 1
South Carolina, SE USA
Spárti 105 B 6 *Eng.* Sparta. S Greece
Spearfish 44 D 3
South Dakota, N USA
Speightstown 55 G 1 W Barbados
Spencer 45 F 3 Iowa, C USA
Spencer Gulf 149 B 6 gulf,
E Indian Ocean
Spenser Mountains 151 C 5
mountain range, South Island,
C New Zealand
Spey 88 C 3 river, NE Scotland, UK
Spijkenisse 86 B 4 SW Netherlands
Spíli 105 C 8 Kriti, SE Greece
Spin Büldak 123 E 5 S Afghanistan
Spitsbergen 83 G 2 island,
NW Svalbard
Split 101 A 8 *It.* Spalato. S Croatia
Spogi 106 D 4 SE Lithuania
Spokane 46 C 2
Washington, NW USA
Spratly Islands 125 E 4 island
group, S South China Sea
Spratly Islands 138 D 2
Chin. Nansha Qundao. Disputed
territory, C South China Sea
Spree 94 D 4 river, E Germany
Springfield 40 C 4 Ohio, NE USA
Springfield 41 G 3 state capital,
Illinois, N USA
Springfield 46 B 3 Oregon, NW USA
Springfield 45 G 5
Missouri, C USA
Spring Garden 59 F 2 NE Guyana
Spring Hill 43 E 4 Florida, SE USA
Springsure 148 D 4 Queensland,
E Australia
Sprottau *see* Szprotawa
Srbroban 100 D 3 *var.*
Bácsszenttamás, *Hung.*
Szenttamás. N Yugoslavia
Srebrenica 100 C 4
E Bosnia & Herzegovina
Sredets 104 E 2 *var.* Sredec;
prev. Syulemeshlii. C Bulgaria
Srednesibirskoye Ploskogor'ye 115
E 3 *var.* Central Siberian Uplands,
Eng. Central Siberian Plateau.
Mountain range,
C Russian Federation
Sremska Mitrovica 100 D 3
Ger. Mitrowitz; *prev.* Mitrovica.
NW Yugoslavia
Srêpôk, Tônle 137 F 5 *var.* Sông
Srepok. River, Cambodia/
Vietnam
Sri Aman 138 C 3 *var.* Bandar Sri
Aman, Simanggang. Borneo,
N Malaysia
Sri Jayawardanapura 132 D 3
W Sri Lanka
Srikakulam 135 F 5 E India

Sri Lanka
132 D 3 Republic of Sri Lanka;
prev. Ceylon. Republic, S Asia

Official name: Democratic Socialist
Republic of Sri Lanka **Date of
formation:** 1948 **Capital:** Colombo
Population:17.9 million **Total Area:**
25,332 sq miles (65,610 sq km)
Languages: Sinhala*, Tamil, English
Religions: Buddhist 70%, Hindu
15%, Christian 8%, Muslim 7%
Ethnic mix: Sinhalese 74%, Tamil
18%, other 8% **Government:**
Multiparty republic
Currency: Rupee = 100 cents

Srinagarind Reservoir 137 C 5 lake,
W Thailand
Stabroek 87 C 5 N Belgium
Stade 94 B 3 NW Germany
Stadskanaal 86 E 2 NE Netherlands
Stafford 89 D 6 W England, UK
Staicele 106 D 3 N Latvia
Stakhanov 109 H 3 E Ukraine
Stalinsk *see* Novokuznetsk
Stalinski Zaliv *see* Varnenski Zaliv
Stalowa Wola 98 E 4 SE Poland
Stamford 41 F 3
Connecticut, NE USA
Stanley 65 D 7 *var.* Port Stanley.
Dependent territory capital,
E Falkland Islands
Stanley *see* Chek Chue
Stanleyville *see* Kisangani
Stann Creek *see* Dangriga
Stanovoy Khrebet 115 F 4
mountain range,
E Russian Federation
Stanthorpe 149 D 5 Queensland,
SE Australia
Staphorst 86 D 3 E Netherlands
Starachowice 98 D 4 SE Poland
Stara Pazova 100 D 3 *Ger.* Altpasua,
Hung. Ópazova. N Yugoslavia
Stara Planina *see* Balkan Mountains
Stara Zagora 104 D 2 *Lat.* Augusta
Trajana. C Bulgaria
Starbuck Island 145 G 3
prev. Volunteer Island. Island,
E Kiribati
Stargard in Pommern *see*
Stargard Szczeciński
Stargard Szczeciński 98 B 3
Ger. Stargard in Pommern.
NW Poland
Starobel'sk *see* Starobil's'k
Starobil's'k 109 H 2 *Rus.*
Starobel'sk. E Ukraine
Starobin *see* Starobyn
Starobyn 107 C 7 *Rus.* Starobin.
S Belarus
Starogard Gdański 98 C 2 *Ger.*
Preussisch-Stargard. N Poland
Starokonstantinov *see*
Starokostyantyniv
Starokostyantyniv 108 D 2 *Rus.*
Starokonstantinov. NW Ukraine
Starominskaya 111 A 7
SW Russian Federation
Starry Oskol 111 B 6
W Russian Federation
Staryya Darohi 107 C 7
Rus. Staryye Dorogi. S Belarus
Staryye Dorogi *see* Staryya Darohi
Staten Island *see* Estados, Isla de los
State of Eritrea *see* Eritrea
Statesboro 43 E 2 Georgia, SE USA
Staunton 41 E 5 Virginia, NE USA
Stavanger 85 A 6 S Norway
St-Avertin 90 B 4 W France
Stavropol' 111 B 7
prev. Voroshilovsk.
SW Russian Federation
Stavropol' *see* Tol'yatti
St-Brieuc 90 A 3 NW France
St-Chamond 91 D 5 E France
St-Claude 91 D 5 *anc.* Condate.
E France
St-Denis 90 C 3 N France
St-Denis 79 H 4 dependent
territory capital, N Réunion
St-Dié 90 E 4 NE France
Steamboat Springs 44 C 4
Colorado, C USA
Steenwijk 86 D 2 N Netherlands
St-Égrève 91 D 5 E France
Steier *see* Steyr

Steinkjer 84 B 4 C Norway
Stejarul *see* Karapelit
Stendal 94 C 3 C Germany
Stephenville 49 G 3 Texas, S USA
Sterling 40 B 3 Illinois, N USA
Sterling 44 D 4 Colorado, C USA
Sterling Heights 40 D 3
  Michigan, N USA
Sterlitamak 111 D 6
  W Russian Federation
St-Étienne 91 C 5 E France
Stettin *see* Szczecin
Stevenage 89 E 6 SE England, UK
Stevens Point 40 B 2
  Wisconsin, N USA
Stewart 36 D 4 British Columbia,
  W Canada
Stewart Island 151 A 8 *var.*
  Sikainana. Island, South Island,
  S New Zealand
Steyr 95 D 6 *var.* Steier. N Austria
St-Flour 91 C 5 C France
St-Gaudens 91 B 6 S France
St-Georges 39 E 4 Québec,
  SE Canada
St-Georges 59 H 3 E French Guiana
Stif *see* Sétif
Stillwater 49 G 1 Oklahoma, C USA
Štip 101 E 6 E Macedonia
Stirling 88 C 4 S Scotland, UK
St-Jean-de-Luz 91 A 6 SW France
St-Jean, Lac 39 E 4 lake, Québec,
  SE Canada
Stjørdal 84 B 4 C Norway
St-Laurent *see* St-Laurent-du-Maroni
St-Laurent-du-Maroni 59 H 3 *var.*
  St.-Laurent. NW French Guiana
St-Lô 90 B 3 *anc.* Briovera, Laudus.
  N France
St-Louis 90 E 4 NE France
St-Louis 74 B 3 NW Senegal
St-Malo 90 B 3 NW France
St-Malo, Golfe de 90 B 3 inlet,
  C English Channel
St-Max 90 D 3 NE France
St-Nazaire 90 A 4 NW France
Stockach 95 B 6 S Germany
Stockholm 85 C 6 country capital,
  C Sweden
Stockmannshof *see* Pļaviņas
Stockton 47 B 6 California, W USA
Stŏeng Trêng 137 D 5 *prev.* Stung
  Treng. N Cambodia
Stoke *see* Stoke-on-Trent
Stoke-on-Trent 89 C 6 *var.* Stoke.
  W England, UK
Stolp *see* Słupsk
Stolpmünde *see* Ustka
St-Omer 90 C 2 N France
Stómio 104 B 4 C Greece
Storebælt 85 B 7 *var.* Store Bælt,
  Storebelt, *Eng.* Great Belt.
  Channel, Baltic Sea/North Sea
Støren 85 B 5 S Norway
Storfjorden 83 G 2 fjord, Barents
  Sea/Norwegian Sea
Storhammer *see* Hamar
Stornoway 88 B 2 island authority
  area capital, NW Scotland, UK
Storsjön 85 B 5 lake, C Sweden
Storuman 84 C 4 lake, N Sweden
Storuman 84 C 4 N Sweden
Stowbtsy 107 C 6 *Pol.* Stolbce,
  Rus. Stolbtsy. C Belarus
St-Paul, Île 141 C 6 *var.* St.Paul
  Island. Island, NE French
  Southern & Antarctic Territories
St-Pierre & Miquelon 39 G 4
  Fr. Îles St-Pierre et Miquelon.
  French Territorial Collectivity,
  NW Atlantic Ocean

St-Pierre et Miquelon, Îles *see*
  St-Pierre and Miquelon
St-Quentin 90 D 3 N France
Strabane 89 B 5 *Ir.* An Srath Bán.
  C Northern Ireland, UK
Strakonice 99 A 5 *Ger.* Strakonitz.
  SW Czech Republic
Strakonitz *see* Strakonice
Stralsund 94 D 2 NE Germany
Stranraer 89 B 5 SW Scotland, UK
Strasbourg 90 E 3 *Ger.* Strassburg;
  anc. Argentoratum. NE France
Strășeni 108 D 4 *var.* Strasheny.
  C Moldova
Strasheny *see* Strășeni
Stratford 150 D 4 North Island,
  C New Zealand
Straubing 95 C 6 SE Germany
Streaky Bay 149 A 6 bay,
  SE Indian Ocean
Strehaia 108 B 5 SW Romania
Strelka 114 D 4
  C Russian Federation
Strofilia *see* Strofyliá
Strofyliá 105 C 5 *var.* Strofilia.
  Évvoia, C Greece
Stromboli, Isola 97 D 6 island,
  S Italy
Stromeferry 88 B 3
  NW Scotland, UK
Strömstad 85 B 6 S Sweden
Strömsund 84 C 4 C Sweden
Struga 101 D 6 SW Macedonia
Struma 104 C 3 *Gk.* Strymónas.
  River, Bulgaria/Greece
Strumica 101 E 6 E Macedonia
Strumyani 104 C 3 SW Bulgaria
Stryy 108 B 2 NW Ukraine
Studholme 151 B 7 South Island,
  SW New Zealand
Stung Treng *see* Stŏeng Trêng
Stupino 111 B 5
  W Russian Federation
Sturgis 44 D 3 South Dakota, N USA
Stuttgart 95 B 6 SW Germany
Stykkishólmur 83 E 5 W Iceland
Styr 108 C 1 river, NW Ukraine
Suakin 72 C 3 *var.* Sawakin.
  NE Sudan
Subačius 106 C 4 NE Lithuania
Subotica 100 D 2 *Ger.* Maria-
  Theresiopel, *Hung.* Szabadka.
  N Yugoslavia
Suceava 108 C 3 *Ger.* Suczawa,
  Hung. Szucsava. NE Romania
Sucre 61 F 4 *hist.* Chuquisaca, La
  Plata. Country capital, S Bolivia
Sudan 74 C 4 physical region,
  W Africa

Sudan
  72 A 4 *Ar.* Jamhuryat es-Sudan,
  Jumhuriyat as-Sudan; *prev.*
  Anglo-Egyptian *Sudan*. Republic,
  NE Africa

Official name: Republic of Sudan
Date of formation: 1956 **Capital:**
Khartoum **Population:** 27.4 million
Total area: 967,493 sq miles
(2,505,815 sq km) **Languages:** Arabic*
Religions: Muslim 70%, traditional
beliefs 20%,*Christian 5%, other 5%
Government: Military regime
Currency: Pound = 100 piastres

Sudbury 38 C 4 Ontario, S Canada
Sudd 73 B 5 wetland, S Sudan
Suddie 59 F 2 NE Guyana
Sudeten 99 C 5 *var.* Sudetes,
  Sudetic Mountains, Cz./Pol.
  Sudety. Mountain range,
  Czech Republic/Poland

Sudong, Pulau 138 A 2 island,
  SW Singapore
Sueca 93 F 3 E Spain
Sue Wood Bay 42 B 5 bay,
  W Atlantic Ocean
Suez 72 B 1 *Ar.* As Suways,
  El Suweis. NE Egypt
Suez Canal 72 C 1 *Ar.* Qanāt as
  Suways. Canal, NE Egypt
Suez, Gulf of 72 B 1 *Ar.* Khalij as
  Suways. Gulf, NW Red Sea
Suffolk 41 F 5 Virginia, NE USA
Suğla Gölü 116 C 4 lake, SW Turkey
Sühbaatar 127 E 1 N Mongolia
Suhl 95 C 5 C Germany
Şuḩār 121 D 5 *var.* Sohar. N Oman
Suixi 129 C 7 S China
Sukabumi 138 C 5 *prev.*
  Soekaboemi. Jawa, C Indonesia
Sukagawa 131 D 5 Honshū,
  C Japan
Sukhumi *see* Sokhumi
Sukkur 134 B 3 SE Pakistan
Sukumo 131 B 7 Shikoku,
  SW Japan
Sulaimān Range 134 C 2 mountain
  range, C Pakistan
Sula, Kepulauan 139 F 4 *prev.*
  Soela, Xulla Islands. Island group,
  E Indonesia
Sulawesi 139 E 4 island,
  C Indonesia
Sulawesi, Laut *see* Celebes Sea
Sullana 60 B 2 NW Peru
Sullivan Island *see* Lanbi Kyun
Sulphur 42 A 3 Louisiana, S USA
Sulphur Springs 49 G 2
  Texas, S USA
Sultānābād *see* Arāk
Sulu Archipelago 139 E 3 island
  group, SW Philippines
Sülüktü *see* Sulyukta
Sulu, Laut *see* Sulu Sea
Sulu Sea 139 E 2 *var.* Laut Sulu.
  Sea, W Pacific Ocean
Sulyukta 123 F 2 *Kir.* Sülüktü.
  SW Kyrgyzstan
Sulz *see* Sulz am Neckar
Sulz am Neckar 95 B 6 *var.* Sulz.
  SW Germany
Sumatera 138 A 4 *Eng.* Sumatra.
  Island, W Indonesia
Sumatra *see* Sumatera
Sumba, Pulau 139 E 5 *Eng.*
  Sandalwood Island; *prev.* Soemba.
  Island, Nusa Tenggara,
  C Indonesia
Sumba, Selat 138 D 5 strait,
  Indian Ocean/Savu Sea
Sumbawanga 73 B 7
  W Tanzania
Sumbay 61 E 4 SE Peru
Sumbe 78 B 2 *var.* N'Gunza,
  Port. Novo Redondo. W Angola
Šumen *see* Shumen
Sumgait *see* Sumqayıt
Summer Lake 46 B 4 lake,
  Oregon, NW USA
Sumqayıt 117 H 2 *Rus.* Sumgait.
  E Azerbaijan
Sumy 109 F 1 NE Ukraine
Suna 73 C 5 S Sudan
Sunbury 149 C 7 Victoria,
  SE Australia
Sun City 88 B 2 Arizona, SW USA
Sunda, Selat 138 B 5 strait,
  Indian Ocean/Pacific Ocean
Sunda Shelf 140 E 4 continental
  shelf, W Pacific Ocean
Sunda Trench 140 D 4 trench,
  NE Indian Ocean

Sunderland 88 D 4 *var.* Wearmouth
  N England, UK
Sundsvall 85 C 5 C Sweden
Sunne 85 B 6 C Sweden
Sunnyside 46 C 2
  Washington, NW USA
Sunnyvale 47 B 6
  California, W USA
Suntar 115 F 3
  E Russian Federation
Sunyani 75 E 5 W Ghana
Suoločielgi *see* Saariselkä
Suomussalmi 84 E 4 E Finland
Suŏng 137 D 6 SE Cambodia
Suoyarvi 110 B 3
  NW Russian Federation
Supérieur, Lac *see* Superior, Lake
Superior 40 A 1 Wisconsin, N USA
Superior, Lake 40 B 1 *Fr.* Lac
  Supérieur. Lake, Canada/USA
Suqrah *see* Şawqirah
Şūr 121 E 5 NE Oman
Surabaya 138 D 5 *prev.* Soerabaja,
  Surabaja. Jawa, C Indonesia
Surakarta 138 C 5 *Eng.* Solo; *prev.*
  Soerakarta. Jawa, C Indonesia
Šurany 99 C 6 *Hung.* Nagysurány.
  SW Slovakia
Sūrat 134 C 4 W India
Suratdhani *see* Surat Thani
Surat Thani 137 C 7 *var.*
  Suratdhani. S Thailand
Surazh 107 E 5 NE Belarus
Surdulica 101 E 5 SE Yugoslavia
Sûre 87 D 7 *var.* Sauer. River,
  W Europe
Surendranagar 134 C 4 W India
Surin 137 D 5 E Thailand

Suriname
  59 G 3 *var.* Surinam; *prev.* Dutch
  Guiana, Netherlands Guiana.
  Republic, NE South America

Official name: Republic of Surinam
Date of formation: 1975 **Capital:**
Paramaribo **Population:** 400,000
Total area: 63,039 sq miles
(163,270 sq km) **Languages:** Dutch*
Pidgin English (Taki-Taki), Hindi,
Javanese, Carib **Religions:** Christian
48%, Hindu 27%, Muslim 20%, other
5% **Ethnic mix:** South Asian 37%,
Creole 31%, Javanese 15%, other
17% **Government:** Multiparty
republic **Currency:** Guilder =
100 cents

Surkhob 123 F 3 river,
  C Tajikistan
Surt 71 G 2 *var.* Sidra, Sirte. N Libya
Surtsey 83 E 5 island, S Iceland
Suruga-wan 131 D 6 bay,
  NW Pacific Ocean
Susa 96 A 2 NW Italy
Sûsah *see* Sousse
Susitna 36 C 3 Alaska, NW USA
Susteren 87 D 5 SE Netherlands
Susuman 115 G 3
  E Russian Federation
Sutlej 134 C 3 river, India/Pakistan
Suur Munamägi 106 D 3 *var.*
  Munamägi, *Ger.* Eier-Berg.
  Mountain, SE Estonia
Suur Väin 106 C 2 *Ger.* Grosser
  Sund. Strait, E Baltic Sea
Suva 145 E 4 country capital,
  Viti Levu, W Fiji
Suwałki 98 E 2 *Lith.* Suvalkai,
  Rus. Suvalki. NE Poland
Suwannee River 43 E 3 river,
  SE USA
Şuwāt 118 D 2 E Syria

ways, Khalīj as *see* Suez, Gulf of
ways, Qanāt as *see* Suez Canal
zhou 129 D 5 *var.* Soochow,
Su-chou, Suchow; *prev.* Wuhsien.
E China
albard 83 G 2 Norwegian
dependency, Arctic Ocean
artisan 84 C 3 glacier, C Norway
ay Riëng 137 D 6 SE Cambodia
eg 85 C 5 C Sweden
enstavik 85 C 5 C Sweden
erdlovsk *see* Yekaterinburg
eti Vrach *see* Sandanski
etlogorsk *see* Svyetlahorsk
etlograd 111 B 7
SW Russian Federation
etlovodsk *see* Svitlovods'k
etozarevo 100 E 4 *var.* Jagodina.
C Yugoslavia
ilengrad 104 D 3 *prev.* Mustafa-
Pasha. SE Bulgaria
isloch' *see* Svislach
itlovods'k 109 E 2
Rus. Svetlovodsk. C Ukraine
obodnyy 115 G 4
SE Russian Federation
yataya Anna Trough 155 H 4
trough, Arctic Ocean
yetlahorsk 107 D 7
Rus. Svetlogorsk. SE Belarus
yakopmund 78 B 3 W Namibia
van Islands *see* Santanilla, Islas
vansea 89 C 7 *Wel.* Abertawe.
S Wales. UK
varzędz 98 C 3 W Poland

aziland
78 D 4 S Monarchy, S Africa

ficial name: Kingdom of
aziland Date of formation: 1968
pital: Mbabane Population:
0,000 Total area: 6,703 sq miles
,360 sq km) Languages: Siswati*,
glish*, Zulu Religions: Christian
%, traditional beliefs 40%
nic mix: Swazi 95%, other 5%
vernment: Executive monarchy
rrency: Lilangeni = 100 cents

eden
84 B 4 *Swe.* Sverige. Monarchy,
N Europe

ficial name: Kingdom of Sweden
te of formation: 1809/1905
pital: Stockholm Population: 8.7
llion Total area: 173,730 sq miles
9,960 sq km) Languages:
edish*, Finnish, Lappish
ligions: Evangelical Lutheran
%, Roman Catholic 2%, other 4%
nic mix: Swedish 87%, Finnish
d Lapp 1%, other European 12%
vernment: Constitutional
narchy Currency: Krona = 100 öre

eetwater 49 F 3 Texas, S USA
idnica 98 B 4 *Ger.* Schweidnitz.
SW Poland
idwin 98 B 2 *Ger.* Schivelbein.
NW Poland
riebodzice 98 B 4 *Ger.* Freiburg
in Schlesien, Swiebodzice.
SW Poland
riebodzin 98 B 3 *Ger.* Schwiebus.
W Poland
riecie 98 C 3 *Ger.* Schwertberg.
N Poland
indon 89 D 7 S England, UK
inemünde *see* Świnoujście
inoujście 98 A 2 *Ger.*
Swinemünde. NW Poland

Switzerland
95 A 7 *Fr.* La Suisse,
Ger. Schweiz, *It.* Svizzera;
anc. Helvetica. Federal republic,
C Europe

Official name: Swiss Confederation
Date of formation: 1815 Capital:
Bern Population: 6.9 million Total
area: 15,940 sq miles (41,290 sq km)
Languages: German*, French*,
Italian* Religions: Roman Catholic
48%, Protestant 44%, other 8%
Ethnic mix: German 65%, French
18%, Italian 10%, other 7%
Government: Federal republic
Currency: Franc = 100 centimes

Syas'stroy 110 B 4
var. S'as'stroj, Sjasstroj.
NW Russian Federation
Sydenham Island *see* Nonouti
Sydney 39 G 4 Nova Scotia,
SE Canada
Sydney 149 D 6 state capital,
New South Wales,
SE Australia
Sydney Island *see* Manra
Sydney Mines 39 G 4
Nova Scotia, SE Canada
Syedpur *see* Saidpur
Syemyezhava 107 C 6
Rus. Semezhevo. C Belarus
Syeverodonets'k 109 H 3
Rus. Severodonetsk. E Ukraine
Syktyvkar 110 D 4 *prev.* Ust'-
Sysol'sk. NW Russian Federation
Sylacauga 42 D 2 Alabama, S USA
Sylhet 135 G 3 NE Bangladesh
Synel'nykove 109 G 3
var. Sinel'nikovo. E Ukraine
Syowa 154 C 2 research station,
Antarctica
Syracuse 41 F 3 New York, NE USA
Syracuse *see* Siracusa
Syr Darya 114 C 5 *var.* Sai Hun,
Sir Darya, Syrdarya, *Kaz.*
Syrdariya, *Rus.* Syrdar'ya,
Uzb. Sirdaryo; *anc.* Jaxartes.
River, C Asia
Syrdar'ya 123 E 2 E Uzbekistan

Syria
118 B 3 *var.* Siria, Syrie, *Ar.*
Al-Jumhūrīyah al-'Arabīyah as-
Sūrīyah, Jumhuriya al-Arabya as-
Suriya, Sūrīya. Republic, SW Asia

Official name: Syrian Arab
Republic Date of formation: 1946
Capital: Damascus Population: 13.8
million Total area: 71,500 sq miles
(185,180 sq km) Languages:
Arabic*, French, Kurdish, Armenian
Religions: Sunni Muslim 74%, other
Muslim 16%, Christian 10%
Ethnic mix: Arab 90%, other 10%
Government: Single-party republic
Currency: Pound = 100 piastres

Syriam 136 B 4 S Myanmar
Syrian Desert 119 D 5
Ar. Ādiyat ash Sham,
Al Ḥamad, Bādiyat ash Shām.
Desert, SW Asia
Sýrna 105 E 7 *var.* Sirna. Island,
Dodekánisos, SE Greece
Syvash, Zatoka 109 F 4 *Rus.* Zaliv
Syvash. Inlet, W Sea of Azov
Syzran' 111 C 6
W Russian Federation
Szamotuły 98 B 3 W Poland
Szczecin 98 B 3 *Eng./Ger.* Stettin.
NW Poland

Szczecinek 98 C 2 *Ger.* Neustettin.
NW Poland
Szczytno 98 D 3 *Ger.* Ortelsburg.
NE Poland
Szeged 99 D 7 *Ger.* Szegedin,
Rom. Seghedin. SE Hungary
Székesfehérvár 99 C 7
Ger. Stuhlweissenberg;
anc. Alba Regia. W Hungary
Szekszárd 99 C 7 S Hungary
Szinna *see* Snina
Szolnok 99 D 7 C Hungary
Szombathely 99 B 6
Ger. Steinamanger; *anc.* Sabaria,
Savaria. W Hungary
Szprotawa 98 B 4 *Ger.* Sprottau.
W Poland

T

Ṭabaqah 118 D 2 N Syria
Tabasará, Serranía de 53 F 5
mountain range, W Panama
Tábor 99 B 5 SW Czech Republic
Tabora 73 B 7 W Tanzania
Tabrīz 120 C 2 *var.* Tauris, Tebriz.
NW Iran
Tabuaeran 145 G 2 *prev.* Fanning
Island. Island, E Kiribati
Tabūk 120 A 4 NW Saudi Arabia
Täby 85 C 6 C Sweden
Tachov 99 A 5 *Ger.* Tachau.
W Czech Republic
Tacloban 139 F 2 *off.* Tacloban City.
Leyte, C Philippines
Tacloban City *see* Tacloban
Tacna 61 E 4 SE Peru
Tacoma 46 B 2 Washington, NW USA
Tacuarembó 64 D 4
prev. San Fructuoso. N Uruguay
Tademaït, Plateau du 70 D 3
plateau, C Algeria
Tādpatri 132 C 2 E India
Taegu 129 E 4 *off.* Taegu-
kwangyŏksi, *var.* Daegu.
Jap. Taikyū. SE South Korea
Taejŏn 129 E 4 *off.* Taejŏn-
kwangyŏksi, *Jap.* Taiden.
C South Korea
Tafí Viejo 64 C 3 NW Argentina
Taganrog 111 A 7
SW Russian Federation
Taganrog, Gulf of 109 G 4
Rus. Taganrogskiy Zaliv,
Ukr. Tahanroz'ka Zatoka. Gulf,
Black Sea/Sea of Azov
Taguatinga 63 F 3 C Brazil
Tagus 92 C 3 *Port.* Rio Tejo, *Sp.*
Río Tajo. River, Portugal/Spain
Tahat 71 E 4 mountain, SE Algeria
Tahiti 145 H 4 island,
W French Polynesia
Tahlequah 49 G 1
Oklahoma, C USA
Tahoe, Lake 47 B 5 lake, W USA
Tahoua 75 F 3 S Niger
T'aichung 129 D 6 *Jap.* Taichou,
Taichū; *prev.* Taiwan. W Taiwan
Taieri 151 B 7 *var.* South Island,
C New Zealand
Taihape 150 D 4 North Island,
C New Zealand
T'ainan 129 D 6 *Jap.* Tainan;
prev. Dainan. SW Taiwan
Tai Pak Wan *see* Discovery Bay
T'aipei 129 D 6 *Jap.* Taihoku;
prev. Daihoku. Country capital,
N Taiwan
Taiping 138 B 3 W Malaysia
Tai Po 128 A 1 N Hong Kong

Taiwan
129 D 6 *var.* Formosa, Formo'sa.
Republic, E Asia

Official name: Republic of China
(Taiwan) Date of formation: 1949
Capital: Taipei Population: 20.8
million Total area: 13,969 sq miles
(36,179 sq km) Languages:
Mandarin* Religions: Buddhist,
Confucianist, Taoist 93%, other 7%
Ethnic mix: Taiwanese 84%,
mainland Chinese 14%, other 2%
Government: Multiparty republic
Currency: New Taiwan $ = 100 cents

Taiwan Strait 125 E 3
var. Formosa Strait, *Chin.* T'aiwan
Haihsia, Taiwan Haixia. Strait,
East China Sea/South China Sea
Taiyuan 128 C 4 *var.* T'ai-yuan,
T'ai-yüan; *prev.* Yangku.
Province capital, N China
Tai Yue Shan *see* Lantau Island
Ta'izz 121 B 7 SW Yemen

Tajikistan
123 E 3 *Rus.* Tadzhikistan,
Taj. Jumhurii Tojikiston; *prev.* Tajik
SSR. Republic, C Asia

Official name: Republic of
Tajikistan Date of formation: 1991
Capital: Dushanbe Population: 5.7
million Total Area: 55,251 sq miles
(143,100 sq km) Languages: Tajik*,
Uzbek, Russian Religions:
Sunni Muslim 85%, Shi'a Muslim
5%, other 10% Ethnic mix: Tajik
62%, Uzbek 24%, Russian 4%, Tartar
2%, other 8% Government:
Single-party republic
Currency: Tajik rouble = 100 kopeks

Tak 136 C 4 *var.* Rahaeng.
W Thailand
Takaoka 131 C 5 Honshū,
SW Japan
Takapuna 150 D 2 North Island,
N New Zealand
Takengon 138 A 3 W Indonesia
Takhiatash *see* Takhiatosh
Takhiatosh 122 C 2 *Rus.* Takhiatash.
W Uzbekistan
Takhtaküpir 122 D 1 *Rus.*
Takhtakupyr. NW Uzbekistan
Takhtakupyr *see* Takhtaküpir
Takikawa 130 D 2 Hokkaidō,
NE Japan
Takli Makan Desert *see*
Taklimakan Shamo
Taklimakan Shamo 126 B 3
Eng. Takli Makan Desert.
Desert, NW China
Takutea 145 G 5 island,
S Cook Islands
Talabriga *see* Aveiro
Talachyn 107 D 6 *Rus.* Tolochin.
NE Belarus
Talamanca, Cordillera de 53 E 5
mountain range, C Costa Rica
Talara 60 B 2 NW Peru
Talas 123 F 4 NW Kyrgyzstan
Talaud, Kepulauan 139 F 3 island
group, E Indonesia
Talavera de la Reina 92 D 3
C Spain
Talcahuano 65 B 5 C Chile
Taldykorgan 114 C 5
Kaz. Taldyqorghan; *prev.*
Taldy-Kurgan. SE Kazakhstan
Taliq-an *see* Tāloqān

Tal'ka 107 D 6 C Belarus
Talkhof *see* Puurmani
Tallahassee 42 D 3
prev. Muskogean. State capital,
Florida, SE USA
Tall Fadghāmī 118 E 2
var. Fadghāmī. NE Syria
Tallinn 106 D 2 *Ger.* Reval,
Rus. Tallin; *prev.* Revel. Country
capital, NW Estonia
Tall Kalakh 118 B 4
var. Tell Kalakh. W Syria
Tallulah 42 B 2 Louisiana, S USA
Tal'ne 109 E 3 *Rus.* Tal'noye.
C Ukraine
Tal'noye *see* Tal'ne
Tāloqān 123 E 3 *var.* Taliq-an.
NE Afghanistan
Talsen *see* Talsi
Talsi 106 C 3 *Ger.* Talsen.
NW Latvia
Taltal 64 B 2 N Chile
Talvik 84 D 2 N Norway
Tamale 75 E 4 C Ghana
Tamana 145 E 3 *prev.* Rotcher
Island. Island, W Kiribati
Tamanrasset 71 E 4
var. Tamenghest. S Algeria
Tamar 89 C 7 river,
SW England, UK
Tamatave *see* Toamasina
Tamazunchale 51 E 4 C Mexico
Tambacounda 74 C 3 SE Senegal
Tambo 148 C 4 Queensland,
C Australia
Tambov 111 B 6
W Russian Federation
Tambura 73 B 5 SW Sudan
Tamchaket *see* Tâmchekkeṭ
Tâmchekkeṭ 74 C 3 *var.* Tamchaket.
S Mauritania
Tamenghest *see* Tamanrasset
Tamiahua, Laguna de 51 F 4 coastal
lagoon, SW Gulf of Mexico
Tam Ky 137 E 5 E Vietnam
Tammerfors *see* Tampere
Tampa 43 E 4 Florida, SE USA
Tampa Bay 43 E 4 bay, Florida,
SE Gulf of Mexico
Tampere 85 D 5 *Swe.* Tammerfors.
SW Finland
Tampico 51 E 3 C Mexico
Tamshiyacu 60 C 1 N Peru
Tamworth 149 D 6
New South Wales, SE Australia
Tana 84 D 2 *var.* Tenojoki,
Fin. Teno, *Lapp.* Dealnu. River,
Finland/Norway
Tana 84 D 2 N Norway
Tanabe 131 C 7 Honshū, SW Japan
Tanaga Island 36 A 3 island,
Alaska, NW USA
T'ana Hāyk' 72 C 4 *var.* Lake Tana.
Lake, NW Ethiopia
Tana, Lake *see* T'ana Hāyk'
Tanami Desert 146 E 3 desert,
Northern Territory, N Australia
Tananarive *see* Antananarivo
Ṭāndârei 108 D 5 E Romania
Tandil 65 D 5 E Argentina
Tando Ādam 134 B 3 *var.* Adam-jo-
Tando. S Pakistan
Tanega-shima 131 B 8 island,
Ōsumi-shotō, SW Japan
Tanen Taunggyi *see* Tane Range
Tane Range 136 B 4 *Bur.* Tanen
Taunggyi. Mountain range,
N Thailand
Tanezrouft 70 D 4 desert,
Algeria/Mali
Tanga 73 C 7 E Tanzania

Tanganyika, Lake 73 B 7 lake,
NE Africa
Tanger 70 C 2 *var.* Tangier, Tangiers,
Fr./Ger. Tanger, *Sp.* Tánger;
anc. Tingis. NW Morocco
Tanggula Shan 126 C 4 *var.* Dangla,
Tangla Range. Mountain range,
W China
Tangier *see* Tanger
Tangiers *see* Tanger
Tangra Yumco 126 B 5
var. Tangro Tso. Lake, W China
Tangro Tso *see* Tangra Yumco
Tangshan 128 D 3 *var.* T'angshan,
T'ang-shan. NE China
Tanimbar, Kepulauan 139 G 5
island group, Maluku,
E Indonesia
Tanna 144 D 5 island, S Vanuatu
Tansen 135 E 3 C Nepal
Tan-Tan 70 B 3 SW Morocco

Tanzania
73 C 7 Swa.Jamhuri ya
Muungano wa Tanzania;
prev. German East Africa,
Tanganyika and Zanzibar.
Republic, NE Africa

Official name: United Republic of
Tanzania **Date of formation:** 1964
Capital: Dodoma **Population:** 28.8
million **Total area:** 364,900 sq miles
(945,090 sq km) **Languages:**
English*, Swahili* **Religions:**
Traditional beliefs 42%, Muslim
31%, Christian 27% **Ethnic mix:** 120
Ethnic Bantu groups 99%, other 1%
Government: Single-party republic
Currency: Shilling = 100 cents

Tao, Ko 137 C 6 island, C Thailand
Taoudenit *see* Taoudenni
Taoudenni 75 E 2 *var.* Taoudenit.
N Mali
Tapa 106 E 2 *Ger.* Taps. NE Estonia
Tapachula 51 G 5 SE Mexico
Tapaiu *see* Gvardeysk
Tapajós 63 E 2 *var.* Tapajóz. River,
NW Brazil
Tapajóz *see* Tapajós
Taps *see* Tapa
Ṭarābulus 71 F 2 *var.* Ṭarābulus
al Gharb; *Eng.* Tripoli. Country
capital, NW Libya
Taraclia 108 D 4 *Rus.* Tarakilya.
S Moldova
Tarakilya *see* Taraclia
Taranaki, Mount 150 D 4 *var.*
Egmont. Mountain, North Island,
C New Zealand
Tarancón 93 E 3 C Spain
Taranto 97 E 5 *var.* Tarentum.
SE Italy
Taranto, Golfo di 97 E 6 *Eng.* Gulf
of Taranto. Gulf, N Ionian Sea
Taranto, Gulf of *see* Taranto, Golfo di
Tarapoto 60 C 2 N Peru
Tarare 91 D 5 E France
Tarascon 91 D 6 SE France
Tarawa Atoll 144 D 2 island,
W Kiribati
Tarazona 93 E 2 NE Spain
Tarbes 91 B 6 *anc.* Bigorra. S France
Tarcoola 149 A 6 South Australia,
S Australia
Taree 149 D 6 New South Wales,
SE Australia
Tarentum *see* Taranto
Târgoviște 108 C 5 *prev.* Tîrgoviște.
S Romania
Targu Jui 108 B 4 *prev.* Tîrgu Jiu.
W Romania

Târgu Mureș 108 B 4
Ger. Neumarkt, *Hung.*
Marosvásárhely; *prev.* Oșorhei,
Tîrgu Mures. C Romania
Târgu-Neamț 108 C 3 *var.* Târgul-
Neamț; *prev.* Tîrgu-Neamț.
NE Romania
Târgu Ocna 108 C 4 *Hung.* Aknavásár;
prev. Tîrgu Ocna. E Romania
Târgu Secuiesc 108 C 4
Ger. Neumarkt, Szekler
Neumarkt, *Hung.* Kezdivásárhely;
prev. Chezdi-Oșorheiu, Târgul-
Săcuiesc, Tîrgu Secuiesc.
E Romania
Tarija 61 G 5 S Bolivia
Tarim 121 C 6 C Yemen
Tarim Basin 126 B 3 *var.* Tarim
Pendi. Basin, NW China
Tarim He 126 B 3 river, NW China
Tarim Pendi *see* Tarim Basin
Tarma 60 C 3 C Peru
Tarn 91 C 6 cultural region, S France
Tarn 91 C 6 river, S France
Târnăveni 108 B 4
Ger. Marteskirch, Martinskirch,
Hung. Dicsőszentmárton; *prev.*
Sînmartin, Tîrnăveni. C Romania
Tarnobrzeg 98 D 4 SE Poland
Tarnów 99 D 5 SE Poland
Taroom 149 D 5 Queensland,
SE Australia
Tarraco *see* Tarragona
Tarragona 93 G 2 *anc.* Tarraco.
E Spain
Tarran Hills 149 C 6 hill range,
New South Wales, C Australia
Tarrasa *see* Terrassa
Tàrrega 93 F 2 *var.* Tarrega.
NE Spain
Tarsus 116 C 4 S Turkey
Tartu 106 E 3 *Ger.* Dorpat; *prev.*
Rus. Yurev, Yuryev. SE Estonia
Tarutao, Ko 137 C 7 island,
S Thailand
Tarvisio 96 D 2 NE Italy
Tarvisium *see* Treviso
Tashkent *see* Toshkent
Tash-Kömür *see* Tash-Kumyr
Tash-Kumyr 123 F 2
Kir. Tash-Kömür. W Kyrgyzstan
Tasikmalaja *see* Tasikmalaya
Tasikmalaya 138 C 5 *prev.*
Tasikmalaja. Jawa, Indonesia
Tasiusaq 82 C 2 *var.* Tasiusak,
Tasiussaq. W Greenland
Tasman Basin 152 C 5 *var.* East
Australian Basin. Undersea basin,
SW Pacific Ocean
Tasman Bay 151 C 5 inlet,
E Tasman Sea
Tasmania 149 B 8 *prev.* Van
Diemen's Land. State,
SE Australia
Tasman Plateau 142 C 5 *var.*
South Tasmania Plateau.
Undersea plateau, S Tasman Sea
Tasman Sea 152 C 5 sea,
SW Pacific Ocean
Tassili N'Ajjer 71 E 4 *var.* Hamada
du Tinghert. Plateau, E Algeria
Tatabánya 99 C 6 NW Hungary
Tathlīth 121 B 6 S Saudi Arabia
Tatra Mountains 99 C 5 *Ger.* Tatra,
Hung. Tátra, Pol./Slvk. Tatry.
Mountain range, Poland/Slovakia
Tatvan 117 F 3 SE Turkey
Tau 145 F 4 *var.* Ta'ū. Island,
E American Samoa

Taumarunui 150 D 4 North Island
C New Zealand
Taungdwingyi 136 B 3 W Myanm
Taunggyi 136 B 3 C Myanmar
Taunton 89 C 7 SW England, UK
Taupo 150 D 3 North Island,
N New Zealand
Taupo, Lake 150 D 3 lake,
North Island, N New Zealand
Tauragė 106 B 4 *Ger.* Tauroggen.
SW Lithuania
Tauranga 150 D 3 North Island,
NE New Zealand
Tauroggen *see* Tauragė
Taurus Mountains *see* Toros Dağla
Tavas 116 B 4 SW Turkey
Tavastehus *see* Hämeenlinna
Tavira 92 C 5 SE Portugal
Tavoy 137 B 5 *var.* Dawei.
SE Myanmar
Tavoy Island *see* Mali Kyun
Ta Waewae Bay 151 A 7 bay,
S Pacific Ocean
Tawakoni, Lake 49 G 2 reservoir,
Texas, S USA
Tawau 138 D 3 Borneo, E Malaysi
Ţawkar *see* Tokar
Tawzar *see* Tozeur
Taxco 51 E 4 *var.* Taxco de Alarcón
S Mexico
Taxco de Alarcón *see* Taxco
Tay 88 C 3 river, C Scotalnd, UK
Taylor 49 G 3 Texas, S USA
Taymā' 120 A 4 NW Saudi Arabia
Taymyr, Ozero 115 E 2 lake,
N Russian Federation
Taymyr, Poluostrov 115 E 2
peninsula, N Russian Federation
Tayshet 115 E 4 S Russian Federatio
T'bilisi 117 G 2 *Eng.* Tiflis. Count
capital, SE Georgia
Tchad, Lac *see* Chad, Lake
Tchien *see* Zwedru
Tczew 98 C 2 *Ger.* Dirschau. N Polan
Te Anau 151 A 7 South Island,
SW New Zealand
Te Anau, Lake 151 A 7 lake,
South Island, SW New Zealand
Teapa 51 G 5 SE Mexico
Teate *see* Chieti
Tebingtinggi 138 B 3 Sumatera,
N Indonesia
Teboe Top 59 G 3 SE Suriname
Techirghiol 108 D 5 E Romania
Tecomán 50 D 4 SW Mexico
Tecpan 51 E 5 *var.* Tecpan de
Galeana. S Mexico
Tecpan de Galeana *see* Tecpan
Tecuci 108 D 4 E Romania
Tedzhen 122 D 3 *Turkm.* Tejen.
S Turkmenistan
Tees 89 D 5 river, N England, UK
Tefé 62 D 2 N Brazil
Tegal 138 C 4 Jawa, C Indonesia
Tegelen 87 D 5 SE Netherlands
Tegucigalpa 52 C 3 country capita
SW Honduras
Tehama *see* Tihāmah
Teheran *see* Tehrān
Tehrān 120 C 3 *var.* Teheran.
Country capital, N Iran
Tehuacán 51 F 4 S Mexico
Tehuantepec 51 F 5 *var.* Santo
Domingo Tehuantepec. SE Mexic
Tehuantepec, Golfo de 51 G 5
Eng. Gulf of Tehuantepec. Gulf,
E Pacific Ocean
Tehuantepec, Gulf of *see*
Tehuantepec, Golfo de
Tehuantepec, Isthmus of *see*
Tehuantepec, Istmo de

huantepec, Istmo de 51 F 5
var. Isthmus of Tehuantepec.
Isthmus, SE Mexico
§en *see* Tedzhen
Kao 150 C 1 North Island,
N New Zealand
kax 51 H 4 *var.* Tekax de Álvaro
Obregón.
SE Mexico
kax de Álvaro Obregón *see* Tekax
keli 114 C 5 SE Kazakhstan
kırdağ 116 A 2 *It.* Rodosto; *anc.*
Bisanthe, Raidestos, Rhaedestus.
NW Turkey
kong, Pulau 138 B 1 island,
E Singapore
Kuiti 150 D 3 North Island,
N New Zealand
la 52 C 2 NW Honduras
l Aviv-Jaffa *see* Tel Aviv-Yafo
l Aviv-Yafo 119 A 6
var. Tel Aviv-Jaffa. C Israel
lish 104 C 2 *var.* Teliš;
prev. Azizie. NW Bulgaria
ll Atlas *see* Atlas Tellien
ll Kalakh *see* Tall Kalakh
lschen *see* Telšiai
lšiai 106 B 3 *Ger.* Telschen.
NW Lithuania
luk Intan 138 B 3 *var.* Telok
Anson, Telok Intan, Teluk Anson.
W Malaysia
ma 75 E 5 SE Ghana
merin 100 D 3 N Yugoslavia
nirtau 114 C 4 *prev.*
Samarkandski, Samarkandskoye.
C Kazakhstan
mpe 48 B 2 Arizona, SW USA
mpio Pausania 97 A 5 W Italy
mple 49 G 3 Texas, S USA
mple Bay 148 C 2 bay,
NW Coral Sea
nryuk 111 A 7
SW Russian Federation
muco 65 B 5 C Chile
muka 151 B 6 South Island,
SW New Zealand
na Kourou 74 D 4 mountain,
SW Burkina
nasserim Range 137 C 6
mountain range, S Myanmar
nenkou 74 D 3 C Mali
nèrè 75 G 2 desert,
Algeria/Niger
nèrè du Tafassâsset 75 G 2
desert, N Niger
nerife 70 A 3 island, Islas
Canarias, SW Spain
ngger Shamo 127 E 3 desert,
N China
ngréla 74 D 4 *var.* Tingréla.
N Ivory Coast
nkodogo 75 E 4 S Burkina
nnant Creek 148 A 3
Northern Territory, C Australia
nnessee 42 C 1 *off.* State of
Tennessee; nickname
Volunteer State. State,
SE USA
nos *see* Tínos
nterfield 149 D 5
New South Wales, SE Australia
n Thousand Islands 43 E 5
island, Florida, SE USA
pelenë 101 C 7 *var.* Tepelena;
It. Tepeleni. S Albania
pic 50 D 4 C Mexico
plice 98 A 4 *Ger.* Teplitz; *prev.*
Teplice-Šanov, Teplitz-Schönau.
NW Czech Republic
quila 50 D 4 SW Mexico
raina 145 G 2 *prev.* Washington
Island. Island, E Kiribati

Teramo 96 D 4 *anc.* Interamna.
C Italy
Tercan 117 E 3 NE Turkey
Terceira 92 A 5 *var.* Ilha Terceira.
Island, W Portugal
Terceira, Ilha *see* Terceira
Terekhovka *see* Tsyerakhowka
Teresina 63 F 2 *var.* Therezina. State
capital, NE Brazil
Termez *see* Termiz
Términos, Laguna de 51 G 4
lagoon, SE Gulf of Mexico
Termiz 123 E 3 *Rus.* Termez.
S Uzbekistan
Termoli 96 D 4 C Italy
Terneuzen 87 B 5 *var.* Neuzen.
SW Netherlands
Terni 96 C 4 *anc.* Interamna Nahars.
C Italy
Ternopil' 108 C 2 *Pol.* Tarnopol,
Rus. Ternopol'. W Ukraine
Terrace Bay 38 B 4 Ontario,
S Canada
Terracina 97 C 5 W Italy
Terranova di Sicilia *see* Gela
Terranova Pausania *see* Olbia
Terrassa 93 G 2 *Cast.* Tarrasa. E Spain
Terre Adélie 154 C 4 French
dependent territory, Antarctica
Terre Neuve *see*
Newfoundland and Labrador
Terre-Neuve *see* Newfoundland
Terschelling 86 C 1 *Fris.* Skylge.
Island, N Netherlands
Teruel 93 F 3 *anc.* Turba. E Spain
Tervel 104 E 1 *prev.* Kurtbunar,
Rom. Curtbunar. NE Bulgaria
Tervueren *see* Tervuren
Tervuren 87 C 6 *var.* Tervueren.
C Belgium
Teseney 72 C 4 *var.* Tessenei. W Eritrea
Tessalit 75 E 2 NE Mali
Tessaoua 75 G 3 S Niger
Tessenderlo 87 C 5 NE Belgium
Tessenei *see* Teseney
Tete 79 E 2 NW Mozambique
Teterow 94 C 3 NE Germany
Tetouan 70 C 2 *var.* Tétouan,
Tetuán. N Morocco
Tetovo 101 D 6 *Alb.* Tetova, Tetovë,
Turk. Kalkandelen. NW Macedonia
Tetschen *see* Děčín
Tevere 96 C 4 *Eng.* Tiber. River, C Italy
Teverya 119 B 5 *var.* Tiberias. N Israel
Texarkana 42 A 2 Arkansas, C USA
Texarkana 49 H 2 Texas, S USA
Texas 49 G 3 *off.* State of Texas;
nickname Lone Star State.
State, S USA
Texas City 49 H 4 Texas, S USA
Texel 86 C 2 island,
NW Netherlands
Texoma, Lake 49 G 2 reservoir,
SW USA
Teziutlán 51 F 4 S Mexico
Thai Binh 136 D 3 N Vietnam

Thailand
137 C 5 *Th.* Prathet Thai;
prev. Siam. Monarchy, SE Asia

Official name: Kingdom of
Thailand **Date of formation:**
1822/1887 **Capital:** Bangkok
Population: 66.9 million **Total Area:**
198,116 sq miles (513,120 sq km)
Languages: Thai*, Chinese, Malay
Religions: Buddhist 95%, Muslim
4%, other 1% **Ethnic mix:** Thai 75%,
Chinese 14%, Malay 4%, other 7%
Government: Constitutional
monarchy **Currency:** Baht = 100 stangs

Thailand, Gulf of 137 C 6 *var.*
Gulf of Siam, *Th.* Ao Thai,
Vtn. Vinh Thai Lan. Gulf,
Pacific Ocean/South China Sea
Thai Nguyên 136 D 3 N Vietnam
Thakhek *see* Thakhèk
Thames 89 D 7 river, S England, UK
Thames 150 D 3 North Island,
N New Zealand
Thăna *see* Thăne
Thăne 134 C 5 *prev.* Thăna. W India
Thanh Hoa 136 D 4 N Vietnam
Thap Put 137 B 7 S Thailand
Thar Desert 134 C 3 *var.* Great
Indian Desert, Indian Desert.
Desert, India/Pakistan
Thásos 104 C 4 Thásos, E Greece
Thásos 104 C 4 island, E Greece
Thaton 136 B 4 SE Myanmar
Thatta 134 B 3 SE Pakistan
Thayetmyo 136 A 4 W Myanmar
The Dalles 46 B 3 Oregon, NW USA
The Flatts Village *see* Flatts Village
The Hague *see* 's-Gravenhage
The Pas 37 F 5 Manitoba,
C Canada
Therezina *see* Teresina
Thérma 105 D 6 Ikaría, SE Greece
Thermaïkós Kólpos 104 B 4 *Eng.*
Thermaic Gulf; *anc.* Thermaicus
Sinus. Gulf, NW Aegean Sea
Thérmo 105 B 5 C Greece
The Rock 93 H 4 E Gibraltar
Thessaloníki 104 B 4 *Eng.* Salonica,
Salonika, *SCr.* Solun,
Turk. Selânik. N Greece
The Valley 55 G 3 dependent
territory capital, E Anguilla
The Village 49 G 1 Oklahoma, C USA
The Woodlands 49 H 4 Texas, S USA
Thiamis *see* Thýamis
Thief River Falls 45 F 1
Minnesota, N USA
Thiers 91 C 5 C France
Thiès 74 B 3 W Senegal
Thikombia *see* Cikobia
Thimphu 135 G 3 *var.* Thimbu;
prev. Tashi Chho Dzong. Country
capital, W Bhutan
Thionville 90 D 3 *var.*
Diedenhofen. NE France
Thíra 105 D 7 Thíra, SE Greece
Thíra 105 D 7 *prev.* Santorini,
Santorini, *anc.* Thera. Island,
Kykládes, SE Greece
Thiruvanathapuram *see* Trivandrum
Tholen 86 B 4 island,
SW Netherlands
Thomasville 42 D 3 Georgia, SE USA
Thompson 37 G 5 Manitoba,
C Canada
Thompson 148 C 3 river, E Australia
Thon Buri 137 C 5 C Thailand
Thonon-les-Bains 91 D 5 E France
Thonze 136 B 4 SW Myanmar
Thorlákshöfn 83 E 5 SW Iceland
Thorn *see* Toruń
Thornton Island *see* Caroline Island
Thorshavn *see* Tórshavn
Thouars 90 B 4 W France
Thoune *see* Thun
Thracian Sea 104 D 4 *Gk.* Thrakikó
Pélagos; *anc.* Thracium Mare. Sea,
SE Greece
Thrakikó Pélagos *see* Thracian Sea
Three Kings Island 150 C 1 island,
North Island, N New Zealand
Thrissur *see* Trichūr
Thun 95 A 7 *Fr.* Thoune.
W Switzerland

Thunder Bay 38 B 4 Ontario,
S Canada
Thuner See 95 A 7 lake,
C Switzerland
Thung Song 137 C 7 *var.*
Cha Mai. S Thailand
Thüringer Wald 95 C 5
Eng. Thuringian Forest.
Mountain range, C Germany
Thuringian Forest *see*
Thüringer Wald
Thurso 88 C 2 N Scotland, UK
Thýamis 104 A 4 *var.* Thiamis.
River, W Greece
Tianjin 128 D 4 NE China
Tianshui 128 B 4 C China
Tiba *see* Chiba
Tiber *see* Tevere
Tiberias *see* Teverya
Tiberias, Lake 119 B 5 *var.*
Chinnereth, Sea of Bahr Tabariya,
Sea of Galilee, *Ar.* Bahrat
Tabariya, *Heb.* Yam Kinneret.
Lake, N Israel
Tibesti 76 C 2 *var.* Tibesti Massif,
Ar. Tibestī. Mountain range,
N Africa
Tibet, Plateau of 126 C 5 plateau,
S Asia
Tibnī *see* At Tibnī
Tiburón, Isla 50 B 2 *var.* Isla del
Tiburón. Island, NW Mexico
Tiburón, Isla del *see* Tiburón, Isla
Tichau *see* Tychy
Tîchît 74 D 2 *var.* Tichitt.
C Mauritania
Tichitt *see* Tîchît
Tichvin *see* Tikhvin
Ticinum *see* Pavia
Ticul 51 H 4 SE Mexico
Tiel 86 C 4 Netherlands
Tienen 87 C 6 *var.* Thienen,
Fr. Tirlemont. C Belgium
Tien Shan 123 G 2 *Chin.* Thian
Shan, Tian Shan, T'ien Shan,
Rus. Tyan Shan, Tian'-Shan'.
Mountain range,
China/Kyrgyzstan
Tierp 85 C 6 C Sweden
Tierra del Fuego 65 B 8 island,
Argentina/Chile
Tiflis *see* T'bilisi
Tifton 43 E 3 Georgia, SE USA
Tighina 108 D 4 *Rus.* Bendery;
prev. Bender, Bendery. E Moldova
Tigris 120 B 2 *Ar.* Dijlah,
Turk. Dicle. River, Iraq/Turkey
Tihāmah 121 B 6 *var.* Tehama.
Plain, Saudi Arabia/Yemen
Tijuana 50 A 1 NW Mexico
Tikhoretsk 111 A 7
SW Russian Federation
Tikhvin 110 B 4 *var.* Tichvin.
NW Russian Federation
Tiki Basin 153 E 3 undersea basin,
S Pacific Ocean
Tiksi 115 F 2 N Russian Federation
Tilburg 86 C 4 S Netherlands
Tillabéri 75 F 3 *var.* Tillabéry.
W Niger
Tillabéry *see* Tillabéri
Tílos 105 E 7 island, Dodekánisos,
SE Greece
Timah, Bukit 138 B 1 hill,
C Singapore
Timaru 151 B 6 South Island,
SW New Zealand
Timbedgha 74 D 3 *var.* Timbédra.
SE Mauritania
Timbédra *see* Timbedgha
Timbuktu *see* Tombouctou

Timétrine 75 E 2 mountain range, C Mali
Timiş 108 A 4 river, W Romania
Timişoara 108 A 4
Ger. Temeschwar, Temeswar, *Hung.* Temesvár; *prev.* Temeschburg. W Romania
Timmins 38 C 4 Ontario, S Canada
Timor 139 F 5 island, Nusa Tenggara, C Indonesia
Timor Sea 152 A 3 sea, E Indian Ocean
Timor Trench *see* Timor Trough
Timor Trough 125 F 5 *var.* Timor Trench. Trough, N Timor Sea
Timrå 85 C 5 C Sweden
Tindouf 70 C 3 W Algeria
Tineo 92 C 1 N Spain
Tinghert, Hamada du *see* Tassili N'Ajjer
Tingo María 60 C 3 C Peru
Tingréla *see* Tengréla
Tinhosa Grande 76 E 2 island, C Sao Tome & Principe
Tinhosa Pequena 76 E 1 island, C Sao Tome & Principe
Tinian 144 B 1 island, S Northern Mariana Islands
Tínos 105 D 6 Tínos, SE Greece
Tínos 105 D 6 *anc.* Tenos. Island, Kykládes, SE Greece
Tinrhert, Hamada de 71 E 3 *var.* Plateau du Tinghert. Plateau, W Algeria
Tipitapa 52 D 3 W Nicaragua
Tirana *see* Tiranë
Tiranë 101 D 6 *var.* Tirana. Country capital, C Albania
Tirasberge 78 B 4 mountain range, SW Namibia
Tiraspol 108 D 4 *Rus.* Tiraspol'. E Moldova
Tiraspol' *see* Tiraspol
Tiree 88 B 3 island, W Scotland, UK
Tîrgovişte *see* Târgovişte
Tîrgu Jiu *see* Targu Jui
Tírnavos *see* Týrnavos
Tirol 95 C 7 *var.* Tyrol, *It.* Tirolo. Cultural region, W Austria
Tirreno, Mare *see* Tyrrhenian Sea
Tiruchchirāppalli 132 C 3 *prev.* Trichinopoly. SE India
Tiruntán 60 C 3 C Peru
Tiruppattūr 132 C 2 SE India
Tisza 81 E 4 *var.* Tisa, Tysa, *Rus.* Tissa. River, E Europe
Tiszakécske 99 D 7 Hungary
Tit 70 D 3 C Algeria
Titano, Monte 96 E 1 mountain, C San Marino
Titicaca, Lake 61 E 4 lake, Bolivia/Peru
Titograd *see* Podgorica
Titose *see* Chitose
Titovo Užice *see* Užice
Titov Veles 101 E 6 C Macedonia
Titu 108 C 5 S Romania
Titule 77 D 5 N Congo (Zaire)
Tiverton 89 C 7 SW England, UK
Tivoli 96 C 4 *anc.* Tiber. C Italy
Tizimín 51 H 3 SE Mexico
Tizi Ouzou 71 E 1 *var.* Tizi-Ouzou. N Algeria
Tizi-Ouzou *see* Tizi Ouzou
Tiznit 70 B 3 SW Morocco
Tjilatjap *see* Cilacap
Tjirebon *see* Cirebon
Tlaquepaque 50 D 4 C Mexico
Tlaxcala 51 E 4 *var.* Tlascala, Tlaxcala de Xicohténcatl. C Mexico

Tlemcen 70 D 2 *var.* Tilimsen, Tlemsen. NW Algeria
Tmassah 71 G 3 C Libya
Toamasina 79 G 3 *var.* Tamatave. E Madagascar
Toba, Danau 138 B 3 lake, Sumatera, W Indonesia
Tobago 55 H 5 island, NE Trinidad & Tobago
Toba Kăkar Range 134 B 2 mountain range, NW Pakistan
Tobol 114 C 4 *Kaz.* Tobyl. River, Kazakhstan/Russian Federation
Tobol'sk 114 C 3 C Russian Federation
Tobyl *see* Tobol
Tocantins 63 F 3 river, N Brazil
Tocoa 52 D 2 N Honduras
Tocopilla 64 B 2 N Chile
Todi 96 C 4 C Italy
Todos os Santos, Baía de 63 G 3 bay, W Atlantic Ocean
Toetoes Bay 151 B 8 bay, SW Pacific Ocean
Tofua 145 E 5 island, C Tonga

Togo 75 E 4 *prev.* French Togoland. Republic, W Africa

Official name: Togolese Republic
Date of formation: 1960 **Capital:** Lomé **Population:** 3.9 million **Total area:** 21,927 sq miles (56,790 sq km) **Languages:** French*, Ewe, Kabye, Gurma **Religions:** Traditional beliefs 70%, Christian 20%, Muslim 10% **Ethnic mix:** Ewe 43%, Kabye 26%, Gurma 16%, other 15% **Government:** Multiparty republic **Currency:** CFA franc = 100 centimes

Toiyabe Range 47 C 5 mountain range, Nevada, W USA
Tokanui 151 B 8 South Island, SW New Zealand
Tokar 72 C 3 *var.* Ţawkar. NE Sudan
Tokat 116 D 3 N Turkey
Tokelau 145 F 3 New Zealand overseas territory, S Pacific Ocean
Tokio *see* Tōkyō
Tokmak 109 G 4 *var.* Velykyy Tokmak. SE Ukraine
Tokmak 123 G 2 *Kir.* Tokmok. N Kyrgyzstan
Tokmok *see* Tokmak
Tokoroa 150 D 3 North Island, N New Zealand
Tokuno-shima 130 A 3 island, Amami-shotō, SW Japan
Tokushima 131 C 7 *var.* Tokusima. Shikoku, SW Japan
Tokusima *see* Tokushima
Tōkyō 131 D 5 country capital, Honshū, S Japan
Tōkyō Bay 130 A 1 bay, NW Pacific Ocean
Toledo 92 D 3 *anc.* Toletum. C Spain
Toledo 40 D 3 Ohio, N USA
Toledo 61 F 4 W Bolivia
Toledo Bend Reservoir 49 H 3 reservoir, SW USA
Toletum *see* Toledo
Toliara 79 F 4 *var.* Toliary; *prev.* Tuléar. SW Madagascar
Tolmin 95 D 8 *Ger.* Tolmein, *It.* Tolmino. W Slovenia
Tolna 99 C 7 *Ger.* Tolnau. S Hungary
Tolnau *see* Tolna
Tolochin *see* Talachyn
Tolo Harbour 128 B 1 NE Hong Kong
Tolosa 93 E 1 N Spain

Tolosa *see* Toulouse
Toluca 51 E 4 *var.* Toluca de Lerdo. S Mexico
Toluca de Lerdo *see* Toluca
Tol'yatti 111 C 6 *prev.* Stavropol'. W Russian Federation
Tomakomai 130 D 2 Hokkaidō, NE Japan
Tomar 92 B 3 W Portugal
Tomaschow *see* Tomaszów Lubelski
Tomaszów Lubelski 98 E 4 *Ger.* Tomaschow. SE Poland
Tomaszów Mazowiecki 98 D 4 *var.* Tomaszów Mazowiecka; *prev.* Tomaszów, *Ger.* Tomaschow. C Poland
Tombigbee River 42 C 3 river, SE USA
Tombouctou 75 E 3 *Eng.* Timbuktu. N Mali
Tombua 78 A 2 *Port.* Porto Alexandre. SW Angola
Tomelloso 93 E 3 C Spain
Tomini, Teluk 139 E 4 *prev.* Teluk Gorontalo. Bay, W Molucca Sea
Tomsk 114 D 4 C Russian Federation
Tonezh *see* Tonyezh

Tonga 145 E 4 *var.* Friendly Islands. Monarchy, S Pacific Ocean

Official name: Kingdom of Tonga
Date of formation: 1970 **Capital:** Nuku'alofa **Population:** 101,000 **Total area:** 290 sq miles (750 sq km) **Languages:** Tongan*, English **Religions:** Protestant 82 Roman Catholic 18% **Ethnic mix:** Tongan 98% other 2% **Government:** Constitutional monarchy **Currency:** Pa'anga = 100 seniti

Tongatapu 145 E 5 island, S Tonga
Tongatapu Group 145 E 5 island group, S Tonga
Tonga Trench 152 D 4 trench, S Pacific Ocean
Tongchuan 128 C 4 C China
Tongeren 87 D 6 *Fr.* Tongres. NE Belgium
Tong Fuk 128 A 2 SW Hong Kong
Tongking, Gulf of 136 E 4 *Chin.* Beibu Wan, *Vtn.* Vinh Băc Bô. Gulf, Pacific Ocean/ South China Sea
Tongliao 127 G 2 N China
Tongres *see* Tongeren
Tongtian He 126 C 4 river, C China
Tonj 73 B 5 SW Sudan
Tônlé Sap 137 D 5 *Eng.* Great Lake. Lake, W Cambodia
Tonyezh 107 C 7 *Rus.* Tonezh. SE Belarus
Tooele 44 B 3 Utah, W USA
Toowoomba 149 E 5 Queensland, E Australia
Topeka 45 F 4 state capital, Kansas, C USA
Toplița 108 C 3 *Ger.* Töplitz, *Hung.* Maroshévíz; *prev.* Oláh-Toplicza, Toplicza, Toplița Română. C Romania
Topol'čany 99 C 6 *Hung.* Nagytapolcsány. W Slovakia
Topolovgrad 104 D 3 *prev.* Kavakli. SE Bulgaria
Top Springs 146 E 3 Northern Territory, N Australia
Torbalı 116 A 4 W Turkey
Torez 109 H 3 SE Ukraine
Torgau 94 D 4 E Germany
Torhout 87 A 5 W Belgium

Torino 96 A 2 *Eng.* Turin. NW Italy
Torneå *see* Tornio
Torneträsk 84 C 3 lake, N Sweden
Tornio 84 D 3 *Swe.* Torneå. NW Finland
Tornionjoki 84 D 3 *var.* Torniojoki. *Swe.* Torneälven. River, Finland/Sweden
Toro 92 D 2 N Spain
Toronto 38 D 5 province capital, Ontario, S Canada
Toropec *see* Toropets
Toropets 110 A 4 *var.* Toropec. W Russian Federation
Toros Dağları 116 C 4 *Eng.* Taurus Mountains. Mountain range, S Turkey
Torquay 89 C 7 SW England, UK
Torre, Alto da 92 C 3 mountain, C Portugal
Torre del Greco 97 D 5 S Italy
Torrejón de Ardoz 93 E 3 C Spain
Torrejón, Embalse de 92 C 3 reservoir, W Spain
Torrelavega 92 D 1 N Spain
Torrens, Lake 149 B 5 salt lake, South Australia, S Australia
Torrente 93 F 3 *var.* Torrent, Torrenti de l'Horta. E Spain
Torreón 50 D 3 C Mexico
Torres Strait 148 C 1 strait, Queensland, Arafura Sea/ Coral Sea
Torres Vedras 92 A 3 W Portugal
Torrington 44 D 3 Wyoming, C US
Tórshavn 83 F 5 *Dan.* Thorshavn. Dependent territory capital, N Faeroe Islands
Tortosa 93 F 2 *anc.* Dertosa. E Spa
Tortue, Montagne 59 H 3 mounta range, C French Guiana
Tortuga, Isla *see* La Tortuga, Isla
Toruń 98 C 3 *Ger.* Thorn. C Polanc
Tõrva 106 D 3 *Ger.* Tõrwa. S Eston
Tõrwa *see* Tõrva
Torzhok 110 B 4 *var.* Toržok. W Russian Federation
Toržok *see* Torzhok
Tosa-wan 131 B 7 bay, NW Pacific Ocean
Toscano, Archipelago 96 B 4 *Eng.* Tuscan Archipelago. Island group, C Italy
Toshkent 123 E 2 *Rus.* Tashkent. Country capital, E Uzbekistan
Totana 93 E 4 SE Spain
Totness 59 G 3 N Suriname
Tottori 131 B 6 Honshū, SW Japar
Touba 74 B 3 W Senegal
Touboro 76 B 4 NE Cameroon
Tougourt 71 E 2 NE Algeria
Toukoto 74 C 3 W Mali
Toul 90 D 3 NE France
Toulon 91 D 6 *anc.* Telo Martius, Tilio Martius. SE France
Toulouse 91 B 6 *anc.* Tolosa. S France
Toungoo 136 B 4 S Myanmar
Touraine 90 B 4 cultural region, C France
Tourane *see* Đă Năng
Tourcoing 90 D 2 N France
Tournai 87 B 6 *var.* Tournay, *Dut.* Doornik; *anc.* Tornacum. SW Belgium
Tournavista 60 C 3 C Peru
Tours 90 A 4 *anc.* Caesarodunum, Turoni. C France
Tovarkovskiy 111 B 5 W Russian Federation
Tower Island *see* Genovesa, Isla

wnshend Island 148 D 4 island, Queensland, E Australia
wnsville 148 D 3 Queensland, NE Australia
woeti Meer see Towuti, Danau
wraghoudī 122 D 4 NW Afghanistan
wson 41 F 4 Maryland, NE USA
wuti, Danau 139 E 4 Dut. Towoeti Meer. Lake, Celebes, C Indonesia
kan He 126 A 3 var. Aksay. River, China/Kyrgyzstan
yama 131 C 5 Honshū, SW Japan
yama-wan 131 B 5 bay, E Sea of Japan
yota 131 C 6 Honshū, SW Japan
zeur 71 E 2 var. Tawzar. W Tunisia
abzon 117 E 2 Eng. Trebizond; anc. Trapezus. NE Turkey
aiskirchen 95 E 6 NE Austria
ajectum ad Rhenum see Utrecht
akai 107 C 5 Ger. Traken, Pol. Troki. SE Lithuania
alee 89 A 6 Ir. Trá Lí. SW Ireland
í Lí see Tralee
ang 137 C 7 S Thailand
ansantarctic Mountains 154 C 3 mountain range, Antarctica
ansylvania 108 B 4 Eng. Ardeal, Transilvania, Ger. Siebenbürgen, Hung. Erdély. Cultural Region, NW Romania
apani 97 B 7 anc. Drepanum. SW Italy
aralgon 149 C 7 Victoria, SE Australia
asimeno, Lago 96 B 3 Eng. Lake of Perugia, Ger. Trasimenischersee. Lake, C Italy
aù see Trogir
aunsee 95 D 6 var. Gmundner See, Eng. Lake Traun. Lake, N Austria
aunstein 95 C 6 SE Germany
averse City 40 C 2 Michigan, N USA
a Vinh 137 E 6 var. Phu Vinh. S Vietnam
avis, Lake 49 F 4 reservoir, Texas, S USA
avnik 100 C 4 C Bosnia & Herzegovina
bovlje 95 E 8 Ger. Trifail. C Slovenia
ebíč 99 B 5 Ger. Trebitsch. S Czech Republic
ebinje 101 C 5 S Bosnia & Herzegovina
ebišov 99 E 6 Hung. Tőketerebes. E Slovakia
ebitsch see Třebíč
ebnitz see Trzebnica
ělazé 90 B 4 NW France
elew 65 C 6 SE Argentina
emelo 87 C 6 C Belgium
enčín 99 C 6 Ger. Trentschin, Hung. Trencsén. W Slovakia
enque Lauquen 64 C 4 E Argentina
ento 96 C 2 Eng. Trent, Ger. Trient; anc.Tridentum. N Italy
enton 41 F 4 state capital, New Jersey, NE USA
es Arroyos 65 D 5 E Argentina
eskavica 100 C 4 mountain range, SE Bosnia & Herzegovina
eviso 96 C 2 anc. Tarvisium. NE Italy
g see Feldkirchen in Kärnten
ichinopoly see Tiruchchirāppalli

Trichūr 132 C 3 var. Thrissur. SW India
Trier 95 A 5 Eng. Treves, Fr. Trèves; anc. Augusta Treverorum. SW Germany
Triesen 94 E 2 SW Liechtenstein
Triesenberg 94 E 2 SW Liechtenstein
Trieste 96 D 2 Slvn. Trst. NE Italy
Trifail see Trbovlje
Trikala 104 B 4 prev. Trikkala. C Greece
Trikkala see Trikala
Trincomalee 132 D 3 var. Trinkomali. NE Sri Lanka
Trinidad 55 H 5 island, C Trinidad & Tobago
Trinidad 64 D 4 SW Uruguay
Trinidad 44 D 5 Colorado, C USA
Trinidad 61 F 3 N Bolivia

Trinidad & Tobago 55 H 5 & Tobago. Republic, SE Caribbean Sea

Official name: Republic of Trinidad and Tobago Date of formation: 1962 Capital: Port-of-Spain Population: 1.3 million Total area: 1,981 sq miles (5,130 sq km) Languages: English* Religions: Christian 58%, Hindu 30%, Muslim 8%, other 4% Ethnic mix: Black 43%, South Asian 40%, mixed 14%, other 3% Government: Multiparty republic Currency: Trin. & Tob. $ = 100 cents

Trinité, Montagnes de la 59 H 3 mountain range, C French Guiana
Trinity River 49 G 3 river, Texas, S USA
Trinkomali see Trincomalee
Tripoli 118 B 4 var. Ţarābulus, Ţarābulus ash Shām, Trāblous; anc. Tripolis. N Lebanon
Tripoli see Ţarābulus
Trípoli 105 B 6 prev. Trípolis. S Greece
Trípolis see Trípoli
Tristan da Cunha 69 A 7 var. Tristan da Cunha Islands. Island group, S Atlantic Ocean
Tristan da Cunha 67 C 6 island, S Atlantic Ocean
Tristan da Cunha Islands see Tristan da Cunha
Trivandrum 132 C 3 var. Thiruvananthapuram. State capital, SW India
Trnava 99 C 6 Ger. Tyrnau, Hung. Nagyszombat. W Slovakia
Trobriand Islands see Kiriwina Islands
Trogir 100 B 4 It. Traù. S Croatia
Troglav 100 B 4 mountain, Bosnia & Herzegovina/Croatia
Troía Península 92 B 4 peninsula, W Portugal
Troisdorf 95 A 5 W Germany
Trois-Rivières 39 E 4 Québec, SE Canada
Trojan see Troyan
Trollhättan 85 B 6 S Sweden
Tromsø 84 C 2 Fin. Tromssa. N Norway
Tromssa see Tromsø
Trondheim 84 B 4 Ger. Drontheim; prev. Nidaros, Trondhjem. S Norway
Trondheimsfjorden 84 A 4 fjord, E North Sea
Troódos Mountains see Troódos
Troppau see Opava
Troy 42 D 3 Alabama, S USA
Troy 41 F 3 New York, NE USA

Troyan 104 C 2 var. Trojan. C Bulgaria
Troyes 90 D 4 anc. Augustobona Tricassium. N France
Trst see Trieste
Trstenik 100 D 4 C Yugoslavia
Trujillo 92 C 3 W Spain
Trujillo 52 D 2 NE Honduras
Trujillo 60 B 3 NW Peru
Trùn 104 B 2 W Bulgaria
Trung Phân 137 E 5 physical region, S Vietnam
Truro 89 C 7 SW England, UK
Truro 39 F 4 Nova Scotia, SE Canada
Trzcianka 98 B 3 Ger. Schönlanke. NW Poland
Trzebnica 98 C 4 Ger. Trebnitz. SW Poland
Tsafjördhur 83 E 4 NW Iceland
Tsalka 117 F 2 SE Georgia
Tsaochuang see Zaozhuang
Tsarevo 104 E 2 var. Mičurin; prev. Michurin. SE Bulgaria
Tschaslau see Čáslav
Tsetserleg 126 D 3 W Mongolia
Tshela 77 B 6 W Congo (Zaire)
Tshikapa 77 C 7 SW Congo (Zaire)
Tshuapa 77 D 6 river, C Congo (Zaire)
Tsodilo Hills 78 C 3 mountain range, NW Botswana
Tsu 131 C 6 var. Tu. Honshū, SW Japan
Tsuen Wan 128 A 1 W Hong Kong
Tsugaru-kaikyō 130 C 3 strait, Pacific Ocean/Sea of Japan
Tsumeb 78 B 3 N Namibia
Tsuruga 131 C 6 var. Turuga. Honshū, SW Japan
Tsuruoka 130 D 4 var. Turuoka. Honshū, C Japan
Tsushima 131 A 7 var. Tsushima-tō, Tusima. Island group, SW Japan
Tsyerakhowka 107 D 8 Rus. Terekhovka. SE Belarus
Tsyurupinsk see Tsyurupyns'k
Tsyurupyns'k 109 F 4 Rus. Tsyurupinsk. S Ukraine
Tu see Tsu
Tuamotu, Îles 145 H 4 var. Tuamotu Islands. Island group, N French Polynesia
Tuamotu Islands see Tuamotu, Îles
Tuapi 53 E 2 NE Nicaragua
Tuapse 111 A 7 SW Russian Federation
Tuba City 48 B 1 Arizona, SW USA
Tubbergen 86 E 3 E Netherlands
Tubeke see Tubize
Tubize 87 B 6 Dut. Tubeke. C Belgium
Tubmanburg 74 C 5 county capital, NW Liberia
Tucker's Town 42 B 5 E Bermuda
Tuckum see Tukums
Tucson 48 B 3 Arizona, SW USA
Tucumán see San Miguel de Tucumán
Tucupita 59 E 2 NE Venezuela
Tucuruí 63 F 2 NE Brazil
Tucuruí, Represa de 63 F 2
Tudela 93 E 2 Basq. Tutera; anc. Tutela. N Spain
Tudmur 101 E 2 var. Tadmur, Tamar, Gk. Palmyra; Bibl. Tadmor. C Syria
Tuen Mun 128 A 1 W Hong Kong
Tuguegarao 139 E 1 Luzon, N Philippines
Tuktoyaktuk 37 E 3 Northwestern Territories, NW Canada

Tukums 106 C 3 Ger. Tuckum. W Latvia
Tula 111 B 5 W Russian Federation
Tulancingo 51 E 4 C Mexico
Tulare 47 C 7 California, W USA
Tulcán 60 B 1 N Ecuador
Tulcea 100 D 5 E Romania
Tul'chin see Tul'chyn
Tul'chyn 108 D 3 Rus. Tul'chin. C Ukraine
Tulia 49 E 2 Texas, S USA
Tulkarm 119 D 7 NW West Bank
Tullahoma 42 D 1 Tennessee, S USA
Tulle 91 C 5 anc. Tutela. C France
Tulln 95 E 6 var. Oberhollabrunn. NE Austria
Tully 148 D 3 Queensland, NE Australia
Tulsa 49 G 1 Oklahoma, C USA
Tuluá 58 B 3 W Colombia
Tulun 115 E 4 S Russian Federation
Tumaco 58 A 4 SW Colombia
Tumba, Lac see Ntomba, Lac
Tumbes 60 B 2 NW Peru
Tumkūr 132 C 2 W India
Tumuc-Humac Mountains 63 E 1 var. Serra Tumucumaque, Port. Serra Tumuc-Humac. Mountain range, N South America
Tunca Nehri see Tundzha
Tunduru 73 C 8 S Tanzania
Tundzha 104 D 3 Turk. Tunca Nehri. River, Bulgaria/Turkey
Tungabhadra Reservoir 132 C 2 lake, S India
Tungsten 37 E 4 Northwestern Territories, W Canada
Tung-t'ing Hu see Dongting Hu
Tunis 71 E 1 var. Tūnis. Country capital, NE Tunisia
Tūnis, Khalīj see Tunis, Golfe de
Tunja 58 B 3 C Colombia
Tuong Buong see Tương Đương
Tương Đương 136 D 4 var. Tuong Buong. N Vietnam
Tüp see Tyup
Tupelo 42 C 2 Mississippi, S USA
Tupiza 61 G 5 S Bolivia
Turabah 121 B 5 W Saudi Arabia
Turangi 150 D 4 North Island, N New Zealand
Turan Lowland 122 C 2 var. Turan Plain, Rus. Turanskaya Nizmennost'. Plain, C Asia
Ţurayf 120 A 3 NW Saudi Arabia
Turba see Teruel
Turda 108 B 4 Ger. Thorenburg, Hung. Torda. NW Romania
Turin see Torino
Turkana, Lake 73 C 6 Eng. Lake Rudolf. Lake, E Africa
Turkestan 114 B 5 Kaz. Türkistan. S Kazakhstan

Tunisia
71 E 2 Ar. Al Jumhūrīyah at Tūnisīyah, Fr. République Tunisienne. Republic, N Africa

Official name: Republic of Tunisia Date of formation: 1956 Capital: Tunis Population: 8.6 million Total area: 63,170 sq miles (163,610 sq km) Languages: Arabic*, French Religions: Muslim 98%, Christian 1%, other 1% Ethnic mix: Arab and Berber 98%, European 1%, other 1% Government: Multiparty republic Currency: Dinar = 1,000 millimes

Turkey
116 B 3 *Turk.* Türkiye Cumhuriyeti. Republic, SW Asia

Official name: Republic of Turkey **Date of formation:** 1923/1939 **Capital:** Ankara **Population:** 63.1 million **Total area:** 300,950 sq miles (779,450 sq km) **Languages:** Turkish*, Kurdish, Arabic **Religions:** Muslim 99%, other 1% **Ethnic mix:** Turkish 80%, Kurdish 17%, other 3% **Government:** Multiparty republic **Currency:** Turkish lira = 100 krural

Turkish Republic of Northern Cyprus 116 C 5 country, SW Asia
Türkistan *see* Turkestan
Türkmen Aylagy *see* Turkmenskiy Zaliv
Turkmenbashi 122 B 2 *prev.* Krasnovodsk. W Turkmenistan

Turkmenistan
122 B 2 *prev.* Turkmenskaya Soviet Socialist Republic. Republic, C Asia

Official name: Republic of Turkmenistan **Date of formation:** 1991 **Capital:** Ashgabat **Population:** 4 million **Total Area:** 188,455 sq miles (488,100 sq km) **Languages:** Turkmen*, Russian, Uzbek **Religions:** Muslim 85%, Eastern Orthodox 10%, other 5% **Ethnic mix:** Turkmen 72%, Russian 9%, Uzbek 9%, other 10% **Government:** Single-party republic **Currency:** Manat = 100 tenge

Turkmenskiy Zaliv 122 B 2 *Turkm.* Türkmen Aylagy. Inlet, S Caspian Sea
Turks & Caicos Islands 55 E 2 UK dependent territory, N Caribbean Sea
Turku 85 D 6 *Swe.* Åbo. SW Finland
Turlock 47 B 5 California, W USA
Turnau *see* Turnov
Turnhout 87 C 5 N Belgium
Turnov 88 A 4 *Ger.* Turnau. N Czech Republic
Turnu Măgurele 108 B 5 *var.* Turnu-Măgurele. S Romania
Turnu Severin *see* Drobeta-Turnu Severin
Turpan 126 C 3 *var.* Turfan. NW China
Turpan Depression 124 C 2 depression, NW China
Turpan Pendi 126 C 3 *Eng.* Turpan Depression. Depression depth, NW China
Türtkül 122 D 2 *prev.* Petroaleksandrovsk, *Rus.* Turtkul'. W Uzbekistan
Turuga *see* Tsuruga
Turuoka *see* Tsuruoka
Tuscaloosa 42 C 2 Alabama, S USA
Tuscan Archipelago *see* Toscano, Archipelago
Tutela *see* Tulle
Tuticorin 132 C 3 SE India
Tutrakan 104 D 1 NE Bulgaria
Tutuila 145 F 4 Island, W American Samoa

Tuvalu
145 E 4 *prev.* The Ellice Islands. Commonwealth republic, C Pacific Ocean

Official name: Tuvalu **Date of formation:** 1978 **Capital:** Fongafale **Population:** 9,000

Total Area: 10 sq miles (26 sq km) **Languages:** Tuvaluan*, Kiribati **Religions:** Protestant 97%, other 3% **Ethnic mix:** Tuvaluan 95% other 5% **Government:** Constitutional monarchy **Currency:** Australian $ = 100 cents

Tuxpan 50 D 4 C Mexico
Tuxpán 51 F 4 *var.* Tuxpán de Rodríguez Cano. E Mexico
Tuxpán de Rodríguez Cano *see* Tuxpán
Tuxtepec 51 F 4 *var.* San Juan Bautista Tuxtepec. S Mexico
Tuxtla 51 G 5 *var.* Tuxtla Gutiérrez. SE Mexico
Tuxtla *see* San Andrés Tuxtla
Tuxtla Gutiérrez *see* Tuxtla
Tuy Hoa 137 E 5 SE Vietnam
Tuz Gölü 116 C 3 lake, C Turkey
Tuzla 100 C 3 NE Bosnia & Herzegovina
Tuz, Lake *see* Tuz Gölü
Tver' 110 B 4 *prev.* Kalinin. W Russian Federation
Twante 136 B 4 S Myanmar
Twin Falls 46 D 4 Idaho, NW USA
Two Thumbs Range 151 B 6 mountain range, South Island, SW New Zealand
Tychy 99 C 5 *Ger.* Tichau. S Poland
Tyler 49 H 3 Texas, S USA
Tynda 115 F 4 SE Russian Federation
Tyne 88 D 4 river, N England, UK
Tyōsi *see* Chōshi
Týrnavos 104 B 4 *var.* Tírnavos. C Greece
Tyrrhenian Sea 97 B 6 *It.* Mare Tirreno. Sea, C Mediterranean Sea
Tyumen' 114 C 3 C Russian Federation
Tyup 123 G 2 *Kir.* Tüp. NE Kyrgyzstan
Tywyn 89 C 6 W Wales, UK
Tzekung *see* Zigong

U

Uaco Cungo 78 B 2 *var.* Waku Kungo, *Port.* Santa Comba. C Angola
UAE *see* United Arab Emirates
Uaupés, Rio *see* Vaupés, Río
Ubangi 77 C 5 *Fr.* Oubangui. River, C Africa
Ube 131 B 7 Honshū, SW Japan
Ubeda 93 E 4 S Spain
Uberaba 63 F 4 SE Brazil
Uberlândia 63 F 4 SE Brazil
Ubin, Pulau 138 B 1 island, NE Singapore
Ubon Ratchathani 137 D 5 *var.* Muang Ubon, Ubol Rajadhani, Ubol Ratchathani, Udon Ratchathani. E Thailand
Ubrique 92 C 5 S Spain
Ubsu-Nur, Ozero *see* Uvs Nuur
Ucayali 60 D 3 river, C Peru
Uchiura-wan 130 D 3 bay, NW Pacific Ocean
Uchkuduk *see* Uchquduq
Uchquduq 122 D 2 *Rus.* Uchkuduk. N Uzbekistan
Udaipur 134 C 4 *prev.* Oodeypore. C India
Uddevalla 85 B 6 S Sweden
Udine 96 D 2 *anc.* Utina. NE Italy
Udintsev Fracture Zone 154 E 5 fracture zone, SE Pacific Ocean
Udipi *see* Udupi

Udon Thani 136 D 4 *var.* Ban Mak Khaeng, Udorndhani. N Thailand
Udupi 132 B 2 *var.* Udipi. SW India
Ueckermünde 94 D 3 NE Germany
Ueda 131 C 5 *var.* Uyeda. Honshū, S Japan
Uele 77 D 5 *var.* Welle. River, N Congo (Zaire)
Uelzen 94 C 3 N Germany
Ufa 111 D 6 W Russian Federation
Ugāle 106 C 3 NW Latvia

Uganda
73 C 6 Republic, NE Africa

Official name: Republic of Uganda **Date of formation:** 1962 **Capital:** Kampala **Population:** 19.2 million **Total area:** 91,073 sq miles (235,880 sq km) **Languages:** English*, Luganda, Nkole, Chiga **Religions:** Christian 66%, traditional beliefs 18%, Muslim 16% **Ethnic mix:** Buganda 18%, Banyoro 14%, Teso 9%, other 59% **Government:** Multiparty republic **Currency:** Shilling = 100 cents

Uglovka 110 B 4 *var.* Okulovka. W Russian Federation
Uíge 78 B 1 *Port.* Carmona, Vila Marechal Carmona. NW Angola
Uinta Mountains 44 B 4 mountain range, Utah, W USA
Uitenhage 78 C 5 S South Africa
Uithoorn 86 C 3 C Netherlands
Ujelang Atoll 144 C 1 *var.* Wujlán. Island, W Marshall Islands
Ujungpandang 139 E 4 *var.* Macassar, Makassar; *prev.* Makasar. Celebes, C Indonesia
UK 89 B 5 *off.* UK of Great Britain and Northern Ireland. Monarchy, NW Europe
Ukhta 110 D 4 *var.* Uchta, Uhta. NW Russian Federation
Ukiah 47 B 5 California, W USA
Ukmergė 106 C 4 *Pol.* Wiłkomierz. C Lithuania

Ukraine
108 C 2 *Rus.* Ukraina, *Ukr.* Ukrayina; *prev.* Ukrainian Soviet Socialist Republic, Ukrainskaya S.S.R. Republic, E Europe

Official name: Ukraine **Date of formation:** 1991 **Capital:** Kiev **Population:** 52.2 million **Total area:** 223,090 sq miles (603,700 sq km) **Languages:** Ukrainian*, Russian, Tartar **Religions:** mostly Ukrainian Orthodox, with Roman Catholic, Protestant and Jewish minorities **Ethnic mix:** Ukrainian 73%, Russian 22%, other (incl. Tartar) 5% **Government:** Multiparty republic **Currency:** Karbovanets (coupons)

Ulaanbaatar 127 E 2 *Eng.* Ulan Bator. Country capital, C Mongolia
Ulaangom 126 C 2 NW Mongolia
Ulan Bator *see* Ulaanbaatar
Ulanhad *see* Chifeng
Ulan-Ude 115 E 4 *prev.* Verkhneudinsk. S Russian Federation
Uldz 127 F 1 river, NE Mongolia
Uleåborg *see* Oulu
Uleälv *see* Oulujoki
Uleträsk *see* Oulujärvi

Ulft 86 E 4 E Netherlands
Ullapool 88 B 3 N Scotland, UK
Ulm 95 B 6 S Germany
Ulsan 128 E 4 *Jap.* Urusan. SE South Korea
Ulster 89 B 5 cultural region, N Ireland
Ulungur Hu 126 C 2 lake, NW China
Uluru 146 E 5 *var.* Ayers Rock. Rock, Northern Territory, C Australia
Ulyanivka 109 E 3 *Rus.* Ul'yanovk, C Ukraine
Ul'yanovka *see* Ulyanivka
Ul'yanovsk 111 C 5 *prev.* Simbirsk. W Russian Federation
Uman' 109 E 3 *Rus.* Uman. C Ukraine
Uman *see* Uman'
Umán 51 G 3 SE Mexico
'Umān, Khalīj *see* Oman, Gulf of
Umbrian-Machigian Mountains se Umbro-Marchigiano, Appennino
Umbro-Marchigiano, Appennino 96 C 4 *Eng.* Umbrian-Machigian Mountains. Mountain range, C Italy
Umeå 84 D 4 N Sweden
Umeälven 84 C 4 river, N Sweden
Umiat 36 D 2 Alaska, NW USA
Umm al Ḩayt, Wādī 121 D 6 *var.* Wādī Amiliayt. River, SW Oman
Umm Durmān *see* Omdurman
Umm Ruwaba 72 B 4 *var.* Umm Ruwābah, Um Ruwāba. C Sudar
Umnak Island 36 A 3 island, Alaska, NW USA
Umtata 78 D 5 SE South Africa
Una 100 B 3 river, Bosnia & Herzegovina/Croatia
Unalaska Island 36 A 3 island, Alaska, NW USA
'Unayzah 120 B 4 C Saudi Arabia
Uncompahgre Peak 44 C 5 mountain, Colorado, C USA
Ungama Bay *see* Formosa Bay
Ungava Bay 39 E 1 bay, W Labrador Sea
Ungava, Péninsule d' 38 D 1 peninsula, Québec, SE Canada
Ungeny *see* Ungheni
Ungheni 108 D 3 *Rus.* Ungeny. W Moldova
Unguja *see* Zanzibar
Üngüz Angyrsyndaky Garagum se Zaunguzskiye Karakumy
Unimak Island 36 B 3 island, Alaska, NW USA
Union 43 E 1 South Carolina, SE USA
Union City 42 C 1 Tennessee, S USA

United Arab Emirates
121 E 5 *Ar.* Al Imārāt al 'Arabiyahal Muttaḩidah, *abbrev.* UAE; *prev.* Trucial States. Federation, SW Asia

Official name: United Arab Emirates **Date of formation:** 1971 **Capital:** Abu Dhabi **Population:** 1.2 million **Total area:** 32,278 sq miles (83,600 sq km) **Languages:** Arabic*, Farsi (Persian), Urdu, Hindi **Religions:** Sunni Muslim 77%, Shi' Muslim 19%, other 4% **Ethnic mix:** South Asian 50%, Emirian 19%, other Arab 23%, other 8% **Government:** Federation of monarch **Currency:** Dirham = 100 fils

nitedKingdom
89 B 5 Monarchy, NW Europe

fficial name: United Kingdom of
reat Britain and Northern Ireland
ate of formation: 1801/1921
apital: London **Population:** 57.8
illion **Total area:** 94,550 sq miles
44,880 sq km) **Languages:** English*
eligions: Protestant 52%, Roman
atholic 9%, Muslim 3%, other 36%
thnic mix: English 81%, Scottish
)%, Welsh 2%,
her 7% **Government:**
onstitutional monarchy
urrency: Pound sterling = 100 pence

nited States of America
var. America, The States
abbrev. USA, U.S, U.S.A.
Federal Republic, North America

fficial name: United States of
merica **Date of formation:**
787/1959 **Capital:** Washington DC
opulation: 265.8 million **Total area:**
,681,760 sq miles (9,372,610 sq km)
anguages: English*, Spanish
eligions: Protestant 56%, Roman
atholic 28%, Jewish 2%, other 14%
thnic mix: White (inc. Hispanic)
3%, Black 13%, other 4%
overnment: Multiparty republic
urrency: US $ = 100 cents

nst 88 D 1 island,
NE Scotland, UK
nye 116 D 2 W Turkey
pala 52 D 4 NW Costa Rica
pata 59 E 2 E Venezuela
pemba, Lake 77 D 7 lake,
SE Congo (Zaire)
pernavik 82 C 2 *var.* Upernivik.
N Greenland
pernivik *see* Upernavik
pington 78 C 4 W South Africa
polu 145 F 4 island, SE Samoa
pper Darby 41 F 4
Pennsylvania, NE USA
pper Klamath Lake 46 B 4 lake,
Oregon, NW USA
pper Lough Erne 89 B 5 lake,
S Northern Ireland, UK
pper Red Lake 45 F 1 lake,
Minnesota, N USA
ppsala 85 C 6 C Sweden
ral 114 B 3 *Kaz.* Zayyq. River, ,
Kazakhstan/Russian Federation
ral Mountains *see* Ural'skiye Gory
ral'sk 114 B 3 *Kaz.* Oral.
NW Kazakhstan
ral'skiye Gory 114 C 3 *var.*
Ural'skiy Khrebet, *Eng.* Ural
Mountains. Mountain range,
Kazakhstan/Russian Federation
raricoera 62 D 1 N Brazil
ra-Tyube *see* Üroteppa
rbandale 45 F 4 Iowa, C USA
reki 117 F 2 W Georgia
ren' 111 C 5
W Russian Federation
rganch 122 D 2 *Rus.* Urgench;
prev. Novo-Urgench.
W Uzbekistan
roševac 101 D 5 *Alb.* Ferizaj.
S Yugoslavia
roteppa 123 E 2 *Rus.* Ura-Tyube.
NW Tajikistan
ruapan 51 E 4 *var.* Uruapan del
Progreso. SW Mexico
ruapan del Progreso *see* Uruapan
ruguai, Rio *see* Uruguay

Uruguay
64 D 4 *off.* Oriental Republic of
Uruguay; *prev.* La Banda Oriental.
Republic, S South America

Official name: Republic of Uruguay
Date of formation: 1828/1909
Capital: Montevideo **Population:** 3.1
million **Total Area:** 68,498 sq miles
(177,410 sq km) **Languages:**
Spanish*, other **Religions:** Roman
Catholic 77%, Protestant 3%, Jewish
2%, other 18% **Ethnic mix:** White
88%, *mestizo* (Euro-Indian) 8%, Black
4% **Government:** Multiparty
republic **Currency:** Peso = 100
centesimos

Uruguay 64 D 3 river, NE Uruguay
Urumaco 58 C 1 NW Venezuela
Ürümqi 126 C 3 *var.* Tihwa,
Urumchi, Urumqi, Urumtsi,
Wu-lu-k'o-mu-shih, Wu-lu-mu-
ch'i; *prev.* Ti-hua. NW China
Urusan *see* Ulsan
Urziceni 108 C 5 SE Romania
Usa 110 F 3 river,
NW Russian Federation
Uşak 116 B 3 *prev.* Ushak.
W Turkey
Ushak *see* Uşak
Ushant *see* Ouessant, Île d'
Ushuaia 65 B 8 S Argentina
Usinsk 110 E 3
NW Russian Federation
Usmas Ezers 106 B 3 lake,
NW Latvia
Usol'ye-Sibirskoye 115 E 4
C Russian Federation
Ussel 91 C 5 C France
Ussuriysk 115 G 5 *prev.* Nikol'sk,
Nikol'sk-Ussuriyskiy, Voroshilov.
SE Russian Federation
Ustica, Isola d' 97 B 6 island, S Italy
Ústí nad Labem 98 A 4 *Ger.* Aussig.
N Czech Republic
Ustinov *see* Izhevsk
Ustka 98 B 2 *Ger.* Stolpmünde.
NW Poland
Ust'-Kamchatsk 115 H 2
NE Russian Federation
Ust'-Kamenogorsk 114 D 5
Kaz. Öskemen. E Kazakhstan
Ust'-Olenëk 115 F 2
N Russian Federation
Ust'-Sysol'sk *see* Syktyvkar
Ustyurt Plateau 122 C 1 *var.* Ust
Ürt, *Uzb.* Ustyurt Platosi. Plateau,
Kazakhstan/Uzbekistan
Usulután 52 C 3 SE El Salvador
Usumacinta 52 A 1 river,
Guatemala/Mexico
Usumbura *see* Bujumbura
Utah 44 B 4 *off.* State of Utah;
nicknames Beehive State, Mormon
State. State, W USA
Utah Lake 44 B 4 lake, W USA
'Uta Vava'u 145 F 4 island, C Tonga
Utena 106 C 4 E Lithuania
Utica 41 F 3 New York, NE USA
Utina *see* Udine
Utrecht 86 C 3 *Lat.* Trajectum ad
Rhenum. C Netherlands
Utsunomiya 131 D 5 *var.*
Utunomiya. Honshū, S Japan
Uttar Pradesh 135 E 3 *prev.* United
Provinces, United Provinces of
Agra and Oudh. State, N India
Utunomiya *see* Utsunomiya
Uulu 106 D 2 SW Estonia

Uummannaq 82 C 3 *var.* Umanak,
Umanaq. Greenland
Uummannarsuaq 82 B 5 *var.*
Nunap Isua, *Dan.* Kap Farvel,
Eng. Cape Farewell. Headland,
S Greenland
Uvalde 49 F 4 Texas, S USA
Uvarovichy 107 D 7 *Rus.*
Uvarovichi. SE Belarus
Uvarovichi *see* Uvarovichy
Uvea, Île 145 E 4 island,
S Wallis & Futuna
Uvs Nuur 126 C 1 *var.* Ozero
Ubsu-Nur. Lake, Mongolia/
Russian Federation
Uyeda *see* Ueda
Uyuni 61 F 5 W Bolivia

Uzbekistan
122 C 1 Republic, C Asia

Official name: Republic of
Uzbekistan **Date of formation:** 1991
Capital: Tashkent **Population:** 21.9
million **Total Area:** 439,733 sq miles
(1,138,910 sq km) **Languages:**
Uzbek*, Russian **Religions:** Muslim
88%, other (mostly Eastern
Orthodox) 12% **Ethnic mix:** Uzbek
71%, Russian 8%, Tajik 5%, Kazakh
4%, other 12% **Government:**
Single-party republic
Currency: Sum = 100 teen

Uzhhorod 108 B 2 *Rus.* Uzhgorod;
prev. Ungvár. W Ukraine
Užice 100 D 4 *prev.* Titovo Užice.
W Yugoslavia

V

Vaal 78 D 4 river, C South Africa
Vaals 87 D 6 SE Netherlands
Vaasa 84 D 4 *Swe.* Vasa; *prev.*
Nikolainkaupunki. W Finland
Vác 99 C 6 *Ger.* Waitzen.
N Hungary
Vacaville 47 B 6 California, W USA
Vadodara 134 C 4 *prev.* Baroda
W India
Vaduz 94 E 2 country capital,
W Liechtenstein
Váh 99 C 5 *Ger.* Waag,
Hung. Vág. River, W Slovakia
Väinameri 106 C 2 *Ger.* Moon-
Sund; *prev.* Muhu Väin. Sea,
E Baltic Sea
Vainode 106 B 3 SW Latvia
Valdaj *see* Valday
Valday 110 B 4 *var.* Valdaj.
W Russian Federation
Valdecañas, Embalse de 92 D 3
reservoir, W Spain
Valdepeñas 93 E 4 C Spain
Valdés, Península 65 C 6 peninsula,
SE Argentina
Valdez 36 C 3 Alaska, NW USA
Valdivia 65 B 5 C Chile
Val-d'Or 38 D 4 Québec, SE Canada
Valdosta 43 E 3 Georgia, SE USA
Valence 91 D 5 *anc.* Valentia,
Valentia Julia, Ventia. E France
Valencia 93 F 3 E Spain
Valencia 58 D 2 N Venezuela
Valencia, Golfo de 93 G 3 *var.*
Gulf of Valencia. Gulf,
W Mediterranean Sea
Valencia, Gulf of *see* Valencia,
Golfo de
Valenciennes 90 D 2 N France
Valera 58 C 2 NW Venezuela
Valetta *see* Valletta

Valga 106 D 3 *Ger.* Walk,
Latv. Valka. S Estonia
Valira 91 A 8 river, Andorra/Spain
Valjevo 100 D 4 W Yugoslavia
Valjok 84 D 2 N Norway
Valka 106 D 3 *Ger.* Walk. N Latvia
Valkenswaard 87 D 5
S Netherlands
Valladolid 92 D 2 NW Spain
Valladolid 51 H 3 SE Mexico
Vall d'Uxó 93 F 3 E Spain
Valle de La Pascua 58 D 2
N Venezuela
Valle del Po *see* Po Valley
Valledupar 58 B 1 N Colombia
Vallejo 47 B 6 California, W USA
Vallenar 64 B 3 N Chile
Valletta 80 D 5 *prev.* Valetta.
Country capital, E Malta
Valley City 45 E 2
North Dakota, N USA
Valls 93 F 2 NE Spain
Valmiera 106 D 3 *Est.* Volmari,
Ger. Wolmar. N Latvia
Valona Bay *see* Vlorës, Gjiri i
Valozhyn 107 C 5 *Pol.* Wołożyn,
Rus. Volozhin. C Belarus
Valparaíso 40 C 3 Indiana, N USA
Valparaíso 64 B 4 C Chile
Valverde del Camino 92 B 4
S Spain
Van 117 F 3 E Turkey
Vanadzor 117 F 2 *prev.* Kirovakan.
N Armenia
Vancouver 37 E 5 British Columbia,
SW Canada
Vancouver 46 B 2
Washington, NW USA
Vancouver Island 36 D 5 island,
SW Canada
Vanda *see* Vantaa
Van Diemen Gulf 146 E 2 gulf,
SW Arafura Sea
Van Diemen's Land *see* Tasmania
Vänern 85 B 6 *Eng.* Lake Vaner;
prev. Lake Vener. Lake, S Sweden
Vangaindrano 79 G 4 S Madagascar
Van Gölü 117 F 3 *var.* Thospitis,
Eng. Lake Van. Salt lake, E Turkey
Van, Lake *see* Van Gölü
Vannes 90 A 4 *anc.* Dariorigum.
NW France
Vantaa 85 D 6 *Swe.* Vanda.
S Finland
Vanua Levu 145 E 4 island, N Fiji

Vanuatu
144 C 4 *prev.* New Hebrides.
Republic, S Pacific Ocean

Official name: Republic of Vanuatu
Date of formation: 1980 **Capital:**
Port-Vila **Population:** 155,000 **Total
Area:** 4,706 sq miles (12,190 sq km)
Languages: Bislama*, English*,
French* **Religions:** Protestant 77%,
Roman Catholic 15%, traditional
beliefs 8% **Ethnic mix:** Ni-Vanuatu
98%, other 2% **Government:**
Multiparty republic
Currency: Vatu - 100 centimes

Vapincum *see* Gap
Varaķļani 106 D 4 C Latvia
Vārānasi 135 E 3 *prev.* Banaras,
Benares, *hist.* Kasi. N India
Varangerfjorden 84 E 2 fjord,
SW Barents Sea
Varangerhalvøya 84 E 1 peninsula,
N Norway
Varaždin 100 B 2 *Ger.* Warasdin,
Hung. Varasd. N Croatia
Varberg 85 B 7 S Sweden

243

Vardar 101 E 6 *Gk.* Axiós. River, Greece/Macedonia
Varde 85 A 7 W Denmark
Varėna 107 B 5 *Pol.* Orany. S Lithuania
Varese 96 B 2 N Italy
Vârful Moldoveanu 108 B 4 *var.* Moldoveanul; *prev.* Vîrful Moldoveanu. Mountain, C Romania
Varkaus 85 E 5 C Finland
Varna 104 E 2 *prev.* Stalin, *anc.* Odessus. NE Bulgaria
Varnenski Zaliv 104 E 2 *prev.* Stalinski Zaliv. Bay, NW Black Sea
Vasilikí 105 A 5 Kríti, SE Greece
Vasilishki 107 B 5 *Pol.* Wasiliszki. W Belarus
Vasil'kov *see* Vasyl'kiv
Vaslui 108 D 4 C Romania
Västerås 85 C 6 C Sweden
Vasyl'kiv 109 E 2 *var.* Vasil'kov. N Ukraine

Vatican City 97 A 7 Papal state, S Europe

Official name: Vatican City State **Date of formation:** 1929 **Capital:** Not applicable **Population:** 1000 **Total area:** 0.17 sq miles (0.44 sq km) **Languages:** Italian*, Latin* **Religions:** Roman Catholic 100% **Ethnic mix:** Italian 90%, Swiss 10% (including the Swiss Guard, which is responsible for papal security) **Government:** Papal Commission **Currency:** Italian lira = 100 centesimi

Vatican City State *see* Vatican City
Vatnajökull 83 E 5 glacier, SE Iceland
Vättern 85 B 6 *Eng.* Lake Vatter; *prev.* Lake Vetter. Lake, S Sweden
Vaupés 58 C 4 *var.* Rio Uaupés. River, Brazil/Colombia
Vava'u Group 143 E 3 island group, N Tonga
Vavuniya 132 D 3 N Sri Lanka
Vawkavysk 107 B 6 *Pol.* Wołkowysk, *Rus.* Volkovysk. W Belarus
Växjö 85 C 7 *var.* Vexiö. S Sweden
Vaygach, Ostrov 110 E 2 Island, NW Russian Federation
Veendam 86 E 2 NE Netherlands
Veenendaal 86 D 4 C Netherlands
Vega 84 B 4 island, C Norway
Veisiejai 107 B 5 S Lithuania
Vejer de la Frontera 92 C 5 S Spain
Veldhoven 87 D 5 S Netherlands
Velebit 100 A 3 mountain range, C Croatia
Velenje 95 E 7 *Ger.* Wöllan. S Slovenia
Velho *see* Porto Velho
Velika Gorica 100 B 2 N Croatia
Velika Morava 100 E 4 *var.* Glavn'a Morava, Morava, *Ger.* Grosse Morava. River, C Yugoslavia
Velika Plana 100 D 4 C Yugoslavia
Velikaya 115 H 2 river, NE Russian Federation
Velike-Luki *see* Velikiye Luki
Velikij Ust'ug *see* Velikiy Ustyug
Velikiye Luki 110 A 4 *var.* Velike-Luki. W Russian Federation
Velikiy Ustyug 110 C 4 *var.* Velikij Ust'ug. NW Russian Federation
Veliko Tŭrnovo 104 D 2 *var.* Veliko Tărnovo; *prev.* Tirnovo, Trnovo, Tŭrnovo. N Bulgaria
Velingrad 104 C 3 SW Bulgaria

Vel'ký Krtíš 99 D 6 S Slovakia
Vellore 132 C 2 SE India
Velsen *see* Velsen-Noord
Velsen-Noord 86 C 3 *var.* Velsen. W Netherlands
Vel'sk 110 C 4 *var.* Velsk. NW Russian Federation
Velsk *see* Vel'sk
Velvendos *see* Velvendós
Velvendós 104 B 4 *var.* Velvendos. N Greece
Velykyy Tokmak *see* Tokmak
Vendée 90 B 4 cultural region, W France
Vendôme 90 B 4 C France
Venezia 96 C 2 *Eng.* Venice, *Fr.* Venise, *Ger.* Venedig; *anc.* Venetia. NE Italy

Venezuela 58 D 2 *prev.* Estados Unidos de Venezuela, United States of Venezuela. Republic, N South America

Official name: Republic of Venezuela **Date of formation:** 1830/1929 **Capital:** Caracas **Population:** 20.6 million **Total area:** 352,143 sq miles (912,050 sq km) **Languages:** Spanish*, Indian languages **Religions:** Roman Catholic 96%, Protestant 2%, other 2% **Ethnic mix:** *mestizo* 67%, White 21%, Black 10%, Indian 2% **Government:** Multiparty republic **Currency:** Bolívar = 100 centimos

Venezuela, Golfo de 58 C 1 *Eng.* Gulf of Maracaibo, Gulf of Venezuela. Gulf, E Caribbean Sea
Venezuelan Basin 66 B 4 undersea basin, W Atlantic Ocean
Venice 43 E 4 Florida, SE USA
Venice 42 C 4 Louisiana, S USA
Venice *see* Venezia
Venice, Gulf of 96 D 2 *It.* Golfo di Venezia, *Slvn.* Beneški Zaliv. Gulf, N Adriatic Sea
Venlo 87 D 5 *prev.* Venloo. SE Netherlands
Venloo *see* Venlo
Venta 106 B 3 *Ger.* Windau. River, Latvia/Lithuania
Ventimiglia 96 A 3 NW Italy
Ventspils 106 B 2 *Ger.* Windau. NW Latvia
Ventura 47 C 7 California, W USA
Vera 64 D 3 NE Argentina
Veracruz 51 F 4 *var.* Veracruz Llave. E Mexico
Veracruz Llave *see* Veracruz
Vercellae *see* Vercelli
Vercelli 96 A 2 *anc.* Vercellae. NW Italy
Verdalsøra 84 B 4 C Norway
Verde, Costa 92 D 1 coastal region, N Spain
Verden 94 B 3 NW Germany
Verkhnedvinsk *see* Vyerkhnyadzvinsk
Verkhneudinsk *see* Ulan-Ude
Verkhoyanskiy Khrebet 115 F 3 mountain range, E Russian Federation
Vermillion 45 F 3 South Dakota, N USA
Vermont 41 F 2 *off.* State of Vermont; nickname Green Mountain State. State, NE USA
Vernal 44 B 4 Utah, W USA
Vernon 49 F 2 Texas, S USA

Vero Beach 43 F 4 Florida, SE USA
Véroia 104 B 4 *var.* Veria, Vérroia, *Turk.* Karaferiye. N Greece
Verona 96 B 2 NE Italy
Versailles 90 C 3 N France
Verulamium *see* St Albans
Verviers 87 D 6 E Belgium
Veselinovo 104 E 2 E Bulgaria
Vesoul 90 D 4 *anc.* Vesulium, Vesulum. E France
Vesterålen 84 B 2 island group, N Norway
Vestfjorden 84 C 3 fjord, E Norwegian Sea
Vestmannaeyjar 83 E 5 S Iceland
Vesuna *see* Périgueux
Vesuvio 97 D 5 *Eng.* Vesuvius. Volcano, S Italy
Vesuvius *see* Vesuvio
Veszprém 99 C 7 *Ger.* Veszprim. W Hungary
Veszprim *see* Veszprém
Vetrino 104 E 2 NE Bulgaria
Vetrino *see* Vyetryna
Veurne 87 A 5 *var.* Furnes. W Belgium
Vexiö *see* Växjö
Vhuru Peak *see* Kilimanjaro
Viacha 61 F 4 W Bolivia
Viana do Castelo 92 B 2 *var.* Viana de Castelo; *anc.* Velobriga. NW Portugal
Vianden 87 D 7 NE Luxembourg
Vianen 86 C 4 C Netherlands
Viangchan 136 D 4 *Eng./Fr.* Vientiane. Country capital, C Laos
Viangphoukha 136 C 3 *var.* Vieng Pou Kha. NW Laos
Viareggio 96 B 3 C Italy
Viborg 85 A 7 NW Denmark
Vic 93 G 2 *var.* Vich; *anc.* Ausa, Vicus Ausonensis. NE Spain
Vicentia *see* Vicenza
Vicenza 96 C 2 *anc.* Vicentia. NE Italy
Vichy 91 C 5 C France
Victor Harbor 149 B 7 South Australia, S Australia
Victoria 36 D 5 province capital, Vancouver Island, SW Canada
Victoria 65 B 5 C Chile
Victoria 149 B 7 state, SE Australia
Victoria 146 C 3 river, Western Australia, N Australia
Victoria 79 H 1 country capital, NE Seychelles
Victoria de Durango *see* Durango
Victoria de las Tunas *see* Las Tunas
Victoria Falls 78 C 3 W Zimbabwe
Victoria Falls 78 C 3 waterfall, Zambia/Zimbabwe
Victoria Harbour 128 A 1 harbor, S Hong Kong
Victoria Island 37 F 3 island, NW Canada
Victoria, Lake 73 B 6 *var.* Victoria Nyanza. Lake, NE Africa
Victoria Land 154 C 4 physical region, Antarctica
Victoria Nyanza *see* Victoria, Lake
Victoria Peak 128 A 2 mountain, S Hong Kong
Victorville 47 C 7 California, W USA
Vicus Elbii *see* Viterbo
Vidalia 43 E 2 Georgia, SE USA
Vidin 104 B 1 *anc.* Bononia. NW Bulgaria
Vidzeme 106 C 3 *Eng.* Livonia. Cultural region, NE Latvia

Vidzy 107 C 5 NW Belarus
Viedma 65 C 5 E Argentina
Vieng Pou Kha *see* Viangphoukha
Vienna *see* Vienne
Vienna *see* Wien
Vienne 91 D 5 *anc.* Vienna. E France
Vienne 91 B 5 river, W France
Vientiane *see* Viangchan
Vierwaldstätter See 95 B 7 *Eng.* Lake of Lucerne. Lake, C Switzerland
Vierzon 90 C 4 C France
Viesíte 106 C 4 *var.* Viesīte, *Ger.* Eckengraf. S Latvia

Vietnam 136 D 4 *Vtn.* Công Hoa Xa Hôi Chu Nghia Viêt Nam, Công Hóa Xã Hôi Chu Nghĩa Viêt Nam. Republic, SE Asia

Official name: Socialist Republic of Viet-Nam **Date of formation:** 1976 **Capital:** Hanoi **Population:** 76.2 million **Total area:** 127,243 sq miles (329,560 sq km) **Languages:** Vietnamese* **Religions:** Buddhist 55%, Roman Catholic 7%, Muslim 1%, other 37% **Ethnic mix:** Vietnamese 88%, Chinese 4%, Thai 2%, other 6% **Government:** Single-party republic **Currency:** Dong = 10 hao = 100 xu

Viêt Tri 136 D 3 *var.* Vietri. N Vietnam
Vieux Fort 55 F 2 S Saint Lucia
Vigo 92 B 2 NW Spain
Viipuri *see* Vyborg
Vijayawāda 132 D 1 *prev.* Bezwada. SE India
Vila *see* Port-Vila
Vila de Moçímboa da Praia *see* Moçímboa da Praia
Vila do Conde 92 B 2 NW Portugal
Vila do Zumbo 78 D 2 *prev.* Vila do Zumbu, Zumbo . NW Mozambique
Vilafranca del Penedès 93 F 2 *var.* Villafranca del Panadés. NE Spain
Vijaka 106 D 4 *Ger.* Marienhausen. NE Latvia
Vilalba 92 C 1 NW Spain
Vila Nova de Gaia 92 B 2 NW Portugal
Vila Nova de Portimão *see* Portimão
Vila Real 92 B 2 *var.* Vila Rial. N Portugal
Vila-real de los Infantes 93 F 3 *var.* Villarreal. E Spain
Vila Rial *see* Vila Real
Vilhelmina 84 C 4 N Sweden
Vilhena 62 D 3 W Brazil
Vília 105 C 5 C Greece
Viljandi 106 D 2 *Ger.* Fellin. E Estonia
Vilkaviškis 106 B 4 *Pol.* Wyłkowyzski. SW Lithuania
Villa Acuña *see* Ciudad Acuña
Villacarrillo 93 E 4 S Spain
Villa Cecilia *see* Ciudad Madero
Villach 95 D 7 *Slvn.* Beljak. S Austria
Villacidro 97 A 5 W Italy
Villa Concepción *see* Concepción
Villa del Pilar *see* Pilar
Villafranca de los Barros 92 C 4 W Spain
Villafranca del Panadés *see* Vilafranca del Penedès
Villahermosa 51 G 4 *prev.* San Juan Bautista. SE Mexico
Villajoyosa 93 F 4 *var.* La Vila Jojosa. E Spain

Villalcampo, Embalse de 92 C 2 reservoir, NW Spain
Villa María 64 C 4 C Argentina
Villa Martín 61 F 5 SW Bolivia
Villanueva 50 D 4 C Mexico
Villanueva de la Serena 92 C 4 W Spain
Villanueva de los Infantes 93 E 4 C Spain
Villa Ojo de Agua 64 C 3 Argentina
Villarreal *see* Vila-real de los Infantes
Villarrica 64 D 2 SE Paraguay
Villavicencio 58 B 3 C Colombia
Villaviciosa 92 D 1 N Spain
Villazón 61 G 5 S Bolivia
Villena 93 E 4 E Spain
Villeneuve d'Ascq 90 D 2 NE France
Villeurbanne 91 D 5 E France
Villingen-Schwenningen 95 B 6 S Germany
Villmanstrand *see* Lappeenranta
Vilnius 107 C 5 *Ger.* Wilna, *Pol.* Wilno; *prev. Rus.* Vilna. Country capital, SE Lithuania
Vil'shanka 109 E 3 *Rus.* Olshanka. C Ukraine
Vilvoorde 87 C 6 *Fr.* Vilvorde. C Belgium
Vilvorde *see* Vilvoorde
Vilyeyka 107 C 5 *Pol.* Wilejka, *Rus.* Vileyka. NW Belarus
Vilyuy 115 F 3 river, C Russian Federation
Viña del Mar 64 B 4 C Chile
Vinaròs 93 F 3 E Spain
Vincennes 40 B 4 Indiana, N USA
Vindhya Mountains *see* Vindhya Range
Vindhya Range 134 D 4 *var.* Vindhya Mountains. Mountain range, N India
Vineland 41 F 4 Delaware, NE USA
Vinh 136 D 4 NE Vietnam
Vinh Loi *see* Bac Liêu
Vinište 104 B 2 *var.* Vinište. NW Bulgaria
Viniste *see* Vinište
Vinita 49 G 1 Oklahoma, C USA
Vinkovci 100 C 3 *Ger.* Winkowitz, *Hung.* Vinkovcze. E Croatia
Vinnitsa *see* Vinnytsya
Vinnytsya 108 D 2 *Rus.* Vinnitsa. C Ukraine
Vinson Massif 154 B 3 mountain, Antarctica
Viranşehir 117 E 4 SE Turkey
Virginia 41 E 5 *off.* Commonwealth of Virginia; *nicknames* Old Dominion, Mother of Presidents, Mother of States. State, E USA
Virginia 45 G 1 Minnesota, N USA
Virginia Beach 41 F 5 Virginia, NE USA
Virgin Islands 55 F 3 *var.* Virgin Islands of the United States; *prev.* Danish West Indies. US unincorporated territory, E Caribbean Sea
Virgin Islands *see* British Virgin Islands
Virôchey 137 E 5 NE Cambodia
Virovitica 100 C 2 *Ger.* Virovititz, *Hung.* Verőcze; *prev. Ger.* Werowitz. NE Croatia
Virton 87 D 8 SE Belgium
Virtsu 106 D 2 *Ger.* Werder. W Estonia
Vis 100 B 4 *It.* Lissa; *anc.* Issa. Island, S Croatia

Vis *see* Fish
Visaginas 106 C 4 *prev.* Sniečkus. E Lithuania
Visakhapatnam 132 D 1 SE India
Visalia 47 C 7 California, W USA
Visby 85 C 7 *Ger.* Wisby. SE Sweden
Viscount Melville Sound 37 F 2 *prev.* Melville Sound. Sound, Arctic Ocean
Visé 87 D 6 E Belgium
Viseu 92 C 3 *prev.* Vizeu. N Portugal
Vişeu de Sus 108 B 3 *var.* Vişeul de Sus, *Ger.* Oberwischau, *Hung.* Felsővisó. N Romania
Visoko 100 C 4 C Bosnia & Herzegovina
Vista 47 C 8 California, W USA
Vistula *see* Wisła
Vistula Lagoon 98 C 2 *Ger.* Frisches Haff, *Pol.* Zalew Wiślany, *Rus.* Vislinskiy Zaliv. Lagoon, S Baltic Sea
Vitebsk *see* Vitsyebsk
Viterbo 96 C 4 *anc.* Vicus Elbii. C Italy
Viti Levu 145 E 4 island, C Fiji
Vitim 115 F 4 river, C Russian Federation
Vitória 63 G 4 state capital, SE Brazil
Vitória da Conquista 63 G 3 E Brazil
Vitoria-Gasteiz 93 E 1 *var.* Vitoria, *Eng.* Vittoria. N Spain
Vitré 90 B 3 NW France
Vitsyebsk 107 E 5 *Rus.* Vitebsk. NE Belarus
Vittoria 97 C 7 SW Italy
Vizeu *see* Viseu
Vizianagaram 132 D 1 *var.* Vizianagram. E India
Vizianagram *see* Vizianagaram
Vjosës, Lumi i 101 C 7 *var.* Vijosa, Vijosë, *Gk.* Aóos. River, Albania/ Greece
Vlaardingen 86 C 4 SW Netherlands
Vladikavkaz 111 B 8 *prev.* Dzaudzhikau, Ordzhonikidze. SW Russian Federation
Vladimir 111 B 5 W Russian Federation
Vladivostok 115 G 5 SE Russian Federation
Vlagtwedde 86 E 2 NE Netherlands
Vlasotince 101 E 5 SE Yugoslavia
Vlieland 86 C 1 *Fris.* Flylân. Island, N Netherlands
Vlijmen 86 C 4 S Netherlands
Vlissingen 87 B 5 *Eng.* Flushing, *Fr.* Flessingue. SW Netherlands
Vlodava *see* Włodawa
Vlorë 101 C 7 *It.* Valona, Vlora; *prev.* Vlonë. SW Albania
Vlorës, Gjiri i 101 C 6 *var.* Valona Bay. S Adriatic Sea
Vlotslavsk *see* Włocławek
Vöcklabruck 95 D 6 NW Austria
Vogel Peak *see* Dimlang
Voiron 91 D 5 E France
Vojvodina 100 D 3 *Ger.* Wojwodina. Cultural region, N Yugoslavia
Volga 111 C 7 river, W Russian Federation
Volgograd 111 B 7 *prev.* Stalingrad, Tsaritsyn. SW Russian Federation
Volkhov 110 B 4 *var.* Volchov, Volnov, NW Russian Federation
Volnovakha 109 G 3 SE Ukraine
Volodymyr-Volyns'kyy 108 C 1 *Pol.* Włodzimierz, *Rus.* Vladimir-Volynskiy. NW Ukraine

Vologda 110 B 4 W Russian Federation
Volokonova 111 A 6 W Russian Federation
Vólos 105 B 5 C Greece
Vol'sk 111 C 6 W Russian Federation
Volta 75 E 4 river, SE Ghana
Volta, Lake 75 E 4 reservoir, SE Ghana
Volturno 97 D 5 river, S Italy
Volunteer Island *see* Starbuck Island
Volzhsk 111 C 5 W Russian Federation
Volzhskiy 111 B 6 SW Russian Federation
Võnnu 106 E 3 *Ger.* Wendau. SE Estonia
Voorst 86 D 3 E Netherlands
Voranava 107 C 5 *Pol.* Werenów, *Rus.* Voronovo. W Belarus
Vorderrhein 95 B 7 river, SE Switzerland
Vóreioi Sporádes 105 C 5 *var.* Vórioi Sporádhes, *Eng.* Northern Sporades. Island group, E Greece
Vorkuta 110 E 3 NW Russian Federation
Vormsi 106 D 2 *var.* Vormsi Saar, *Ger.* Worms, *Swe.* Ormsö. Island, W Estonia
Voronezh 111 B 6 W Russian Federation
Voroshilovsk *see* Stavropol'
Vorskla 109 F 2 river, C Ukraine
Võrtsjärv 106 D 3 *Ger.* Wirz-See. Lake, SE Estonia
Võru 106 D 3 *Ger.* Werro. SE Estonia
Vosges 90 E 4 mountain range, NE France
Vostochno-Sibirskoye More 115 G 1 *Eng.* East Siberian Sea. Sea, Arctic Ocean
Vostok 154 C 3 research station, Antarctica
Vostok Island 145 G 3 *var.* Vostok Island; *prev.* Stavers Island. Island, E Kiribati
Voznesens'k 109 E 3 *Rus.* Voznesensk. S Ukraine
Voznesensk *see* Voznesens'k
Vraca *see* Vratsa
Vrangelya, Ostrov 115 G 1 *Eng.* Wrangel Island. Island, NE Russian Federation
Vranje 101 E 5 SE Yugoslavia
Vranov nad Topl'ou 99 E 5 *var.* Vranov, *Hung.* Varannó. E Slovakia
Vratsa 104 C 2 *var.* Vraca. NW Bulgaria
Vrbas 100 C 3 river, N Bosnia & Herzegovina
Vrbas 100 D 3 N Yugoslavia
Vršac 100 E 3 *Ger.* Werschetz, *Hung.* Versecz. NE Yugoslavia
Vsetín 101 D 5 *Ger.* Wsetin. E Czech Republic
Vučitrn 101 D 5 C Yugoslavia
Vukovar 100 D 3 *Hung.* Vukovár. E Croatia
Vukovár *see* Vukovar
Vulcan 37 E 5 Alberta, SW Canada
Vulcan 108 B 4 *Hung.* Zsilyvajdevulkán; *prev.* Crivadia Vulcanului, Vaidei, *Hung.* Sily-Vajdej, Vajdej. W Romania
Vulcano, Isola 97 C 7 island, S Italy
Vung Tau 137 E 6 *prev. Fr.* Cap Saint-Jacques, *Eng.* Cape Saint Jacques. S Vietnam

Vyatka 111 C 5 *var.* V'atka, Viatka. River, NW Russian Federation
Vyatka *see* Kirov
Vyborg 110 B 3 *Fin.* Viipuri. NW Russian Federation
Vyerkhnyadzvinsk 107 D 5 *Rus.* Verkhnedvinsk. N Belarus
Vyetryna 107 D 5 *Rus.* Vetrino. N Belarus
Vynohradiv 108 B 3 *Cz.* Sevluš, *Hung.* Nagyszöllös, *Rus.* Vinogradov; *prev.* Sevlyush. W Ukraine
Vytegra 110 B 4 NW Russian Federation

W

Wa 75 E 4 NW Ghana
Waal 86 D 4 river, S Netherlands
Wabash River 40 B 5 river, NE USA
Waco 49 G 3 Texas, S USA
Waddān 71 F 3 NW Libya
Waddeneilanden 86 C 1 *Eng.* West Frisian Islands. Island group, N Netherlands
Waddenzee 86 C 2 *var.* Wadden Zee, *Eng.* Wadden Sea. Sea, E North Sea
Waddington, Mount 36 D 5 mountain, SW Canada
Wādī as Sīr 119 B 6 *var.* Wadi es Sir. NW Jordan
Wadi es Sir *see* Wādī as Sīr
Wadi Halfa 72 B 3 *var.* Wādī Ḥalfā'. N Sudan
Wādī Ḥalfā' *see* Wadi Halfa
Wādī Mūsā 119 B 7 *var.* Petra. S Jordan
Wad Madanī *see* Wad Medani
Wad Medani 72 C 4 *var.* Wad Madanī. C Sudan
Wagadugu *see* Ouagadougou
Wagga Wagga 149 C 7 New South Wales, SE Australia
Wagin 147 B 7 Western Australia, SW Australia
Wāh 134 C 1 NE Pakistan
Wahai 139 F 4 Pulau Seram, E Indonesia
Wahiawa 47 A 8 *Haw.* Wahiawā. Hawaii, W USA
Wahiawā *see* Wahiawa
Wahpeton 45 F 2 North Dakota, N USA
Waiau 151 C 5 river, South Island, New Zealand
Waigeo, Pulau 139 G 4 island, Maluka, E Indonesia
Waikaremoana, Lake 150 E 4 lake, North Island, NE New Zealand
Wailuku 47 B 8 Hawaii, W USA
Waimate 151 B 7 South Island, SW New Zealand
Waiouru 150 D 4 North Island, C New Zealand
Waipara 151 C 6 South Island, C New Zealand
Waipawa 150 E 4 North Island, NE New Zealand
Waipukurau 150 E 4 North Island, NE New Zealand
Wairau 151 C 5 river, South Island, C New Zealand
Wairoa 150 D 2 river, North Island, N New Zealand
Wairoa 150 E 4 North Island, NE New Zealand
Waitaki 151 B 7 river, South Island, SW New Zealand
Waitara 150 D 4 North Island, C New Zealand

Waitzen *see* Vác
Waiuku 150 D 3 North Island,
  N New Zealand
Wakasa-wan 131 C 6 bay,
  SE Sea of Japan
Wakatipu, Lake 151 A 7 lake,
  South Island, SW New Zealand
Wakayama 131 C 6 Honshū,
  SW Japan
Wake Island 142 D 1 US
  unincorporated territory,
  W Pacific Ocean
Wakkanai 130 C 1 Hokkaidō,
  NE Japan
Wałbrzych 98 B 4 *Ger.* Waldenburg,
  Waldenburg in Schlesien.
  SW Poland
Walcourt 87 C 7 S Belgium
Wałcz 98 B 3 *Ger.* Deutsch Krone.
  NW Poland
Wales 89 C 6 *Wel.* Cymru.
  National region, UK
Wales 36 C 2 Alaska, NW USA
Walgett 149 D 5 New South Wales,
  SE Australia
Walk *see* Valka
Walker Lake 47 C 6 lake,
  Nevada, W USA
Wallaby Island 148 C 2 island,
  Queensland, N Australia
Wallachia 108 B 5 *var.* Walachia,
  Ger. Walachei, *Rom.* Valachia.
  Cultural region, S Romania
Wallal Downs 146 B 3 W Australia
Walla Walla 46 C 2 Washington,
  NW USA
Wallis & Futuna 145 F 4
  Fr. Territoire de Wallis et Futuna.
  French overseas territory,
  S Pacific Ocean
Wallis et Futuna, Territoire de *see*
  Wallis and Futuna
Walnut Ridge 42 B 1
  Arkansas, C USA
Walvisbaai *see* Walvis Bay
Walvis Bay 78 B 4 *Afr.* Walvisbaai.
  W Namibia
Walvis Bay 78 B 4 bay,
  W Atlantic Ocean
Walvish Ridge *see* Walvis Ridge
Walvis Ridge 67 D 6 *var.* Walvish
  Ridge. Undersea ridge,
  E Atlantic Ocean
Wanaka 151 B 7 South Island,
  SW New Zealand
Wanaka, Lake 151 B 6 lake,
  South Island, SW New Zealand
Wandel Sea 83 F 1 sea,
  Arctic Ocean
Wanganui 150 D 4 North Island,
  C New Zealand
Wangaratta 149 C 7 Victoria,
  SE Australia
Wankie *see* Hwange
Wanlaweyn 73 D 6 *var.* Wanle
  Weyn, *It.* Uanle Uen. SW Somalia
Wanxian 129 B 5 C China
Warburg 94 B 4 W Germany
Ware 37 E 4 British Columbia,
  W Canada
Waremme 87 C 6 E Belgium
Waren 94 C 3 NE Germany
Wargla *see* Ouargla
Warnemünde 94 C 2 NE Germany
Warnes 61 G 4 C Bolivia
Warrego 149 D 5 river, New South
  Wales/Queensland, E Australia
Warrego Range 148 D 4 mountain
  range, E Australia
Warren 40 D 4 Ohio, N USA
Warren 40 D 3 Michigan, N USA
Warri 75 F 5 S Nigeria

Warrnambool 149 B 7 Victoria,
  SE Australia
Warsaw *see* Warszawa
Warszawa 98 D 3 *Eng.* Warsaw,
  Ger. Warschau, *Rus.* Varshava.
  Country capital, C Poland
Warta 98 C 4 *Ger.* Warthe. River,
  W Poland
Warthe *see* Warta
Warwick 149 D 5 Queensland,
  E Australia
Washington 40 D 4
  Pennsylvania, NE USA
Washington 46 B 2 *off.* State of
  Washington; *nicknames* Chinook
  State, Evergreen State. State,
  NW USA
Washington D.C. 41 E 4 country
  capital, District of Columbia,
  NE USA
Washington Island *see* Teraina
Washington Land 82 D 1 physical
  region, NW Greenland
Wash, The 89 E 6 inlet,
  SW North Sea
Waspam 53 E 2 *var.* Waspán.
  NE Nicaragua
Waspán *see* Waspam
Watampone 139 E 4 *var.* Bone.
  Sulawesi, C Indonesia
Watenstedt-Salzgitter *see* Salzgitter
Waterbury 41 G 3
  Connecticut, NE USA
Waterford 89 B 6 *Ir.* Port Láirge.
  S Ireland
Waterloo 45 G 3 Iowa, C USA
Watertown 41 F 2
  New York, NE USA
Watertown 45 E 2
  South Dakota, N USA
Waterville 41 G 2 Maine, NE USA
Watford 89 E 7 SE England, UK
Watlings Island *see* San Salvador
Watsa 77 E 5 NE Congo (Zaire)
Watsonville 47 B 6
  California, W USA
Wau 73 B 5 *var.* Wāw. S Sudan
Waukegan 40 B 3 Illinois, N USA
Waukesha 40 B 3
  Wisconsin, N USA
Wausau 40 B 2 Wisconsin, N USA
Wave Hill 146 E 3 N Australia
Waverly 45 G 3 Iowa, C USA
Wavre 87 C 6 C Belgium
Wāw *see* Wau
Wawa 38 C 4 Ontario, S Canada
Waycross 43 E 3 Georgia, SE USA
Wearmouth *see* Sunderland
Weatherford 49 F 1
  Oklahoma, C USA
Webster City 45 F 3 Iowa, C USA
Weddell Plain 154 A 2 abyssal
  plain, SW Atlantic Ocean
Weddell Sea 154 B 2 sea,
  SW Atlantic Ocean
Weener 94 A 3 NW Germany
Weert 87 D 5 SE Netherlands
Weesp 86 C 3 C Netherlands
Węgorzewo 98 D 2 *Ger.* Angerburg.
  NE Poland
Weimar 94 C 4 C Germany
Weissenburg 95 C 6 SE Germany
Weissenstein *see* Paide
Wejherowo 98 C 2 NW Poland
Welchman Hall 55 G 1 C Barbados
Weldiya 72 C 4 *var.* Waldia,
  It. Valdia. N Ethiopia
Welkom 78 D 4 C South Africa
Welle *see* Uele
Wellesley Islands 148 B 2 island
  group, N Australia

Wellington 151 D 5 country capital,
  North Island, C New Zealand
Wellington 45 F 5 Kansas, C USA
Wellington *see* Wellington, Isla
Wellington, Isla 65 B 7 *var.*
  Wellington. Island, S Chile
Wellsford 150 D 2 North Island,
  N New Zealand
Wells, Lake 147 C 5 lake, Western
  Australia, C Australia
Wels 95 D 6 *anc.* Ovilava. N Austria
Wemmel 87 B 6 C Belgium
Wenatchee 46 C 2 Washington,
  NW USA
Wenchi 75 E 4 W Ghana
Wen-chou *see* Wenzhou
Wendau *see* Võnnu
Wenden *see* Cēsis
Wenmen Island *see* Wolf, Isla
Wentworth 149 B 6 New South
  Wales, SE Australia
Wenzhou 129 D 5 *var.* Wen-chou.
  E China
Werda 78 C 4 S Botswana
Werder *see* Virtsu
Werkendam 86 C 4 S Netherlands
Werro *see* Võru
Wesenberg *see* Rakvere
Wessel Islands 148 B 1 island
  group, N Australia
West Antarctica *see*
  Lesser Antarctica
West Australian Basin *see*
  Wharton Basin
West Bank 119 D 6 disputed region,
  SW Asia
West Bend 40 B 3 Wisconsin, N USA
West Bengal 135 F 4 state, NE India
West Caroline Basin 152 B 3
  undersea basin, SW Pacific Ocean
West Caroline Islands 144 B 2
  island group, C Micronesia
West Des Moines 45 F 4
  Iowa, C USA
Westerland 94 B 2 N Germany
Western Australia 146 C 4 state,
  W Australia
Western Carpathians *see* Carpaţii
  Occidentali
Western Dvina 106 D 4 *Bel.* Dzvina,
  Ger. Düna, *Latv.* Daugava,
  Rus. Zapadnaya Dvina. River,
  Asia/Europe
Western Ghats 132 B 1
  mountain range, SW India
Western Isles *see* Outer Hebrides
Western Punjab *see* Punjab
Western Sahara 70 B 4 territory of
  NW Africa, occupied by Morocco
  from 1976
Western Samoa *see* Samoa
Western Sayans *see*
  Zapadnyy Sayan
Western Sierra Madre *see*
  Madre Occidental, Sierra
Westerschelde 87 B 5 *Eng.* Western
  Scheldt; *prev.* Honte. Channel,
  S North Sea
Westerville 40 C 4 Ohio, N USA
West European Basin 66 C 3
  undersea basin, N Atlantic Ocean
Westfalen 94 A 4 cultural region,
  W Germany
West Falkland 65 C 7
  var. Gran Malvina. Island,
  W Falkland Islands
West Fargo 45 F 2
  North Dakota, N USA
West Frisian Islands *see*
  Waddeneilanden
West Indies 66 A 4 island group,
  W Atlantic Ocean

Westliche Morava *see*
  Zapadna Morava
Weston-super-Mare 89 D 7
  SW England, UK
West Palm Beach 43 F 5
  Florida, SE USA
Westport 151 C 5
  South Island, C New Zealand
West Punjab *see* Punjab
West Siberian Plain *see*
  Zapadno-Sibirskaya Ravnina
West Virginia 40 D 4 *off.* State of
  West Virginia; nickname
  Mountain State. State, E USA
Wetar, Pulau 138 D 5 island,
  E Indonesia
Wetzlar 95 B 5 W Germany
Wevok 36 C 2 *var.* Wewuk.
  Alaska, NW USA
Wewuk *see* Wevok
Wexford 89 B 6 *Ir.* Loch Garman.
  SE Ireland
Weyburn 37 F 5 Saskatchewan,
  S Canada
Weymouth 89 D 7 S England, UK
Weymouth 41 G 3
  Massachusetts, NE USA
Weymouth, Cape 148 C 2 headland
  Queensland, NE Australia
Wezep 86 D 3 E Netherlands
Whakatane 150 E 3
  North Island, NE New Zealand
Whale Cove 37 G 4 Northwest
  Territories, C Canada
Whangarei 150 D 2 North Island,
  N New Zealand
Wharton Basin 141 D 5 *var.* West
  Australian Basin. Undersea basin
  E Indian Ocean
Whataroa 151 B 6 South Island,
  SW New Zealand
Wheatland 44 D 3 Wyoming, C USA
Wheeling 40 D 4
  West Virginia, NE USA
Whitby 89 D 5 N England, UK
Whitefish 44 B 1 Montana, NW USA
Whitehaven 89 C 5
  NW England, UK
Whitehorse 36 D 4 territory capital
  Yukon Territory, W Canada
White Lake 42 A 3 lake,
  Louisiana, S USA
White Mountains 41 G 2
  mountain range, USA
White Nile 72 B 4 *Ar.* Al Baḥr al
  Abyaḍ, An Nīl al Abyaḍ, Bahr el
  Jebel. River, SE Sudan
White River 44 D 3 river,
  South Dakota, N USA
White Sea *see* Beloye More
White Volta 75 E 4 *var.* Nakambé,
  Fr. Volta Blanche. River,
  Burkina/Ghana
Whitewater Bay 43 E 5 bay,
  Florida, SE Gulf of Mexico
Whitianga 150 D 2 North Island,
  N New Zealand
Whitney, Mount 47 C 6 mountain,
  California, W USA
Whitsunday Island 148 D 3 island,
  Queensland, E Australia
Whyalla 149 A 6 South Australia,
  S Australia
Wichita 45 F 5 Kansas, C USA
Wichita Falls 49 F 2 Texas, S USA
Wichita River 49 F 2 river,
  Texas, S USA
Wicklow Mountains 89 B 6
  Ir. Sléibhte Chill Mhantáin.
  Mountain range, E Ireland
Wiehl 94 A 4 W Germany
Wieliczka 99 D 5 S Poland

ieluń 98 C 4 C Poland
ien 95 E 6 Eng. Vienna,
Hung. Bécs, Slvk. Vídeö, Slvn.
Dunaj; anc. Vindobona.
Country capital, NE Austria
iener Neustadt 95 E 6 E Austria
ierden 86 E 3 E Netherlands
iesbaden 95 B 5 W Germany
ight, Isle of 89 D 7 island,
S England, UK
igorna Ceaster see Worcester
ijchen 86 D 4 SE Netherlands
ijk bij Duurstede 86 D 4
C Netherlands
ilberforce, Cape 148 B 1
headland, Northern Territory,
N Australia
ilcannia 149 C 6
New South Wales, SE Australia
ilhelm, Mount 144 B 3 mountain,
New Guinea, C Papua New Guinea
ilhelm-Pieck-Stadt see Guben
ilhelmshaven 94 B 3 NW Germany
ilkes Barre 41 F 3
Pennsylvania, NE USA
ilkes Fracture Zone 153 F 3
fracture zone, E Pacific Ocean
ilkes Land 154 D 4 physical
region, Antarctica
ilkes Rise see Wilkes Guyot
ilkomierz see Ukmergė
illebroek 87 C 5 C Belgium
illemstad 55 E 5 dependent
territory capital,
C Netherlands Antilles
illeroo 146 E 2 N Australia
illiston 44 D 1
North Dakota, N USA
ilmington 43 F 2
North Carolina, SE USA
ilmington 41 F 4
Delaware, NE USA
ilrijk 87 C 5 N Belgium
inchester 89 D 7
hist. Wintanceaster, Lat. Venta
Belgarum. S England, UK
inchester 41 E 4 Virginia, NE USA
indau see Venta
indhoek 78 B 3 Ger. Windhuk.
Country capital, C Namibia
indhuk see Windhoek
indsor 89 D 7 S England, UK
indsor 38 C 5 Ontario, S Canada
indsor 41 G 3 Connecticut, NE USA
indward Islands 55 H 4 island
group, SE Caribbean Sea
indward Islands see
Barlavento, Ilhas de
indward Passage 54 D 3
Sp. Paso de los Vientos. Channel,
N Caribbean Sea
inisk 38 C 2 river, Ontario,
S Canada
inisk 38 C 2 Ontario, C Canada
innebago, Lake 40 B 2 lake,
Wisconsin, N USA
inning 146 A 4 W Australia
innipeg 37 G 5 province capital,
Manitoba, S Canada
innipeg, Lake 37 G 5 lake,
Manitoba, C Canada
innipesaukee, Lake 41 G 2 lake,
New Hampshire, NE USA
inona 38 C 3 Minnesota, N USA
inschoten 86 E 2 NE Netherlands
insen 94 B 3 N Germany
inslow 48 B 2 Arizona, SW USA
inston Salem 43 E 1 North
Carolina, SE USA
insum 86 D 1 NE Netherlands

Winter Haven 43 E 4 Florida, SE USA
Winterswijk 86 E 4 E Netherlands
Winterthur 95 B 7 NE Switzerland
Winton 151 A 7 South Island,
SW New Zealand
Winton 148 C 4 Queensland,
E Australia
Wirz-See see Võrtsjärv
Wisby see Visby
Wisconsin 40 A 2 off. State of
Wisconsin; nickname Badger
State. State, N USA
Wisconsin Rapids 40 B 2
Wisconsin, N USA
Wisconsin River 40 B 3 river,
Wisconsin, N USA
Wisła 98 D 4 Eng. Vistula,
Ger. Weichsel. River, C Poland
Wismar 94 C 2 N Germany
Wittenberge 94 C 3 N Germany
Wittlich 95 A 5 SW Germany
Wittstock 94 C 3 NE Germany
W.J.van Blommesteinmeer 59 G 3
reservoir, E Suriname
Władysławowo 98 C 2 N Poland
Włocławek 98 C 3 Ger./Rus.
Vlotslavsk. C Poland
Włodawa 98 E 4 Rus. Vlodava.
SE Poland
Wodonga 149 C 7 Victoria,
SE Australia
Wodzisław Śląski 99 C 5
Ger. Loslau. S Poland
Wojewodina see Vojvodina
Woking 89 E 7 SE England, UK
Wolf, Isla 60 A 4 var. Wenmen
Island. Island, Galapagos Islands,
E Pacific Ocean
Wolfsburg 94 C 3 N Germany
Wolgast 94 D 2 NE Germany
Wöllan see Velenje
Wollaston Lake 37 F 4
Saskatchewan, C Canada
Wollongong 149 D 6
New South Wales, SE Australia
Wolvega 86 D 2 Fris. Wolvegea.
N Netherlands
Wolvegea see Wolvega
Wolverhampton 89 C 6
W England, UK
Wonowon 37 E 4 British Columbia,
W Canada
Wŏnsan 128 E 3 SE North Korea
Woodburn 46 B 3 Oregon, NW USA
Woodland 47 B 5 California, W USA
Woodruff 40 B 2 Wisconsin, N USA
Woods, Lake of the 38 B 3 Fr. Lac
des Bois. Lake, Canada/USA
Woodville 150 D 4 North Island,
C New Zealand
Woodward 49 F 1 Oklahoma, C USA
Wooramel 147 A 5 W Australia
Worcester 89 C 6 hist. Wigorna
Ceaster. W England, UK
Worcester 41 G 3
Massachusetts, NE USA
Worcester 78 C 5 SW South Africa
Workington 89 C 5 NW England, UK
Worland 44 C 3 Wyoming, C USA
Worms 95 B 5 anc. Augusta
Vangionum, Borbetomagus,
Wormatia. SW Germany
Worthington 45 F 3
Minnesota, N USA
Wotje Atoll 144 D 1 var. Wōjjä.
Island, E Marshall Islands
Woudrichem 86 C 4 S Netherlands
Wrangel Island see
Vrangelya, Ostrov

Wrangel Plain 155 G 2 abyssal
plain, Arctic Ocean
Wreck Reef 148 F 4 reef, W Coral Sea
Wrocław 98 C 4 Eng./Ger. Breslau.
SW Poland
Września 98 C 3 C Poland
Wsetin see Vsetín
Wuday 'ah 121 C 6 S Saudi Arabia
Wuhai 127 E 3 N China
Wuhan 129 C 5 var. Han-kou,
Han-k'ou, Hanyang, Wuchang,
Wu-han; prev. Hankow.
Province capital, C China
Wuhu 129 D 5 var. Wu-na-mu.
E China
Wujlān see Ujelang Atoll
Wukari 75 G 5 E Nigeria
Wuliang Shan 129 A 6 mountain
range, S China
Wu-na-mu see Wuhu
Wuppertal 94 A 4 prev. Barmen-
Elberfeld. W Germany
Würzburg 95 B 5 SW Germany
Wuxi 129 D 5 var. Wuhsi, Wu-hsi,
Wusih. E China
Wye 89 C 6 Wel. Gwy. River,
England/Wales, UK
Wyłkowyszki see Vilkaviškis
Wyndham 146 D 2 Western
Australia, W Australia
Wyoming 40 C 3 Michigan, N USA
Wyoming 44 B 3 off. State of
Wyoming; nickname Equality
State. State, C USA
Wyszków 98 D 3 Ger. Probstberg.
C Poland

X

Xaçmaz 117 H 2 Rus. Khachmas.
N Azerbaijan
Xai-Xai 79 E 4 prev. João Belo, Vila
de João Bel. S Mozambique
Xam Nua 136 D 3 var. Sam Neua.
NE Laos
Xankändi 117 G 3 Rus. Khankendi;
prev. Stepanakert. SW Azerbaijan
Xánthi 104 C 3 NE Greece
Xátiva 93 F 4 var. Jativa; anc.
Setabis. E Spain
Xiaguan 129 A 6 S China
Xiamen 129 D 6 var. Hsia-men;
prev. Amoy. SE China
Xi'an 128 C 4 var. Changan,
Hsi-an Sian, Sian, Signan,
Siking,Singan, Xian. Province
capital, C China
Xiang see Hunan
Xiangkhoang 136 D 4 var. Xieng
Khouang. E Laos
Xiangtan 129 C 5 var. Hsiang-t'an,
Siangtan. S China
Xianning 129 C 5 C China
Xiao Hinggan Ling 128 E 2
Eng. Lesser Khingan Range.
Mountain range, NE China
Xichang 129 B 5 C China
Xieng Khouang see Pèk
Xieng Ngeun see
Muong Xiang Ngeun
Xifeng 128 B 4 N China
Xigazê 126 C 4 var. Jih-k'a-tse,
Shigatse, Xigaze. W China
Xi Jiang 129 C 3 var. Hsi Chiang,
Eng. West River. River, S China
Xilin Hot 127 F 2 var. Abagnar Qi.
NE China
Xilokastro see Xylókastro
Xingu 63 E 2 river, C Brazil
Xingxingxia 126 D 3 C China

Xining 127 E 4 var. Hsining,
Hsi-ning, Sining. C China
Xinjiang Uygur Zizhiqu 126 B 3
var. Sinkiang, Sinkiang Uighur,
Sinkiang Uighur Autonomous
Region, Xin, Xinjiang.
Autonomous region, NW China
Xinpu see Lianyungang
Xinxiang 128 C 4 NE China
Xinyang 129 C 5 var. Hsin-yang,
Sinyang. C China
Xinzo de Limia 92 C 2 NW Spain
Xizang Zizhiqu 126 B 4 var. Thibet,
Xizang, Chin. Sitsang, Eng. Tibet.
Autonomous region, W China
Xolotlán see Managua, Lago de
Xuguit Qi 127 F 1
var. Yakeshi. N China
Xuwen 129 C 7 S China
Xuzhou 128 D 4 var. Hsu-chou,
Suchow, Tongshan;
prev. T'ung-shan. E China
Xylókastro 105 B 6
var. Xilokastro. S Greece

Y

Ya'an 129 B 5 var. Yaan. C China
Yaan see Ya'an
Yabēlo 73 C 5 S Ethiopia
Yablis 52 E 2 NE Nicaragua
Yablonovyy Khrebet 115 F 4
mountain range,
C Russian Federation
Yafran 71 F 2 NW Libya
Yaghan Basin 67 B 7
undersea basin, SE Pacific Ocean
Yagotin see Yahotyn
Yahotyn 109 E 2 Rus. Yagotin.
N Ukraine
Yahualica 50 D 4 SW Mexico
Yakeshi see Xuguit Qi
Yakima 46 B 2 Washington, NW USA
Yakima River 46 B 2 river,
Washington, NW USA
Yakoruda 104 C 3 SW Bulgaria
Yaku-shima 131 B 8 island,
Ösumi-shotó, SW Japan
Yakutat 36 C 4 Alaska, NW USA
Yakutsk 115 F 3
E Russian Federation
Yakymivka 109 F 4 SE Ukraine
Yala 137 C 7 S Thailand
Yalizava 107 D 6 Rus. Yelizovo.
E Belarus
Yalong Jiang 129 A 5 river, C China
Yalova 116 B 3 NW Turkey
Yalpuh, Ozero see Yalpuh, Ozero
Yalpuh, Ozero 108 D 4 Rus. Ozero
Yalpug. Lake, SW Ukraine
Yalta 109 F 5 S Ukraine
Yalu 128 E 2 Chin. Yalu Jiang,
Jap. Oryokko, Kor. Amnok-kang.
River, China/North Korea
Yamaguchi 131 B 7 var. Yamaguti.
Honshū, SW Japan
Yamaguti see Yamaguchi
Yamal, Poluostrov 114 D 2
peninsula, N Russian Federation
Yambio 73 B 5 var. Yambiyo.
S Sudan
Yambiyo see Yambio
Yambol 104 D 2 var. Jambol,
Turk. Yanboli. E Bulgaria
Yamdena, Pulau 139 G 5 island,
Kepulauan Tanimbar, E Indonesia
Yamoussoukro 74 D 5 country
capital, C Ivory Coast
Yana 115 F 2 river,
N Russian Federation

Yanaul 111 D 5
W Russian Federation
Yanbu' al Bahr 121 A 5
W Saudi Arabia
Yangambi 77 D 5 N Congo (Zaire)
Yangchow see Yangzhou
Yangiyŭl 123 E 2 Rus. Yangiyul'.
E Uzbekistan
Yangiyul' see Yangiyŭl
Yangon 136 B 4 var. Rangoon.
Country capital, S Myanmar
Yangtze 129 B 5 var. Chang Jiang,
Yangtze Kiang. River, C China
Yangzhou 129 D 5 var. Yangchow.
NE China
Yankton 45 E 3
South Dakota, N USA
Yantai 128 D 4 var. Yan-t'ai;
prev. Chefoo, Chih-fu. E China
Yaoundé 77 B 5 var. Yaunde.
Country capital, S Cameroon
Yap 144 A 1 state, W Micronesia
Yapanskoye More see Japan, Sea of
Yapen, Pulau 139 G 4 prev. Japen.
Island, E Indonesia
Yap Trough see Yap Trench
Yaqui, Río 50 B 2 river, NW Mexico
Yaransk 111 C 5 var. Jaransk.
NW Russian Federation
Yarega 110 D 4 var. Jarega.
NW Russian Federation
Yarkant see Shache
Yarmouth 39 F 5
Nova Scotia, SE Canada
Yarmouth see Great Yarmouth
Yaroslavl' 110 B 4 var. Jaroslavl.
W Russian Federation
Yarumal 58 B 2 NW Colombia
Yasyel'da 107 B 7 river, SW Belarus
Yatsushiro 131 A 7 var. Yatusiro.
Kyūshū, SW Japan
Yatusiro see Yatsushiro
Yaunde see Yaoundé
Yavarí 56 B 3 var. Javari. River,
C Brazil
Yavarí see Javari
Yaviza 53 H 5 SE Panama
Yavoriv 108 B 2 Pol. Jaworów,
Rus. Yavorov. NW Ukraine
Yazd 120 D 3 var. Yezd. C Iran
Yazd-e Khvāst 120 D 3 C Iran
Yazoo City 42 B 2 Mississippi, S USA
Yding Skovhøj 85 A 7 hill,
C Denmark
Ýdra 105 C 6 var. Ídhra. S Greece
Ye 137 B 5 SE Myanmar
Yecheng 126 A 3 var. Kargilik.
NW China
Yeeda 146 C 3 NW Australia
Yefremov 111 B 5
W Russian Federation
Yei 73 B 5 S Sudan
Yelizovo see Yalizava
Yell 88 D 1 island, NE Scotland, UK
Yellowknife 37 E 4 territory
capital, Northwest Territories,
W Canada
Yellow River 124 D 2 river, C China
Yellow River see Huang He
Yellow Sea 128 D 4 Chin. Huang
Hai, Kor. Hwang-Hae. Sea,
NW Pacific Ocean
Yellowstone River 44 C 2 river,
NW USA
Yel'sk 107 C 8 SE Belarus
Yelwa 75 F 4 W Nigeria

Yemassee 43 E 2
South Carolina, SE USA

Yemen 121 C 7 Ar. Al Jumhuriyah al
Yamaniyah, Al Yaman. Republic,
SW Asia

Official name: Republic of Yemen
Date of formation: 1990 **Capital:**
Sana **Population:** 13 million **Total
area:** 203,849 sq miles
(527,970 sq km) **Languages:** Arabic*
Religions: Sunni Muslim 55%, Shi'a
Muslim 42%, other 3% **Ethnic mix:**
Arab 95%, Afro-Arab 3%, South
Asian, African, European 2%
Government: Multiparty republic
Currency: Rial (North), Dinar
(South) - both are legal currency

Yemva 110 D 4 var. Železnodorožny,
Zeleznodorožnyj; prev.
Zheleznodorozhnyy.
NW Russian Federation
Yenakiyeve 109 G 3 Rus.
Yenakiyevo; prev. Ordzhonikidze,
Rykovo. E Ukraine
Yenangyaung 136 A 3
W Myanmar
Yendi 75 E 4 NE Ghana
Yengisar 126 A 3 NW China
Yenipazar see Novi Pazar
Yenisey 114 D 3 river,
Mongolia / Russian Federation
Yeovil 89 D 7 S England, UK
Yeppon 148 D 4 Queensland,
E Australia
Yerevan 117 G 3 var. Erevan,
Eng. Erivan. Country capital,
C Armenia
Yermak 114 C 4 Kaz. Ermak.
NE Kazakhstan
Yerushalayim see Jerusalem
Yeu, Île d' 90 A 4 island,
NW France
Yevlakh see Yevlax
Yevlax 117 G 2 Rus. Yevlakh.
C Azerbaijan
Yevpatoriya 109 F 5 S Ukraine
Yezd see Yazd
Yezerishche see Yezyaryshcha
Yezyaryshcha 107 E 5
Rus. Yezerishche. NE Belarus
Yiannitsá see Giannitsá
Yichang 129 C 5 C China
Yıldizeli 116 D 3 N Turkey
Yinchuan 128 B 4 var. Yinch'uan,
Yin-ch'uan, Yinchwan.
Autonomous region capital
N China
Yingcheng 128 E 3 C China
Yining 126 B 2 var. I-ning, Uigh.
Gulja, Kuldja. NW China
Yin Shan 127 E 3 mountain range,
N China
Yof 74 B 3 W Senegal
Yogyakarta 138 C 5 prev.
Djokjakarta, Jogjakarta,
Jokyakarta. Jawa, C Indonesia
Yokohama 131 D 5 Honshū, S Japan
Yokote 130 D 4 Honshū, C Japan
Yola 75 H 4 E Nigeria
Yonago 131 B 6 Honshū, SW Japan
Yong'an 129 D 6 var. Yongan.
SE China
Yongan see Yong'an
Yonkers 41 F 4 New York, NE USA
Yonne 90 C 4 river, C France
Yopal 58 C 3 var. El Yopal.
C Colombia
York 89 D 5 anc. Eboracum,
Eburacum. N England, UK

York 45 E 4 Nebraska, C USA
York, Cape 148 C 1 headland,
Queensland, NE Australia
Yorkton 37 F 5 Saskatchewan,
S Canada
Yoro 52 C 2 C Honduras
Yoshkar-Ola 111 C 5
W Russian Federation
Youngstown 40 D 4 Ohio, N USA
Ypres see Ieper
Ysabel see IJssel
Yuba City 47 B 5 California, W USA
Yucatán, Canal de see
Yucatan Channel
Yucatan Channel 54 A 2 Sp. Canal
de Yucatán. Channel Caribbean
Sea / Gulf of Mexico
Yucatan Peninsula see
Yucatán, Península de
Yucatán, Península de 51 H 4
Eng. Yucatan Peninsula.
Peninsula, Guatemala / Mexico
Yuci 128 C 4 NE China
Yuen Long 128 A 1 NW Hong Kong
Yueyang 129 C 5 S China

Yugoslavia
100 D 4 SCr. Jugoslavija,
Savezna Republika Jugoslavija.
Federal republic, SE Europe
See also Serbia, Montenegro

Official name: Federal Republic of
Yugoslavia **Date of formation:** 1992
Capital: Belgrade **Population:** 10.6
million **Total area:** 39,449 sq miles
(102,173 sq km) **Languages:**
Serbian*, Croatian **Religions:**
Orthodox Catholic 65%, Muslim
19%, other 16% **Ethnic mix:** Serb
63%, Albanian 14%, Montenegrin
6%, other 17% **Government**
Multiparty republic: Currency:
Dinar = 100 para

Yukhavichy 107 D 5
Rus. Yukhovichi. N Belarus
Yukhovichi see Yukhavichy
Yukon River 36 D 3 river,
Canada / USA
Yukon Territory 36 D 3
var. Yukon, Fr. Territoire du
Yukon. Territory, NW Canada
Yulin 129 C 6 S China
Yuma 48 A 2 Arizona, SW USA
Yumen 128 A 3 var.
Lao-chün-miao, Laojunmiao,
Yümen, Yu-men. N China
Yunjinghong see Jinghong
Yunnan 129 A 6 var. Yun, Yünna,
Yun-nan. Province, SW China
Yuruá, Río see Juruá
Yushu 126 D 4 C China
Yuty 64 D 3 S Paraguay
Yuzhno-Sakhalinsk 115 H 4
Jap. Toyohara; prev.
Vladimirovka. Ostrov Sakhalin,
SE Russian Federation
Yuzhnyy Bug see Pivdennyy Buh
Yylanly see Il'yaly

Z

Zaandam see Zaanstad
Zaanstad 86 C 3 prev. Zaandam.
C Netherlands
Zabaykal'sk 115 F 5
S Russian Federation
Zabīd 121 B 7 W Yemen
Ząbkowice Śląskie 98 C 4
var. Ząbkowice, Ger. Frankenstein,
Frankenstein in Schlesien.
SW Poland

Zábřeh 99 B 5 Ger. Hohenstadt.
E Czech Republic
Zacapa 52 B 2 E Guatemala
Zacatecas 50 D 3 C Mexico
Zacatepec 51 E 4 S Mexico
Zacháro 105 B 6 var. Zakháro.
S Greece
Zadar 100 A 3 It. Zara; anc. Iader.
W Croatia
Zadetkyi Kyun 137 B 6 island,
S Myanmar
Zafra 92 C 4 W Spain
Zagazig 72 B 1 var. Az Zaqāzīq.
N Egypt
Zagreb 100 B 2 Ger. Agram,
Hung. Zágráb. Country capital,
N Croatia
Zágros, Kuhhā-ye 120 C 3
Eng. Zagros Mountains.
Mountain range, W Iran
Zagros Mountains see Zágros,
Kuhhā-ye
Zāhedān 120 E 4 var. Zahidan;
prev. Duzdab. SE Iran
Zahlah see Zahlé
Zahlé 118 B 4 var. Zahlah.
C Lebanon
Záhony 99 E 6 NE Hungary
Zaire 78 C 1 prev. Congo. Province:
NW Angola
Zaire see Congo (Zaire)
Zaječar 100 E 4 E Yugoslavia
Zakataly see Zaqatala
Zākhō 120 B 2 var. Zākhū. N Iraq
Zākhū see Zākhō
Zákynthos 105 A 6 var. Zákinthos,
It. Zante. Island, W Greece
Zalantun see Butha Qi
Zalău 108 B 3 Ger. Waltenberg,
Hung. Zilah; prev. Zillenmarkt.
NW Romania
Zalim 121 B 5 W Saudi Arabia
Zaliv Syvash see Syvash, Zatoka
`Zalni Pjašaci see Zlatni Pyasŭtsi
Zambesi Canyon see Zambezi
Canyon
Zambesi 78 D 2 var. Zambesi,
Port. Zambeze. River, S Africa
Zambezi 78 C 2 W Zambia

Zambia
78 C 2 prev. Northern Rhodesia.
Republic, S Africa

Official name: Republic of Zambia
Date of formation: 1964 **Capital:**
Lusaka **Population:** 8.9 million **Total**
area: 290,563 sq miles (752,610 sq km)
Languages: English*, Bemba, Tonga
Nyanja **Religions:** Christian 63%,
traditional beliefs 35%, other 2%
Ethnic mix: Bemba 36%, Maravi
18%, Tonga 15%, other 31%
Government: Multiparty republic
Currency: Kwacha = 100 ngwee

Zamboanga 139 E 3 off.
Zamboanga City. Mindanao,
S Philippines
Zamboanga City see Zamboanga
Zambrów 98 E 3 E Poland
Zamora 92 D 2 NW Spain
Zamora de Hidalgo 50 D 4
SW Mexico
Zamość 98 E 4 Rus. Zamostye.
SE Poland
Zamostye see Zamość
Zanda X 126 A 4 W China
Zanjān 120 C 2 var. Zenjan, Zinjan.
NW Iran
Zanthus 147 C 6 S Australia
Zanzibar 73 D 7 Swa. Unguja.
Island, E Tanzania

Zanzibar 73 D 7 E Tanzania
Zaozhuang 128 D 4
  var. Tsaochuang. E China
Zapadna Morava 100 D 4
  Ger. Westliche Morava. River,
  C Yugoslavia
Zapadnaya Dvina 110 A 4
  W Russian Federation
Zapadno-Sibirskaya Ravnina 114 D
  3 *Eng.* West Siberian Plain. Plain,
  Kazakhstan/Russian Federation
Zapadnyy Sayan 114 D 4 *Eng.*
  Western Sayans. Mountain range,
  C Russian Federation
Zapala 65 B 5 W Argentina
Zapiola Ridge 67 B 6 undersea
  ridge, SW Atlantic Ocean
Zapolyarnyy 110 C 2
  var. Zapol'arnyj, Zapoljarny.
  NW Russian Federation
Zaporizhzhya 109 G 3
  Rus. Zaporozh'ye; *prev.*
  Aleksandrovsk. SE Ukraine
Zapotiltic 50 D 4 SW Mexico
Zaqatala 117 G 2 *Rus.* Zakataly.
  NW Azerbaijan
Zara 116 D 3 C Turkey
Zarafshan *see* Zarafshon
Zarafshon 122 D 2 *Rus.* Zarafshan.
  N Uzbekistan
Zarafshon *see* Zeravshan
Zaragoza 93 F 2 *Eng.* Saragossa;
  anc. Caesaraugusta, Salduba.
  NE Spain
Zarand 120 D 3 C Iran
Zaranj 122 D 5 SW Afghanistan
Zarasai 106 C 4 E Lithuania
Zárate 64 D 4 *prev.* General José
  F.Uriburu. E Argentina
Zarautz 93 E 1 *var.* Zarauz. N Spain
Zarauz *see* Zarautz
Zaraza 59 E 2 N Venezuela
Zarghūn Shahr 122 D 5
  SE Afghanistan
Zaria 75 G 4 C Nigeria
Zarós 105 D 8 Kríti, SE Greece
Zarqa *see* Az Zarqā'
Żary 98 B 4 *Ger.* Sorau, Sorau in der
  Niederlausitz. W Poland
Zavertse *see* Zawiercie
Zavet 104 D 1 NE Bulgaria
Zavidovići 100 C 3
  N Bosnia & Herzegovina
Zawiercie 98 C 4 *Rus.* Zavertse.
  S Poland
Zaysan Köl *see* Zaysan, Ozero
Zaysan, Ozero 114 D 5 *Kaz.* Zaysan
  Köl. Lake, E Kazakhstan
Zayyq *see* Ural
Zbarazh 108 C 2 W Ukraine
Zduńska Wola 98 C 4 C Poland
Zēbāk 123 F 3 NE Afghanistan
Zeebrugge 87 A 5 NW Belgium
Zeewolde 86 D 3 C Netherlands
Zefat 119 B 5 *var.* Safed, *Ar.* Safad.
  N Israel
Zeila *see* Saylac
Zeist 86 C 4 C Netherlands
Zele 87 B 5 NW Belgium
Zelenoborski *see* Zelenoborskiy
Zelenoborskiy 110 C 2
  var. Zelenoborski.
  NW Russian Federation
Zelenodol'sk 111 C 5
  W Russian Federation
Zelenograd 111 B 5
  W Russian Federation

Zelenogradsk 106 A 4 *var.* Kranz,
  Ger. Cranz. W Russian Federation
Železnodorožny *see* Yemva
Zelle *see* Celle
Zel'va 107 B 6 *Pol.* Zelwa. W Belarus
Zelwa *see* Zel'va
Zelzate 87 B 5 *var.* Selzaete.
  NW Belgium
Žemaičių Aukštumas 106 B 3
  physical region, W Lithuania
Zemst 87 C 6 C Belgium
Zemun 100 D 3 N Yugoslavia
Zenica 100 C 4
  C Bosnia & Herzegovina
Zenta *see* Senta
Žepa 100 C 4
  SE Bosnia & Herzegovina
Zeravshan 123 E 3 *Taj./Uzb.*
  Zarafshon. River,
  Tajikistan/Uzbekistan
Zevenaar 86 D 4 SE Netherlands
Zevenbergen 86 C 4 S Netherlands
Zgierz 98 C 4 *Ger.* Neuhof,
  Rus. Zgerzh. C Poland
Zgorzelec 98 B 4 *Ger.* Görlitz.
  SW Poland
Zhabinka 107 A 6 *Pol.* Żabinka.
  SW Belarus
Zhambyl 114 C 5 *prev.* Aulie
  Ataprev, Auliye-Ata, Džambul,
  Dzhambul. S Kazakhstan
Zhangaözen *see* Novyy Uzen'
Zhangaqazaly *see* Novokazalinsk
Zhangjiakou 128 C 3 *var.*
  Changkiakow, Zhang-chia-k'ou,
  Eng. Kalgan; *prev.* Wanchuan.
  NE China
Zhangzhou 129 D 6 SE China
Zhanjiang 129 C 7 *var.* Chanchiang,
  Chan-chiang, *Cant.* Tsamkong,
  Fr. Fort-Bayard. S China
Zhaoqing 129 C 6 SE China
Zhdanov *see* Mariupol'
Zhejiang 129 D 5 *var.* Che-chiang,
  Chekiang, Zhe. Province, E China
Zhelezndoroznyy 106 A 4
  Ger. Gerdauen.
  W Russian Federation
Zheleznogorsk 111 A 5
  W Russian Federation
Zhëltyye Vody *see* Zhovti Vody
Zhengzhou 128 C 4 *var.* Ch'eng-
  chou, Chengchow; *prev.*
  Chenghsien. Province capital,
  C China
Zhezkazgan 114 C 4 *var.*
  Džezkazgan, *Kaz.* Zhezqazghan;
  prev. Dzhezkazgan. C Kazakhstan
Zhitkovichi *see* Zhytkavichy
Zhitomir *see* Zhytomyr
Zhmerinka *see* Zhmerynka
Zhmerynka 108 D 2 *Rus.*
  Zhmerinka. C Ukraine
Zhodino *see* Zhodzina
Zhodzina 107 D 6 *Rus.* Zhodino.
  C Belarus
Zhovkva 108 C 2 *Pol.* `Żółkiew,
  Rus.Zholkev, Zholkva;
  prev. Nesterov. NW Ukraine
Zhovti Vody 109 F 3 *Rus.* Zhëltyye
  Vody. C Ukraine
Zhovtnewe 109 E 4
  Rus. Zhovtnevoye. S Ukraine
Zhovtnevoye *see* Zhovtnewe
Zhydachiv 108 C 2 *Pol.* Żydaczów,
  Rus. Zhidachov. NW Ukraine
Zhytkavichy 107 C 7
  Rus. Zhitkovichi. SE Belarus
Zhytomyr 108 D 2 *Rus.* Zhitomir.
  NW Ukraine
Zibo 128 D 4 *var.* Chang-tien,
  Zhangdian. E China

Zichenau *see* Ciechanów
Zielona Góra 98 B 4 *Ger.* Grünberg,
  Grünberg in Schlesien,
  Grüneberg. W Poland
Zierikzee 86 B 4 SW Netherlands
Zigong 129 B 5 *var.* Tzekung.
  SW China
Ziguinchor 74 B 4 SW Senegal
Žilina 99 C 5 *Ger.* Sillein,
  Hung. Zsolna. NW Slovakia
Zillertaler Alpen 95 C 7
  Eng. Zillertal Alps, *It.* Alpi
  Aurine. Mountain range,
  Austria/Italy

Zimbabwe
  78 D 3 *prev.* Rhodesia. Republic,
  S Africa

Official name: Republic of
Zimbabwe **Date of formation:** 1980
Capital: Harare **Population:** 10.9
million **Total area:** 150,800 sq miles
(390,580 sq km) **Languages:**
English*, Shona, Ndebele **Religions:**
Syncretic (Christian and traditional
beliefs) 50%, Christian 26%,
traditional beliefs 24% **Ethnic mix:**
Shona 71%, Ndebele 16%, other 11%,
White, Asian 2% **Government:**
Multiparty republic **Currency:**
Zimbabwe $ = 100 cents

Zimnicea 108 C 5 S Romania
Zimovniki 111 B 7
  SW Russian Federation
Zinder 75 G 3 S Niger
Zintenhof *see* Sindi
Zipaquirá 58 B 3 C Colombia
Zittau 94 D 4 E Germany
Zlatni Pyasŭti 104 E 2 *var.* `Załni
  Pjasăci. NE Bulgaria
Zlín 99 C 5 *prev.* Gottwaldov.
  SE Czech Republic
Złotów 98 C 3 NW Poland
Znaim *see* Znojmo
Znamenka *see* Znam''yanka
Znam''yanka 109 E 3
  Rus. Znamenka. C Ukraine
Žnin 98 C 3 W Poland
Znojmo 99 B 5 *Ger.* Znaim.
  S Czech Republic
Zoetermeer 86 C 4 W Netherlands
Zolochev *see* Zolochiv
Zolochiv 108 C 2 *Pol.* Złoczów,
  Rus. Zolochev. W Ukraine
Zolochiv 109 G 2 *Rus.* Zolochev.
  E Ukraine
Zolote 109 H 3 *Rus.* Zolotoye.
  E Ukraine
Zolotonosha 109 E 2 C Ukraine
Zolotoye *see* Zolote
Zomba 79 E 2 S Malawi
Zombor *see* Sombor
Zongo 77 C 5 N Congo (Zaire)
Zonguldak 116 C 2 NW Turkey
Zonhoven 87 D 6 NE Belgium
Zoppot *see* Sopot
Żory 99 C 5 *var.* Zory, *Ger.* Sohrau.
  S Poland
Zouar 76 C 1 N Chad
Zouérat 74 C 2 *var.* Zouérate,
  Zouïrât. N Mauritania
Zrenjanin 100 D 3
  Ger. Grossbetschkerek, *Hung.*
  Nagybecskerek; *prev.* Petrovgrad,
  Veliki Bečkerek. N Yugoslavia
Zsupanya *see* Županja
Zugspitze 95 C 7 mountain,
  S Germany
Zuid-Beveland 87 B 5 *var.* South
  Beveland. Island, SW Netherlands
Zuider Zee *see* IJsselmeer

Zuidhorn 86 E 1 NE Netherlands
Zuidlaren 86 E 2 NE Netherlands
Zujevka *see* Zuyevka
Zula 72 D 4 E Eritrea
Zumbo *see* Vila do Zumbo
Zundert 87 C 5 S Netherlands
Zunyi 129 B 5 S China
Županja 100 C 3 *Hung.* Zsupanja.
  E Croatia
Zürich 95 B 7 *Eng./Fr.* Zurich,
  It. Zurigo. N Switzerland
Zurich, Lake *see* Zürichsee
Zürichsee 95 B 7 *Eng.* Lake Zurich.
  Lake, NE Switzerland
Zutphen 86 D 3 E Netherlands
Zuwārah 71 F 2 NW Libya
Zuyevka 111 D 5 *var.* Zujevka.
  NW Russian Federation
Zvenigorodka *see* Zvenyhorodka
Zvenyhorodka 109 E 2 *Rus.*
  Zvenigorodka. C Ukraine
Zvishavane 78 D 3 *prev.* Shabani.
  S Zimbabwe
Zvolen 99 C 6 *Ger.* Altsohl, *Hung.*
  Zólyom. C Slovakia
Zvornik 100 C 4
  E Bosnia & Herzegovina
Zwedru 74 D 5 *var.* Tchien.
  E Liberia
Zwettl 95 E 6 N Austria
Zwevegem 87 A 6 W Belgium
Zwickau 95 C 5 E Germany
Zwiesel 95 D 6 SE Germany
Zwolle 86 D 3 E Netherlands
Zyōetsu *see* Jōetsu
Zyryanovsk 114 D 5 E Kazakhstan

MAP FINDER

NORTH & WEST ASIA 112-113

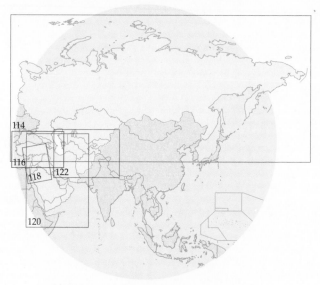

114
116
118
122
120

SOUTH & EAST ASIA 124-125

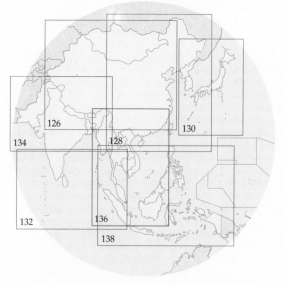

126
134
128
130
132
136
138